Preventing Corporate Corruption

Stefano Manacorda • Francesco Centonze
Gabrio Forti
Editors

Preventing Corporate Corruption

The Anti-Bribery Compliance Model

With the participation
and support of

eni
eni.com

Springer

Editors
Stefano Manacorda
Dipartimento di Giurisprudenza
Seconda Universita di Napoli
Santa Maria Capua Vetere
Italy

Gabrio Forti
Facoltà di Giurisprudenza
Università Cattolica del Sacro Cuore
Milan
Italy

Francesco Centonze
Facoltà di Economia e Giurisprudenza
Università Cattolica del Sacro Cuore
Piacenza
Italy

ISBN 978-3-319-04479-8 ISBN 978-3-319-04480-4 (eBook)
DOI 10.1007/978-3-319-04480-4
Springer Cham Heidelberg New York Dordrecht London

Library of Congress Control Number: 2014935960

Printed on acid-free paper

Springer is part of Springer Science+Business Media (www.springer.com)

Preface

This book is the result of an international research project on the topic of bribery and the private sector, and specifically on the role of compliance programs. The project began in January 2012 under the auspices of the United Nations Office on Drugs and Crime (UNODC), and involved the participation of an international team of prominent academic institutions, working under the coordination of the International Scientific and Professional Advisory Council of the United Nations (ISPAC), and in cooperation with Eni.

The ambitious goal for the project was to design and make available a unique Anti-Bribery Compliance Model (an "ABC Model"), based on the results of a serious effort to integrate international best practice in anti-corruption policy with a new set of maximum standards drawn from a combination of empirical observation, concrete business experience, theoretical research and comparative analysis of legal systems and case law. The ABC Model published in this book has therefore been designed to serve as the most advanced set of guidelines for multinational companies in complying with anti-corruption laws, while also comprising a new benchmark for use by national legislators—endorsed by international institutions, and consistent with the United Nations Convention against Corruption (UNCAC)—in assessing the liability of corporations in the event of corruption.

The aim of this research is to develop and promote new preventive and enforcement strategies against corruption in the context of partnerships between the public and private sectors. To this end, four academic institutions were selected based on their scientific expertise and record of research in the field of corporate criminal liability: Equipe Internormativités dans l'espace pénal, Collège de France, Paris; Centro Studi "Federico Stella" sulla Giustizia penale e la Politica criminale, Università Cattolica del Sacro Cuore di Milano in partnership with LUISS in Rome; the School of Criminology and Criminal Justice, Northeastern University, Boston; and Instituto de Derecho penal Europeo e Internacional, Universidad de Castilla-la-Mancha. Eni then offered its support for this work, through making a contribution to the study based on its expertise in the field of anti-bribery practices.

This challenging research project has offered the unique opportunity for establishing a wider discussion forum focused on the development of innovative instruments to combat bribery and corruption, whose results were set forth during the Conference on International Strategies Against Corruption held in Courmayeur from the 14th to the 16th of December 2012. The primary outcomes of this lively debate are presented in this volume. Indeed, the present work is divided in five main parts. The first section offers a comprehensive overview of the juridical issues and recent approaches that have led to the conception of the "ABC Model". Without purporting to be exhaustive, it is sufficient here to highlight some of the contributions included therein. The opening article written by Stefano Manacorda illustrates the aims of the research conducted to draft the ABC model and proposes a complete depiction of the initiatives that have been established at international level to fight corruption. Furthermore, Francesco Centonze analyses the model of public-private partnerships in the prevention of this criminal phenomenon presenting an extensive illustration of a "hybrid governance" system and examining the valuable role that incentives play in the field. From the same perspective, the contribution of Adán Nieto Martín concerns the functions that internal investigations, whistle-blowing and cooperation serve in the criminal proceedings carried out to prosecute wrongdoers for perpetrating bribery or corruption. The second and the third part of this work present respectively the ABC model, at which the ensuing passages of this preface are extensively dedicated, and an analysis of the practical functioning of compliance programs with a focus on the oil and gas sector. The reasons behind the selection of such business sector are clearly illustrated in the article written by Stefania Giavazzi, where it is highlighted that it represents one of the most significant as well as at high risk sectors in relation to corruption. The fourth section of the volume offers a detailed outline of the international legal framework currently adopted in this field that, as it is underlined in the work of Juliette Tricot, presents a two-faced nature. On one hand, the number and diversity of norms, actions and initiatives at global or regional levels are commonly presented as a success story; whilst, on the other, the international legal framework on corruption reveals a complex and evolving picture and several doubts have arisen on its effectiveness. The articles contained in this part of the book concern *inter alia*, the anti-bribery self-regulation instruments adopted by corporations, the function assumed in this field by the G20 Anti-Corruption Working Group, the input into the discussion made by the B20 Task Groups on Anti-Corruption and Transparency and the important role assumed by the World Bank and the International Chamber of Commerce in the fight against corruption. Finally, the last section of the volume is entirely dedicated to the presentation of the contributions focused on the legal instruments developed in several domestic jurisdictions in order to combat such a criminal phenomenon. In particular, it is offers an analysis of the US Foreign Corrupt Practices Act 1977, the UK Bribery Act 2010, and the legal framework currently implemented in Italy, Swizerland, France, Canada, Australia and China. Coming back to ABC model, which represents the final output of the research project, it can be defined as an exhaustive, innovative model, drawing on a combination of practical experience and theoretical research, with direct implications for corporate compliance practice.

From a practical perspective, the ABC Model stands out as a forward-looking anti-bribery compliance instrument, incorporating not only a compendium of the most widely recognized examples of best practice, but also a set of new tools, original solutions and clear stances on some of the most controversial issues in the anti-corruption compliance debate. Its most innovative features include: unambiguous regulation of facilitation payments, political contributions and private commercial bribery; the integration of an ad hoc, dedicated Anti-Corruption Unit within the company structure; the provision of compulsory principles and rules for corporate governance, organizational structures, and decision-making processes; detailed provisions and procedures for the implementation and monitoring of the program; and a clear categorization for violations of the program and the concomitant disciplinary sanctions. All of these will contribute to making the ABC Model one new leading standard in anti-corruption compliance for years to come and an adaptable normative framework as well, being ready to adjust to the changing conditions of a quite complex regulative and economic environment as well as to the inputs which grow from an ever flourishing theoretical debate.

However advanced and ingenious any compliance model may be devised, and vitally needed for the prevention of corruption in the private sector and in society as a whole, it must account for the sheer reality that any actor, private or public, is no more living in a Newtonian era, namely expecting to solve or alleviate the problem of corruption in the corporate world single-acting solely on the political, administrative, economic, financial or market environments. Due to the intertwined causal chains and feedbacks which make corruption so complex a phenomenon to deal with at any level, the most suitable strategy must target it through a multiple approach, where private and public sectors act and regulate according to the firm awareness that any lack of integrity, any patent and undue inequality and any conflict of interest growing in one of them is bound to permanently damage the other. As Michael Sandel (Justice 2009) puts it, our societies suffer from a dearth of attention to inequality (and, we could also say, to one of its most powerful preparatory steps: conflict of interest) and one very important reason to worry about this neglectfulness is that the yawning of a huge gap between rich and poor (as confirmed for various European countries by recent data developed from the Gini coefficient, used as a measure of inequality of income or wealth) undermines the solidarity required by democratic citizenship, bringing to the secession by the privileged from public institutions and facilities, and thus to a kind of cultural and human desertification of those institutions that once gathered people together and served as informal schools of civic virtue. In few words: in the (not so) long run, it brings to what has been aptly called the hollowing out of the public realm and, we could add, the hollowing out of any persistent rule of law, as applied to public as well as private actors.

Inequality and conflict of interest being the most powerful breeding grounds of corruption (besides being conversely its further damaging outcomes), targeting them at any level, in the public as well as in the private sector, should be the primary way to break the vicious circles of the ever expanding corrupt flow. A serious crack-down on conflicts of interest appears to be the primary step towards prevention of State capture, the most noxious kind of corruption from which a large part of administrative, political and private corruptions ‘trickle down’. Albeit difficult, this is not a mission impossible, and in any case it is an inescapable one for any anticorruption policy bent on achieving good integrity standards and not merely interested in exhibiting its self-righteousness or in selling junk reforms to easily distracted (or contented) audiences.

In this direction the ABC Model sounds as a quite promising step, being bent on preventing, among many other generative forces of corruption, corporate conflicts of interest (B.2.2) and thus countering the blurring of any divide between public and private sectors, which marks the extreme evolutionary stage of illicit practices—where the same distinction of roles between briber and bribee is dissolved—and the almost irreversible planting of the 'cancer' of corruption in the pith and marrow of society.

Due to the unique methodology adopted for this volume, the ABC Model is immediately applicable, anywhere, and by any company operating at the multinational level—since it stems from the business experience of a prominent multinational corporation and takes advantage of the empirical studies and surveys conducted during the preliminary stage of the project.

At the same time, the ABC Model is an instrument with global reach and multiple potential applications: on one hand, there is scope for implementing its policies in companies from all nations and in all industries, since those policies are based on a comprehensive and transversal risk analysis, are consistent with the UNCAC and are endorsed by UNODC; in addition, the model is intended to serve as a tool of harmonization among States, by establishing a new standard for the legal requirements and judicial criteria in assessing companies' liability in cases of bribery.

The project would not have been possible without the support of many institutions and the dedication of some extraordinary people. As editors, we wish to express our warm gratitude to Dimitri Vlassis, chief of the Corruption and Economic Crime Branch of UNODC, who initially discussed this initiative with Professor Stefano Manacorda, as well as to Camilla Beria di Argentine, Director General of CNPDS/ISPAC, who enthusiastically agreed to undertake this work. The research program, and the present publication, would have never come into being without the invaluable support of Johanna Caputi-Mallmann at the secretariat of CNPDS/ISPAC, who assisted the whole group with great patience and competence. We also owe sincere thanks to Ben Young and his team at Babel Editing for their careful work in reviewing the manuscript and to Costantino Grasso for his assistance in reviewing the whole manuscript. We also wish to thank Eni for its material support, which in our view itself represents an example of best practice in public–private partnerships in the area of anti-corruption policies. The Courmayeur Mont Blanc Foundation and its chairman, Lodovico Passerin d'Entrèves, also deserve special thanks for having hosted and sponsored the International Conference on *International Strategies Against Corruption: Public–Private Partnership and Criminal Policy*.

Last, but not least, we express our appreciation to Springer, our publisher.

19th November 2013

Stefano Manacorda
Francesco Centonze
Gabrio Forti

Contents

Contributors

Ursula Cassani University of Geneva, Geneva, Switzerland

Francesco Centonze CSGP—Università Cattolica del Sacro Cuore, Piacenza, Italy

Francesca Cottone Eni Legal Department, Rome, Italy

Michele De Rosa Eni Legal Department, Rome, Italy

Vincenzo Dell'Osso CSGP—Università Cattolica del Sacro Cuore, Milan, Italy

V-Tsien Fan Northeastern University, Boston, USA

Gabrio Forti Università Cattolica del Sacro Cuore, Milan, Italy

Stefania Giavazzi CSGP—Università Cattolica del Sacro Cuore, Milan, Italy

John R. Heilbrunn Colorado School of Mines, Golden, Colorado, USA

Paul Kett UK Ministry of Justice, London, UK

Stefano Manacorda University of Naples II, Naples, Italy

Massimo Mantovani Eni Legal Department, Rome, Italy

Marta Muñoz de Morales University of Castilla-la-Mancha, Ciudad Real, Spain

Adán Nieto Martín University of Castilla-la-Mancha, Ciudad Real, Spain

Alessia Paludi LUISS Guido Carli University, Rome, Italy

Mark Pieth University of Basel, Faculty of Law, Basel, Switzerland

John Sandage United Nations Office on Drugs and Crime-UNODC, Vienna, Austria

Juliette Tricot University Paris Ouest Nanterre La Défense, Paris, France

François Vincke International Chamber of Commerce-ICC, Paris, France

Dimitri Vlassis United Nations Office on Drugs and Crime-UNODC, Vienna, Austria

Celia Wells University of Bristol, Bristol, United Kingdom

Mattia Zecca LUISS Guido Carli University, Rome, Italy

Stephen Zimmermann The World Bank, Washington, DC, USA

Part I
Moving Towards the ABC Model: A General Overview

Chapter 1
Towards an Anti-Bribery Compliance Model: Methods and Strategies for a "Hybrid Normativity"

Stefano Manacorda

Contents

S. Manacorda (✉)
Dipartimento di Giurisprudenza, University of Naples II, Naples, Italy
e-mail: stefano.manacorda@unina2.it

S. Manacorda et al. (eds.), *Preventing Corporate Corruption*,
DOI 10.1007/978-3-319-04480-4_1,

1.1 Introduction: Meaning and Purposes of an Anti-Bribery Compliance Model

This research project on drafting an anti-bribery compliance model (ABC model), conducted by several academic institutions and supported by the private sector under the auspices of the UN Office for Drugs and Crime, aims to elaborate an appropriate set of tools for tackling bribery to be used in structuring criminal-policy responses, at both the national and the international level.[1]

From a social and from an economic point of view it is widely recognized that corruption is no longer a local matter but a global criminal phenomenon that deeply affects political and administrative structures, as well as the fundamental rights of individuals (Borghi and Meyer-Bisch 1995; Delmas-Marty and Manacorda 2000; Broersma and Nelen 2010). In particular, the UN General Assembly, in Resolution 55/61 of 4 December 2000, recognized that an effective international legal instrument against corruption was needed. On this basis the United Nations Convention against Corruption (UNCAC), the main text designed to fulfill this purpose, was adopted by Resolution 58/4 on 31 October 2003.[2]

Taking into consideration the need to refine existing instruments in order to permit a global fight against corruption, the core of the proposal discussed here can be summarized as: *a unique anti-bribery compliance model which will be functionally linked with an effective corporate corruption liability regime, consistent with the principles set forth in conventional legal texts and in particular with the UNCAC.* With this in mind, the end product of the project will serve as a resource for future harmonization and cooperation initiatives promoted by international organizations working in this area.

Schematically, the proposal is based on *three pillars:*

- The elaboration of a common standard for anti-bribery compliance programs, which will ultimately serve as a model for corporations
- The acknowledgment within domestic criminal law systems of self-regulation as an instrument for assessing the liability of corporations in cases of corruption
- The endorsement of such compliance programs at the international level

[1] This proposal is the result of a wide international research project on the topic Bribery and the Private Sector, and specifically on the role of compliance programs in this area. This project, which started in 2012, involved the participation of four prominent academic institutions under the coordination of ISPAC (the four institutions being: Equipe Internormativités dans l'espace pénal,Collège de France, Paris; Centro "Federico Stella,"sulla giustizia penale e la politica criminale (CSGP), Università Cattolica del Sacro Cuore, Milan, in partnership with LUISS in Rome; the School of Criminology and Criminal Justice, Northeastern University, Boston; Instituto de Derecho penal Europeo e Internacional, Universidad de Castilla-la-Mancha) and in cooperation with Eni.

[2] Conference Proceedings, Courmayeur, 15–17 December 2006, organized by CNPDS/ ISPAC in collaboration with the United Nations Office on Drugs and Crime (UNODC) and the Fondazione Courmayeur (Milan 2007). See also Passas and Vlassis 2007; On the OECD convention, see Pieth et al. 2007 (and in particular Pieth's Introduction to that volume); Leventhal 2008.

The inclusion of the aforesaid compliance rules in a normative text, which should be a source of international law, should on the one hand favor their adoption by multinational enterprises with the aim of crime prevention, and on the other hand bind states to acknowledge the relevance of the compliance model in criminal investigations and proceedings that are conducted in order to evaluate the liability of corporations.

For ease of exposition, the anti-bribery compliance model will here be referred to in abbreviated form: the *ABC model*. This abbreviation will also highlight the *basic* role the model is called upon to play in the self-regulation mechanisms of enterprises and, at the same time, in the establishment of an effective and fair criminal policy that aims to repress corruption as perpetrated by transnational corporations.

1.2 A New Step in International Criminal-Policy Responses Against Corruption?

Within this framework, the first question to be addressed concerns whether we now have a particular opportunity to establish new international responses to corruption and to set stricter rules and regulations for corporations. The response could, at first sight, appear negative: This is a field in which repeated interventions in favor of criminalization have been made in recent decades. Emblematic of this trend is the considerable number of international texts adopted in order to address this phenomenon—a number far in excess of the measures adopted to combat other offenses.

A brief presentation of the initiatives that have been undertaken at the international level in recent decades confirms the idea that the field of responses to corruption has been characterized by an "international inflationary spiral of criminalization" (Pieth and Eigen 1998; Manacorda 1999; Tricot 2001; Mongillo 2012; Terracino 2012).

The *first phase* dates back to the 1970s when the Foreign Corrupt Practices Act (FCPA) was adopted in the USA; but attempts to scale up and implement this strategy internationally—in particular by means of the 1976 adoption by the Organisation for Economic Co-operation and Development (OECD) of the Guidelines for Multinational Enterprises—did not succeed.[3] The reasons for this failure have been thoroughly analyzed in academic debates and are essentially attributable to the persisting and widespread opinion—among economic operators, and not uncommonly among government officials as well—that the payment of bribes in order to obtain contracts in foreign markets is a necessary, if not altogether legitimate, act.

The *second phase* in the establishment of a worldwide set of tools to fight corruption dates back to the 1990s, when a proliferation of international conventions

[3] See, among others, Greanias and Windsor 1982; Deming 2010.

and other texts (recommendations, guidelines, common actions, and so on) gave rise to a very rich but uncoordinated legal framework. It was not until the historic adoption of the OECD Convention on Combating Bribery of Foreign Public Officials in International Business Transactions (1997) that a significant number of acts began being issued from various sources. This convention was grounded on the assumption that bribery is a criminal phenomenon which corrupts and hinders free competition. It was within this complex panorama that the UNCAC, as well as certain other regional[4] and subregional conventions designed to prevent and combat corruption, stand out as being more relevant than the rest. Concerning soft-law legal instruments, one might mention—besides the other initiatives taken by the OECD[5]—the well-known Partnering Against Corruption Initiative (PACI) and the International Chamber of Commerce (ICC) texts.[6]

Almost 20 years after the commencement of this impressive normative wave, the question is whether we are now seeing a *third phase* of anticorruption policies, or whether we can at least agree on the advisability of taking a further step towards the prevention and punishment of bribery perpetrated at the international level. There are various reasons to answer this in the positive.

Some of these reasons are empirical in nature: The real extent of corrupt practices is still obscure, due to the impressive—and probably increasing—darkness which surrounds such acts; indeed, it is precisely the bilateral nature of the corrupt agreement that makes the phenomenon at once secret and endemic. While recent judicial cases have forced corporations to devote enormous amounts of financial resources to fines and settlements, they also provide clear evidence of the resilience

---

[4] See the Inter-American Convention against Corruption, adopted by the Organization of American States on 29 March 1996; the Convention on the Fight against Corruption involving Officials of the European Communities or Officials of Member States of the European Union, adopted by the Council of the European Union on 26 May 1997; the Convention on Combating Bribery of Foreign Public Officials in International Business Transactions, adopted by the Organisation for Economic Cooperation and Development on 21 November 1997; the Criminal Law Convention on Corruption, adopted by the Committee of Ministers of the Council of Europe on 27 January 1999; the Civil Law Convention on Corruption, adopted by the Committee of Ministers of the Council of Europe on 4 November 1999; the African Union Convention on Preventing and Combating Corruption, adopted by the Heads of State and Government of the African Union on 12 July 2003; and the Framework Decision 2003/568/JHA of 22 July 2003 on combating corruption in the private sector.

[5] Concerning the OECD see: Guidelines for Multinational Enterprises (1976, revised in 2011); Recommendation on Improving Ethical Conduct in the Public Service (1998); Recommendation for Managing Conflict of Interest in the Public Service (2003); Recommendation on Bribery and Export Credits (2006); Recommendation on Enhancing Integrity in Public Procurement (2008); Recommendation for Further Combating Bribery of Foreign Public Officials in International Business Transactions (2009); Recommendation on Tax Measures for Further Combating Bribery of Foreign Public Officials in International Business Transactions (2009); Due Diligence Guidance for Responsible Supply Chains of Minerals from Conflict-Affected and High-Risk Areas (2011).

[6] Concerning the ICC see: Fighting Corruption: A Corporate Practices Manual (1999, revised in 2003); Combating Extortion and Bribery: Rules of Conduct and Recommendations (2005); ICC Guidelines on Whistleblowing (2008); Guidelines on Agents, Intermediaries, and Other Third Parties (2010); Rules on Combating Corruption (as revised in 2011): Anti-corruption Clause (2012).

and diffuseness of the phenomenon. Moreover, the economic and social costs of corruption (Rose-Ackerman 1999; Robinson 1998; Kimberly 1997; Moody-Stuart 1997; Ward 1989) make it increasingly unacceptable for civil society and corporations alike, particularly during the post-2008 financial crisis (Button 2011).

Notwithstanding the proliferation of texts, corruption represents a field in which punitive responses have demonstrated the highest levels of inefficacy. As already mentioned, dozens of documents have been adopted in the last 20 years at both the global and the regional level. But the different conventions are neither the expression of a unified philosophy nor do they combine into a systematic structure. Even the UNCAC, the sole text with the potential to assume the role of a universally accepted norm, does not have the will to impose itself hierarchically on all other normative texts. Moreover, the transposition of complex and heterogeneous normative texts has been realized slowly, and still reveals persistent differences from a comparative point of view. Even where the process of implementation has been completed, national criminal law responses against bribery have not significantly evolved—with the exception of the area of transnational corruption, and rather more indirectly by means of refining notions of seizure and the progressive establishment of criminal corporate liability.

These weaknesses in the existing legal framework, combined with new emerging risks, call for a renewed effort to identify appropriate and effective criminal-policy strategies. Improving the legal tools adopted in the international sphere to counter bribery of national and foreign officials, as perpetrated by individuals acting on behalf of corporations, should be one of the main objectives of legal scholars, private-sector actors, and public organizations alike.

1.3 The Current Picture: An "Integrated Criminal Policy" Against Corruption

1.3.1 Hard-Law Versus Soft-Law Sources

During recent decades, the kinds of corrupt practices to which the above-mentioned complex network of international texts relate have taken center stage in the elaboration of advanced normative models. The efforts to tackle such corruption have become the favored venue for the development of an integrated criminal policy (*gesamte Strafrechtwissenschaft*, following the traditional formula: see von Liszt 1883), in which recourse is made to several types of remedy which are *complementary* to one another. In a very schematic way, the following conceptual pairings can be seen within current criminal policy: (a) hard law and soft law, (b) public and private initiatives, (c) preventive and punitive dimensions.

In relation to the first aspect, which concerns the nature of the legal sources, we may note the significant heterogeneity of the international rules currently in force. As we have already seen, the normative texts framed over the last 20 years sometimes have a binding nature (*hard law*), while on other occasions—and more innovatively—they have a merely exhortative nature (*soft law*). Hard law constitutes the pillar on which criminalization is traditionally based, and is conceived as the imposition of mandatory bounds (from the international system to states; from states to individuals); soft law, conversely, has begun to penetrate into crime-fighting strategies only recently, and its efficacy is derived more from its persuasive force.[7]

International law which has been elaborated for tackling the phenomena of corruption shows a strong divergence on this point: mostly, it has recourse to binding instruments. Among the highest-level mandatory measures, one finds certain international conventions that establish obligations on states not only to adopt preventive and repressive measures, but also to set up review mechanisms designed to constantly monitor the development of domestic legislation and the effective implementation of the convention, along with recourse to some forms of sanction in case of failure to comply with conventional rules.[8]

There are also mechanisms other than peer review which are used to monitor and ensure compliance with internationally agreed policies: These include judicial proceedings whose final outcomes, unlike peer review, are issued by a superior authority and are legally binding; fact-finding missions that are carried out by independent bodies, such as commissions of experts appointed by international organizations, in order to conduct specific investigations on-site; and reporting and data collection, which comprises an obligation to periodically report to an independent body whose duty it is to analyze the submitted data.

1.3.1.1 Review Mechanisms

It is well known that the OECD convention procedures had established their primacy in the field of review mechanisms, and were succeeded a few years later by the analogous mechanism provided by the UNCAC. Within this framework, *peer review* can be defined as the systematic scrutiny and evaluation of the performance of a state by other states, with the ultimate goal of helping the reviewed state to comply with established standards and principles (Pagani 2002).

The examination is conducted on a non-adversarial basis, and it relies heavily on mutual trust among the states involved in the review. The effectiveness of peer

[7] See Hachez et al. 2013, and in particular, Bernardi's essay "Réflexions sur les rapports entre droit pénal et soft-law" in that volume.

[8] At the regional level, there are currently several different mechanisms to review the implementation of anticorruption treaties. The first anticorruption follow-up mechanism was established by the OECD convention: In this framework, country monitoring is carried out by the OECD Working Group on Bribery (WGB). The Council of Europe's anticorruption conventions are monitored by the Group of States against Corruption (GRECO). Mechanisms for follow-up on implementation of the IACAC, called MESICIC, and other peer-review mechanisms of the African Union Convention, and the SADC Protocol (e.g., the Advisory Board on Corruption and APRM), have recently been established. See Terracino 2012, pp. 297–324.

review relies on "peer pressure," that is the influence exerted over the state that is under scrutiny by the peers during the review.

The OECD Peer-Review Monitoring System

Article 12 of the OECD Convention on Combating Bribery of Foreign Public Officials in International Business Transactions provides that:

The Parties shall co-operate in carrying out a programme of systematic follow-up to monitor and promote the full implementation of this Convention. Unless otherwise decided by consensus of the Parties, this shall be done in the framework of the OECD Working Group on Bribery in International Business Transactions.

By means of this provision, an apparently rigorous system of multilateral surveillance has thus been established to foster the effectiveness of the convention and its related instruments. The system was developed drawing on experiences gained through OECD accession procedures, UN human rights audits, and the mutual evaluation procedures of the OECD's Financial Action Task Force. The peer-review monitoring system is conducted in three phases. The first phase, which includes elements of both self and mutual evaluation, is dedicated to the evaluation of the legal texts adopted by member states in order to implement the OECD Anti-Bribery Convention and, in particular, to verify whether the legal measures adopted by the state meet the standards set by the convention. During the second phase, which also includes elements of both self and mutual evaluation, the Working Group on Bribery studies the structures put in place to enforce the laws and rules implementing the convention and assesses their application in practice. The third phase consists in evaluating the progress made by parties on weaknesses identified during the second phase by means of a constant cycle of peer review that involves systematic on-site visits and a more focused assessment mechanism that includes the participation of more experienced prosecutors on country review teams and encourages civil society participation. At the end of each phase the working group adopts a report on country performance that includes possible recommendations.

Although there is no other international organization in which the practice of peer review has been so extensively developed as the OECD, this technique is also used by other intergovernmental organizations and within different international programs. For instance, peer review has also been developed within the World Trade Organization under the Trade Policy Review Mechanism. Moreover, in the European Union framework, peer review is used in relation to national labor market policies in order to identify good practices and assess their transferability. In the field of corruption, the UNCAC has more recently introduced a similar mechanism.

The Mechanism for the Review of Implementation of the United Nations Convention against Corruption[9]

The Conference of the States Parties to the United Nations Convention against Corruption, recalling Article 63(1) of the convention, which provides that the aforesaid conference has been established in order to "improve the capacity of and cooperation between States Parties to achieve the objectives set forth in this Convention and to promote and review its implementation," and Article 63(7), which provides that: "the Conference of the States Parties shall

[9] Vlassis 2012; Schultz 2010. Norway submitted an amendment in order to develop a much more rigorous monitoring mechanism and set out innovative methods for addressing noncompliance with the Convention, including positive (targeted technical assistance) and negative (suspension of the state party from the Convention) measures. However, this proposal was not accepted. See Webb 2005.

establish, if it deems it necessary, any appropriate mechanism or body to assist in the effective implementation of the Convention," adopted, during its third session held in Doha (Qatar) in November 2009, Resolution 3/1 providing the Mechanism for the Review of Implementation of the UNCAC. In particular, the conference has developed the review mechanism on a non-adversarial and non-punitive basis providing that each State party shall be reviewed by two other States parties, one of which shall be from the same geographical region as the State under review and have a similar legal system: Under the guiding principles it is provided that the mechanism, inter alia, shall be: "transparent, efficient, non-intrusive, inclusive and impartial; not produce any form of ranking; non-adversarial and non-punitive; of a technical nature" and it "shall not serve as an instrument for interfering in the domestic affairs of States parties but shall respect the principles of equality and sovereignty." The review will be conducted by governmental experts appointed by each State party. At the final stage of the country review process the governmental experts shall prepare a country review report, which shall identify successes, good practices, and challenges and make observations for the further implementation of the convention. The review mechanism provides that each review phase shall be composed of two review cycles of 5 years each and that ordinarily the review of all states that are parties at the start of a review cycle should be completed before a new review cycle begins. The first cycle will cover Chap. III and IV (criminalization/law enforcement, and international cooperation), while the second will cover Chap. II and V (preventive measures and asset recovery). As of 4 October 2012, 157 countries are involved in the review mechanism either as countries under review or as reviewing countries. Notwithstanding that it is still in its embryonic stage, the review mechanism has already enhanced the ability of the international community to assess progress in implementation of the convention and created a framework in which states are able to cooperate in sharing their best practices and identifying thematic areas for further actions. Moreover, the review process could also have an indirect positive impact within the state under review. However, the monitoring mechanism has some weakness: The reports need only be submitted every 5 years and there is no mention of on-site visits or other means of verifying the accuracy of the country reports; the role of civil society is weak; and no methods for effectively addressing noncompliance with the convention have been established.

1.3.1.2 Guidelines

On the opposite side of the hierarchical scale of norms, one finds a wide range of instruments which are more flexible and non-compulsive, and which we can generically designate as *soft law*. Although criminal justice systems are conceived of as carrying imperative force, the need to "level the playing field" has given an increasing role to soft-law instruments in the field of anticorruption (Pieth and Aiolfi 2003). Arguably, soft law can lack the clarity and precision that is needed to provide a predictable and reliable framework for action; however, it has other positive effects. Recently, legal doctrine has recognized some of the main positive aspects of the recourse to soft law at the international level:

> The greater flexibility of non-binding legal instruments allows for renegotiation or modification of agreements as circumstances change.... Soft law, given its simplicity and speed might be motivated by the desire to avoid formal and visible pledges by states, to avoid ratification or other cumbersome domestic procedures (in case of amendments, etc.), or to induce even the least committed states to participate.... In principle, soft law permits the Participation of all interested parties in the process of transnational law-making. Increased openness allows

> for more active participation of non-state actors, promotes transparency, enhances agenda setting, and facilitates the diffusion of knowledge. (Trubek et al. 2005, p. 12)

The OECD Guidelines for Multinational Enterprises, revised in 2011 and complementing the OECD convention are clear examples of such an approach.[10]

The OECD Guidelines for Multinational Enterprises

In June 1976, the OECD adopted the Declaration on International Investment and Multinational Enterprises. The declaration provides for three "complementary and inter-connected" statements of policy with respect to voluntary, nonbinding Guidelines for Multinational Enterprises and it also includes agreements on consultation procedures and periodic review by the member countries. The guidelines are divided into seven specific sections, covering general business policies, disclosure of information, competition, financing, taxation, employment and industrial relations, and science and technology. The guidelines were updated in 2011 for the fifth time since they were first adopted. The guidelines are defined as far-reaching recommendations addressed by governments to multinational enterprises operating in or from adhering countries. The aim of the guidelines is to promote economic, social, and environmental progress by establishing concepts and principles for responsible business conduct that could aid to:

Ensure that the operation of [multinational enterprises] is in harmony with government policies, to strengthen the basis of mutual confidence between enterprises and the societies in which they operate, to help improve the foreign investment climate and to enhance the contribution to sustainable development made by multinational enterprises. (Preface, para. 1)

While the guidelines' recommendations are voluntary for companies, adhering governments are committed to promoting them among multinational enterprises that operate in or from their territories. The guidelines incorporate a broad range of influences that may not be specifically acknowledged in the text and commentaries. In particular, in relation to corruption, the guidelines have been influenced by many international instruments such as, inter alia, the United Nations Convention against Corruption, the OECD anticorruption instruments, the African Union Convention on Preventing and Combating Corruption, and the reports issued by the International Chamber of Commerce. Section no. 6 of the guidelines deals with combating bribery and offers six recommendations for enterprises that share such an aim. As a single example, Section no. 6 provides that enterprises should: "Ensure that remuneration of agents is appropriate and for legitimate services only; enhance the transparency of their activities in the fight against bribery and extortion; promote employee awareness of and compliance with company policies on such criminal conducts; not make illegal contributions to candidates for public office or to political parties or to other political organisations."

1.3.2 Public Versus Private Initiatives

A second element that contributes to defining international anticorruption strategies is the recourse to *public and private initiatives*. Although such initiatives have traditionally been encapsulated in anticorruption policies, there is real scope for innovative practice in engaging with the private sector (Peters et al. 2009). This is manifest in Article 12 of the UNCAC (private sector), stating that:

> 1. Each State Party shall take measures, in accordance with the fundamental principles of its domestic law, to prevent corruption involving the private sector, enhance account-

[10] Plaine 1977; Santner 2011. For a critical point of view see Hägg 1984.

ing and auditing standards in the private sector and, where appropriate, provide effective, proportionate and dissuasive civil, administrative or criminal penalties for failure to comply with such measures. 2. Measures to achieve these ends may include, inter alia: (a) Promoting cooperation between law enforcement agencies and relevant private entities; (b) *Promoting the development of standards and procedures designed to safeguard the integrity of relevant private entities*, including *codes of conduct* for the correct, honourable and proper performance of the activities of business and all relevant professions and the prevention of conflicts of interest, and for the promotion of the use of good commercial practices among businesses and in the contractual relations of businesses with the State....

In the field of criminal law, the hetero-regulation that has been established at international level and has been implemented by states, has traditionally played a predominant role (Pieth 2007, 2012; see also Pieth and Aiolfi 2003). Private- or self-regulation is adopted by large corporations or representatives of enterprises for which the same rules are designed, and it is becoming increasingly widespread, in part as a response to calls made at the international level by the Global Compact, the World Economic Forum, and the B20/G20. All these international initiatives establish a clear set of markers demonstrating that commercial bribery is no longer seen as acceptable and, at the same time, that the task of resolving the problem falls as much to companies as it does to governments.

The UN Global Compact

Launched in July 2000, the UN Global Compact is a strategic policy initiative for businesses that are committed to aligning their operations and strategies with ten universally accepted principles in the areas of human rights, labor, environment, and anticorruption. With more than 8,500 signatories in over 135 countries, the UN Global Compact is the world's largest voluntary corporate sustainability initiative.[11] The UN Global Compact is not a regulatory instrument, but rather a voluntary initiative that relies on public accountability, transparency, and disclosure to complement regulation and to provide a space for innovation and collective action. The program could be defined as at once global and local, private and public, voluntary yet accountable. Indeed, it requires a commitment signed by the company's chief executive, and endorsed by the highest-level governance body. Under the Corporate Commitment, the company is expected to fulfill various duties, for instance: making the UN Global Compact and its principles an integral part of business strategy, day-to-day operations, and organizational culture; or integrating in the company's annual report a description of the ways in which the program has been implemented. Moreover, upon joining the UN Global Compact, companies are required to make a regular annual contribution to support the work of the UN Global Compact office. Finally, the Global Compact incorporates a transparency and accountability policy known as the Communication on Progress (COP). The annual posting of a COP is an important demonstration of a participant's commitment to the program and its principles. Participating companies are required to follow this policy as a commitment to transparency, and disclosure is critical to the success of the initiative. Failure to communicate will result in a change in participant status and possible expulsion. Concerning the 10th Principle against Corruption, during the 7th Meeting of the Global Compact Working Group, the Global Compact and UN Office on Drugs and Crime (UNODC) jointly launched a new web-based e-learning tool on anticorruption.

[11] On the origins of the Global Compact, see McIntosh et al. 2003. On the fact that the new emphasis on drafting international law against corrupt practices has triggered a significant response by multinational companies, see Cockcroft 2010.

Moreover, during the 11th meeting of the Global Compact Working Group participants discussed the business perspective on how to integrate good governance and anticorruption into the post-2015 Development Agenda. Therefore, a call to action statement was issued urging governments to promote anticorruption measures and implement related policies to establish systems of good governance.

The Partnering Against Corruption Initiative (PACI)
In 2004, the World Economic Forum developed the PACI. The initiative asks business leaders to sign a set of principles, thereby committing to a zero tolerance policy towards bribery and corruption and agreeing to establish an internal anticorruption program. PACI Members are companies that support the PACI Principles for Countering Bribery, derived from Transparency International's Business Principles for Countering Bribery. Historically focused on improving compliance practices, PACI has been devoting growing efforts to fostering a high-level dialogue between business and governments on key corruption challenges. The work of PACI is guided by two objectives: to help set the global anticorruption agenda at a strategic policy level, and to drive change in key markets through targeted initiatives and partnerships. PACI's Good Practice Guidelines were issued in January 2013. These guidelines are designed to help organizations conduct third-party due diligence with a view to mitigating the risk of becoming involved in corruption through their third parties (e.g., agents, suppliers, joint-ventures).

The Business 20
The Business 20 (B20) is an event which takes place in conjunction with the G20 summit. The purpose of this meeting is to create a forum where the international business community may convey its opinion on the most relevant and current issues. In particular, this aim is achieved by developing recommendations and issuing relevant commitments from business leaders and business organizations. The B20 summit is currently focused upon 12 topics, which are crucial to the business community and which correspond with the priorities for the G20. The presidents of the business confederations of the G20 countries, as well as 120 CEOs and chairmen from a number of global companies, are gathered in 12 working groups which are cochaired by a company CEO and a president of a business organization. These teams work together in order to elaborate concrete recommendations that are then presented to heads of state and government to be taken into account in the G20 final conclusions. The involvement of such a rich panel of prominent business leaders—across regions and industries—provides adequate expertise and legitimacy to express views of the business community as a whole.
In relation to corruption, in 2013 the Task Force on Improving Transparency and Anti-corruption agreed to concentrate on issues of serious concern to the business community, for which businesses could, and indeed should, be part of the solution. The recommendations elaborated by the working group were restricted to two major concerns: (1) how business can combat and resist the solicitation of bribes, especially when bidding in public tenders; and (2) the ability, as companies, to guarantee the highest standards of integrity of their own employees, and to build the capacity of dealers, distributors, and suppliers to aspire to similar standards.
The recent work of the B20 summit has highlighted that the new method to promote transparency and counter corruption requires collective action, that is, a complex, multifaceted, cross-sector alliance aimed at reducing corruption in the markets. Such an action consists in the adoption of various measures ranging from codes of conduct between companies in particular industries to integrity pacts between companies and governments around public tenders.

1.3.3 Preventive Versus Punitive Measures

Corruption has become an area in which it is appropriate to test forms of intervention that are complementary or alternative to criminalization. This is a result of the paradox that within this field there is an abundance of punitive measures, but these have demonstrated a high level of inefficacy. The alternative modes of intervention are characterized by a combination of punitive and preventive measures,[12] and also include responses of a civil and administrative nature which are aimed at reparation and prevention. Such rules have inspired recent amendments to the domestic legislation of some states that have demonstrated higher levels of sensitivity towards the adoption of crime-prevention strategies.

1.3.3.1 Civil Remedies

Certain provisions of the UNCAC, as well as the Council of Europe Civil Law Convention on Corruption and the ICC Anti-corruption Clause, have established civil remedies in order to fight corruption.

The Civil Law Convention on Corruption[13]

Adopted within the Council of Europe, the Civil Law Convention on Corruption represents the first attempt to define common international rules in the field of civil law and corruption. As provided by Article 1, the convention requires that each contracting party "Shall provide in its internal law for effective remedies for persons who have suffered damage as a result of acts of corruption, to enable them to defend their rights and interests, including the possibility of obtaining compensation for damage."

For instance, the convention requires the parties to establish in their domestic law: appropriate measures to allow persons who have suffered damage as a result of corruption to claim compensation for such damage (Articles 3 and 4); appropriate procedures to allow persons who have suffered damage as a result of an act of corruption perpetrated by a public official in the exercise of their functions to claim for compensation from the state (Article 5); the possibility for all parties to a contract whose consent has been undermined by an act of corruption to be able to apply to the court for the contract to be declared void (Article 8); and appropriate protection of whistle-blowers (Article 9). As provided by Article 14, the Group of States against Corruption (GRECO) will monitor the implementation of the convention by the parties.

---

[12] See, among others, Forti 1997; Palazzo 2011.

[13] The Civil Law Convention on Corruption (CETS No. 174) was opened for signature in Strasbourg on 4 November 1999 and entered into force on 1 November 2003 after 14 ratifications. As stated by the explanatory report to the draft of the Civil Law Convention on Corruption issued on 9 July 1999 by the GMC: "the Council of Europe became strongly interested in the international fight against corruption because of the obvious threat corruption poses to the basic principles this Organisation stands for: the rule of law, the stability of democratic institutions, human rights and social and economic progress."

The ICC Anti-corruption Clause

The International Chamber of Commerce (ICC) is a very active body in the field of combating corruption. In 1977, the ICC published the first edition of the ICC Rules of Conduct to Combat Extortion and Bribery, which contained strong measures to end both bribery and extortion. These rules have been updated regularly since then and continue to be an important tool for fighting corruption today. Another relevant anticorruption tool developed by the ICC is the ICC Anti-corruption Clause. The clause provides a contractual basis for parties to commit to complying with ICC's voluntary Rules on Combating Corruption or to implement a corporate anticorruption compliance program. It is intended to apply to any contract that incorporates it either by reference or in full. The general aim of the clause is to provide parties with a contractual provision that will reassure them about the integrity of their counterparts during the term of the contract. Therefore, the clause represents a civil law tool whose aim is to support the anticorruption compliance programs in creating something we can define as *contractual compliance*. In practice, if a party becomes aware that the other party has committed any breach of the clause, it will notify the other party accordingly. A party invoking corruption must bring evidence that corruption is at stake. Concerning the degree of evidence required, it will be sufficient to prove that suspicions of corruption are not invoked in a vexatious or otherwise unjustified manner. In order to ensure to the highest degree possible the continuity of a contract, the allegedly noncomplying party will be allowed to remedy the situation to the maximum extent possible. The nature and quantity of the remedial measures required of the party subject to the allegation will depend on the circumstances of the case in question (e.g., on the gravity of the infringement). Necessary remedial action might include providing cooperation in evidentiary action in conducting an examination or calling for an external audit of the incident, issuing warnings, reorganizing work, terminating subcontracts, or correcting the detrimental economic effect on the other party, e.g., adjusting the amount of the price of the contract. Where a remedy is not or cannot be taken, the party allegedly in breach may invoke a defense by proving that it had, by the time the evidence of breach had arisen, put into place adequate anticorruption preventive measures. If the party allegedly infringing the provisions does not remedy the situation within a reasonable period of time and no defense of preventive measures is effectively invoked, the other party will have the right, at its discretion, to suspend the contract or terminate it. Parties refer all disputes related to the contractual consequences of any alleged noncompliance with the clause to the entity provided for in the dispute resolution provisions of the contract, such as an arbitral tribunal.

1.3.3.2 Administrative and Criminal Measures

The purpose of the UNCAC is to promote and strengthen measures to combat corruption. Chap. II "mandates States Parties to develop a coordinated approach to corruption, which includes developing and maintaining effective policies for dealing with corruption and for implementing the various measures identified in it," and Chap. III "requires States Parties either to 'adopt' or to 'consider adopting' a range of criminal offences" (Nicholls et al. 2011, p. 392, 420).

The United Nation Convention against Corruption

In its 8 chapters and 71 articles, the UNCAC obliges the states parties to implement a wide and detailed range of anticorruption measures through their laws, institutions, and practices. The UNCAC is a very active body in the field of combating corruption, and can be defined as the most wide-ranging instrument to date that covers the three major aspects of fighting corruption: prevention, criminalization, and international cooperation and asset recovery.

Chapter II of the convention (from Article 5 to 14) is entirely dedicated to preventive measures. As a matter of fact, of all existing anticorruption conventions, the UNCAC has the most extensive provisions on preventive measures in the public and private sectors. Indeed, the convention recognizes that preventive measures, such as institutional and systemic barriers, represent a crucial factor in fighting corruption (see Larson 2011). Article 5 (1) introduces Chap. II of the convention, requiring states to: "Develop and implement or maintain effective, coordinated anticorruption policies that promote the participation of society and reflect the principles of the rule of law, proper management of public affairs and public property, integrity, transparency and accountability." The convention then provides a wide range of measures which aim to enact and implement legislation and administrative regulations that are capable of preventing corrupt practices. Such a list of preventive measures includes, inter alia, the introduction of ombudsman systems, whistle-blower protection laws, transparent rules of procurement and accounting, freedom-of-information laws, auditing and internal-control requirements for public and private entities, and anti-money-laundering regimes. Moreover, the convention expressly recognizes the importance of the role that civil society plays in preventing corruption; in relation to that Article 13 provides that "Each State Party shall take appropriate measures…to promote the active participation of individuals and groups outside the public sector, such as civil society, non-governmental organisations and community-based organisations, in the prevention of and the fight against corruption." In addition, in accordance with Article 6 of the convention, anticorruption oversight bodies should be established. These institutions should play a relevant part in the development or review of policy guidelines, in a combined effort with agencies and civil society.

1.4 One Step Further: The ABC Model as "Normative Hybridization"

Given this framework, the specific proposal arising from the present research is to elaborate a normative mechanism which effects an interpenetration of different areas and strategies of intervention, thereby overcoming the traditional opposing alternatives.

The key element to be taken into account is that macro-corruption cannot effectively be tackled without recourse to a certain form of *liability of legal entities*. Such a proposal could benefit from the increasing orientation of international law towards the repression of crimes perpetrated by multinational enterprises, and particularly by the recent developments aiming at making them liable for any gross violations of human rights (Kamminga and Zia-Zarifi 2000; Jagers 2002; Alston 2005; Clapham 2006; De Schutter 2006; Zerk 2006; Koebele 2009; Huisman 2010; Martin-Chenut 2013). Today, the focus is essentially on gross violations of human rights (some of which could be defined as international crimes) committed by corporations in critical zones. This criminal behavior is related, in particular, to certain forms of cooperation between multinational corporations and certain military and dictatorial regimes. Such illicit cooperation usually consists of, on the one hand, drawing economic advantage from acts of state violence, and, on the other, facilitating the international crimes committed by such regimes by supplying the material tools necessary to perpetrate the abuses, or even by directly participating in repression. The sanctions adopted by the various legal systems in reaction to such phenomena are very different. One possible approach is that adopted by US district courts, which is grounded on the Alien Tort Claims Act (e.g., the cases *Unocal, Shell, Chevron, South African Apartheid,* and *Chiquita Brands International*).

Although the ABC model is directed at multinational corporations, which are the main actors in the mechanisms of corruption, it is intended to create an innovative corruption-fighting strategy which is characterized by a combined methodological approach. In brief, the underlying idea is that an integrated policy grounded on mere complementarity among different legal tools should be superseded by a holistic approach giving rise to a mechanism of "normative hybridization," in which prevention and punishment, hetero-regulation and self-regulation, public and private initiatives are all merged together in a sole legal instrument. The term "hybridization" is used, although in a different sense, by a number of scholars working on legal pluralism. (See particularly Delmas-Marty (2003, p. 13, 2009, p. 164). See also Trubek et al. 2005). As such, the integration of tools for addressing corruption should be replaced by a more consistent policy based around the central animating concept of *hybridization.*

From a conceptual point of view, this proposal is closely linked with the development of legal theories concerning the emerging role of flexible norms besides the more classical "rigid" ones (Thibierge 2009; Hachez et al. 2013), a phenomenon that takes place even in the field of criminal law, traditionally considered to be one of the most imperative areas of law. The ABC model—the specific proposal hereby presented—should thus be suited to encapsulate different modalities of intervention against corruption and their corresponding philosophies, which so far have been disjointed. It is reasonable to expect that such a development of criminal-policy strategies of intervention could lead to an increase in the efficacy of anticorruption measures.

As a consequence of hybrid normativity, *all of the features of the anticorruption strategies analyzed in the sections above should be reflected in the ABC model in a combined way*. It is an intrinsic feature of the proposed model that it is able to transcend the traditional *gaps* between: hetero-regulation and self-regulation (allowing partnership, in its various forms, between private and public initiatives in the drafting, enforcing, and controlling phases); hard law and soft law (providing a double level of implementation, which binds states and urges corporations to comply with international standards); and prevention and punishment (providing a preventive system that also has punitive effects for the accused company in the enforcement phase).

1.4.1 Combining Hetero-Regulation and Self-Regulation

The elaboration of a model aimed at combining hetero-regulation and self-regulation constitutes the first evolutionary step in this strategy for fighting corruption. Such a development imposes a new archetype of partnership between public and private sectors, in which regulations are not imposed directly on enterprises from the top (*top-down approach*), but are elaborated by corporations themselves (*bottom-up approach*).

Nevertheless, if the starting point in the elaboration of an adequate anticorruption model is taken to be the analysis of the framework of rules arising from corporations themselves, considered as a typical outcome of self-regulation, the rules that should eventually be applied to multinational corporations must not constitute a mere synthesis of the existing self-regulations, but must represent something more, reflecting the choices of criminal policy made by public authorities.

The risks arising from assigning such a role to corporations, and particularly to multinationals, must not be underestimated. Large private companies may be able to influence the elaboration of the norms, especially through international initiatives which are solicited by private or public institutions. The proposed method would assure a better final result, however, since corporations would not be left alone in deciding the final contents of the norm.

Therefore, the process of establishing effective and innovative anticorruption regulation requires that the relationship between public and private sectors cannot be seen in terms of mere contrast, and not even in terms of complementariness, but has to be the result of an *interaction* between them. This interaction brings the relationship between public and private sectors into balance by enhancing collaboration and discouraging conflict. This interaction is devised to contribute to a practical and also theoretical elaboration of criminal-policy strategies for fighting corruption.

From this point of view, the ABC model represents the technical expression of this new methodology because it has been conceived via considering, in a dynamic way, the organizational reality of multinational enterprises (related to the organization both of single corporations and the wider business sectors in which they operate), without having recourse to top-down control in search of an effective and global strategy against corruption.

Such a mechanism—which works according to a "circular" logic, binding the ascending phase (from private to public) to the descending phase (from public to private)—might be designed to operate over time by means of "normative valves for interaction," consisting, for instance, of committees devoted to regularly updating the model.

1.4.2 Integrating Hard Law and Soft Law

In the descending phase (the *top-down approach*), the implementation of the model will be realized through a normative hybridization between *hard law* and *soft law*. Framing a criminal policy which can effectively combat corruption calls for innovative reconsideration of the relationship between these two approaches to law. Hard law and soft law must merge, by means of normative hybridization, into a single legal instrument, which is, on the one hand, capable of constituting a binding text for states when adopting criminal law measures and, on the other, capable of being used autonomously by corporations as a point of reference in tailoring their anticorruption compliance models.

A suitable tool for such an initiative will be a legal instrument of international origin and conventional nature, which is designed both to bind states and, at the same time, to urge multinational enterprises to develop internal anticorruption rules. The ABC model has thus been conceived to function as a double-edged weapon: With respect to economic entities, the model would limit itself to proposing a compliance scheme that corporations will be free to adopt if they wish (albeit under the pressure of incentives); in relation to states, however, the model should be binding, in order to guarantee its correct and effective adoption within their domestic criminal law systems.

1.4.3 Merging Preventive and Punitive Measures

Finally, the relationship between prevention and punishment should be revised. In the logic of subsidiarity and *extrema ratio*, the recourse to criminal law instruments appears justified only where the available non-criminal sanctions are inadequate to effectively safeguard protected values. Concerning the function of punishment, the recourse to criminal sanctions by a legislator is justified only in so far as their general preventative purpose, and especially its positive component, is fulfilled—namely, the capacity to discourage other multinational corporations from committing crimes by defining both protected values and prohibited behaviors.

Following the example set by those national legal systems which have adopted a mechanism for corporate liability grounded on the lack of organizational schemes, we here propose a sort of reversal of levels: from punishment with preventative effects to *prevention with punitive effects*. The adoption of compliance programs can mitigate sanctions and even exempt a corporation from criminal liability, and so their influence extends into the penal field.

In conclusion, the ABC model is designed to become the proper tool for a hybrid criminal policy and for a global strategy in the fight against bribery, overcoming the difficulties arising from the fragmentation of the existing legal framework. The initial intuition of the research group has therefore been vindicated, having revealed a useful instrument for breaking through the impasse that currently characterizes the fight against corruption. In order to achieve a successful result, *normative hybridization must be pursued at every single phase: in drafting the compliance, in implementing it, and finally in enforcing it.*

1.5 Drafting the ABC Model: Coordinated Self-Regulation

In starting with the drafting process, it is necessary to proceed via a preliminary analysis of the preventive measures that have been already set up by multinational enterprises. Indeed, an assessment of previous experiences is a necessary precursor to the identification of the best actions to develop subsequently.[14] This perspective forms part of the *bottom-up approach*: It brings in corporations to participate in the identification of *best practices* and objectives for fighting corruption.

Major corporations have already taken significant steps in the direction of adopting and implementing effective anti-bribery self-regulation and measures, in particular through auditing and specialized control units. This development has occurred primarily in the last 10 years, as a result of judicial charges of corruption and as a way to reduce the risks and costs of criminal administrative liability. The effectiveness of this exercise depends on a corporation's capacity to adopt and implement self-regulation codes, establishing both prohibitions and procedures. Compliance programs can make a substantial contribution to the prevention of bribery by: mapping the risk incurred by corporations, defining prohibited behaviors and the concomitant obligations for managers and employees, establishing rules for internal accounting and external relations, setting alerting and reporting procedures, providing internal monitoring and control, and establishing disciplinary sanctions or other responses in case of violations.

The methodological paradigm which induced the research group to favor such a research procedure is represented by a survey conducted under the auspices of the UNODC on Global Fortune 500 companies that was able to identify general rules of conduct against bribery.

Anticorruption policies and measures of Fortune Global 500[15]

> This compendium, compiled by UNODC and PricewaterhouseCoopers, looks at what companies in the Fortune 500 Global Index (2008) are doing to fight corruption. It highlights a range of measures, and different approaches. While there is no one-size-fits-all, businesses should not go below international standards contained in the United Nations Convention against Corruption. For example, a facilitation payment is simply another term for a bribe, yet some companies allow them up to certain threshold or under certain circumstances—or even consider them tax deductible. Some companies provide whistleblowers full anonymity, others promise that such employees will not be exposed to retaliation. Greater harmonization is needed, in line with international standards, to protect businesses and their employees against corruption. Having collected existing practices, the next step is to highlight good practices and have them widely applied. That means that leaders and managers must set the tone from the top by enforcing a zero-tolerance policy, and checks and balances must be put in place to strengthen integrity and minimize wrong-doing. The Third session of the Conference of the States Parties to the UN anticorruption Convention, to be held in Doha in November 2009, is a golden opportunity to strengthen corporate responsibility in line with the world's only universal anti-corruption instrument. The private sector has a lot to lose from corruption, and has considerable leverage to stop it. Based on the experience collected in this report, companies should be in a better position to do their part to say "NO" to corruption.

---

[14] "In the context of our research, best practice consists in the process of developing and following efficient and effective standard rules to prevent corruption," Giavazzi, "The Anti-Corruption Compliance Program Benchmarking Assessment in the Oil and Gas Industry: Methodology and Achievements," in this volume.

[15] See "Anti-corruption policies and measures of the Fortune Global 500," United Nations Office on Drugs and Crime (UNODC), http://www.unodc.org/unodc/en/corruption/anti-corruption-policies-and-measures-of-the-fortune-global-500.html, accessed 11 July 2013.

Rigorous theoretical and practical analyses, however, must be based on precise and detailed information on specific internal rules and procedures, in turn allowing researchers to identify concrete results arising from these self-regulatory frameworks. Information is needed on the organizational details of corporations and the practices they employ in discovering and preventing bribery. To this end, the research team conducted an empirical analysis of the anticorruption self-regulation applied by corporations, with the aim of producing a picture of recent trends and best practices adopted by major market players for dealing with the most common corrupt practices in their business sector.

The research team focused on the oil and gas sectors, which—together with logistics and defense—comprise the major areas in which bribery is a particular concern. A detailed questionnaire was administered to the largest corporations in the field.[16] The research unit asked a large number of questions to multinational companies operating in the oil and gas industries, on the following topics:

a. General information on the group
b. Anticorruption compliance programs
c. Facilitation payments
d. Gifts/benefits/hospitality
e. Political or charitable contributions/donations
f. Sponsorship activities
g. Business partners
h. Other aspects of their anticorruption compliance programs

The responses given by multinational companies were extensively analyzed,[17] summarizing the main results arrived at by the research team.

This survey represents only the first step in the work of the research project: the aim of this exercise is not simply to engage in passive acknowledgment of the practices of multinational companies, but to consolidate and extend our knowledge, frame new policy proposals, and implement the corresponding approaches. Although the ABC model has been elaborated via a bottom-up approach, it is not a mere synthesis of extent self-regulation, but constitutes an innovative compliance program which has been conceived in order to address the specific aims of criminal policy for fighting corruption. Self-regulation is the *base* of the legal process, but it has been integrated and corrected in order to achieve a more balanced result.

In this context, the ABC model intends to be a benchmark for assessing the effectiveness of existing programs for the prevention of bribery, and at the same time to provide a model for corporations that wish to introduce or develop their own internal compliance programs. The model is to serve as an instrument of harmonization for anticorruption programs at the international level (a *common standard*) and

[16] See the Appendix for the text of the questionnaire. For discussion of results see Giavazzi, "The Anti-Corruption Compliance Program Benchmarking Assessment in the Oil and Gas Industry: Methodology and Achievements," in this volume.

[17] See Giavazzi, "The Anti-Corruption Compliance Program Benchmarking Assessment in the Oil and Gas Industry: Methodology and Achievements," in this volume.

is designed to act as a *meta-model* (a model for the models), that is, an international standard with which other organizational anticorruption models developed by multinational enterprises have to comply.

1.6 Implementing the ABC Model: "A Double Track" for States and Corporations

With regards to implementing the ABC model, harmonization is achieved by combining the contents of different regulatory standards as well as various normative tools. Implementing the ABC model thus needs—as already mentioned—a "double track" approach, in which hard-law and soft-law instruments, designed to operate in relation to states and corporations respectively, are merged.

In order to be adopted and effectively implemented by corporations, the ABC model must be *endorsed at the international level*. This is for various reasons. First, private actors should not be left alone in the fight against corruption; on the contrary, they should be supported and encouraged in their commitment to reducing corruption and in building an organization that is compliant with the law. Second, multinational companies need to be able to "go for a single standard," since their operational nature is an obstacle to enacting differing standards under one roof (Pieth 2011).

Nevertheless, harmonized compliance does not mean uniformity. A compliance program must be a suit which is tailor-made: it must be perfectly adapted to the specifications of each corporation. Hence, the ABC model needs to be implemented flexibly, through specific internal rules and procedures, in order that corporations should be interested in adopting it.

As our text states:

> The ABC Model has been conceived as a universal and flexible anti-corruption instrument that can be adapted to a variety of different organizational structures each time a bribery-related risk is faced. This ABC Model has therefore been designed for all those business organizations, entities, and professional associations operating in a multinational environment which carry out activities in areas considered at risk of corruption.[18]
> [I]t is advisable that the ABC Program be adopted across the group worldwide. This adoption may be undertaken in two different ways: firstly, the company may decide to extend its own ABC Program to all the subsidiaries regardless of the geographical areas (a "precautionary approach"); alternatively, the company may decide to adapt the ABC Program to better fit structural and operational differences.[19]

In either case, the ABC program must be in compliance with the applicable local anti-bribery and corruption laws, which may impose *stricter or different requirements* (such as requesting the use of local contractors). In this case, the company or

[18] "The ABC-Model," Sect. 1.3, in this volume.

[19] "The ABC-Model," Sect. A.2.3.1, in this volume.

its subsidiaries may implement stricter or different provisions to reflect the requirements of the applicable local laws.

Several options are available for the harmonization of the ABC model at the international level. The first option consists in assigning the task of recommending the adoption of an ABC model to private international organizations representing the interests of corporations. As our research has shown, such a solution is not totally novel within the current legal framework. At the national level, private associations of industrial or commercial companies have sometimes conceived compliance models for specific sectors, for instance in the pharmaceuticals industry. Similarly, at the international level, a number of initiatives, standards, and principles have been developed over the years by private actors (e.g., associations of firms, NGOs, businesses, and so on), such as the 2008 Bali Business Declaration and the PACI Principles for Countering Bribery.

The theoretical model under which such experiences have been elaborated recalls the Transnational Private Regulation system (TPR), which has already been used in several areas (e.g., in exploiting limited resources such as fishing). This model, however, has been subject to criticism both in terms of legitimacy and effectiveness:

> Transnational Private Regulation (TPR) constitutes a new body of rules, practices and processes, created primarily by private actors, firms, NGOs, independent experts (like technical standard-setters and epistemic communities), either: exercising autonomous regulatory power or implementing delegated power, conferred by international law or by national legislation. Its recent growth reflects (A) a reallocation of regulatory power from the domestic to the global sphere and (B) a redistribution between public and private regulators. When in place, TPR produces strong distributive effects both among private actors and between them and national states. It differs both from global public regulation and from conventional forms of private rule-making identifiable with the law merchant. The main differences concern both actors and effects. TPR differs from international regulation primarily because rule-making is not based on states' legislation. It is rather centred around private actors, interplaying with international organizations (IO) and intergovernmental organizations (IGO). This is not to say that states do not take part in and are not affected by TPR. TPR emphasizes to a greater extent the role of the state as a rule-taker as opposed to a rule maker. It produces direct effects on participants to the regime without the need for states' legislative intermediation. However, it still lacks a comprehensive and integrated set of common principles. The toolbox of regulatory instruments differs significantly from that developed in the domain of public international law. Private regulatory regimes are specific sectors, driven by different constituencies often conflicting because they protect divergent interests. Standards are generally stricter than those defined by international public organizations, when they exist. The complementariness between public and private often encompasses multiple standards, where the public provides minimum mandatory common standards and the private voluntary stricter ones. (Scott et al. 2011)

A second option, which is the core of our proposal, consists in delegating to international organizations the task of recommending to corporations—in their capacities as emerging subjects of international law—that they engage in the adoption of such rules, while also encouraging and prompting states to put pressure on corporations (see the following paragraph). The present research has noted that regional and international organizations have already started adopting international models and principles of compliance for corporations that are seriously committed to preventing misconduct in transnational economic transactions. This represents a sign of acknowledgment of the importance of corporate governance in tackling bribery. Prime examples of such intervention are represented by the OECD Principles of Corporate Governance, Guidelines for Multinational Enterprises, and Good Practice Guidance on Internal Controls, Ethics, and Compliance, all adopted on 18 February 2010.

Today the UNODC seems to be in a position to promote such an initiative on a universal scale. In this context the UN Global Compact, appointed and chaired by the UN secretary-general, has already played a prominent role by adopting tools such as those represented by the Reporting Guidance on the 10th Principle against Corruption, and Fighting Corruption in the Supply Chain: A Guide for Customers and Suppliers.

Fighting Corruption in the Supply Chain: A Guide for Customers and Suppliers

This guide has been conceived by the United Nations Global Compact 10th Principle Working Group as an essential resource to help companies reduce corruption risks in their supply chains. The guide outlines why businesses must join the fight against corruption and provides pragmatic advice on addressing this complex challenge. The guide is structured into an introduction, followed by three sections and addenda. The introduction as well as the first two sections outline the business case for fighting corruption in the supply chain, and provide a framework for customer–supplier engagement on these issues. The final section and addenda, which are designed for program administrators and technical personnel, offer detailed guidance on common supply-chain corruption scenarios and a set of tools for fighting corruption. In particular, the addenda contain a series of tools for fighting corruption in the supply chain: Code of Conduct for Suppliers; Anti-Corruption Contract Language; Due Diligence Protocol; Supplier Questionnaire; Anti-Corruption Education and Communication for Suppliers; and Anti-Corruption Resources.

The Reporting Guidance on the 10th Principle against Corruption

The guidance was elaborated over the course of 15 months (from September 2008 until November 2009) by a taskforce which included nongovernmental organizations, anticorruption experts, and business practitioners appointed by the Global Compact Working Group on the 10th Principle against Corruption. It has been conceived as a tool to give practical guidance to corporations as they report on their efforts. The reporting guidance provides a comprehensive set of reporting elements designed to help any organization by identifying the components of a comprehensive anticorruption program; giving practical examples on how and what to report, including references to indicators from other initiatives; and providing a clear and easy-to-use format to structure and facilitate the reporting of anticorruption activities in the annual Communication on Progress.

Although it opts for this second mode of intervention, the research team recognizes that a "double track" approach must be followed in implementing the ABC model. First, an *international convention* (hard law) should bind states to give legal acknowledgment of the effective and correct implementation of the model within their domestic criminal law systems. Second, the ABC model constitutes the framework of a *compliance program* that multinational enterprises are free to adopt. Therefore, a legal instrument of international source and conventional nature, which is designed to bind states, should encourage and indeed urge multinational enterprises to develop internal anticorruption rules. This decision to merge hard-law instruments with soft-law instruments represents a new logic of criminal policy in the global fight against corruption.

Concerning corporations, since the ABC model is not a binding instrument for corporations but represents a simple soft-law tool, the research team took the decision to introduce—where weak points still to be worked out have appeared—the highest standard arising from existing best practice. In other terms, it provides *maximum rules* to be included in the internal compliance programs: Corporations are free to decide to introduce less detailed or more stringent rules in order to prevent corruption at the internal level, but they are invited to consider the higher existing standard.

One example of such a recourse to best practices can be seen in relation to so-called facilitation payments: in this case a decision has been made to include this conduct on the list of illicit behaviors (Pieth 2011, p. 68; see also Fox 2010; Jordan 2011; Peeler and Pulley 2011; Strauss 2013), despite the fact that the illicit nature of this conduct is not yet recognized in all legal systems. On the basis of the ABC model, facilitation payments can be tolerated only when acting under necessity. As is clearly stated:

> For reasons based on comparative analyses of the different legislation in this respect, it is strongly advised to forbid facilitation payments, whether directly or through third parties and even if they are nominal in amount and/or common in a particular country
> ….
> However, it must be recognized that demands for facilitation payments are often backed by a form of extortion, and that in exceptional circumstances resistance may not be feasible. As employee safety is a primary concern, payments made as a result of extortion or under duress to protect "life, limb, or liberty" or personal safety may be considered a justifiable exception. In such circumstances, the company, as part of its ABC Program, may accept that employees will need to use their best judgment, as long as they report it and provide absolute transparency as to the circumstances surrounding the payment shortly after the incident has occurred. All personnel must report to their line manager and the ACU at the earliest opportunity regarding any incident where they felt forced to make a facilitation payment.
> The payment must be accurately and transparently recorded in the financial records.[20]

Similarly, following the current trend at the international level, the bribery of private individuals has been included among the list of illicit behaviors, going beyond the bribery of public officials (Forti 2003), notwithstanding the fact that Article 15 of UNCAC only considers such a provision as being facultative.

Finally, the ABC model proposes the establishment of an anti-corruption unit:

> It is recommended to establish a special internal body with specialized expertises and exclusive competence in the anti-corruption matter. The Board of Directors (or the meeting of shareholders) shall nominate a dedicated body or Committee. For the purpose of this Model, the body is the Anti-corruption Unit (also ACU). The ACU shall also assume the role of Ethics Officer with reference to the ACCP Program.

[20] "The ABC Model," Sect. B.3.1, in this volume.

In contrast, when addressed to states the ABC model is a binding instrument and establishes minimum rules, as we will see in the following paragraph.

1.7 Enforcing the ABC Model: Incentives and Criminal Law Responses

As a third complementary driving idea of the research, soft law—one of the main pieces of the global policy strategy—has to be coordinated with national legal responses and, more precisely, *must be acknowledged by domestic criminal law*. There will be no successful self-regulation, even in the case of strong recommendations by international organizations, if the effective and correct implementation of the ABC model does not produce any consequences in terms of criminal law and procedure.

Such a result calls for a return to the traditional hard-law approach: The research team has suggested the adoption of an international legal instrument (a convention) addressing itself to states and asking for their formal acknowledgement of the legal value of compliance programs, insofar as they correspond to the ABC model and are correctly adopted and implemented.

Taking into account the persistent domestic dimension of criminal law, the proposal calls upon national legislators to give importance to the appropriate incorporation of anti-bribery compliance principles in their legislation. These principles could serve as criteria to assess liability of corporations or to determine appropriate sentencing for violations.

In several domestic legal systems, it is already the case that the adoption of organizational compliance and ethics models, or the commitment to implement them, can mitigate sanctions and even exempt an organization from liability. The linchpin of the model that has been proposed is the carrot-and-stick approach, even if the picture, at the European and international level, still appears to be complex and heterogeneous. (For comparative studies see Zapatero 2012; Gobert and Pascal 2011; Stanislas et al. 2008.)

From a theoretical point of view, the possibility of mitigation or exemption from liability based on a commitment to compliance is consistent with the idea that companies can only be held liable for bribery occurring as a consequence of inadequate organization and deficient accounting systems, which are unsuitable to prevent the commission of crimes. From a practical point of view, the proposed solution creates incentives for compliant corporations in terms of both avoiding negative consequences and achieving positive results, resulting in strengthened prevention.

The researchers therefore focused on a wider range of countries, including those with "advanced" legal systems where the criminal law impact of compliance is legally binding (such as the USA, Italy, and Australia), as well as more traditional ones where such an evolution has taken place in other fields such as environmental law or competition law, or as a result of the impact of the judiciary (Spain, France, and China). The solution—establishing a close link between compliance programs and anti-bribery criminal law enforcement—is gaining increasing importance at the international level but still needs to be strengthened. This link has been highlighted in the recent OECD guidelines underlining the importance of systems based on strict liability, where compliance seems to be a mitigating factor (US), and of systems based on a "failure to prevent" approach, where compliance is a full defense (the UK) (Pieth 2011, p. 28).

With regards to the UN, the UNCAC already admits that a certain weight should be given to cooperative companies. Article 39(2), concerning the cooperation between national authorities and the private sector, states that:

> Each State Party shall consider encouraging…to report to the national investigating and prosecuting authorities the commission of an offence established in accordance with this Convention.

Consequently, the time has arrived to assign liability to legal entities, as foreseen in Article 26 of the UNCAC, based on their own behavior and internal organizational structures.

Starting from this comparative and international legal assessment, the research team proposes to attribute a *criminal relevance to the compliance program* adopted by corporations. This solution constitutes a perspective already adopted within the legal systems of some states. The idea is to promote a new harmonization phase of domestic legal systems aimed at the global extension of a preventive model that also has effects on punishment.

In particular, the effects of the proper implementation of the ABC model can be both substantial and procedural. From a substantial point of view, the adoption of such a program can constitute either: (1) a defense; (2) a mitigating factor; or (3) a defense or a mitigating factor depending on whether the adoption of the model occurred respectively before or after the commission of the offense (Walsh and Pyrich 1995; Fatino 2002). The latter option is preferable because it urges companies to preemptively adopt an effective anticorruption compliance program. From a procedural point of view, the adoption of such a model can produce the following effects: (1) exclusion, discontinuation, or suspension of prosecution; and (2) suspension of the criminal proceeding/trial with the possibility of its further suppression (Wellner 2005).

1.8 Concluding Remarks

The main aim of the research group, as presented along with supportive scholarly material in this volume, is the elaboration of a suitable anticorruption compliance model, functionally linked with an effective corporate corruption liability regime and consistent with the principles set forth in the UNCAC.

As the ABC model has been conceived, regulation would not be imposed directly on enterprises from the top, but would be elaborated through taking corporations' existing policies into consideration. However, the model would not be a mere combination of existing self-regulations, but would include criminal-policy recommendations framed on the basis of multiple assessments, and would include best practice guidelines. An international convention should bind states to give legal acknowledgment, within their domestic criminal law systems, of the value of effective and correct implementation of the model. National legislators should be internationally obliged to give incentives to compliant corporations, while corporations should be encouraged to comply with anticorruption standards in order to avoid or mitigate criminal sanctions.

By virtue of such features, which represent a synthesis of the various strategies developed so far, the ABC model constitutes the result of a process of elaboration aiming to obtain the hybridization of traditional approaches. Its adoption would allow us to bridge the traditional gaps between hetero-regulation and self-regulation, hard law and soft law, and prevention and punishment, in the drafting, enforcing, and controlling phases. The ABC model has all the makings of a point of reference for multinational corporations, and of a common standard in establishing guidelines for international institutions.

References

Alston, P. (2005). *Non-state actors and human rights*. New York: Oxford University Press.

Borghi, M., & Meyer-Bisch, P. (Eds.). (1995). *La corruption l'envers des droits de l'homme*. Fribourg: Éditions Universitaires.

Broersma, M., & Nelen, H. (Eds.). (2010). *Corruption and human rights: Interdisciplinary perspectives*. Cambridge: Intersentia.

Button, M. (2011). Editorial: Fraud, corruption and the financial crisis. *International Journal of Law, Crime and Justice, 39*(3), 137–139.

Clapham, A. (2006). *Human rights obligations of non-state actors*. Oxford: Oxford University Press.

Cockcroft, L. (2010). Global corruption: An untamed hydra. *World Policy Journal, 27*(1), 21–28.

De Schutter, O. (2006). *Transnational corporations and human rights*. Portland: Hart Publishing.

Delmas-Marty, M. (2003). The contribution of comparative law to a pluralist conception of international criminal law. *Journal of International Criminal Justice, 1*(1), 13–25.

Delmas-Marty, M. (2009). *Ordering pluralism: A conceptual framework for understanding the transnational legal world*. Oxford: Hart Publishing.

Delmas-Marty, M., & Manacorda, S. (2000). Corruption: A challenge to the rule of law and democratic society. In P. Bernasconi (Ed.), *Responding to corruption* (pp. 401–424). Napoli: Istituto Italiano per gli Studi Filosofici.

Deming, S. H. (2010). *The Foreign Corrupt Practices Act and the new international norms*. Chicago: American Bar Association.

Fatino, J. F. (2002). Corporate compliance programs: An approach to avoid or minimize criminal and civil liability. *Drake Law Review, 51,* 81–105.

Forti, G. (1997). Unicità o ripetibilità della corruzione sistemica? Il ruolo della sanzione penale in una prevenzione "sostenibile" dei crimini politico-amministrativi. *Rivista trimestrale di diritto penale dell'economia, 4*.

Forti, G. (2003). La corruzione tra privati nell'orbita di disciplina della corruzione pubblica: Un contributo di tematizzazione. *Rivista italiana di diritto e procedura penale, 46*(4), 1115–1163.

Fox, T. R. (2010). The end of the FCPA facilitation payment exception? FCPA Compliance and Ethics Blog, 11 November 2010. http://tfoxlaw.wordpress.com/2010/11/11/the-end-of-the-fcpa-facilitation-payment-exception/. Accessed 4 Sept 2009.

Gobert, J., & Pascal, A.-M. (2011). *European developments in corporate criminal liability*. London: Routledge.

Greanias, G. C., & Windsor, D. (1982). *The Foreign Corrupt Practices Act: Anatomy of a statute*. Lexington: LexingtonBooks.

Hachez, I., Cartuyvels, Y., Dumont, H., Gérard, P., Ost, F., & van de Kerchove, M. (Eds.). (2013). *Les sources du droit revisitées. Volume 2: Normes internes infraconstitutionnelles*. Bruxelles: Presses des Facultés Universitaires de Saint Louis.

Hägg, C. (1984). The OECD Guidelines for Multinational Enterprises. *Journal of Business Ethics, 3*, 71–76.

Huisman, W. (2010). *Business as usual? The involvement of corporations with international crimes*. The Hague: Boom Legal Publishers.

Jagers, N. (2002). *Corporate human rights obligations: In search of accountability*. Antwerp: Intersentia.

Jordan, J. (2011). The OECD's call for an end to "corrosive" facilitation payments and the international focus on the facilitation payments exception under the Foreign Corrupt Practices Act. *University of Pennsylvania Journal of Business Law, 13*(4), 881–925.

Kamminga, M. T., & Zia-Zarifi, S. (2000). *Liability of multinational corporation under international law*. The Hague: Kluwer Law International.

Kimberly, A. E. (1997). *Corruption and the global economy*. Washington: Institute for International Economics.

Koebele, M. (2009). *Corporate responsibility under the Alien Tort Statute: Enforcement of international law through US torts law*. Leiden: Martinus Nijhoff Publishers.

Larson, E. N. (2011). The United Nations Convention against Corruption. In L. Achathaler et al. (Eds.), *Korruptionsbekämpfung als Globale Herausforderung: Beiträgeaus Praxis und Wissenschaft*. Heidelberg: VS Verlag für Sozialwissenschaften.

Leventhal, R. (2008). International legal standards on corruption. Proceeding of the Annual Meeting. *American Society of International Law, 102*, 203.

Manacorda, S. (1999). *La corruzione internazionale del pubblico agente. Linee dell'indagine penalistica*. Napoli: Jovene.

Martin-Chenut, K. (2013). Droits de l'homme et responsabilité des entreprises: Les Principes Directeurs des Nations Unies. In G. Giudicelli-Delage et al. (Eds.), *Responsabilité pénale des personnes morales: Perspectives européennes et internationales*. Paris: Société de Législation Comparée.

McIntosh, M., Thomas, R., Leipziger, D., & Coleman, G. (2003). *Living corporate citizenship: Strategic routes to socially responsible business*. London: Financial Times Management.

Mongillo, V. (2012). *La corruzione trasfera interna e dimensione internazionale. Effetti, potenzialità e limiti di un diritto penale "multilivello" dallo Stato-nazione alla globalizzazione*. Napoli: Edizioni Scientifiche Italiane.

Moody-Stuart, G. (1997). *Grand corruption: How business bribes damage developing countries*. Oxford: WorldView.

Nicholls, C., Daniel, T., Bacarese, A., & Hatchard, J. (2011). *Corruption and misuse of public office*. New York: Oxford University Press.

Pagani, F. (2002). Peer review as a tool for co-operation and change—An analysis of an OECD working method. *African Security Review, 11*(4), 15–24.

Palazzo, F. (Ed.). (2011). *Corruzione pubblica. Repressione penale e prevenzione amministrativa*. Firenze: Firenze University Press.

Passas, N., & Vlassis, D. (2007). *The United Nations Convention against Corruption as a way of life*. Milano: ISPAC.

Peeler, M. S., & Pulley, J. C. (2011). Internationalizing the FCPA: Ending the facilitation payments exception and U.S. anti-corruption hypocrisy. In M. A. Srere et al. (Eds.), *International Bribery: FCPA update*. Wayne: Andrews Publications.

Peters, A., Koechlin, L., Förster, T., & Zinkernagel, G. F. (Eds.). (2009). *Non-state actors as standard setters*. Cambridge: Cambridge University Press.

Pieth, M. (2007). Multistakeholder initiatives to combat money laundering and bribery. In C. Brütsch et al. (Eds.), *Law and legalization in transnational relations* (pp. 81-100). New York: Routledge.
Pieth, M. (2011). *Harmonising anti-corruption compliance: The OECD Good Practice Guidance 2010*. Zurich: Dike Verlag AG.
Pieth, M. (2012). *Collective action: Innovative strategies to prevent corruption*. Zurich: Dike Verlag AG.
Pieth, M., & Aiolfi, G. (2003). *Anti-money laundering: Leveling the playing field*. Basel: Basel Institute of Governance.
Pieth, M., & Eigen, P. (Eds.). (1998). *Korruption im internationalen Geschäftsverkehr: Bestandsaufnahme, Bekämpfung, Prävention*. Basel: Helbing & Lichtenhahn.
Pieth, M., Low, L. A., & Cullen, P. J. (2007). *The OECD Convention on Bribery: A Commentary*. Cambridge: Cambridge University Press.
Plaine, D. J. (1977). The OECD Guidelines for Multinational Enterprises. *International Lawyer, 11*(2), 339.
Robinson, M. (Ed.). (1998). *Corruption and development*. New York: Frank Cass Publishers.
Rose-Ackerman, S. (1999). *Corruption and government: Causes, consequences and reform*. Cambridge: Cambridge University Press.
Santner, A. L. (2011). A soft-law mechanism for corporate responsibility: How the updated OECD guidelines for multinational enterprises promote business for the future. *The George Washington International Law Review, 43*(2), 375.
Schultz, J. L. (2010). The UNCAC compliance review in Kenya: Process and prospects. *U4 Practice Insight, 3, 1.*
Scott, C., Cafaggi, F., & Senden, L. (2011). The conceptual and constitutional challenge of transnational private regulation. *Journal of Law and Society, 38*(1), 1–19.
Stanislas, A., Colette-Baseqz, N., & Nihoul, M. (2008). *Le responsabilité pénale des personnes morales en Europe*. Bruxelles: La Charte.
Strauss, E. N. (2013). "Easing out" the FCPA facilitation payment exception. *Boston University Law Review, 93*(1), 235–273.
Terracino, J. B. (2012). *The international legal framework against corruption: State's obligations to prevent and repress corruption*. Cambridge: Intersentia.
Thibierge, C. (2009). *La force normative: Naissance d'un concept*. Paris: LGDJ.
Tricot, J. (2001). Inventaire des instruments internationaux de lutte contre la corruption: Le processus de construction du cadre juridique international. In M. Delmas-Marty (Ed.), *Vers des principes directeurs de droit pénal, Volume VII: Les processus d'internationalisation*. Paris: Maison des Sciences de l'Homme.
Trubek, D. M., Cottrell, P., & Nance, M. (2005). "Soft Law," "Hard Law," and European integration: Toward a theory of hybridity. *University of Wisconsin Law School, Legal Studies Research Papers Series*, 1002.
Vlassis, D. (2012). The United Nations convention against corruption: A successful example of international action against economic crime. *Temida, 15*(2), 61–70.
von Liszt, F. (1883). Der Zweckgedanke im Strafrecht. *Zeitschrift fuer die gesamte Strafrechtswissenschaft, 3*, 83.
Walsh, C. J., & Pyrich, A. (1995). Corporate compliance programs as a defense to criminal liability: Can a corporation save its soul? *Rutgers Law Review, 47*, 605–691.
Ward, P. M. (1989). *Corruption, development and inequality: Soft touch or hard graft*. London: Routledge.
Webb, P. (2005). The United Nations convention against corruption—global achievement or missed opportunity? *Journal of International Economic Law, 8*(1), 191–229.
Wellner, P. A. (2005). Effective compliance programs and corporate criminal prosecutions. *Cardozo Law Review, 27*(1).
Zapatero, L. A. (2012). La responsabilità penale delle persone giuridiche nella penisola iberica. In A. Fiorella et al. (Eds.), *Corporate criminal liability and compliance programs: First colloquium, Sapienza University of Rome 12–14 May 2011*. Napoli: Jovene.
Zerk, J. (2006). *Multinationals and corporate social responsibility*. Cambridge: Cambridge University Press.

Chapter 2
The Universal Approach of the United Nations Convention Against Corruption

John Sandage

The role of the United Nations Office on Drugs and Crime (UNODC) is to build a world safer from drugs, crime, and terrorism. In doing so, one of our key targets must be corruption.

Corruption has a devastating impact on development. It is estimated that up to US$ 40 billion is stolen from developing countries every year, robbing citizens of better education, better health care, and better lives, and denying them hope for a better future. Corruption breeds more corruption and facilitates other crimes. It undermines democracy and weakens good governance and the rule of law. It squanders precious resources and talent, keeping countries from fulfilling their potential. And in the worst case, it costs lives.

The impact of corruption on the private sector is also considerable. Corruption stifles economic growth, distorts competition, and presents serious legal and reputational risks. It keeps investors away, acting as a hidden "tax" or illegal overhead charge, and thereby increasing costs for companies and further down the chain, their consumers.

But during the last decade, we have experienced a positive change in the attitudes towards corruption. Whereas once the question was to bribe or not to bribe, there is now a broad consensus that bribery and corruption are no longer acceptable forms of doing business. The world has embraced the notion of a level playing field for all, and more and more people and societies are rejecting individual gains, in favor of universal principles of accountability, fairness, transparency, and equality.

One reason for this change is the existence of the United Nations Convention Against Corruption (UNCAC). UNCAC is the only universal legal anticorruption instrument. It embodies innovative and globally accepted anticorruption standards applicable to both the public and private sectors and provides a comprehensive approach to preventing and combating corruption. With 164 states parties, UNCAC has great potential for universal adherence in the not-too-distant future. Calls encouraging countries that are not yet parties to the convention to ratify or accede to

J. Sandage (✉)
United Nations Office on Drugs and Crime-UNODC, Vienna, Austria
e-mail: john.sandage@unodc.org

S. Manacorda et al. (eds.), *Preventing Corporate Corruption*,
DOI 10.1007/978-3-319-04480-4_2, © Springer International Publishing Switzerland 2014

it have been made by all major fora, including the General Assembly, the G8, and the G20.

While ratification is essential, it is only the first step. Governments around the world are engaged in earnest in the implementation of the convention. There has also been significant progress with the landmark implementation review mechanism, which was introduced in 2010. Countries are treating the review process very seriously, and with considerable enthusiasm. One hundred and fifty-seven countries have been involved in the review mechanism, either as reviewing countries or under review themselves. Furthermore, the majority of the countries have demonstrated their willingness to take full advantage of the review mechanism, including its optional features, and to carry out the reviews in a transparent and inclusive manner. For example, to date a large number of states have involved the private sector in reviews: seven in the first 2 years involved the private sector in the self-assessment stage, 21 involved the private sector in the country visit stage.

Yet governments cannot win the fight against corruption alone. Preventing and combating corruption is the shared responsibility of every sector of society, and UNODC welcomes the fact that the private sector has added its own powerful voice to those who wish to eradicate this crime. Already during the Second conference of the States Parties to UNCAC, held in Bali in 2008, representatives of the business community, including the United Nations Global Compact, the International Chamber of Commerce, the World Economic Forum/Partnering Against Corruption Initiative, and Transparency International, adopted the so-called Bali Business Declaration. The declaration recorded the business community's commitment to work towards the alignment of existing business principles with the fundamental values enshrined in UNCAC; to ensure that anticorruption policies and strategies include effective whistle-blower protection; to ensure due diligence in the selection of agents and intermediaries and to address effectively facilitation payments; to work towards developing mechanisms to review companies' compliance with realigned business principles; and to strengthen public–private partnerships for combating corruption in business.

The role of the private sector is thus critical. And the private sector has come to realize that the fight against corruption is a win–win situation: By developing strong internal anticorruption policies and measures and by supporting countries in developing and strengthening their public anticorruption infrastructure, the business community can help create a transparent and strong global economy and prosperous societies, which contributes toward a level playing field.

Business thrives where laws are defined clearly and applied all-inclusively. We are currently seeing that the desired *level* playing field is becoming a *legislated* playing field. Again, one of the main reasons is the UNCAC, which requires states parties to take a series of measures that, together, lay the foundation for free and fair markets and sustainable economic development.

One of the main provisions of the convention in this regard is Article 12, which calls on states parties to prevent corruption involving the private sector, to enhance accounting and auditing standards in the private sector, and to provide effective, proportionate, and dissuasive civil, administrative, or criminal penalties for failure to comply with such measures. In Article 26, UNCAC makes it obligatory to establish criminal, civil, or administrative liability of legal persons and to make such liability independent of the criminal liability of the natural persons committing an offence of corruption. Furthermore, Article 39 calls on states parties to encourage cooperation between national investigating and prosecuting authorities and entities of the private sector.

Four years ago, UNODC, in partnership with PricewaterhouseCoopers, collated the existing anticorruption practices and measures of the Fortune Global 500 companies. In this context, it became clear that greater harmonization is needed, in line with international standards, to protect businesses and their employees against corruption. For example, a facilitation payment is just a fancy word for a bribe, yet some companies still allow them up to a certain threshold or under certain circumstances—or even consider them tax deductible. Some companies provide whistle-blowers full anonymity while others promise that such employees will not be exposed to retaliation.

When Dimitri Vlassis, Chief of the Corruption and Economic Crime Branch of the UNODC, and Professor Stefano Manacorda of the International Scientific and Professional Advisory Council (ISPAC) discussed the findings of this report, they agreed that more analytical work was needed. The private sector is facing new innovations and challenges due to a complex and ever-evolving international regulatory anticorruption framework. On the one hand, it has become subject to direct liability for the commission of corruption offences. On the other, it is more and more called upon directly to engage in the prevention of and fight against international corruption. UNODC thus welcomes that ISPAC, with the support of ENI S.p.A., is now making a serious effort to collect the best practices of anticorruption policy at the international level. The research aims at assembling concrete experiences of bribery, misconduct, and anticorruption policies in the international fora, in order to achieve more satisfying results at the criminal policy level. This will also support the efforts to coordinate and harmonize anticorruption compliance programs at the international level. UNODC is delighted to support this important and timely initiative.

Preventive action in the private and public sectors is a key driver for change. There is a lot that we can and must do together. I conclude by providing some information on the work of UNODC in strengthening integrity in and with the private sector.

UNODC, together with the Organization for Economic Cooperation and Development (OECD) and the World Bank, is developing a practical handbook for businesses that will bring together guidelines and related material on private sector anticorruption compliance.

We are implementing a number of public–private partnership projects. These projects aim at reducing vulnerabilities to corruption in public procurement systems; creating legal incentives for corporate integrity and cooperation; and developing an outreach and communication program for UNCAC, targeted at the private sector.

We are also about to launch a certificate course and different language versions of the e-learning tool for the private sector, which was developed jointly with the

UN Global Compact. The e-learning tool is publicly accessible from our website free of charge, and has already had 600,000 hits in the first year of its use.

UNODC is addressing the issue of corruption in the context of major public events, such as the Olympic Games. The private sector has a major role to play in this regard, both as service providers and through sponsorships and hospitality arrangements. Through UNCAC, we are identifying good practices and helping organizers mitigate the risk associated with such events.

Another fundamental area for UNODC is education. We need to educate the young on fairness and integrity today, so that we can have ethical leaders tomorrow. Our approach is twofold: First, focus on tertiary education through the development of anticorruption curricula for law schools and business schools. Second, embed the values and ethics of UNCAC in younger children by teaching the values that are the bedrock of the convention. The Anticorruption Academic Initiative, which brings together academics and other practitioners from around the world, will launch a menu of topics and academic resources on anticorruption on our website by the end of 2012.

UNODC is also closely involved in both the G20 and the B20 process. I am pleased to note that UNCAC has received a lot of recognition in both contexts, and just recently the G20 governments reiterated their commitment to the ratification and full implementation of the convention against corruption. They also welcomed continuing engagement from the B20 in the fight against corruption and, in accordance with the Terms of Reference of the review mechanism, committed to involve the private sector and civil society in the UNCAC review process.

We all share the same world, the same values—and the same problems. Therefore, UNODC considers public–private partnerships crucial to preventing and combating corruption. To tackle the problem effectively, we must also share the same solutions.

Chapter 3
The Private Sector Role in the Fight Against Corruption

Massimo Mantovani

Contents

3.1 Introduction

When discussing corruption and anticorruption compliance in the business community, we want to hear, and indeed to repeat, phrases such as:

> International corruption is an intolerable impediment to the efficiency of business and to fair competition. Our organization is committed to ensuring effective compliance with all anticorruption laws applicable to our business.

The issue of the private sector's role in the fight against corruption has a number of different aspects. Some of the most relevant are:

- Internal anti-bribery programs
- Collective actions
- Self-reporting and cooperation with authorities

It is also important to underline the role of the private sector in international fora such as the B20, the Extractive Industries Transparency Initiative (EITI), the UN Global Compact, and many others.

M. Mantovani (✉)
Eni Legal Department, Rome, Italy
e-mail: massimo.mantovani@eni.com

S. Manacorda et al. (eds.), *Preventing Corporate Corruption*,
DOI 10.1007/978-3-319-04480-4_3,

3.2 Internal Anti-bribery Compliance Programs: General

There is an increasing demand for the adoption of internal anti-bribery programs. Key aspects of such programs are:

a. A risk assessment to identify the key business areas with higher exposure to the risk of corruption
b. A tailor-made set of process rules for areas identified with relevant red flags
c. An internal training program on anticorruption and a clear top-level commitment message—"We will not tolerate!"
d. Continuous monitoring of the correct adoption of the program
e. Appropriate disciplinary measures for inappropriate behavior

In addition, it is important to set up an internal anticorruption unit to supervise the activities set out in the anti-bribery program.

These programs have the ambitious goal of neutralizing the risk of corrupt conduct in which employees or company representatives can be consciously or unconsciously involved, and they have a significant positive impact in greatly reducing the risk of such conduct. When building an anti-bribery program a company must look at the relevant regulatory framework, at international sector best practice, and at its own personal "history."

In Italy, pursuant to the Legislative Decree of 8 June 2001, n. 231, it is essential not only that the "organization and management models" are suited to preventing the commission of the relevant crimes, but they have also to be "effectively applied"; if this were to be the case the relevant company may benefit for an exemption of liability. In the UK, the UK Bribery Act established that the failure to adopt an anticorruption model is itself a crime and that the adoption of an adequate anticorruption compliance program represents an exemption from corporate liability. In the USA, the adoption of an anticorruption model represents the central element for potential mitigations of consequences in cases of unlawful conduct.

3.3 The Requirements for Anti-bribery Compliance Models: Red Flags and the Internal Anti-bribery Unit

An adequate anti-bribery model has as a starting point a specific risk assessment of the relevant business activities of the company and the consequent definition of internal control standard for the areas considered at risk: the identification and management of specific pre-identified "red flags" for each business activity are therefore critical.

Red flags, in particular, are essential in two distinct phases: initially, in the due diligence activities on contractual counterparties that must be performed prior to the conclusion of agreements, whether they are intermediary, joint venture, transfer of assets, consulting services, brokerage agreements, etc. (in this respect it is necessary that the anti-bribery program pre-identifies and lists the various types of red flags relevant for the different business activities to be analyzed); and after the conclusion of an agreement, in the phase of contractual management (e.g., *whistle-blowing* reports of anomalies, such as the sudden growth of orders or commissions or rough handling of potential dysfunctions, or the detected absence of proper functioning of the internal control tools).

In addition to the fundamental issue of "red flags," another key issue is the setting up of an internal anticorruption support unit with the following characteristics:

- Has to be centrally controlled in order to enhance and guarantee independence from the business units
- Has to provide preventive specialized assistance in the field of anti-bribery to the company's business units
- Has to check that the anti-bribery program is updated to the relevant regulatory framework, to the international best practice (in particular with reference to the relevant sector of business activity), and on a lesson-learned basis with respect to events in which the company or the business community in general has been involved (even with respect to criminal judicial proceedings)
- Has to periodically report information about its activities to the relevant company supervisory and control entities
- Has to coordinate and supervise the anti-bribery training of employees, counterparties, partners, and contractors in the field of anticorruption and management of activities at risk
- Has to be involved in the most delicate phases, such as the analysis of due diligence and red flags
- Has to manage or at least be involved in the management of whistle-blowing reports and red flags in relation to bribery concerns (forensic investigations)

3.4 The Growing Importance of Best Practice and International Comparison

In defining an anti-bribery program, reference to international standards and best practices is fundamental. Currently key international references are:

1. The twelve principles established by the OECD on 18 February 2010 in the document "Good Practice Guidance on Internal Controls, Ethics and Compliance," adopted in implementation of the Recommendation of the Council for Further Combating Bribery of Foreign Public Officials
2. The six principles established for compliance with the UK Bribery Act of 4 April 2010—"GUIDANCE about procedures which relevant commercial organizations can put into place to prevent persons associated with them from bribing"
3. The seven principles (so-called seven pillars) indicated by the US Sentencing Commission for Compliance with the Foreign Corruption Practice Act in the document of 1 November 2010, "Federal Sentencing Guidelines Manual, Chapter 8, Part B, Effective compliance and ethics programs"

At the international level the number of fora increase, both spontaneous and organized, in particular in the field of industrial activity, which through the exchange of experience plays a fundamental role in the assessment of suitability of the model based on codes of conduct and best practices. It is now generally considered that a model in accordance with them may be presumed suitable; a constant exchange of information between major business players on the respective systems and compliance with anti-bribery rules is now common practice. There are also fora of great importance, such as the UN Global Compact and the PACI (Partnering Against Corruption) organized by the WEF, in addition to the fundamental role of ICC in Paris and of UNODC and the OECD, which have an ongoing and useful dialogue with the business world on compliance programs in particular. Most notably, major corporations are getting together on anti-bribery issues; not only to learn from each other and identify common solutions and uniform anti-bribery programs, but also, and more importantly, major corporations understand that they have a pivotal role to play in anti-bribery, specifically through requesting clear commitment and training on anti-bribery from their chain of suppliers.

3.5 Collective Action

What is collective action and what are its advantages for business participants? In taking collective action, companies join forces with each other, as well as with governments and civil society organizations, to create a fair and equal market and to minimize the opportunities for, and risks of, corruption. Collective action is a process of cooperation between various stakeholders that aims at jointly countering corruption. Through such alliances of like-minded business people, a specific problem or a range of problems can be approached from multiple angles and resolved, and the impact of individual actions increased.[1]

The idea is therefore simple: Get together with your competitors, with other civil society stakeholders, and local authorities. Then:

1. Create tools to deal with and/or mitigate the risk of corruption.
2. Create and maintain a uniform approach to compliance programs among your competitors, dealing with business partners, and reacting to red flags.
3. Improve the regulatory framework and best practice relating to anticorruption.

Collective action is more than risk mitigation: Corporations are not simply trying to avoid involvement in corrupt schemes by adopting and maintaining appropriate compliance and training programs. Rather, they are aiming at changing their business environments.

The variety of methods of collective action demonstrates that there is growing momentum in this area and increasing interest among businesses in becoming involved in such initiatives. Underlining the importance that business is giving to

[1] See "Counselor Corruption (2010).

collective action, the recommendations of the B20 in Los Cabos included the promotion, extension, and implementation of collective action and sectoral initiatives.[2]

Collective action has several important advantages for business. First, in an increasingly global market, it helps create and maintain a level playing field, thereby enabling business to compete fairly. Second, it seeks to increase transparency and accountability, thereby improving public trust in business. Third, it ensures that business acts in conformity with the legal framework, and can even contribute to changes in the regulatory system. Fourth, it leads to improved efficiency and helps avoid overcharging for products and services, thereby driving investment in new

---

[2] See "B20 Task Force Recommendations (2012). The recommendation states:

A number of Collective Action and Sectoral initiatives have been launched in recent years to address problems linked to specific country or regional contexts and industry sectors. Experiences from these initiatives should be pooled together to replicate their successes and address their weaknesses. Additional efforts are needed to increase the number of companies participating in these initiatives and to address the issue of solicitation of bribes by public officials. Collective Action initiatives in specific country contexts have proven to be most successful when (a) they were developed bottom-up addressing a specific local issue, (b) there was a strong collaboration between government and the private sector with tangible mechanisms such as a clear code of conduct that was widely disseminated and supported by a monitoring system, (c) the initiative was recognized, incentivized and supported by the public sector at the top level, and (d) when the initiative was driven by a champion that was recognized by the public and the private sectors.

a. *Business-driven actions*
   The business community should:
   - Invite all private sector participants in their value chains to join existing Collective Action initiatives in their respective industry sectors and/or initiate multi-sector initiatives in their respective countries of origin and in all countries in which they operate. Business associations should encourage and promote the adoption by members of effective compliance programs, and provide capacity building assistance to facilitate their development.
   - Create a central hub with a user-friendly interface that leverages key tools from the Internet (e.g., videos, social networks) to document, measure and share existing Collective Action and Sectoral initiatives across industry sectors and countries. The head of such hub should possess a breadth of experience in anti-corruption, including direct past experience in a Collective Action initiative.
b. Government-driven actions
   Governments should:
   - Foster the adoption of codes of conduct and other available tools to private sector participants through the appointment of Local Program Managers, charged with promoting codes and driving their implementation at country level, and of a Global Program Manager, charged with administering communication activities and executing the roll-out of these codes and tools. Governments should encourage state-owned enterprises to fully participate in these efforts.
   - Establish appropriate forms of "High Level Reporting Mechanisms" to address allegations of solicitation of bribes by public officials. In particular, governments should ensure the involvement of top authorities and set up such a mechanism in close cooperation with the support of the private sector and civil society. A pilot project could be set up in a country willing to test such a mechanism.
c. Joint public-private actions
   Governments and business should:
   - Generate public-private partnerships to address the need to untangle the root causes of corruption. To monitor such partnerships, a neutral secretariat function should be established with senior level recognition and involvement from both the public and the private sectors.

technology and innovation. Fifth, collective action is one of the means by which business may effectively contribute to reducing the market's capacity for corruption. A less corrupt business environment results in more opportunities for business.

The final recommendation of the anti-bribery working group of the B20 in June 2013 in St Petersburg, Russia, concluded:

> We recommend that the G20 governments and B20 companies should continue to support the establishment, by the end of 2013, of a Collective Action Hub to share best practices throughout the G20 countries and beyond.

As such, the B20 forum agreed that it would be beneficial to establish an entity which could be the recognized repository of best practices on collective action; a "counselor" or "advisor" to business, government, and civil society on how to structure and implement collective action strategies in order to accomplish their stated goals. Accordingly, the B20 working group has paved the way for a Collective Action Hub that will shortly start its activity. No doubt it will become a fundamental tool for the private sector fight against corruption.

3.6 Cooperation with the Authorities

In a global market with global market players, cooperation among authorities is fundamental. Cooperation between the private sector and the authorities is also key, in particular during the investigation phase. How can we enhance such cooperation, and why is it important?

Companies as well as authorities can benefit from self-reporting of corruption incidents. Benefits of self-reporting for companies include:

- Internal controls: Sending a clear message to company employees, setting the "tone from the top" that corruption will not be tolerated
- Reduced sanctions: Increasing the chances that the authorities will allow the company to lead the investigation (often in consultation with the government authority) resulting in less disruption to the company's business

Benefits for the authorities of self-reporting by companies include:

- Identifying and remediating unlawful conduct that the government may not otherwise discover
- Saving government resources by relying on companies to bear the cost of the investigations

However, under the current international framework, there are not clear and uniform incentives for corporations to cooperate and self-report. There are, instead, obstacles for companies which seek to self-report the corrupt behavior of employees. For example, there are concerns over whether self-reports might be used in other jurisdictions, leading to cross-border concurrent liabilities—in effect, people paying twice for the same offense. There is no helpful international framework that guarantees international cooperation or mitigates the potential for duplicative fines.

The issue of enhancing the dialogue between the private sector and the authorities was also central to the B20 recommendation in St. Petersburg in June 2013:

> A regulatory framework which encourages incentives for self-reporting, strengthens international coordination and harmonisation and avoids multiple sanctions will go a long way towards improving cooperation between regulatory authorities and the private sector, and ultimately reducing corruption. The Task Force has identified a number of issues for more in-depth consultations between the Task Force and ACWG:
>
> - Establishment of a clear framework for addressing multiple jurisdiction issues through the full implementation of Article 4.3 of the OECD Convention and Articles 47, 48 and 49 of UNCAC in national legislations. Exploration of ways and means of preventing or mitigating the risk of duplication of financial sanctions in the case of cross-border concurrent liabilities (in particular with respect of disgorgement of profit); and the possibility of recognition of the validity of global settlements;
> - Assessment of the feasibility of alternative means of settlement such as Deferred Prosecution Agreements (DPA), and Non Prosecution Agreements (NPA) that could incentivize self-reporting;
> - Exploration of measures to further incentivize self-reporting, such as a reduction of financial penalties and guaranteeing a certain level of confidentiality;
> - Examination of leniency mechanisms (such as the leniency programmes provided for in the case of cartels) to be defined on the basis of clear parameters and with clear benefits;
> - Identification of benefits and clear limitations of liability to corporations that have initiated autonomous internal investigations prior to self-reporting or that carry out such internal investigation in consultation with national authorities (with consequent savings of government resources by relying on companies' investigations carried out at their own cost).
> - Exploration of the potential for companies which are effectively co-operating with authorities or have self-reported to be exempted from interim measures such as injunctions, monitoring, or debarment which may be proclaimed pending the outcome of the investigations.
> - Exploration of the possibility to improve the use of civil recovery orders as an incentive for self-reporting as opposed to criminal sanctions.
> - Exploration of the feasibility of including in national laws the validity of compliance defence, with clearly defined limitations of liability, as a means to mitigate or exclude liability in cases where anti-corruption programs are in place, and supported by independent third-party assurance.

Companies do want to take an active role in the fight against corruption, and if incentivized they can do more. To be clear, to incentivize a corporation does not mean to avoid imposing sanctions where applicable. Sanctions are and will remain the most powerful tool in the fight against corruption. However, such a tool has not proved to be sufficient. If we want to be successful in this fight we must also increase the efforts of the private sector in the fight against corruption and in particular increase the number of corporations that are ready to do so. A balanced and clear incentive system could achieve this.[3]

---

[3] With regard to incentives, two significant projects are due concurrent with the publication of this volume: (a) a report by the Humboldt Viadrina School of Governance, Germany, on Motivating Business to Counter Corruption, that will also include a significant international survey and (b) a position paper coordinated by the works stream 4 of the B20 2013 working group on anti-bribery that will be presented at the Fifth Session of the Conference of the States Parties to the United Nations Convention against Corruption (Panama, 25–29 November 2013).

References

B20 Task Force Recommendations. (June 2012). B20 Business Summit. http://b20.org/documentos/B20-Complete-Report.pdf. Accessed 16 July 2013.

Counselor Corruption. (2010). The UN global compact. http://www.unglobalcompact.org/docs/issues_doc/Anti-Corruption/CollectiveAction2010.pdf. Accessed 16 July 2013.

Chapter 4
Public–Private Partnerships and Agency Problems: The Use of Incentives in Strategies to Combat Corruption

Francesco Centonze

Contents

4.1 Public–Private Partnerships and the Delegation of Corruption Prevention Tasks to Entities

The various international efforts to combat corporate crime, and corruption in particular, generally share a clear criminal policy strategy. This strategy is to encourage corporations, which are closer to the sources of risk, to take upon themselves the task of preventing criminal acts that may occur within the organization (Pieth 2010, p. 891). Preventing corporate crime therefore requires putting into place, alongside the traditional punishment model which focuses on deterring individuals, a more efficient "public–private partnership" (Hefendehl 2007, p. 846) which transforms the role of the corporation in the criminal justice process "from potential criminal target to branch office of the prosecutor whose role it is to partner with prosecutors in investigating and prosecuting business crimes" (First 2010, p. 97).

F. Centonze (✉)
Centro Studi "Federico Stella" sulla giustizia penale e la politica criminale (CSGP), Università Cattolica del Sacro Cuore, Piacenza, Italy
e-mail: francesco.centonze@unicatt.it

S. Manacorda et al. (eds.), *Preventing Corporate Corruption*,
DOI 10.1007/978-3-319-04480-4_4, © Springer International Publishing Switzerland 2014

Thus, at the root of this cooperation between public institutions and corporations is an awareness of the weakness of the state's monopoly in preventing business crimes and, above all, as far as we are concerned here, in preventing corruption linked to international investments.

What we are seeing at the criminal policy level is actually a reflection of a more general "new division of labor between state and society" (Levi-Faur 2005, p. 13) in which the former, by abandoning *direct* regulation, has given rise to a gradual privatization and delegation to non-state actors. We have seen a gradual decline in traditional state regulation systems based on "command and control" in favor of regimes of *indirect* regulation where the use of administrative agencies is favored, new categories of controllers are created, internal structures of governance are formalized, and self-regulatory regimes are encouraged (Baldwin et al. 2012, pp. 108, 146; Carrigan and Coglianese 2011, p. 107).

The state therefore *transfers* to private organizations a portion of its control (Bamberger 2006, p. 380), withdrawing from the direct regulation of economic life (Power 2007, p. 36; Lobel 2004, p. 262; Dorf and Sabel 1998, p. 270; Cunningham 2004, p. 269) and "encouraging self-regulatory and compliance strategies on the part of non-state actors" (Forti 2007, p. 639).

The latter, in turn, take on new tasks (and the resulting responsibilities) since they "possess information and knowledge of the sector in which they operate, or oversee" (Ferrarese 2010, pp. 7, 52, 58).

Contemporary society is therefore a "regulatory society" in which "regulation is not 'centered' on the state, but instead is 'decentered,' diffused throughout society" (Black 2002; Hutter 2006, p. 3).[1]

The role of the state, in this context, is to delegate to corporations and business organizations and take on "meta-regulation" tasks, i.e., to regulate self-regulation. There has been a "proliferation of different forms of regulation (whether tools of state law or non-law mechanisms) each regulating one another" (Parker 2007, p. 207; Braithwaite 2003, p. 1; Coglianese and Lazer 2003, p. 691). In short, there has been a "re-invention of governance" which attributes to the state solely the role of "monitor of last resort" (Power 1997, p. 66) and to internal controls the function of the regulatory instruments necessary to manage risk (Power 2007, p. 48).

This "hybrid governance" (Braithwaite 2006, p. 408), which has also been implemented in the fight against international corruption, can be described as an agency relationship, in which "one or more persons (the principal(s)) engage another person (the agent) to perform some service on their behalf which involves delegating some decision-making authority to the agent" (Jensen and Meckling 1976, p. 308).

Thus, according to this scheme, the state embodies the role of the principal enlisting private organizations (its agents) to perform activities to prevent business crimes.

The first set of problems inherent in this relationship, as in all agency relationships, arises primarily because the principal cannot, normally, directly monitor the agent's activity (so called agency problems), (Laffont 2003; Posner 2000, p. 4). The

[1] Hutter uses the expression "fragmented regulation."

principal is hampered by a structural limitation in knowledge due to an information shift towards the agent, which instead has a private wealth of knowledge that it can hide or not share with the principal (this has given rise, in the economic literature, to the issue of "adverse selection" or "hidden knowledge"). In any case, the agent may therefore act without being monitored by the principal ("moral hazard" or "hidden action;" Laffont and Martimort 2002).

The second issue, which is crucial in the management of the relationship between the principal (the public authority) and the agent (the private organization), is the potential difference in objectives that may put the delegator at odds with the delegate. For example, the goal of preventing organized criminal action may be disregarded by members of the corporation who act illegally with the intention perhaps of benefiting the corporation and/or its members ("unethical pro-organizational behavior") (Umphress and Bingham 2011, p. 621).

Given the information asymmetry and the potential conflict of interests between the principal and agent, the principal's problem is to "design a compensation and control (monitoring) system that attracts and retains good agents and motivates them to behave appropriately (in the principal's interest)" (Milgrom and Roberts 1988, p. 155; Kraakman et al. 2009, p. 35).[2] The agent will therefore normally be willing to actively pursue the principal's objectives (in our case, the prevention of corruption) only if it receives an adequate return. This is why the agency relationship between public and private implies an architecture of incentives to the agent for it to carry out the preventive tasks transferred by the principal in an effective manner.

Similarly, the model of public–private partnerships in the prevention of corruption is grounded on the effective functioning of increasingly varied incentives to cooperate. On the one hand, there are incentives devised by public authorities and by national legislatures, also on the basis of supranational legislation, to promote the organization's commitment to prevention; and on the other there are incentives designed by the organization to promote compliance by its managers and employees with corporate rules.

As we will see, the two systems are in a relationship of mutual subjective and objective interference: subjectively, with regard to those actors required both to respond to the requirements of external incentives and to promote the internal incentives; objectively, with reference to the link between internal procedures and the public regulation of incentives.

Before going on to describe the various types, purposes, and sources of incentives, it must be emphasized that the public–private partnership rests on two key, highly problematic assumptions which we must deal with, albeit briefly.

The first assumption, which will be analyzed in the next section, is that individuals and organizations both act on the basis of "instrumental reasons," i.e., that human and organizational behavior is motivated and driven, at least in part, by the presence of (positive or negative) incentives. Rewards and sanctions can be

[2] Milgrom and Roberts (1988) note that "the problem lies in motivating the agent to act in the principal's interest rather than simply in the agent's own interest."

considered effective only by attributing "a high degree of rationality on the part of corporations and the claim that, specifically, managements within these can identify and act upon rational corporate self-interest" (Tombs and Whyte 2013) (infra, Sect. 4.2). The second assumption is that self-regulatory rules and compliance programs are actually effective in preventing deviant action (infra, Sect. 4.3).

4.2 Instrumental Motivations and Relational Incentives

Identifying the factors that lead people to conform to a normative system or to cooperate in an organization is crucial to assessing the potential and the limitations of a regulation model centered on positive and negative incentives. Incentives are "external prompts to which the individual responds. Individuals are assumed to be passive and to act in response to incentives in their environment. But human agency is much more complicated than that" (Grant 2012, p. 33). It is therefore clear that a "narrow view of human motivation may severely limit progress in understanding incentives" (Fehr and Falk 2002, p. 688).

In fact, while toning down the "myth" of self-interest and the rational actor as maximizer of utility model, behavioral scientists—though they do not question the fact that human decisions are largely guided by instrumental motivations and therefore by the desire to maximize rewards and minimize losses—emphasize the role of "intrinsic motivations" in complying with a system of rules. It has been noted that "one is said to be intrinsically motivated to perform an activity when one receives no apparent reward except the activity itself" (Deci 1971, p. 105, as cited in Atiq 2014, p. 1080). Conversely, extrinsic motivation is the recognition that a certain behavior is driven by external factors, such as the incentives that make a particular behavior more attractive through the promise of rewards or the threat of sanctions (Atiq 2014, p. 1080; Feldman 2011, p. 11).

At the same time, in answering the question *why people cooperate,* a recent study emphasizes the "social motivations" that encourage the individual to comply with rules (Tyler 2011, p. 28):[3] these include individual attitudes; principles, and informal rules that have arisen in a situation; the authority and legitimacy of the rules and procedures imposed; and the relationships of trust (Jackson et al. 2012, p. 1051).[4]

In the case of this last motivation, it has also been noted that a crucial psychological mechanism in creating cooperation models based on social motivations is "trust responsiveness," according to which "an explicit act of trust has the pecu-

[3] Tyler (2011) also notes that "research suggests that incentives and sanctions frequently do shape the level of cooperative behavior that occurs in organizational settings."

[4] Jackson et al. (2012) argue that "legitimacy is the belief that the law and agents of the law are rightful holders of authority; that they have the right to dictate appropriate behavior and are entitled to be obeyed; and that laws should be obeyed simply because that is the right thing to do".

liarity of 'inducing' or 'eliciting,' to some degree, a trustworthy response. Trust is said to be responsive or self-fulfilling." Trustful actions motivate people "to reward such trustfulness," making them behave trustworthily, even though such a behavior implies "some material cost" (Pelligra, forthcoming).

As has been pointed out, trust "appears to be motivationally self-enforcing: it does not serve just to give trustor and trustee greater confidence in one another—specifically, in one another's loyalty or virtue or prudence—it also has the effect of binding them more closely with each another" (Pettit 1995, pp. 202, 218).

An act of trust can therefore be considered, in terms of trust responsiveness, a relational incentive that can be an important tool to encourage adherence to the rule (Kahan 2002). In short, in a "self-sustaining atmosphere of trust, reliance on costly incentive schemes becomes less necessary" (Kahan 2002).

Possible evidence of the validity of these assertions comes from cognitive psychology studies on compliance without pressure, i.e., those behaviors characterized by "positive and costly responses to a certain request or expectation, despite all absence of coercion" (Pelligra 2007, p. 239). In this regard "several studies have found that increasing the feeling of freedom acts as a facilitator of commitment towards the expected behavior" and that the "evocation of freedom might decrease the weight of external factors and increase the weight of internal ones" (Gueguen and Pascual 2005, p. 301).

Recent studies play down the efficacy even of monetary incentives, arguing that at least three important human motives interact with these incentives: "the motive to reciprocate, the desire for social approval and the desire to work on interesting tasks." According to this study, there are "powerful non-pecuniary motives" that "also shape human behavior" (Fehr and Falk 2002, p. 689). Proof that economic incentives are not decisive in inducing behavior consistent with the rules comes from an empirical study on the relationship between monetary rewards and reporting. It shows that "in laws which are likely to trigger strong internal ethical motivation, offering monetary awards may be unnecessary or, worse yet, counterproductive. In such circumstances, in which legal violation is generally perceived as morally offensive, creating a duty to report may be sufficient" (Feldman and Lobel 2010, p. 1151).

By way of an initial conclusion, therefore, the construction of a system of incentives in the context of an agency relationship should consider that awards and sanctions are certainly necessary tools to motivate agents to cooperate, but must be supplemented by a more realistic understanding of the agent's behavioral patterns. When it comes to deciding whether, to achieve a certain goal, it is more appropriate to use a system of incentives or use other means such as "persuasion" or "coercion," "the justification of the choice of incentives must include an assessment of their effectiveness in meeting that goal relative to the alternative" (Grant 2012, p. 69). The problem is, therefore, to concretely evaluate the effectiveness of the incentive proposed and other possible instruments available to the principal: "incentives should not be the only tool in the policymaker's toolbox" (Grant 2012, p. 139).

After examining the role of instrumental motivations in compliance with certain behavioral models, albeit in a necessarily brief manner, let us now analyze the second underlying assumption in a system of prevention of wrongdoing based on the mechanism of incentives, namely the preventive capability of self-regulatory models in legal entities.

4.3 The Efficacy of Compliance Programs in Crime Prevention and the Reasons Why Organizations Choose Cooperation

This problem must be addressed first because the public–private partnership to prevent corruption rests on the assumption that delegating to private organizations is to be encouraged because self-regulation models are effective tools, especially for the purposes of preventing wrongdoing.

The question arises from a number of concerns about the well foundedness of this principle. There are those who claim that there is very little evidence for the assumption that internal compliance structures really reduce the incidence of wrongdoing within an entity. Indeed, "a growing body of evidence indicates that internal compliance structures do not deter prohibited conduct within firms and may largely serve a window-dressing function that provides both market legitimacy and reduced legal liability" (Krawiec 2003, p. 491; see also Parker and Nielsen 2006, p. 487; Khanna 2003, p. 1231). In short, a compliance system may be nothing more than cosmetic and may only make compliance monitoring professionals richer while having virtually no impact on actual prevention.

As a German scholar has recently written, there is growing "disenchantment" with the effectiveness of compliance which "in many cases has only had a window-dressing function, and has not led to any real change in business culture" (Schünemann 2005, p. 361; Schünemann 2008, p. 444; Sieber 2008, p. 449).

In the USA literature there is even talk of a "paradox of compliance," identifying a "moral hazard" in the adoption of good compliant behavior patterns by firms as mere insurance against the risk of a criminal investigation. Precisely because they are "insured" (against legal risk) corporations appear to pay much less attention to actually preventing unlawful conduct within the organization (hence the moral hazard), with the obvious potential consequence of a (paradoxical) *increase* in wrongdoing (Laufer 1999, p. 1405).

These are very serious arguments against the effectiveness of compliance programs which, furthermore, raise doubts that business organizations may be induced to cooperate by the desire for external legitimacy rather than by an actual aspiration for legality in the business environment. The phenomenon is well known in organization theory studies that have investigated the relationship between "isomorphism" and external "legitimacy" (Powell and Di Maggio 1991).

The former (isomorphism) refers to the process by which entities belonging to the same type tend to resemble each other by adopting similar structures, strategies, and processes. Organizations are driven by public opinion, politics, laws, and courts "to incorporate the practices and procedures defined by prevailing rationalized concepts of organizational work and institutionalized in society." Isomorphic processes are the result of creating "rationalized myths," i.e., rules that are not based on empirical evidence obtained through the scientific method, but which are legitimized by the belief that they are effective or by their official recognition by legislative or judicial authorities.

Organizations which conform in this manner "increase their legitimacy and their survival prospects," and this, it should be noted, is "independent of the immediate efficacy of the acquired practices and procedures." Indeed, "conformity to institutionalized rules often conflicts sharply with efficiency criteria" (Meyer and Rowan 1991, p. 41).

The key point is that:

> by designing a formal structure that adheres to the prescriptions of myths in the institutional environment, an organization demonstrates that it is acting on collectively valued purposes in a proper and adequate manner. The incorporation of institutionalized elements provides an account of its activities that protects the organization from having its conduct questioned. The organization becomes, in a word, legitimate, and it uses its legitimacy to strengthen its support and secure its survival. (Meyer and Rowan 1991, p. 50)

So, in our specific context, social and institutional expectations about the need to create formal structures of control, to be displayed publicly, legitimize an organization in the eyes of its shareholders, the public, and the state. Ultimately, it is the incorporation of "structures with high ceremonial value" which confer credibility on the organization.

Conversely, however:

> organizations that omit environmentally legitimated elements of structure or create unique structures lack acceptable legitimated accounts of their activities. Such organizations are more vulnerable to claims that they are negligent, irrational, or unnecessary. (Meyer and Rowan 1991, p. 50)

On the other hand, it is precisely the indirect governance method that requires formalized and public control models: in essence, we have complex "control of control" circuits. The monitoring carried out by the internal principals must in turn be audited: "the audit explosion is to do with the need to install a *publicly auditable* self-inspecting capacity which attempts to link ideals of accountability to those of self-learning" (Power 1997, p. 67).

The risk, however, is that the controls are designed more on the basis of how they can be audited than on the basis of their actual effectiveness. There is a substantial difference between effective and auditable control. A corporation may have a more effective but less auditable internal control system, or controls that are less effective but more auditable. However, behind this option there lies a paradox: the less we trust those whose behavior we wish to monitor by increasing surveillance systems, the more we will tend to produce auditable controls. But the "infallibility complex" associated with these checks will lead us to adopt controls that can be audited rather than controls that are really effective (Cunningham 2004, p. 269).

The problem is that the very adherence to the "myths" of the institutional environment can turn controls into "a cosmetic practice which hides real risk…. Where the audit process is defensively legalized there is a risk of relying too heavily on an industry of empty comfort certificates" (Power 1997, p. 123). According to Power, this is the typical product of the "audit society," i.e., "a society that endangers itself because it invests too heavily in shallow rituals of verification at the expense of other forms of organizational intelligence. In providing a lens for regulatory thought and action audit threatens to become a form of learned ignorance" (Power 1997, p. 123).

These observations are extremely useful in understanding the limits of compliance and the risks of uncritical trust in the preventive virtues of public–private partnerships. However, the fact remains that corporations are still "uniquely positioned to intervene ex ante to deter crime through their ability to structure compensation and promotion policies so as to make crime less profitable" (Arlen 2012, p. 144). This is the crucial reason why preventive tasks should be delegated to corporations.

So, while extremely problematic, and despite the above-mentioned reservations, the underlying assumption concerning the preventive effectiveness of organization models remains valid. It is now time to consider public–private partnerships and examine, in depth, the incentives that the principal can use to encourage compliance.

4.4 "Carrots versus Sticks" in the Public–Private Partnership: Source, Form, and Purpose of the Incentives

Let us now move on to analyze the various incentives, distinguishing them according to their source, purpose, and form.

As regards source, we can distinguish between incentives promoted by the organization and incentives provided by the public sphere: the former are to be found in a corporation's self-regulatory structure, in the rules and procedures that are the result of private initiative, whereas the latter are the product of international institutions, of state law (which in turn may pass legislation under the impulse of supranational law) and of the administrative authorities responsible for overseeing the various markets (such as the Securities and Exchange commission (SEC) or the Department of Justice (DOJ) in the USA).

These are distinct, but communicating sources: the *agent*'s self-regulated rules are drawn up according to the indications set by the *principal,* i.e., public institutions. For example, under Italian law, the provisions contained in Art. 6 of legislative decree No. 231 of 2001 require, as a key element of a compliance program, the establishment of a disciplinary system which must be actually implemented by the entity according to its own rules. The same also applies under US law where:

> the organization's compliance and ethics program shall be promoted and enforced consistently throughout the organization through…appropriate disciplinary measures for engaging in criminal conduct and for failing to take reasonable steps to prevent or detect criminal conduct.[5]

[5] US Sentencing Guidelines § 8B2.1(b)(6) (2011).

The diversity of the receivers and the purpose of the incentives follow from the variety of the sources. Incentives promoted by the organization are directed only at its members and may concern both compliance with self-regulation rules and the reporting of any violations of the organizational model. Incentives based on an institutional source, whose purpose instead is to ensure compliance by the organization and self-reporting by its members, are therefore aimed at both entities and natural persons. From the perspective of the former, these include all the different measures intended to encourage the entity, especially through its management, to faithfully comply with the state's delegation of crime-prevention tasks. In this regard there has been considerable debate, which will be explored in detail later, on "compliance defense," i.e., on the possible need to encourage the virtuous organization to comply by assuring a comprehensive and secure exemption from liability for a crime committed by an employee or a representative (see Sect. 5.1). At the same time, self-reporting incentives targeted at members of the organization may also be built in. A case in point in this regard is the monetary compensation and protection provided by the Dodd–Frank Act, which will also be discussed later (infra, Sect. 5.2).

Let us now consider the issue of the form of the incentives. Traditionally the most commonly used incentives are the negative ones, i.e., based on the threat of a sanction: the factor driving the recipient of the incentive is the fear of being subjected to a punishment and suffering the stigmatizing effect inherent in the sanction (Bobbio 1968, p. 530).

However, there are also positive incentives, conversely characterized by the promise of a reward on the occurrence of a desired behavior (Ormerod 2005).[6] In the scheme of positive incentives, upon verification of the proper conduct an *award is made,* which, even when it is of material value, always possesses:

> a symbolic component, which is the outward sign, the public testimony of acknowledgement. The award expresses a positive evaluation of the person or behavior and is directed at each single individual as a stimulus and acknowledgment of extraordinary conduct, special aptitude or effort. (Facchi 1995, p. 175)

The key issue at present is to find the right mix between the two forms of incentive.

Although legal systems have sometimes used positive incentives, it must be recognized, in the words of Norberto Bobbio, that the dominant conception of the law has for a long time been a repressive one. "The law is prevalently considered a coercive system, thus establishing a necessary, indissoluble link between law and coercion" (Bobbio 2007, p. 8).[7]

In fact, the traditional focus on negative incentives—on the stick, the sanction—conveys "an extremely simplified image of the law" which, especially with the

[6] Ormerod notes that "'negative' incentives are those that deter and prevent crime—the probability and severity of punishment. 'Positive' incentives are those that encourage people to take up legitimate work instead of crime" (Ormerod 2005, p. 35).

[7] Beccaria underlines that "yet another method of preventing crimes is to reward virtue. Upon this subject the laws of all nations are silent. If the rewards proposed by academies for the discovery of useful truths have increased our knowledge, and multiplied good books, is it not probable that rewards, distributed by the beneficent hand of a sovereign, would also multiply virtuous actions" (Beccaria 2004, p. 62).

advent of "post-liberal" constitutions, has been comprehensively challenged by a school of thought that emphasizes the "promotional function" of the legal order. The change in perspective is significant: "it marks the transition from passive monitoring, which is more concerned with discouraging harm doing than encouraging beneficial actions, to active monitoring, which is concerned with promoting beneficial actions more than discouraging harmful actions". We can therefore distinguish "a legal system based on protection/repression from a legal system based on promotion. The former focuses on socially undesirable behaviors, so its primary purpose is to prevent their occurrence as much as possible; the latter focuses mainly on socially desired behaviors, so its purpose is to encourage their performance even by those who are most reluctant" (Bobbio 2007, p. 15).

In view also of the human, economic, and social costs usually resulting from the use of sanctions and the limited effectiveness of the instruments of punishment, the prospect of positive incentives is now beginning, despite the obvious ease of use of negative incentives, to be adopted more frequently.

Let us consider, for example, § 8B2.1, "effective compliance and ethics program," in the US Sentencing Guidelines, which encourages entities to promote and enforce compliance programs not only through adequate disciplinary measures, but also through "appropriate incentives to perform in accordance with the compliance and ethics program."[8]

The importance of a system of incentives, including financial ones, has also been highlighted at the European level. The draft regulation proposal issued by the European Commission in October 2011 on the abuse of privileged information and market abuse (Market Abuse Regulation) establishes, among other things, a system aimed at encouraging the reporting of possible violations of the rules. It requires, in particular, that member states on the one hand offer protection to whistle-blowers from possible retaliation, while on the other hand safeguard those accused of crimes (Art. 29, para. 1). The regulation expressly recognizes the possibility of granting monetary incentives to anyone who reports irregularities, as long as they provide new information (whose disclosure is not already compulsory pursuant to a legal obligation) and that such information leads to the imposition of administrative or criminal law sanctions (Art. 29, para. 2; Fleischer and Schmolke 2012).[9]

[8] "The organization's compliance and ethics program shall be promoted and enforced consistently throughout the organization through (A) *appropriate incentives* to perform in accordance with the compliance and ethics program; and (B) *appropriate disciplinary measures* for engaging in criminal conduct and for failing to take reasonable steps to prevent or detect criminal conduct." US Sentencing Guidelines § 8B2.1.

[9] ECGI, Law Working Paper No. 189/2012. Art. 29 on Reporting of Violations prescribes that "1. Member States shall put in place effective mechanisms to encourage reporting of breaches of this Regulation to competent authorities.... 2. Financial incentives to persons who offer salient information about potential breaches of this Regulation may be granted in conformity with national law where such persons do not have a pre-existing legal or contractual duty to report such information, that the information is new, and it results in the imposition of an administrative sanction or measure or a criminal sanction for a breach of this Regulation."

Italy's security authority, CONSOB, has expressed "support for the approach indicated by the European Commission, which has successfully been in force in other EU countries for some time," while stressing that it is essential "that the matter be organized so as to limit grassing up, and more generally, the risk of the improper use of reporting" (Salini 2012).

We have already considered the limitations of the effectiveness of monetary incentives (supra, Sect. 4.2), and will return later to the risks associated with this type of incentive. For the present let us continue to analyze incentives for preventing criminal conduct from the institutional perspective, i.e., public sphere incentives to organizations (infra, Sect. 5.1.) and individuals (infra, Sect. 5.2).

4.5 The Institutional Perspective: Incentives to the Entity

4.5.1 Compliance Incentives and the Entity's Residual Liability Risk

Let us now return to the heart of the public–private partnership in preventing international corruption and, hence, to the question of the benefits that organizations (through their management decisions) can obtain from scrupulously performing the preventive tasks. In the agency relationship, the problem, as we have said, lies in motivating the agent to act in the interest of the principal, and not only in his/her own interest, because "the agent…would rather not go to the effort unless she is compensated for that effort" (Posner 2000, p. 4).

So, how can the principal, the legal system, reward an agent's compliance efforts? Further, what characteristics should the benefits offered to the virtuous organization have in order to minimize agency costs and therefore reduce the risk of the agent's ineffectiveness? Finally, to what extent does the state rely on the organization properly performing the preventive tasks?

In the context of the public–private partnership, the public authority seeks to minimize agency costs. Therefore, as it is not able to constantly monitor the work of the non-state actor, it is ready to reward the organization only on the basis of the results achieved in the prevention and disclosure of criminal acts: it is the "output of the agent" that counts and, therefore, if the organization proves it has been virtuous, it can enjoy the benefits provided. For its part, the organization will be willing to cooperate only if its aversion to risk is properly taken into account—the public authority should therefore "insure" the organization against any "unlucky outcomes" (Posner 2000).[10]

[10] Posner notes that "principals want to minimize agency costs (and the agent wants the principal to minimize agency costs, to the extent that she will share the savings). There are two main ways of doing this. The first is…design a contract that makes compensation depend on the output of the agent. As output rises, so should compensation. Notice that the principal does not need to know the actual level of effort; he simply looks at the amount of output, which should be easily verifiable.

The problem of possible unlucky outcomes seems to be particularly prominent in international corruption. Indeed, as one American scholar who has explored these issues at length writes: "doing business in international markets often requires hiring local workers who are products of different cultures and experiences, speak different languages, and are located in different time zones from corporate headquarters." Even with more effective compliance policies and procedures "the practical reality of monitoring and supervising this vast and various network of individuals is difficult and even gold standard compliance policies and procedures are not foolproof" (Koehler 2012, p. 609).

It is therefore necessary to determine which system of incentives will most encourage the organization to faithfully perform its preventive duties and ensure that "those making decisions for the organization will cooperate, even if it means that some constituents (employees or, perhaps, current shareholders) suffer" (First 2010, p. 39).

In this regard, two models will be compared very briefly. The first is the "full defense" model, which was also adopted in Sect. 7 of the UK Bribery Act 2010, for commercial organizations which can prove that although a bribery payment was made, adequate procedures were nevertheless implemented to prevent wrongdoing. The need to encourage the organization's compliance while at the same insuring against an "isolated incident of bribery" is expressed very clearly by the UK Ministry of Justice which, in the guidelines to the Bribery Act, specifies that "in order to achieve an appropriate balance," English law has decided to grant the organization a full defense because "no bribery prevention regime will be capable of preventing bribery at all times" (Ministry of Justice, UK, 2011). We do not intend to explore in depth here how the rules of this defense are applied, nor the differences between the UK and similar legal systems.

Let us instead consider the second model of incentives as exemplified, among others, by US law. The key feature of the US system is the sentencing phase. It is at this stage of the proceedings, following the finding of liability, that a whole series of factors, which are predefined and codified in the Sentencing Guidelines, come into play. If these factors are present, the organization may obtain a significant reduction in the monetary sanction (potentially as much as 95 %). The mitigating factors can include the fact that the legal entity has adopted an effective compliance and ethics program, and that it has demonstrated a culture of compliance through self-reporting, cooperation with authorities, and acceptance of responsibility (US Sentencing Guidelines, p. 489). Sentencing is, in short, the moment in the proceedings against the organization in which the public–private partnership becomes evident, and in which the business's active role in crime control is encouraged.

The US legal system is therefore reluctant to recognize the exemption of liability as an incentive, except in deferred prosecution agreements and non-prosecution agreements. In these forms of negotiation, the prosecutor plays—to use the

The problem is that if the agent is risk-averse—and this will almost always be the case—the agent will demand insurance against unlucky outcomes. So the principal might offer a mixed contract containing both insurance and incentives" (Posner 2000, p. 5).

terminology of the agency relationship—the role of principal with respect to the corporation under investigation, which becomes his *agent* (Arlen 2012, p. 144; Epstein 2011, p. 38).[11] Here too:

> these agreements are tools to ensure that the agent's conduct is aligned with the principal's interests by memorializing the various obligations of the corporation-agent and the prosecutor principal and providing enforcement mechanisms for the agent's breach. (First 2010, p. 63)[12]

To conclude on this point, the problem is as follows: on the one hand, we should recognize that in order to really encourage the agent to pursue the interests of the principal, a system of incentives should ensure full exclusion of liability if the organization complies with prevention tasks and none of the models considered guarantees such an outcome (Weissmann and Newman 2007).[13] On the other hand, however, there seems to be no alternative to entrusting to the courts the retrospective assessment of the organization's commitment to prevention:

> whether an organization had adequate procedures in place to prevent bribery in the context of a particular prosecution is a matter that can only be resolved by the courts taking into account the particular facts and circumstances of the case. (UK Bribery Act 2010)

Therefore, the corporation, which, despite having done its best to fulfill what the legal system has delegated to it, receives no guarantees that its commitment will be fully recognized and has no means to neutralize the risk of suffering the consequences of wrongdoing by one of its members.

To overcome this structural limit in the public–private partnership, a certification of compliance programs has been proposed to exempt corporations ex-ante—a sort of "Papal Bull" (Matus Acuña 2013, p. 151).

A system to validate organizational models has recently been introduced, for example in Chilean law,[14] which, however, does not explicitly state the effect that

---

[11] In this regard, we may underline that deferred prosecution agreements have also been recently introduced in the UK by the Crime and Courts Act 2013, Schedule 17.

[12] First notes that it is also possible that "these agreements may be prone to breakdowns or failures because some of the agents making these agreements were lawbreakers in the first place, who cooperate only because they were caught or were about to be caught. This concern for ensuring against bad faith behavior from lawbreakers may explain the much-criticized provisions in the deferred prosecution agreements that give the Department the unilateral right to revoke the agreement in the event of a breach" (First 2010, p. 89).

[13] The authors underline that the "incentive would be all the greater…where the establishment of an effective compliance program would serve to shield the company from criminal prosecution and the vagaries of individual criminal prosecutors" (Weissmann and Newman 2007, p. 433).

[14] Article 4, Ley No. 20393/2009 prescribes that "las personas jurídicas podrán obtener la certificación de la adopción eimplementación de su modelo de prevención de delitos. En el certificado constará que dicho modelo contempla todos los requisitos establecidos en los numerales 1), 2) y 3) anteriores, en relación a la situación, tamaño, giro, nivel de ingresos y complejidad de la persona jurídica. Los certificados podrán ser expedidos por empresas de auditoría externa, sociedades clasificadoras de riesgo u otras entidades registradas ante la Superintendencia de Valores y Seguros que puedan cumplir esta labor, de conformidad a la normativa que, para estos efectos, establezca el mencionado organismo fiscalizador."

such a certificate would have on the organization's liability. Commentators have suggested it would simply be a "proof of the entity's good conduct which can justify a mitigation of the criminal liability" (Matus Acuña 2013, p. 151).

However, a certification system, which has already been debated in Italy, is unable to offer an adequate solution to the problem, even if it envisaged exemption from liability. First, there would be the problem of increased red tape: the system would, in fact, run "the risk of becoming too rigidly associated with the time period of effectiveness of each certification," given "the very real possibility that the risks assessment within the organization will change as a result of changes in the organization and in its activity" (Flick 2010, p. 1294). Secondly, it would be difficult to actually limit the model's certification to the period before the criminal act occurred. There would always be a need for the courts to verify ex-post the validity of such a certification (Flick 2010, p. 1300). Finally, there is also the risk that it will all lead to a "market of certifications" created by corporate consultants who would not hesitate to offer the corporation an insurance against possible sanctions (Martin 2013, p. 25).

4.5.2 Self-Reporting Incentives: The Individual and the Organization

It is therefore unlikely that the law will provide, even to the most scrupulous organization, a blank delegation that will protect it from the risk of criminal prosecution, thus suggesting a lack of confidence in the non-state actor's capacity for prevention.

Evidence of the legal system's distrust towards business organizations can be found in the legislative framework of incentives for self-reporting, where the current debate is mainly focused on the appropriateness of providing a monetary reward to anyone who reports wrongdoing. This would be a further step in the classic "carrot and stick" approach, transforming it into a "carrot-for-the-whistle-blower, stick-for-the-corporation approach" (Ashcroft et al. 2011, p. 379; Gonzalez 2010, p. 338).[15]

The reason is clear: the principal (the public authority) is highly skeptical about the possibility of creating a virtuous information channel between the corporation and the public authorities and, as a result, offers members of the organization the possibility of circumventing the internal controls to provide any news of wrongdoing directly to investigators.

Let us first consider the legal system that is currently experimenting most with the use of such incentives, namely the USA. We will not deal with how the measures were developed and the problems that have arisen over time in implementing them, but proceed directly to the most recent legislation, to be found in the Dodd–Frank

[15] Gonzalez notes that "some commentators have argued that this type of private-public partnership is often good for both the informants and the government. Private individuals reap monetary profits from pointing out federal violations to the relevant government agency. Regulators obtain information that they otherwise would not know about, develop stronger cases against bad actors, and more efficiently use scarce investigative and litigation resources."

Act of 2010 which, in addition to strengthening the anti-retaliation protection for whistle-blowers, has developed a detailed system of monetary rewards.

Under this Act, the whistle-blower must contribute to the disclosure of wrongdoing by providing "original information," i.e., information "derived from the independent knowledge or analysis of [the] whistle-blower," and not yet known to the SEC. In exchange, the whistle-blower has the right to obtain a reward calculated at between 10 and 30 % of the sanction imposed and actually paid, but only in the event that the information allows the SEC to apply a financial penalty of over US$ 1 million.

The bounty can reach quite considerable figures, particularly in the case of international corruption, where the sanctions applied are typically extremely high:

> Take, for example, the SEC's recent $ 1.6 billion settlement with Siemens AG (Siemens), the electronics and engineering conglomerate, involving charges that Siemens violated the Foreign Corrupt Practices Act (FCPA) in 2010. Under the bounty provisions of the Dodd-Frank Act, an individual who reported to the SEC that Siemens had engaged in a "systematic practice of paying bribes to foreign government officials to obtain business" would stand to gain an award of a minimum of $ 160 million to a maximum of $ 480 million. (Hartmann 2011, p. 1304)

We will not go into the details of the legislation or the implementing regulations issued by the SEC,[16] nor consider the main differences from earlier legal provisions related to incentives for whistle-blowing. We shall instead address the question of the balance between the different interests involved: on the one hand, the aim of more effectively preventing and acting against wrongdoing in the corporate context, on the other hand, the aim of minimizing any ensuing collateral damage.

At a pragmatic level, it is worth noting the results achieved, in some contexts, by such reward mechanisms (Ferziger and Currell 1999, p. 1143)[17] and the preventive efficacy of a system in which every potential perpetrator of a criminal act knows he may be monitored by an indeterminate number of observers ready to betray him for money. Therefore, since it is very difficult to counter the interest of the individual to report, the only real way forward for corporations that want to avoid adverse effects would be to make every effort to prevent wrongdoing by individuals belonging to it by, for example, investing in an effective organizational model.

However, this system of incentives has been variously criticized. In addition to a historical argument taken from delation during the fascist regime (Franzinelli 2012, p. 163), the important warnings of Cesare Beccaria may be reminded Cesare Beccaria also warned:

> He who has strength to defend himself will not purchase the assistance of another. Besides, such an edict confounds all the ideas of virtue and morality, already too wavering in the mind of man. At one time treachery is punished by the laws, at another encouraged. With one hand the legislator strengthens the ties of kindred and friendship, and with the other rewards the violation of both. Always in contradiction with himself, now he invites the suspecting minds of men to mutual confidence, and now he plants distrust in every heart. To prevent one crime he gives birth to a thousand. Such are the expedients of weak nations, whose laws are like temporary repairs to a tottering fabric. (Beccaria 2004)

---

[16] Adopted rules to implement a Whistle-blower Incentives & Protection Program, May 2011.

[17] In this chapter it is highlighted that whistle-blowing plays an important part in the fight led by the US government against tax evasion.

Even today, however, moral counter-arguments are not infrequent (Gonzalez 2010, p. 339).[18] There are also those who point out the risk that even within an organization one ends up encouraging a pernicious culture of suspicion which undermines trust and respect among colleagues and employees: if "the very social fabric is not to be worn dangerously thin," then "the means of mutual trust and care need to be shored up, not further eroded" (Lyon 2003, p. 61).

Furthermore, it has been claimed, as mentioned previously, that the use of such monetary incentives may end up having almost paradoxical consequences:

> [I]f the incentives created by the Act crowd out ethical motives to blow the whistle on wrongdoing—a serious possibility, as the evidence suggests—it renders persons engaged in commerce even more beholden to financial interest; a fact that might be genuinely regrettable to them. By shutting down a means for cultivating a sense of commercial decency, the law diminishes ethical behavior for its own sake. (Atiq 2014, p. 20)

There is also the risk of an exponential growth in irrelevant information being given about acts that are not unlawful, or even worse, in untruthful reports. This might occur because the huge bounties would lead many employees to adopt a "lottery mentality," whereby whistle-blowing is "a chance to instantly win economic success" (Hartmann 2011, p. 1305). What is more, given the time constraints within which a report must be undersigned, and the originality of the information necessary to obtain a reward, the whistle-blower may be overcome by a sense of urgency, leading him to file a report in the absence of evidence.

Another implication is related to the mechanism for calculating the reward and the US$ 1 million threshold established for the reward. It would be in the whistle-blower's interest to wait until the criminal act had reached proportions that will maximize his reward, rather than report everything as soon as he discovers it. The paradox is that individuals who previously would have immediately reported an offense out of a sense of duty would now have an incentive not to do so.

Then there is the role of the lawyers: the Dodd–Frank Act has already given rise to a flourishing whistle-blowing "industry" made up of lawyers who, in the pursuit of the very high fees that the adjudication of a reward can command, encourage their potential clients to sign a report.

In relation to our subject, one of the most negative aspects of this system (unlike the *qui tam* model, as some studies have shown)[19] is that it has seriously affected, if

[18] Gonzalez notes that: "bounty programs raise important moral and ethical questions irrespective of their alleged economic efficiencies. They are socially and politically dangerous because many people do not believe it is best to monetarily reward an informant, whatever the public benefit the informant may be providing. This philosophy was best exemplified during the 1998 debates regarding whether to discontinue the IRS whistleblower program. At that time, Senator Harry Reid of Nevada called for an end to the IRS whistleblower program. He termed it the 'Snitch Program' and the 'Award for Rats Program.' He argued to end the program on moral grounds. Senator Reid's effort failed, but the sentiment he expressed is one many people in American society agree with" (Gonzalez 2010, p. 339).

[19] According to a 2010 study, almost 90% of subjects who started a *qui tam* action, prescribed by the False Claim Act, had first tried to solve the problem internally through reporting systems (Impact of Qui Tam Laws 2010, p. 4).

not killed "at birth," the internal reporting systems set up by all the major corporations for their employees in the past few years, in the light of the Sarbanes-Oxley Act.[20] Indeed:

> not only will the lottery mentality drive employees to report truthful but frivolous claims of fraud and other improper conduct, but it will encourage the employee to file the claim with the SEC or CFTC first, rather than reporting internally through the corporation's internal procedures or guidelines…. Given the significant monetary awards that employees can now receive under the Dodd-Frank Act, the employee is more likely to report externally first. Therefore, the ethics and compliance programs of reporting fraud internally could be significantly undermined. (Hartmann 2011, p. 1307)

This type of incentive, therefore, compromises the smooth functioning of compliance programs and ends up transferring the management of "red flags" outside the corporation.

Despite the fact that today's professionals, in designing compliance programs, recommend corporations to improve their internal reporting systems and encourage employees to use them, it is clear that no corporation will ever be able to offer the rewards that the US government provides to whistle-blowers (Ashcroft et al. 2011, p. 407).

The SEC has attempted to remedy this situation by adopting an implementing regulation of the reform (US SEC 2011). The commission decided to grant the reward even if the whistle-blower initially reports internally (and the corporation later reports the episode to the SEC), or to award it if the whistle-blower reports internally first and then to the SEC within 120 days. In addition, the criteria for determining the amount due have been modified, with the reward increasing when the whistle-blower participates in the internal system for reporting and decreasing when it interferes with this system.

In essence, these measures would, on the one hand, allow the whistle-blower to first use the internal reporting system without excluding access to the reward provided for by law, and on the other encourage the corporation to report to the SEC in order to stop the whistle-blower from doing so beforehand.

However, these measures are not considered sufficient. Indeed, they have been the subject of much criticism, primarily because internal reporting is not considered "a prerequisite to obtaining whistle-blower award bounties." The lack of mandatory internal reporting seems to:

> encourage whistleblowers to bypass internal compliance programs; undermine the ability of an organization to detect, investigate, and remediate securities violations, particularly as to those complaints over which the [SEC] has no jurisdiction or that are too small for the [SEC] to investigate; create adverse incentives for whistleblowers to see their corporations sanctioned or to delay reporting potential violations; and reduce the incentive for corporations to establish and maintain effective internal compliance programs. (Ashcroft et al. 2011, p. 386)

As a result of such criticism, there has been no shortage of reform proposals based on the idea that "a whistle-blower who provides information to the government

---

[20] 15 U.S.C. § 78j-1(m) (4) (2006). For citations, see Sarbanes-Oxley Act (2006).

does so in lieu of offering the same to an internal compliance department which might very well be in a position to quickly investigate and, if necessary, remedy the illegality" (Ashcroft et al. 2011, p. 393).

Would it not be more appropriate to shift the incentives towards reporting to internal control bodies, at least in the first instance? Indeed, it has been pointed out that the costs resulting from the exponential growth of inquiries and disputes with government agencies, even for alleged violations or unfounded claims, "may also end up creating more problems for the legal community and law-abiding corporations" (Hartmann 2011, p. 1312).

Another issue is the possibility of directly rewarding the organization for self-reporting. This could be based on the so-called Cernobbio project, developed in 1994 at the height of the *Tangentopoli* scandal by a group of Italian lawyers. In order to encourage reporting, they proposed the introduction of grounds for non-punishment of the offender who had been the first to report an episode of corruption within 3 months of its commission (before the crime had been entered in the general register against his name) and who provided useful information to identify the other culprits. This was clearly intended to break the bond of silence between the corrupted and corruptor.

In the case of corporate liability, it could also be established that the legal entity whose employee or representative has committed an act of bribery (national or international) is not punishable if it reports the wrongdoing, provides useful information to identify the other culprits, and makes available any profit from the criminal act, before news of the act comes to the attention of the judicial authority or, in any case, within 3 months of its occurrence.

This kind of reward-based legislation—if also adopted at an international level—could trigger a self-reporting race between corporations that are party to wrongdoing, immediately creating strong incentives for cooperation.

Before moving on to consider the organization's perspective and the issue of incentives to individuals in the organization, it is worth devoting attention to what has now become a crucial problem in the fight against international corruption, i.e., disincentives to prevent wrongdoing generated by parallel proceedings in different countries for the same criminal act.

4.5.3 Disincentives to Compliance and Reporting: The Problem of International Double Jeopardy

The extraterritorial application of criminal laws related to international corruption, exacerbated by ever-wider US jurisdiction, raises, in the absence of international regulation mechanisms, the real risk of a proliferation of proceedings in several countries against the same person and involving the same episodes of corruption (Van Alstine 2012, p. 1331).[21] Thus, "the worthy goal of combating trade-distorting

[21] According to Van Alstine "many of the criminal sanctions imposed by the United States (most often through settlements with the corporate entities) cover actions that other member states to the

bribery has the potential to collide with fundamental notions of fairness, and in particular with the intuition that a person should not be subject to successive prosecutions for essentially the same criminal act" (Van Alstine 2012, p. 1332).

There is, in other words, a conflict between the need to ensure the prohibition of double jeopardy as "a fundamental individual right intended to ensure international legal certainty and jurisdiction, and the fulfillment of various claims of territorial sovereignty arising from the convergence over the same criminal act of competing jurisdictions based on crimes of an extraterritorial nature" (Galantini 2005, p. 1567).

The problem—which affects both natural persons and legal persons—does not only concern new trials in the presence of a final ruling, but also many parallel criminal proceedings (the so-called international *lis pendens*). There is no doubt, in fact, that *lis pendens* "has considerable ability to infringe individual rights and fundamental values that go well beyond endangering the right to legal certainty and infringing the rights of an individual against whom a certain jurisdictional judgment has become enforceable" (Luparia 2010, p. 340).

As regards this chapter, concern about parallel *in idem* proceedings against the legal person is also due to the negative effects that this phenomenon is likely to have on the prevention model in the corporate context and, in particular, on the use of incentives that various legal systems offer organizations to bring wrongdoing to light and cooperate with judicial authorities. Indeed, faced with the increasing prospect of parallel criminal proceedings in different jurisdictions for the same criminal act, the corporation may choose not to take advantage of these incentives for fear that self-reporting may trigger further investigations in other jurisdictions (Herbel et al. 2011; Dunn 2012).[22]

Given the complexity of the topic, this is not the place to consider it at length. It must, nonetheless, be noted that the construction of a system of incentives to combat international corruption may be compromised by the failure to recognize *non bis in idem* as a binding principle of international law.

We conclude this chapter by looking at the functioning of incentives to individuals in the organization.

4.6 The Entity's Perspective: Incentives to Individuals in the Organization.

The problem of incentives offered by the organization to the individual is a vast issue involving business economics, organization theory, labor law, and psychology.

Strangely, while legal commentators have debated at length on codes of conduct, as well as on the formalization of compliance programs and reporting systems, they

---

OECD Convention were prosecuting or had already punished" (Van Alstine 2012, p. 1331).

[22] Dunn notes: "the potential for double jeopardy may also deter companies from coming forward to disclose bribery violations in the first place if an admission in one jurisdiction, rather than helping to close a matter, only exposes a company to further liability elsewhere."

have devoted little attention to the construction of a system of incentives within the organization.

Yet the first attempt to construct a general theory of incentives in an organization—a study in 1938 entitled *The Functions of the Executive*—offered insights of great interest. The author of the work, Chester Barnard, after a long career as a manager, in particular as President of the New Jersey Bell Telephone Company, theorized the fundamental importance of an "economy of incentives" in organizations. According to him: "inadequate incentives mean dissolution, or changes of organization purpose, or failure of cooperation" (Barnard 1968, p. 139).

In relation to preventing business crimes and corruption, we should first understand the purpose of the incentives an organization must develop. The organization may have at least three objectives: to encourage compliance of individual conduct with the organization's rules and principles; to promote reporting, by the individual involved, of potential or actual infringements of the set of regulations; and to encourage reporting of wrongdoing, related to the organization's activities, by third parties.

The problem with regard to achieving these objectives is how to balance positive and negative incentives. The latter are frequent in self-regulatory models also because they have been imposed by various national legislations. For example, the US Sentencing Guidelines underline the need to have "appropriate disciplinary measures for engaging in criminal conduct and for failing to take reasonable steps to prevent or detect criminal conduct," while Italian law requires "a disciplinary system to punish failure to comply with the organizational and control model."

Such disciplinary systems can therefore be constructed to punish violation of compliance program rules, including, more specifically, failure to report infringements of self-regulatory codes, failure to have in place suitable precautions to prevent or reduce wrongdoing, and the infringement of non-retaliation policies to protect whistle-blowers.

The problem is that even in a complex organization, negative incentives must be used with great caution, while taking account of the potential counterproductive effects of an approach based purely on blame. In this regard, Catino has analyzed the "institutional dilemma of blame" that must be solved by organizations in identifying the "trade-off between blaming people" for unlawful conduct and "learning from such acts (e.g., understanding organizational factors that caused a specific event)." The problem is that "individuals in organizations may be reluctant to report negative information, especially when this can lead to disciplinary sanctions…. The politics of blame can therefore discourage operators from reporting problems and errors" (Catino 2013, p. 180).

No less problematic in the organizational context are the incentives of awards and rewards. These tools have already been tested in attempts to encourage managers and employees to be more productive through higher wage or bonus systems. It is widely acknowledged that "people tend to do what gets rewarded. This is how organizations communicate what management values most highly. Employees look to see who gets promoted and who gets passed over, who gets the bonus and who is ignored. The use of rewards is one of an organization's most effective communications tools" (Murphy 2012, p. 17).

Certainly, these awards can have a strong symbolic value in publicly reaffirming the corporation's positive evaluation of behavior which complies with a legal system's rules and principles. The awards may vary from incentives to carry out with the utmost diligence the procedures required by compliance program and to report practices that do not conform to the rules, to incentives to report violations by third parties and possible faults in the organizational model.

We should, however, be aware that in building a balanced internal architecture of incentives, the recognition of awards and rewards (including money) may have some drawbacks. As Dan Kahan says in his chapter on collective action, firstly:

> the simple existence of an incentive scheme can be seen as a cue that other individuals are not inclined to cooperate voluntarily: if they were, incentives would be unnecessary. This inference can in turn trigger a reciprocal disposition to withhold voluntary cooperation thereby undercutting, if not wholly displacing, the force of the incentive. (Kahan 2002, p. 2).

Paradoxically, therefore, a set of positive incentives could end up compromising voluntary compliance with the organization's rules (Atiq 2014, p. 1070).[23] In addition:

> the existence of incentives can mask voluntary contributions to public goods, thereby diluting the power of such contributions to trigger reciprocal cooperation. Relatedly, incentives can crowd out dispositions such as altruism by extinguishing the opportunity of individuals to demonstrate (to themselves and to others) that they are willing to sacrifice material gain for the public good. (Kahan 2002, p. 2)

It has also been observed that incentives, if designed to encourage reporting of the unlawful conduct of third parties, could erode the precious trust relationships constructed within an organization (supra, Sect. 2). Indeed they "can create a situation where people come to construe their responsibilities to the organization and its common enterprise narrowly," abandoning the cultivation of a team spirit and undermining altruism, reciprocity, and other non-self-interested motives (Grant 2012, p. 69).

Finally, positive incentives should be applied with great care due to their potential counterproductive effects with respect to optimal prevention. One recent example of this can be found in the OSHA's *Memorandum on Employer Safety Incentive and Disincentive: Policies and Practices* (OSHA 2012), in which the American agency asks employers to use great caution in initiating programs that may indirectly induce employees not to report accidents; indeed it refers to positive incentives, such as the promise of a bonus to the team which had no injured members in a certain period of time, or the inclusion of a prize for all employees who were not injured in the previous year. In such cases "if the incentive is great enough that its loss dissuades reasonable workers from reporting injuries, the program would result in the employer's failure to record injuries that it is required to record" (OSHA 2012).

Recalling these considerations which recommend a sensible use of incentives, it becomes clear why Chester Barnard emphasized the particular importance, for

[23] Atiq noted that "when extrinsic legal considerations become a person's reasons for acting, they deprive her of the experience of desiring personal achievement, knowledge, general welfare for their own sake—an experience that…is crucial to the fortification of intrinsic motivation. The resulting erosion in virtue generates a real risk of impoverishing the lives of individuals and the relations they hope to realize with their fellows" (Atiq 2014, pp. 123, p. 1097).

the purposes of cooperation, of "non-materialistic" incentives and, among these, the "ideal benefaction" which might be considered the "most powerful" and "most neglected" of stimuli (Barnard 1968, p. 139).

In this respect, a prominent place should be attributed to communion incentives i.e., "solidarity, social integration, the gregarious instinct, or social security…: the need for communion is a basis of informal organization that is essential to the operation of every formal organization" (Barnard 1968, p. 148). On the other hand, Barnard goes on to say, "many of the most effective and powerful organizations are built up on incentives in which the materialistic elements, above bare subsistence, are either relatively lacking or absolutely absent" (Barnard 1968, p. 144).[24]

The crucial problem in the organizational context is therefore to create the conditions "to capture a person's internalization and acceptance of the organization's rules, regulations, and procedures, which results in a scrupulous adherence to them, even when no one observes or monitors compliance" (Podsakoff et al. 2000, p. 517). How this goal is to be achieved is, however, still being debated. The scrupulous balancing of positive and negative incentives in the organization is a necessary but not at all sufficient step.

References

Arlen, J. (2012). Corporate criminal liability: Theory and evidence. In A. Harel & N. Hylton (Eds.), *Research handbook on the economics of criminal law*. Cheltenham: Edward Elgar Publishing.

Ashcroft, J., Hanaway, C., & Greim, C. L. O. (2011). Whistleblowers cash in, unwary corporations pay. *Hofstra Law Review, 40,* 367–409.

Atiq, E. H. (2014). Why motives matter: Reframing the crowding out effect of legal incentives. *Yale Law Journal*, 123(4).

Baldwin, R., Cave, M., & Lodge, M. (2012). *Understanding regulation: Theory, strategy, and practice*. Oxford: Oxford University Press.

Bamberger, K. A. (2006). Regulation as delegation: Private firms, decisionmaking, and accountability in the administrative state. *Duke Law Journal, 56*(2), 377–468.

Barnard, C. I. (1968). *The functions of the executive*. Cambridge: Harvard University Press.

Beccaria, C. (2004) [1764]. *Of crimes and punishments*. Whitefish: Kessinger Publishing.

Black, J. (2002). Critical reflections on regulation. *Australian Journal of Legal Philosophy, 27*(1), 1–35

Bobbio, N. (1968). Sanzione. In Novissimo Digesto Italiano, XVL, Torino: Utet.

Bobbio, N. (2007). *La funzione promozionale del diritto (orig. 1969). In N. Bobbio, Dalla struttura alla funzione. Nuovi studi di teoria del diritto*. Rome: Laterza.

Braithwaite, J. (2003). Meta-risk management and responsive regulation for tax system integrity. *Law & Policy, 25*(1), 1–16.

Braithwaite, J. (2006). The regulatory state? In A. W. R. Roderick et al. (Eds.), *The Oxford handbook of political institutions*. New York: Oxford University Press.

Carrigan, C., & Coglianese, C. (2011). The politics of regulation: From new institutionalism to new governance. *Annual Review of Political Science, 14,* 107–129.

Catino, M. (2013). *Organizational myopia: Problems of rationality and foresight in organizations*. Cambridge: Cambridge University Press.

[24] The author quotes the examples of military, religious, and even political organizations!

Coglianese, C., & Lazer, D. (2003). Management-based regulation: Prescribing private management to achieve public goals. *Law & Society Review, 37*(4), 691–730.
Cunningham, L. A. (2004). The appeal and limits of internal controls to fight fraud, terrorism, other ills. *Journal of Corporation Law, 29,* 267–336.
Deci, E. L. (1971). Effects of externally mediated rewards on intrinsic motivation, 18 *J. Personality & Soc. Psychol.*, 105.
Dorf, M. C., & Sabel, C. F. (1998). A constitution of democratic experimentalism. *Columbia Law Review, 98*(2), 267–473.
Dunn, C. (2012). Can't they cooperate? *Corporate Counsel.* http://www.law.com/corporatecounsel/PubArticleCC.jsp?id=1202541462077&Cant_They_Cooperate. Accessed 16 July 2013.
Epstein, R. A. (2011). Deferred prosecution agreements on trial. In A. S. Barkow & R. E. Barkow (Eds.), *Prosecutors in the boardroom: Using criminal law to regulate corporate conduct.* New York: New York University Press.
Facchi, A. (1995). *Diritto e ricompense. Ricostruzione storica di un'idea.* Torino: Giappichelli.
Fehr, E., & Falk, A. (2002). Psychological foundations of incentives. *European Economic Review, 46,* 687–724.
Feldman, Y. (2011). The complexity of disentangling intrinsic and extrinsic compliance motivations: Theoretical and empirical insights from the behavioral analysis of law. *Washington University Journal of Law and Policy, 35,* 11–48.
Feldman, Y., & Lobel, O. (2010). The incentives matrix: The comparative effectiveness of rewards, liabilities, duties, and protections for reporting illegality. *Texas Law Review, 88,* 1151–1211.
Ferrarese, M. R. (2010). *La governance tra politica e diritto. Bologna.* Italy: Il Mulino.
Ferziger, M. J., & Currell, D. G. (1999). Snitching for dollars: The economics and public policy of federal civil bounty programs. *University of Illinois Law Review, 1999,* 1141–1208.
First, H. (2010). Branch office of the prosecutor: The new role of the corporation in business crime prosecutions. *North Carolina Law Review, 89,* 23.
Fleischer, H., & Schmolke, K. U. (2012). Financial incentives for whistleblowers in European capital markets law? Legal policy considerations on the reform of the market abuse regime. *European Company Law, 9*(5), 250–259.
Flick, G. M. (2010). Le prospettive di modifica del d.lgs.231/2001 in materia di responsabilità amministrativa degli enti: un rimedio peggiore al male. *Rivista delle società, 55*(6), 1294–1306.
Forti, G. (2007). La "chiara luce della verità" e "l'ignoranza del pericolo." Riflessioni penalistiche sul principio di precauzione. In M. Bertolino & G. Forti (Eds.), *Scritti per Federico Stella* (p. 639). Napoli: Jovene.
Franzinelli, M. (2012) *Delatori. Spie e confidenti anonimi: L'arma segreta del regime fascista,* Feltrinelli.
Galantini, N. (2005). Evoluzione del principio del ne bis in idem europeo tra norme convenzionali e norme interne di attuazione. *Diritto penale e processo*, 12, 1567.
Gonzalez, J. S. (2010). A pot of gold at the end of the rainbow: An economic incentives-based approach to OSHA whistleblowing. *The Employee Rights and Employment Policy Journal, 14,* 325.
Grant, R. W. (2012). *Strings attached: Untangling the ethics of incentives.* Princeton: Princeton University Press.
Gueguen, N., & Pascual, A. (2005). Improving the response rate to a street survey: An evaluation of the "But you are free to accept or to refuse" technique. *The Psychological Record, 55*(2), 297–303.
Hartmann, L. M. (2011). Whistle while you work: The fairytale-like whistleblower provisions of the Dodd-Frank Act and the emergence of "Greedy," the eighth dwarf. *Mercer Law Review, 62,* 1279–1313.
Hefendehl, R. (2007). Außerstrafrechtliche und strafrechtliche Instrumentarien zur Eindämmung der Wirtschaftskriminalität. *Zeitschrift für die gesamte Strafrechtswissenschaft, 119*(4), 816–847.
Herbel, P., Hess, B., & Mantovani, M. (2011). Double jeopardy: Finding a balance in enforcement actions for companies. *Legalweek.com* (24 November).

Hutter, B. M. (2006). The role of non-state actors in regulation. Discussion Paper No. 37. London School of Economics.

Impact of Qui Tam Laws on Internal Compliance: A Report to the Securities Exchange Commission (2010). National Whistleblower Center. http://www.whistleblowers.org/index.php?option=com_content&task=view&id=1169. Accessed 16 July 2013.

Jackson, J., Bradford, B., Hough, M., Myhill, A., Quinton, P., & Tyler, T. R. (2012). Why do people comply with the law? Legitimacy and the influence of legal institutions. *British Journal of Criminology, 52*(6), 1051–1071.

Jensen, M. C., & Meckling, W. H. (1976). Theory of the firm: Managerial behavior, agency costs and ownership structure. *Journal of Financial Economics, 3*(4), 305–360.

Kahan, D. M. (2002). The logic of reciprocity: Trust, collective action, and law. John M. Olin Center for Studies in Law, Economics, and Public Policy Working Papers, Paper 281.

Khanna, V. S. (2003). Should the behavior of top management matter? *Georgetown Law Journal, 91,* 1231.

Koehler, M. (2012). Revisiting a foreign corrupt practices act compliance defense. *Wisconsin Law Review, 2,* 609–659.

Kraakman, R., Davies, P., Hansmann, H., Hertig, G., Hopt, K., Kanda, H., & Rock, E. (2009). *The anatomy of corporate law: A comparative and functional approach* (2nd ed). Oxford: Oxford University Press.

Krawiec, K. D. (2003). Cosmetic compliance and the failure of negotiated governance. *Washington University Law Quarterly, 81,* 487–544.

Laffont, J. J. (2003). *The principal–agent model: The economic theory of incentives*. Cheltenham: Edward Elgar Publishing.

Laffont, J. J., & Martimort, D. (2002). *The theory of incentives: The principal-agent model*. Princeton: Princeton University Press.

Laufer, W. S. (1999). Corporate liability, risk shifting, and the paradox of compliance. *Vanderbilt Law Review, 52,* 1341–1420.

Levi-Faur, D. (2005). The global diffusion of regulatory capitalism. *The Annals of the American Academy of Political and Social Science, 598*(1), 12–32.

Lobel, O. (2004). The renew deal: The fall of regulation and the rise of governance in contemporary legal thought. *Minnesota Law Review, 89,* 7–27.

Luparia, L. (2010). Bis de eadem re ne sit actio: Premesse per uno studio sulla litispendenza penale internazionale. In P. Corso & E. Zanetti (Eds.), *Studi in onore di Mario Pisani, v. 2*. Piacenza: CELT.

Lyon, D. (2003). *Surveillance after September 11*. New York: Blackwell Publishing.

Martin, A. N. (2013). Introduccíon. In L. Arroyo Zapatero & A. Nieto Martin (Eds.), *El derecho penal economico en la era compliance*. Valencia: Tirant lo Blanch.

Matus Acuña, J. P. (2013). La Certification de los programas de cumplimiento. In L. Arroyo Zapatero & A. N. Martin (Eds.), *El derecho penal economico en la era compliance*. Valencia: Tirant lo Blanch.

Meyer, J. W., & Rowan, B. (1991). Institutionalized organizations: Formal structure as myth and ceremony. In W.W. Powell & P.J. Di Maggio (Eds.), *The New Institutionalism in Organizational Analysis*. Chicago: University of Chicago Press.

Milgrom, P., & Roberts, J. (1988). An economic approach to influence activities in organizations. *American Journal of Sociology, 94,* 154–179.

Ministry of Justice (UK) (2011). Guidance about procedures which relevant commercial organisations can put into place to prevent persons associated with them from bribing (section 9 of the Bribery Act 2010). http://www.justice.gov.uk/guidance/docs/bribery-act-2010-guidance.pdf. Accessed 16 July 2013.

Murphy, J. (2012). Using incentives in your compliance and ethics program. *Society of Corporate Compliance and Ethics*.

Ormerod, P. (2005). *Crime: Economic incentives and social networks*. London: Institute of Economic Affairs.

OSHA [Occupational Safety and Health Organization] (2012). Employer safety incentive and disincentive. Policies and Practices Memorandum, 2012. www.osha.gov/as/opa/whistleblower-memo.html. Accessed 16 July 2013.

Parker, C. (2007). Meta-regulation: Legal accountability for corporate social responsibility. In D. McBarnet, A. Voiculescu & T. Campbell (Eds.), *The new corporate accountability: Corporate social responsibility and the law*. Cambridge: Cambridge University Press.
Parker, C., & Nielsen, V. L. (2006). Do businesses take compliance systems seriously? An empirical study of the implementation of trade practices compliance systems in Australia. *Melbourne University Law Review, 30,* 441–494.
Pelligra, V. (2007). *I paradossi della fiducia. Scelte razionali e dinamiche interpersonali*. Bologna: Il Mulino.
Pelligra, V. (Forthcoming). Promoting trust through institutional design. In S. Bartolini, L. Bruni, & P. L. Porta (Eds.), *Policies for happiness*. Oxford: Oxford University Press.
Pettit, P. (1995). The cunning of trust. *Philosophy and Public Affairs, 24*(3), 202–225.
Pieth, M. (2010). *Co-Regulierung im Wirtschaftsstrafrecht*. Heidelberg: C.F. Müller.
Podsakoff, P. M., MacKenzie, S. B., Paine, J. B., & Bachrach, D. G. (2000). Organizational citizenship behaviors: A critical review of the theoretical and empirical literature and suggestions for future research. *Journal of Management, 26*(3), 513–563.
Posner, E. (2000). Agency models in law and economy. *Chicago John M. Olin Law & Economics Working Paper*, 92.
Powell, W. W., & Di Maggio, P. J. (1991). *The new institutionalism in organizational analysis*. Chicago: University of Chicago Press.
Power, M. (1997). *The audit society: Rituals of verification*. New York: Oxford University Press.
Power, M. (2007). *Organized uncertainty: Designing a world of risk management*. New York: Oxford University Press.
Salini, C. (2012). General Secretary of CONSOB. Speech at Senato della Repubblica, 13 June 2012.
Sarbanes-Oxley Act. (2006). U.S. Government Printing Office. http://www.gpo.gov/fdsys/pkg/PLAW-107publ204/pdf/PLAW-107publ204.pdf. Accessed 16 July 2013.
Schünemann, B. (2005). Brennpunkte des Strafrechts in der Entwickelten Industriegesellschaft. In B. Schünemann, W. Bottke, & R. Hefendehl (Eds.), *Empirische und dogmatische Fundamente, kriminalpolitischer Impetus. Symposium für Bernd Schünemann zum 60*. Geburtstag. Koìln: Carl Heymanns.
Schünemann, B. (2008). Strafrechtliche Sanktionen gegen Wirtschaftsunternehmen? In U. Sieber, G. Dannecker, U. Kindhäuser, J. Vogel & T. Walter (Eds.), *Strafrecht und Wirtschaftsstrafrecht. Dogmatik, Rechtsvergleich, Rechtstatsachen. Festschrift für Klaus Tiedemann zum 70. Geburtstag*. Koìln: Carl Heymanns.
Sieber, U. (2008). Compliance-Programme im Unternehmensstrafrecht. Ein neues Konzept zur Kontrolle von Wirtschaftskriminalität. In U. Sieber, G. Dannecker, U. Kindhäuser, J. Vogel, & T. Walter (Eds.), *Strafrecht und Wirtschaftsstrafrecht. Dogmatik, Rechtsvergleich, Rechtstatsachen. Festschrift für Klaus Tiedemann zum 70. Geburtstag*. Koìln: Carl Heymanns.
Tombs, S., & Whyte, D. (2013). The myths and realities of deterrence in workplace safety regulation. *British Journal of Criminology, 53*(5), 746–763.
Tyler, T. R. (2011). *Why people cooperate: The role of social motivations*. Princeton: Princeton University Press.
Umphress, E. E., & Bingham, J. B. (2011). When employees do bad things for good reasons: Examining unethical pro-organizational behaviors. *Organization Science, 22*(3), 621–640.
U.S. Sentencing Guidelines § 8B2.1(b)(6). (2011). USSC Guidelines Manual, United States Sentencing Commission. http://www.ussc.gov/. Accessed 16 July 2013.
US SEC [US Securities and Exchange Commission]. (2011). Implementation of the whistleblower provisions of Section 21F of the Securities Exchange Act of 1934, US Securities and Exchange Commission. http://www.sec.gov/rules/final/2011/34–64545.pdf. Accessed 16 July 2013.
Van Alstine, M. (2012). Treaty double jeopardy: The OECD Anti-Bribery Convention and the FCPA. *Ohio State Law Journal, 73*(5), 1321.
Weissmann, A., & Newman, D. (2007). Rethinking criminal corporate liability. *Indiana Law Journal, 82*(2), 411–451.

Chapter 5
Internal Investigations, Whistle-Blowing, and Cooperation: The Struggle for Information in the Criminal Process

Adán Nieto Martín

Contents

5.1 The Criminal Process as a Struggle for Information

The criminal process can be seen as a battle in which two sides fight fiercely for control of information. On the one hand, the public prosecutor, the police, and the administrative authorities attempt to secure information which will destroy the presumption of innocence and result in the imposition of a sanction; on the other, the person under investigation tries to control the flow of information that reaches the accuser, or tries to limit this information to that which is convenient to the defendant.

This battle has rules. Public investigators must obtain information through legally established means of investigation, always respecting the fundamental rights of the person under investigation. Breaking these rules leads to the inadmissibility of any resultant evidence, including any secondary evidence that was derived directly from it. With the aim of preserving the presumption of innocence, the accused is allowed to hide information which may be prejudicial to him. According to principle *nemo tenetur se ipse accusare*, any kind of coercion applied to the accused with the

A. N. Martín (✉)
University of Castilla-la-Mancha, Ciudad Real, Spain
e-mail: adan.nieto@uclm.es

S. Manacorda et al. (eds.), *Preventing Corporate Corruption*,
DOI 10.1007/978-3-319-04480-4_5, © Springer International Publishing Switzerland 2014

aim of obtaining information is considered illicit.[1] Another key rule in the struggle for information is the prohibition against starting an investigation unless there is reasonable doubt as to whether an offense has been committed. Prospective or fishing investigations have serious constitutional problems. These three rules are part of the core of the criminal process in a state ruled by the rule of law.

Beyond the rules concerning the main adversaries (prosecution and defense), there are others concerning third parties. For example, the criminal process forces the witnesses—under threat of penalties for false statements or obstruction of justice—to truthfully provide as much information as they can. But in some cases there are also rules that protect the right to noncollaboration by third parties. These may apply in the case of witnesses with specific connections to the accused, such as close family members, and—of greater interest here—lawyers, by means of the privilege of professional secrecy.

The norms by which the rule of law limits the manner in which information can be garnered during the criminal process entail significant costs for the prosecution in obtaining the evidence necessary to support their case. The cost of obtaining information depends on the visibility of the crime, as well as its characteristics. Costs are lower in homicides than in so-called victimless crime such as corruption or anticompetitive practices, which have a very high unrecorded crime rate. If the offense has been committed within an organization, the cost of access to information increases, since organizations are especially skilled in the protection and concealment of information (Vaughan 1999, p. 277, 1998, p. 23).

Investigation costs are also higher in transnational crimes. *Ius puniendi,* with the exception of some regional spaces such as the EU, is still basically national. However, states do have jurisdiction to prescribe punishment for some behaviors which are committed beyond their borders, as it occurs with corruption in international transactions. Nevertheless, their jurisdiction to enforce is still purely national. States cannot investigate or execute sanctions in other member states. To this end, they need judicial cooperation, which increases the cost of accessing information significantly.[2]

As can be seen, the costs of investigating cases of economic crimes—which are usually victimless, take place inside organizations, and increasingly have a transnational nature—are high. That is why contemporary criminal policy has incorporated a set of strategies to increase the efficacy of such investigations, thus reducing the cost of obtaining information. Although they have different origins, these strategies are linked and can be applied jointly.

Criminal liability of legal persons aims, among other things, to reduce the costs of preventing corporate crime and of obtaining information pertinent to a case. The

[1] In economic criminal law, the most complicated problems regarding this fundamental right emerge when the public administration, as part of its powers of investigation, obliges corporations to hand over documents which they are legally obliged to produce. An analysis of this problem from a European perspective can be found in Nieto Martin and Blumenberg 2010, p. 397–420.

[2] With regards to judicial cooperation in economic crimes, see Nelles 2006, p. 632; Zagaris 2010, p. 218–427.

punishment of legal entities strives to motivate them to implement compliance programs.[3] Most legal systems provide an important set of incentives to implement compliance programs for uncovering, investigating, and, if necessary, imposing sanctions for offenses committed within the company. These incentives reward confession and collaboration with the criminal process through a significant reduction in any subsequent sanction. However, the most powerful and efficient incentives are those which exist within the criminal process. Through a reward-based usage of the nonmandatory prosecution principle, public prosecutors do not prosecute companies that cooperate effectively with the investigation. Such "carrots" are very attractive for corporations, since they can thereby avoid long criminal proceedings and the shame of sitting in the dock—which can cause considerable reputational damage, especially to major companies quoted on public stock markets. For these reasons, procedural incentives work much better than those located within substantive criminal law, regardless of whether they reduce or exclude the liability of the entity.[4]

It is important to point out that, generally, "carrots" awarded to companies that confess or collaborate do not depend on whether the company had a preexisting compliance program or not. A company can take advantage of the "carrots" even if its previous corporate policy boosted the likelihood of offenses being committed. The system does not require verification that the corporation's collaboration or reporting was the result of a compliance program. In terms of reducing costs, this decision is beneficial since it opens the doors for any company to collaborate, regardless of its previous behavior. Nevertheless, it also has perverse effects: It seems to encourage companies to be unconcerned about prevention, instead surrendering unconditionally, when necessary, to the prosecutor, giving him whatever information he may require.[5]

A second cost-cutting strategy is the encouragement of whistle-blowing. Several methods are available to this end. The first is the protection of the whistle-blower, achieved by establishing criminal sanctions for any kind of threats or intimidation made against him or her.[6] The second is the creation of obligations to report, as is

[3] See the recent analysis of different justifications in Artaza Varela 2013, p. 45–74; Ortiz de Urbina 2012, p. 227. Regarding the original North American incentive model, the Guidelines for Sentencing Organizational Offenders, based on the "carrot and stick" strategy, see Swenson 1998, p. 27.

[4] For an overview of different strategies in the fight against corporate crime in the USA, as well as the underlying changes in incentive policy (where the benefits they may confer have shifted from the determination of the penalty to the procedural field), see Griffin 2007, p. 311.

[5] For a general discussion of the different situations this strategy can produce, see Laufer 2008, p. 99.

[6] This was the first path followed by whistle-blowing laws. The most draconian sanctions are foreseen in the § 806 SOA, regarding criminal protection: see Rodríguez Yagüe 2006, p. 447; Ragués i Vallès 2006, p. 3. Firstly, the protection of whistle-blowers depends on whether the employee's behavior was appropriate with respect to labor and criminal law. With regards to the former, see for example Article 9 of the French Act n° 2007/1598, 13 November 2007, reforming the *Code du Travail* in order to ensure the protection of whistle-blowers in the workplace. The situation is not so positive, for example, in Switzerland, where whistle-blowing can even be considered a disclosure of trade secrets offense, as happened in the recent *Falciani* case.

stipulated in securities market legislation, where securities agencies are forced to report any transaction which raises suspicions of market abuse (Article 83 *quater* LMV) or money laundering.[7] The OECD also encourages auditors and tax administrations[8] to blow the whistle when they discover any fact in the company which may provide evidence of the payment of bribes.[9] Another even more efficient way to encourage whistle-blowing is simply to pay them. The Dodd-Frank Act offers whistle-blowers 30 % of the amount recovered by the state in fraud cases amounting to more than a million dollars.[10]

An intelligent system used to encourage claims is, without a doubt, the leniency programs which are used in competition law.[11] This model of collaboration offers stronger incentives, such as a reduction of the sanction, to those who are first to report an offense or those who provide more or more detailed information. Leniency programs are based on a competition between the companies that have participated in an anticompetitive agreement: only the first to provide information will receive the benefits of cooperation.

However, this strategy is not exclusive to competition law. Most legal systems dealing with liability of legal entities have created the conditions for this kind of race between natural and legal persons, in order to be first to reach the "carrots" associated with collaboration. In cases of corruption in Spain, for example, if the legal person reports first, the mitigating circumstances provided in the Criminal Code[12] or in Article 787.8 Code of Criminal Procedure will be applied (Gascón Inchausti 2012, p. 16). If, instead, the employee is faster and reveals the facts first (Article 426 Criminal Code), the company will have no opportunity to collaborate.[13]

Whistle-blowing channels and internal investigations[14] are the main elements of a compliance program, allowing the corporation to take advantage of the incentives

---

[7] Regarding this model, see Vogel 2007, p. 731; Nieto Martín 2010, p. 315.

[8] See, for example, in Germany, § 4 Abs. 5, n° 10, sentence 3 of the EStG, which obliges tax authorities to inform the public prosecutor about any facts that might provide evidence of bribery.

[9] OECD 2009: "Member countries should require the external auditor who discovers indications of a suspected act of bribery of a foreign public official to report this discovery to management and, as appropriate, to corporate monitoring bodies."

[10] According to the Wallstreet Reform and Consumer Protection Act, 21 July 2010, Sects. 992 and 748, incentives have been established by the SEC in the Bounty Program. Before the Dodd-Frank Act, the Federal False Claims Act paid whistle-blowers in cases of fraud against public administration. Regarding this and other US laws which offer these kind of incentives, see Schemmel et al. 2008, p. 182; González de León Berini 2013, p. 131, 137.

[11] See Thomas 2012, p. 11; Holmes 2010. With regards to the possibility of using them in other sectors, e.g., corruption, see Tarun and Tomczak 2010, p. 153.

[12] On mitigating circumstances, see Gómez-Aller 2011, p. 1885; Bajo Fernández et al. 2012, p. 193; and Goena Vives 2013, p. 229.

[13] On German regulations on whistle-blowing (§ 46 b StGB) and its implications for compliance, see Dann 2010, p. 30.

[14] On internal investigations in general, see Molo et al. 2008; on EU countries, see Moosmayer and Hartwig 2012. Regarding Article 31bis of the Spanish Criminal Code, see Bajo Fernández et al. 2012, p. 190; Gascón Inchausti 2012, p. 119. An introduction to its legal problems can be found in Moosmayer 2013, p. 137.

that state legislation offers. These tools also enable the corporation to control information and facts relevant to offenses that have been committed within it. Control is the key to success in an efficient criminal defense (Sahan 2012, p. 171). Corporations are interested in knowing about any criminal behavior in order to access the incentives the state offers to encourage cooperation: Any intelligent corporation also wants to know what is happening at home, rather than being made aware of it through the media or a judicial notice (Schemmel et al. 2008, p. 74). This kind of knowledge has considerable advantages. The first is that the company can start to prepare a suitable defense strategy. Having this information, the company can decide what the most convenient approach is: cooperating or concealing the information. If the company decides to cooperate, and does so early in the process, the company's version of events will be the first to emerge and so, to a certain extent, it can guide the development of the investigation. Furthermore, cooperation can lead to a shorter legal process, and in this way reputational costs can be avoided. Swift provision of evidence by the corporation can also help avoid certain investigative acts (such as the seizure of records, the sealing off of IT equipment, and so on) that can affect a company's business activities.

The aim of this chapter is primarily to identify the dangers to basic fundamental rights arising from this struggle for control of information rooted in the encouragement of collaboration and the use of tools such as whistle-blowing channels and internal investigations.

The paradigmatic example of how fundamental rights can be affected is the case of the USA, where public prosecutors require the corporation's "full collaboration" in return for nonprosecution (Gómez Jara 2008, p. 298; Zabala López-Gómez 2008, pp. 7062–7065). This practice has proven dangerous both for corporations' and employees' defense rights. Internal investigations and whistle-blowing channels also affect other rights, such as the right to privacy of communications, or the employee's right not to incriminate himself. A corporation carrying out an internal investigation can access employees' communications (through their corporate emails, records of phone calls, or websites accessed) more easily than a public prosecutor or judge can. Safeguards—and thus costs—for accessing this information within the company are lower than in the criminal process. The existence of these threats to fundamental rights therefore requires new safeguards and limits. The effective prosecution of economic and corruption offenses committed within big companies of course depends upon the scenario of collaboration between corporations and the state, but such a strategy requires the reinforcement of some basic guarantees within the criminal process, such as the right not to incriminate oneself, in order to keep in balance the forces that characterize the criminal process.

5.2 Whistle-Blowing Channels and Internal Amnesty Programs

Whistle-blowing channels are one of the main pillars of a compliance program. That is why all guidelines, both public[15] and private,[16] on compliance programs require their implementation. From the point of view of corporations, an efficient whistle-blowing channel is necessary for controlling information. If the whistle-blower decides to offer his information directly to the prosecutor, the corporation begins the criminal process at a disadvantage. The implementation of a whistle-blowing channel can, in fact, be very easy; what is more difficult is implementing a channel which is effective.

The first condition for making an effective whistle-blowing channel is that it must be integrated into an efficient compliance system. A whistle-blowing system will not work if employees think that the compliance program is there merely for show. Employees are unlikely to blow the whistle if the widespread perception is that the compliance system is just for show, since it could mean taking a risk for no possible benefit. That is why the first requirement of an effective whistle-blowing channel is that employees and managers feel engaged and committed to the implementation of a culture of legality (Nieto Martín 2008, p. 257; Schemmel et al. 2008, p. 77; Ragués i Vallès 2013, p. 161).

The second condition for the effective functioning of a channel is that it provides security for whistle-blowers. The channel will not work if the potential whistle-blower is not certain of his rights, or of the commitment undertaken by the company in dealing with whistle-blowers. It is therefore helpful if the company implements a formal complaint system as part of its internal regulation. This task is, in part, easy to accomplish, and in fact the vast majority of major corporations have a whistle-blowing channel in place already.[17] Among all the elements integrated within a compliance program, the whistle-blowing channel is the one which has received the greatest attention by lawmakers. Labor and personal data protection laws provide

[15] See, for example, in the USA, US Sentencing Commission, *Organizational Guidelines—USSC Guidelines Manual*—§ 8 A1.2.3, available at http://www.ussc.gov/Guidelines/Organizational_Guidelines/index.cfm, accessed 16 July 2013. Similarly in the UK, see Ministry of Justice, *The Bribery Act 2010—Guidance—Principle 1 Proportionate Procedures, 22,* http://www.justice.gov.uk/downloads/legislation/bribery-act-2010-guidance.pdf, accessed 16 July 2013.

[16] See, for example, in Italy, the compliance model proposed by Confindustria, *Linee Guida per la costruzione dei modelli di organizzazione, gestione e controllo ex D.Lgs. n. 231/2001, 45.*, http://www.confindustria.it/Aree/lineeg.nsf/(WebDataIST)?OpenView&MenuID=572E9F6FDD21F-CBCC1256F90002FB00E. Accessed 16 July 2013. Regarding whistle-blowing channels, see the International Chamber of Commerce (ICC) Sweden, *ICC Guidelines on Whistleblowing,* http://www.icc.se/mutor/whistleblowing.pdf, accessed 16 July 2013.

[17] In the Spanish case, see Emisores Españoles, *Grupo de trabajo sobre responsabilidad penal de las personas jurídicas, Informe Final −12 de diciembre de 2012, 37.* http://www.emisoresespanoles.es/wp-content/uploads/2013/04/Responsabilidad-Penal-Personas-Juridicas-Informe-final.pdf, accessed 16 July 2013. Here, it is shown that almost 100 % of corporations studied had a whistle-blowing channel.ʃ

the basic normative framework for establishing complaint channels.[18] In the EU, the recommendations of data protection authorities are very important.[19] However, there are two areas in which these recommendations provide no clear indications: how one defines the concepts of reporting in good and bad faith, and the options available for systems supporting anonymous or confidential complaints.

To identify in each case what a complaint in good faith would be, the corporation must decide what level of commitment to the truth is asked of whistle-blowers. If the whistle-blower is required to be completely sure of the facts, avoiding any report of false rumors, there will be very few complaints, and these will rarely concern the senior hierarchy since it has more power to conceal information. Therefore, in defining a complaint in good faith, it is better to opt for subjective criteria, regardless of whether the whistle-blower can verify the facts.[20] What is important is the existence of a reasonable belief, a set of circumstances—regardless of whether the facts can be verified or not—from which wrongdoing can be inferred.[21]

Opting for a standard which does not require from the whistle-blower an especial commitment to verifying the truth involves greater risks to the corporation's reputation. Nevertheless, these can be offset if the whistle-blowing channel is integrated into an efficient and formalized compliance program. In this context, employees are aware that false complaints driven by revenge or harassment are going to be punished, and they also know that their complaint is going to be investigated prior to making any decision that could damage a third party.

Opting to increase the efficacy of the whistle-blowing channel could lead to a preference for an anonymous complaints system over a confidential one.[22] The level of risk that an anonymous complaint entails for the whistle-blower is significantly lower than that entailed by a confidential complaint.[23] As the reader may know, the

[18] With regards to these labor issues in Spanish doctrine, see Goñi Sein 2011, p. 320; Nieto Martín 2012, p. 105. In Germany, where doctrine has addressed this issue on many occasions, see Maschmann 2012, p. 98; Schemmel et al. 2008, p. 233; Fritz 2009, p. 111. A comparison between German—and European—law and US law can be found in Graser 2000.

[19] Article 29 Working Party; see the European Commission, Opinion 1/2006 on the application of EU data protection rules to internal whistle-blowing schemes in the fields of accounting, internal accounting controls, auditing matters, fight against bribery, banking and financial crime, adopted on 1 February 2006, http://ec.europa.eu/justice/policies/privacy/docs/wpdocs/2006/wp117_en.pdf, accessed 16 July 2013. The Spanish agency on data protection is even more strict on some points: see Agencia Española de Protección de Datos, Creación de sistemas de denuncias internas en las empresas (mecanismos de "whistleblowing"), http://www.agpd.es/portalwebAGPD/canaldocumentacion/informes_juridicos/otras_cuestiones/common/pdfs/2007-0128_Creaci-oo-n-de-sistemas-de-denuncias-internas-en-las-empresas-mecanismos-de-whistleblowing.pdf, accessed 16 July 2013.

[20] About the importance of the "if in doubt, report" approach in the Australian law on whistle-blowing, see Brawn 2008.

[21] Regarding the UK and the Public Interest Disclosure Act, 1998, which enshrined the *reasonable belief* standard, see Gobert and Punch 2000, p. 36.

[22] On anonymous reports, see Fritz 2009, p. 111; Maschmann 2012, p. 99; Ragués i Vallès 2013, p. 181.

[23] On weighing up the advantages of both systems, see Schemmel et al. 2008, p. 178.

Sarbanes–Oxley Act[24] opted for anonymous complaints. As a result, large quoted companies in Europe had to opt for anonymity, which was not welcomed by European data protection authorities.[25] The choice between anonymity and confidentiality depends on the compliance model that the company wants to employ. From this point of view, confidentiality fits better with a compliance program based on values such as transparency and dialogue, and which is guided by ethical principles (Nieto Martín 2012, p. 38). This model is the one expressly proposed by the guidelines in the USA and is more commonly used by companies.[26]

In fact, anonymity is not necessarily more efficient than confidentiality. Even if the company opts for confidentiality, it cannot "close its eyes" to well-founded anonymous complaints with a high probability of being true. However, the company can and must remain inactive when the complaint contains mere rumors. On the other hand, as we have already seen, whistle-blowing systems based on confidentiality need a lower level of commitment to the truth from the whistle-blower, so almost every complaint must initiate a preliminary investigation at the very least. Confidential complaints have *per se* more credibility than anonymous ones,[27] since there is a person responsible for the content who risks facing criminal, civil, or disciplinary sanctions if the complaint is found to be absolutely false.

Protection of whistle-blowers and an efficient compliance program are, as has been seen, decisive factors in the healthy functioning of a channel, but in some cases stronger incentives are needed. This usually happens when the whistle-blower is somehow involved in the infringement that he is going to report. The usual image of whistle-blowers is of someone who has information about someone *else's* wrongdoing; however, those who are participants in the infringement usually have more and higher-quality information. As mentioned above, in many countries, criminal law has established a competition between the natural person liable for the infringement and the legal entity, encouraging both to confess their liability. In this race for collaboration, the mitigation of or exemption from liability is reserved for the first to provide evidence and collaborate.

So if the corporation wants to encourage the best-informed whistle-blowers to come forward, it needs to create its own system of internal "carrots" through a

---

[24] Sect. 301 SOA. Regarding this matter, see among others Schemmel et al. 2008, p. 69.

[25] See Not. 25, Article 29 Working Party; see also European Commission, Opinion 1/2006 (n. 21 to this chapter).

[26] The review of the guidelines performed in 2004 established expressly that in addition to implementing elements of their compliance program, the corporation should "otherwise promote an organizational culture that encourages ethical conduct and a commitment to compliance with the law." This aspect was especially emphasized by the Report of the Ad Hoc Advisory Group on the Organizational Guidelines: see The US Sentencing Commission, *Report of the Ad Hoc Advisory Group on the Organizational Sentencing Guidelines,* http://www.ussc.gov/Guidelines/Organizational_Guidelines/Special_Reports/Advisory_Group_Organizational_Guidelines.cfm, accessed 16 July 2013. Regarding this, see Kaplan and Murphy 2009, § 7. On the distinction between compliance programs based on ethical values and those aimed at the formal compliance of law, see Treviño and Weaver 2002, p. 89.

[27] It could be useful to consider the jurisprudential criteria establishing when an anonymous report can initiate the criminal process: see Gascón Inchausti 2012, p. 128.

program of "internal amnesty."[28] The company obviously cannot promise whistle-blowers that they will not be criminally punished. But it certainly can offer not to take internal measures against them (dismissal, claim for damages, etc.), to bear the costs of the employee's defense, and, where allowed, to pay any resultant fines. If such internal "carrots" prove to be more appetizing than the public ones, the company will obtain the whistle-blower's information first and can use it at its convenience in their defense strategy.

Internal amnesties are, however, delicate tools. If they are perceived by employees and the board as unjustified, the credibility of the internal compliance program can be undermined. When disclosure is used in criminal law, the best informed tend to be the most powerful people within the organization. That means prizes for high-level employees and blame for those in the lower levels of the organization hierarchy. There can also be an economic cost to the company which must be justified: for example, when the company decides not to press charges against the employee who is responsible for the wrongdoing, which, in some legal systems, can itself be considered an offense (*Untreue*).

5.3 The Ombudsman and Self-Auditing Privileges

Information obtained via a whistle-blowing channel is extremely "juicy." If the channel works properly, accessing its content can provide an entire history of the entity's criminal wrongdoing. To access the information held in a major company's whistle-blowing channel is the dream of any public investigator. Because of that, companies face a difficult balancing act. On the one hand, to demonstrate that their whistle-blowing system works—which is a good indication of the effectiveness of their compliance system—the company should keep a record of complaints and investigations carried out. But on the other hand, the most compliant companies run the risk that they might be required to surrender this information by a judge or public prosecutor, or that it should be accessed from within the company's buildings.

The problem arises in more concrete terms with regard to the identity of possible whistle-blowers (Schemmel et al. 2008, p. 301). If the whistle-blower's identity is confidential, the person in charge of the hotline must conceal this information from third parties, both inside and outside the company. However, it is unclear whether this confidentiality works as well in situations involving a judge or public prosecutor, who may be very interested in knowing the whistle-blower's identity. This risk makes for a strong disincentive: Whistle-blowers will not usually want to get involved in legal proceedings or participate in them as a witness, even if as a protected witness.

In fact, both issues lead to a common problem: the confidentiality of information generated by the company with the purpose of creating and improving its compliance system. To have an efficient compliance program, it is necessary to undertake

[28] Regarding internal amnesties, see Breßler et al. 2009, p. 721; Weiße 2012, p. 58.

a risk mapping in which the corporation's most risky activities are identified. It is also necessary to ensure ongoing self-assessment of the system in order to bring to light any mistakes and correct them. As a result, operating an efficient compliance program involves generating information which may be sensitive, and thus tempting for any public investigator.

In the EU, the European Court of Justice (ECJ) decision in *Akzo Nobel Chemicals Ltd.* case provides a clear example of this situation.[29] Since the adoption of Regulation 1/2003 on competition law,[30] the European Commission has insisted upon the importance of corporations having compliance programs which deal with this matter. Before then, companies could use the mechanism of previous notifications in order to determine whether an agreement was forbidden or not. Once this system was removed, corporate compliance programs had to shoulder the task of indicating to employees precisely which conducts are illicit.[31] In *Akzo,* the ECJ granted permission for the commission, through its powers of investigation, to access any documentation used by the company for the implementation of its compliance program, even including emails exchanged with the company's lawyer and notes taken during the meetings (Schemmel et al. 2008, p. 303).

This problem, in all of its forms, illustrates the scenario of the struggle for information and offers a clear view of the need to create new rules to govern it. The importance of whistle-blowers, and of compliance programs generally, in preventing economic criminality makes it necessary to establish some kind of guarantee to protect sensitive information from the demands of judges and prosecutors. Failure to provide such a guarantee discourages whistle-blowers and corporations from coming forward. The most compliant companies will always retain highly sensitive information which can be accessed by prosecutors and public agencies. Destroying the information once it has been used is an option that does not suit the logic of the system. Documents used for identifying corporate risks and the records of the whistle-blowing channel will also be needed, should the company be accused of any criminal offense, in order to enable it to demonstrate that it has an active compliance program.

While this matter has barely been addressed in EU countries,[32] US law and jurisprudence some time ago established the so-called self-auditing privilege (Kaplan

[29] Judgment of the ECJ (Grand Chamber), 14.9.2010, case C-550/07 P. 14.9.2010.

[30] See EUR-Lex, Access to European Union law, Council Regulation (EC) No 1/2003 of 16 December 2002 on the implementation of the rules on competition laid down in Articles 81 and 82 of the Treaty, 1–25, http://eur-lex.europa.eu/LexUriServ/LexUriServ.do?uri=OJ:L:2003:001:0001:0025:EN:PDF, accessed 16 July 2013.

[31] See The European Association of Chemical Distributors (Fecc), *Compliance matters: What companies can do better to respect EU competition rules,* November 2011, http://www.fecc.org/fecc/images/stories/downloads/NEWS/compliance_matters_en.pdf, accessed 16 July 2013.

[32] See, for example, Schemmel et al. 2008, 311, which mentions the possibility of having an outsourced lawyer or ombudsman in charge of the whistle-blowing channel, admitting however that the client–attorney privilege also has important limitations on this point. In Germany, the judgment of Ladgerichts Hamburg has been specially important (NJW, no. 3501 (2011), pp. 942 ff.). The relevant facts are the following: The Monitoring Council of the HSH Nordbak asked a law firm to

and Murphy 2009, § 5.38) and its offshoot, the "ombudsman privilege" (Kaplan andMurphy 2009, § 13: 24 et sEq.). The self-auditing privilegeprevents public prosecutors and judges from demanding documents generated by the compliance program that deals with improving it, while the ombudsman privilege works mainly in those cases in which an ombudsman acts as a mediator in the corporation (Spanheimer 2012, p. 659). However, confidentiality is also needed if the ombudsman is the person in charge of receiving complaints and advising employees on the legality of certain behaviors.

In both cases, the ombudsman privilege is a different right from the client–attorney privilege. There is no need for a lawyer, and documents need not be directly related to the right to defense. These circumstances allow the judge to modulate its extension, weighing the public interest and the interests of all parties in the process. As a result, these legal privileges are only admitted in concrete cases in which the interests being protected take precedence over the public interest in having all information made available through the criminal process.[33]

When designing these new legal privileges, or when seeking a balance between public and corporate interest, attention must be paid to the configuration of the compliance organs within the corporation. The principal characteristic of compliance organs should be their independence from the company's centers of power, and the only aim should be the efficiency of the compliance system. Such is, for instance, the Italian model (*organism di vigilanza*).[34] The design of these new rights must be such that it encourages this kind of compliance body. By way of example, in contrast to what the ECJ proposed in *Akzo,* the criterion for granting or not granting such a privilege should not be the existence of an external lawyer but the independence of the compliance body. For this reason, the privilege should not be granted to an internal lawyer, who is another part of the corporation's systems of production, but to the corporation's compliance body, which should be operating independently.

5.4 Internal Investigations and the Criminal Process

With regard to whistle-blowing channels, there is a general agreement that internal investigations are an essential part of compliance programs.[35] Internal investigations help to detect any shortcomings in the preventive systems and correct them; they also enable any infringements of the company's ethical code to be punished.

carry out an internal investigation on some millionaire loans that the board of directors had awarded. The results of the investigations were given to the prosecutor and he then asked the company to provide other documentation of the investigation (for example, the proceedings of the interviews carried out). When the lawyers declined to hand over this information, the prosecutor ordered it. The court refused the lawyers' claims, invoking the client–attorney privilege. The argument was that the legal privilege only applies in the framework of the criminal process.

[33] For a comparison with the other privileges, see Kaplan and Murphy 2009, § 5.38, p. 5–75.

[34] See Mongillo 2012, p. 57.

[35] See Moosmayer 2013, p. 137.

But beyond this internal function, what really matters is to determine what the relationship between internal investigations and the criminal process is or must be.

Within the framework of collaboration and the battle for information, internal investigations mean the privatization of the criminal process.[36] In this regard, the experience of the USA is especially significant. After Enron and the other scandals of the early twenty-first century, the US Department of Justice (DOJ) decided to establish a more aggressive policy of prosecution which prioritized the punishment of individuals over legal entities. Due to this, corporations changed from being the object of criminal process to becoming—compulsorily—a means of investigation, allies of the public prosecutor in obtaining evidence against natural persons. This new strategy in the fight against corporate crime was enshrined in the well-known Thompson Memorandum in 2003.[37] The function of this memorandum and its successive updates is to guide public prosecutors in the use of their discretionary power to indict companies. One of the principal criteria is the need for corporations to cooperate fully in the criminal process, in order to identify the individual(s) liable. This total cooperation means, among other things, that the corporation must provide all the information relevant to the case that it has in its possession, even information that may be protected by client–attorney privilege. Full cooperation also involves renouncing any common strategy of defense with the accused employees, including not bearing the costs of their legal defense. But what is most important here is that nonprosecution agreements usually require the company to carry out an internal investigation under the direction of a lawyer appointed by the prosecutor, who must be paid by the company, and whose work will not be protected by the client–attorney privilege.

Despite these strict conditions for corporations wishing to reap the benefits of cooperation, in most cases they have acceded to the demands. The fear of becoming involved in a lengthy and costly criminal process leads companies to accept almost any agreement, even if it includes a pecuniary sanction, the appointment of a curator in charge of monitoring changes in the compliance system, or the removal of company managers.

Aside from this, what is of interest here is that internal investigations according to the US system are, in fact, public investigations which are paid for by the corporation and conducted by the prosecutor. In Europe, this privatization has not happened in such a radical way. Criminal systems in most (but not all) countries have established incentives that make it attractive for corporations to collaborate with

[36] For the USA, see especially Griffin 2007, p. 313 and 341. Regarding the investigation of KPMG for tax fraud, see First 2010, p. 23. In the case of Europe, see Reeb 2012, p. 41; Montiel 2012, p. 188.

[37] Memorandum from Larry D. Thompson, Deputy Attorney Gen, to US Attorneys, Regarding Principles of Federal Prosecutions of Business Organizations. See University of Albany, *Principles of Federal Prosecution of Business Organizations Memorandum from Larry D. Thompson, Deputy Attorney General to Heads of Department Components US Attorney—January 20, 2003*, http://www.albany.edu/acc/courses/acc695spring2008/thompson%20memo.pdf, accessed 16 July 2013.

the prosecutor. In spite of this, up to the present a director for the investigation has never been imposed, and the client–attorney privilege has never been suspended.

Such aggressiveness means only that problems are quantitatively but not qualitatively different. In other words, the root of the matter remains the same: Through the incentives policy, the prosecutor and the judge retain the possibility of changing the legal framework which governs the obtaining of information in the criminal process. Internal investigations are ruled by labor law, not by criminal procedural law, and they concern the employer–employee relationship, not the relationship between the state and the citizen under investigation (Hamm 2010, p. 1332). This leads to a significant saving in the cost of obtaining information. In internal investigations, the investigator acts with the mandate of the corporations' management and, consequently, on behalf of it. Thus, the relationship with the employees when the investigator is questioning them or accessing their emails is that of labor law.[38]

If, as in the *Siemens* case (Graeff et al. 2009; Weidenfeld 2011), an investigation must be carried out in several countries, the private investigator acts as an international prosecutor. Since the investigation is still internal, and consequently is not the manifestation of the *ius puniendi* of any state, the investigator can conduct simultaneous searches of multiple company offices around the world, question employees, or carry out any other acts of investigation. In other words, the investigator can circumvent all restrictions of judicial cooperation. This strategy can be decisive in the fight against international corruption. It is not a matter of asking for the collaboration of a third state (which may have a weak judicial system) in which the corruption has taken place. Instead, it is a question of requiring the multinational company to investigate its operations in that state and, in return for some incentives, provide any incriminating evidence against the individuals involved (Hart-Hönig 2009; Nieto Martín 2013).

In addition to the above-mentioned tensions, internal investigations cause another disruption to the rules of criminal process under the rule of law. As was said before, a fundamental feature of the criminal process is that it can only start if there is prima facie evidence of wrongdoing. Under the rule of law, prosecutors cannot act on mere suspicion. But this limitation does not apply in internal investigations, which can start much earlier, based on mere rumors made known via the whistle-blowing channel, or even through fishing investigations which are purely preventive.

Once problems have been presented, the question is how to avoid the imbalances which internal investigations cause in the framework of rules and guarantees that shape the struggle for information in criminal law.

[38] Regarding the different steps within an internal investigation and how to organize them, see Moosmayer and Hartwig 2012, p. 106. Biegelman and Biegelman 2010, Chap. 12, is also very instructive.

5.5 Internal Investigation and the Corporation's Right of Defense

When analyzing the legitimacy of internal investigations, it should be first pointed out that when a legal entity faces criminal proceedings due to some wrongdoing which is being investigated by an internal investigation, this investigation can be used by the company as part of their right of defense. Proper defense of a corporation entails that the company must have the opportunity to create its own version of the facts. This problem does not exist—or is not as serious—with regard to natural persons; but it is essential in the case of legal entities. The version of the facts which the corporation regards as more congenial may not correspond to the managers' and employees' versions. Conflicts of interests can easily arise. For this reason, it is generally necessary to carry out an internal investigation before designing the corporate strategy of defense: for example, before deciding whether the company will opt for cooperation, or maintain a strategy in accordance with the strategy of any of employees embroiled in the case.[39]

Since internal investigations are an expression of the corporation's right of defense, the US model of total cooperation is questionable from a constitutional perspective. In this model, cooperation means renouncing the right of defense, so the choice of the lawyer in charge of conducting the investigation and protecting the client–attorney privilege is important. In this respect, after *Stein v. USA,*[40] the requirement of total cooperation seemed to ease off. Although this decision addressed only one aspect of the right of defense—the choice of lawyer—its outcomes can be easily extrapolated. Pressures from the system of super-collaboration, established in the post-Enron era, override the most basic rights of defense, for example, the client–attorney privilege (legal privilege and work-product doctrine). The DOJ's latest guidelines to prosecutors have reduced the requirements of cooperation and even presented a draft law with the intention of properly protecting the client–attorney privilege.[41]

In Europe, the assault on company information has taken place in a much more subtle—but also questionable—way. The ECJ, in the above-mentioned *Akzo* case,[42] declared that internal lawyers are not protected by the client–attorney privilege.[43] The court's main argument was that an in-house lawyer does not have the same status of independence as an external lawyer. Although the decision concerns EU competition law, it can be taken as a European benchmark. The European Court of Human Rights (ECHR), the ECJ, and the national Constitutional Courts work together to give effect to fundamental rights. The *Akzo* ruling means that public

[39] Regarding the legitimacy of internal investigations, see Reeb 2012, p. 58.

[40] Stein v. USA, 440 F. Sup. 2006.

[41] Griffin 2007, p. 59. See especially the draft law: Attorney–Client Privilege Protection Act of 2008, 10th Congress 2d Session s. 3217, presented by Senator Specter.

[42] Judgment of the ECJ (Grand Chamber), 14.9.2010, case C-550/07 P. Among several comments on the judgment, see Pérez Fernández 2011; Rodríguez-Piñero y Bravo-Ferrer 2011, p. 7685.

[43] For a comparison of the USA and the EU, see Mackintosh and Angus 2004, p. 31.

investigators—regardless whether they are prosecutors, agencies, or the European Commission—will have no difficulty accessing the content of internal investigations carried out by a company's in-house lawyers or its auditing department.

In fact, there is an easy way for corporations to prevent access to such information: hiring an external lawyer to carry out the investigation and, for added security, giving him or his office custody of the results and any related documents. But this solution, besides being expensive, is also uncertain, since an internal investigation can hardly be carried out efficiently by a stranger who does not know the structure of the company. It requires the collaboration of the internal staff—including lawyers—even if they are not protected by legal privilege.[44] If employees are not subject to any right of confidentiality, the public prosecutor may call them as witnesses in order to access company information.[45] On this point, American legal constructs—legal privilege, work-product doctrine, the self-auditing privilege—are much more protective of the corporation's rights of defense with regard to internal investigations than European jurisprudence. *Akzo* opens the door to new ways of accessing corporate information.

Given that limiting internal investigations through super-cooperation is a violation of the right of defense, forbidding them—as has been proposed in some jurisdictions—is also unconstitutional. This temptation can arise in continental criminal law, in which the public prosecutor is considered the "owner of the investigation" and any other parallel investigation is regarded with suspicion.[46] In fact, there can be good reasons for limiting internal investigations that take place at the same time as criminal proceedings. Internal investigations can interfere with the ultimate object of the criminal process: uncovering the truth. For example, if the company questions essential witnesses or even the suspects, it could make the subsequent investigation by the public prosecutor less effective. Likewise, if employees' communications are accessed in violation of their fundamental rights, it could invalidate essential evidence. It may also be that information retrieved from computers during the internal investigation is accessed improperly, such that doubts can arise about its authenticity in subsequent criminal proceedings.

To avoid tensions arising between internal investigations (under the company's right to defense) and an effective criminal process, there are several solutions available. For instance, where appropriate, the company must report the existence of an internal investigation to the public prosecutor and, as far as possible, coordinate both investigations, or at least obtain the prosecutor's authorization for certain actions.[47] Another way is to review the current offenses of obstruction of justice in

[44] On the role of the in-house lawyer during investigation and as a part of the investigation team, see Moosmayer 2013, p. 128.

[45] See Beulke et al. 2009, p. 23. Regarding the lawyer, it may be necessary to distinguish between two possible scenarios: where the corporate lawyer is, in fact, acting as a lawyer, and where he is acting as a legal adviser. In the latter case, according to the proportionality principle, legal privilege can be restricted.

[46] Regarding how to coordinate public and private investigations, see Hartwig and Moosmayer 2012, p. 33.

[47] In this regard, Hartwig and Moosmayer 2012, p. 33.

the light of that tension. The company could be punished, for example, for reckless destruction of evidence.[48] In the Spanish Criminal Code, these offenses have a very limited scope: they have very little capacity to punish any obstruction of a public investigation caused by an internal one. The opposite model can be found in US criminal law, where there is a widely recognized offense of obstruction of justice that includes the sorts of situation which can arise when internal investigations are implemented concurrently with criminal proceedings.

5.6 Internal Investigations and the Employees' Right to Defense

The most worrying dangers of internal investigations are those concerning the rights of people under investigation—that is, the company employees. It is they who experience the transformation of their procedural rights of defense into rights and duties derived from their employment contract. The rules of corporate cooperation are aimed not only at the punishment of legal entities but also of the individuals involved. The new style of aggressive prosecutions initiated after Enron is, in fact, characterized by seeking individuals who can be held liable, through applying pressure on the company to cooperate. This marks an important change of course in relation to criminal policy in the USA in the 1970s and 1980s, which opted to hold corporations liable rather than individuals (Griffin 2007, pp. 314–316; First 2010, p. 81).

With regard to employees' rights, there are two main areas of danger that derive from the two most important means of investigations. Interviewing and questioning are essential tools, but can also violate the employee's right not to incriminate himself. The second area of danger concerns the right to privacy, the secrecy of communications, and personal data protection. A very common means of investigation is, for example, to review the emails sent and received by the employee from the corporation's computers, search their office, check their call records, and so on.

5.6.1 The Right Not to Incriminate Oneself and Internal Investigations

In an interview carried out within the framework of an internal investigation, the person under investigation is an employee who must render an account of his work activities to the employer (Griffin 2007, p. 353; Reeb 2012, p. 95). Providing information on his work activities is part of the employee's obligations, and the employer has a right to this information. The right not to incriminate oneself has no meaning in this context (Fritz and Nolden 2010, p. 170); the employee interviewed must col-

[48] Cf. Hartwig and Moosmayer 2012, p. 34.

laborate by providing all the information he has under his contractual relationship with the employer. Noncompliance with this obligation can lead to disciplinary proceedings, including the dismissal of the employee. In fact, many internal investigations have been developed according to the concept of "talk or walk."[49] When a corporation carries out an internal investigation, for example, in order to comply with an agreement with the prosecutor, it means that the employee faces a choice of either informing, and thus contributing to his own incrimination, or being fired.

With the objective of easing this tension, some nuanced interpretations have been allowed. For instance, a distinction has been made between information arising directly from the tasks the employee is contractually required to carry out, and information that he may have had access to through his work (Fritz and Nolden 2010, p. 170). While in the first case the right not to testify is not subject to conditions, in the second case the obligation to inform—derived from good faith—would be subject to weighting, meaning that the employee would have the right to remain silent if, by answering the employer's question, he might incriminate himself. Another distinction has been made with the purpose of reducing areas of tension between internal investigations and employees' rights: that is, the distinction between investigations aimed at improving the compliance system (which may be carried out even if there is no known wrongdoing), and investigations that are intended to uncover wrongdoing, punish the employees involved, and demonstrate collaboration with a public investigation (Maschmann 2012, p. 95). The conflict between internal investigations and employees' rights appears only in the latter case; in investigations aimed at improving the system, the employee will always be obliged to testify.

None of these proposals completely solves the problem. The distinction between obligations directly stipulated in the employment contract and the obligations derived from its interpretation in the light of good faith are all very well from a theoretical point of view. However, from a practical perspective such distinctions do not necessarily provide any solution. If the employee does not provide all the information in his possession, he may lose the employer's confidence; as a result, the employer may consider him no longer to be the right person for the position, and fire him.

Also, the distinction between reactive and proactive[50] investigations is not always useful. At the beginning of an investigation, the corporation's intention is not always clear. A proactive investigation, similar to an internal audit, can become a reactive investigation if in the course of the investigation a wrongdoing is uncovered (Green and Podgor 2013, p. 76). Regardless of the kind of investigation, practical experience also shows that when an employee testifies, he is usually confident that the corporation will be on his side and will defend his interests. In fact, this has traditionally been the most common strategy of defense. Until recently, the company would align its strategy with the strategy of the employees who had committed offenses for its benefit, bearing the costs of their legal defense, sometimes even

[49] Broadly regarding these questions, see Green and Podgor 2013, p. 73; Cummings 2007, p. 670.

[50] Regarding the equivalent distinction between internal audit and internal investigation, see Bührer 2012, p. 106.

sharing the same lawyer. In such a situation, an employee acting in good faith may provide information that could harm him should the corporation eventually decide to collaborate with the court.

Other solutions may be attempted in order to solve, or ease, the tension between the right not to incriminate oneself and the contractual obligation to inform. In all internal investigations, regardless of their nature, the employee must be clearly informed about his legal situation, his rights, and above all about the possible uses of any information he provides by the company, before being interviewed. This "Corporate Miranda,"[51] so named for its similarities with the reading of rights to the detainee, must make clear that the person carrying out the investigation represents only the corporation's interests.

The origin of this practice is the well-known Upjohn[52] doctrine. In this decision, the US Supreme Court established that employees' statements, regardless of their position within the company, were protected by the client–attorney privilege. This meant that prosecutors could not access information provided by employees, as was common up until then. But it also meant that the corporation had the right to waive their legal privilege and hand over information to the prosecutors. The solution provided for protecting employees was precisely to recognize the need to fully inform them as to their legal rights before commencing any interview.

In fact, the "Corporate Miranda" does not avoid the tension referred to above, but it does, at least, legitimize a company wishing to contribute information gathered from employees to the criminal process. Considered from another perspective, however, it could be argued that such information was obtained misleadingly by the company; in other words, that the employer behaved dishonestly with respect to the employee, failing to comply with his duties as an employer (Green and Podgor 2013, p. 93). This opens the door to claims that the information was obtained in violation of the right not to incriminate oneself and, thus, does not respect the fundamental rights of the employee.

Beyond the "Corporate Miranda," the corporation has other ways to avoid conflict between employment obligations and the right not to testify. The above-mentioned amnesty programs are one option. The legal entity can commit not to impose any disciplinary measures or, at least, not to dismiss employees if they cooperate openly with the investigation. In fact, the company can even commit to withhold information in the criminal process. This can be a good solution in cases where the employee has not played a significant role in the criminal offense and does not hold a high position within the corporate hierarchy.

But, above all, when resolving such conflicts, it is important not to forget that compliance programs are based on the promotion of ethical values, which require

[51] An example can be found in Biegelman and Biegelman 2010, p. 304; see also American Bar Association (ABA), Upjohn Warnings: Recommended Best Practices when Corporate Counsel Interacts with Corporate Employees—ABA WCCC Working Group, 17 July 2009, http://meetings.abanet.org/webupload/commupload/CR301000/newsletterpubs/ABAUpjohnTaskForceReport.pdf, accessed 16 July 2013.

[52] Upjohn v. US, 449 U.S. (1981).

a healthy environment in terms of labor relations, preventing the corporation from becoming a "police state." For this reason, the basic principles of the rule of law should be recognized in corporate regulation of internal investigations. It is not possible to implement a code based on ethical values if, during the internal investigations, the basic guarantees of the rule of law—such as the right of defense and the right not to incriminate oneself—are not respected.[53]

If ethical compliance programs are the most efficient way to achieve this, criminal, procedural, and substantive law must promote this model. Public investigations can benefit from internal investigations, but this should not mean that the basic safeguards of criminal law be voided. This means that collaboration should open the door to the principle of nonmandatory prosecution. Collaboration cannot involve the company playing "dirty tricks" on employees or coercing them with threats of dismissal or disciplinary sanctions, such that they renounce their right not to testify. Incentives in criminal law must aim to obtain information while ensuring that internal investigations are carried out within an acceptable framework of guarantees. To put it another way, systems of incentives can prove counterproductive to internal compliance systems, which must be based on a culture of loyalty and dialogue between the company and the employees (Griffin 2007, p. 333, 337).

5.6.2 Privacy of Communications and Internal Investigations

One of the most commonly used methods in internal investigations is accessing employees' corporate communications. In extensive internal investigations, a huge number of emails, electronic files, and call records are reviewed. If the company collaborates with the public investigator, the saving in costs is considerable. However, what is significant is that this access to information takes place in a legal framework which is different from the legal framework of the criminal process. The corporation is the owner of the computers and other technology used by employees in order to do their job. This situation allows the company to define their terms of use from the outset, and subsequently check the way in which they have been used.[54]

[53] Nieto Martín 2012, p 38; Montiel 2012, p. 193. The need for adapting internal investigations to the guarantees of due process has been supported by a document presented on this topic in the German Bar Association, Bundesrechtsanwaltskammer (BRAK-Stellungnahme-Nr. 35/2010, Thesen der Bundesrechtsanwaltskammer zum Unternehmensanwalt im Strafrecht, November 2010), Thesis nº 3: (2) The corporate lawyer will comply with the general rules and standards derived from the rule of law in the internal investigations, especially during the employees' interviews. (3) The corporate lawyer will carry out the investigation without affecting the quality and utility of evidence.

[54] On this matter, see, e.g., Peccorella and Di Ponti 2010, p. 583; Vitaletti 2012, p. 111; Maschmann 2012, p. 85; Mengel 2009, p. 109. Regarding the possible offenses that the corporation can commit during these investigations, see Reeb 2012, p. 77.

In most EU countries, in line with the ECHR jurisprudence, the "expectation of privacy"[55] has been settled upon as a basic principle on this matter. The corporation has the right to access the content of communications made through corporate-owned machines and stored on its computer hard disks, so long as employees have been clearly warned that these machines can only be used for employment purposes and thus have no expectation of privacy. Although all the nuances and unsolved problems related to this jurisprudence cannot be explored here, what is important to highlight is that when an expectation of privacy exists, access to emails and call records is a violation of the fundamental right to privacy.

Such violation has consequences in the criminal process, where the use of such evidence must be forbidden. In other words, the doctrine on forbidden evidence must remain constant regardless of whether the violation of fundamental rights happened during a public or private internal investigation.[56] Logically, the right to privacy and to secrecy of communications have a different intensity in the framework of state–citizen and employer–employee relationships. Nevertheless, once the violation has been determined, consequences must be similar.

5.7 Conclusions

Two principal conclusions can be drawn from the discussion in this chapter. The first regards the corporate side of things. To be efficient, cooperation, investigation, and whistle-blowing channels must be embedded in a compliance system based on ethical values. The basic guarantees of the criminal process and respect for fundamental rights are the basis of the legal system, and also of any public or private ethical system. It follows that compliance programs must respect these guarantees too. More concretely, corporate regulation on whistle-blowing and internal investigation must be inspired by the basic safeguards of the rule of law, along with logical interpretation and necessary nuances.

The *ius puniendi* must operate in accordance with these guarantees. This involves designing and using the state "carrots" system in a manner that does not violate them. This means that complaints and provision of information cannot be encouraged at any price, regardless of the consequences. To reduce economic criminality, companies cannot become a panopticon—that is to say, totalizing institutions which extract information from their employees at any price. In short, compliance and criminal processes must share certain values and guarantees. According to this principle, cooperation, confession, and compliance programs should not be considered in isolation as grounds for attenuating or excluding liability. As has been seen, separating collaboration from an effective compliance system can lead to perverse effects on fundamental rights. For this reason, collaboration and confession should

[55] As well as the reference included in n. 30, above, see Alcácer Guirao (2013); Martín 2012, p. 111, and Rodríguez Sanz de Galdeano 2011, p. 358.

[56] In favor of applying theory on forbidden evidence, see Reeb 2012, p. 109.

not mitigate or exclude liability unless they are the result of an effective compliance program. Companies which do not actively pursue a culture of compliance should not gain advantage from collaboration, except in very specific cases (for example, when the collaboration involves only senior executives). The ex ante separation between collaboration and compliance presents a risk to fundamental rights and may place limits on the corporation's enthusiasm to implement an effective compliance program.

Secondly, it is not simply a matter of encouraging any kind of compliance, but of creating an effective compliance system. In such a system, violations of fundamental rights during an internal investigation should be penalized and, generally, criminal law must be used to encourage corporations to establish compliance programs sustained by ethical values. Information obtained by the company through serious violations of employees' rights must be left out of the criminal process. This rule has a dissuasive effect: Corporations will not reap the benefits of collaboration if the information they supply in the criminal process was obtained in violation of employees' rights.

Finally, serious consideration must also be given to privileges—that is, corporations' right to prevent public investigators from accessing certain information. Creating a good compliance program involves self-assessment, being aware of potential flaws, learning from mistakes, and creating a favorable environment for internal dialogue, where problems in compliance can be exposed in order to correct them. Logically, this activity generates highly sensitive information which public investigators should be forbidden to access.

References

Alcácer Guirao, R. (2013). Cumplimiento penal por la persona jurídica y Derechos fundamentales: la intimidad como límite a la vigilancia empresarial. In *Diario La Ley*, no. 8053.

Artaza Varela, O. (2013). *La empresa como sujeto de imputación de responsabilidad penal: fundamentos y límites*. Madrid: Marcial Pons.

Bajo Fernández, M., Feijoo Sánchez, B. J., & Gómez-Jara Díez, C. (2012). *Tratado de responsabilidad penal de las personas jurídicas*. Navarra: Civitas Ediciones, S.L.

Beulke, W., Swoboda, S., & Lüdke, I. (2009). *Unternehmen im Fadenkreuz: Über den Umfang anwaltlicher Privilegien von Syndici—Rechtsabteilungen im Ermittlungsverfahren*. Berlin: Müller.

Biegelman, M. T., & Biegelman, D. R. (2010). *Foreign Corrupt Practices Act compliance guidebook: Protecting your organization from bribery and corruption*. New York: Wiley.

Brown, A. J. (2008). *Whistleblowing in the Australian public sector: Enhancing the theory and practice of internal witness management in public sector organizations*. Canberra: The Australian National University Press.

Breßler, S., Kuhnke, M., Schulz, S., & Stein, R. (2009). Inhalte und Grenzen von Amnestien bei Internal Investigations. *Neue Zeitschrift für Gesellschaftsrecht, 19*.

Bührer, R. (2012). Einrichtungeiner internen Untersuchungsabteilung und deren Prozesse. In K. Moosmayer & N. Hartwig (Eds.), *Interne Untersuchungen*. Munich: Beck.

Cummings, L. P. (2007). The ethical mine field: Corporate internal investigations and individual assertions of the attorney client privilege. *West Virginia Law Review, 109*.

Dann, M. (2010). Die neue Kronzeugenregelung: ein Störfaktor aus Compliance-Sicht? *Corporate Compliance Zeitschrif, 1.*
First, H. (2010). Branch office of the prosecutor: The new role of the corporation in bussines crime prosecutions. *North Carolina Law Review, 89.*
Fritz, H. (2009). Whistleblowing-Denunziation oder Wettbewerbsvorteil?. In F. Maschmann (Ed.), *Corporate Compliance und Arbeitsrecht*. Berlin: Nomos.
Fritz, H., & Nolden, D. (2010). Unterrichtungspflichten und Einsichtsrechte des Arbeitnehmers. *Corporate Compliance Zeitschrift, 5.*
Gobert, J., & Punch, M. (2000). Whistleblowers, the public interest, and the Public Interest Disclosure Act 1998. *The Modern Law Review, 63*(1).
Goena Vives, B. (2013). Capítulo 9. La Atenuante De Colaboración. In J. Silva Sánchez (Ed.) *Criminalidad de empresa y compliance. Prevención y reacciones corporativas*. Barcelona: Atelier Libros Jurídicos.
Gómez Jara, C. (2008). La incidencia de la autorregulación en el debate legislativo y doctrinal actual sobre la responsabilidad penal de las personas jurídicas. In L. Arroyo Jimenez & A. Nieto Martín (Eds.), *Autorregulación y Sanciones*. Valladolid: Lex Nova.
Gómez-Aller, J. D. (2011). Responsabilidad penal de las personas jurídicas. In I. Ortiz de Urbina (Ed.) *Memento Penal Económico y de la Empresa 2011–2012*. Madrid: Ediciones Francis Lefebvre.
Goñi Sein, J. L. (2011). Sistemas de denuncia interna de irregularidades (Whistleblowing). In J. L. Goñi Sein (Ed.), *Ética empresarial y Códigos de Conducta*. La Rozas: La Ley.
González de León Berini, A. (2013). El Criminal Compliance En La Reforma Norteamericana De La Dodd-Frank Act. In J. Silva Sánchez (Ed.), *Criminalidad de empresa y compliance: Prevención y reacciones corporativas*. Barcelona: Atelier Colección.
Graeff, P., Schröder, K., & Wolf, S. (2009). *Der Korruptionsfall Siemens. Analysen und praxisnahe Folgerungen des wissenschaftlichen Arbeitskreises von Transparecy International Deutschland*. Berlin: Nomos.
Graser, D. (2000). *Whistleblowing: Arbeitnehmeranzeigen im US-amerikanischen und Deutschen Recht*. New York: Peter Lang Publishing.
Green, B. A., & Podgor, E. S. (2013). Unregulated internal investigations: Achieving fairness for corporate constituents. *Boston College Law Review, 54.*
Griffin, L. K. (2007). Compelled cooperation and the new corporate criminal procedure. *New York University Law Review, 82*(2).
Hamm, R. (2010). Compliance vor Recht? *Neue Juristische Wochenschrift, 19.*
Hart-Hönig, K. (2009). Verteidigung von Unternehmen und Compliance im globalisierten Strafrecht. Rechtstaatlich problematische Verschärfung von Haftungsrisiken – exemplarisch skizziert anhand der Verfolgung von Korruption und Kartellrechtsverstössen unter europäischen und US-amerikanischem Einfluss. In *Strafverteidigung im Rechtsstaat, Deutscher Anwaltverein Arbeitsgemeinschaft Strafrecht*. Berlin: Nomos.
Hartwig, N., & Moosmayer, K. (Eds.). (2012). *Interne Untersuchungen*. Munich: Beck.
Holmes, S. (Ed.). (2010). *The international comparative legal guide to cartels & leniency 2011: A practical cross-border insight into cartels and leniency*. London: Global Legal Group Ltd.
Gascón Inchausti, F. (2012). *Proceso penal y persona jurídica*. Madrid: Marcial Pons.
Kaplan J. M., & Murphy, J. E. (2009). *Compliance programs and the corporate sentencing guidelines*, revised edition, 2009–2010 supplement. New York: Thomson Reuters West.
Laufer, W. S. (2008). *Corporate bodies and guilty minds: The failure of corporate criminal liability*. Chicago: University of Chicago Press.
Mackintosh, J. T., & Angus, K. M. (2004). Conflict in confidentiality: How EU laws leave in-house counsel outside the privilege. *The International Lawyer, 38*(1).
Martín, V. G. (2012). Compliance und Arbeitnehmenrecht. In L. Kuhlen; H. Kudlich & I. Ortiz de Urbina (Hrsg.), *Compliance und Strafrecht (Schriften zum Wirtschaftsstrafrecht)*. Heidelberg: Müller Jur. Vlg. C.F.

Maschmann, F. (2012). Compliance und Mitarbeitrrecht. In L. Kuhlen; H. Kudlich & I. Ortiz de Urbina (Hrsg.), *Compliance und Strafrecht (Schriften zum Wirtschaftsstrafrecht)*. Heidelberg: Müller Jur. Vlg. C.F.
Mengel, A. (2009). *Compliance und Arbeitsrecht*. Munich: Beck.
Molo, S. F., Tarun, R. W., & Webb, D. K. (2008). *Corporate internal investigations*. New York: Law Journal Press.
Mongillo, V. (2012). The supervisory body (organismo di vigilanza) under Legislative Decree n[a] 231/2001. In A. Fiorella (Ed.), *Liability ex crimine of legal entities in member states*. Napoli: Jovene Editore.
Montiel, J. P. (2012). Unternehmerische Selbstreiningung. In L. Kuhlen; H. Kudlich & I. Ortiz de Urbina (Hrsg.), *Compliance und Strafrecht (Schriften zum Wirtschaftsstrafrecht*. Heidelberg: Müller Jur. Vlg. C.F.
Moosmayer, K. & N. Hartwig. (2012). Interne Untersuchungen. Praxisleitfaden für Unternehmen. München: C.H. Beck.
Moosmayer, K. (2013). Investigaciones internas: una introducción a sus problemas esenciales. In L. Arroyo Zapatero & A. Nieto Martín (Eds.), *El Derecho penal económico en la era compliance*. Valencia: Titant lo Blanch.
Nelles, U. (2006). Grenzüberschreitende Strafverteidigung. In K. Volk (Ed.), *Münchener Anwaltshandbuch Verteidigung in Wirtschafts- und Steuerstrafsachen*. München: Beck.
Nieto Martín, A. (2008). *La responsabilidad penal de las personas jurídicas: un modelo legislativo*. Madrid: Iustel.
Nieto Martín, A. (2010). El abuso de mercado: un nuevo paradigma en el Derecho penal económico europeo. In J.R. Serrano-Piedecasas & E. Demetrio (Dirs), *El derecho penal económico y empresarial ante los desafíos de la sociedad mundial del riesgo*. Madrid: Colex.
Nieto Martín, A. (2012). Grundlegende Probleme von Compliance und Strafrecht. In Serrano-Piedecasas et al. (Eds.), *El derecho penal económico y empresarial ante los desafíos de la sociedad mundial del riesgo*. Heidelberg: Müller Jur. Vlg. C.F.
Nieto Martín, A. (2013). Criminal liability of legal entities: Opportunities and challenges for judicial cooperation. In A. Fiorella (Ed.), *Corporate criminal liability and compliance programs* (Vol. 2). Napoli: Jovene Editore.
Nieto Martín, A., & Blumenberg, A. (2010). Nemo tenetur se ipsum accusare en el Derecho penal económico europeo. In L. M. Díez-Picazo (Ed.), *Los derechos fundamentales en el Derecho penal europeo* (pp. 397–420). Pamplona: Civitas–Thomson Reuters.
OECD (2009). Recommendation of the Council for Further Combating Bribery of Foreign Public Officials in International Business Transactions – 29 November 2009. Website of the OECD. http://www.oecd.org/investment/anti-bribery/anti-briberyconvention/44176910.pdf. Accessed 28 June 2013.
Ortiz de Urbina, I. (2012). Strafrechtliche Sanktionen gegen Unternehmen in Spanien. In L. Kuhlen; H. Kudlich & I. Ortiz de Urbina (Hrsg.), *Compliance und Strafrecht (Schriften zum Wirtschaftsstrafrecht)*. Heidelberg: Müller Jur. Vlg. C.F.
Peccorella, C., & Di Ponti, R. (2010). Privacy y control del correo y de la navegación por la Red en el puesto de trabajo. In J. B. Reig (Ed.), *La protección jurídica de la intimidad*. Madrid: Iustel.
Pérez Fernández, P. (2011). ¿Cómo casan las limitaciones al secreto profesional de los abogados de empresa y el cumplimiento de la normativa por parte de las empresas? Comentario a la Sentencia del TJCE en el caso Akzo Nobel Chemicals y otros/Comisión, de 14 de septiembre de 2010 (asunto C-550/07). *Revista General de Derecho Penal*, 15.
Ragués i Vallès, R. (2006). *¿Héroes o traidores?: La protección de los informantes internos (whistleblowers) como estrategia político-criminal*. Indret: Revista para el Análisis del Derecho.
Ragués i Vallès, R. (2013). Capítulo 7: Los procedimientos internos de denuncia como medida de prevención de delitos en la empresa. In J. Silva Sánchez (Ed.), *Criminalidad de empresa y compliance: Prevención y reacciones corporativas*. Barcelona: Atelier Colección.
Reeb, P. (2012). *Internal Investigations. Neue Tendenzen privater Ermittlungen*. Berlin: Duncker & Humblot.

Rodríguez Sanz de Galdeano, B. (2011). La regulación, mediante códigos, del uso y control de los medios informáticos y de comunicaciones puestos a disposición del trabajador y de las secciones sindicales. In J. L. Goñi Sein (Ed.), *Ética empresarial y Códigos de Conducta*. La Rozas: La Ley.

Rodríguez Yagüe, C. (2006). La protección de los Whistleblowers por el ordenamiento español: aspectos sustantivos y procesales. In L. Arroyo Zapatero & A. Nieto Martín (coords.), *Fraude y Corrupción en el Derecho Penal Económico Europeo: Eurodelitos de Corrupción y Fraude*. Cuenca: Ediciones de la Univesidad de Castilla-La Mancha.

Rodríguez-Piñero y Bravo-Ferrer, M. (2011). El secreto profesional del abogado interno y la STJUE Akzo de 14 de septiembre de 2010. *Diario La Ley*, no. 7685.

Sahan, O. (2012). Unternehmensinterne Untersuchungen aus rechtsanwaltlicher Perspektive. In L. Kuhlen; H. Kudlich & I. Ortiz de Urbina (Hrsg.), *Compliance und Strafrecht (Schriften zum Wirtschaftsstrafrecht*. Heidelberg: Müller Jur. Vlg. C.F.

Schemmel, A., Ruhmannseder, F., & Witzigmann, T. (2008). *Hinweisgebersysteme: Implementierung im Unternehmen*. Heidelberg: Müller Jur. Vlg. C.F.

Spanheimer, R. (2012). Justification for creating an ombudsman privilege in today's society. *Marquette Law Review*, *96*(2).

Swenson, W. (1998). The organizational guidelines' "carrots and stick" philosophy, and their focus on "effective" compliance. In R. P. Conaboy (Ed.), *Corporate crime in america: Strengthening the "good citizen" corporation*. Darby: Diane Publishing.

Tarun, R. W., & Tomczak, P. P. (2010). Introductory essay: A proposal for a United States Department of Justice Foreign Corrupt Practices Act leniency policy. *American Criminal Law Review, 47*.

Thomas, S. (2012). Guilty of a fault that one has not committed: The limits of the group-based sanction policy carried out by the Commission and the European courts in EU antitrust law. *Journal of European Competition Law & Practice, 3*(1).

Treviño, L. K., & Weaver, G. R. (2002). *Managing ethics in business organizations*. Stanford: Stanford University Press.

Vaughan, D. (1999). The dark side of organizations: Mistake, misconduct, and disaster. *Annual Review of Sociology, 25*.

Vaughan, D. (1998). Rational choice, situated action, and the social control of organizations. *Law & Society Review, 32*(1).

Vitaletti, M. (2012). Compliance programmes and labor law. In A. Fiorella (Ed.), *Liability ex crimine of legal entities in member states*. Napoli: Jovene Editore.

Vogel, J. (2007). Wertpapierhandelsstrafrecht—Vorschein eines neuen Strafrechtsmodells? In G. Jakobs (Ed.), *Festschrift für Günther Jakobs: zum 70. Geburtstag am 26. Juli 2007*. Berlin: Heymann.

Weidenfeld, U. (2011). *Nütztliche Aufwendungen? Deer Fall Siemens und die Lehren für das Unternhemen, die Industrie und Gesellschaft*. München: Piper.

Weiße, M. (Ed.) (2012). *Interne Untersuchungen*. Munich: Beck.

Zabala López-Gómez, C. (2008). La responsabilidad penal de las sociedades cotizadas en Estados Unidos de América en la época post-Enron: los pactos de no acusar y de retraso en la acusación. *Diario La Ley*, nos. 7062–7065

Zagaris, B. (2010). *International white collar crime: Cases and materials*. New York: Cambridge University Press.

Chapter 6
Collective Action and Corruption

Mark Pieth

Contents

M. Pieth (✉)
University of Basel, Faculty of Law, Peter Merian-Weg 8,
CH-4002, Basel, Switzerland
e-mail: Mark.Pieth@unibas.ch

S. Manacorda et al. (eds.), *Preventing Corporate Corruption*,
DOI 10.1007/978-3-319-04480-4_6,

6.1 Introduction

The term collective action has long been used in economics and the social sciences to address the difficulties associated with jointly accessing public goods: Citizens are sometimes expected to refrain from individually profitable actions for the sake of the common good. And yet, individual self-interest usually prevails.[1] With *The Logic of Collective Action* (Olson 1965), Mancur Olson founded the theory of collective action, though some of the underlying ideas are much older (Hardin 2012, p. 3). Economists have employed game analysis (Holzinger 2003, p. 4) to explore aspects of the prisoner's dilemma (Hardin 2012, p. 26; Reuben 2003; Sandler 2010, p. 40). From this perspective, corruption is a typical collective action problem (Brütsch and Lehmkuhl 2007, p. 12; Kingston 2005; Mostipan 2009). Kingston puts it rather bluntly when he says:

> The citizens or firms dealing with a corrupt government official would all benefit from an agreement not to pay bribes, but each has an incentive to pay bribes to try to get preferential treatment. (Kingston 2005)

His fellow academics have put forward several models to overcome collective action impediments,[2] also in the area of corruption (Kingston 2005; Mostipan 2009). They attempt, among other things, to neutralize the free-rider problem (Hardin 2012).

In the area of combating corruption, the topic of collective action has transitioned from being a major academic think piece into a very concrete policy issue: Collective action is now a kind of catchall term for industry standards, multi-stakeholder initiatives, and public–private partnerships (PPPs; Pieth 2007, p. 81). It may take on the form of an anticorruption declaration,[3] an Integrity Pact (or an "Island of Integrity"; see Wiehen 1999a, 1999b),a principle-based initiative (WBI 2008, Slide 33), or, even, a certifying effort (WBI 2008, Slide 34). The World Bank Institute (WBI), in its Fighting Corruption Through Collective Action, A Guide for Business, defines—and justifies—"collective action" as:

> a collaborative and sustained process of cooperation amongst stakeholders. It increases the impact and credibility of individual action, brings vulnerable individual players into an alliance of like-minded organizations and levels the playing field between competitors. Collective action can complement or temporarily substitute for and strengthen weak local laws and anti-corruption practices. (WBI 2008, Slide 4)

Its main significance is as a way out of serious dilemmas in international business. Over the last two decades, states and international organizations have promulgated

[1] On the problem of collective action in general, see Bandiera et al. (2005); Holzinger (2003); Kingston (2005); Olson (1965); Reuben (2003); and Zürn (1998, p. 154). On citizens refraining from individually profitable actions for the sake of the common good, see Bandiera et al. (2005, p. 2). On prevalence of self-interest, see Holzinger (2003, p. 2).

[2] See Olson (1965). See also Bandiera, Barankay, and Rasul (2005); Hardin (2012); Holzinger (2003); Nielsen (2009); Reuben (2003); and Sandler (2010, p. 4).

[3] This was the goal of early collective action initiatives in the power systems and the defense industries between 2000 and 2003.

regulatory standards in the areas of environmental protection, labor relations, and safety, as well as on the "macro crimes" of illegal trusts, money laundering, embargo breaches, and corruption. Since the turn of this century, they have dramatically stepped up law enforcement on international commercial corruption in particular. Multinational enterprises (MNEs) and small- and medium-sized enterprises (SMEs) alike face considerable risks when caught bribing foreign public officials. And yet, they find themselves in a tight spot in many areas of the world where corruption remains endemic and they are regularly confronted with extortionate demands. On the one hand, if they give in to solicitation they may face legal action in the "victim country" or their country of domicile. Since solicitation is not a valid excuse,[4] a defense of extortion will only be heard in extreme cases of physical threat (Murphy 2011, p. 136; Pieth 2011, p. 70). On the other hand, if they take the ethical high road they could easily lose business. Now, commercially strong players may be well connected in the "victim country"—even in places with particularly bad reputations—and they may be able to resist the challenge by escalating the issue appropriately. Typically, however, even large companies are uneasy about "going it alone." They are uncertain whether their competitors are following the same virtuous path and they are aware they may be sidelined by ministers "on the take" and replaced by less scrupulous suppliers. This is what collective action theorists meant by defection (Mostipan 2009, p. 6, referring to Olson 1965). In such circumstances, collective action—be it a common standard among competitors, a joint démarche to government, or a bidders' anticorruption pledge—could be used to escape the dilemma collectively.

6.2 The Historical Background

6.2.1 Deregulation and Reregulation

Ironically, new international forms of regulation were themselves responses to new forms of deregulation. With increasing economic, political, and social globalization during the 1970s and 1980s, national governments and international organizations (including the Bretton Woods institutions) promoted the goals of market liberalization and privatization (Jenkins 2001, p. 1). It rapidly became apparent, however, that nation states, especially in the South, were unable to protect themselves against abuses by MNEs, which were typically domiciled in the North. Environmental catastrophes, child labor, and corruption were commonplace (Haufler 2001, p. 11; Jenkins 2001, p. 2). Increasing criticism by civil society groups prompted international organizations to opt for reregulation of a different kind: international behavioral standards (such as the Organisation for Economic Co-operation and Development's (OECD)

[4] See Recommendation of the Council for Further Combating Bribery of Foreign Public Officials in International Business Transactions—November 26, 2009, OECD, Annex I.A, http://www.oecd.org/investment/anti-bribery/anti-briberyconvention/44176910.pdf, accessed 20 July 2013.

Guidelines for Multinationals),[5] coupled with industry self-regulation. Self-regulation was considered cheaper, more flexible, and less burdensome than public regulation.[6] However, it too soon emerged as insufficient to deal with the formidable international challenges. Among other things, transnational economic and organized criminals were making use of the newly guaranteed free movement of people, goods, and capital.

6.2.2 Coregulation

Supplanting traditional command-and-control-style regulation (Black 2001) was "coregulation" (Black 2001; Haufler 2001, p. 12; Pieth 2007, p. 94). A hybrid system of regulation (Brütsch and Lehmkuhl 2007, p. 23),it is made up of international "hard" and "soft" law standards that are set, implemented, and monitored by state and non-state actors, including both private sector and civil society organizations (Peters et al. 2009). It quickly became the regulatory model of choice for nation states. Researchers talk of the law of cooperation replacing the law of coexistence among states in a world of increased international legalization (Brütsch and Lehmkuhl 2007, p. 13). Monitoring by peers and third parties is now a regular element of regulation both between states and among companies.

6.2.3 Regulating Corruption

As for corruption, a new phase of regulation followed the end of the Cold War and the opening of new markets in the former second and third worlds. In view of the upcoming redistribution of markets, major economic players (states and corporations) were not content to allow access to be influenced by unfair trade practices, such as corruption. Increasingly, states used task forces to focus on specific topics and to circumvent cumbersome negotiation procedures (Pieth 2007, p. 94). Alongside traditional conventions and dispute settlement procedures, new international instruments began to appear. The radical change was first apparent in regulations on the financial sector, particularly the soft law standards and peer pressure enforcement mechanisms of the Financial Action Task Force (FATF). What started as an effort to reduce money laundering,[7] was rapidly extended to the financing of

[5] In particular, see Annex 1, Guidelines for Multinational Enterprises, OECD Declaration and Decisions on International Investment and Multinational Enterprises, OECD, http://www.oecd.org/daf/inv/investment-policy/oecddeclarationoninternationalinvestmentandmultinationalenterprises.htm, accessed 20 July 2013.

[6] On advantages, see Black (2001); see also the introduction to Brütsch and Lehmkuhl (2007). On disadvantages, see Black (2001); Jenkins (2001, p. 26); Klauser (1994, p. 53); Pieth (2007, p. 94); Ruch (2004, p. 373).

[7] FATF 40 Recommendations (FATF 1990). For all FATF recommendations, see the FATF Recommendations, Financial Action Task Force, http://www.fatf-gafi.org/topics/fatfrecommendations/, accessed 20 July 2013.

terrorism,[8] corruption-related money laundering,[9] and, eventually, financial flows from tax fraud.[10] When tackling corruption after 1989,[11] the OECD broadly copied the FATF methodology. The OECD Working Group on Bribery (OECD-WGB) opted to develop an actual convention on criminalization, the OECD Anti-Bribery Convention (OECD-ABC)[12] and a recommendation for related matters in 1997.[13] Both the FATF and the OECD-WGB used peer review aggressively (Bonucci 2007, p. 445). Regional organizations in Europe[14] and the Americas[15] soon followed suit, as did the UN, ultimately, with its 2003 Convention against Corruption (UNCAC).[16]

6.2.4 Ensuring Enforcement

The various monitoring mechanisms have adopted a variety of styles, the OECD-WGB probably being the most outspoken and undiplomatic. Since its goals are most directly linked to the competition agenda, it assesses how countries deal with specific cases, as well as their laws and levels of awareness. Even though the OECD-WGB is not an international court, it can require states, through the responsible law enforcement agencies, to tell their peers why they have not opened or why they have closed a particular case. If there is no reasonable explanation for the state's decision to close an individual case (such as a lack of evidence, lapse of time, or lack of jurisdiction), and a cluster of such allegations are not followed up, the effectiveness of the country's system will be put into question (see, e.g., OECD 2012). A country may even be put on probation and forced to explain at regular intervals (e.g., every 6 months) how its cases are advancing.[17] As a last resort, the group can ask a country to reopen a specific case that has been closed and can threaten trade sanctions in the event of noncompliance (see, e.g., OECD 2008).

[8] FATF, IX Special Recommendations (FATF 2002). For all FATF recommendations, see http://www.fatf-gafi.org/topics/fatfrecommendations/.

[9] From the second 1996 edition of the FATF 40 Recommendations, http://www.fatf-gafi.org/topics/fatfrecommendations/.

[10] For all FATF recommendations, see The FATF Recommendations, FATF website, http://www.fatf-gafi.org/topics/fatfrecommendations/, accessed 20 July 2013.

[11] See the introduction to *The OECD Convention on Bribery* (Pieth et al. 2007, p. 11).

[12] Convention on Combating Bribery of Foreign Public Officials in International Business Transactions, Paris, 17 December 1997, in force 15 February 1999, (1998) 37 ILM 1.

[13] Revised Recommendation of the Council on Combating Bribery in International Business Transactions, 23 May 1997 reprinted (1997) 36 ILM 1061.

[14] Council of Europe: Criminal Law Convention on Corruption, Strasbourg, 27 January 1999 in force 1 July 2002, 2216 UNTS 225, 173 ETS. See also Civil Law Convention on Corruption, Strasbourg, 4 November 1999, in force 1 November 2003, 2246 UNTS 3, 174 ETS.

[15] Organization of American States: Inter-American Convention Against Corruption, Caracas, 29 March 1996, in force 6 March 1997, (1996) 35 ILM 724.

[16] United Nations Convention Against Corruption, New York, 31 October 2003, in force 14 December 2005, 2349 UNTS 41 (2004) 43 ILM 37.

[17] OECD 2005. See, further, Pieth et al. (2007, p. 36).

With increased pressure for implementation on states has come a dramatic increase in the risk to companies of enforcement. It should be no surprise that the private sector is itself becoming more active in combating corruption. First, it is very much interested in extending the anticorruption standards to other exporting nations, especially Brazil, Russia, India, and China (the BRIC countries). Here, the G20 format is proving very handy.[18] Second, the private sector has become even more insistent than the peer countries that anticorruption standards are applied equally. Third, companies have acknowledged that they are dependent on the evolution of a reliable body of common standards.[19]

6.2.5 Corporate Motives?

Companies have complex motivations for entering into particular collective action initiatives. Industry representatives usually emphasize the need to create "a level playing field for commerce" and "prevent regulatory arbitrage." However, collective risk management is always, at least in part, expectation management: With similar levels of regulation among all competitors, companies are also better able to limit costs. Also, members of the "club of the virtuous" may hope to be rewarded for their efforts with preferential treatment, e.g., in public procurement processes (by definition, they pose a lower risk to potential "victim states"). In all, there could be a strong business case (Mostipan 2009, p. 6; Sandler 2010, p. 44) for collectively combating corruption. Once again, this is a clear reference back to the theory of collective action, where ways are sought to exclude free riders from benefits (Reuben 2003, p. 7).

6.3 Early Experiments

The history of early experiments with collective action in relation to corruption and money laundering is far from straightforward: It is a story of early success and failure, and renewed efforts.

[18] See Letter of the B20 Working Group on Improving Transparency and Anti-Corruption to President of Mexico, Felipe Calderón Hinojosa, Chair of the G20 Nations for the Los Cabos Summit, June 2012, International Chamber of Commerce (ICC), http://www.iccwbo.org/, accessed 20 July 2013.

[19] See B20 Task Force Recommendations, June 2012, website of the B20, http://b20.org/documentos/B20-Complete-Report.pdf, accessed 20 July 2013.

6.3.1 *Early Success: Wolfsberg*

During the 1990s, regulation of the financial industries dramatically increased, anti-money laundering standards abounding in particular. For banks, it seemed that regulators had gone out of control. It was as if they were continuously raising the bar for compliance without really understanding the challenges for business. And, though complaints about singling out by regulators were rife, competitors had not yet considered the possibility of sitting down together and drafting an anti-money laundering compact of their own. Indeed, when civil society organizations[20] and far-sighted bankers first raised the idea, most executives responded semiautomatically with concerns about breaching laws on anticompetitive trusts. Perhaps this was a self-protective reflex, aimed at preventing their institutions from rushing prematurely into an ill-considered adventure. The common efforts were, nonetheless, the starting point for an initiative that served as a pattern for collective action initiatives to come: the Wolfsberg Banking Group.[21]

Initially, Wolfsberg's standards were relatively simple. They did not really go beyond what regulators had already decided. However, the activation of the private sector was a sensation in itself, drawing close to 200 journalists to a press conference.[22] The fact that banks—so frequently criticized for laundering drug money and hiding dictator's loot—would go on the offensive was apparently spectacular in 2000.

The group met intensively and produced further compacts. It rapidly established itself as a crucial industry reference group for regulators and international public bodies, not unlike the FATF. Now, beyond its internal meetings, the Wolfsberg Group even holds an annual "Wolfsberg Forum," inviting all relevant regulators and competitors to participate and comment on its annual catalogue of working documents. Thus, with time, the Wolfsberg Group matured into a strong self-regulatory body of the financial sector, one capable of dealing with issues of money laundering, the financing of terrorism, corruption, and embargo busting.[23]

6.3.2 *Failed First Attempts at Anticorruption Collective Action*

Shortly after the Wolfsberg success, similar groups formed around the issue of corruption. One needs to keep in mind that the US law on foreign bribery, the Foreign

[20] The Basel Institute on Governance and TI.

[21] See Anti-Money Laundering Principles, Wolfsberg AML Principles, http://www.wolfsberg-principles.com/, accessed 20 July 2013, at 243. See further Pieth and Aiolfi 2003, 243.

[22] The original principles were made public in a well-attended press conference in Zurich on 30 October 2000.

[23] See Wolfsberg Statement on the Suppression of the Financing of Terrorism 2002, and Wolfsberg Anti-Corruption Guidance 2011, Wolfsberg AML Principles, available at http://www.wolfsberg-principles.com/standards.html, accessed 20 July 2013.

Corrupt Practices Act (FCPA),[24] had been in force since 1977, but that it had taken until 1997 for states to agree to enlarge its scope through the instruments of the OECD. State parties to the OECD-ABC[25] and the related recommendation[26] were just about to enact laws on foreign bribery when these groups formed. The common denominator with the Wolfsberg Group was, then, the threat of intense cross-border public regulation; this motivated key players in certain industries to jointly formulate detailed standards.

Between 2000 and 2003, companies in the defense and the power systems sectors made early and impressive attempts to harmonize their compliance systems. In both sectors, groups labored for 2–3 years. However, distrust remained strong and public enforcement weak. In contrast to the financial sector, where regulators were already hitting noncompliant companies with heavy penalties, companies in these other industries were initially able to play a double game: They had incentive enough to say the right things and have convincing compliance systems on paper; but they also maintained impressive slush funds, just in case the anticorruption initiatives did not really take off and they needed to bribe their way into contracts again. So, a European version[27] of the successful US defense integrity initiative[28] was derailed by the BAE scandal (Pieth 2011, p. 19, with further references); only several years later, was a new—and genuinely transnational—text adopted.[29] Similarly, a power systems initiative stalled shortly before signature, General Electric voicing particular concerns about the depth of commitment on the part of its colleagues.[30]

6.4 Public–Private Partnerships: The Extractive Industries Transparency Initiative (EITI)

In the meantime, it had also rapidly become obvious that combating corruption from the supply side alone might not work since it hit at soft targets (companies and their employees), but it missed the recipients (the demand side of corruption) and the financial intermediaries. In particular, oil-producing states and their officials were identified as major contributors to the corruption cycle. The idea that oil com-

---

[24] Pub. L. No. 95–213, 21, 91 Stat. 1494 (FCPA 1977); Pub. L. No. 100–148, 102 Stat. 1107 (FCPA 1988); Pub. L. No. 105–366, 112 Stat. 3302 (FCPA 1998).

[25] Convention on Combating Bribery of Foreign Public Officials in International Business Transactions, Paris, 17 December 1997.

[26] Revised Recommendation of the Council on Combating Bribery in International Business Transactions, 23 May 1997.

[27] The Clovis Principles for the Defence Industry, Paris 2007.

[28] See DII Principles, Defense Industry Initiative on Business Ethics and Conduct (DII), http://www.dii.org/about-us/dii-principles, accessed 20 July 2013.

[29] See International Forum on Business Ethical Conduct for the Aerospace and Defense Industry (IFBEC), IFBEC website, http://ifbec.info/, accessed 20 July 2013.

[30] The trust generated through this original process was lost when misconduct by major competitors became obvious.

panies (and mining corporations) would publicly declare what they had paid into the budgets of the producing state ("publish what you pay") was a major contribution to public accountability in these states. The Extractive Industries Transparency Initiative (EITI) was then one of the first major PPPs in combating corruption. Governments of the North and the South, as well as corporations active in the entire sector, were linked up with the help of mediators from civil society (Brew and Moberg 2006, p. 128).

6.4.1 A Generic Intermezzo

After the failure of the first initiatives in defense and heavy industry, new initiatives maintained the need for common standards as the fundamental point of departure. Rather than develop new codes, however, they went back to the generic, older texts, especially the ICC Rules of Conduct[31] and the TI Business Principles.[32]

The generic industry standards for companies were gradually overtaken by a new generation of public regulations: national standards on corporate liability. These began to integrate the notion of a "sound compliance program," as defined by the US Sentencing Commission's (USSC) Guidelines,[33] and, later, the guidance that accompanied the UK Bribery Act 2010 (O'Shea 2011, p. 371). Spanning these efforts, the OECD Council enacted a Good Practice Guidance on Internal Controls, Ethics, and Compliance.[34] The US Department of Justice is currently working on a new FCPA Guidance in an effort to neutralize criticism from US companies[35] and comply with the recommendations of the OECD-WGB in its third phase evaluation (OECD 2010, 23 ff.). Together with detailed benchmarking by the compliance industry, these standards are rapidly congealing into a coherent body of rules. The rules themselves are no longer center stage: As major companies have harmonized their approaches to compliance, implementation and application, particularly in difficult business environments, is now at the forefront of collective action.

---

[31] See ICC Rules of Conduct and Recommendations to Combat Extortion and Bribery (2005 Edition), International Chamber of Commerce (ICC), http://www.iccwbo.org/Advocacy-Codes-and-Rules/Document-centre/2004/ICC-Rules-of-Conduct-and-Recommendations-to-Combat-Extortion-and-Bribery-%282005-Edition%29/, accessed 20 July 2013.

[32] See Business Principles for Countering Bribery, Transparency International (TI), http://archive.transparency.org/global_priorities/private_sector/business_principles, accessed 20 July 2013.

[33] See Guidelines Manual, 15 September 2009, United States Sentencing Commission (USSC), http://www.ussc.gov/, accessed 20 July 2013.

[34] OECD Recommendation 2009, Annex II: Good Practice Guidance on Internal Controls, Ethics, and Compliance, http://www.oecd.org/investment/anti-bribery/anti-briberyconvention/44176910.pdf.

[35] In particular, the US Chamber of Commerce 2011. See also Peter J. Henning, Taking aim at the Foreign Corrupt Practices Act, *New York Times*, http://dealbook.nytimes.com/2012/04/30/taking-aim-at-the-foreign-corrupt-practices-act/, accessed 20 July 2013.

6.5 Methods and Challenges

6.5.1 Initiating Collective Action

In thinking about the possibilities for future collective action, one needs to consider why companies do not end up cooperating on their own. The answer is relatively simple: Competitors usually trust each other little and they usually fear being perceived as "trusting" each other too much. In other words, many companies are wary of anticorruption compacts lest they be regarded as engaging in anticompetitive behavior.

Now, their fears are baseless if the goal is genuinely to reduce the risk of bribery. The contrary is true, since collective action allows companies to focus on price and quality once more. But, trade associations, the traditional mediators, have generally failed to take on the role of bringing companies together (Kingston 2005, p. 12; Mostipan 2009, p. 10). In my experience, they may be too slow and too risk averse. They typically represent a broader range of companies, beyond those interested in demanding a common solution to bribery and extortion.[36] Repeatedly, therefore, collective action has been promoted first by an ad hoc group of representatives from one or more nongovernmental organizations (NGOs), together with select private-sector protagonists.[37]

These consortia perform a crucial task in the early days of a collective action initiative by bringing together a group of industry representatives that is able to generate its own momentum.

The first moves are extremely sensitive. Though there is no set model for success, the civil society representatives frequently need to obtain the support of at least one industry champion.[38] Together, they attempt to convince other major players to participate. At the outset, the participants avoid committing to anything beyond a preliminary exchange of views. It takes time to convince the participants of the benefits of the initiative, and much depends on the subtlety of the mediators (Brew and Moberg 2006, p. 132). Once the initiative has taken off, however, the collaboration is publicized and corporate exponents take their share of the responsibility (Pieth and Aiolfi 2003, p. 267). In the meantime, it is also the task of the NGO representatives to ensure that the members of the group do not embark on anticompetitive behavior.

Thus, in starting a particular collective action initiative, the key factor is not (simply) the size of the group (Bandiera et al. 2005, p. 15; Holzinger 2003, p. 18; Nielsen 2009), as frequently suggested in academic debates about the conditions for overcoming collective action problems (Sandler 2010, p. 40). It is assumed that a few, especially strong, players achieve more than a multitude of small actors—the

[36] Such business associations are frequently shy of initiating a process, even if they may want to take it over once it is running (see, e.g., the defense industries).

[37] For example, Wolfsberg, PACI, and the aeronautics industries.

[38] Siemens, TNT, or UBS in their respective contexts, to name just a few.

larger the number, the greater the risk of truancy. Really, the challenges to collective action are concrete and tangible.

6.5.2 *Contents*

The substantive contents of the initiatives have evolved with the methodology of collective action. Originally, the fine-tuning of public standards that aimed at leveling commercial playing fields was at the forefront.[39] Later, collective action initiatives became more refined, being expanded to involve the public sector[40] in public procurement pledges and so-called Integrity Pacts (Wiehen 1999a, 1999b), among other things. These were intended to ensure that sound competitive practices became more relevant. More recently still, competitors have begun finding new creative uses for collective action, mutually opening their whistleblower hotlines to each other, for example. Finally, several initiatives are directed at certifying business behavior.[41]

6.5.3 *Major Challenges*

There are still major challenges to collective action, however. Its informality is a particular impediment. Most initiatives have their basis in soft law and are only concluded among private operators, public players getting involved only occasionally. So, collective action initiatives typically suffer from the same deficiencies as self-regulation initiatives: It is unclear who is supposed to ensure that commitments are implemented.

6.6 Recent Examples

6.6.1 *Categorizing Collective Action*

Over the last decade, an entire spectrum of local, regional, and global collective action initiatives on corruption has emerged. They have been divided by the WBI into four categories:

[39] Such as the early efforts in the power systems sector or the TI's Business Principles, (http://archive.transparency.org/global_priorities/private_sector/business_principles), or the PACI Principles.

[40] See, e.g., the EITI, discussed further in Brew and Moberg (2006, p. 128).

[41] For example, The Makati Business Club's activities in the Philippines under the Siemens Integrity Initiative, Siemens Integrity Initiative Slide Presentation, First Funding Round, February 2012, Slide 20.

- Anticorruption declarations
- Principle-based initiatives
- Integrity Pacts
- Certifying business coalitions

Pioneered by the NGO Transparency International (TI) sometime back, these very concrete forms of collective action are usually tied to specific contracts and monitored by civil society organizations.

6.6.2 *Back to Sector-wide Initiatives*

The time is also ripe for a fresh look at sector-wide collective action initiatives against corruption. Regulation has intensified to a point that noncompliance and law enforcement are perceived as real legal and reputational risks to corporations. They are now especially interested in reducing risks and leveling playing fields in emerging markets, such as Russia, Nigeria, Angola, China, and the Middle East.

Industry-specific groups are concentrating on particular topics: "facilitation payments" at customs in the logistics and transport industry; "offsets" in the defense industry and, to give another example, "signature bonuses" in the oil and gas industry.

Industry-specific groups are developing an overall interest in crosscutting issues, like the obligation to hire intermediaries, a so-called sponsor (particularly in the Middle East), or the problem of the solicitation of bribes.

6.6.3 *Activating Creativity*

The future for collective action lies in addressing very real challenges with creative means, including the use of information technology. Some such initiatives have emerged; two examples are mentioned here:

6.6.4 *Logistics and Transport*

Recently, major express carriers agreed to cooperate with the World Customs Organisation (WCO) and the People's Republic of Vietnam in the introduction of an electronic customs procedure. The collaboration was facilitated by the World Economic Forum's Partnering Against Corruption Initiative (PACI) and the Basel Institute on Governance, two civil society organizations. The new customs procedure, which is endorsed by the logistics and transportation industry, is more efficient than the existing manual process and far less vulnerable to misuse for rent seeking. Therefore, it is an indirect means of reducing corruption, in the form of facilitation payments at customs. On the basis of the experiences gathered during the pilot study, it is thought that the procedure may be used in other emerging markets.[42]

6.6.5 *High-Level Reporting Mechanisms (HLRM)*

The idea of "High-Level Reporting Mechanisms" (HLRMs) was born originally of discussions between general counsels of the largest heavy industries (power systems) groups, which was mediated by the Basel Institute on Governance. Frequently, even large companies find themselves confronted with outright extortion and, in some of the most difficult markets, are uneasy with escalating the matter individually. Hence, participants suggested the creation of ombudsman offices close to heads of government or heads of state. The organization of the structure would obviously be a matter for each country. The central idea, though, is not primarily of a law enforcement agency. Rather, from a company perspective, a complaint to the ombudsman would be a last-ditch effort at corruption prevention.

With the help of TI-USA, the idea was picked up and developed beyond one sector. The OECD agreed to act as a platform to promote the concept. The G20 countries and their B20 business representatives expressed their interest in this initiative at the summits of Cannes and Los Cabos in 2011 and 2012, respectively. Colombia is the current pilot country, and has developed a concept in which complaints of solicitation trigger increased due diligence in specific procurement procedures.

6.6.6 *The Current Policy Discourse on Collective Action*

I mentioned that collective action has moved from being one of the most challenging problems in economics and the social sciences (Reuben 2003, p. 1)—an academic riddle—to being an eminently practical challenge for a diverse range of actors interested in combating corruption. For the private sector, collective action offers a way out of very concrete dilemmas. The private sector is most interested in collective action initiatives that are already underway and that could yet be created. The issue is no longer how to prevent free riders. It is highly likely that noncompliant companies will be caught by law enforcement, especially if their competitors are ready to denounce them. The challenge is now to develop a reliable methodology for initiating and supporting collective action and to map and categorize the complex patchwork of current initiatives.

In G20 states, public and private sector policy groups, especially the B20,[43] are currently promoting the creation of a network ("hub") and web-based resources to

[42] World Economic Forum, PACI Annual Report 2010, Case Study 1, 13.

[43] See The B20 Task Force Recommendations, June 2012, http://b20.org/documentos/B20-Complete-Report.pdf.

collect and offer information about existing initiatives. So far, two such attempts to create a "hub" for collective action initiatives stand out.

First, the WBI's 2008 guide for business on collective action (WBI 2008) contained a log of collective action case studies.

Second, together with actors from the private sector, the Basel Institute on Governance is establishing an International Center on Collective Action (ICCA).[44] A network of organizations active on collective action and anticorruption work, the ICCA is currently developing IT tools to provide business with information about collective action drawn from network members. The ICCA is already providing assistance in setting up concrete collective action initiatives and is using its experiences as the basis for further research.[45]

6.7 Concluding Remarks

The current interest in collective action as a means for combating corruption is a response to a drastic increase in regulatory risks for corporations. The topic has emancipated itself from the classic debates about "collective action problems," "free riders," and "prisoners' dilemmas." It is a complex form of hybrid regulation (coregulation) in which public and private sanctions together form a strong incentive to behave. The motivation for companies to participate in collective action on anticorruption reflects their wish to escape from the trap of extortion, as well as their desire to earn recognition for their efforts to comply.

Promoting collective action is a crucial element in a wider strategy of combating corruption. It is about moving from talk to action. The private sector is taking its share of responsibility and control over the anticorruption agenda. Civil society is there to foster, mediate, and monitor this development.[46]

References

Bandiera, O., Barankay, I., & Rasul, I. (2005). Cooperation in collective action—2005. Manuscript, London School of Economics. http://econ.lse.ac.uk/staff/bandiera/collective.pdf. Accessed 20 July 2013.

Black, J. (2001). Decentring regulation: Understanding the role of regulation and self-regulation in a "post-regulatory world." *Current Legal Problems, 54*(1), 103–146.

[44] See International Centre for Collective Action (ICCA), ICCA website, http://www.collective-action.com/, accessed 20 July 2013.

[45] The ICCA has received seed funding from the Siemens Integrity Initiative.

[46] This chapter was originally published as Working Paper Series 13, Basel Institute on Governance, September 2012. It was reprinted in Mark Pieth (Ed.), *Collective Action—Innovative Strategies to Prevent Corruption* (DIKE AG, October 2012, ISBN 978-3-0371-474-0; www.dike.ch). It is reprinted here with permission.

Bonucci, N. (2007). Art. 12: Monitoring and follow-up. In M. Pieth, L. A. Low, & P. J. Cullen (Eds.), *The OECD convention on Bribery: A commentary*. Cambridge: Cambridge University Press.

Brew, P., & Moberg, J. (2006). The power of joining forces—The case for collective action in fighting corruption. In B. Errath (Ed.), *Business against corruption: Case stories and examples, UN global compact*. http://www.unglobalcompact.org/docs/issues_doc/7.7/BACbookFINAL.pdf. Accessed 20 July 2013.

Brütsch, C., & Lehmkuhl, D. (2007). *Law and legalization in transnational relations*. Oxford: Routledge.

FATF [Financial Action Task Force] (1990). The 40 recommendations of the FATF. 1st ed., Paris. http://www.fatf-gafi.org/topics/fatfrecommendations/. Accessed 20 July 2013.

FATF [Financial Action Task Force] (2002). IX special recommendations. 1st ed., Paris. http://www.fatf-gafi.org/topics/fatfrecommendations/. Accessed 20 July 2013.

Hardin, R. (2012). The free rider problem. In E. N. Zalta (Ed.), *The stanford encyclopedia of philosophy* (Online encyclopedia, Summer 2012 edition). http://plato.stanford.edu/archives/sum2012/entries/free-rider/. Accessed 20 July 2013.

Haufler, V. (2001). A public role for the private sector: Industry self-regulation in a global economy. *Carnegie endowment for international peace*. http://carnegieendowment.org/2001/08/14/public-role-for-private-sector-%20industry-self-regulation-in-global-economy/apt. Accessed 20 July 2013.

Holzinger, K. (2003). The problem of collective action: A new approach—2003. Max Planck Institute for Research on Collective Goods. http://www.coll.mpg.de/publications/problems-collective-action-new-approach. Accessed 20 July 2013.

Jenkins, R. (2001). Corporate codes of conduct: Self-regulation in a global economy. Technology, Business and Society Programme Paper 2 (2001), UN Research Institute for Social Development. http://www.social-standards.info/inhalte/texte_grundlagen/jenkins_coc.pdf. Accessed 20 July 2013.

Kingston, C. (2005). Social capital and corruption: Theory, and evidence from India—2005. Amherst College. https://www3.amherst.edu/~cgkingston/India.pdf. Accessed 20 July 2013.

Klauser, P. (1994). Selbstregulierung versus staatliche Regulierung. In *Ein schweizerisches Börsengesetz im Europäischen Kontext, Tagungsband*. Basel: Europa Institut an der Universität Basel.

Mostipan, I. (2009). Private sector–led collective fight against corruption in transition countries. Second prize in an essay competition of the World Bank Institute. World Bank Institute.

Murphy, A. G. (2011). *Foreign corrupt practices act, a practical resource for managers and executives*. Hoboken: John Wiley & Sons.

Nielsen, M. (2009). The logic of collective action—2009. Michael Nielsen, website. http://michaelnielsen.org/blog/the-logic-of-collective-action/. Accessed 20 July 2013.

O'Shea, E. (2011). *The Bribery act 2010, a practical guide*. London: Jordans.

OECD (2008). United Kingdom: Phase 2bis—Report on the application of the Convention on Combating Bribery of Foreign Public Officials in International Business Transactions and the 1997 Recommendation on Combating Bribery in International Business Transactions. OECD. http://www.oecd.org/investment/anti-bribery/anti-briberyconvention/41515077.pdf. Accessed 20 July 2013.

OECD (2010). Phase 3 report on implementing the OECD anti-bribery convention in the United States. OECD. http://www.oecd.org/unitedstates/UnitedStatesphase3reportEN.pdf. Accessed 20 July 2013.

OECD (2012). Sweden: Phase 3—Final Report. Report on the implementation and application of the Convention on Combating Bribery of Foreign Public Officials in International Business Transactions and the 2009 Recommendations on Further Combating Bribery. OECD. http://search.oecd.org/officialdocuments/displaydocumentpdf/?cote=DAF/INV/BR%282012%2915/FINAL&docLanguage=En. Accessed 20 July 2013.

Olson, M. (1965). *The logic of collective action*. Harvard: Harvard University Press.

Peters, A., Koechlin, L., Förster, T., & Zinkernagel, G. F. (2009). *Non-state actors as standard setters*. Cambridge: Cambridge University Press.

Pieth, M. (2007). Multi-stakeholder initiatives to combat money laundering and bribery. In B. Christian et al. (Eds.), *Law and legalization in transnational relations* (pp. 81–100). Oxford: Routledge.

Pieth, M. (2011). *Harmonizing anti-corruption compliance, the OECD Good Practice Guidance 2010*. Zurich: Dike.

Pieth, M., & Aiolfi, G. (2003). The private sector becomes active: The Wolfsberg process. In A. Clark & P. Burrell (Eds.), *A practitioner's guide to international money laundering law and regulation*. London: Thomson Reuters.

Pieth, M. et al. (Eds.), (2007). *The OECD convention on bribery, a commentary*. Cambridge: Cambridge University Press.

Reuben, E. (2003). The evolution of theories of collective action—2003. Tinbergen Institute. http://www.ereuben.net/research/MPhilThesis.pdf. Accessed 20 July 2013.

Ruch, A. (2004) Regulierungsfragen der Gentechnologie und des Internet. *Zeitschrift für Schweizerisches Recht, 4*(2), 373.

Sandler, T. (2010). Overcoming global and regional collective action impediments. *Global Policy, 1*(1), 40–50.

Wiehen, M. (1999a). Transparency International. In P. Mark et al. (Eds.), *Korruption im internationalen Geschäftsverkehr:Bestandsaufnahme, Bekämpfung, Prävention*. Neuwied: Luchterhand.

Wiehen, M. (1999b). Auftragsvergabe. In P. Mark et al. (Eds.), *Korruption im internationalen Ges chäftsverkehr:Bestandsaufnahme, Bekämpfung, Prävention*. Neuwied: Luchterhand.

World Bank Institute (2008). Fighting Corruption through collective action, a guide for business. World Bank. http://info.worldbank.org/etools/docs/antic/Whole_guide_Oct.pdf. Accessed 20 July 2013.

Zürn, M. (1998). *Regieren jenseits des nationalen Staates. Globalisierung und De-nationalisierung als Chance, Suhrkamp*. Frankfurt: Suhrkamp Verlag.

Part II
The ABC Model

Chapter 7
The ABC Model: The General Framework for an Anti-Bribery Compliance Program

Stefania Giavazzi, with the support of Francesca Cottone and Michele De Rosa

Contents

This chapter has been drafted by Stefania Giavazzi (CSGP—Università Cattolica del Sacro Cuore, Milan) with the support of Francesca Cottone and Michele De Rosa (Eni legal compliance), under the supervision of Stefano Manacorda (ISPAC—Collège de France).

S. Giavazzi (✉)
Centro Studi "Federico Stella" sulla giustizia penale e la politica criminale (CSGP)
Università Cattolica del Sacro Cuore, Milan, Italy
e-mail: stefania.giavazzi@unicatt.it

F. Cottone
Eni Legal Department, Rome, Italy
e-mail: francesca.cottone@eni.com

M. De Rosa
Eni Legal Department, Rome, Italy
e-mail: michele.derosa@eni.com

S. Manacorda et al. (eds.), *Preventing Corporate Corruption*,
DOI 10.1007/978-3-319-04480-4_7, © Springer International Publishing Switzerland 2014

7.1 The Nature and Value of an Anti-Bribery Compliance Model

7.1.1 The Genesis of the Anti-Bribery Compliance Model

The ABC Model is a tool with which corporations can prevent and combat corruption at an international level.

The aim of this chapter and of the following Chap. 8 is to establish an appropriate set of compliance tools and policies aimed at combating corruption at both national and international level.

The proposal is the result of a wide-ranging international research project on the topic of "Bribery and the Private Sector," initiated in 2012, which involved the participation of prominent academic institutions under the coordination of International Scientific and Professional Advisory Council (ISPAC) (Equipe Internormativités dans l'espace pénal—Collège de France in Paris; Centro studi "Federico Stella" (CSGP)—Università Cattolica del Sacro Cuore, Milan; LUISS Guido Carli University, Rome; School of Criminology and Criminal Justice—Northeastern University in Boston; Instituto de Derecho Europeo Internacional—Universidas of Castilla-la-Mancha) in cooperation with Eni, under the auspices of the United Nations Office for Drugs and Crime.

The core of the proposal expounded here is represented by a unique anti-bribery compliance set of rules (the ABC Model and the ABC Program), to be taken into account when establishing a corporate corruption liability regime which is consistent with the principles set forth in the conventional legal texts, and in particular with the United Nations Convention Against Corruption (UNCAC). The ABC Model should then be acknowledged within domestic *criminal law* systems of regulation as an instrument for assessing the liability of corporations in case of corruption, and should be endorsed at *international level.*

The ABC Model describes the scope and value of the approach and the national and international legal frameworks which the model must abide by.

The ABC Model also represents prerequisite of the proposed ABC Program[1], which contains three sections: (a) key elements, (b) anticorruption compliance rules, and (c) reporting violations, incentives, and the disciplinary system.

This ABC Model and the ABC Program are intended to be a point of reference and a good practice guide for corporations, providing a common standard approach based on existing international guidelines.

[1] See Chap. 8 in Part II of this volume.

7.1.2 The Scope of the Anti-Bribery Compliance Model and the Anti-Bribery Compliance Program

The ABC Program is a part of the ABC Model and provides a system of anti-bribery regulations for corporations operating at an international level.

The main purpose of the ABC Model is to provide a general framework for a system of anti-bribery regulations (the ABC Program) that a company should design and implement in order to prevent corruption and promote ethics and transparency in performing its business activities.

The ABC Program is a *specific part* of the ABC Model. It provides an extensive list of measures which may be included in anticorruption compliance programs adopted by corporations operating in a multinational environment.

The ABC Program[2] provides guidelines to enable corporations to:

- Detect situations and areas of activities where corruption has occurred or may occur, i.e., high-risk conduct
- Manage activities identified as "at risk"
- Train company personnel considered to be at risk
- Implement appropriate precautions when dealing with third parties identified as "at risk"
- Identify and manage red flags
- Adopt appropriate measures to prevent corruption and deal with wrongdoings

7.1.3 The Value of the Anti-Bribery Compliance Model

The ABC Model is addressed both to corporations and states in order to harmonize criminal law systems.

An international instrument which could have the nature of a convention, should be directed towards both urging multinational enterprises and encouraging states in order that they develop internal anticorruption rules.

Indeed, the ABC Model has been conceived to function as a double-edged weapon: Towards economic entities, the model would limit itself to proposing a compliance scheme that corporations will be *free to adopt or not* (under the pressure of incentives); whereas in relation to states, the model aims to *harmonize* the criminal

[2] See Chap. 8 in Part II of this volume.

law systems so as to be considered as a fundamental element in assessing corporate liability.

7.1.4 The Target Entities of the Anti-Bribery Compliance Model

The ABC Model can be adopted by all corporations, adapting it to their size, structure, and level of corruption risk.

The ABC Model has been conceived as a universal and flexible anticorruption instrument that can be adapted to a variety of different organizational structures each time a bribery-related risk is faced. This ABC Model has therefore been designed for all those business organizations, entities, and professional associations operating in a multinational environment which carry out activities in areas considered at risk of corruption. Enterprises, entities, and associations are included in the scope of this ABC Model irrespective of their:

- *Size and dimension:* Even though the controls presented in the model address risks that generally pertain to multinational entities, small and medium enterprises may face some degree of bribery-related risk, and should adopt measures to detect and prevent any risk of misconduct by adapting the ABC Model in accordance to the risk assessment performed.
- *Shareholding structure:* Bribery risk exists in both publicly owned companies and privately held companies, which therefore have equal need for internal controls and the adoption of an ABC program.

7.1.5 The Background to the Anti-Bribery Compliance Model

The ABC Model takes as a reference point the current international anticorruption standards, international best practice, and the compliance programs implemented by a number of corporations operating in the oil and gas sector.

The ABC Model has been drafted on the basis of the results of all the research units which took part in this project. Each applying their own expertise, the research units analyzed all the current research and evidence concerning the ideal content of an ABC model.

The ABC Program reflects contemporary anticorruption standards and international best practices in developing and implementing an adequate and effective anticorruption program.

As regards the legal framework, the proposed ABC Program[3] takes into consideration the current international anticorruption standards that have been defined by national legislation and international guidelines and conventions (see Sect. 2 of this chapter on the general framework of the ABC Model).

Concerning best practice, we have considered in some detail the results of the research on legal frameworks and of an *empirical survey* in the oil and gas sector, which took an in-depth and comprehensive look at the content of the ABC programs which have been implemented by a number of corporations operating in this area. In particular, the survey has identified best practice for compliance in specific at-risk areas and in the "operation" of the compliance program. The benchmark assessment that has been undertaken thus plays a significant role in the identification of the best practices employed to prevent and detect corruption.

The role of best practice in the field of international anticorruption compliance appears particularly significant where there is a lack of international common and mandatory regulation. At the very least, the draft of the ABC Program contains the minimum standard rules. In some instances, the proposed measures represent more than the minimum standard that is generally required to prevent corruption. That is because in some areas, best practice, when put to the test, has revealed its weak points, and the model is thus framed with a view to improving the actual compliance approach.

In other sectors, it is not yet possible to identify best practice or a common approach. In these circumstances, the measures that have been suggested can be considered a template ABC program based on the experience of corporations; in other cases, the proposal is based on case law studies, in the sense that courts have highlighted the importance of adopting policies to regulate certain high-risk activities.

7.1.6 The Main Features of the Anti-Bribery Compliance Program

The ABC Program aims to fulfill the following criteria: adequacy (ability to prevent corruption), specificity (adaptation to the specificities of the corporation), and effectiveness (effective implementation and ongoing monitoring).

The ABC Model requires that an ABC program be implemented following the completion of an appropriate risk assessment. The corruption risk assessment is a necessary first step to developing any anticorruption compliance program, and companies should finish this assessment before determining what policies to include in their ABC program.

[3] See Chap. 8 in Part II of this volume.

The proposed ABC Program[4] aims to fulfill the following criteria:

- *Adequacy:* The adequacy of the ABC Program depends on its ability to prevent corruption. This ability is connected to the decision-making process, to the existence of preventive and detective control mechanisms capable of identifying transactions at risk and conducts relevant to the risk assessment, and to the establishment of appropriate urgent measures to be taken in case such circumstances arise. The adequacy of the ABC Program depends also upon the appropriateness of the tools that have been adopted for identifying "corruption warning signs." For this reason, an ABC program must provide for an appropriate and immediate response to any "red flags" that may arise.
- *Specificity:* The ABC Program has to be adapted to the specificities of each company. It must be tailored to the company's specific business and take into account particular risks that are associated with that business, regulating "high risk" activities which are most likely to involve corruption. Therefore, the ABC Program must be proportionate and constructed based on the type of activities that are carried out, as well as on the company's characteristics, size, and history especially where a company has in the past been subject to allegations of misconduct or corruption. This requires an in-depth understanding of the company's business model, including its products and services, third-party agents, customers, government interactions, and industrial and geographical risk. The context in which a company operates must therefore be taken into consideration in order to identify and elaborate the processes of making and implementing decisions, the managing of financial resources, the duty of disclosure, and the disciplinary system.
- *Effective implementation:* The ABC Program can only be efficiently implemented if it is effectively applied, if its application is regularly monitored, and if a credible mechanism is established to receive, investigate, and determine the authenticity of complaints. The *effective implementation* of the ABC Program also entails its constant adaptation to the characteristics of the company's structure and its business activities; it must be allowed to evolve over time. It must be dynamic, periodically reviewed, and open to amendment whenever violations are discovered and consequent gaps are identified, or whenever changes occur in the company's business or its organizational structure. Therefore, all events that change the company's risk index must be evaluated in order to successfully adapt the ABC Program through updating.

  Finally, in order to build an adequate, specific, and efficiently implemented ABC program, it is recommended that it also be implemented in the local language so that employees in foreign subsidiaries can access and understand it.

[4] See Chap. 8 in Part II of this volume.

7.1.7 The Structure of the Anti-Bribery Compliance Program

The scheme for the ABC Program is structured as follows:

a. *How the ABC Program Operates:* zero-tolerance approach to corruption, risk assessment, design, approval and implementation of the ABC Program in the company and in its subsidiaries, training of the personnel at risk, monitoring and updating of the ABC Program
b. *Compliance Rules:* appropriate measures for managing risk-related activities and processes, and guidance on how to recognize and deal with the main risks of bribery and corruption
c. *Procedures to Detect and Manage Violations to the ABC Program and the Disciplinary System:* reporting violations or suspected violations, incentives for employees' active participation, disciplinary sanctions, and remedial activities.

7.2 General Framework of the Anti-Bribery Compliance Model

7.2.1 Legal References

7.2.1.1 National Laws

The role and legal value of the compliance programs may vary according to different legislations. Even inside a given country, the compliance program may be built differently depending on several factors, including case-law experiences. The ABC Program takes into consideration the current legal framework as defined by national legislation, as well as the case-law experience in some countries, selected on the basis of the different role played by the compliance program in the model of imputation. The countries involved in the study belong both to the common law tradition (UK, USA, Australia, and Canada), to the civil law tradition (Italy, France, and Switzerland), and to other traditions (China).[5]

7.2.1.2 International Conventions

The international regulatory framework consists in a significant number of conventions specifically dedicated to the fight against corruption.

Such conventions do not refer directly to compliance programs: They outline the general framework of the types of conduct that have to be opposed with "effective, proportionate, and dissuasive" sanctions against individuals and corporations,

[5] For more details see the chapters in Part V of this volume.

whereas the model of imputation of responsibility to corporations is left to the discretion of the member states.

However, for corporations that operate at the international level, the international conventions represent a constant point of reference for individuating types of illicit conduct, thus providing as the basis for the standard of compliance as well as for the use of common concepts and definitions in the negotiations of contracts, procedures, or other legal instruments.[6]

The ABC Model takes into account the following list of international conventions on corruption.

America *Organización de los Estados Americanos (OEA): Inter-American Convention Against Corruption (29 March 1996)* The convention covers corruption in the public sector, both in demand and supply. It gives a wide and inclusive interpretation of what constitutes "corruption offences" including bribery (domestic and foreign), illicit enrichment, and money laundering and concealment of property. It includes preventive measures (creating and enforcing codes of conduct for public officials), criminalization and regional assistance cooperation measures, as well as provisions on recovery of assets. Obligations towards the convention are a combination of mandatory and discretionary provisions.

Europe

European Union (EU) *1997 EU Convention on the Fight Against Corruption Involving Officials of the European Communities or Officials of Member States of the EU:* The EU convention targets corruption involving a public official. Its main aim is to secure that EU members' criminal provisions against corruption also cover bribery involving public officials from other EU countries or public officials of the European Communities. The convention also prescribes that, for bribery committed by private companies, those companies' management shall be criminally liable for acts of corruption committed by persons under their supervision. It requires the liability of legal persons.

2003 Framework Decision on Combating Corruption in the Private Sector: The framework decision covers corruption committed entirely within the private sector, that is, between two commercial entities. Its aim is to establish a common definition of corruption in the private sector and the penalties applicable.

Council of Europe *Council of Europe Criminal Law Convention:* The convention covers the public sector and private sector (private-to-private) corruption and also a broad range of offences including bribery (domestic and foreign), trading in influence, and money laundering and accounting offences. A provision is dedicated to corporate liability.

Council of Europe Civil Convention: The first attempt to define common international rules in the field of civil law and corruption, it provides for compensation for damages as a result of acts of corruption.

[6] For more details see the chapters in Part IV of this volume.

Africa *South African Development Protocol against Corruption (SADC):* Adopted in 2001 by all 14 SADC members, the protocol provides both preventive and enforcement mechanisms. Preventive measures include the development of a code of conduct for public officials, transparency, and establishment of anticorruption agencies. In line with the Organisation for Economic Co-operation and Development (OECD) Convention, the protocol criminalizes the bribing of public foreign officials. It also addresses the issue of money laundering by allowing for seizure of the proceeds of the crime. The protocol also sets out an implementation mechanism.

African Union Convention on Preventing and Combating Corruption: Adopted in 2003, the convention has been ratified by 53 African countries. It covers the public and the private sector. Offences covered are bribery (domestic or foreign), diversion of property by public officials, trading in influence, illicit enrichment, money laundering, and concealment of property. All provisions are mandatory including those on private-to-private corruption. The convention provides for prevention, criminalization, regional cooperation, and mutual legal assistance as well as the recovery of assets.

OECD *OECD Convention on Combating Bribery of Foreign Public Officials in International Business Transactions:* After entering into force in 1999, the OECD convention has been implemented in 40 countries, including five non-OECD members (Argentina, Brazil, Bulgaria, Russian Federation, and South Africa). The convention focuses exclusively on the supply side of the bribery of public foreign officials. It requires the liability of legal persons.

UN *UNCAC:* The UNCAC was adopted in Merida in 2003 and came into force in 2005. As of July 2013, UNCAC has 140 signatories and 167 parties. UNCAC includes preventive measures, including model preventive policies that are directed at both the public and private sectors. It covers a wide range of offences including bribery, domestic and foreign; embezzlement; trading in influence; and concealment and laundering of the proceeds of corruption. It provides for a provision on the liability of legal persons. Asset recovery has been stated explicitly as a fundamental principle of the convention. The convention combines mandatory and discretionary provisions.

7.2.2 International Guidelines and the Emerging Role of Anti-Bribery Compliance Programs

Anticorruption compliance goes far beyond the current law of any specific country and is not limited to the provision of legally binding international conventions.

Anticorruption compliance is defined by a broader body of international recommendations, guidelines, and principles that aim, along with the legal regime, at defining the common worldwide standard in an environment where the line between public and private actions is blurred. The guidelines attached to certain domestic statutes that are also particularly relevant at an international level for their extraterritorial jurisdiction (such as the Foreign Corrupt Practices Act, FCPA and the Bribery Act, BA) play an important role in the definition of the compliance standard for corporations.

Analyzing this body of rules, it is certainly possible to make a distinction between initiatives taken by the public sector (international organizations or national states) for the private sector such as the Good Practice Guidance on Internal Controls, Ethics and Compliance, adopted 18 February 2010 in implementation of the recommendation by the OECD Council for Further Combating Bribery of Foreign Public Officials, and initiatives born from the private sector for the private sector itself, such as the Partnering Against Corruption Initiative (PACI), a global platform developed by the private sector for the promotion of anticorruption compliance programs.

In particular, the chronological order of those initiatives shows, on one side, the growing (self-)involvement of the private sector in the area of anticorruption policies and programs and, on the other, a tendency towards the generalization of the private initiatives of specific or sector-based fora into the global forum, and from traditional initiatives to innovative proposals.

In all their forms, however, the international guidelines increasingly take into account the important role of compliance programs in the prevention of corruption, describing and detailing the requirements that such programs need to have to be in line with international best practices.

It is for all these reasons that the ABC Model also takes into account the following international guidelines.

OECD Guidelines for Multinational Enterprises: The OECD Guidelines for Multinational Enterprises, updated in 2011 for the fifth time since they were adopted in 1976, are recommendations addressed by governments to multinational enterprises operating in or from adhering countries. They provide voluntary principles and standards for responsible business conduct in areas such as employment and industrial relations, human rights, environment, information disclosure, combating bribery, consumer interests, science and technology, competition, and taxation.

OECD Recommendation for Further Combating Bribery: Released by the OECD on 9 December 2009, the Recommendation for Further Combating Bribery includes the Good Practice Guidance on Internal Controls, Ethics, and Compliance.

ICC Rules for Combating Corruption: The 2011 edition of the ICC Rules for Combating Corruption consists of three parts: Part I states the rules proper; Part II deals with policies which enterprises should enact to support compliance with the rules; and Part III lists the suggested elements of an effective corporate compliance program.

ICC Handbook: Fighting Corruption Divided into three parts, the 2008 edition of Fighting Corruption details the international legal framework necessary for self-regulation and management initiatives, including whistle-blowing and compliance by small- to medium-sized enterprises.

ICC Guidelines on Agents, Intermediaries and Other Third Parties: These ICC guidelines of November 2010 provide companies with advice on how to choose and manage third parties and address the desirable features of a due diligence process.

ICC Guidelines on Whistleblowing: The purpose of the ICC Guidelines on Whistleblowing, adopted in June 2008, is to help companies establish and implement internal whistle-blowing programs by setting forth practical indications that can serve as a useful point of reference, while meeting, as far as possible, the objections formulated in certain countries about some aspects of a whistle-blowing system.

ICC Anti-corruption Clause: The ICC Anti-corruption Clause issued in October 2012 is for companies to include in their agreements, whereby they undertake to comply with the ICC Rules on Combating Corruption or commit to put in place and maintain an anticorruption compliance program.

Transparency International Business Principles for Countering Bribery Partnering Against Corruption Initiative: The Transparency International Business Principles for Countering Bribery provide a framework for companies to develop comprehensive anti-bribery programs. It reflects recent developments in anti-bribery practice worldwide and incorporates approaches by business, academia, and civil society. Since its initial publication in 2003, the Business Principles have been used by many leading companies around the world to benchmark their own anti-bribery policies and procedures and have also served as a solid basis for the development of other anti-bribery codes and voluntary initiatives. The principles are, at present, under revision through public consultation among the participants of PACI.

The World Bank Institute (WBI) *2008 Guide for Business on Collective Action:* The WBI 2008 Guide on Fighting Corruption through Collective Action explains collective action, its benefits, and how to use it. It defines "collective action" as a collaborative and sustained process of cooperation among stakeholders that increases the impact and credibility of individual action, brings vulnerable individual players into an alliance of like-minded organizations and levels the playing field between competitors. Collective action is conceived as a mechanism that can complement or temporarily substitute for and strengthen weak local laws and anticorruption practices.

The Tenth Principle of the UN Global Compact: The UN Global Compact is a strategic policy initiative for businesses that are committed to aligning their operations and strategies with ten universally accepted principles in the areas of human rights, labor, environment, and anticorruption. The adoption of the tenth principle commits UN Global Compact participants not only to avoid bribery, extortion, and other forms of corruption, but also to develop policies and concrete programs to address corruption. The UNCAC is the underlying legal instrument for the tenth principle against corruption.

The PACI—Principles on Countering Bribery: PACI is a multinational task force of companies working with the World Economic Forum, Transparency International, and the Basel Institute of Governance, which promote the fight against corruption.

The PACI Principles provide a framework for good business practices and risk-management strategies for countering bribery, through the commitment of a zero-tolerance policy and the adoption of an effective internal compliance program. In particular, the principles give concrete indications regarding the procedures that an effective compliance program requires and on the implementation, review, and communication of the program.

7.2.3 Corporate Ethical Business Principles and Ethical Values

The ABC Program is part of the corporation's environment of integrity, which is led by its code of ethics.

Given the close and important relationship between compliance and ethics, it is recommended that the anticorruption compliance program is created and implemented in tandem with the goal of establishing and advancing an overall environment of *ethical behavior* and *integrity*.

The ABC Program should then be inspired by the principles described in the company's code of ethics, and compliance with the anticorruption rules should have a prominent place in the company's code of ethics and in overall corporate compliance issues.

The benefits of undertaking such an approach include defining desirable organizational values, promoting achievement, preventing undesired conduct, preserving the organization's reputation, avoiding the risk of blacklisting, building employee and organizational sensitivity, identifying and resolving ethical dilemmas and scenarios, and infusing ethics into business practice, specifically in the role of top management and leadership, strategy, decision making, and organizational processes.

Accordingly, ethical factors that may be considered ancillary principles to anticorruption measures include at least the following:

- Reinforcing an approach of *fair competition* and free enterprise while preserving the organization's profit-making and economic goals
- Establishing a culture of professionalism, equality, safety, and protection of privacy in conducting business operations
- Promoting a culture of honesty, integrity, transparency, and respect throughout the organization
- Contributing to sustainable development and protection of the environment, human rights, and communities where business is conducted, optimizing positive impacts and minimizing negative impacts
- Encouraging responsibility to shareholders and stakeholders, including customers, employees, suppliers, partners, contractors, creditors, governments, and society
- Encouraging open discussion of ethics and values with a corresponding reward system

Though it is an important part of an anticorruption compliance program, a code of ethics setting out general principles of conduct is not sufficient, and nor can it be used in place of a compliance program. Companies whose anticorruption compliance program is reduced to a simple code of ethics are considered to have a weak ABC program or none at all.

7.2.4 *Type of Offences*

For the purpose of the present ABC Model, the term *corruption* has the meaning set forth below.

The Company Prohibits: to any officer, director, employee, agent, stockholder thereof acting on behalf of the company, or to any other person who performs services for or on behalf of the company

The offering, Promising, Giving, Paying/ Accepting any request Directly or through a third party	Of any financial advantage Or other advantage of any kind	To/from any	Public official Political party Official thereof or candidate for political office Official of a public international organization

with the intention of:

- influencing any act or decision of such official, whether or not in his official capacity;
- inducing such official to do or omit to do any act in violation of the lawful duty of such official;
- securing any improper advantage in the conduct of business;
- inducing such official to use his influence with a foreign government, a public international organization, or instrumentalities thereof to affect or influence any act or decision of such government, organization, or instrumentality;
- rewarding such official with an undue advantage for any act or decision he has already taken in relation with his public position.

The company also prohibits the *complicity in,* including incitement, aiding and abetting, or authorization of an act of bribery as described above, or any attempt to execute such act of bribery.

The company also prohibits offering, promising, giving, paying (or authorizing anyone to offer, promise, give, or pay), directly or through a third party, of a financial advantage or other advantage of any kind to any person in order that he/she abuse his/her real or supposed *influence* with a public official, a political party, or an official of a public international organization, with a view to obtaining an undue advantage for the original instigator of the act or for any other person.

The company also prohibits any act of *private commercial bribery*. For the purpose of this model, it is forbidden:

To any officer, director, employee, agent, stockholder thereof acting on behalf of the company, or to any other person who performs services for or on behalf of the company	(a)	The promise, offering, or giving, directly or indirectly, of an undue advantage to any person who directs or works, in any capacity, for a private sector entity, for the person himself or herself or for another person, in order that he or she, in breach of his or her duties, act or refrain from acting
	(b)	The solicitation or acceptance, directly or indirectly, of an undue advantage by any person who directs or works, in any capacity, for a private sector entity, for the person himself or herself or for another person, in order that he or she, in breach of his or her duties, act or refrain from acting

Chapter 8
The ABC Program: An Anti-Bribery Compliance Program Recommended to Corporations Operating in a Multinational Environment

Stefania Giavazzi, with the support of Francesca Cottone and Michele De Rosa

Contents

This chapter has been drafted by Stefania Giavazzi (CSGP—Università Cattolica del Sacro Cuore, Milan) with the support of Francesca Cottone and Michele De Rosa (Eni legal compliance), under the supervision of Stefano Manacorda (ISPAC—Collège de France)

S. Giavazzi (✉)
Facoltà di Giurisprudenza
Centro Studi "Federico Stella" sulla giustizia penale e la politica criminale (CSGP)
Università Cattolica del Sacro Cuore, Milan, Italy
e-mail: stefania.giavazzi@unicatt.it

F. Cottone
Eni Legal Department, Rome, Italy
e-mail: francesca.cottone@eni.com

M. De Rosa
Eni Legal Department, Rome, Italy
e-mail: michele.derosa@eni.com

S. Manacorda et al. (eds.), *Preventing Corporate Corruption*,
DOI 10.1007/978-3-319-04480-4_8, © Springer International Publishing Switzerland 2014

8.1 Section A: Key Elements of the Anti-Bribery Compliance Program

8.1.1 Introduction: Zero-Tolerance Approach

- The ABC Program is based on the "zero-tolerance" approach and has implications for the "Tone at the Top": The company's top management must be personally committed in the fight against corruption.

8.1.1.1 Zero Tolerance

In developing and implementing an Anti-Bribery Compliance (ABC) Program which is able to effectively combat the risk of corruption, the company has to actively promote its adoption of a *zero-tolerance* approach to bribery and corruption.

This means that the company shall prohibit all company personnel and all persons acting on their behalf or in their interests (without exception), all illegitimate favors, collusion, and requests, both direct and/or through third parties, for the purpose of any benefit for themselves or for others. This also requires the company to denounce all forms of corruption, public and private, with no exceptions.

8.1.1.2 Tone at the Top

In observance of the principle of *zero tolerance,* the top management of the company, regardless of the size of the organization, has to personally commit itself in the fight against corruption (the so-called *Tone at the Top*) through:

- Increasing awareness of possible corrupt activities.
- Strong, explicit, and visible support in the fight against corruption.

The Tone at the Top requires that the top management within the company establish a culture of anticorruption compliance, not only by the implementation and adoption of the ABC Program by the board of directors, but also through a diffusion process, to all staff and commercial partners, of clear, unambiguous, and regularly repeated messages (e.g., in annual reports, employee newsletters, at annual meetings, management conferences, retreats, and employee gatherings).

Top-level commitment should be explicit in a *statement* prefacing the ABC Program, signed by the company's CEO or president. Such a declaration should clearly define and communicate the company's zero tolerance of bribery and underline the following issues:

- The company management's commitment to do business in an ethical manner.
- The prohibition of giving or receiving bribes in any form both to public officials and private parties.
- The requirement of mandatory compliance with the ABC Program for all company personnel and all other interested parties.
- The statement that no questionable or illegal practice can ever be justified or tolerated because it is "customary" in the business or countries where the company operates.
- The statement that no performance goal should be imposed or accepted if it can be achieved only by compromising ethical standards.
- The statement that no company personnel will be subject to sanctions or to any other adverse consequence for refusing to carry out behavior prohibited by the ABC Program, even if such refusal leads to a loss of business.

Public reporting on anticorruption commitments also increases the credibility of an anticorruption message.

8.1.2 Design and Adoption of the ABC Program

- An adequate ABC Program requires a preliminary corruption risk assessment.
- The corruption risk assessment is a tool to identify which of the company's activities pose risks of corruption.
- Once the ABC Program has been designed on the basis of the results of the risk assessment, it must be approved by the board of directors (or by the corresponding structure) both within the company and in its subsidiaries.

In order to strengthen the implementation of the "zero-tolerance" principle and in order to constitute a system of rules and controls for the prevention of crimes of corruption, the company must adopt and implement an adequate and effective ABC Program.

In addition to the Tone at the Top, essential steps and requirements of an ABC Program are the following:

- Conducting a corruption risk assessment.
- Adopting and implementing an ABC Program based on risk and on due diligence activities of third parties.
- Conducting an anticorruption compliance communication and training.
- Monitoring the implementation of the ABC Program.
- Periodically reassessing risk and continuous updating.
- Ensuring transparency and implementing accounting policies.
- Establishing an Anticorruption Unit (ACU; see Sect. 8.1.6).

In the following subsections, these essential steps and requirements will be described.

8.1.2.1 The Risk-Assessment Process

The risk-assessment process includes risk prevention, which, through identification, assessment, management, and monitoring of the major risks, contributes to support informed decision making. Effective corruption risk assessment means understanding the company, and the environments in which it operates, in both the public and private sector. Effective corruption risk assessment should not be an isolated event, but it depends on companies' risk profiles and resources.

In order to develop a strong ABC Program, the company must provide a *comprehensive assessment of potential bribery and corruption-specific risks,* both existing and emerging.

The goals of this corruption *risk assessment* are to:

- *Identify areas of business and activities that are at risk* of corruption due to the company's size, the nature of the company's operations, the degree of the business relationship with governmental entities, the use of agents and intermediaries

and potential business partners, the countries where it does business, the regulatory environment, and any other relevant factors.
- *Evaluate and analyze the risks identified and prioritize all relevant risks of corruption* which would have the greatest impact on company business and are most likely to occur, and thus require devoting greater attention and resources.
- Carry out *a gap analysis of the current internal standard of procedures, systems, and controls:* identify what policies and controls the company has in place to mitigate the corruption risks and analyze the adequacy of such policies and controls.
- Undertake a *root cause analysis* of internal and external causes in relation to past incidents and near misses (if known).

The *risk-assessment process* should consider external and internal risk factors. External risks may include:

- Company's *business sector risk:* Some sectors are riskier than others, as based on the data from reliable surveys (e.g., the Index of Bribery in the Business Sector conducted by Transparency International within the framework of the Bribe Payers Index survey).
- Company's customers.
- Company's *business partners:* use of consultants, intermediaries, or business partnerships when doing business, and use of other third parties acting on the company's behalf.
- Transaction risks.
- Potential direct *contact with foreign officials* (customs agents, business licensing officials, government employees, and local political officials).
- Company's *geographic location:* In particular, prior to starting up activities in new countries, there should be a general requirement that an assessment should be carried out to show to what extent the business, political, and social environment in the country is characterized by unethical or corrupt practices. Reference should be made to reputable information sources and indicators, such as Transparency International's Corruption Perception Index, as well as mapping the existence of potential weaknesses and exposure to corruption.

Internal risk factors may include:

- Deficiencies in employee awareness and/or employee training.
- Lack of clear policies or procedures related to activities at risk, such as hospitality and promotional expenditures, due diligence, and mergers or acquisitions.
- Lack of a well-communicated anticorruption policy specifically addressed to company personnel and third-party agents.
- Lack of a clear anticorruption message from the top management.
- Ineffective or nonexistent procedures in place to monitor employees, third-party agents, and distributors for compliance, anti-bribery laws, or the company's code of conduct.
- Lack of clear *financial controls.*
- Prior enforcement failures or prior criminal records related to corruption.
- A bonus culture that rewards excessive risk taking.

The company must provide *documentary evidence* of the risk assessment, maintaining accurate documentation on its process and conclusions, and must update the risk assessment on a periodic basis to reflect the risks and risk appetite of the company's organization; for example, when an incident is uncovered, the impact of that incident on the risk-assessment framework should be taken into consideration, and similarly when the company begins to do business in a new country.

8.1.2.2 Approval and Adoption of the Anti-Bribery Compliance Program

Once the ABC Program has been organized on the basis of the results of the risk assessment, it must be approved and reviewed by a board of directors' resolution both in the company and in the subsidiaries (i.e., any entity that is controlled by the company), or by the corresponding body/structure/role when the governance of the subsidiary does not include such a board.

The board of directors also nominates the ACU (see Sect. 8.1.6).

The adoption and enforcement of the ABC Program is mandatory for the company and for all its subsidiaries on a worldwide basis.

All associated internal regulations, policies, and procedures must be considered integral parts of the ABC Program.

8.1.2.3 Implementation of the Anti-Bribery Compliance Program

- The ABC Program must be extended to all the company's subsidiaries.
- The ABC Program must be compliant with the local anticorruption laws where they impose stricter or different requirements.
- The ABC Program should be extended to entities in which the company has a noncontrolling interest, on the basis of a best-efforts approach.

Local Adaptation

The case law in this area clearly demonstrates that parent companies may be held responsible for the wrongdoings of their subsidiaries. For this reason, it is advisable that the ABC Program be adopted across the group worldwide. This adoption may be undertaken in two different ways: Firstly, the company may decide to extend its own ABC Program to all the subsidiaries regardless of the geographical areas (a "precautionary approach"); alternatively, the company may decide to adapt the ABC Program to better fit structural and operational differences.

In either case, the ABC Program must be in compliance with the applicable local anti-bribery and corruption laws, which may impose *stricter or different requirements* (such as requesting the use of local contractors). In this case, the company or its subsidiaries may implement stricter or different provisions to reflect the requirements of the applicable local laws.

Implementation Modalities in Subsidiaries (at Group Level)

As mentioned above, the ABC Program should require each subsidiary to adopt the ABC Program by the board of directors (or the corresponding body) within a time period established by the company.

The subsidiaries may be allowed to adopt and implement additional internal regulations and/or associated procedures, if needed, to address specific risks or applicable local laws.

In defining and implementing their own regulations and associated procedures, the subsidiaries may consult with the ACU (see Sect. 8.1.6).

All subsidiaries must report the date of approval of their anti-bribery regulations and their implementation plan to the company. Every significant delay in the implementation of the ABC Program must be communicated to the ACU, explaining the reasons for the delay.

The company and its subsidiaries must take care to observe all local employment and privacy procedural prerequisites before rolling out the ABC Program and the associated regulations and procedures.

Implementation Modalities in Entities in Which the Company Has a Noncontrolling Interest

It is recommended that the company use its influence to cause *entities in which it has a noncontrolling* interest to meet the standards set out in its ABC Program, by adopting and maintaining an adequate internal control system which is consistent with the requirements established by anticorruption laws.

In any case, the representatives appointed by the company in such entities shall use their best efforts to cause the standards set out in this ABC Program to be adopted.

Relevant circumstances include the degree of company's ownership or controlling stake in the entity.

Associated Activities in Implementing the Anti-Bribery Compliance Program

The company board and senior management is responsible for implementing and maintaining the anticorruption principles and rules throughout the corporation, and for reviewing these principles and rules and keeping them up to date.

In order to maintain control over the implementation process, a detailed *implementation timetable* shall be drafted to consider, as a minimum, the following issues:

- The rollout of policies and procedures.
- Training activities.
- Monitoring system.

Appropriate procedures may be adopted to outline frameworks, for example: (1) *risk assessment processes,* to ensure that the ABC Program keeps up with changes in the organization and new areas at risk; (2) *internal self-review and reporting,* to monitor the risks and the adequacy of anticorruption rules; and (3) *procedures to manage incidents.*

The ACU (see Sect. 8.1.6) has the role of guaranteeing *active oversight* of the implementation phase of the ABC Program.

Company personnel, each in their area of competence, are responsible for:

- Reading and complying with the ABC Program.
- Taking responsibility for the prevention, detection, and reporting of bribery and corruption.

Company personnel, each in their area of competence, are responsible for embedding ABC Program policies and rules into business activities and the existing operating procedures (editing them with specific reference to the ABC Program). Therefore, preexisting policies and procedures should then be revisited in light of the risk-assessment process. For this purpose, it may be appropriate for business units to analyze the type and level of risks that their activities face, with coordination and cooperation between compliance, audit, and legal functions.

The company should encourage synergy between the ABC Program and other internal operating rules and procedures.

8.1.3 Communication and Training

- The content and value of the ABC Program must be known and understood by all its recipients; to this end, the ABC Program must be clear, easily understandable, and always accessible.
- Training on the ABC Program is mandatory for all at-risk personnel and the company's and its subsidiaries' directors.
- Training must be tailored to the type of recipient.
- The company may consider training sessions for high-risk third parties, as appropriate to the nature of the relationship and the corruption risks involved.

8.1.3.1 Communication and Accessibility

The company should develop effective *communication planning* to make the ABC Program known to all recipients.

The company must also ensure that all recipients have received and read the ABC Program, using the most appropriate procedures and in conformity with local standards and customs.

In the phase of first implementation, a copy of the ABC Program can be distributed to all employees, officers, and directors (e.g., in welcome packs or with pay slips). Subsequently, all personnel shall receive a copy of the ABC Program within a reasonable period of time after being hired or given new responsibilities. The ABC

Program, as amended from time to time, is intended, where possible, to be enforceable as part of each employee's employment contract.

A certification or an equivalent document that each employee has read and understood the ABC Program should be a mandatory requirement.

Management and senior staff at all levels are responsible for ensuring that those reporting to them are made aware of and understand the content and importance of the ABC Program.

The company must also ensure that all recipients have understood the content of the ABC Program. The ABC Program must be clear and easily understandable (including to non-jurists) and, when necessary, it may need to be translated into the languages of the countries where the company has significant operations.

The ABC Program must also provide guidance to employees on how to seek help in case of doubts on its interpretation or importance. It may be useful to put in place an informal consultation process or mechanism that all recipients of the ABC Program can readily avail themselves of, should they wish to seek clarification and advice in particular situations.

The ABC Program must be always accessible for consultation by all directors, officers, and other employees at all times. To facilitate this, the ABC Program may be posted on the company intranet site.

The ABC Program may also be freely downloaded from the company's website and advertised to the company's customers.

Policies and procedures related to the ABC Program should be internally communicated on an ongoing basis.

8.1.3.2 Training

The company must establish organizational consensus and awareness.

All recipients of the ABC Program must clearly understand and be aware of the different types of offences, the risks related to them, corporate responsibilities, the actions to be taken in order to prevent bribery, and the potential sanctions and other adverse consequences (both for the corporate and individual) in case of violation of the ABC Program and anti-bribery laws.

Training on the ABC Program and anti-bribery laws is *mandatory* for all at-risk personnel, company, and subsidiaries' directors, and it must be periodically *updated*.

At-risk personnel must be preliminarily identified by the company in the light of their roles and involvement in at-risk activities or as regards internal control issues.

Consideration should be given to training third parties. All third parties should reach a basic level of awareness by being provided with information on anticorruption laws and on the company's ABC Program through printed courses and/or web-based training programs. For *high-risk third parties* (see Sect. "General Provisions"), the company may consider running training sessions, as appropriate to the nature of the third party and the work they undertake for, or on behalf of, the company.

In defining and implementing the anticorruption training program, the Human Resources Department (or another authorized corporate unit or department) should consult with the ACU (see Sect. 8.1.6) for appropriate support and guidance in terms of the contents of the training materials and the carrying out of the training.

The contents and extent of training should be defined according to the following criteria:

- The role of the person in the company organization in terms of authority and powers.
- The role of the person in terms of relationship with public officials and other third parties, such as vendors and clients.
- Regard to the areas within which a subject/individual operates and the tasks they undertake on behalf of the company.
- The subject/individual's reporting obligations arising from the implementation of the ABC Program.

The training program should cover at least the following:

- National and international anticorruption laws.
- Sanctions, other adverse consequences (such as fines, debarment, imprisonment, impact on share price) and reputational issues.
- All the contents of the ABC Program, its nature, and importance.
- Associated policies and procedures.
- Approval requirements and record keeping.
- Internal control and monitoring practices.
- Reporting obligations and their timing.
- Instructions to recognize the importance of red flags and avoid ethically questionable actions.
- Responsibilities for adherence to anticorruption policies and procedures.

Training can be provided in a variety of ways. *Basic training* is normally appropriate only for employees who have minimal authority or minimal interaction with corruption risks. *In-depth and customized training programs* must be conducted for all employees who may be especially exposed to corruption in their work, such as employees in procurement and contract functions, senior advisers, and staff functions (legal, audit, finance), employees seconded into a joint venture or "mixed" company, and all employees located in geographic areas where the risk of corruption is high.

For senior management, country general managers, compliance officers, sales, legal, financial, accounting, and audit personnel, *periodic live anticorruption training* is suggested as one of the most appropriate training options.

Workshops run by legal experts to train middle managers in identifying the risks associated with their decisions and for senior managers who interface with government are also suggested as a best practice.

It is also recommended that employees be offered examples of problematic situations and appropriate guidance on how to deal with criticalities (such as payments to and by sales representatives and other agents; gifts, entertainment, and travel allowances; political contributions and facilitation payments) through case studies or frequently asked questions. It is recommended that practical guidance be provided on how to deal with recognized areas of risk, or that there be systematic intranet sharing of best practices.

At-risk personnel shall be responsible for keeping their training up to date; each manager is responsible for ensuring that all at-risk personnel under his or her supervision complete and update training periodically.

It is recommended that the company provides for an *assessment of the effectiveness* of the training. The minimum requirement for a meaningful training assessment includes a scoring test during or at the end of the training session to ensure that the employee has learned the required concepts. The results of such testing also provide important feedback regarding the content of the training materials and where the training needs to be clarified, enhanced, or improved.

The company must keep records of anticorruption training attendance and the names and titles of participants, the results of the self-testing, copies of training materials, and the dates of the training, in compliance with the applicable labor, privacy, or other laws. The company should also ensure the constant updating of training, especially in the case of significant changes to the organization or regulatory framework, or in case a new risk arises.

8.1.4 Monitoring—Enhancements—Follow-up

8.1.4.1 Monitoring: Roles and Responsibilities

- The ABC Program must be constantly monitored.
- To this end, it is necessary to establish: (1) a reporting system to monitor and oversee risks, to allow directors to intervene and prevent wrongdoings, and to notify them of cases of fraudulent or criminal conduct and (2) an ongoing plan of regular audits to check the effective implementation of the program.

The ACU (see Sect. 8.1.6) is responsible for monitoring the ABC Program and must periodically review it to ensure that it remains maximally effective. In general, the ACU must discharge the critical ongoing monitoring and surveillance function of the ABC Program.

Managers of business units are responsible for supervising their staff and for taking steps to prevent, detect, and report potential violations.

All recipients are responsible, in their respective areas of competence, for doing business in compliance with the ABC Program.

The board of directors has the overall and final responsibility for the functioning of the ABC Program and for ensuring that the ABC Program complies with legal and ethical obligations.

8.1.4.2 Reporting Duties

The company should ensure that reporting mechanisms are put in place to ensure that the top management, the board of directors, and eventually the control bodies are informed of all important and relevant information that will allow them, within their roles, to take appropriate and proportionate actions and decisions.

The ABC Program needs to be monitored through a *periodic reporting system* that is able to:

- Create a clear reporting mechanism to monitor and oversee risks.
- Create a mechanism to check compliance with the ABC Program.
- Allow directors to intervene and prevent wrongdoings.
- Notify cases of fraudulent or criminal conduct (see Sect. 8.3.1.1).

The ABC Program must ensure that the reporting mechanism exists *even in the absence of red flags*.

The ABC Program should clearly set out the duty on all recipients to convey all information concerning compliance with the rules imposed by the ABC Program itself to the ACU. In particular, the company should establish a *reporting system* requiring that the ACU is regularly informed by the business units in relation to, at least, the following key indicators:

- Aspects or events of corporate activities that could expose the company to the risk of corruption.
- Particularly high-risk third-party relationships within the scope of high-risk transactions.
- Any extraordinary company transactions.
- Need for modification to policies or procedures associated with the ABC Program.
- All behaviors that are not in line with the principles of conduct foreseen by the ABC Program.
- Sanctions issued to the company by the authorities supervising public procurement.
- Critical issues that emerge over the course of the relationship with public officials or public service employees.
- Proceedings and/or notifications from judicial police departments, or any other authority, indicating investigations that are underway for corruption, also regarding unknown persons.
- Rulings regarding the application of disbursements and utilization of government grants.
- Requests for legal assistance submitted by managers and/or employees regarding proceedings by judicial authorities relative to corruption.
- Information relative to any disciplinary proceedings that have been executed and the eventual sanctions imposed pursuant to the ABC Program (including provisions toward employees).
- Organizational modifications.

- Any direct or indirect request by a public official or private parties for payment (including a facilitation payment), gifts, travel, meals or entertainment, employment, investment opportunities, personal discounts, or other personal benefits.
- Specific reports requested by the compliance rules of the ABC Program (gifts, hospitality, sponsorship, donations, acquisition, and disposals).
- Training programs.
- Critical factors in implementing the ABC Program in subsidiaries.

The ACU must be appropriately notified by employees, corporate bodies, service companies, consultants, and business partners *regarding events that could generate responsibilities for the company*. For requirements related to notifying criminal conduct or violations to the ABC Program, see Sect. 8.3.1.1.

Internal regulations associated with the ABC Program can more specifically address:

- The company functions, department, or office in charge of mandatory information flows.
- The recipients of mandatory information flows.
- The format of the report and the information it should contain.

8.1.4.3 Regular Audits

An *internal control system* needs to be designed to ensure compliance with ethics and the policies prescribed by the ABC Program. Therefore, anticorruption controls should be included within the audit plan.

In all circumstances, a *direct information flow* to the ACU must be guaranteed.

It is important for the company to appoint experienced internal auditors who understand, are trained in, and regularly focus on anticorruption issues. It could be also useful to appoint *regional compliance officers or auditors*.

Reviews and other audit activities should refer to *global anticorruption compliance,* the internal regulations and procedures that are ancillary to this, the *legal framework,* and the *control system* designed to ensure that process-related activities are performed and controlled in accordance with the objectives set by management.

Usually, these controls should include:

- Assigning powers and tasks at different levels, in keeping with the required degrees of responsibility, with special emphasis on key tasks and their assignment to qualified people.
- Assuring the principle of segregation of duties.
- The reporting process.
- Performing follow-up of previous internal audit examinations.
- Reviewing documentation of the decision-making processes at senior level concerning operations or transactions at risk of corruption.
- Controls to help ensure that books and records are properly kept and that any irregularities which may indicate that bribes are being paid are identified.

- Reviewing transaction files and financial records concerning operations or transactions at risk of corruption.
- Reviewing operations, also using attorneys or regular outside auditors.
- Reviewing large operations in high-risk countries, as well as tracking and analyzing money flows.
- Reviewing (also through random interviews with supervisory and field personnel) the adequacy of policies and procedures in relation to areas where there are significant risks of corruption.
- Reviewing agreements with, payments to, and expenses related to third parties covered by the ABC Program (see Sect. 8.2.3.3).
- Routine compliance and/or internal audit checks of higher-risk third-party payments to ensure there is appropriate supporting documentation and adequate justification to pay.
- Checking bank account reconciliations.

Full cooperation with auditors is required of all company employees and third parties covered by the ABC Program.

Periodic *risk assessments* or spot audits in a limited number of foreign countries or activities at risk may also be conducted to identify issues and present suggestions that regular audits may miss.

A program of external compliance audits of company subsidiaries across the world could allow the company to assess implementation of its ABC Program by its subsidiaries and identify potential areas of improvement.

It may be also useful for the company to monitor public disclosures by competitors which could entail an industry-wide investigation, or identify gaps or improvements in areas at risk.

Anticorruption policies and procedures may need to be adapted in light of any gaps highlighted.

Internal audit and independent auditors should then recommend enhancements to the ABC Program on the basis of emerging best practices. If gaps or weaknesses are identified, regular and adequate feedback should be given to management on the basis of the internal control results.

Executives are expected to follow up audit findings (even on the basis of proposals from the ACU) by correcting errors and weaknesses in the control system identified by the auditors.

8.1.5 Update and Review of the Anti-Bribery Compliance Program

- When reports and audits identify potential weaknesses, the ABC Program must be reviewed and updated in order to fill the gaps.
- An updating of the ABC Program shall also be considered in the event of changes in the company's organization or to the legal framework.

Regular assessment of the ABC Program is essential to ensure it remains up to date and as effective as possible. The ABC Program should regularly be reviewed, re-valuated, and updated to reflect any:

- Modifications in the legal framework as well as in international best practice
- Changes in the company's asset organization or in the company's activities at risk
- Need to improve the internal control system
- Violations that have demonstrated the ineffectiveness of the ABC Program

The ABC Program should provide that the ACU is the unit in charge of making proposals for modifications to the ABC Program to the board of directors, where the latter has the responsibility for approving the ABC Program as well as any further modifications.

Compliance monitoring activities and internal audit reviews should determine not only whether the anticorruption procedures have been followed, but also whether they are effective. Controls aimed at identifying potential weaknesses in the ABC Program should therefore be developed and documented.

As regards potential vulnerability, controls might include periodic testing and validation, review of available metrics, and design of self-assessment forms and exercises performed as part of the corruption and bribery risk assessment.

Reassessment of the global *corruption risks* is suggested every 3–5 years in order to make sure that the ABC Program is in line with the modifications as listed above. If the business changes significantly or any other relevant changes occur, it may be prudent to make a reassessment at that stage in order to identify and deal with any new corruption risk. Larger organizations and those engaging in high-risk activities should consider external verification or performance evaluation led by independent counsel, who may confirm whether the steps taken in terms of compliance are appropriate and thorough. Some useful indicators of performance may include:

- The number of policies and procedures promulgated or revised, in connection with the activities and processes identified as at risk.
- The number of third parties that have passed or failed the request to adopt anti-corruption regulations.
- The effectiveness of the "Tone at the Top," such as the number of "town hall" meetings on compliance issues.
- The tracking of implementation of audit recommendations.
- Statistics on employee disciplinary sanctions.
- The number of red flags reported.
- Employee questions related to compliance.
- The number of training meetings conducted.

8.1.6 The Anti-Corruption Unit (ACU)

- In order to ensure efficient implementation of the ABC Program, the company should establish a dedicated internal unit (in this model called the ACU).
- The ACU must be independent and autonomous with respect to any external and internal influences; its role should be clearly focused on anticorruption issues.

In order to ensure an efficient implementation of the ABC Program, it is recommended that a special internal unit be established with specialized expertise and exclusive competence with respect to anticorruption matters. The board of directors should be the body which establishes such a unit. For the purposes of this model, this unit will be referred to as the ACU.

To ensure that the ACU works in an effective manner, a number of crucial aspects have to be established, including the procedural framework to ensure independence, reporting arrangements, and resourcing.

The ACU should report directly to the board of directors or to the CEO whenever necessary.

Basic Requirements for the ACU

Independence and Autonomy In order that it properly exercises its activities, the ACU must be guarded against inappropriate external as well as internal influences and must carry out its activity in the absence of conflicts of interest. Consequently, it is recommended that the appointment in the ACU of company personnel who have previously worked in offices exposed to corruption risk be carefully evaluated. The company must supply the ACU with adequate financial resources, commensurate to the company's size and risk profile.

Expertise and Qualification The members of the ACU must be properly trained and qualified in this matter and competent to carry out the functions assigned to them.

Adequate Number of Resources The amount of resources devoted to compliance will depend on the company's size, complexity, industry, geographical areas of operation, and the risks associated with the business; these resources have to be sufficient and proportionate to ensure that the company's ABC Program is implemented effectively.

ACU Powers and Duties

The ACU must receive full cooperation from all company functions in order to be provided with all the information, data, and company documents which are relevant and required for performing its duties.

In general, it is the duty of the ACU to provide expert assistance in the field of anticorruption in relation to operational activities managed by the company and its subsidiaries.

Notwithstanding the above, the powers and duties of the ACU can be grouped into the following areas: (1) implementation, monitoring, and updating; (2) dissemination and training; (3) support to the business units; (4) investigation; and (5) reporting.

Implementation, Monitoring, and Updating

- Implementing the ABC Program and adequate monitoring of its adoption and implementation by the company and its subsidiaries.
- Overseeing the effectiveness and adequacy of the ABC Program in terms of its effective capability for preventing corruption.
- Liaising with corporate operative functions in order to enhance the monitoring of activities relative to the procedures established by the ABC Program.
- Monitoring the need for updating the ABC Program, in the light of any change in the company organization or the legislative framework.
- Verifying the company's compliance with the methods and procedures required by the ABC Program, revealing any eventual behavioral gaps that might emerge from the analyses of the periodic information flows.
- Receiving recommendations relating to proposed enhancements of the ABC Program from the business units, the internal audit, and independent auditors, on the basis of emerging best practices or if gaps or weaknesses are identified.
- Submitting proposals to the corporate bodies with regard to the possible need for *updating* the existing ABC Program through appropriate amendments and/or integrations, as a consequence of significant violations to the requirements of the ABC Program, important changes to the structure or business activities of the company, and/or as a result of legislative changes.
- Being entitled to participate in ethics and ABC Program network meetings to ensure continuous improvements in the ABC Program through comparison with international best practice.

Dissemination and Training

- Ensuring the effective dissemination and communication of knowledge about anticorruption laws applicable to the company and its personnel, and of the ABC Program.
- Supporting the Human Resources Department to create and to provide anticorruption training programs to all at-risk employees.
- Overseeing the training programs.
- Supporting the company in order to define the content of periodic communications aimed at providing the company's personnel with the necessary sensibility and knowledge of the ABC Program's requirements.

Support to the Business Units

- Being involved in the due diligence process when an anticorruption perspective is required and providing an evaluation of potential counterparts in key risk areas (joint-venture partner, agent, intermediary, sponsorship, etc.) on the basis of the outcome of the due diligence carried out by the business units.
- Evaluating any deviation, in a given set of circumstances, from the terms set out in the ABC Program.

- Supporting the company's representatives in applying the relevant internal anti-corruption rules.
- Proposing/supplementing/amending the relevant anticorruption contractual clauses.
- Interpreting the relevant legislation (with the assistance of or in collaboration with the company legal office/department) and verifying the adequacy of the ABC Program regarding such provisions of law.
- Supplying on-demand interpretation of anticorruption laws and relevant policies.

Reporting The ACU must submit a periodic report on its monitoring activity to the board of directors or to the chief executive officer. The ACU shall also receive periodic reports prepared by the ACUs or similar units of the subsidiaries and periodic reporting flows from business units (see Sect. 8.1.4.2).

Investigating The ACU plays an important role in the conducting of internal investigations into possible violations of anticorruption laws and of the ABC Program. These investigations may arise from information gathered through its monitoring and surveillance role, or may be referred from business units or other areas, or result from whistle-blowing reports, litigation, or otherwise, complying with its role to manage reported violations (see Sect. 8.3.1.3).
When criminal conduct has been alleged or detected, the ACU shall take reasonable steps to prevent further similar conduct, including proposing any necessary modifications to the ABC Program.

For the purpose of investigation, the ACU may avail itself of the company's internal audit function and compliance officers or of external auditors.

Liaison with the organization's internal audit system and compliance officers is likely to be of great help to the ACU with the exercise of all its duties.

8.2 Section B: Anticorruption Compliance Rules

8.2.1 Applicability

- The ABC Program applies to all the company's employees and to all members of corporate bodies.
- Specific requirements should be adopted to make at-risk third parties compliant with the company's ABC Program.

The ABC Program applies to all employees at all levels and grades, including senior managers, officers, directors (whether permanent, fixed term, or temporary), trainees, and casual staff, *wherever located.*

The ABC Program applies to all members of corporate bodies (board of directors, members of the statutory auditors, etc.).

The company should require that the third parties identified as at risk must comply with the principles of the ABC Program. Alternatively, the third parties at risk may be required to declare to have in place, and maintain throughout the terms of the contract, their *own anticorruption regulations* to ensure compliance with the anticorruption laws (in such cases a proper preliminary assessment by the company of the counterpart's compliance program should be conducted). In both cases, the appropriate company's protection clauses should be included in all contracts signed with at-risk third parties (see Sect. "General Provisions"). Third parties at risk include the following:

- Consultants
- Agents
- Distributors
- Dealers and franchisees
- Brokers
- Lobbyists
- Intermediaries
- Supply-chain members
- Joint-venture partners

8.2.2 *Basic Requirements*

As part of its ABC Program the company has to: (1) ensure transparent decision-making processes and segregation of duties; (2) make impartial decisions and avoid potential conflicts of interest; (3) keep accurate and up-to-date accounting records; (4) implement appropriate internal administrative and financial controls.

8.2.2.1 Company Organizational Structure and Decision-Making Process

As part of an ABC Program, the company has to set out a virtuous organizational structure and transparent decision-making processes. In order to implement these aspects, a number of preliminary activities must be put in place.

The company must be equipped with organizational instruments (such as organization charts, organizational communications, policies and procedures, etc.) based, at least, upon the following general principles:

- Awareness within the company about roles, powers, and responsibilities.
- Clear and formal definition of roles, functions, and representative powers.
- Clear description of the lines of reporting (an easily identifiable organizational chart)
- Traceability of decision-making processes.

- Adequacy of the level of authorization and delegation of powers and tasks.
- Monitoring of the services to be performed by third parties on behalf of the company.

Appropriate procedures need also to be adopted to regulate the decision-making process. The following basic principles may be suggested as guidance:

- *Segregation of duties:* There must be segregation of duties between executing parties, controlling parties, and authorizing parties; in a specific process, individual phases should be identified and governed in a consistent way within management, with a consequent limitation of enforcement discretion, ensuring the traceability of the decision process.
- Identification of *key functions* in any single process.
- Identification of *individuals* who shall be vested with the power to bind the company.
- *Record keeping* of the whole decision-making process.

Specific requirements should also be implemented in case of transfer of powers and functions, i.e., in case of:

- *Delegation of authority*—the internal act of conferring functions and duties, reflected in the system of organizational communications.
- *Power of attorney*—the unilateral legal document by which the company assigns power of representation to third parties.

8.2.2.2 Conflicts of Interest

Conflict of interest occurs when a situation or activity can interfere with the company's ability to make impartial decisions in its best interests and in full accordance with its principles, or in general with its ability to fully comply with its functions and responsibilities.

Any situation that may constitute or give rise to a conflict of interest shall be immediately reported to one's superior within management, or to the body one belongs to. Furthermore, the party concerned shall abstain from taking part in the operational/decision-making process, and the relevant superior within management, or the relevant body, shall:

- Identify the operational solutions suitable for ensuring, in the specific case, transparency and fairness of behavior in the performance of activities.
- Transmit to the parties concerned—and for information to one's superior—the necessary written instructions.
- File the received and transmitted documentation.

The ABC Program should explicitly forbid employees and representatives from:

- *Using* their office, confidential information, assets, or other resources for personal gain or for the advantage of others with whom they are related or associated.

- Having a financial interest in a supplier competitor or customer involved in the company's decisions relating to, or of relevance, to them.
- Delegating relations with government agencies to consultants or third parties that may create conflicts of interest.

To avoid possible conflicts of interest as identified above, it is suggested that former public officials shall not be hired or engaged in any capacity before a reasonable period has elapsed after their leaving office, if their contemplated activity or employment relates to the functions held or supervised during their tenure.

Appropriate procedures need to be in place for action when a conflict of interest (a conflict between competing interests which may impair the ability to make objective unbiased business decisions) is likely to occur or has already been detected. For example, the company could include clauses in the agreement by which the counterparts state that no conflict is in place, and that the company reserves the right to terminate the contract in the event that it becomes aware of any conflicts of interest (associated with a full indemnification right).

8.2.2.3 Accounting Policies

The ABC Program should require the company to keep accurate and updated accounting records of each business transaction, reflecting completely and transparently the facts of each of them, and the nature, amount, and frequency of accounting operations, in reasonable detail.

All financial information must have adequate supporting documents issued in line with the applicable legislation and the internal control system.

All book entries and related informative documentation have to be at disposal of the external auditor for the audit activities. Internal *financial controls* should be developed, documented, maintained, and continually enhanced to help make sure that all payments are accurately *recorded* in the company's books and records in accordance with applicable regulatory requirements.

8.2.2.4 Record Keeping

The principle according to which all payments and transactions of the company must be recorded accurately in the relevant company's books and records applies to all transactions and expenses, whether or not they are material in an accounting sense.

The company shall establish and maintain adequate internal accounting controls sufficient to provide reasonable assurances that:

- Transactions are executed in accordance with management's general or specific authorization.
- Transactions are recorded to allow the preparation of financial statements in compliance with the generally accepted accounting principles and to maintain accountability for all corporate assets.

The system of internal controls is intended to provide reasonable assurance of the reduction to a low (remote) level of risk that misstatements, caused by errors or fraud in amounts that would be material in relation to the annual financial statements or interim reports, may occur and not be detected on a timely basis.

The system of internal controls related to financial information consists of specific controls and pervasive controls.

Specific controls are performed during the normal course of operations to prevent, identify, and correct errors and frauds. Typically, these controls include: checks of accounting records documentation, issuance of authorizations, reconciliation between internal and external information, and consistency checks.

Pervasive controls ensure that process activities are performed and controlled in accordance with the objectives set by management. The principal types of pervasive controls include the assignment of powers and tasks at different levels, and the identification and segregation of incompatible activities/duties. This type of control involves the separation between the individuals that perform tasks, those who control them, and those who authorize them.

Special attention should be paid to those areas that may directly affect anticorruption provisions, such as procurements, agents, consultants, intermediaries, and other third-party business payees, the offering and receiving of corporate gifts, entertainment, hospitality, travel, and promotional expenses. In particular, the company should establish and maintain *registers* of certain matters related to the main activities at risk as proposed in Sect. B of this model.

The original documentation related to the approvals released and the controls carried out must be kept by the company for a reasonable period of time and in accordance with the requirements of the applicable legislation.

All book records must be made available to the internal audit every time a control is required.

8.2.2.5 Payment Mechanisms

As part of its ABC Program, the company must implement internal administrative and financial controls that reduce the risk of improper payments (check issuance, wire transfers, petty cash controls).

As a general rule, the company should require that payments are allowed only on the basis of a contractual relationship and the remuneration to be paid shall be exclusively proportionate to the services to be rendered and described in the contract.

In particular, payments shall not be allowed:

- In cash.
- To a numbered account.
- To an account held in the name of a person other than the counterparty.
- To a third country other than one of the parties or where the contract has to be performed.

All *fees* paid to third parties must represent appropriate, justifiable, and proportionate remuneration and be commercially reasonable under the circumstances. Payments must be subject to the control that the service has been rendered and/or that the conditions foreseen in the agreement concerning the payment of fees have been met. Particular attention must be paid to situations where a significant change in payment or other material terms of an agreement occurs.

The purpose and traceability of the expenses must be guaranteed. The early payment of the fee (that is, before the complete execution of the contract terms) may be allowed only in specific cases (properly motivated and stated in the contract) and, in any event, only for a part of the entire amount.

Unusually high and/or undocumented commissions, fees, or expenses should be carefully reviewed to determine if such payments are justified on commercial grounds.

One or more of the following actions may help to guard the company against risks:

- Requiring documentation or justification before paying unusual or excessive expenses.
- Terminating or suspending the execution of the agreement or payment where there is a suspicion that it has involved or will involve illicit or questionable payments or gifts (see Sect. 8.2.3.3).

Possible corrupt payments made to most vendors and consultants may be detected through standard forms of due diligence and forensic auditing. The internal audit procedure must include the objective of learning the identities of all beneficiary owners and actual control persons of shell companies, holding companies, trusts, charities, and other sources or destinations of funds.

8.2.3 Corruption At-Risk Activities

8.2.3.1 Facilitation Payments

- Facilitation payments are small amounts of money paid to government officials in order to facilitate routine government actions.
- Although there is no uniform approach in legislation, it is strongly advised to forbid facilitation payments.
- Only payments made under duress to protect personal safety may be considered a justifiable exception.

Facilitation payments are a form of payment involving a small amount of money given to a government official with the purpose of expediting, facilitating, or securing the performance of routine governmental action or necessary action by the public official for providing services to which one is legally entitled without any payment (e.g., processing a visa, customs invoice, or other government paperwork), and not to obtain or retain business or any other undue advantage. They are sometimes referred to as "speed" or "grease" payments. They are typically demanded by low-level officials.

Examples of "routine government action" include:

- Obtaining licenses, permits, or other official documents.
- Processing government paperwork, such as visas to cross borders or work orders.
- Obtaining permits to transport goods across borders/clear goods through customs.
- Providing police protection or other security.
- Providing mail pick-up and delivery services.
- Scheduling inspections associated with contract performance.
- Scheduling inspections related to the transit of goods.
- Providing telephone services.
- Providing access to power and water supply.
- Loading and unloading cargo.

For reasons based on comparative analyses of the different legislation in this respect, it is strongly advised to forbid facilitation payments, whether directly or through third parties and even if they are nominal in amount and/or common in a particular country.

By adopting this approach, the company accepts that their refusal to make such payments now considered illicit in most legislation—may lead to commercial delays, for example in the processing of government paperwork, and that there may be a commercial cost to the company attributable to this policy.

However, it must be recognized that demands for facilitation payments are often backed by a form of extortion, and that in exceptional circumstances resistance may not be feasible. As employee safety is a primary concern, payments made as a result of extortion or under duress to protect "life, limb, or liberty" or personal safety may be considered a justifiable exception. In such circumstances, the company, as part of its ABC Program, may accept that employees will need to use their best judgment, as long as they report it and provide absolute transparency as to the circumstances surrounding the payment shortly after the incident has occurred. All personnel must report to their line manager and the ACU at the earliest opportunity regarding any incident where they felt forced to make a facilitation payment.

The payment must be accurately and transparently recorded in the financial records.

8.2.3.2 Gifts, Hospitality, and Promotional Expenses

- Gifts, hospitality, and promotional expenses are permitted only if made strictly according to the ABC Program's requirements and guidance.
- Gifts, hospitality, and promotional expenses made or received must be always properly recorded.
- Company personnel who are offered gifts, hospitality, and promotional expenses not in accordance with the ABC Program's requirements shall reject them and inform the direct supervisor and/or the ACU

Gifts, hospitality, and promotional expenses are considered to be normal marketing activities and, when made correctly, are parts of acceptable business behavior. However, these may be, or may appear to be, bribes if they are provided with the intent of (or may be judged by an independent third party as provided with the intent of) obtaining an improper commercial or other advantage or exercising an improper influence.

Therefore, the provision or receipt of gifts, hospitality, and promotional expenses should be permitted only in keeping with the requirements of the company's ABC Program.

The company should determine as part of its ABC Program whether the gift, hospitality, or promotional expense envisaged is appropriate or whether it is unreasonable, improper, or even illegal. Special rules shall apply where public officials are involved.

The term "gifts" includes all gifts of products, services, cash or cash equivalents (such as checks, travelers checks, gift cards, gift certificates, vouchers, loans, and shares), and all business courtesies, gratuities, discounts, favors, and other things of value for which the recipient does not pay the fair value.

The term "hospitality" includes all meals, drinks, entertainment, recreation (such as tickets or invitations to sporting or cultural events), travel, accommodation (such as hotel stays), and other forms of hospitality which are of value and for which the recipient does not pay the fair value.

The term "promotional expenses" includes any other expenditure, such as travel and accommodation expenses that relate to the promotion, demonstration, or explanation of products or services.

Any gift, hospitality, or promotional expenses for a family member or designee of a public official or of a private party that was proposed at the request of a public official or as a result of the recipient's relationship with a public official must be treated as a benefit to that public official or private party and is therefore subject to the restrictions provided by the ABC Program.

Prohibitions

Gifts, hospitality, or promotional expenses should *never be acceptable,* irrespective of value, if:

- They are in breach of any applicable laws or regulations, including local laws.
- They are given or received to gain an improper advantage, or motivated by a desire to exert improper influence or by the expectation of reciprocity.
- They are in cash or an equivalent.
- They are not tasteful and commensurate with generally accepted standards for professional courtesy.
- They are not reasonable in terms of type, value, and frequency of provision with reference to the context (including local cultural sensitivities).
- They are not given in bona fide (that is, they are given with an intention other than to build or maintain legitimate business relations or offer normal courtesy).

Therefore:

(i) The intention behind the provision and timing of gifts, hospitality, or promotional expenses should always be considered.
(ii) It is always forbidden to provide gifts or promotional expenses to public officials for the purpose of influencing them in the performance of their official functions with the intention of obtaining or retaining business or an advantage in the conduct of business, or to "facilitate" or expedite a routine procedure for the company, for personnel, or for family, friends, associates or acquaintances, or any other person. This is irrespective of whether the public official actually performs the function illegally, unethically, in bad faith, not impartially, or in breach of a position of trust.
(iii) Company personnel must never seek to avoid any requirement set out in the ABC Program regarding any gift, hospitality, or other promotional expense by paying for it personally.
(iv) Company personnel must not actively solicit, request, or demand any form of gift, hospitality, or promotional expense from any person or organization.

Guidance on Gifts, Hospitality, and Promotional Expenses
The giving or receipt of gifts and hospitality *is permitted,* if the following requirements are met:

- They are in the context of a commercial courtesy.
- They are made in connection with a business purpose.
- They cannot be construed by an impartial observer as aimed at obtaining undue advantages or influencing a decision.
- They are given openly, not secretly.
- They are of a reasonable amount/value.

Promotional expenses, in particular, may be considered *reasonable* and *in bona fide* when they are directly related to:

- The promotion, demonstration, or explanation of products or services.
- The execution or performance of a contract with a government or government agency.
- Attendance at educational seminars or workshops.
- Developing or maintaining cordial business relationships.

Promotional expenses must be recorded with sufficient detail and be supported by appropriate documentation.

The company may pay for meals, entertainment, and/or travel only for those invitees whose participation is directly related to, and necessary for, the company's legitimate business purposes. The company should not provide money for invitees to make their own meal, entertainment, or travel arrangements. If travel is required for a third party to participate in a business event, no side trips unrelated to the business event should be provided. The company should also set out:

- A value level above which a gift or any financial advantage or other benefit offered to, or received by, the company personnel must be reported to the direct supervisor of the personnel in question.
- A value level for offers of gifts above which the personnel must seek prior approval from a senior official before accepting.

Best practice suggests that the offer or receipt of anything of value to or from any public official needs *prior approval* in writing by the direct supervisor, depending on the value. When providing approval, the aggregate value of gifts, hospitality, and promotional expenses provided to a public official over recent months will be considered. This "value level" may be set by the company taking into consideration the characteristics of the relevant country (average cost of living, economic factors, etc.).

Gifts and other benefits made or received must be always *recorded* accurately and transparently in a register established within the company which provides sufficient information and documentation, including, at least: each recipient's name and title, the name and title of each beneficiary, description of the benefit, currency value (actual or estimated), acceptance and refusal and relevant reasons.

Registers of gifts and hospitality should record hospitality and gifts both offered and accepted. Guidance should also be given about how registers are maintained within the company and how personnel should make entries in the record.

Company personnel who *receive offers* of gifts, hospitality, financial advantages, or other benefits that cannot be considered a low-value commercial courtesy shall reject them and immediately inform the direct supervisor and/or the ACU.

In specific cases, any deviation from the terms set out in this subsection must be subject to a preliminary evaluation by the ACU on the basis of a written and detailed note submitted by the relevant business unit.

In order to ensure that the provisions relating to gifts or other similar benefits are appropriate, applicable, and in full compliance with applicable local anti-bribery and corruption laws which may impose stricter requirements, it may be necessary for them to be supplemented for certain countries or territories.

8.2.3.3 Third Parties

General Provisions

- A third party who acts in the interest or on behalf of the company or who is likely to have relevant contact with a public official in his/her work is considered at risk.
- In order to prevent corruption risks in this area, the ABC Program requires: preengagement due diligence on third parties at risk; contractual protection clauses; post-engagement monitoring; controls on payments.

All relationships with third parties must be established with maximum correctness and transparency, with respect for the law, the code of conduct, the company's ABC Program, and internal procedures.

The company should first *identify* the different types of third parties which the company does business with, categorize them as high- or low-risk relationships, and analyze risks posed by any category, in order to determine which category warrants enhanced action to mitigate corruption risks. In general, where the third party is a person who acts in the interest or on behalf of the company or is likely to have relevant contact with a public official in the course of his/her work (i.e., joint-venture partners, intermediaries, consultants, distributors, dealers, agents, franchisees, etc.), the third party may be considered at "high risk."

It is suggested that company maintain a *database* of all of the categories listed as being at risk.

The company should require that the third parties identified as "at risk" must comply with the principles of the ABC Program. Alternatively, the third parties at risk may be required to declare to have in place, and maintain throughout the duration of the contract, their *own anticorruption regulations* to ensure compliance with anticorruption laws (in such cases a proper preliminary assessment from the company regarding the counterpart's compliance program should be conducted). The third party shall meet at least the standards set out below.

To avoid or mitigate corruption risks posed by the relationship with *third parties identified at risk,* the ABC Program should include the following rules:

- Due diligence and approval procedures.
- Contracting clauses with anti-bribery representations and warranties and other vendor requirements such as certifications and anticorruption training.
- Post-engagement monitoring.
- Review and approval of special payments.

Due Diligence and Approval

- Preengagement due diligence shall be conducted using a risk-based approach.
- Red flags resulting from the due diligence process shall be properly assessed and, where required, actions to mitigate the relevant risks shall be recommended by the ACU.

The ABC Program should require that the company establish a due diligence agenda when it engages with third parties.

In particular, the ABC Program must require *preengagement due diligence* to be performed before the execution of the agreement, as well as contractual protection and *post-engagement monitoring* activities to be performed during the life of an agreement with all third parties who (1) perform services for or on behalf of the company, or (2) are likely to have relevant contact with a public official in the course of their work.

The *preengagement due diligence* should be based on the third party's risk profile, so as to help identify potential conflicts of interest and other adverse relationships that could put the company at risk of corruption.

The due diligence must be performed according to Appendix 1. The nature and extent of the due diligence depends on the third parties' risk profile, i.e., comprehensive data about a third party's chain of ownership and activities must be collected when engaging with a high-risk partner.

Local laws protecting *privacy* must also be taken into consideration in carrying out the research. During the due diligence process, circumstances that lead to concerns that corruption may take place (red flags) may arise. Examples of red flags are provided in Appendix 2.

The ACU may consider, upon the detailed written request of the interested company business unit, to perform a reduced due diligence when certain circumstances exist, such as a longstanding working relationship with the partner, recognized standing, demonstrated reliability, or the excellent ethical reputation of the relevant third party.

The results of the due diligence, including the evidence of any red flags, should be included in a *due diligence report* which shall be submitted to the ACU, which will evaluate the results of due diligence and—if necessary—suggest any possible solutions. The ACU shall also assess what, if any, further due diligence should be undertaken.

The due diligence report should be prepared in order to document all the findings, specifying areas of uncertainty, noting any red flags, and drawing conclusions with respect to potential risks for the company. Once all the information has been gathered and if the company decides to proceed with the business relationship, a robust *approval process* for hiring the third party should then be set out. Decisions to decline a potential business partner relationship should be adequately recorded, such that they can support/establish that the company takes its ABC Program seriously.

The Agreement and the Relevant Anticorruption Clauses

- The contract regulating the relationship with at-risk third parties shall include such provisions as are necessary to protect the company from corruption risks associated with the counterparty's improper conduct.

All third parties at risk must enter into written agreements before doing any work for or on behalf of the company and may be paid only in accordance with the terms and conditions provided in the agreement. In particular, the agreements should at least include the following compliance provisions.

Representations and Warranties

- The obligation to act in full compliance with all applicable anticorruption laws and other relevant laws as well as with anticorruption clauses.
- The commitment of the third party to comply with the company's ABC Program or to put in place and maintain throughout the term of the relationship its own anti-bribery compliance regulations.
- The declaration from the third party that neither it, nor its owners/directors/employees or their family members are public officials (or disclosure of any such condition to be properly assessed by the company).
- The commitment to inform promptly if, after the execution of the agreement, it or its owners, directors, or employees or their family members are appointed as public officials (such information to be properly assessed by the company).
- The requirement of proper record keeping, as well as provisions addressing the implementation of internal accounting controls.
- The obligation to report promptly to the company any request or demand for any undue financial or other advantage of any kind received by the third party in connection with the performance of the contract.
- In case of subcontracting: (1) Obtain the company's prior approval before appointing any subcontractor and (2) ensure that any subcontractor performing services in connection with the contract does so only on the basis of a written contract which imposes on and secures from such party terms equivalent to those imposed on the third party.

Audit Rights The company's right to perform compliance audits, including in the event that the company has a reasonable belief that the counterparty may have violated the anticorruption laws or any anticorruption contractual obligations.

Termination Rights It is suggested that the agreements provide the company with the right to terminate or suspend the execution of the agreement or payment and to receive compensation for damages as a result of any breach of the obligations, representations, and warranties referred to above and/or violation of anticorruption laws.

Monitoring the Third Party's Activities

- Adequate monitoring during the performance phase of the contract is recommended; in case of red flags, the ACU must be immediately informed.

Post-engagement monitoring should be conducted during the life of the relationship. These activities should at least consist in:

- Adequately and continuously monitoring the services provided by the third party to verify the correct execution of the contract.

- Monitoring that the third party always acts in compliance with anticorruption laws, the anticorruption regulation that applies to the contract, and the provisions of the contract.
- Identifying any possible red flags in the activities carried out by the third party.
- Immediately notifying the company's ACU of any discrepancy, gap, or suspected violation.

For *higher-risk relationships,* the monitoring might include site visits, forensic financial statement reviews, and investigative procedures.

Payments to Third Parties and Record Keeping Billing (or methods of payment) and the payments mechanism shall comply with the requirements described in Sects. 8.2.2.4 and 8.2.2.5.

Intermediaries and Consultants

- Intermediaries and consultants shall be considered as "high risk" third parties.
- The ABC Program provides specific requirements in terms of selection, internal approvals, and contractual protection clauses.

In addition to the general provisions set out in Sect. "General Provisions", specific measures may be implemented for intermediaries and consultants.

Taking into consideration the high-risk level in hiring intermediaries and consultants the company should set out a robust *approval process* for such initiatives.

Intermediaries and consultants must be *selected* according to a specific internal procedure, providing for an appropriate level of due diligence, which should establish or ensure the following minimum checks:

- Outstanding reputation for honesty, correct business practices, and high ethical standing.
- When the intermediary or consultant is a company, the fact that it has been recently incorporated represents a red flag.
- Whether the intermediary or consultant has any links to public officials directly or indirectly involved with the activities carried out by the company and/or with the activities to be carried out by the intermediary or consultant.
- Whether the intermediary or consultant has been subject to any allegations, investigations, and/or convictions relating to bribery or corruption, or to other criminal activities.
- The ability of the intermediary or consultant to provide services that meet high standards not only in terms of quality, innovation, and cost, but also in terms of ethical conduct, with particular emphasis on respect for transparency and correctness in business affairs.

The company should be particularly cautious when intermediaries or consultants are suggested to them by government officials, especially when the government official is in a position to affect the company's business or when it has been convicted or involved in judicial investigations for corruption in the past.

As general best practice, negotiation of the relevant contract should only commence once the due diligence process has been completed.

Agreements with intermediaries and consultants must be negotiated, entered into, and managed in compliance with the general provisions described in Sect. "General Provisions". Best practice suggests that contracts should *also* contain:

- A description of the service to be provided by the intermediary or the consultant.
- A requirement that the intermediary or the consultant shall at all times comply with the anticorruption laws and shall have and maintain in place throughout the duration of the intermediary agreement its own regulations to ensure compliance.
- A requirement to promptly report to the company any request or demand for any undue financial or other advantage of any kind received in connection with the performance of the intermediary or the consultant agreement.
- A requirement that the intermediary or the consultant shall ensure that any person associated with the intermediary or the consultant and who is performing services in connection with the intermediary or the consultant agreement does so only on the basis of a written contract which imposes on and secures from such persons terms equivalent to those imposed on the intermediary or the consultant.
- The amount of the compensation, which must be proportional to the subject matter of the agreement, to the experience of the intermediary or the consultant, and to the country where the services will be carried out.
- The intermediary or the consultant's representation and covenant that the compensation payable pursuant to the intermediary or the consultant agreement shall be used solely as payment for its professional services and that no part thereof shall be given to a public official or private party or to any of his/her family members, for corrupt purposes, or to the counterparty with which the company wishes to conclude the deal, nor in violation of applicable laws.
- A prohibition of the intermediary or the consultant transferring, either directly or indirectly, its compensation to directors, officers, members of corporate bodies, company employees, or any of their family members.
- The billing terms (or method for payment) and payment terms, taking into account that: (1) payment shall not be made to a party other than the intermediary or the consultant or to a country other than the country of one of the parties or where the agreement shall be implemented; (2) payment shall be subject to the conclusion of the contract to which the intermediary's service refers, or, for the consultants, the early payment of the fee may be allowed before the complete execution of the contract terms only in specific cases (properly motivated and stated in the contract), and in any event only for a part of the entire amount; (3) payment shall be made directly and exclusively into the registered account of the intermediary or the consultant and never to numbered accounts or in cash.

- The intermediary or the consultant's commitment to notify the company of any changes that have occurred in its ownership and/or in respect of the representations provided to the company during the selection phase.
- The company's right to carry out an audit of the intermediary or the consultant and to terminate the agreement in case of a change of control of the intermediary or the consultant
- A clause providing for the non-transferability of the agreement.
- The company's right to terminate the agreement and to interrupt the payment and to receive compensation for damages in case of breach of the obligations, representations, and warranties referred to above and/or violation of the anticorruption laws or the internal regulations regarding the intermediary or consultant agreement.
- The intermediary or consultant's representation and covenant that, at the time of signing of the agreement and for as long as the agreement is in effect, neither he/she nor his/her family members, nor, where the intermediary or the consultant is a company, its owners, directors, employees, nor the company itself, are public officials.

8.2.3.4 Joint Ventures

- The company may be liable for the conduct of the joint-venture partner or the partners thereof.
- Where the company has control of the joint venture, the company's representative should ensure the joint-venture partner adopts its own ABC Program.
- Where the company is not in control of the joint venture, the company's representative must use his best efforts to cause the joint-venture partner to adopt the ABC Program.
- The company's representative has the duty to constantly monitor the joint venture's at-risk activities.

In addition to the general provisions for managing the relationship with third parties described in Sect. "General Provisions", specific measures may be implemented for joint-venture partners.

Although there is a wide variance in how joint ventures can be structured, certain joint-venture partners may be considered high-risk third parties by the scope of the ABC Program.

When the company has a *majority interest* and the control of the joint venture, it should ensure the joint venture complies with its ABC Program.

When the company is not the *controlling partner,* it must take steps to cause joint ventures to adopt an ABC program for the prevention of corruption, or at least to implement an adequate internal control system which is consistent with the requirements established by anticorruption laws.

Specific *internal regulations* should be set out by the company to govern joint-venture agreements. Best practice suggests that internal regulations on joint ventures must be compliant with the following minimum standards:

- The joint-venture partners shall only be entities who are well known.
- The joint-venture partners shall be reliable and have outstanding reputations for honesty and correct business practices.
- A documented and appropriate level of due diligence review should be carried out on each joint-venture partner and on the contractual arrangements for the operations of the joint venture.

In negotiating the *joint-venture agreement,* especially those involving national companies, the company shall also make its best efforts to include in such agreements the following provisions:

- The commitment by the joint venture's operator to adopt and the commitment by each partner to cause the joint venture to adopt an effective and appropriate internal control system and a compliance program for the prevention of corruption.
- The commitment by the joint venture's operator to act and the commitment by each partner to cause the joint venture to act in compliance with the anticorruption laws, the internal control system and the compliance program.
- Clauses requiring proper record keeping, as well as provisions addressing the implementation of internal accounting controls.
- The right to audit books and records for compliance with the anti-bribery and corruption clauses in the event that the company has a reasonable belief that the joint venture or the joint-venture operator (in its activities directly or indirectly related to the joint venture) may have violated anticorruption laws or paid some form of bribe.
- The right of withdrawal from the joint venture and to receive compensation for damages in the event of breach of the anticorruption obligations of the joint-venture agreement or in the event of violations of the anticorruption laws or of related policy in the joint venture.

Once a joint venture is established, the company must continue to monitor joint-venture activities and the activities of joint-venture partners to ensure continuing compliance with applicable laws and the joint-venture agreement.

The implementation and the monitoring of the joint-venture activities are the responsibility of the company's representative, who shall be selected from among individuals with adequate seniority levels and outstanding reputations for honesty and correct business practices, as well as competence in the field of internal control systems.

The company's representative is responsible for:

- Ascertaining and ensuring that the joint venture, the operator of the joint venture, and the partners always operate the joint venture according to the criteria of maximum diligence, honesty, transparency, integrity, and compliance with the laws and the joint venture's internal control system and compliance program.
- Monitoring, with the support of the ACU, the adequacy and effectiveness of the internal control system and compliance program adopted by the joint venture.

- Monitoring the relationships with the joint venture's clients/counterparties, especially when they are public entities.
- Monitoring, in particular, the relevance, pertinence, necessity, legality, and correct execution of any agreement with intermediaries or business partners that will act on behalf of the joint venture.
- Drafting a periodical report regarding the activities carried out based on the preceding points and to be submitted to the ACU.

In particular, if the company's representative reveals the absence of specific internal procedures, or the noncompliance of such procedures, he or she shall ensure that the joint venture controlled by the company adopts the ABC Program and shall propose the adoption of the ABC Program to the joint venture not controlled by the company.

Some warning signs that the company should be aware of, or that should warrant further investigation, may be:

- Excessive, false, or inadequately described payment requests.
- Unusual or overly generous contracts or subcontracts.
- Unusual or incomplete documentation.
- Other unusual arrangements.

The company's representative in the joint venture must promptly inform the ACU in relation to any news concerning an investigation or ascertained violation of anticorruption laws by the joint-venture operator, the joint-venture partners, their owners, members of their corporate bodies, or their representatives in the joint venture.

8.2.3.5 Political Contributions

- Political contributions might be used for corruptive purposes; for this reason, the ABC Program suggests prohibiting any direct or indirect political contributions, or, at least, to impose strict requirements.

Political contributions may present a risk of consequent liability as they may be perceived as bribes. In fact, they may be used with the intention of influencing business or official decisions or gaining a commercial or other advantage such as to win a contract, obtain a permit or license, or shape legislation favorable to the company's business.

Prohibition and Guidance Best practice suggests prohibiting any direct or indirect contributions in whatever form to political parties, movements, committees, political organizations and trade unions, their representatives and candidates.

Where the company allows political contributions, it should ensure that appropriate assessment and authorization processes are set up within its organization in order to avoid the risk of improper influence.

The legitimacy of the contribution under the applicable laws is required and contributions must be properly and transparently recorded in the company's books and records.

In case of any doubts, the company's legal department and/or the ACU must be consulted at a preliminary stage.

8.2.3.6 Charitable Contributions/Donations

- In order to avoid improper uses of charitable contributions and donations, they should be made strictly in accordance with the ABC Program requirements and guidance.
- The ABC Program also requires the company to check that the payments have been used exclusively for the intended purpose of the charitable contribution/donation.

The offering or making of charitable donations may constitute bribery when done with the intention of influencing business or official decisions or gaining a commercial or other advantage.

Even if a public official or private party does not receive a direct economic benefit, a charitable contribution made in exchange for obtaining or retaining business or to secure an improper advantage could be construed as an unlawful act under anticorruption laws. This may be the case, for example, where a donation is made to a "charity" which is controlled by a public official who is in a position to make decisions affecting the company. Moreover, donations to government agencies and government instrumentalities present the risk of funds or something of value being diverted for the personal use or benefit of a public official or private party.

For these reasons, it is necessary to carry out preliminarily checks on the legitimacy of the contribution under the applicable laws.

Grants and donations can only be given if the company does not receive, and is not perceived to receive, any tangible consideration in return.

Money should always be given to a charitable organization and not to an individual.

Guidance on Charitable Contributions All charitable contributions must comply with the following minimum standards:

- All contributions must be approved by senior management, with evidence provided of the nature and scope of the individual contribution.
- The beneficiary entity must show that it has all relevant certifications and has satisfied all requirements for operating in compliance with applicable laws.
- An adequate due diligence review on the beneficiary entity must be carried out.

- Contributions shall be made only in favor of well-known, reliable entities with outstanding reputations for honesty and correct business practices and which have not been recently incorporated.
- Contributions must be properly and transparently recorded in the company's books and records.
- The beneficiary entity shall guarantee that contributions received are recorded properly and transparently in its own books and records.

The company shall also verify that payments have been used exclusively for the purpose for which they were made.

Billing (or methods of payment) and payments to the beneficiary entity must comply with the rules described in Sect. 8.2.2.5.

Record keeping must comply with the rules described in Sect. 8.2.2.4.

A similar procedure should also be set out for the *offset commitments* required by many governments, such as investments devoted to social welfare.

Companies involved in offset commitments should establish clear rules to that effect in their agreements with governments and should institute a strict due diligence review, an approval process, and a monitoring process for any offset partners, similar to those in place for dealing with very high-risk third parties.

8.2.3.7 Sponsorship Activities

- Sponsorship activities might be used for corruptive purposes; for this reason, they should be carried out strictly in accordance with the ABC Program's requirements and guidance.

Sponsorship activities may also raise anticorruption issues; therefore, all sponsorship activities must be approved for anticorruption compliance purposes in accordance with internal regulations concerning the request for, and authorization, stipulation, and management of sponsorship agreements.

Any sponsorship activity must be compliant with the following minimum standards:

- Preliminarily checks on the legitimacy of the initiative under the applicable laws and an adequate due diligence review on the potential partner of the sponsorship agreement must be carried out.
- All initiatives must be approved by senior management, with evidence provided regarding the nature and scope of the individual initiative.
- Partners under sponsorship shall only be well-known, reliable entities or individuals.

- In case of companies, a sponsorship partner must prove that it has all relevant certifications and has satisfied all requirements for operating in compliance with applicable laws.

The sponsorship must be regulated by a written agreement with the beneficiary entity. Sponsorship agreements must be negotiated, entered into, and managed in compliance with the general provisions described in Sect. "General Provisions" for high-risk third parties.

Best practice suggests that sponsorship agreements should *also* contain:

- A declaration from the counterparty that the amount paid by the company shall be used solely as payment for the counterparty's services and that these sums shall never be given to a public official or a private party for corrupt purposes or transferred, either directly or indirectly, to members of the company's corporate bodies, directors, or employees.
- A declaration from the counterparty that neither the counterparty, nor its owners, directors, or employees are public officials.
- The commitment of the counterparty to comply with the applicable laws, the anticorruption laws, and the anticorruption provisions of the relevant sponsorship agreement.
- The billing terms (or method of payment) and payment terms, taking into account that such payments can be made exclusively to the counterparty and in the country of the counterparty's incorporation, exclusively into the account registered to the counterparty as indicated in the agreement, and never to numbered accounts or in cash.
- The currency and the amount paid pursuant to the sponsorship agreement.
- The counterparty's commitment to record the amount received properly and transparently in its own books and records.
- The company's right to terminate the agreement and to interrupt the payment and to receive compensation for damages in case of breach of the obligations, representations, and warranties referred to above and/or violation of the anticorruption laws or the internal regulations on sponsorship agreements.
- The company's right to carry out an audit on the counterparty in the event that company has a reasonable belief that the counterparty may have violated the compliance-related provisions of the relevant policy and/or of the agreement.

The amount paid according to the sponsorship agreement must be recorded properly and transparently in the company's books and records.

Payments must be made exclusively as indicated in the sponsorship agreement, subject to verification that the service has been rendered.

Payments to the counterparty must comply with the rules described in Sect. 8.2.2.5. Record keeping must comply with the rules described in Sect. 8.2.2.4.

Appropriate monitoring and checks shall be made by the company as regards the effective performance of the sponsorship initiative, in line with the contractual terms and conditions.

8.2.3.8 Mergers and Acquisitions

- The company may be liable for pre-acquisition corrupt activities pertaining to the counterparty or the target entity. To mitigate the risk, the ABC Program provides specific requirements to protect the company: (1) a preliminary anticorruption due diligence on the counterpart and on the target; (2) adequate representations, warranties, and covenants in the relevant sale and purchase agreement; and (3) a plan to implement the ABC Program in the target as part of the company's post-acquisition integration plan.

The company should develop specific procedures for anticorruption due diligence in any merger or acquisition project, including thorough examination of the seller or buyer, the target, and the target's activities at risk, so as to avoid inheriting liability. The company should set out a robust *approval process* for any acquisition or merger operation.

The due diligence process shall be coordinated by the departments identified as responsible for performing it in order to evaluate the reliability of the target. The due diligence report must contain:

- The names of the persons who have carried out the due diligence procedures.
- The specific checks conducted and their respective outcomes.
- The conclusions and recommendations made.
- Any contractual provision to be proposed to the counterparty.

In relation to any proposed acquisition or disposals, the ACU must be consulted as far in advance as possible.

Whenever an acquisition is made, a plan to comply with the ABC Program must be part of the company's *post-acquisition integration plan:* following the closing of the transaction, the acquiring company should put anticorruption compliance high on its integration plan and conduct further risk assessment to ensure it has a good grasp of the corruption risks posed by the new organization, and is addressing them.

All costs and charges, revenues and proceeds, receipts and payments have to be entered into the financial records in timely, complete, and accurate form, with adequate supporting documents issued in conformity with any applicable legislation and the relevant internal control system provisions. All book entries and related documentation have to be available to the external auditor for audit activities.

8.2.3.9 Human Resources Management

- As part of the selection process of company personnel, specific checks should be made on the candidate to the extent allowed by the applicable laws.
- Personnel remuneration policy should comply with realistic and consistent targets.

Best practice suggests that the ABC Program adopt strict rules to regulate the selection of personnel, providing for certain anti-bribery requirements in order to protect the company from any corruption risks.

In particular, the company's internal regulations should, to the extent allowed by the applicable labor and privacy laws, provide for reference checks and appropriate questions regarding:

- Any criminal record or indictment of the individual.
- Any civil or pending investigations relating to unethical or illegal activities of the individual, in accordance with and as permitted by applicable laws.
- Any relationships with public officials or representatives of private entities who, respectively, perform duties or carry out activities in relation to the activities of the company.

Particular caution must be adopted when dealing with candidates that:

- Have relevant contact with public officials that are in a position to exercise influence on the company's activities.
- Supervise employees or business partners likely to have such contact.
- Are involved with financial control issues or other activities covered by anticorruption laws.

Finally, specific rules must be adopted by the company to regulate the *remuneration* of personnel and directors, and when dealing with the management business objectives, the following must be taken into consideration:

- Any compensation system to reward employees must comply with realistic targets.
- Any compensation system must be consistent with the tasks and the activities performed and the responsibilities accordingly entrusted.
- Incentives for personnel should be predetermined through clear and precise quantitative and qualitative criteria.

It is furthermore suggested that a section of the management objectives be dedicated to targets and behavior pertaining to integrity and ethics.

8.2.3.10 Contractors and Subcontractors: The Supply Chain

- Corporations may be liable for the conduct of contractors and subcontractors; in order to mitigate the relevant risks, the ABC Program imposes strict requirements on their selection process and in monitoring their activities.

The company must develop internal procedures which promote and maintain the highest standards of integrity in all activities performed for procurement of goods and services.

The company should define the reference principles and the methodology for an assessment of risks with regards to potential vendors and regulate the operating procedures for the management of a due diligence process.

In consideration of the anticorruption risks that are particularly high within the *procurement process* and other activities which pertain to it (e.g., the vendor selection and qualification process, awarding of contracts, authorization to subcontract, monitoring of contractors' ethical requirements), the company must set out a framework which ensures transparency and fairness by adopting measures aimed at encouraging such behavior and requesting that potential partners declare their identities. The company must implement stringent qualification and selection processes aimed at verifying the technical expertise and the ethical, economical, and financial competence of its partners, while minimizing the risks involved in operating with third parties.

In accordance with the above, the company shall carry out *due diligence* on third parties, analyzing the main characteristics of the vendor/candidate company, such as the vendor's financial position, the shareholding structure, and the control chain of the vendor/candidate company.

In case the information that has been collected is insufficient or incomplete, the vendor/company being analyzed shall be asked to provide a self-certification in which the shareholding structure and the control chain are detailed, for further compliance verifications in relation to the information already acquired.

If compatible with the provisions of the law in force, the company must exclude a vendor/candidate company from being registered in the vendor database, as well as from qualification activities and/or from the awarding/amendment of contracts and/or from the authorization to subcontract, in the following cases:

- Absence of information regarding the shareholding structure.
- Absence of information regarding the control chain sufficient to trace the beneficiary or owner of the company in question.
- Identification of significant risks as determined by negative outcomes during due diligence activities: for example, an economic-financial situation that seriously compromises the company, a turnover or organizational size (number of employees) that is not consistent with the aim of the contract, having been sentenced for relevant offences, etc.

However, in exceptional cases and whenever required and justified by business criticalities, the company may derogate the said prohibition by a specific authorization procedure.

The company must conduct these activities in accordance with the following principles and requirements:

- Personnel involved in procurement activities are to be trained in anticorruption policies.
- Employees are required always to operate as a team of at least two and never to meet with suppliers alone at key contract milestones.
- The roles and responsibilities of the main parties involved in the procurement process are clearly identified.
- The qualification process for vendors is subject to clear and objective rules.

- The awarding of contracts is open, fair, and transparent.
- Procurement reporting and document management is clearly defined.
- Standard documents and other requirements are established for prequalification, qualification, bidding, contract assignment, and contractual terms and conditions.
- Before, during, and after a bidding process, gifts, entertainment, sponsorship, and donation activities are prohibited or strictly regulated (see previous subsections).
- Monitoring responsibilities shall be assigned with the aim of checking the compliance of vendors and subvendors with respect to the qualification, contractual, and ethical standards, as well as with the applicable laws, including anticorruption laws.
- Monitoring systems shall provide for the immediate and adequate reaction by and protection of the company in case of red flags, including suspension or termination of the contract (associated with indemnification rights), and suspension or debarment or blacklisting of vendors/subvendors.
- The qualification process (and relevant assessment) shall be periodically repeated (after a period of 2 or 3 years, depending on the risk level of the vendor).

In the case of *subcontracting,* the agreement with the contractor should include provisions requiring the contractor to:

- Obtain the company's prior approval of any subcontractor (such as subagent, subrepresentative, subconsultant, or any other similar third party) in accordance with the company's internal rules.
- Ensure that any subcontractor performing services in connection with the contract does so only on the basis of a written contract which imposes terms on the subcontractor that are equivalent to those imposed on the contractor.

8.3 Section C: Reporting Violations—Incentives—Disciplinary System

8.3.1 Procedures to Detect and Manage Violations

8.3.1.1 Reporting Violations or Suspected Violations: How to Raise a Concern

- Violations or suspected violations of the ABC Program must be reported immediately to the employee's direct supervisor and/or the ACU and, in any case, through the dedicated whistle-blowing channels.
- Any employee who submits a report in good faith will not be suspended, threatened, harassed, or discriminated against.

Specific procedures for deterring, detecting, and dealing with incidents of misconduct need to be implemented by the company, ensuring the respect of the following rules.

All the recipients of the ABC Program who become aware that an actual or suspected breach of the ABC Program or of any associated procedures has occurred or may occur in the future have *the duty to raise a concern* as soon as possible. Doubts as to whether a particular act constitutes bribery or corruption, or is relevant to the ABC Program, should be raised with line manager or the ACU or through the confidential helpline.

The company should encourage concerns about any issue or suspicion of malpractice at the earliest possible stage.

As part of its ABC Program, the company is required to employ all possible means to motivate participants to reveal knowledge of malpractice that would otherwise remain undisclosed, and to establish adequate rules and procedures to facilitate personnel to make such reports.

Generally, experience has shown that differentiating the lines of the reporting system encourages the disclosure of any potential violations.

The company should provide employees and third parties with the opportunity to make a report through a dedicated channel, anonymously.

Any suspected violation of the ABC Program must therefore be reported immediately to *one or more* of the following:

- The employee's direct supervisor or the business partner's primary contact. In terms of implementing this requirement, a clear chart of reporting roles and responsibilities (local, regional, headquarters)—that is, who is to be notified of suspected violations—is a useful tool.
- The ACU.

And, in any case, through the dedicated channels, also anonymously, such as mail, e-mail, fax numbers, voicemail, and online Web addresses (whistle-blowing helpline).The implementation of a hotline or other proper reporting mechanism is mandatory. This should be well publicized. All third parties are encouraged to raise concerns about any issue or suspicion of violation at the earliest opportunity possible.

The company should ensure that concerns and documents thereby received are properly evaluated, and results should be reported to the corporate control functions and bodies.

Internal regulations should ensure the appropriate safeguarding and storage of the relevant data and documentation, as well as clearly identifying the relevant roles/functions that have access to the record of concerns and are charged with taking action.

The company must ensure that company personnel are not suspended, threatened, harassed, or discriminated against, in any manner, based upon lawful and good-faith reporting activity.

8.3.1.2 Whistle-Blower Protection

- No employee may suffer any detrimental treatment as a result of refusing to take part in bribery or corruption, or because of reporting in good-faith violations or suspicions of violation.

The company must encourage openness, and should support anyone who raises genuine concerns in good faith, even if they turn out to be mistaken.

The protection of witnesses, experts, and victims is an important complementary activity of the ABC Program.

Close attention must be paid to the *security* and *confidentiality* of any reporting through the establishment of a system that ensures that those who report suspicions of corruption and malpractice in good faith are fully protected against open or disguised reprisals.

The company guarantees to keep *confidential* the identity of the whistle-blower, except for legal obligations and as regards protecting the rights of the company and relevant persons accused in mala fide.

No one may suffer any *detrimental treatment* as a result of refusing to take part in bribery or corruption, or for reporting in good faith their suspicion that an actual or potential bribery or other corruption offence has taken place, or may take place in the future.

Detrimental treatment includes: any form of retaliation or penalty, dismissal, disciplinary action, threats, or other unfavorable treatment connected with raising a concern, as well as disguised discrimination and damage to a whistle-blower's career at any time in the future, as a result of their having made allegations of corruption.

Therefore, the employee will not be discharged, demoted, suspended, threatened, harassed, or discriminated against, in any manner, based upon any lawful reporting activity made in good faith.

8.3.1.3 Mechanisms for Processing Suspected Violations

- The internal audit function, the ACU, and the Human Resources Department (or other relevant departments) must verify and investigate allegations concerning violations and consult with each other to identify the proper course of action.
- Investigations can be conducted internally, or by external experts as a guarantee of independence or in case of a need for particular expertise.
- The ABC Program sets out the minimum standard rules and criteria to conduct the investigation.

The company has the duty to appropriately investigate all complaints, although not every reported incident requires the company to respond with an exhaustive, unlimited, and disruptive global investigation.

The internal audit, the ACU, and the Human Resources Department (or other internal unit, committee, or department designated to this end) are responsible for the receipt, verification, and investigation of allegations and will consult with each other to identify the proper course of action. These corporate bodies will consider the nature of the wrongdoing and ensure that a reasonable review is conducted into relevant matters.

Some basic principles should guide the internal investigation process:

- It should not be a partial or judgmental fact-gathering process.
- It must be in compliance with local laws.
- It must guarantee the right to be heard before the end of the investigation and the right to consult the case files and to have a lawyer.
- If the company's policies and practices for handling internal investigations do not give those involved or the whistle-blowers comfort in the objectivity and sincerity of the process, then they are less likely to rely on the company and let the internal investigation take its course before reporting the matter outside of the company.
- With due respect to the self-defense principle, the company's cooperation with public authorities does not necessarily mean "corporate employees' cooperation."

Failure to cooperate fully and openly with any internal investigation into alleged or suspected bribery, corrupt activity, or breach of the ABC Program may lead to disciplinary action.

Internal guidelines need to be designed in order to prepare for and conduct the internal investigation, taking into consideration the following steps and rules.

Investigative Plan The ACU, in cooperation with the legal department or the compliance officer, frames the investigative plan.

The Investigative Team The internal audit, the ACU, and the Human Resources Department (or other corporate bodies) will ensure communication channels are well maintained, documents received are monitored, and the results reported to the appropriate corporate control functions and bodies.

Depending on the circumstances, investigations can be conducted internally or by external experts, whether as a guarantee of independence or as an assurance of the company's ability to staff a large-scale, long-term, global investigation.

The company is responsible for hiring external experts with high-level and certified investigation skills. Investigators who possess qualifications such as Certified Fraud Examiner, Certified Compliance and Ethics Professional, and Certified Public Accountant are of added value. Depending on the circumstances, it is important to ensure that the investigators have the language skills, experience, and/or expertise relevant to the country and regional legal system in question.

The company should require that investigators engaged in investigation activities fulfill the following duties:

- Conduct investigations with honesty and integrity.
- Use only investigative techniques in line with the applicable laws, approved by the company and always to the highest professional standards.
- Safeguard all evidence obtained in investigations, etc.

Interviews with Witnesses All potential witnesses and subjects under investigation must be identified.

Employees must be informed about the consequences of the interview, that is, the company's right to use and disclose anything said during the interview.

Employees must be informed that attorneys representing the company are not representing them.

At least two interviewers should participate, in order to provide greater protection from allegations of fabricated investigator misconduct by subjects.

Interviewers must take copious notes, or where possible record interviews on tape.

All interviews should be conducted with regard to the local legal requirements.

Preserving Documentary and Electronic Information Company personnel who are known to have data and information related to the potential wrongdoing must be notified that no documents can be destroyed (this includes e-mail and electronic files on computers and similar storage devices). To collect everything pertaining to the matter, it is suggested that the company should:

- Aim to collect all the information filed on desktop computers, laptops, and company computers that employees may have in their homes, etc.
- Preserve information filed on backup drives, online and in cloud storage, and portable storage devices including USB drives
- Capture instant messages retained by the organization
- Gather hardcopy documents (i.e., documents concerning the money trail of corrupt payments and how they were accounted for in the company's books and records)

The company should nevertheless consider that in certain countries, privacy restrictions prohibit the capture and review of employees' e-mail. Therefore, a preliminary legislation check must be performed to avoid any legal consequences for the company itself.

Decision on Self-disclosure The company policy should define when—or whether—an internal investigation resulting in solid evidence of violations is to be voluntarily reported to public authorities.

When the information gathered as part of an internal investigation is intended to be used before a court or prosecutor's office, internal investigations must be conducted in compliance with the following rights:

- The *secrecy* of employee communications and their *privacy:* Access to the employee's inbox, the content of communications, data traffic, visited websites, e-mail folders, etc., must be pursued with due respect for fundamental rights. In any case, a preliminary legislation check must be performed to avoid any legal consequences for the company.

- The right not to testify against oneself may prevail over the employer's right to know the activity of the employee during working hours. Employees are obliged to declare those aspects related to their activities to the extent that they are not in conflict with the right to self-defense.

8.3.1.4 Incentives

- Incentives should be established by the company to support its ABC Program. Such incentives may include financial and nonfinancial rewards.

All aspects of human resources management, such as recruitment, promotion, and performance reviews, should reflect the company's commitment to the zero-tolerance policy on corruption.

Human resource practices should involve schemes that concretely reward integrity. To this end, in the evaluation of personnel performance, the company should consider measuring the achievement of targets in relation to the *way* the targets have been met.

Companies should also consider establishing *incentive schemes* to support the acceptance of their ABC Program and anticorruption practices. Such incentives can include financial and nonfinancial rewards for the employee's active participation in the enhancement of the company's policies and regulations, for instance in the case of reporting of irregularities or violations.

In order to reinforce the ABC Program, the company may also consider the inclusion of compliance as a component of board of directors' or managerial staff compensation. Specifically, failure to reach compliance targets can reduce the board of directors' or managerial staff's personal bonuses by up to a certain predetermined percentage.

The company could also include ABC Program compliance as part of the regular performance evaluation of its compliance and control system.

8.3.2 Disciplinary System

- It is mandatory for the company to adopt a disciplinary system as part of its ABC Program.
- Proportionate and dissuasive disciplinary sanctions for company personnel, and appropriate measures for third parties, must be defined and applied in case of violations.
- A remediation system is mandatory to prevent the recurrence of the violation and to improve the ABC Program.

8.3.2.1 Purpose of the Disciplinary System

In the event of violation of the rules set out in the ABC Program, it is mandatory for the company to adopt appropriate sanctions.

The framing of a suitable disciplinary system is an essential requisite for avoiding or reducing corporate liability.

In any case, the right of the company to be fully indemnified against damage costs caused by unfaithful employees' conduct is not prejudiced.

8.3.2.2 Violations

The following forms of behavior represent possible violations of the ABC Program by employees:

- Violating anticorruption laws.
- Failure to comply with any ABC Program requirement.
- Unreasonable failure to detect or report misconduct.
- Failure to conduct or complete mandatory training.
- Failure by supervisors to detect misconduct or to correct it, despite having knowledge of the conduct.
- Failure by internal control bodies to proceed with mandatory controls required by the ABC Program.
- False statements or false documentation related to at-risk activities.
- Assisting others in violating ABC Program rules.
- Removing, destroying, or falsifying documentation in order to avoid controls.
- Making false statements during internal investigations.
- Retaliating against others who report a violation.
- Not collaborating with the ACU.

Any of the above examples of violations should be subject to a *disciplinary action.*

Other possible violations will be evaluated according to the concrete circumstances in order to apply the most suitable and effective sanctions.

Ignorance of ABC Program rules and/or local law is not an excuse for failure to comply.

8.3.2.3 Disciplinary Sanctions

Management, in conjunction with the Human Resources Department and the Legal/Compliance Department, and/or other appointed corporate units/departments, is responsible for determining any appropriate disciplinary action in accordance with local labor laws.

The company must provide for sanctions taking into account the gravity of the offence or behavior in question.

Employees Failure by any employee to comply with the ABC Program will subject the *employee*—including supervisors who ignore or fail to detect misconduct or who have knowledge of the conduct and fail to correct it—to disciplinary action in accordance with local laws and bargain agreements, up to and including termination from employment.

Board of Directors In the event of a violation committed by one or more board members, the company should take suitable action, summoning a shareholders' meeting in order to adopt the appropriate measures (penalties, revocation, etc.) permitted by national corporate law.

Contractual Partner As part of its ABC Program, the company must take appropriate measures against third parties whose actions are found to violate the rules applicable to them or to have committed corruption offences, in accordance with specific contractual clauses included in the relevant agreements.

Contracts entered into by the company with third parties should therefore include specific provisions to ensure compliance and to allow the company to undertake appropriate remedies.

Standard contractual clauses may include specific penalties, the termination of the contract, and claims for damages.

8.3.2.4 Remediation Activity

The ABC Program should require remediation activities to minimize the recurrence of improper acts. In this respect, the company should maintain a post-investigation action plan specifying objectives, action steps, responsible persons, and commitment dates.

After discovering the misconduct, the company must be proactive. In particular, and especially upon the request of the ACU, the company must evaluate whether a revision of the ABC Program or enhancements to internal regulations would help to prevent the recurrence of the violation. If so, the company should then reconsider and revise internal procedures and controls to make sure that an adequate system is in place. Breakdowns in internal controls should be fully remedied.

Appendix 1: Due Diligence Guidelines

In order to identify and document any reference to unethical or suspicious conduct by a potential third party—including relationships with public officials and any information inconsistent with that actually provided by the third party—the third party's ownership structure and the information collected shall be reviewed and verified as per the following guidelines. The following is intended to adumbrate the appropriate steps. Further investigations may be opportune in certain circumstances.

Identification of relevant names As a first step, begin by examining registrations and other documents to identify the full name of the third party, any entity linked to the third party (e.g., holding companies, subsidiaries, branches, and affiliates), and third party's principals.

Registry of companies Most official registries of companies and other organizations make their records available to the public in some form. Check ownership of companies, date of incorporation, directorships, accounts, and other relevant official documentation. Furthermore, if the owner is a trust company, check ownership of this company.

Financial references Request that the official registries provide the financial statements (including the balance sheet and profit and loss statements) for the last 3 years of the third party's activities as well as of related entities (in particular, holdings and subsidiaries), and review them in order to verify, when possible, the information provided by the third party. If audited financial records for the previous 3 years are not available, a third-party financial referee may be requested to state the duration of the relationship and provide an opinion of reliability, financial capabilities, and probity.

Qualifications and membership of professional bodies Review the curricula vitae provided by the third party regarding the third party's principals and regarding managers, executives, or key employees related to the contractual activity to be performed by the third party, and verify, when possible, the information disclosed. In particular, the experience and qualifications of such people should be verified through search of the registry of companies as regards the third party, as well as relevant professional associations, Internet resources, or by contacting former employers when deemed useful or necessary. Most educational or professional bodies will confirm qualifications—especially if the prospective employer or contractor is able to produce an authorizing letter from the individual or company concerned. It is important to view originals of certificates issued by official bodies and, where these bodies are not well known, to assess the authenticity of the issuing body.

Electoral documentation, documentation referring to the business practices at the level of local public administration, and so on Local public administration and business libraries will make available public records of individuals (e.g., from the electoral roll) and businesses (e.g., from local business directories, etc.). Verify that the third party is registered at the address given.

Criminal records Check criminal records for the third party and related entities (parent companies, subsidiaries, branches, and affiliates), the third party's principals and key management personnel (if legally permissible in the country concerned).

Lists of debarred or restricted parties Information is available on some websites, and also via media searches, regarding companies and individuals barred from entering into local, national, or international contracts. One such website with a list of individuals and companies debarred for having been judged to have committed acts of bribery or corruption in bid processes is the World Bank site: http://www.worldbank.org/html/opr/procure/debarr.html

Credit rating There are a large number of international and local commercial organizations offering a credit rating service on individuals and organizations on a fee-paying basis. There are facilities available to check on bankruptcy or insolvency of individuals or companies. These will either be registers available to public scrutiny or listings made available on the Internet.

Business history Using the Internet, financial statements, or other sources determine the business history and experience of the third party. In this respect, also verify the business history and experience as presented by the third party itself.

The third party's experience with the company Review the list of agreements the third party currently has with the company or has had in the past, if any. Subsequently, contact the company's key personnel responsible for managing each agreement, in order to request documentation on previous third-party due diligence reviews, if made, and information regarding the third party's conduct in the execution of such agreements, as well as any red flags or problems that may have arisen in connection to them.

Media search Simple and cost-effective, the use of free and/or subscription databases to research the third party is recommended. If the third party has a website, this should be examined, as should useful government sites dealing with anti-cartel or antifraud activities, etc. Search for each name on a suitable Internet search engine. If the results are unreasonably large, click "search within results" (or equivalent functionality) and use appropriate terms to narrow the search, such as "bribe," "crime," "charge," "corrupt," "fraud," "slush fund," "black money," "money laundering." Search within the results using the filtering terms individually. If the results remain unreasonably large, use specification of the country to further narrow the search. Review the results list, identifying and printing any articles that implicate the third party, related entities, or the third party's principals, in inappropriate activity, as well as those which indicate government services/employment or ties to the government or public officials, or that provide information that appears inconsistent with the information obtained by the third party. Verify, if possible, such information through other sources (including embassies, consulates, international exchange agencies, etc.).

Anticorruption measures Search the third party or related companies' official website for codes, procedures, or policies addressing business ethics, anticorruption compliance, and entertainment or gifts for clients or public officials.

Appendix 2: Red Flags

The following are some of the red flags that may signal corruption and so should be considered in conducting due diligence (although the presence of one or more red flags does not mean that unlawful conduct has already occurred or indeed will occur, it does require more in-depth investigation as well as the implementation of safeguards):

- The circumstances in which the third party was identified or introduced are unusual or abnormal (e.g., the third party was the only available option; was introduced by someone who may have a conflict of interest; was strongly recommended by a third party, someone in public government, or a public official; was involved or proposed for no apparent good reason, etc.).
- The third party pursues commercial activities in a country or in an industrial sector known for bribery and corruption (it should be noted that the energy, construction, and engineering sectors are among those with a very high risk of corruption). In terms of risk of corruption in the country in question, one of the most relevant indexes to which the company may refer is the Corruption Perceptions Index published by Transparency International.
- The third party or any of its principals is domiciled and/or is a resident of a so-called tax haven or of a country with a high rate of corruption.
- The third party, if a company, has an unusual corporate structure or was only recently incorporated.
- The third party is duly registered but does not appear to undertake any business; it has no, or few, personnel, and the commercial address is only a "post-office box."
- The third party is owned by or employs a public official or a public official's family member.
- The third party or any of its principals has a conflict of interest, has a questionable reputation, has been accused, prosecuted, or convicted (especially in case of bribery-related offences, money laundering, or fraud), or has been debarred or blacklisted.
- A different third party states that the third party has stipulated or may stipulate "special agreements" relative to decision-making or operational processes in the contract with the company.
- The third party refuses to guarantee compliance with the anticorruption laws.
- The third party does not have an adequate internal control system nor adequate procedures for the prevention or identification of crimes of corruption, or refuses to implement them.
- The third party refuses to provide the information requested during the due diligence process.
- The third party's business does not seem to be consistent with services required by the contract with the company.
- The third party does not have adequate resources to execute the contractual service, or its financial situation (capital invested and turnover) is questionable (e.g., annual turnover/net assets are lower than the services provided, the company shows significant losses, financial statements are not subject to independent audit, there are discrepancies or inconsistencies in the financial statements).
- The third party has little/no experience in relation to the contractual services required.
- According to the terms of the agreement, the operation involves a public official or a public entity with a reputation for corruption or who requests a payment or gift.

- The third party requires that payments stipulated in the agreement with the company are paid (1) in cash, (2) to an entity or an individual different from the third party, (3) to a bank account in a country which is neither the third party's country of residence nor of commercial operations, or (4) to a numbered bank account.
- The third party requests an increase in the fee, or a discount, for reasons not arising from modifications of the contract conditions during the course of the negotiations.
- The third party requests an unusual operational structure, inclusion of incorrect or unnecessary cost items, or false documentation.
- Contrary to the terms expressly provided for in the contract with the company, the third party requests payment in advance or prior to conclusion of the project.
- The third party does not provide the service directly but through one or more companies or other third parties.
- The third party requests unusually high payments or payments that seem excessive and disproportionate in relation to the service.
- The third party requests reimbursement of expenses that are undocumented or poorly documented.
- The third party provides information that is incomplete or inaccurate following a request for information in relation to false invoices or other documentation.
- The laws of the country impose limitations in relation to the form or amount of the compensation.

The list of red flags provided above is not exhaustive. Other circumstances can arise that may lead to concerns regarding risks of corruption. Company personnel who learn of circumstances that suggest the possibility of corruption must immediately refer their discovery to the ACU.

Part III
Background Analysis for the ABC Model: Compliance Programs in Practice

Chapter 9
The Anticorruption Compliance Program Benchmarking Assessment in the Oil and Gas Industry: Methodology and Achievements

Stefania Giavazzi

Contents

9.1 The Scope of the Survey

The primary purpose of this section of the research was to provide an empirical analysis of recent trends and best practice as adopted by major market players in dealing with the most common forms of corruption in their business sectors. As a reliable source of data for this analysis, the research unit chose the anticorruption self-regulation applied by corporations with specific reference to multinational companies operating in the oil and gas industry. This business sector was selected because this is a highly significant sector which also faces high corruption risks, as is indicated by the legal background to our research project and the evidence from case law studies (see chapters in Part 5 of this volume). As a matter of fact, it is characteristic of oil and gas multinational companies that they carry out operations worldwide, including in high-risk geographical areas, and that they normally deal with all the potential risks connected with typical corruption practices.

Data were collected primarily through a tailored questionnaire, filled in by each company involved in the research, which maps out the scope, value, and content of the oil and gas companies' anticorruption compliance programs. The questionnaire proposed stemmed from some general questions:

- Does the geographical area play a role in the formalization of anticorruption compliance programs? Are they actually enforced or just window dressing, and

S. Giavazzi (✉)
Facoltà di Giurisprudenza Centro Studi "Federico Stella" sulla giustizia penale e la politica criminale (CSGP), Università Cattolica del Sacro Cuore, Milan, Italy
e-mail: stefania.giavazzi@unicatt.it

S. Manacorda et al. (eds.), *Preventing Corporate Corruption*,
DOI 10.1007/978-3-319-04480-4_9, © Springer International Publishing Switzerland 2014

are there significant variations from country to country (even within a single company)?
- Are anticorruption compliance programs consistent with international (and other) standards?
- What lessons can we draw from corporations' experience?

Although our empirical research was confined to a single business sector, we tried where possible to generalize the results, on the grounds that risk areas and preventive rules of conduct share common standards. More specifically, the aim of the proposed survey was to develop a deep understanding of the content of the anticorruption compliance programs implemented by corporations, in order to identify best practices in specific areas at risk and in the "operation" of the program. The role of best practice in the field of anticorruption international compliance is particularly significant due to the lack of common and mandatory international regulations. Although corporations have many international guidelines and national regulations available to them, technically speaking the rules adopted in preventing corruption go beyond so-called regulatory compliance (which describes the goals achieved by corporations in their efforts to ensure that personnel are aware of and take steps to comply with relevant laws and regulations). In this context, rather than conforming to specific laws, "compliance" means conforming to rules, policies, or standards so that the best practice becomes the real reference system. "Best practice" can be defined as a methodology or technique which is proven to lead reliably to a desired outcome, and, since its results consistently exceed those achieved by other means, can therefore be used as a benchmark. In the context of our research, best practice consists in the process of developing and following efficient and effective standard rules to prevent corruption.

In order to achieve a complete benchmark, the following elements of anticorruption compliance programs were investigated: the preliminary processes (i.e., risk assessment, gap analysis); the program adoption process; the implementation, enforcement, and control procedures (monitoring systems, transmission of data, audit activities); the existence of a committee or other internal bodies responsible for monitoring the program; systems for reporting violations or suspected violations; procedures for dealing with violations (remediation); disciplinary or other sanctions in cases of infringement; the rules of conduct for facilitation payments, gifts, benefits, hospitality; political contributions; charitable contributions and donations; sponsorship activities; relationships with business partners.

It is our view that the benchmark assessment thus achieved plays a significant role in the identification of both the *minimum* and the *maximum standard rules* for the prevention and detection of corruption. The benchmark also represents a requirement for the final output of the research, that is, a draft of an antibribery compliance program (ABC program) which can be adopted by all corporations at international level. In fact, the ABC program expounded in this volume contains the minimum standard rules and proposes some new standard rules in those areas where best practice does not exist, or where it has proved to be weak when put to the test, with a view to improving the actual compliance approach.

9.2 Methodology

The questionnaire was sent to a selected number of companies operating in the oil and gas industry. The research unit first selected the most representative multinational companies within this industry and, subsequently, identified the function inside the organization which was in charge of the aspects addressed in this research and thus deemed responsible for filling in the questionnaire. The questionnaire was sent to approximately 15 companies worldwide, and each was invited to take part in the project by collecting data; obviously, the participating companies were advised that the answers provided would be treated in confidence and reported only as ancillary data in the final report. Few questionnaires were returned. In some cases, the corporation did not give us any reason for declining our invitation. On the basis of these limited levels of participation, we drew the preliminary conclusion that, possibly, no anticorruption compliance program existed in some companies, or that because compliance is still viewed as a private matter, many companies would rather not disclose detailed information about their anticorruption programs. Of course, this is just speculation and is not based on objective data. Yet, the low number of answers we received is a symptom of the necessity of our approach, the target of which is the strengthening of the role of the private sector: Private regulation has to be considered and recognized as part of the public strategy for preventing and fighting corruption through the process of sharing best practices and experiences. This conclusion seems to be confirmed by the fact that, before filling in the questionnaire, we asked the participants to decide whether they preferred to remain anonymous or be listed as participants in this survey. Every company (with the exception of Eni) decided to remain anonymous. We also offered each company the opportunity to add comments, information, documentation, or details of internal procedures which they considered of relevance in describing their anticorruption compliance program. Only one company sent us its antibribery and corruption manual, although they asked to us keep this confidential.

Our sample thus consisted of five multinational companies. One is based in the USA, while the others are based in different European countries. The sample, although limited, is representative of the world's major geographical areas. Four companies declared that they operate in each of the following areas: Europe, North America, South America, Middle East, North Africa, Sub-Saharan Africa, and Asia Oceania; one company operates only in Europe, North America, South America, and the Middle East. Although Asia was not formally represented, most of the companies declared that they had subsidiaries there.

As regards the size of the companies, the sample is representative of different sizes of multinational companies: Three declared that they had more than 400 subsidiaries and two had between 251 and 400; three companies declared that they had more than 90,000 employees at group level, one employed between 60,000 and 90,000, and one employed between 25,000 and 40,000.

The research unit decided to analyze the outcome data in accordance with two different rubrics. Our initial mapping schedule simply collected the results: We checked and recorded the answers to each question for each company, also considering open questions (where companies had the opportunity to indicate alternative answers in the final option "other"). This approach avoided the loss of data and made that data more easily available. Our second mapping schedule aggregated and processed the results on topics of interest. This second option allowed us to interrogate the data as regards the percentage of positive or negative answers on specific issues, and to draw some relevant conclusions on the best practices that can be adopted.

9.3 Achievements and Comments

All the companies taking part in the survey declared that they had implemented an anticorruption compliance program and answered almost all the questions. Here we set out the major facets of the survey.

1. In the general part of the questionnaire, we asked whether the compliance program adopted aims to prevent and fight corruption in both the *public and private sectors*. All of the respondents confirmed that this was the case. Considering the nature of the respondents' business activity, carried out internationally, this result is probably due to the requirement to comply with the provisions of the UK Bribery Act; in any case, it is undeniable that best practice suggests that the rules should also be extended to the private sector.
2. With reference to geographical implementation, all the respondents confirmed that their anticorruption compliance program had been implemented on a *worldwide basis* (one respondent specified that the worldwide implementation was limited to the business entities actually controlled by the company). This result shows that within the same group, the anticorruption compliance program has the same content all over the world, with no variation or adjustment from country to country. The survey therefore suggests that the best practice is the creation of a single worldwide, extended corporate program. We can conclude that the rules are not usually tailored to reflect the specifications of particular markets, regions, and functions involved in business activity: The content is the same for all group's entities and individuals, wherever they are located; the program does not reflect specific issues such as the characteristics of the local marketplace or the entity's local organization. This datum does not exclude the possibility that in *applying* the program worldwide, companies may take the diverse legal and cultural environments in which they operate into consideration; in fact, it goes without saying that corruption procedures must be appropriate, applicable, and in full compliance with applicable local laws, which may impose stricter requirements.
3. Another significant question concerned the role of *guidelines indicated by international institutions or associations*. Four of the respondents confirmed that their anticorruption compliance program is based on organizations' guidelines: Each of the companies mentioned international institutions and industry associations; three referred to NGO guidelines; two indicated national public institutions; one

made reference to the International Chamber of Commerce. In two cases, the companies added references which had not been mentioned in the question: In particular, the Federal Sentencing Guidelines, Transparency International, and the principles of an anticorruption program under the UK Bribery Act. All of the respondents declared that their anticorruption compliance program was *inspired by* one of the guidelines adopted by *international institutions*; all the respondents mentioned the United Nations convention against corruption. Furthermore, all the companies involved declared that their anticorruption compliance program *explicitly refers* to one of the listed instruments/guidelines. Despite this, only the OECD was mentioned by all the respondents; two companies also mentioned Global Compact, two also indicated the International Chamber of Commerce, and only one mentioned the World Bank. Three also declared that they took part in international public or private campaigns or initiatives against bribery; in this regard, the United Nations Global Compact, the World Economic Forum Principles for Countering Bribery, Transparency International, the Extractive Industries Transparency Initiative, PACI, IBA, and the B20 were mentioned.

By way of a general statement, we could say that, on the one hand, the anticorruption compliance programs adopted by respondents seem to be generally consistent with international standards. On the other hand, none of the international references prevail, nor has any of them been recognized as the main framework, with the exception of the OECD guidelines. Therefore, the conclusion we draw is that the international institutions and associations sources appear to be very fragmentary, and do not represent common, clear, and shared guidance.

4. Let us now examine the merits of the content of the anticorruption compliance programs. There is a general convergence on the question of the program being based on a preliminary *risk-assessment* process, while there are some relevant differences as regards *monitoring activity*.

   Firstly, we checked the *implementation phase*. Responses to the question "Who is responsible for monitoring the implementation of your company's compliance program?" are reported in Table 9.1.

   The internal audit function was identified as the corporate body which is most involved in the implementation stage, but it is worth noting that Eni has created a specific antibribery legal unit. It is also remarkable that a company decided to monitor the implementation through professional compliance officers operating in each corporate unit of the group: The result of this is that local supervision takes place in addition to central supervision.

   After this initial implementation stage, the compliance program is *monitored* through a periodic reporting system which is run monthly, quarterly, 6 monthly, or yearly (we obtained widely differing answers concerning the frequency of reporting activity). All companies therefore guarantee a reasonable circulation of information and a regular reporting system, even in the absence of red flags. However, different approaches were identified with respect to both the choice of the function responsible for monitoring the day-by-day operating of the program, and to the elements of the monitoring system. Concerning the frequency of auditing activities, different answers were given: On one approach, frequency

Table 9.1 Who is responsible for monitoring the implementation of your company's compliance program?

Subject	Percentage
Board of directors	60
Chief executive officer	60
Internal audit	80
Compliance officer	60
Ethics committee	40
Others: Compliance professionals in each organization	20
Others: Business integrity committee (management committee), Corporate and social responsibility committee (board committee), Legal department, Anticorruption legal support unit	40

is linked to the internal audit annual schedule; another approach is based on a need-to basis; the last is based on a predetermined and fixed frequency (quarterly, every 3 years).

The respondents also differed as regards which corporate body has to be notified about the periodic report on monitoring activity. As a matter of fact, all the options proposed in the questionnaire were selected: Board of directors, Chief executive officer, Chief financial officer, Chief operating officer, Internal audit, Ethics committee, and others: Audit and risk supervision committee, Compliance policy committee audit. It would appear that this divergence is not simply a question of terminology, because all these functions (Internal audit, Compliance officers, Ethics committee, or a specific antibribery unit) differ substantially as regards their role, their powers, and their competence. We can therefore probably affirm that there is neither a best practice nor a common approach to the building and operating of the monitoring system. What we can infer from this data is only that monitoring is an ongoing activity often directly embedded within the controls system, but that companies also seem to take suboptimal monitoring by managers or other responsible individuals into consideration. Finally, two companies declared that they notify the board of directors of the periodic report on monitoring activity. Even though this practice is not adopted by all the companies in our sample, it should be embraced as a good standard rule, in order to guarantee that the board receives timely and accurate information, sufficient to allow the board to make informed judgments concerning the corporation's compliance with anticorruption laws.

It is interesting to note that three of the companies also make provision for an *external assessment* of their anticorruption program; one respondent declared that they proceed with this assessment on an annual basis, another one occasionally (i.e., once in the last 5 years), and another only when necessary. Furthermore, all the companies declared that they require an *audit on the degree/extent to which their own rules are violated,* but there was no common indication concerning who should be appointed to carry this out. In fact, the internal audit and external auditors are equally selected, while one company indicated that this procedure is carried out by the Ethics Committee. Therefore, it is common

Table 9.2 Fields of activity subject to anticorruption rules

Activity	Percentage
Whistle-blowing reports	100
Political contributions	100
Charitable contributions	100
Sponsorship activities	100
Gifts/hospitality/travel expenses	100
Joint ventures agreements	100
Intermediaries agreements	100
Consultants agreements	80
Acquisitions and disposals	80
Facilitation payments	100
Selection of personnel	100
Training of personnel	100
Disciplinary actions/contractual remedies for breach of anticorruption compliance program	100
Communication of the anticorruption compliance program to stakeholders/business partners	100
Record keeping & internal controls	100
Others (please specify): conflicts of interest, contractors and suppliers appointment of external lawyers	40

practice to regularly review, revaluate, and modify the program, along with anticorruption related issues, developments, and best practices.

5. As far as *precautionary protocols* are concerned, our sample declared, as expected, that rules were implemented with respect to the fields of activity listed in Table 9.2.
Only one respondent affirmed that its anticorruption compliance program does not cover all of the listed categories and, in particular, that it excludes *consultant agreements* and *acquisitions and disposals*, while three companies mentioned categories which are not listed in the question: Conflicts of interest, appointment of external lawyers, contractors and suppliers.
6. As regards *red flags,* all of the sample declared that they have a reporting requirement in place, which applies both to employees and to business partners, in case of suspected violations of the anticorruption compliance program or anticorruption laws. However, when asked to whom the suspected violations should be reported, the answers were rather dissimilar. This is probably due to the fact that multiple channels are available for reporting concerns, and no single channel seems to be the clearly preferred option. Furthermore, some of these channels can easily coexist. The violation can thus be indiscriminately reported to any of the following subjects or channels: manager/supervisor, another senior officer (e.g., human resources or legal representative, compliance officer), hotline, helpline. The business partners' preferred channel is instead the contract owner.

Table 9.3 Reporting of red flags in 2010 and 2011

Red flags	Percentage
None	20
Less than 10	20
Less than 20	–
More than 20	40
No answer	20

Not every company answered the question concerning *how many red flags* were reported in 2010 and 2011. The responses of the four companies which gave answers are indicated in Table 9.3.

Only one company registered no red flags, while two declared that more than twenty red flags had been reported in only 2 years. Although we are not in a position to assess the validity of the red flags, what we can infer from this data is that the reporting system seems to work quite properly.

All the companies have a mechanism for processing suspected violations reported by employees or third parties. Once again, when we asked who is responsible for managing the violation (or suspected violation), responses varied significantly. Four companies indicated the Ethics Committee, though not as the sole owner of the process; other functions were in fact equally mentioned. The functions/subjects referenced with the greatest frequency were the Human Resources Department and the Legal Department, immediately followed by the Audit and Risk Committee, the Corporate Social Responsibility Committee, the Chief Ethics and Compliance Officer, the Compliance Officer, and the Investigations Unit. It is difficult to evaluate these results. However, it appears that despite differences in terminology, some functions are fundamentally equivalent, and that the decision to create *an independent specific committee* (the Chief Ethics and Compliance Officer, the Ethics Committee, the Corporate Social Responsibility Committee, the Investigation Unit) is the option most commonly chosen.

There is also a potentially interesting correlation between this answer and the one given when asked for an indication concerning the body or department responsible for giving *support and interpretation* for the compliance program or anticorruption laws. We can infer from the answers received that the function/unit/body which manages the violations or the suspected violations does not correspond to the one which provides support for personnel when there is cause for doubt. In fact, the Compliance Officer and the Legal Department were the two functions most frequently selected as occupying the latter role, and these are not necessarily involved in the process of dealing with violations.

7. In case of *violation,* all of the sample declared that measures are in place to prevent the reported violation from occurring again, and that the company's anticorruption compliance program provides for *disciplinary actions*. As expected, the number of reported violations does not correspond to the number of disciplinary sanctions. With the exception of one company, all the others answered the question concerning how many disciplinary sanctions were taken in 2011. The percentage results are set out in Table 9.4.

Table 9.4 Number of disciplinary sanctions taken in 2011

Disciplinary sanctions	Percentage
None	20
Less than 5	–
Less than 10	40
More than 10	20
No answer	20

Table 9.5 To whom does your company provide training on its antibribery compliance program?

Training activities	Percentage
Directors	80
Senior management	80
Middle management	80
All employees	60
Business partners	60
Other (please specify): contractors	20
Other (please specify): all employees exposed to bribery risk/all at-risk personnel	40

All the companies consider the *implementation* of measures to prevent the reoccurrence of the reported violation to be an important issue; it is best practice to reassess and adapt the program as necessary, to ensure the effectiveness of the company's internal controls and compliance measures.

8. All the companies provide for *training activities* as part of their anticorruption compliance program. We should emphasize that training is provided for different categories of subject, as set out in Table 9.5.
   Training programs are provided for *all employees* by three of the companies, while other companies provide "tailored" training programs, depending on the role of the person in the company organization in terms of levels of authority and power (directors and managers are always covered), or the risk level of the areas where the subject operates.
   It is worth noting that some companies also provide training to third parties (business partners and contractors). This last datum is quite unexpected, since we can hardly imagine how this kind of training can be concretely offered and how the company can impose a training program upon independent subjects. However, it is an option that should be considered as a good standard rule for improving preventive measures against corruption.
9. With a view to investigating the rules of conduct adopted, we first asked whether the company explicitly forbids *facilitation payments*. Two companies answered that they do not forbid facilitation payments. The other three forbid them: For one of these companies, the prohibition is absolute, and for the remaining two the prohibition allows for exceptions due to health or safety reasons only. This clearly reflects the different approaches to the legal background concerning this matter: According to the legislation in some states and the OECD convention, facilitation payments are not considered bribery (they are one of the unsettled

Table 9.6 Are employees permitted to receive gifts, hospitality, or other benefits from public officials as passive bribery?

Answer	Percentage
Yes	–
No	40
Yes, depending on stated criteria	60

questions of Sect. 9, meaning that the convention does not establish them as an offence), while in other states they are forbidden.

10. We then asked questions about *gifts, hospitality, or other benefits offered to and received from* public officials. It is significant that only one company declared that it does not authorize the provision of gifts, hospitality, or other benefits to public officials. All the others answered that the offer is permitted *depending on stated criteria.* In three cases, criteria were specified: One company said that the authorization is subject to a general rule (do not offer/accept gifts and hospitality if it influences/appears to influence a business decision or is on the "black list") and to specific rules: gifts and hospitality with value less than a monetary threshold may be offered to a government official, while special procedures are required (registration, prior management approval and legal/compliance review, additional documentation under defined circumstances) before offering gifts and hospitality with value greater than a single monetary threshold. A second company specified that gifts or any other financial benefits can be offered only in the context of a commercial courtesy and if they are reasonable and bona fide; a third company specified that they only have severe controls concerning hospitality for government officials.
    It is worth noting that all the companies which permit the provision of gifts, hospitality, or other benefits to public officials declared that they have financial limits: Some companies have both a single monetary threshold and a cumulative monetary threshold; in contrast, other companies adopt a general rule, such that the amount must be proportionate to the recipient, reasonable and with a legitimate business purpose.
    As regards the question of whether employees are permitted to *receive* gifts, hospitality, or other benefits *from* public officials as passive bribery, our sample answered as shown in Table 9.6.
    Another best practice seems to be that whenever a public official is involved, special procedures (prior management approval, registration) apply before offering or receiving gifts and hospitality. Three companies stated that in any case the company requires *reporting of requests* from public officials for gifts, hospitality, or other benefits, while another one makes the reporting subject to the circumstance that requests are unreasonable or not bona fide (Table 9.7).
    Four of the companies in the sample also require employees to *record* the receipt of gifts, hospitality, or other benefits from public officials in a *register.*
    As regards this field of our enquiry, the conclusion is that all companies apply the general principle not to offer/accept gifts and hospitality from/to a public official if it influences/appears to influence a business decision. In all other

Table 9.7 Does the company requires reporting of requests from public officials for gifts, hospitality, or other benefits?

Answer	Percentage
Yes	60
No answer	20
Only if such requests are unreasonable or not bona fide	20

Table 9.8 Where does the responsible unit or department principally reside?

Location	Percentage
Corporate headquarters	100
Subsidiary	50
Field/local office	50

circumstances, the best practice is to *authorize* the provision or receipt of gifts, hospitality, or other benefits to or from a public official depending on stated criteria. However, there is no convergence about the authorization criteria or about the procedures for reporting and recording the activities.

11. Another section of the survey was dedicated to gifts, hospitality, or other benefits to third parties. First, we enquired about the permission to offer benefits to *third parties*. In this case, only one company answered negatively, in contrast with the other four, although the latter make permission subject to *stated criteria*. We also asked each company to specify whether it requires *approval* to provide gifts, hospitality, or other benefits and, if positive, which unit or department is responsible for this. One company answered that the responsibility to approve the provision lies exclusively with line management, two indicated that responsibility lies with the line management and the compliance unit or department (Ethics and compliance office, with legal counsel review and support under defined circumstances); the last company indicated that the legal unit and the compliance office or department is responsible. We also asked for the principal location of the responsible unit or department. With the exception of one company (which answered only corporate headquarters), the others indicated multiple choices, as shown in Table 9.8.

    The companies declared that they set financial limits on these kinds of benefits for third parties. With one exception, these limits are approximately equivalent to the monetary threshold fixed for public officials.

    We then investigated whether the provision to third parties needs to be reported. One company answered that they must always be reported, two of them answered that it depends on stated criteria, and the last answered that no report is ever required. It is worth pointing out that no common rule exists in connection with entries. Only one company requires that *provisions* to third parties are *recorded* in a register in any case. The other companies answered as reported in Table 9.9.

    The *register,* where it exists, may be kept at headquarters, with a subsidiary, or at another office.

Table 9.9 Are employees required to record in a register the provision of gifts/hospitality/other benefits to third parties?

Answer	Percentage
Yes (always, even though refused)	20
Yes (sometimes, depending on the value or other stated criteria) (please specify): registration and approval required where value exceeds a fixed limits	20
Yes (sometimes, depending on the value or other stated criteria): companies do not specify	40
No answer (company does not permit the provision)	20

Table 9.10 Are employees permitted to receive gifts, hospitality, or other benefits from third parties?

Answer	Percentage
Yes (always)	20
Yes (depending on the value or other stated criteria)	40
No	20
No answer	20

The question whether the employees are permitted *to receive* gifts, hospitality, or other benefits from third parties was answered by our sample as set out in Table 9.10.

Once again, all the companies apply the principle *not to accept* gifts and hospitality if this influences/appears to influence a business decision. Four of the companies also affirmed that they set financial limits on the value of the benefits their employees are allowed to receive. Authorization to receive gifts, hospitality, or other benefits is generally required. The unit/function who approves the request is the line management (two cases), the legal unit (one case), or the business unit manager (one case). The requirement to *report* these benefits is, in general, a non-mandatory one, although it depends on stated criteria. However, four companies require that their employees *record* the receipt of gifts, hospitality, or other benefits from third parties in a register. The register is kept by the CEO, the Human Resources Department, or the Ethics or Compliance unit or department; therefore, it is usually kept at the corporate headquarters. Once again, no convergence or common approach for the authorization and reporting of activities exists in connection with entries.

12. A different perception of risk emerges as regards rules concerning *political contributions* and *charitable contributions/donations*. Companies generally do not permit political contributions, as represented in Table 9.11, while they permit charitable contributions depending on stated criteria, as shown in Table 9.12.

According to best practices, charitable contributions require approval while completely different answers are given concerning who is *responsible* for this authorization; all the following units or departments are mentioned: Line management, Finance unit or department, Human Resource unit or department,

Table 9.11 Does the company permit contributions to political parties, movements, committees, political organizations, or trade unions?

Political contributions	Percentage
Yes	–
Yes, depending on stated criteria (please specify): the company does not permit political contributions except those mandated by applicable law and regulations	20
Yes, depending on stated criteria (please specify): company does not specify	20
No	60

Table 9.12 Does the company permit charitable donations?

Charitable contributions	Percentage
Yes	50
Yes, depending on stated criteria (please specify): company does not specify	20
Yes, depending on stated criteria (please specify): the charitable contributions must be compliant with the provision of the anticorruption compliance program	20
Yes, depending on stated criteria (please specify): funding is legitimate, not made to improperly influence a business outcome; proposed recipient is a legitimate organization and due diligence is conducted accordingly; red flags are resolved prior to commitment	20
No	–

Legal unit or department, Compliance unit or Department, Board of Directors, Ethics and Compliance Office, CEO.

Finally, all companies involved adopt the following two anticorruption rules: *Due diligence* is performed on the entity which receives the charitable contribution and *restrictions on methods and terms of payment* are provided in favor of the entity which receives the contribution. As far as the second rule is concerned, payments in cash are always forbidden; as a general rule, payments to a numbered account or to an account held in the name of a person other than the contractor are also forbidden.

We can therefore argue that for the prevention of corruption related to this activity at risk, due diligence and restrictions on payments are best practice.

13. As regards *sponsorship initiatives,* all companies adopt a procedure requiring specific *approval* in order to proceed, although widely different answers were given as to which unit, department, or subject is responsible for authorizing such initiatives. The following subjects are equally mentioned: line management, Compliance unit or department, Legal unit or department, Human Resource unit or department, Ethics and Compliance Office, Public Affairs, CEO, Government Affairs department.

All companies involved adopted the following two rules: *Due diligence* is performed on the entity which solicits the sponsorship and *restrictions on methods*

Table 9.13 Does the company require or encourage any of the following persons to have or to implement/adopt certain compliance programs to counter bribery/corruption?

Subject	Percentage
Intermediaries	100
Consultants	100
Contractors	100
Joint venture partners	100
Business partners (including agents, distributors, dealers and franchisees)	100
Other (please specify): subcontractors	40
Other (please specify): advisors, suppliers	20

and terms of payment applied to the counterparty of a sponsorship agreement. As to the second rule, payments in cash are always forbidden; as a general rule, payments to a numbered account or to an account held in the name of a person other than the contractor are forbidden.

Again, due diligence and restrictions on payments can be considered as best practice in preventing corruption related to this activity.

14. The questionnaire also investigated the relationship with *business partners* in depth. First of all, we asked whether the company's anticorruption compliance program requires or encourages any of the following persons to have or implement/adopt certain compliance programs to counter bribery/corruption.

All the categories explicitly listed are covered by all the companies in the sample, while three new categories were added by the respondents (as "Other"), as set out in Table 9.13.

We then asked whether subsidiaries require approval to sign a contract with business partners. The answers are summarized in Table 9.14.

Once again, there is no convergence about the subject who gives approval: Local subsidiary's top management, Direct Supervisor, Headquarters management, line management, and Ethics and Compliance Office are all mentioned.

All of the companies in the sample declared that their anticorruption compliance programs require *due diligence* on intermediaries, consultants, contractors, and joint venture partners. One company specified that a risk-based approach for all potential and existing intermediaries, consultants, contractors, joint venture partners, and business partners can be considered the main rule adopted. Four of the companies also declared that they maintain a *database* of all of the categories listed above.

There can be no doubt about the requirement, as a minimum standard practice, to ask third parties *to adopt a program* against corruption and to perform *due diligence* on intermediaries, consultants, contractors, joint venture partners, and also on other business partners.

As a matter of best practice, *subsidiaries* also require approval to sign contracts with the majority of business partners; the power is assigned to local subsidiary's top management (100% of positive answers) or to headquarters' management (60% of positive answers) or to the direct supervisor (60% of positive answers), depending upon the internal procurement system.

Table 9.14 Which of the following third parties do subsidiaries require approval to sign contracts with?

Subject	Percentage
Intermediaries	100
Consultants	100
Contractors	100
Joint venture partners	100
Business partners (including agents, distributors, dealers and franchisees)	80
Other (please specify)	–

Table 9.15 For which of the following third parties does your company provide standard protection clauses in agreements?

Subject	Percentage
Intermediaries	100
Consultants	100
Contractors	100
Joint venture partners	100
Business partners (including agents, distributors, dealers and franchisees)	100
Other (please specify): sponsorship partners	20

Another area of investigation concerned the existence of *protection clauses* in the agreements with business partners. This provision is universally applied, as reported in Table 9.15.

Significant data emerged about the content of these compliance clauses: only one company did not answer this question. The answers led us to conclude that some of the listed clauses are quite common, while there are many other clauses which can be considered relevant. Table 9.16 shows the results.

We also inquired about the existence of restrictions on *methods and terms of payment* applied to business partners. The answers given are positive in 100% of the sample for all the categories listed: Intermediaries, consultants, contractors, and joint ventures partners; for other business partners, responses were 80% positive. In all cases, payment either in cash or to an account held in the name of a person other than the contractor is forbidden, but the prohibition on paying to a numbered account is less frequently implemented in this case (two out of the five respondents declared that they did not adopt this rule).

15. A specific section of the questionnaire was dedicated to *joint ventures*. First of all, we asked whether the company's anticorruption compliance program requires the joint venture entity (or the third party operator) to apply or to adopt/implement certain compliance programs to counter corruption. All the respondents gave positive answers in this respect, even though in half of the cases the requirement is not absolute but applied only to those joint ventures in which the company exercises control. In any event, each company's anticorruption compliance program encourages the joint venture vehicle/entity in which the company does not exercise control (or in which there is a third party

Table 9.16 Common antibribery compliance clauses

Clause	Percentage
Prohibition to make undue payments to public officials	60
Prohibition to make undue payments to third parties	60
Right to terminate or suspend the execution of the agreement in case of breach of the obligations	60
Right to receive compensation for damages in case of breach of the obligations	60
Right to audit the contractor in case of a reasonable suspicion of violation of the compliance program provisions and/or anticorruption laws	60
Extension of clauses over subcontractors	20
Other (please specify): veto right over the other partners' decisions concerning conclusion of agreements; measures of protection in case of change of partner's ownership/control; prior written approval of (the company) before transferring of contractual interests; partners' commitments in relation to adoption, implementation, and constant monitoring of an adequate internal control system and compliance program	20
Other (please specify): Obligation to comply with antibribery laws, including the US FCPA and the UK Bribery Act	20
No answer	20

operator) to apply or adopt or implement certain compliance programs to counter corruption.

As regards the *monitoring* of joint ventures, all of the sample affirmed that this is a requirement, although the type of monitoring is not equivalent. For example, the replies to the question whether the company requires its joint venture representatives to *report* on their monitoring activities are summarized in Table 9.17.

When reporting is mandatory, different subjects may be notified. All the following units, departments or functions are mentioned by the respondents: Line Management, Legal Unit or Department, Compliance Unit or Department, Human Resource Unit or department, finance unit or department, ethics and compliance office, and anticorruption legal support unit.

16. In cases of *acquisition or disposal,* all companies require *due diligence* on the acquired company or on the purchaser as part of their anticorruption compliance program.
17. As a general rule, all companies declared that they include questions regarding the employee's *personal relationship* with public officials in employment applications as part of their anticorruption compliance program. Therefore, this kind of rule must be considered as best practice.
18. The anticorruption compliance program is generally considered an asset in terms of marketing strategy (there was only one negative answer on this issue), and it is also generally advertised to the company's customers (positive answers to this question prevailed).

Table 9.17 Does the company require its joint ventures representatives to report on their monitoring activities on the joint ventures?

Clause	Percentage
No	20
Yes (Please specify in which circumstances): risk-based approach to general monitoring/reporting; annual bribery and corruption statement	20
Yes (Please specify in which circumstances): regular periodic reporting	20
Yes (Please specify in which circumstances): company does not specify	40

9.4 Conclusion

The results set out above deserve some general comments.

Even though the questionnaire was not focused on how the anticorruption compliance program regulates corruption among private parties, all the anticorruption compliance programs investigated consider both corruption among private parties and passive bribery (requesting or agreeing to receive or accepting a bribe). As for passive corruption, the survey provides a solid answer: Passive bribery is considered as relevant as active bribery. As for corruption among private parties, all the anticorruption compliance programs investigated regulate the relationships, transactions, and payments involving third parties in detail.

Another general consideration concerns the approach to compliance in this matter, which seems to be substantially identical across the respondents. The most significant differences arise in connection with the corporate functions/units/departments in charge of managing the implementation of the anticorruption compliance program. On the basis of the results of this survey, we can note that no common standard rule exists, except for the fact that the option of assigning responsibility for the implementation to executive functions or directly to the top management is never envisaged. Apparently, the idea of assigning this responsibility to an internal and independent committee (meaning that they have no personal or professional involvement with or allegiance to the area under control prevails). The survey is not even useful in detecting to whom (within the organization) the monitoring of the anticorruption compliance program should be delegated. The most interesting solution seems to be the idea of creating *an anticorruption unit* or committee, a specific body dedicated to supporting all the activities related to the anticorruption compliance and to guaranteeing the active supervision of the compliance program, as well as a regular consideration of its suitability, adequacy, and effectiveness. Considering the complexity of changing the inertia generated by preexisting unsuccessful practices, the establishment of a new specific dedicated unit could demonstrate a new commitment to the fight against corruption. This body/unit seems to be a good point of reference, at least for both the monitoring of day-by-day activity (including periodic reporting on activities at risk and internal audit reports) and the updating activity, due to its skills and role in the organization; however, we cannot exclude the opportunity of also assigning to the unit the role of evaluating and managing the red flags, and also supporting all the company personnel in case of ethical dilemmas or doubts about the interpretation of the law. Relatedly, it is interesting to note that the survey highlighted the option of a corporate security department/business integrity department, which would be responsible for the detection and reporting of suspicious fraudulent activities. This responsibility is normally attributed to preexisting corporate units or departments (legal, human resources), so the alternative option of creating a specialized department acting as the custodian of the incident procedure and internal investigations of violations is quite an innovation.

The lack of common practice can also be observed with respect to the unit or department responsible for authorizing or approving single transactions or operations at risk. In fact, it seems impossible to identify a common approach to the matter: sometimes this role is played by supervision or compliance units and at other times by operative offices; sometimes supervision is centralized, and sometimes it operates at a local level (some evidence, for example, emerges about the use of regional compliance officers). Finally, as regards monitoring, the use of independent audits on the anticorruption compliance program carried out by independent counsels and auditors is not indicated as normal practice.

As expected, the rules of conduct concern more or less the same areas at risk. The only areas for which there is no general convergence are facilitation payments, meaning that not all the companies have a specific prohibition in place, and the activities related to consultancy agreements, acquisitions and disposals, conflicts of interest, and contractors and suppliers, meaning that not all companies adopt specific rules for preventing corruption in those at-risk areas. More surprisingly, the area of contractors and suppliers is not always covered by anticorruption rules, considering that procurement is acknowledged to be a process vulnerable to corruption. The same consideration can be noted for the area of acquisitions and disposals.

Getting to the heart of the rules, we should emphasize that only one company stated that it never authorizes the provision of gifts, hospitality, or other benefits to public officials and to third parties. All the others answered that the offer is permitted depending on stated criteria. A similar conclusion can probably be drawn with reference to facilitation payments and political contributions, for although these activities entail direct contact with public officials, in many circumstances they can be authorized, or are permitted under strict controls (preapproval by the CCO is mentioned by one company).

The majority of companies also allow employees to receive benefits from public officials depending on stated criteria, which are similar, but less stringent for third parties. In fact, companies generally require the *reporting* of the provision to public officials in all circumstances, while in the case of third parties the requirement is not always mandatory. The practice of *recording* the provision or receipt of gifts, hospitality, or other benefits (both from third parties and public officials) in a register generally depends on the value of the benefit or other stated criteria. In this field of investigation, we can conclude that no minimum standard emerges, although a common approach can be identified. The survey confirms that direct contact with public officials is still considered to involve the highest risk and to be the activity requiring the strictest controls, while a broader degree of freedom seems to exist in offering and receiving gifts or other benefits to or from private parties.

Another consideration relates to the very high perception of the risk posed by third parties acting on behalf of the company or who are likely to have relevant contact with a public official in the course of their work. Accordingly, this is the area where a common best practice can be observed and preventive measures and controls seem to be more stringent. This last conclusion is also confirmed by the data concerning training programs, considered mandatory for business partners by three of the five companies in the sample. The preengagement due diligence (used to check risks related to intermediaries, consultants, business partners, contractors, and joint ventures partners) is undoubtedly the most implemented procedure in the prevention and detection of corruption relating to this area. An important role in this preventing action is nonetheless generally assigned to clauses in agreements signed with third parties. Besides this, the survey highlighted a minimum standard on the nature, type, and content of these clauses.

Due diligence is also used to check risks related to beneficiary entities in donations and sponsorship. The data confirms that the companies investigated seem to be fully aware that even if a public official does not receive a direct economic benefit, a legitimate contribution made in exchange for obtaining or retaining business or to secure an improper advantage could be construed as an unlawful payment under anticorruption laws.

The commitment by the joint venture's operator to adopt an effective and appropriate anticorruption compliance program, together with due diligence on the partners, are the rules generally applied to prevent criminal conduct in joint ventures agreements. The survey confirms that these relationships may generate anticorruption issues and that companies are fully conscious that they may be held liable for corrupt acts by business partners.

As regards the preventing rules in all the areas at risk, an important role is also played by strict controls on payments and by the requirements of prior approval, reporting, and recordkeeping. The reporting and recording requirements are not generally mandatory for all the activities or transactions at risk, but they depend on stated criteria, while a minimum standard emerges on the restrictions on methods and terms of payments. The survey confirms, in particular, that anticorruption compliance programs give special attention to the detection of corrupt payments and to the remuneration criteria applied to third parties.

Chapter 10
Empirical Features of International Bribery Practice: Evidence from Foreign Corrupt Practices Act Enforcement Actions

Vincenzo Dell'Osso

Contents

10.1 Introduction

In the field of criminal law, the discussion among scholars and policy makers on the definition of bribery focuses on the kind of conduct that must be criminalized, and the best way to build a general definition broad enough to distill into a simple formula all the ways in which bribery occurs in practice.

Despite the long debate on this problem, defining bribery has been deemed an "almost indomitable" issue (Forti 2003, p. 157), wrapped up in an intricate debate that de-

V. Dell'Osso (✉)
Centro Studi "Federico Stella" sulla giustizia penale e la politica criminale (CSGP), Università Cattolica del Sacro Cuore, Milan, Italy
e-mail: vincenzo.dellosso@unicatt.it

S. Manacorda et al. (eds.), *Preventing Corporate Corruption,*
DOI 10.1007/978-3-319-04480-4_10,

pends on moral beliefs and political considerations (Géneaux 2004, p. 13) and conducted between philosophers, jurists, sociologists, and economists (Shihata 1997, p. 12).

Many approaches have been proposed, each of them focusing on one specific element of the crime. The UK Law Commission, in the preliminary works that eventually led to the introduction of the Bribery Act in 2010, found no fewer than five distinct models for framing the definition of the offense, depending on how the nature of the wrong is identified (Law Commission 2011, p. 26). Each of these models emphasizes one key element of the crime, i.e., one of the "common dimensions" (Rabl 2008, p. 23) that might be derived from all the given definitions (Law Commission 2011, p. 26).

In the *Principal–Agent Model,* the center of attention is on the betrayal of the principal's trust in his or her agent's loyalty; the *Improper Payment Model* focuses on the receipt of an undue payment by a person whose official or contractual position makes that payment improper; the *Improper Influence Model* emphasizes the influence of the bribery on how the agent carries out his or her official duties; while the *Improper Conduct Model* identifies the very nature of the wrong with the acceptance of a payment in return for contravening a duty.

Finally, the commission identifies a *Market Model,* which focuses attention on how the act of bribery causes distortions in the operation of an existing market. After all, bribery can itself be described as a specific market that results from "demand—the bribe taker—and supply—the bribe giver" (Calderon et al. 2009, p. 319). This particular model is very important from the perspective of the present research project, because any company must pay attention precisely to the features of the supply side of such transactions, in order to prevent the crime from being committed.

In spite of the vast literature that exists on the above theoretical models, for a multinational company seeking to build an effective compliance program, knowledge of legal definitions and the speculative framework is only a starting point; it is a necessary but still insufficient condition. Apart from the scope of the criminal offense in a given state or group of states, the person in charge of designing new preventive corporate structures and practices needs to know everything about the concrete ways in which bribery can occur in the real world: how and why misconduct begins, who is usually responsible, which kinds of sectors are at risk, how the offender can hide the illicit payments, etc.

This pragmatic knowledge is essential to the risk-assessment process, which represents the "basis of every serious *ethics and compliance programme*" (Pieth 2011, p. 53): Without deep knowledge of all the empirical circumstances in which bribery can mature and eventually occur, it would be impossible to map the risk to the company's functions and activities.

Deep knowledge of the empirical features of bribery practices is also essential for the creation of policies and procedures. Obviously, a compliance program is not only a set of rules which reiterates the prohibition of a type of conduct already criminalized by the law; it must also establish a detailed set of procedures that specifically addresses bribery by contemplating all activities within which it could take place. Such misconduct would then be prevented by providing an organizational modus operandi that aims to remove all opportunities to commit the crime in question.

Together with a wide-reaching corporate culture built on strong ethics, such preventive procedures are the core element of every compliance program. Again, to be able to design and implement such procedures, companies first need comprehensive knowledge of how managers and employees usually engage in, conceal, and benefit from a bribery agreement with a foreign official.

For these reasons—and considering the absence of such a systematization in international studies to date—during the preparatory work for the creation of the Anti-Bribery Compliance Model (ABC Model), the research group felt it necessary to clearly summarize the main empirical features of bribery practices. My purpose was then to review the modus operandi of individuals and organizations involved in public bribery cases, together with any other relevant elements of criminal schemes which, on assessment, could serve as a factual basis for the creation of a universal model for a compliance program.

As is often the case in empirical studies on bribery, the first problem I faced when conducting my research was to find a reliable source of data, given that secrecy and concealment are central characteristics of this specific kind of crime (Forti 2007, p. 139), together with a widespread failure to identify any concrete victim (Spahn 2010, p. 861).

In this regard, the present contribution is based on an analysis of data and information from selected enforcement actions arising from the US Foreign Corrupt Practices Act (FCPA), and therefore deals with the bribery of foreign public agents. Section 3 examines the nature and the value of the most common kinds of bribes paid to public officials, before moving on to an assessment of the briber's pursued advantage in Sect. 4. Section 5 examines the financial aspects of bribery: how money is collected, how it is transferred to the bribee, and how the paper trail is concealed. Section 6 deals with the qualifications and functions of public officials who receive bribes, and with the recurrent issue of kickbacks paid to employees of state-owned enterprises. Section 7 illustrates the role played in bribery schemes by intermediaries, while Sect. 8 assesses the position and functions of individual wrongdoers within a company's organizational structure. The last part of the study, Sect. 9, gives an overview of the ways in which bribery cases commonly come to the attention of enforcement agencies.

Before starting to illustrate and classify the findings of my research, I must first summarize the main features of the information sources I relied on, and then consider the issues and questions that may arise as a result of their usage in empirical research.

10.2 Data Sources: FCPA Enforcement Action Documents, Their Limitations and Their Relevance

This research is primarily based on official documentation related to the US Department of Justice (DOJ) and Securities and Exchange Commission (SEC) enforcement actions arising from the violation of anti-bribery regulations, together with books and record provisions of the FCPA.[1] This material is the most noteworthy existing official documentation on international bribery investigations, since no other country can boast such long and wide-ranging enforcement activity in this field, nor such easy access to the related documents.[2]

However, in spite of the huge number of investigations into FCPA violations run by the enforcement agencies in the last decade, an examination of FCPA case law reveals surprisingly few decisions throughout the country.[3] This is due to the fact that business organizations have historically been reluctant to challenge the enforcement agencies' aggressive prosecution theories in FCPA cases (Koehler 2010a, p. 406). Instead, they have preferred to resolve investigations through the negotiation of non-prosecution agreements (NPAs), deferred prosecution agreements (DPAs), plea agreements, or SEC settlements. This state of affairs has led to a general lack of impartial rulings in FCPA cases, which has implications for the trustworthiness of the facts as described in the collected documents.

Such agreements are "privately negotiated; entered into in the context of the enforcement agencies possessing substantial 'carrots' and 'sticks'; motivated by issues other than law and facts; and subject to little or no judicial scrutiny" (Koehler 2010a, p. 907). More importantly, for our purposes, "there is no judicial scrutiny in most FCPA enforcement actions of whether factual evidence exists to support each of the legal elements of an FCPA violation" (Koehler 2010b, p. 406). It is therefore important to devote some attention to the nature and limitations of the documents used in this research.

Most of the present study is based upon information arising from statements of facts included in NPAs and DPAs. These are tools for the exercise of prosecutorial discretion, traditionally used to divert juvenile and first-offender street criminals from traditional criminal justice processing (DOJ 1997, 9–22.010), and transferred during the 1990s to corporate offenders. In the aftermath of the collapse of Arthur Andersen, in order to avoid the collateral consequences to innocent stakeholders of prosecuting companies, DPAs and NPAs have become a very common means of concluding corporate criminal investigations, with an extremely high concentration of these agreements in FCPA cases (Hall 2009, p. 128; Henning 2007, p. 315. See also Hall 2009, p. 135; Finder et al. 2009; Mark 2012, p. 435; Spivack and Raman 2008, p. 176). These tools take the form of formal settlement agreements between the DOJ and a corporate entity, and they differ from one another only in terms of their details.

A DPA is usually accompanied by the simultaneous filing of a criminal case in the form of an indictment or criminal information. While the DOJ holds the exer-

---

[1] 15 U.S.C. §§ 78dd-1, et seq. See "Prohibited Foreign Trade Practices by Issuers," US Government Printing Office, http://www.gpo.gov/fdsys/granule/USCODE-2010-title15/USCODE-2010-title15-chap2B-sec78dd-1/content-detail.html, accessed 28 June 2013.

[2] Most of the documents related to the FCPA cases are available on the DOJ and SEC websites. See "Foreign Corrupt Practices Act," Department of Justice (DOJ), accessed 28 June 2013, www.justice.gov/criminal/fraud/fcpa/ and "Spotlight on Foreign Corrupt Practices Act," US Securities and Exchange Commission (SEC), www.sec.gov/spotlight/fcpa.shtml, accessed 28 June 2013.

[3] In these terms, see USA v. Kozeny, 493 F. Supp. 2d 693, 697 (S.D.N.Y. 2007).

cise of the criminal action in abeyance, the corporate defendant generally admits the wrongdoing as set forth in an attached statement of facts and agrees to pay a fine, make some restitution, and enact a number of compliance reforms, as well as undertaking not to violate the applicable laws and regulations (Hall 2009, p. 123). If the terms of the DPA are satisfied at the end of the agreed period (usually from 2 to 4 years), the DOJ dismisses the charges against the defendant; otherwise, the company will face prosecution both for the original indictment and for the new violations, as well as additional exposure for violating the same DPA.

As specifically addressed by the new corporate charging policy released in 2008 (Finder et al. 2009, p. 4), using a DPA instead of prosecuting a company depends on nine factors, among them the company's timely and voluntary disclosure of the offense and the presence and effectiveness of a preexisting compliance program (DOJ 1997, 9–28.300).

In the case of NPAs, on the other hand, no charges are filed, and the breach of the agreement does not allow the DOJ to prosecute the company for the original violation that triggered the settlements. NPAs usually take the form of a letter from the DOJ—which commits itself not to criminally prosecute the organization—to the company's lawyer, and generally also include a statement of facts.

No formal rules exist to guide the choice between a DPA and an NPA. As some authors have observed, the DOJ seems to prefer NPAs when success at trial seems less likely, when the company is less morally culpable, or when it wants to "reward" a company for its voluntary disclosure or remedial actions (Hall 2009, p. 125).

In spite of the formal nature of their negotiated instruments, DPAs and NPAs have been widely criticized due to the prosecutor's ability to unilaterally impose the conditions of the agreement on the corporate defendant, which is coerced into accepting the settlement in order to avoid the collateral consequences of a criminal prosecution (Greenblum 2005, p. 1886). A variety of expressions have been used to describe this, from the "'proverbial gun' to the company's head"[4] to the "sword of Damocles" (Greenblum 2005, p. 1884), all underlining the fact that the company "may be under intense pressure to resolve the investigation" (Hall 2009, p. 141), and that the fear of consequences that may be the difference between bankruptcy and survival increases the incentive to do whatever is necessary to have prosecution deferred (Greenblum 2005, p. 1886). This can result in heightened tensions between the company and its employees (Thompson and Yong 2012, p. 522), especially where prosecutors design deals in pursuit of the "divide and conquer" strategy often used in major white-collar criminal actions (Hall 2009, p. 170).

In this scenario, it is reasonable to raise concerns about the practice of scapegoating, by which "corporations find and offer up lower echelon officials to prosecutors in order to save the firm" (Oesterle 2004, p. 480; see also Orland 2006, p. 47). Wray and Hur describe the risk as follows:

> This phenomenon, the argument goes, motivates companies to quickly interview, terminate, and incriminate as many employees as possible, in a zeal to impress the government—even where careful consideration of the facts would not otherwise warrant it. At times, the

[4] USA v. Stein, 435 F. Supp. 2d 330, 336 (S.D.N.Y. 2006).

> interests of companies—who are eager to demonstrate genuine cooperation to prosecutors—are in tension with the interests of individual employees. This has led some outside counsel and some boards or audit committees to pursue a strategy of aggressively selling management up the river. (Wray and Hur 2006, p. 47)

Moreover, it should be taken into account that such settlements are subject to poor or no judicial oversight. As a private agreement, an NPA is not subject to court approval, and therefore there is absolutely no judicial scrutiny of it. Consequently, as has been argued, "there is no independent review of the statement of facts to determine if evidence exists to support the essential elements of the crime 'alleged' or to determine whether valid and legitimate defenses are relevant to the 'alleged' conduct" (Koehler 2010a, p. 935).

DPAs, meanwhile, are filed in a court and are subject to judicial approval. Nonetheless, in view of a recent survey by the US Government Accountability Office (2009), "judges routinely 'rubber-stamp' DPAs without inquiring into whether factual evidence exists to support the essential elements of the crime 'alleged' or to determine whether valid and legitimate defenses are relevant to the 'alleged' conduct" (Koehler 2010a, p. 936). Such criticism must therefore be taken into account when evaluating the reliability of the statement of facts attached to the agreement, even where this has been acknowledged as accurate by the corporate defendant.

Similar warnings apply to other documents consulted, such as those related to plea agreements. These are the outcome of a process of negotiation where, upon the defendant's plea of guilty or nolo contendere to a charged offense or to a lesser or related offense, the prosecutor will take a certain position with respect to the sentence to be imposed (DOJ 1997, 9–27.400) For corporate defendants, the Principles of Federal Prosecution of Business Organizations specifically establish that "[i]n negotiating plea agreements with corporations, as with individuals, prosecutors should generally seek a plea to the most serious, readily provable offense charged" (DOJ 1997, 9–28.1300).

Unlike DPAs and NPAs, a plea of guilty is subject to a judicial review of the factual evidence. As stated in Rule 11(b)(3) of the US Federal Rules of Criminal Procedures, before the court accepts a plea of guilty, it "must determine that there is a factual basis for the plea" (US Courts 2010). Nevertheless, even in this case some authors have raised doubts about the significance of the judicial scrutiny, asserting that "judges commonly rubber-stamp the plea deal negotiated by the DOJ and a business entity" (Koehler 2010a, p. 939).

The final data source on which this chapter is based is SEC enforcement actions. The SEC is responsible for the civil enforcement of both the anti-bribery and accounting provision with respect to issuers (OECD 2004, p. 29). The SEC can seek the application of a civil monetary sanction, the disgorgement of ill-gotten profits, an injunction, or a cease and desist order prohibiting current and future violations of the same provision of the law. As a general rule, if the SEC concludes that a securities law has been violated, it may bring an action in federal court (necessary if it is seeking the application of a sanction) or in an administrative proceeding against the violators.

Like DOJ investigations, SEC investigations into FCPA violations are often resolved by means of a settlement between the SEC and the defendant, with the consequence that the independent check by federal judges that is required in order to impose a monetary sanction is once again largely absent (Koehler 2010a, p. 943).

What is more, SEC settlements have the peculiarity that the defendant is allowed—according to the common formula used in the agreements—to consent "without admitting or denying the allegations of the complaint."[5] The complaint is the common formal document that contains the charges and a description of the incriminated actions. Due to this "neither admit nor deny" policy, the reliability of SEC complaints is very limited.

As a result, I have relied more on the statements of facts from DPAs and NPAs, which have usually been acknowledged as truthful by the private party. Nonetheless, it has not been possible to completely disregard SEC investigation documents, as in many cases they provide detailed descriptions of the modus operandi of the alleged wrongdoing, especially with regard to the record of the improper payments on the company's books, since it is the SEC that enforces the FCPA's record-keeping and accounting provisions (OECD 2004, p. 29). The information drawn from these documents is therefore only relevant on a hypothetical basis, and to the extent to which they are consistent with other findings.

For all the above reasons, facts drawn from all the documents examined for this study cannot be said to be proven *beyond reasonable doubt*. Strictly speaking, it has to be accepted that the data I must rely on are not completely trustworthy. As such, it can only form the basis of a descriptive study, and does not enable us to reach definitive conclusions on the modus operandi of international bribery actors.

Furthermore, the available data represent a preselected set of information: It has been filtered by two US enforcement agencies, and less evident or otherwise different forms of bribery may have slipped through their net. According to this perspective, rather than painting a clear picture of the empirical features of foreign bribery, these data provide deep insight into what the DOJ and SEC consider these to be, and in particular into those violations that the agencies were able to investigate. The selective decisions of enforcement agencies would surely represent a very interesting object of investigation, which nevertheless lies outside the scope of this research.

As set forth above, the purpose of this study is to provide an empirical basis for the design and construction of an effective anti-bribery compliance program by depicting all the relevant forms in which public bribery manifests itself in international business transactions. The vigorous renewed enforcement of the 1977 FCPA which began during the 2000s has yielded more than a decade's worth of materials which, despite their limitations, represent an outstanding opportunity for corruption scholars, who constantly grapple with the "dark number" of cases characterizing this criminal phenomenon. As has already happened in other historical and geographical

[5] However, the SEC has recently announced its intention to reconsider its policies, limiting the possibility of including such provisions to certain kinds of settlements. In addition, since 2011 the Commission has started to resolve FCPA cases through enforcement tools traditionally used by the DOJ, such as DPAs and NPAs.

contexts with regard to domestic corruption, and thanks to other important judicial campaigns,[6] such materials offer an invaluable source of information that can potentially shed light on the dark side of international bribery practices.

The following sections are therefore devoted to discussing the main features of international bribery practice, as they arise from an analysis of more recent FCPA enforcement actions.

10.3 Nature and Value of the Bribe

The first assessed feature corresponds to the nature of the core element of this type of crime, the bribe, which is usually defined in criminal law provisions to include any kind of advantage or benefit, irrespective of whether it has actually been given, or only promised.

In practice, bribes can take several forms; in the majority of cases, however, they merely consist of money. As observed in an OECD report, "money is always of interest because it is rapid, simple and practical. Also, the bribee need not wait for the bribe to be valuable as would be the case for stamps given to a stamp collector, for instance" (OECD 2009, p. 47). Thus, almost nine times out of ten, the bribes described in the data sources took the form of a sum of cash, mostly as the only kind of improper advantage, but sometimes in conjunction with other types of benefits.

Nevertheless, cash payments may present some inconvenience, especially because of the intensification of controls over financial resources both by internal bodies and governmental control agencies. Today, cash expenditure needs to be strongly justified, creating the need for the recipient of the bribe to launder the proceeds of the crime. As a result, the data include several examples of bribery agreements based on forms of compensation other than a direct cash payment.

One of the most common kinds of kickback is the covering of travel expenses (DOJ and SEC 2012). In the *Aon* case, for example, the company was investigated for covering travel expenses for public officials and their family members from a range of countries, together with cash payments through intermediaries.[7] Likewise, the SEC and the DOJ allege that the telecommunication company UTStarcom paid for hundreds of trips for employees of Chinese state-owned telecommunication companies that were their customers.[8] The value of the trips totaled millions of

[6] This is the case, for example, with Italy's "Mani Pulite" (Clean Hands) investigation into the "Tangentopoli" scandal in the early 1990s, which Vannucci has said "represented an extraordinary and maybe unique *source of information* on the features of hidden trades and of the underworld ties between political powers and business actors." Indeed, the information revealed by it benefited scholars so greatly that "thanks to the huge amount of empirical data made available by the criminal investigations, in the last decade knowledge of the mechanisms and dynamics of bribery have increased enormously" (Vannucci 2003, p. 5).

[7] Statement of facts in Non-Prosecution Agreement, *In Re Aon Corp.*, 4 ff. (For full citations, see *infra*, Table of PCPA Enforcement Actions.)

[8] Complaint, *SEC v. UTStarcom, Inc.*, 3 ff.

dollars, mostly spent on tourist destinations such as Las Vegas, Hawaii, and New York, and recorded as overseas "training."

> In fact, however, no training occurred on many of these purported "training" trips. Instead, the customers' employees visited popular tourist destinations where UTSI had no facilities. For example, UTS-China paid for customer employees to travel to Hawaii, Las Vegas and New York. UTS-China's senior management believed that providing the purported "training" trips was necessary in order to obtain and retain the systems contracts.
>
> Between 2002 and 2007, UTSI spent nearly $ 7 million on approximately 225 trips for customer employees pursuant to training provisions in systems contracts entered into between UTS-China and government-controlled municipal or provincial telecommunications companies. In connection with at least 10 of these systems contracts, UTS-China paid and improperly accounted for approximately $ 670,000 as training expenses.[9]

Las Vegas appears to be a particularly desirable destination for corrupt foreign public officials: According to enforcement agencies, trips there were also covered, for example, by Siemens Medical Solutions for Chinese officials in connection with the sales of medical equipment to five state-owned hospitals,[10] and to employees of various state-owned entities by Control Components, which also allegedly paid for first-class air fares to Hawaii and private boat trips.[11] Travel expenses have also purportedly been covered by Johnson & Johnson for publicly employed Romanian healthcare providers,[12] by Alcatel for Costa Rican government officials,[13] and by DaimlerChrysler China for Chinese government officials.[14]

Occasionally, covering travel costs constitutes just a part of a larger set of goods and entertainment that allows foreign officials to reach and maintain luxury lifestyles. Agents of an American company, for example, were accused of having paid millions of dollars in cash, Ferrari cars, yachts, and Mediterranean cruises to employees of Mexico's Comisión Federal de Electricidad in order to get contracts with two public customers (nevertheless, the charges were later dismissed).[15] In Indonesia, Daimler furnished public officials with gifts, trips, and entertainment, such as Mercedes cars, access to golf clubs, and wedding gifts.[16]

Corrupt officials at the highest level of the hierarchy in the public sector usually crave luxury items, a situation foreign companies often take advantage of. This is the case, for example, with the British company BAE Systems, which is believed to have paid an Arab prince with trips, security, real estate, and cars amounting to a total value of US$ 5 million;[17] or with the Mercator Corporation, which allegedly

---

[9] Statement of facts in Non-Prosecution Agreement, *In Re UTStarcom Inc.*

[10] Complaint, *SEC v. Siemens Aktiengesellschaft*, 24.

[11] Criminal Information, *USA v. Control Components*.

[12] Statement of facts in Deferred Prosecution Agreement, *USA v. Johnson & Johnson*, 25.

[13] Statement of facts in Deferred Prosecution Agreement, *USA v. Alcatel-Lucent*, SA, 23.

[14] Statement of facts in Deferred Prosecution Agreement, *USA v. DaimlerChrysler China Ltd.*, 3.

[15] See Indictment, *USA v. Aguilar, et al.*

[16] Statement of facts in Deferred Prosecution Agreement, *USA v. Daimler AG*, 53.

[17] Information, *USA v. BAE Sys. Plc.*, 12.

bought jewelry, private ships, and snow-scooters worth a total of US$ 80 million for the president of Kazakhstan and other officials.[18]

Another common form of compensation is the offering of full employment to the bribee's family members, or even to the corrupt official him- or herself. This was the case with Latin Node, which made an illicit payment of US$ 1 million to an employee of Hondutel, the state-owned Honduras telecommunications company, and eventually hired him as head of business development for Latin America and the Caribbean.[19] In Thailand and in China, UTStarcom is alleged not only to have provided employment, but also to have falsified personnel recordings so as to enable beneficiaries to obtain permanent residency in the USA.[20]

Another benefit that has been promised to corrupt officials is the covering of course tuition fees and expenses. In addition to many cash payments, for example, in at least two cases Control Components allegedly paid college tuition fees for public officials.[21] Similarly, UTStarcom allegedly covered all the costs for Chinese public officials to attend university management courses in the USA in areas unrelated to its real business.[22]

Another important factor is the size of the bribe relative to the expected economic benefit for the bribing company. In this matter, I must stress that it is not always possible to estimate the exact value either of the undue advantage offered to the public agent, especially when the benefits are immaterial, or of that gained by the briber, which can be very hard to estimate, particularly in those cases where the public agent puts his or her functions at the briber's disposal for an indefinite set of needs.

However, when the awarding of a contract with a public customer or any other quantifiable advantage is at stake, the bribe size is typically determined as a percentage of the value of the contract or the advantage itself. According to OECD experts, "bribes in transnational business may range from 5 to 25 % or even more. It would seem that for military supplies the bribe may reach 30 % in the Gulf region, 10 % in Africa, 5–20 % in Latin America and 5 % in Taiwan" (OECD 2007, p. 47). This reflects a trend identified over a decade ago, when observers noted that from an old standard of 5 %, bribe sizes had crept up to the range of 20–30 % (Andelman 1998, p. 50).

Using data collected by TRACE International and published in the *TRACE Compendium* (TRACE 2013), I calculated the average benefit–bribe ratio for 18 of the FCPA cases and obtained a mean of 20 %, although the standard deviation (which measures the degree of spread among the set of values) is quite high (21.7 %).

Usually, bribes are of a smaller amount: This was the case, for example, for bribes allegedly paid by Saint Regis University in Liberia (1.9 %); ABB in Mexico (2.1 %) and Iraq (7.8 %); Siemens in Venezuela (2.6 %), Russia (2.7 %), and Iraq (4.4 %); and Daimler in Latvia (6 %). An amount closer to the mean was purportedly

[18] Indictment, *USA v. Giffen*.

[19] Information, *USA v. Latin Node, Inc.*, 7 ff.

[20] Complaint, *SEC v. UTStarcom, Inc.*, 1 ff.

[21] Criminal Information, *USA v. Control Components*, 9.

[22] Complaint, *SEC v. UTStarcom, Inc.*

paid by Control Components (14.7 %), Helmerich & Payne in Venezuela (15 %), and by Alcatel in its widespread bribery practices (16.6 %). Obviously, in some other instances I found ratios over the average: for example, American Rice in Haiti (33 %) and Alcatel in Costa Rica (43 %).

10.4 The Briber's Pursued Advantage

In more than seven out of ten of the observed cases, the briber's intention was to secure contracts with public customers, and in one case out of ten the briber sought to make adjustments to certain aspects of an existing contractual relationship. Although the value of the public tender varies considerably from case to case, most of the examined contracts were worth several million dollars, and the contractor stood to gain profits of more than one million.

This suggests that, in international business, bribery takes place more often in the context of works and supplies of significant economic impact. Public procurements move huge sums of money, estimated at 15 % of the OECD countries' GDP, and even at higher proportions in many non-OECD countries (OECD 2007, p. 3). Beyond this, only economic operations which guarantee a healthy return on investment justify the costs and the risks that a company has to face in order to expand its business in foreign markets.

However, the impact of control agency selection processes should not be underestimated, as these usually seek to optimize their resources by investigating only the most relevant and evident cases. In fact, the criminalization process as determined by the public authorities' investigative and allocative choices is a significant influence factor on recorded criminality: It constitutes one of the filters that contribute to the so-called funnel effect, i.e., the process of criminal selection that allows the majority of crimes to remain hidden (Forti 2000, p. 63, 403; see also Davigo and Mannozzi 2007, p. 117).

Another relevant aspect is the specific type of public procurement deal that is typically corrupt. Despite the limitations of the data outlined above, the cases studied nonetheless reveal that most corrupt public procurement processes concern the sale of goods or services, while a minor but still relevant part involves public works.

An example of the former is the case of a Delaware-based chemical company that allegedly offered and paid money to Indonesian government officials to secure a contract for the supply of a chemical additive for gasoline, TEL, to state-owned enterprises. According to the SEC complaint,

> Aside from its illicit conduct in Iraq, Innospec also paid bribes to Indonesian government officials from at least 2000 through 2005 in order to win contracts for the sale of TEL to state owned oil and gas companies in Indonesia. The bribes were made through Indonesian Agent and totaled approximately $ 2,883,507. Innospec's revenues in connection with the illicit bribes were approximately $ 48,571,937 and profits were $ 21,506,610.[23]

[23] Complaint, *SEC v. Innospec, Inc.*, 13.

The case history is full of other examples of contract-related corrupt payments: BAE Systems was investigated by the UK Serious Fraud Office for bribes to secure a contract for the supply of a radar defense system for an international airport in Tanzania (SFO 2010); the German company Daimler is accused of having made hundreds of improper payments in at least 22 countries to assist in securing contracts with government customers for the purchase of vehicles;[24] and Johnson & Johnson has been investigated for bribes paid by intermediaries to a Greek surgeon to secure the sale of the company's medical devices to public hospitals.[25]

In this regard, one of the most varied cases is that of Siemens, which has been involved in a wide variety of corrupt supply contracts:

> Among the transactions on which Siemens paid bribes were those to design and build metro transit lines in Venezuela; metro trains and signaling devices in China; power plants in Israel; high voltage transmission lines in China; mobile telephone networks in Bangladesh; telecommunications projects in Nigeria; national identity cards in Argentina; medical devices in Vietnam, China, and Russia; traffic control systems in Russia; refineries in Mexico; and mobile communications networks in Vietnam. Siemens also paid kickbacks to Iraqi ministries in connection with sales of power stations and equipment to Iraq under the United Nations Oil for Food Program. Siemens earned over $ 1.1 billion in profits on these fourteen categories of transactions that comprised 332 individual projects or individual sales.[26]

My survey of the data revealed corrupt agreements to be frequent among public contracts for major engineering and construction projects. This is the case, for example, with the TSKJ joint venture, which was involved in a bribery scheme in Nigeria in connection with contracts to design and build liquefied natural gas production plants on Bonny Island;[27] with the Texas-based Willbros company, the managers of which allegedly bribed public officials in order to win two pipeline construction projects in Nigeria and a contract to rehabilitate a pipeline in Ecuador;[28] and with Control Components, which has been accused of bribing public officials to win contracts for the Chunxiao Gas Complex Development in China and the Wolsong and YNG projects in Korea.[29]

The fact that bribery and corruption in general are commonplace in major infrastructure projects around the world has recently been confirmed by Flybjerg and Molloy, who studied the causes of the recurrent economic underperformance of this kind of project. They recognized that "corruption, in this broader sense, has strong explanatory potential for understanding the systematic underestimation of costs and overestimation of benefits observed…over the time" (Flybjerg and Molloy 2011, p. 90).

---

[24] Statement of facts in Deferred Prosecution Agreement, *USA v. Daimler AG*, 3.

[25] Statement of facts in Deferred Prosecution Agreement, *USA v. Johnson & Johnson.*

[26] Complaint, *SEC v. Siemens Aktiengesellschaft*, 2.

[27] Statement of acts in Plea Agreement, *USA v. Kellogg Brown & Root LLC.*

[28] Statement of facts in Deferred Prosecution Agreement, *USA v. Willbros Group, Inc. and Willbros International, Inc.*

[29] Criminal Information, *USA v. Control Components*, 18 ff.

In the rest of the cases observed, the briber pursued a tax benefit by securing favorable results of tax controls or assessments,[30] or by declaring false information to national customs inspectors concerning quantities of imported goods.[31] A further widespread form of corruption is the practice of bribing customs officers in order to import irregular goods and equipment by obtaining only partial controls,[32] or simply to facilitate custom procedures.[33] In this way, the company is able to import goods that other competitors cannot import.

> From at least 2004 through 2008, H&P Argentina paid Argentine customs officials approximately $ 166,000 to improperly secure customs clearance for equipment and materials. In return for the improper payments, the Argentine customs officials permitted the importation and exportation of equipment and materials without required certifications, permitted the importation of such equipment and materials at a lower duty rate than was properly applicable, and allowed the importation of materials that could not be imported under Argentine law.[34]

In this kind of scheme, the improper payment is usually solicited by the custom officials, as in the Pride International case:

> On or about December 13, 2004, Mexican customs officials inspected port facilities leased by Pride Mexico. During the inspection, the officials claimed that Pride Mexico had violated customs rules due to the presence of certain equipment on board a Pride Mexico supply boat that had not been properly reported to customs.
>
> On or about December 13, 2004, and, again, on or about December 14, 2004, the Mexico Customs Official advised the Logistics Coordinator and Country Manager 2 that a payment of $ 10,000 to the customs official could assist the company with avoiding taxes and penalties for the alleged violations that had been discovered during the inspection.[35]

Elsewhere, improper payments have been offered with the intention of securing the purchase of a public company subject to privatization, as in the Bourke case (DOJ 2005), or to obtain accreditation from a foreign government for a sham university, as in the Saint Regis University case.[36]

In another noteworthy example, in Indonesia, Monsanto allegedly sought to influence national legislation by bribing a senior Indonesian environmental officer so

---

[30] Statement of facts in Deferred Prosecution Agreement, *USA v. Tidewater Marine Int'l, Inc.*

[31] See "Order instituting public proceedings pursuant to Sect. 21c of the securities exchange act of 1934, making findings and imposing a cease-and-desist order, in the matter of American rice," US Securities and Exchange Commission (SEC), 2013, http://www.sec.gov/litigation/admin/34-47286.htm, accessed June 28.

[32] Statement of facts in Deferred Prosecution Agreement, *USA v. Pride International, Inc.*, 19; statement of facts in Non-Prosecution Agreement, *In Re Hemlerich & Paine*, 2; statement of facts in Deferred Prosecution Agreement, USA v. *Tidewater Marine Int'l, Inc.*, 23.

[33] Statement of facts in Deferred Prosecution Agreement, *USA v. Shell Nigeria Exploration and Production Company Ltd.*

[34] Statement of facts in Non-Prosecution Agreement, *In Re Helmerich & Paine*, 2.

[35] Statement of facts in Deferred Prosecution Agreement, *USA v. Pride International, Inc.*, 19.

[36] Plea Agreement, *USAs v. Novak.*

that he would repeal an environmental impact study requirement that was making it difficult for the company to sell its genetically modified crops in that country.[37]

Another interesting aspect is the type of industrial sectors typically involved in bribery schemes. OECD experts identify energy, exploitation of mineral resources, major construction or infrastructure projects, telecommunications, and the arms sector as among the most exposed to the risk of bribery (OECD 2007, p. 27). In turn, the qualified economic actors interviewed for Transparency International's 2008 *Bribe payers survey* perceive the most affected sectors to be public works contracts and construction, oil and gas, mining, real estate and property development, and heavy manufacturing (Transparency International 2008, p. 10). The 2011 survey showed a similar scenario, citing the most corrupt sectors to be those involving public contracts and utilities, real estate, property, legal and business services, oil and gas, and mining (Transparency International 2011, p. 14).

It is evident that the most exposed sectors are those characterized by high-value investments, and where relevant discretionary decisions and regulations are made by government institutions: "vast, highly centralized and capital-intensive new projects," it has been noted, "give decision-makers opportunities to reap hidden commissions, exert bureaucratic control and acquire political prestige" (OECD 2007, p. 47).

The empirical research I conducted into FCPA records gives evidence of bribery in the telecommunications, energy, medical and pharmaceutical, public transport, technology and IT, military, chemical, insurance, and food sectors.

In many of the cases described above, there were no specific indications of supposedly corrupt actions on the part of the public official. Rather, the bribee is expected to undertake all measures necessary for the briber to achieve their final goal, which often means securing a public contract, extending a contract, or increasing payments from the public customer. Sometimes the improper payment is believed to have been offered to achieve a competitive advantage, such as by obtaining confidential or classified information,[38] an unfavorable test result for competitor products,[39] an adjustment in the rules of a public tender (DOJ 2005), or discounted fees to use public infrastructures.[40] Finally, there are cases in which bribes were intended to persuade bribees to hide past corrupt conduct.[41]

---

[37] Complaint, *SEC v. Monsanto Co.*, 4 ff.

[38] Statement of facts in Deferred Prosecution Agreement, *USA v. Alcatel-Lucent, SA*, 24.

[39] Criminal Information, *USA v. Innospec, Inc.*, 8.

[40] Criminal Information, *USA v. Latin Node, Inc.*

[41] Statement of facts in Deferred Prosecution Agreement, *USA v. Willbros Group, Inc. and Willbros International, Inc.*; statement of offense, *USA v. Siemens S.A. (Argentina).*

10.5 Bribery Payments and Related Financial Issues

Every unlawful payment to a public official in the execution of a bribery agreement must be concealed from the eyes of both internal controls and public control agencies. As set forth by OECD experts, multiple methods are currently used to hide bribes, including "cash payments, payments disguised as consulting fees, remuneration of false services, overpayment of goods and services, subcontracting, delivery of materials for the private benefit of an agent, payments to a front company owned by the bribee or to the bribee's hidden accounts or to a third party beneficiary" (OECD 2007, p. 48). Equally varied are the techniques used to hide the funds collected to pay bribes, transfer these funds to the bribee, and record the payment in the company's books. The following subsections examine each of these aspects.

10.5.1 Collection of Sums for Bribery

A widespread method for collecting the financial resources necessary for bribing a public officer consists of creating so-called slush funds, usually stored in an unrecorded bank account located in offshore financial centers so as to hide the account owner's identity.

The use of slush funds dates to the origin of foreign bribery practices. In 1973, the US Office of the Watergate Special Prosecutor and the SEC investigations into the Watergate scandal revealed that many US companies maintained slush funds not only to finance contributions to domestic political campaigns, but also to bribe foreign officials (Weismann 2009, p. 615; Spalding 2010, p. 351; Brown 2001, p. 239; Lindsey 2009, p. 959).

These funds, as revealed by OECD experts, "are frequently opened in financial centres—often offshore—where secrecy is granted thanks to domestic bank and tax regulations. Furthermore, examples illustrate that the transfer of funds through various financial centres or the investment into complex financial products help hide both funds to be used as bribes, and the proceeds of bribery crimes" (OECD 2007, p. 50). Relying on slush funds entails some unquestionable advantages for bribers, such as having a reserve account ready to be used in any circumstances. For example, slush funds were widely used in the Siemens worldwide bribery scandal.[42]

However, the availability of a slush fund implies preparation and anticipation of future needs, often at a moment when the request of the public official is still unknown. Slush fund creation and administration requires specific accounting knowledge and the participation of individuals who have access to the company's financial resources, who must engage in false accounting and establish off-the-books accounts (OECD 2007, p. 50). In addition, slush funds may be discovered by internal and external control bodies, exposing those who created them and endangering the entire bribery operation.

[42] Complaint, *SEC v. Siemens Aktiengesellschaft*, passim.

Given the risks that slush funds entail, funds for bribes may be kept in the form of cash, as in the case of the bribes paid by Willbros to Nigerian officials.[43] Alternatively, other methods are often used to collect the necessary sums of money *after* the corrupt agreement with the public officer has been stipulated, often with his or her active assistance. A frequent method used to this end is the overpricing of services provided to the public customer. This was the case, for example, for EvoBus GmbH, a wholly owned subsidiary of Daimler AG that purportedly paid bribes to members of Riga City Council in order to obtain a contract for the sale of buses. Accordingly to the DOJ, "EvoBus paid these bribes to members of the Riga City Council, at least in part, by inflating the purchase price of the buses and kicking back the price increases to individual members of the City Council in the form of 'commissions.'"[44]

The same allegedly occurred with another subsidiary of Daimler, the Moscow-based Mercedes-Benz Russia SAO, which "sometimes made improper payments to government officials in Russia to secure business by over-invoicing the customer and paying the excess amount back to the government officials."[45] The same method was allegedly employed by a number of other companies, such as Control Components, employees of which made corrupt payments by inflating the fee paid by CCI,[46] and in certain other cases related to the Oil for Food program scandal.[47]

Yet another method of collecting funds is for the briber to ask for an intragroup loan between parent companies and their subsidiaries or joint venture partners, as in the cases of Siemens in Argentina[48] or of Willbros in Nigeria;[49] or to use money stored in funds originally assigned to other purposes, as in the case of Aon in Costa Rica.[50]

However, the most popular method is undoubtedly the use of company financial resources to cover apparently legitimate expenses, corresponding to invoices submitted by third parties for totally or partially sham services. These will usually consist of consultancy (covered in detail in Sect. 7) or other kinds of services, as in case of ABB in Mexico, where third parties submitted invoices for "technical service" and "maintenance support services,"[51] or the Daimler scandal in Vietnam, where the company paid for "broker commission."[52]

---

[43] Statement of facts in Deferred Prosecution Agreement, *USA v. Willbros Group, Inc. and Willbros International, Inc.*, 12.

[44] Statement of facts in Deferred Prosecution Agreement, *USA v. Daimler AG*, 47.

[45] Statement of offense, *USA v. DaimlerChrysler Automotive Russia SAO*, 3.

[46] Statement of facts in Plea Agreement, *USA v. Control Components*, 7.

[47] See, for example, the Azko Nobel case, in which the supplier submitted its contract with an inflated price of 10 % to the UN for approval: Complaint, *SEC v. Akzo Nobel N.V.*, 5.

[48] Statement of offense, *USA v. Siemens S.A. (Argentina),* 14.

[49] Statement of facts in Deferred Prosecution Agreement, *USA v. Willbros Group, Inc. and Willbros International, Inc.*, 13.

[50] Statement of facts in Non-Prosecution Agreement, *In Re Aon Corp.*

[51] Superseding Criminal Information, *USA v. Basurto, 6.*

[52] Statement of facts in Deferred Prosecution Agreement, *USA v. Daimler AG*, 28 ff.

Other methods employed to raise funds for bribery are further described in the next section, where I consider the means used to funnel improper payments to corrupt public officials.

10.5.2 Methods for Transferring the Money to the Public Official

Every unlawful payment to a public official in the execution of a bribery agreement must be concealed from the eyes of both internal controls and public control agencies. As set forth by OECD experts, multiple methods are currently used to hide bribes, including "cash payments, payments disguised as consulting fees, remuneration of false services, overpayment of goods and services, subcontracting, delivery of materials for the private benefit of an agent, payments to a front company owned by the bribee or to the bribee's hidden accounts or to a third party beneficiary" (OECD 2007, p. 48).

Money paid as bribes is generally transferred from the company to third parties, which operate as intermediaries with the public official. As we will see in Sect. 7 below, which is dedicated to intermediaries, in most cases the third party appears to be a consultant or a consultancy,[53] which may even transfer the money to another consultant before allowing the public official to receive it. But the money can be also channeled through a customs broker—especially when a customs officer has to be bribed[54]—or a shell company incorporated in a third country.[55]

Bribes can be delivered by local subsidiaries' employees: In these cases, cash payments are usual,[56] and by preference are made by splitting up the whole sum into numerous smaller amounts.[57] In some of the cases I examined, the payments originated directly from bank accounts belonging to the parent company or a subsidiary;[58] however, in order to conceal the nature of the transaction, third-party accounts (TPAs) are also used.[59]

Companies may avail themselves of different methods at the same time. According to the SEC, to execute the 4,283 improper payments in its global bribery practice, Siemens relied mostly on sham consultancy agreements (US$ 982.7 million), but it also made use of slush funds held by ex-managers, third parties, or affiliated companies (US$ 211 million); cash distributed by the "cash desk" of the Siemens

---

[53] See statement of facts in Deferred Prosecution Agreement, *USA v. Alacatel Lucent S.A*, 34; statement of facts in Deferred Prosecution Agreement, *USA v. Willbros Group, Inc. and Willbros International, Inc., 6; Complaint, SEC v. Sharef et al.*, 11.

[54] Indictment, *USA v. Kay*, 3.

[55] Statement of facts in Deferred Prosecution Agreement, *USA v. Daimler AG*, 27.

[56] Complaint, SEC v. *Siemens Aktiengesellschaft*; statement of offense, *USAv. DaimlerChrysler Automotive Russia SAO*; see "Order instituting public proceedings, imposing a cease-and-desist order, in the matter of American rice," http://www.sec.gov/litigation/admin/34-47286.htm.

[57] Statement of facts in Non-Prosecution Agreement, *In Re Helmerich & Payne, Inc.*, 2.

[58] Criminal Information, *USAv. Latin Node, Inc*; Statement of facts in Deferred Prosecution Agreement, *USA v. Daimler AG; statement of offense, USA v. Siemens S.A.* (Argentina).

[59] Statement of facts in Deferred Prosecution Agreement, *USA v. Daimler AG*.

Real Estate Group to employees, who physically transported the money across borders (US$ 160 million); and internal accounts, originally created for intragroup transfers (US$ 16.2 million).[60]

A good example of a company using a range of such methods is Siemens in Argentina, as alleged by the DOJ and the SEC. According to the SEC claims, executives of the local Siemens subsidiary were looking for a way to execute the promised payments of US$ 27 million to intermediaries, but matters were complicated by the fact that the project involved in the bribery agreement (known as the "DNI Contract") had already been terminated by the Argentine government, and thus Siemens officials lacked a plausible business justification for transferring the money.[61]

As a result, Siemens officials purportedly used a diversified strategy over the course of many years, which included four different methods of making illicit payments. The first tranche of a US$ 5.2 million payment to Argentine officials was allegedly routed through an intermediary in Uruguay. With the help of employees of Siemens Business Services (SBS), the Siemens operating group responsible for managing the DNI Contract, company officials generated a series of fictitious documents to facilitate the payment and to obscure the audit trail.

> In the summer of 2002, defendant [S] had [B] and a subordinate SBS employee sign a backdated consulting agreement with Meder Holding Corporation S.A. ("Meder"), a Uruguay front company controlled by the Project Group [i.e., the intermediary with the public official]. [S] also instructed the SBS employee to sign backdated invoices from Meder totaling approximately $ 5.2 million.
>
> In May 2002, defendant [T] sent [S] the Meder invoices, which were backdated to 2001 and early 2002. The invoices were purportedly for "market development in Chile and Uruguay" and included wire transfer instructions to a Standard Chartered bank account in New York. The references to "market development in Chile and Uruguay" were false. The payments were not made in connection with any such work.[62]

The payment of the second tranche implied the direct involvement of a Siemens managing board member (Officer A) and a senior executive of Siemens Argentina (Agent B) in order to seek and secure the cooperation of another headquarter division (PTD), completely extraneous to the DNI project. The plan included the signing of another sham consulting agreement and an infra-group operation, and deserves to be described in greater detail:

> In or about May 2003, at the direction of Officer A, PTD agreed to cooperate to provide funds for the payments to the Argentine Consulting Group [i.e., the intermediary with the public official] through an audit-obscured channel, despite the fact that PTD had no business role in connection with the national identity card project.
>
> On or about April 2, 2003, Agent B sent an email to senior employees of Lincas, an entity frequently used by Siemens entities as a conduit for improperly recorded payments, stating that PTD had determined it was "necessary to transfer an agreement for US$ 7 million to South America." Agent B's email indicated that with Officer A's approval, Agent B developed a two-part "solution" for raising the funds: (1) Agent B's corporate entity, Consulting

[60] Complaint, SEC v. *Siemens Aktiengesellschaft*, 11 ff.

[61] Complaint, *SEC v. Sharef et al.*, 16.

[62] Complaint, *SEC v. Sharef et al.*, 15–16.

> Firm B, would increase its commission by 4–5 % on an unrelated PTD project outside of Argentina; and (2) Lincas would increase the "service fee" that it owed to Consulting Firm B on the project.
>
> In or about late April 2003, Agent B, at the direction of Argentina Executive A, deposited $ 7,000,000 in four installments into an account in Nassau, Bahamas, in the name of Consulting Firm C. Agent B divided the payments into installments to minimize potential compliance red flags.
>
> In or about May 2003, a PTD accounting and controlling employee wrote in an email that according to "discussions with [Officer A]," PTD would receive € 7,100,000 in credits. These funds were intended to reimburse PTD for fronting the money used for the Argentina payments.
>
> In or about July 2003, after Agent B received a call from a PTD senior manager asking for an additional $ 2,500,000 for the Argentina project, Agent B deposited $ 2,500,000 in three installments into an account in Nassau, Bahamas, in the name of Consulting Firm D. Agent B again divided the payments into installments to minimize potential compliance red flags. Ultimately, PTD received credits from SBS totaling € 9.6 million for these transactions.
>
> On or about October 7, 2003, Agent B signed an agreement between Consulting Firm B and PTD for purported "troubleshooting" tasks on the unrelated PTD project outside of Argentina. The agreement contained neither a detailed explanation of services to be provided, nor a set amount to be paid. Agent B received approximately € 4,300,000 under this agreement as part of his reimbursement for the $ 9,500,000 he had paid to the Nassau, Bahamas accounts in April and July 2003.[63]

The third tranche of payments once again involved the submission of fabricated invoices for consulting services, based on a backdated sham consulting agreement.[64]

The last method is perhaps the most original and, from a preventive point of view, it draws attention to an issue often neglected by anti-bribery compliance programs. The strategy consisted of simulating an international arbitration initiated by a consulting company, MFast, against Siemens, to recover the US$ 27 million that Siemens supposedly owed as a result of a sham consulting agreement signed while the DNI Contract was being executed. After the claim had been filed, the two parties promptly reached an agreement to settle the dispute, creating an apparently legitimate basis for a payment that had no legal reason to be made.

> On March 15, 2005, MFast initiated a private arbitration proceeding against SBS with the International Chamber of Commerce ("ICC") in Zurich, Switzerland, to recover the $ 27 million in bribe payments that it had been promised for Argentine officials under the corrupt contract it signed with SBS in January 2001. Siemens did not attempt to defend the ICC arbitration on the grounds that the MFast contract was part of an illegal bribery scheme involving the DNI Contract. Nor did Siemens reveal that the ICC arbitration was a sham proceeding concocted by defendants [U. S.] and [C. S.] during their meeting in New York. Instead, once the arbitration commenced, Siemens' management withheld any evidence of corruption from the ICC proceeding and quickly settled with MFast. The settlement kept the MFast bribery scheme from coming to light and thereby endangering the hundreds of millions of dollars at stake in the then-pending ICSID arbitration….
>
> On November 9, 2006, despite knowing that the sole purpose of the MFast contract was to funnel bribes to Argentine government officials, Siemens' management settled the ICC arbitration by agreeing to pay MFast $ 8.8 million. Payment was made in January 2007.

---

[63] Statement of offense, *USA v. Siemens S.A. (Argentina)*, paras. u–z.

[64] Complaint, *SEC v. Sharef et al.*, 19.

> The $ 8.8 million payment was itself a bribe designed to satisfy defendant [C. S.] and the Argentine government officials who were owed money, and to keep them from revealing the extensive bribery surrounding the DNI Contract. The settlement agreement with MFast expressly barred [C. S.] and his associates from "involv[ing] themselves in [the ICSID Arbitration Proceedings], either directly or indirectly, or in any other manner influenc[ing] said proceedings, even if only by passing on information…." The settlement agreement also barred [C. S.] and his associates from serving as witnesses in the ICSID proceedings.[65]

The Daimler case is also noteworthy for the light it sheds on the range of payment methods a company can use to bribe a public official. In their allegation, the enforcement agencies describe a widespread bribery scheme especially based upon the use of *internen Fremdkonten* (TPAs), a number of bank accounts maintained as receivable ledger accounts on the company's books. These TPAs were controlled by third parties outside the company or by Daimler's own subsidiaries and affiliates and, according to the DOJ, were used to "facilitate the making of improper payments and the provision of gifts to foreign government officials":

> Funds were credited to these accounts through price inclusions, discounts, rebates, and other mechanisms. Although these accounts appeared in DAIMLER's books and records, they were accounted for improperly and were not subject to normal auditing or other financial controls. Moreover, certain accounts remained "off the books" of those DAIMLER affiliates on whose behalf DAIMLER maintained the accounts….
>
> Prior to 2002, DAIMLER's TPA policies permitted DAIMLER employees to make cash disbursements which were deducted from ledger balances on the TPAs. The cash was disbursed from a corporate "cash desk" located at a Daimler manufacturing facility in Stuttgart, Germany. In some instances, DAIMLER employees then took the cash and transported it to other countries, where the funds were used to pay bribes to governmental officials.[66]

At the end of the 1990s, after Daimler had been subjected to both German and US laws prohibiting foreign bribery, the company's head of internal audits expressed concerns about the potential legal consequences of the continuation of traditional bribery practices when doing business in foreign countries. In order to prevent the risk of violating the law, he recommended the company "close all TPAs unless they met due diligence requirements"[67] and commissioned an investigation into the risk of bribery in foreign markets. Indeed, during the investigation, authorities came into possession of a document written by an employee of this same internal audit department. Usually referred to as the "Useful Expenditures Document," it is particularly interesting because it sets forth in detail the ways in which Daimler's internal audit department was aware that employees had made and could make bribe payments. As reported in the criminal information, the methods were as follows:

1. Cash payments from secret accounts
2. Payment for fictitious shipments or artificial invoices
3. Payment for fictitious services, such as phony consulting services

---

[65] Complaint, *SEC v. Sharef et al.*, 21–22.

[66] Statement of facts in Deferred Prosecution Agreement, *USA v. Daimler AG*, 4–5.

[67] Statement of facts in Deferred Prosecution Agreement, *USA v. Daimler AG*, 6.

4. Granting credits without justification
5. Waiving claims/charges or collection
6. Entering into fictitious employment relationships
7. Taking cash from employees' own accounts through a false declaration that the funds would be used in the private sector
8. Personally delivering cash inside or outside the country of the "home country national"
9. Granting an "agency commission" to decision makers or through "third party agency commissions to persons closely associated with the decision maker who will pass on the funds in whole or in part"
10. Granting "donations" to institutions that the decision-maker is interested in supporting
11. "Price surcharges" charged to TPAs and used for useful expenditures
12. Using the "grey market for corruption purposes"
13. Using countries with strict banking secrecy laws or weak regulations over cash deposits
14. Granting special terms for Daimler products and services, such as special discounts[68]

Even more interestingly, the author of the Useful Expenditures Document assessed the risk of detection for each form of payment.

> Under the section of the document discussing "payment of fictitious 'services'" through artificial invoices or consulting services, the document reflected that this is a "relatively easy" method of committing bribery provided that the "entrepreneurial status of the partner is plausible and the fictitious 'fees' are within plausible range." The document also reflected that the probability of discovery was low "especially if a foreign company acts as service provider, which may also assume the function of corruption intermediary," but that this particular "type of bribery is comparatively expensive for the paying party [i.e., DAIMLER] due to the participation of the state on the side of the recipient." Significantly, the document noted that the payment of "useful expenditures" through these methods was subject to criminal prosecution in countries such as the United States.[69]

This brief examination of the methods commonly used in bribery practice reveals how vital the regulation of financial resource management is for every compliance program.

The submission of invoices for phony consulting services is certainly one of the most widely used methods of concealing bribe payments (Johansen 2010, p. 86), and has proven hard for internal audit departments to address. This is especially true for those companies that do business all over the world and operate in several markets, since they constantly need the support of external advisors and third parties to carry out their legitimate operations.

Nevertheless, handling the issue of sham consulting agreements alone is not enough to prevent bribery: As this section has demonstrated, there are a variety of

[68] See Criminal Information, USA v. *Daimler AG*, ¶ 20.

[69] Criminal Information, USA v. *Daimler AG*, ¶ 21.

possible methods for paying bribes, and these change all the time to evade discovery by internal compliance controls.

10.5.3 How Payments are Recorded in Accounting and Financial Statement Books

Every payment made using a company's financial resources has to be recorded in its accounting books. In a bribery scheme, this is a very complex, sensitive issue, because the record could give rise to a so-called red flag, i.e., a specific warning sign that triggers a report obligation to the internal controls.

This issue is also very important for law enforcement agencies. This is the case not only from an investigative point of view—since vague or suspect records often conceal illegal payments—but also from a prosecution perspective, because false accounting records often constitute an autonomous offense according to FCPA books and records provisions, allowing agencies to prosecute the briber even if not all elements of the bribery scheme have been proven.

The potential for this kind of incrimination to expand the jurisdiction over foreign bribery cases is well known. Indeed, false recording in a foreign subsidiary's books can easily trigger liability on the part of the parent company when the subsidiary's financial statements are included in the consolidated year-end financial statements filed by the holding company.

Recording a bribery payment necessitates finding a way of concealing its true nature and misleading controls by ascribing some other legitimate reason to it. In most of the cases studied, improper payments were recorded as "commissions" or "payments" for consulting,[70] after sales services,[71] technical services and maintenance support services,[72] urgent processing or customs processing,[73] fees, commissions and legal services,[74] and broker commission.[75] In other cases, more generic terms like "expenses," "costs," or "payments" were used (costs of sales[76] and electricity maintenance expenses,[77] for example; elsewhere, training expenses were used to cover entertainment travel, and marketing expenses for university tuition fees[78]).

---

[70] See, for example, statement of facts in Deferred Prosecution Agreement, *USA v. Daimler AG,* 46; statement of facts in Deferred Prosecution Agreement, *USA v. Alcatel-Lucent, SA,* 20; statement of offense, *USA v. Siemens S.A. (Argentina)*; Indictment, *USA v. Esquenazi, et al.,* 8.

[71] Criminal Information, *USA v. Innospec, Inc.*, 24; Complaint, *SEC v. ABB, Ltd.,* 12.

[72] Superseding Criminal Information, *USA v. Basurto,* 6.

[73] Cease and Desist Order, *SEC v. Helmerich & Payne, Inc.,* 4.

[74] Statement of facts in Plea Agreement, *USA v. Baker Hughes Svcs. Int'l,* 12.

[75] Statement of facts in Deferred Prosecution Agreement, *USA v. Daimler AG,* 28 ff.

[76] See "Order instituting public proceedings, imposing a cease-and-desist order, in the matter of American rice," SEC.

[77] Complaint, *SEC v. Pride International, Inc.,* 8.

[78] Complaint, *SEC v. UTStarcom, Inc.,* 1 ff.

Other descriptions included royalties,[79] platform fees and prepaid expenses,[80] extra costs and extraordinary expenses,[81] and bonus payments.[82]

A variety of expressions are generally used in the same case. This was allegedly the case with Alcor, a subsidiary of the Delaware-based company Innospec, which was reported on by the DOJ in the criminal information as follows:

> In order to conceal the kickback payments to the Iraqi government for contracts under the OFFP on the books and records of Alcor, on or around December 19, 2001, January 19, 2002, and February 11, 2002; [agent A] sent Alcor invoices misrepresenting the kickbacks on Contracts 803584, 930208, and 930299 as "remuneration for after sales services."
>
> In order to conceal the payments to the Iraqi officials on orders under the 2004 Long Term Purchase Agreement on the books and records of Alcor, Alcor recorded the payments to reimburse [agent A] for the bribes as "commissions."
>
> Based on [agent A]'s false invoices, from in or around 2001 to in or around 2008, Alcor improperly characterized the kickback and bribe reimbursement payments to [agent A] as "commissions" and "sales promotion expenditures" on its books and records.[83]

In some other cases even vaguer terms were used, such as special discounts, *nützliche Aufwendungen* (meaning "useful" or "necessary" payments[84]), additional assessment,[85] miscellaneous expenses,[86] extra amount, or special arrangement fees.[87] These expenses are almost always recorded together with the relative invoices submitted by the same sham provider;[88] in some instances, however, the invoices are allegedly forged by the bribing company itself.[89]

Finally, in two cases the payments were recorded as loans.[90]

---

79 Statement of facts in Deferred Prosecution Agreement, *USA v. Biomet, Inc.*, 16.

80 Complaint, *SEC v. Willbros Group, Inc.*, 14.

81 Cease and Desist Order, *SEC v. Helmerich & Payne, Inc.*, 3.

82 Complaint, SEC v. *Siemens Aktiengesellschaft*, 9.

83 Criminal Information, *USA v. Innospec, Inc.*, 24.

84 Statement of facts in Deferred Prosecution Agreement, *USA v. Daimler AG*, 2.

85 Cease and Desist Order, *SEC v. Helmerich & Payne, Inc.*, 3.

86 Complaint, *SEC v. Pride International, Inc.*, 8.

87 Statement of facts in Deferred Prosecution Agreement, *USA v. Maxwell Technologies Inc.*, 24.

88 Complaint, *SEC v. ABB, Ltd.*, 5 ff.; Cease and Desist Order, *SEC v. Helmerich & Payne, Inc.*, 3; statement of facts in Deferred Prosecution Agreement, *USA v. Alcatel-Lucent, SA*, 16; statement of facts in Non-Prosecution Agreement, *In Re Faro Technologies, Inc.*, 4; statement of facts in Deferred Prosecution Agreement, *USA v. Biomet, Inc.*, 15 ff.; statement of facts in Non-Prosecution Agreement, *In Re Westinghouse Air Brake Technologies Corporation*, 5.

89 Complaint, *SEC v. Sharef et al.*,15; Complaint, *SEC v. Avery Dennison Corp.*, 6.

90 Complaint, *SEC v. Willbros Group, Inc.*, 9; Indictment, *USA v. Giffen*, 24.

10.6 The Position of the Corrupt Official and the Problem of State-Owned Enterprises

According to the OECD Convention on Combating Bribery of Foreign Public Officials in International Business Transactions, as well as to national legislations (exceptions include German law—see Sect. 299(3) of the German Criminal Code), foreign bribery is prohibited only when it is public bribery, i.e., when the bribee is a public official. As a consequence, one of the most troublesome obstacles to the application of anti-bribery laws is verifying whether the bribee can be considered a public official by the relevant law.

Article 4(a) of the OECD convention defines a foreign public official as "any person holding a legislative, administrative or judicial office of a foreign country, whether appointed or elected; any person exercising a public function for a foreign country, including for a public agency or public enterprise; and any official or agent of a public international organization" (OECD 2011, p. 7). The same is established in Article 2 of the United Nations Convention against Corruption (UNCAC), which also includes anyone holding an executive office in its definition of a foreign public official (UNODC 2004, pp. 7–8).[91]

Some of the elements of the definition are explained in more detail in the Commentaries to the OECD convention, where *public function* is described as "any activity in the public interest, delegated by a foreign country, such as the performance of a task delegated by it in connection with public procurement," while *public agency* is understood as "an entity constituted under public law to carry out specific tasks in the public interest" (OECD 1997, p. 3).

Each category included in the two definitions has been found in the selected case law. Surprisingly, very few cases involved improper payments to national legislators and judges. In terms of legislators, I found the Alcatel cases in Taiwan and Costa Rica,[92] and the Bellsouth Corporation case, in which officials of its Nicaraguan subsidiary allegedly retained the consultancy services of the wife of a member of the local legislative committee responsible for overseeing telecommunications in the country.[93] On the other hand, only in the Pride case did the bribee have a judicial qualification, being a member of an Indian administrative court, the Customs, Excise and Gold Appellate Tribunal.[94]

The most commonly bribed officers are, by far, members of the government or administrative and public agency officers. In some cases, the bribee is even the

[91] See also UNODC 2006: "[t]he word 'executive' is understood to encompass the military branch, where appropriate (A/58/422/Add.1, para. 2). Another interpretative note indicates that the term 'office' is understood to encompass offices at all levels and subdivisions of government from national to local. In States where subnational governmental units (for example, provincial, municipal and local) of a self-governing nature exist, including States where such bodies are not deemed to form a part of the State, 'office' may be understood by the States concerned to encompass those levels also" (11, ¶ 28).

[92] Statement of facts in Deferred Prosecution Agreement, *USA v. Alcatel-Lucent, SA.*, 19 and 28.

[93] Complaint, *SEC v. BellSouth Corp.*

[94] Statement of facts in Deferred Prosecution Agreement, *USA v. Pride International, Inc.*, 17.

head of state or government: Such was the case for the former president of Costa Rica, who was sentenced in his country in the Alcatel trial.[95] Siemens has also been charged for bribes paid to the Bangladeshi prime minister's son and for kickbacks paid to secure a public contract in Argentina, where, according to the SEC, bribees included the former president of the republic.[96]

In many other cases, bribes were allegedly paid to high-level ministry officials,[97] representatives of subnational governmental units,[98] diplomatic representatives,[99] and other government officials.[100]

Consistent with the findings described above in the section on the briber's pursued goals, most bribed public officials had power over the purchasing decisions of public agencies and companies, allowing them to influence tenders for public contracts. Examples of public agencies or instrumentalities involved include the National Telecommunications Commission, the government agency regulating the telecommunications sector in Honduras;[101] the General State Tax Inspection Office within the Ministry of Finance of the Republic of Azerbaijan;[102] the Nigerian Customs Service, a Nigerian government agency within the Ministry of Finance of the Federal Republic of Nigeria;[103] the Mexican Customs Service;[104] the Taiwan Railway Administration, the authority responsible for managing, maintaining, and running passenger freight services on Taiwan's railroad lines;[105] Kyrgyz Tamekisi, the government agency responsible for the management and control of the government-owned share of tobacco-processing facilities throughout Kyrgyzstan;[106] the Nigerian police force;[107] and the army of Ghana.[108]

---

[95] Sentenced to jail in April 2011 by the Tribunal de Hacienda, Segundo circuito penal de San José en Goicoechea, he was later acquitted on appeal because of the statute of limitations. See "Tribunal absuelve a Miguel Ángel Rodríguez por prescripción de sentencia," *El Financiero,* 21 December 2012.

[96] Complaint, SEC v. Siemens Aktiengesellschaft, 19; Complaint, SEC v. Sharef et al., 9.

[97] Statement of facts in Deferred Prosecution Agreement, *USA v. Daimler AG,* 55; Complaint, *SEC v. Innospec, Inc.*

[98] Statement of facts in Deferred Prosecution Agreement, *USA v. Daimler AG,* passim.

[99] Statement of facts in Deferred Prosecution Agreement, *USA v. Daimler AG,* 43; Superseding Information, *USA v. Novak.*

[100] Statement of facts in Deferred Prosecution Agreement, *USA v. Daimler AG,* 4; statement of facts in Deferred Prosecution Agreement, *USA v. JGC Corp.,* 5; statement of facts in Deferred Prosecution Agreement, *USA v. Alcatel-Lucent, SA.*, 8.

[101] Statement of facts in Deferred Prosecution Agreement, *USA v. Alcatel-Lucent, SA,* 7.

[102] Statement of facts in Deferred Prosecution Agreement, *USA v. Tidewater Marine Int'l Inc.*, 9.

[103] Complaint, *SEC v. Pride International, Inc.,* 13; statement of facts in Deferred Prosecution Agreement, *USA v. Shell Nigeria Exploration and Production Company Ltd.*, 2; statement of facts in Deferred Prosecution Agreement, *USA v. Tidewater Marine Int'l, Inc.,* 8.

[104] Statement of facts in Deferred Prosecution Agreement, *USA v. Pride International, Inc.*, 9.

[105] Statement of facts in Deferred Prosecution Agreement, *USA v. Alcatel-Lucent, SA.*, 10.

[106] Statement of facts in Non-Prosecution Agreement, *In Re Alliance One International, Inc.*, 4.

[107] Statement of facts in Deferred Prosecution Agreement, *USA v. Daimler AG,* 41.

[108] Statement of facts in Deferred Prosecution Agreement, *USA v. Daimler AG,* 45.

As already observed, in many cases the bribee was a customs officer,[109] a health care provider working in a publicly owned hospital,[110] or a tax inspector.[111] Moreover, in a relevant number of cases the bribee had no formal public function, but was a leader or a high-level representative of a political party.[112]

However, the types of public officials most frequently involved in the selected FCPA actions are managers and employees of foreign state-owned or state-controlled enterprises (SOEs). Koehler observes that "the majority of 2009 FCPA enforcement actions (as well as others in recent years) have absolutely nothing to do with such government officials," but rather with employees of SOEs (2010b, p. 389).

This category is more problematic than those explored above, since not all countries address it in the same way, and because it marks the boundary line between public corruption (punishable in practically every country) and private commercial bribery (not always considered illegal, especially if committed abroad).

In relation to this issue, the OECD convention commentaries state that "[a] 'public enterprise' is any enterprise, regardless of its legal form, over which a government, or governments, may, directly or indirectly, exercise a dominant influence. This is deemed to be the case, inter alia, when the government or governments hold the majority of the enterprise's subscribed capital, control the majority of votes attaching to shares issued by the enterprise or can appoint a majority of the members of the enterprise's administrative or managerial body or supervisory board" (OECD 1997, p. 3).

The wide variety of SOEs that appear in the case history are set out in Table 10.1, which summarizes the information reported in the enforcement action documentation.[113]

One of the most noteworthy cases is the TSKJ joint venture in Nigeria, in which the enforcing agencies deemed employees of Nigeria LNG Limited (NLNG) to be

[109] See "Order instituting public proceedings, imposing a cease-and-desist order, in the matter of American rice," SEC; statement of facts in Non-Prosecution Agreement, *In Re Helmerich & Payne, Inc.*, 2.

[110] Statement of facts in Deferred Prosecution Agreement, *USA v. Johnson & Johnson*; Complaint, *SEC v. Siemens Aktiengesellschaft,* 24.

[111] Statement of facts in Non-Prosecution Agreement, *In Re Alliance One International, Inc.*, 6; statement of facts in Deferred Prosecution Agreement, *USA v Tidewater Marine Int'l, Inc.*, 8; Complaint, *SEC v Pride International, Inc.*, 11; Statement of facts in Deferred Prosecution Agreement, *USA Daimler AG,* 52.

[112] Statement of facts in Deferred Prosecution Agreement, *USA v. Magyar Telekom, Plc.*, 7; statement of facts in Deferred Prosecution Agreement, *USA sv. Daimler AG,* 48; statement of facts in Deferred Prosecution Agreement, *USA v. Snamprogetti Netherlands B.V.*, 8.

[113] Clearly, the features of the SOEs presented in the sample are determined by the FCPA definition of foreign official, which is described by the law as "any officer or employee of a foreign government or any department, agency, or instrumentality thereof, or of a public international organization, or any person acting in an official capacity for or on behalf of any such government or department, agency, or instrumentality, or for or on behalf of any such public international organization" (§ 78dd-1–f); and therefore on the interpretation of the term *instrumentality*, which is believed to include "government-owned or government-controlled companies" (see Jury Instructions, *USA v. Bourke,* 27).

Table 10.1 The variety of SOEs that appear in the case history

Case/company	Description of the SOE
Aon (Costa Rica)	Instituto Nacional de Seguros, Costa Rica's state-owned insurance company, had a monopoly over the Costa Rican insurance industry. INS was created by Act No. 12 of October 30, 1924, with the aim of meeting the protection needs of Costa Rican society. All insurance agreements in Costa Rica, including the reinsurance contracts that Aon Limited assisted in obtaining to insure Costa Rican entities, were required to be issued through INS. The head of INS was appointed by the president of Costa Rica[a]
Alcatel (Costa Rica)	Instituto Costarricense de Electricidad S.A., a wholly state-owned telecommunications authority in Costa Rica responsible for awarding and administering public tenders for telecommunications contracts. ICE was governed by a seven-member board of directors that evaluated and approved, on behalf of the government of Costa Rica, all bid proposals submitted by telecommunications companies[b]
Alcatel (Malaysia)	Telekom Malaysia Berhad (Telekom Malaysia) was a state-owned and controlled telecommunications provider in Malaysia, responsible for awarding telecommunications contracts. The Malaysian Ministry of Finance owned approximately 43 % of Telekom Malaysia's shares, had veto power over all major expenditures, and made important operational decisions. The government owned its interest in Telekom Malaysia through the minister of finance, who had the status of a "special shareholder." Most senior Telekom Malaysia officers were political appointees, including the chairman and director, the chairman of the board of the tender committee, and the executive director[c]
Alliance One (Tahilandia)	Thailand Tobacco Monopoly (TTM), established in 1943 by the government of Thailand to manage and control the government-owned tobacco industry in Thailand. The TTM supervised the cultivation of domestic tobacco crops, purchased imported tobacco, and manufactured cigarettes and other tobacco products[d]
Avery Dennison Corp.	Henan Luqiao, a state-owned enterprise[e]
Bridgestone	Latin American government officials employed at state-owned entities, including an employee of Petroleo Mexicanos (PEMEX)[f]
Control Components, Inc.	State-owned customers included, but were not limited to, Jiangsu Nuclear Power Corporation (JNPC) (China), Guohua Electric Power (China), China Petroleum Materials and Equipment Corporation (CPMEC), PetroChina, Dongfang Electric Corporation (China), China National Offshore Oil Corporation (CNOOC), Korea Hydro and Nuclear Power (KHNP), Petronas (Malaysia), and National Petroleum Construction Company (NPCC) (United Arab Emirates)[g]
Daimler (China)	Changqing Petroleum, a Chinese state-owned entity in the energy sector[h]
Daimler (Croatia)	IM Metal, a Croatian government-controlled and partially owned former weapons manufacturer, and an instrumentality of the Croatian government[i]
Daimler (Indonesia)	Perum Dari, Indonesian state-owned bus company[j]
Daimler (Vietnam)	Saigon Passenger Transport Company (Saigon Bus), a governmental entity in Vietnam[k]
Haiti Teleco case	Telecommunications D'Haiti (Haiti Teleco) was the Republic of Haiti's state-owned national telecommunications company. Haiti Teleco was the only provider of noncellular telephone service to and from Haiti. Various international telecommunications companies contracted with Haiti Teleco to allow those companies' customers to make calls to Haiti, paying a set rate for each minute of calls[l]

Table 10.1 (continued)

Case/company	Description of the SOE
Latin Node (Honduras)	Hondutel, the Honduran government-owned telecommunications company[m]
Latin Node (Yemen)	TeleYemen, the Yemeni government-owned telecommunications company[n]
Magyar Telekom/ Deutsche Telecom (Montenegro)	Now known as Crnogorski Telekom, Telekom Crne Gore A.D. (TCG) and its mobile company subsidiary were the Montenegrin state-owned fixed-line and cellular telecommunications companies[o]
Pride (Venezuela)	Petroleos de Venezuela S.A. (PDVSA) was a Venezuelan state-owned oil company, established in 1975 as an agency and instrumentality of the government to manage and control the exploration, production, refinement, and transport of oil, as well as the exploration and production of natural gas, in Venezuela[p]
Siemens (Israel)	State-owned Israel Electric Company[q]
Siemens (Italy)	ENEL, an energy company partly owned by the Italian government[r]
TSKJ joint venture	The Nigerian National Petroleum Corporation (NNPC) was a Nigerian government-owned company charged with the development of Nigeria's oil and gas wealth and regulation of the country's oil and gas industry. NNPC was a shareholder in certain joint ventures with multinational oil companies
	Nigeria LNG Limited (NLNG) was created by the Nigerian government to develop the Bonny Island Project and was the entity that awarded the related EPC contracts. The largest shareholder of NLNG was NNPC, which owned 49 % of NLNG. The other owners of NLNG were multinational oil companies[s]
Willbros (Ecuador)	PetroEcuador was Ecuador's state-owned oil and gas company, and PetroComercial was a subsidiary of PetroEcuador engaged in the transportation and commercialization of refined gas products[t]
Utstarcom, Inc.	Government-controlled municipal and provincial telecommunications companies in China;[u] government-controlled telecommunications company in Thailand[v]

[a] Statement of facts in Non-Prosecution Agreement, *In Re Aon Corp.,* 2
[b] Statement of facts in Deferred Prosecution Agreement, *USA v. Alcatel-Lucent SA.,* 6
[c] Statement of facts in Deferred Prosecution Agreement, *USA v. Alcatel-Lucent SA,* 9
[d] Statement of facts in Non-Prosecution Agreements, *In Re Alliance One International, Inc*
[e] Complaint, *SEC v. Avery Dennison Corp.,* 4
[f] Plea Agreement, *USA v. Bridgestone Corp.,* 8 ff
[g] Indictment, 6, *USA v. Stuart Carson et al.,* No cr-00077-JVS (C.D. Ca. April 8 2009)
[h] Statement of facts in Deferred Prosecution Agreement, *USA v. Daimler AG,* 24
[i] Statement of facts in Deferred Prosecution Agreement, *USA v. Daimler AG,* 55
[j] Criminal Information, *USA v. Daimler AG,* 43
[k] Statement of facts in Deferred Prosecution Agreement, *USA v. Daimler AG,* 30
[l] Criminal Information, *USA v. Diaz,* 2
[m] Criminal Information, *USA v. Latin Node, Inc,* 2
[n] Criminal Information, *USA v. Latin Node, Inc.,* 3
[o] Information, *USA v. Magyar Telekom, Plc.,* 4
[p] Statement of facts in Deferred Prosecution Agreement, *USA v. Pride International, Inc.,* 8
[q] Complaint, *SEC v. Siemens Aktiengesellschaft,* 17
[r] Complaint, *SEC v. Siemens Aktiengesellschaft,* 8
[s] Indictment, *USA v. Tesler et al.,* 7
[t] Criminal Information, *USA v. Willbros Group, Inc. and Willbros International, Inc.,* 3
[u] Statement of facts in Non-Prosecution Agreement, *In Re UTStarcom Inc.,* 1
[v] Complaint, *SEC v. UTStarcom, Inc.,* 5

public officials, despite the fact that 51 % of NLNG was owned by a consortium of private multinational oil companies (Koehler 2010b, p. 412).

Equally interesting is the Siemens case in Italy: While the Italian court deemed the employees of Enelpower to be "public officials" under its criminal code,[114] the German court established that the enterprise, although state owned, was not to be considered a public company due to the normal commercial basis that characterized its operations.[115]

In this regard, the Commentaries to the OECD convention clarify that "[a]n official of a public enterprise shall be deemed to perform a public function unless the enterprise operates on a normal commercial basis in the relevant market, i.e., on a basis which is substantially equivalent to that of a private enterprise, without preferential subsidies or other privileges."

In such an unclear legal context, it is helpful to establish a set of factual indicators that are as objective as possible, to allow anybody to clearly distinguish between public and private entities. On this matter, it might be useful to refer to judicial pronunciations in two FCPA cases.

In the Lindsey case (Koehler 2012, p. 4), Judge Matz listed some of the features that combine to identify a public official:

- The entity provides a service to the citizens—indeed, in many cases to all the inhabitants—of the jurisdiction.
- The key officers and directors of the entity are, or are appointed by, government officials.
- The entity is financed, at least in large measure, through governmental appropriations or through revenues obtained as a result of government-mandated taxes, licenses, fees or royalties, such as entrance fees to a national park.
- The entity is vested with and exercises exclusive or controlling power to administer its designated functions.
- The entity is widely perceived and understood to be performing official (i.e., governmental) functions.[116]

In the Control Components case, Judge Selna concluded that recognizing whether someone is a "foreign official" is a factual matter that those assigned to the jury must decide on the basis of the following criteria:

> An instrumentality of a foreign government is any entity through which a foreign government achieves a governmental end or purpose, and can include state-owned entities. In determining whether an entity is an instrumentality of a foreign government, you should consider the following, none of which is exclusive:
>
> 1. the circumstances surrounding the entity's creation;
> 2. the foreign government's characterization of the entity, and whether the entity is widely perceived and understood to be performing official (i.e., governmental) functions;
> 3. whether the governmental end or purpose sought to be achieved is expressed in the policies of the foreign government;

[114] See *Tribunale di Milano*, Giudice per le indagini preliminari Salvini, ordinanza, 27 April 2004.

[115] See *Bundesgerichtshof*, 2 StR 587/07–29 August 2008 (LG Darmstadt).

[116] See Criminal Minutes—General, *USA v. Aguilar, et al.*, 9.

4. the degree of the foreign government's control over the entity, including the foreign government's power to appoint key directors or officers of the entity;
5. the purpose of the entity's activities, including whether the entity provides a service to the citizens of the jurisdiction;
6. the entity's obligations and privileges under the foreign country's law, including whether the entity exercises exclusive or controlling power to administer its designated functions;
7. the status of employees under the foreign government's law, including whether the employees are considered public employees or civil servants;
8. the extent of the foreign government's ownership of the entity, including the level of financial support by the foreign government (e.g., subsidies, special tax treatment, and loans);

These factors are not exclusive, and no single factor is dispositive. In addition, in order to conclude that an entity is an instrumentality of a foreign government, you need not find that all of the factors listed above weigh in favor of such a determination.[117]

10.7 The Use of Intermediaries

A very common feature of foreign bribery case law is the presence of an intermediary, also known as a sponsor or middleman (OECD 2007, p. 38), who usually acts on behalf of the briber or the bribee, or as an instrument of both parties.

The use of intermediaries is habitual among private companies, which hire them to carry out various legitimate services such as dealing with bureaucratic rules, conducting market research, carrying out sales and after-sales services, and taking care of necessary logistical arrangements. Even more frequent is the use of intermediaries in international business transactions, where the enterprises "find themselves in unfamiliar environments with a wide variety of cultural, legal, financial and accounting complexities and obligations" (OECD 2009, p. 5), and where direct representation in the operating market is not always possible. Furthermore, in some countries, hiring a local agent is a legal requirement for foreign companies wishing to operate there (Koehler 2010b, p. 399).

Nevertheless, intermediaries also act in bribery exchanges. In these cases, it has been said that the briber "generally seeks to obscure his or her own identity and expects the intermediary to hold the bribery act and purpose at an arm's-length distance … to reduce the potential frictions and misunderstandings as well as to establish hidden financial circuits in order to prevent judicial complications" (OECD 2007, p. 39). The same can be said for the intermediaries appointed by the bribee.

However, intermediaries often also play a more sophisticated role in corrupt systems. Indeed, as clarified by Della Porta and Vannucci, the middleman "represents a sort of *lubricating oil*, able to arrange meetings and agreements that, in his absence, would be otherwise impossible due to the lack of confidence and the dearth of infor-

[117] See Criminal Minutes—General, *USA v. Stuart Carson et al.*, 5.

mation about the partner characteristics or the quality of the exchanged resources" (2007, p. 148; my translation).

The middleman, it has been argued, knows the level of honesty or corruptness of individual public officers, as well as their price, allowing the client to avoid "the risk of offering bribe to an honest officer and risk of offering to a corrupted officer an amount of bribe lower than his reservation price" (Bayar 2005, p. 277). Della Porta and Vannucci observe that the intermediary's presence is crucial in illegal agreements, where the "inability to appeal to tribunals in order to obtain compliance with the agreements, the risk connected with the identification of the counterparties willing to close a deal, the circumstance that the latter have no scruples and are disposed to violate the law, the difficulties in the collection of information, everything boosts mistrust and uncertainty" (Della Porta and Vannucci 2007, p. 148).

Due the kind of role they play in a bribery scheme, individual intermediaries must have two essential characteristics: On one hand, they need to have "good contacts with persons involved in the attribution of a contract" (OECD 2007, p. 39) or at least with individuals who have an influential position; on the other hand, they must have "the ability to provoke confidence in the others...thus creating expectations of mutual compliance between...clients" (Della Porta and Vanucci 2007, p. 149). This is exemplified by the Siemens case, in which the company allegedly hired both a group of consultants and the former CEO of the Argentinian subsidiary due to the network of contacts that he had developed during his mandate over the previous two decades.[118]

OECD experts catalogue the types of intermediaries involved in bribery cases into three groups: the official's family, friends, and other third persons; intermediaries who do not provide any identifiable service; and intermediaries who provide a combination of legitimate and illegitimate goods and services (OECD 2009, p. 6).

Official's family, friends, and other third persons. In this case, the intermediary is usually nothing but a means for channeling the payment: The company knows the identity of the foreign public official and agrees directly with him or her on the amount of the bribe and the services that the officer will provide. The payment is then made through the intermediary's bank account and justified in the accounting books in one of the ways described above.

Intermediaries of this sort were allegedly used by Siemens in Nigeria,[119] as well as in many other cases.[120]

Intermediaries who do not provide any identifiable service. Often, the middleman is a professional who is officially hired by the company but does not provide any identifiable services other than those necessary for the negotiation and execu-

---

[118] Complaint, *SEC v. Sharef et al.*, 5.

[119] Complaint, *SEC v. Siemens Aktiengesellschaft*, 20.

[120] Statement of facts in Plea Agreement, *USA v. Baker Hughes Svcs. Int'l.*, 6; Information, *USA v. Latin Node, Inc.*, 6 ff.; statement of facts in Deferred Prosecution Agreement, *USA v. Alcatel Lucent S.A*, 21; see "Order instituting public proceedings, imposing a cease-and-desist order, in the matter of American rice," http://www.sec.gov/litigation/admin/34-47286.htm; statement of facts in Deferred Prosecution Agreement, *USA v. Daimler AG*, 19, 25, and 27.

tion of the corrupt agreement. As already shown, this scheme allows the intermediaries to charge the company by raising invoices for sham services so that the illicit payment can be safely recorded in the company's accounting books.

OECD experts explicitly refer to the Siemens case, in which "a Hong Kong–based consultant was hired to work on a power plant contract" even though it was "a clothing company with no expertise in the power generation industry"; in the same case, a Russian consultant was found producing bogus work products, such as a sham traffic study (OECD 2009, p. 7). The OECD final report also refers to the Baker Hughes case, where a local subsidiary entered into a sales representation agreement with a consultant, even though he never provided any services.[121]

Intermediaries who provide a combination of legitimate and illegitimate goods and services. The third category includes intermediaries who perform legitimate services, and can in addition potentially carry out acts of bribery on behalf of their client. In such cases, "the contract price includes the real value of the transaction, the bribe and a percentage fee for the agent" (OECD 2009, p. 8).

Intermediaries can act as natural[122] or legal[123] persons, and can be based in the bribee's country or in the briber's. Sometimes the intermediary could be a shell entity, based in a third country, as purportedly occurred in the cases of Comverse and Mercator Corp.[124] As was set out above, the intermediary can run the negotiation with the public official,[125] as in the case of the Project Group hired by Siemens Argentina, or he can merely serve as a channel for transferring the bribe to the corrupted officer.[126]

[121] Statement of facts in Plea Agreement, *USA v. Baker Hughes Svcs. Int'l.,* 8.

[122] Plea Agreement, *USA v. Tesler*; Statement of facts in Deferred Prosecution Agreement, *USA v. Daimler AG,* 27; statement of facts in Deferred Prosecution Agreement, *USA versus Willbros Group, Inc. and Willbros International, Inc.*, 7.

[123] Superseding Criminal Information, *USA v. Basurto,* 6; statement of facts in Deferred Prosecution Agreement, *USA v. Alcatel-Lucent, SA,* 8 f.; Information, *USA v. BAE Sys. Plc.,* 8; statement of facts in Plea Agreement, *USA v. Baker Hughes Svcs. Int'l.,* 6; Complaint, *SEC v. Comverse Technology, Inc.,* 1; statement of facts in Deferred Prosecution Agreement, *USA v. Daimler AG,* 48; statement of facts in Deferred Prosecution Agreement, *USA v. Willbros Group, Inc. and Willbros International, Inc.,* 6.

[124] Complaint, *SEC v. Comverse Technology, Inc., 4; Indictment, USA v. Giffen,* 11.

[125] Complaint, *SEC v. Akzo Nobel N.V.,* 6; statement of facts in Non-Prosecution Agreement, *In Re Alliance One International, Inc.,* 12; Complaint, *SEC v. Pride International, Inc.,* 15.

[126] Complaint, *SEC v. ABB, Ltd.,* 4; statement of facts in Deferred Prosecution Agreement, *USA v. Alacatel Lucent S.A,* 31; see "Order instituting public proceedings, imposing a cease-and-desist order, in the matter of American rice," http://www.sec.gov/litigation/admin/34-47286.htm; Information, *USA v. BAE Sys. Plc.*, 13; statement of facts in Plea Agreement, *USA v. Baker Hughes Svcs. Int'l.,* 6; Complaint, *SEC v. Comverse Technology, Inc.,* 1.

The most widely used types of intermediaries are consultants[127] and local agents,[128] but the case history also includes accountancy firms,[129] travel agencies,[130] custom brokers,[131] marketing advisers,[132] and subcontractors.[133] Another recurrent method is the use of outside legal counsel fees to disguise bribery payments to public officials as legitimate disbursements.[134]

A remarkable case in this regard is that of Siemens in Argentina, both for the role allegedly played by the former local subsidiary's CEO, said to have been recruited to facilitate the payment of bribes because of his longstanding connections in Argentina,[135] and for the creation of a team of consultants known as the Project Group or the Argentine Consulting Group, which also allegedly included company employees. As reported in the statement of offense, "the Argentine Consulting Group received improperly recorded corrupt payments from Siemens Argentina and its affiliates in connection with the national identity card project, and passed along some portion of those payments to Argentine officials in exchange for improper advantages for SIEMENS ARGENTINA and/or its affiliates."[136]

According to the SEC, the Project Group conducted the negotiation with high-ranking government officials on behalf of Siemens, and was also used as a means of funneling the corrupt payments. The SEC summarizes the facts as follows:

> The Project Group, headquartered in Central and South America, was an informal designation for a collection of entities that served as intermediaries through which Siemens made corrupt payments to Argentine government officials. The Project Group was led and controlled by [C. S.] and included his family members and close associates as principals. The Project Group was created to coordinate the DNI Contract bribe payments and to provide a single point of contact for Siemens in negotiating its bribe payments to Argentine government officials.[137]

[127] Statement of facts in Deferred Prosecution Agreement, *USA v. Alcatel Lucent S.A.*, 34; statement of facts in Deferred Prosecution Agreement, *USA v. Willbros Group, Inc. and Willbros International, Inc.*, 6; Complaint, *SEC v. Sharef et al.*, 11.

[128] Statement of facts in Non-Prosecution Agreement, *In Re Alliance One International, Inc.*, 12; Complaint, *SEC v. ABB, Ltd.*, 4; Plea Agreement, *USA v. Bridgestone Corp.*, 8 ff.; statement of facts in Deferred Prosecution Agreement, *USA v. Daimler AG*, 48; Information, *USA v. Innospec, Inc.*, 2.

[129] Complaint for Permanent Injunction Relief, *USA and SEC. v. KPMG Siddharta Siddharta & Harsono et al.*

[130] Complaint, *SEC v. UTStarcom, Inc.*, 3.

[131] Indictment, *USA s v. Kay*, 3.

[132] Information, *USA v. BAE Sys. Plc.*, 7.

[133] Statement of facts in Deferred Prosecution Agreement, *USA v. Shell Nigeria Exploration and Production Company Ltd.*, 9.

[134] Plea Agreement, *USA v. Tesler*. See also the cases cited in Cregar 2011, 1.

[135] Complaint, *SEC v. Sharef et al.*, 5.

[136] Statement of offense, *USA v. Siemens S.A. (Argentina)*, 4.

[137] Complaint, *SEC v. Sharef et al.*, 8.

The leader of the Project Group, C.S., had been a board member of Siemens Argentina before resigning from the company to be rehired as an outside business consultant.

> In fact, [C.S.]'s primary role was to serve as a payment intermediary between Siemens and Argentine government officials in connection with the DNI Contract. While purporting to act as a business consultant for Siemens Argentina, [C.S.] paid bribes to Argentine government officials on Siemens' behalf.[138]

The Project Group allegedly played a driving role in the bribery scheme, even paying the bribe to public officials in advance, and continuing to serve as an intermediary after the cancellation of the contract.

> Notwithstanding the DNI Contract's cancellation, defendant [C.S.] and the Project Group advised Siemens that the Argentine government officials who had helped Siemens secure the DNI Contract still expected to be paid the bribes they had been promised but had not yet received. [C.S.] also demanded that he be reimbursed for the bribes that he had advanced to government officials on Siemens' behalf. If the payment demands were not met, [C.S.] threatened to go public with corruption allegations against Siemens.[139]

Equally noteworthy is the Daimler case, in which a multitude of third parties were involved, many of them located in the UA.[140]

When a bribery scheme is carried out using intermediaries, questions arise about the extent of knowledge required for the company's managers to be charged. This issue was discussed by the court in the Bourke case, in which the judges deemed the defendants to have arranged a situation of "conscious avoidance," through which "Bourke enabled himself to participate in a bribery scheme without acquiring actual knowledge of the specific conduct at issue" (Koehler 2012, p. 5).

Ultimately, the risk that a foreign consultant or agent may lead to the company becoming involved in an act of bribery reveals the importance for any company hiring such people to carry out accurate due diligence and constantly monitor their activities.

10.8 The Role of the Individual in Bribing Organizations

Assessing the specific role of individuals in bribery schemes is not easy, considering that FCPA actions are largely limited to corporate enforcement: "of the 11 corporate FCPA enforcement actions brought by DOJ in 2011, only three (27 %) have resulted, at present, in related enforcement actions against company employees. Likewise, of the 13 corporate FCPA enforcement actions brought by the SEC in 2011, only two (15 %) have resulted, at present, in related enforcement actions against company employees" (Koehler 2012, p. 3).

[138] Complaint, *SEC v. Sharef et al.*, 8.

[139] Complaint, SEC v. Sharef et al., 12.

[140] Statement of facts in Deferred Prosecution Agreement, *USA v. Daimler AG*. See, for example, page 75, regarding Biotop Group, a Delaware corporation.

However, between 2008 and 2011, approximately 62 individuals were incriminated for an FCPA or related violation, 54 of them as the principal briber, and the rest for their role as intermediaries. These enforcement actions provide useful insights into the role of individuals where bribery occurs within a complex organization.

In bribery cases, experts usually assume that top management is involved. As stated in the OECD report, "experts shared the view that the person paying the bribe rarely acts alone. They suggested that knowledge by senior management and the company's board may be assumed for high value transactions. It can also be presumed that the briber's employer organises the bribe as the contract awarded will benefit the entire company" (OECD 2007, p. 48).

My research seems to confirm this hypothesis: Of 54 individuals charged as bribers, 21 were members of the board of directors or shareholders, and in another 24 cases the individuals were senior managers, including company presidents, CEOs, CFOs, and vice presidents. Examples of such cases include Nature's Sunshine (president, CEO, and CFO),[141] American Rice (president),[142] Terra Telecommunication Corp. (president and executive vice president),[143] Innospec (CEO),[144] Latin Node (CEO and vice-president),[145] KBR (CEO),[146] and Siemens (CFO).[147]

Other senior managers implicated in bribery schemes are often in charge of sales of business development, as set out in Table 10.2.

Equally frequent are cases involving those in financial resources and control management positions, reported in Table 10.3.

Indeed, a much greater range of information could be obtained from the analysis of these cases, which thus constitute an important subject for future studies. It would be very important, for example, to assess the specific role played by each individual in the decision-making process that led to a bribe being paid, with the purpose of identifying the risk of corruption along the chain of command. However, the available documents may not always allow for such assessments.

Analysis of the individuals investigated and sentenced might also further understanding of how responsibility for the crime is distributed between the parent company and local subsidiaries, where present. In my research, I observed that in 43 cases out of 54, the individual charged held a position in the parent company, and that he or she was an employee of a subsidiary in just nine cases. Another interesting feature is that in nine cases the defendant had been the parent company's manager in charge of the country or the geographical zone where the bribery took place.[148]

---

[141] See Complaint, *SEC v. Nature's Sunshine Products, Inc. et al.*

[142] Superseding Indictment, *USA v. Kay and Murphy*.

[143] See Indictment, *USA v. Joel Esquenazi, et al.*

[144] Complaint, *SEC v. Jennings*.

[145] Indictment, *USA v. Granados et al.*

[146] Information, *USA v. Stanley*.

[147] Complaint, *SEC v. Siemens Aktiengesellschaft,* 9.

[148] See SEC v. Elkin et al.; SEC v. Meza; USA v. Carson et al.; USA v. Amoako; SEC v. Summers; USA v. Kay and Murphy; USA v. Young.

Table 10.2 Senior managers implicated in bribery schemes

Case/firm	Position
Armor Holding	Vice president for international sales[a]
Control Component	Vice president for sales in Europe, the Middle East, Africa[b]
Control Component	Director of sales for CCI China and Taiwan[c]
Control Component	Director of worldwide factory sales[d]
Dimon (Alliance)	Senior vice president of sales[e]
Faro Tecnologies	Director of Asia-Pacific sales[f]
Innospec (agent)	Business director[g]
ITXC Corp.	Executive vice president of global sales[h]
KBR (TSKJ)	Commercial vice president[i]
Latin Node	Vice president of business development[j]
Latin Node	Chief commercial officer[k]
Pacific Consolidated	Director of sales and marketing[l]

[a] See *USA v. Bistrong*
[b] See *USA v. Carson et al*
[c] See *USA v. Carson et al*
[d] See *USA v. Covino*
[e] See *SEC v. Elkin et al.*
[f] See *SEC v. Meza*
[g] See *SEC. v. Turner et al*
[h] See *USA v. Ott*
[i] See *USA v. Chodan et al*
[j] See *USA v. Caceres et al*
[k] See *USA v. Vasquez*
[l] See *USA v. Smith*

Table 10.3 Cases involving managers in financial resources and control management positions

Case/firm	Position
Control component	Finance director[a]
Dimon (Alliance)	Corporate controller[b]
Dimon (Alliance)	Regional financial director[c]
Innospec	CEO and CFO[d]
Latin node	CFO[e]
Nature's sunshine	CFO[f]
Siemens	CFO Siemens Business Services[g]
Terra Telecom. Corp	Controller[h]
Willbros	Accounting employee[i]

[a] See *USA v. Morlok*
[b] See *SEC v. Elkin et al*
[c] See *SEC v. Elkin et al*
[d] See *SEC v. Jennings*
[e] See *USA v. Salvoch*
[f] See *SEC v. Nature's Sunshine Products, Inc. et al*
[g] See *SEC v. Sharef et al*
[h] See *USA v. Perez*
[i] See *SEC v. Willbros Group, Inc*

This information calls for recognition of the significant role played by the parent company in the country of origin, even when the company carries out its operations in the host country through a local subsidiary. All the same, the data might also be explained by reference to the selection process operated by enforcement agencies in their application of the relevant law.

10.9 How the Conduct was Discovered

In most of the cases studied, the discovery of the bribery was prompted by a so-called trigger event which drew the attention of law enforcement agencies and regulatory authorities. A relevant number of cases were first discovered thanks to the voluntarily disclosure of the company itself, which had usually acquired knowledge of the wrongdoing through an internal investigation and later disclosed it to the DOJ or SEC. This process was mostly the result of the "carrot and stick" approach that shapes the Principles of Federal Prosecution of Business Organization and the US Sentencing Guidelines for Organizations, although some scholars have expressed doubts about how convenient it is for a company to submit a self-disclosure (Koehler 2012, p. 2).[149]

For example, in the case of UTStarcom, after the company's audit committee learned of alleged bribe payments in Mongolia, it conducted an internal investigation into potential FCPA violations throughout its operations worldwide, and later disclosed its findings to the DOJ and the SEC.[150] In the American Rice case, the existence of improper payment practices was discovered by the new board that was nominated after the company's bankruptcy, who decided to fire the consultants and the vice president of operations and to disclose the misconduct to the DOJ and the SEC.[151] Another company that decided to disclose violations of the FCPA to the DOJ and the SEC was Pride International. The company describes how the facts where discovered and disclosed as follows:

> During the course of an internal audit and investigation relating to certain of our Latin American operations, our management and internal audit department received allegations of improper payments to foreign government officials. In February 2006, the Audit Committee of our Board of Directors assumed direct responsibility over the investigation and retained independent outside counsel to investigate the allegations, as well as corresponding accounting entries and internal control issues, and to advise the Audit Committee.

[149] See also Koehler (2010a, 926n63): "voluntary disclosure means a company's lawyer picks up the phone and calls the DOJ to schedule a meeting during which the lawyer will disclose conduct that could potentially implicate the FCPA even though the enforcement agencies, in many cases, would never find out about the conduct."

[150] Complaint, *SEC v. UTStarcom, Inc.*; statement of facts in Non-Prosecution Agreement, *In Re UTStarcom Inc.*

[151] See "Order instituting public proceedings, imposing a cease-and-desist order, in the matter of American rice," SEC.

> The investigation, which is continuing, has found evidence suggesting that payments, which may violate the U.S. Foreign Corrupt Practices Act, were made to government officials in Venezuela and Mexico aggregating less than $ 1 million….
>
> We voluntarily disclosed information relating to the initial allegations and other information found in the investigation and compliance review to the DOJ and the SEC, and we have cooperated and continue to cooperate with these authorities.[152]

Sometimes, the trigger event is an internal report submitted by an employee. The case of Helmerich & Payne (H&P) in Argentina shows how this can occur, and emphasizes the multiple purposes that anti-bribery communications and training can serve within a corporate compliance program.

> In early 2008, as part of an effort to improve compliance with the FCPA, H&P designed and implemented a stand-alone set of FCPA policies and procedures. In conjunction with this effort, H&P also designed and conducted worldwide FCPA training for its key employees. At one such training session in May 2008, an employee voluntarily disclosed that potentially improper payments had been made by H&P Argentina, through a customs broker, to Argentine customs officials. This information was relayed to H&P's corporate headquarters in Oklahoma, and came to the attention of H&P's general counsel in July 2008. In response, H&P hired outside FCPA counsel and independent forensic accountants to conduct an internal investigation of its subsidiaries' customs payment practices in a number of Latin American countries.[153]

A major source of information might now be represented by whistle-blower revelations, especially after the introduction of significant bounty provisions in 2010 with the approval of the Dodd-Frank Act.[154] It would obviously be premature to expect to find evidence of these new provisions having taken effect. At this moment, we can only rely on the information disclosed by the SEC in its 2012 Annual Report, which makes mention of 115 whistle-blower tips received from all over the world about FCPA violations in the 2012 fiscal year (SEC 2012, Appendix A).

In any case, whistle-blower revelations led to FCPA investigations even before the introduction of the Dodd-Frank Act. This occurred, for example, in the BAE Systems case, where "a whistleblower's 2004 claim that the company had a $ 120 million bribery fund to facilitate defense contracts triggered the U.K. Serious Fraud Office's investigation" (Ryznar and Korkor 2011, p. 415).

The SEC investigations into the Daimler case also originated from a whistle-blower revelation. The information is reported as follows by the company itself:

---

[152] See *Notes to Unaudited Consolidated Financial Statements,* in Pride International Inc., Quarterly Report Pursuant to Sect. 13 or 15(d) of the Securities Exchange Act of 1934 for the Quarterly Period ended September 30, 2009, dated November 2, 2009, 24.

[153] Cease and Desist Order, *SEC v. Helmerich & Payne, Inc.*

[154] See Sect. 922 of the Dodd-Frank Wall Street Reform and Consumer Protection Act that, among other things, added Sect. 21(F)(3), entitled "Securities Whistleblower Incentives and Protection," to the Securities Exchange Act of 1934. The amendment directs the SEC to make monetary awards to eligible individuals who voluntarily provide original information that leads to successful SEC enforcement actions resulting in the imposition of monetary sanctions over $ 1 million (SEC 2012, Appendix A).

> In August 2004, the Securities and Exchange Commission ("SEC") notified DaimlerChrysler AG that it has opened an investigation relating to our compliance with the U.S. Foreign Corrupt Practices Act. The investigation follows the filing of a "whistleblower" complaint with the U.S. Department of Labor ("DOL") under the Sarbanes-Oxley Act by a former employee of our wholly-owned subsidiary DaimlerChrysler Corporation whose employment was terminated in 2004. The terminated employee filed a lawsuit against DaimlerChrysler Corporation in the U.S. District Court for the Eastern District of Michigan in September 2004 which contains substantially the same allegations as in the DOL complaint and additional allegations relating to other federal and state law claims arising from the termination. In November, the DOL dismissed the complaint because it found no reasonable cause to believe that the employee was terminated in violation of the Sarbanes-Oxley Act. DaimlerChrysler is providing information to the SEC in cooperation with its investigation.[155]

In some instances, the misconduct was discovered through an undercover investigation. In the Tannenbaum case, for example, after receiving information from a confidential informant, an FBI special agent posing as a foreign government procurement official arranged a meeting with the businessman. As reported in the complaint, during this meeting the defendant "offered to make a payment to the [Special Agent], who was posing as an official of the Government of Argentina, to obtain business, namely, a contract for the sale of a garbage incinerator to the Government of Argentina."[156] Undercover agents operated also in the Saint Regis University investigation.[157]

The largest FCPA undercover sting investigation, however, was the one that led to the arrest of more than 20 individuals in 2010. The DOJ and FBI orchestrated a large-scale scheme in which undercover agents posed as representatives and sales agents of the minister of defense of an African country. The operation caused the defendants to enter into a corruption agreement with the presumed ministerial representative to secure contracts for the sale of military and law enforcement equipment. As stated in the DOJ press release:

> The indictments allege that the defendants engaged in a scheme to pay bribes to the minister of defense for a country in Africa. In fact, the scheme was part of the undercover operation, with no actual involvement from any minister of defense. As part of the undercover operation, the defendants allegedly agreed to pay a 20 % "commission" to a sales agent who the defendants believed represented the minister of defense for a country in Africa in order to win a portion of a $ 15 million deal to outfit the country's presidential guard. In reality, the "sales agent" was an undercover FBI agent. The defendants were told that half of that "commission" would be paid directly to the minister of defense. The defendants allegedly agreed to create two price quotations in connection with the deals, with one quote representing the true cost of the goods and the second quote representing the true cost, plus the 20 % "commission." The defendants also allegedly agreed to engage in a small "test" deal to show the minister of defense that he would personally receive the 10 % bribe. (DOJ 2010)

---

[155] See "Notes to Consolidated Financial Statements," in DaimlerChrysler AG and Subsidiaries, Annual Report Pursuant to Sect. 13 or 15(D) of the Securities Exchange Act of 1934 for the Fiscal Year Ended December 31, 2004, 73.

[156] See Complaint, *USA v. Tannenbaum*.

[157] See Indictment, *USA v. Randock et al.*

Nevertheless, it must be highlighted that the entire investigation raised concerns about how the case was investigated and how the prosecutors handled informants and evidence. In fact, the trials against the defendants eventually resulted in the government filing a motion to dismiss, resolving what the judge has defined as "a long and sad chapter in the annals of white collar criminal enforcement."[158]

Finally, in addition to FCPA violations, many cases involved charges for the offense of money laundering. This supports the opinion that the systems implemented by national legislators and private entities in the last decades to prevent money laundering might have a primary role in the detection and reduction of bribery practices on both the demand and supply sides of the corrupt relationship (Sharman and Chaikin 2009, p. 27).

10.10 Final Remarks

To design an effective set of organizational anti-bribery measures and rules, it is essential to acquire full knowledge of the empirical features of bribery practices. As bribery, like most criminal phenomena, cannot be directly observed, I decided to analyze documents related to FCPA enforcement actions, with the aim of determining the most common features of multinational corporations' practices in bribing foreign public officials. Despite the limitations that characterized the chosen source of information, as accounted for in the opening section, I believe such empirical analysis and systematization can serve as useful tools in the creation of a compliance program.

The purpose of this chapter was therefore to draw from this kind of investigation all the elements of international bribery that must be taken into account when designing new preventive corporate structures and practices.

I began by discussing the nature and value of the bribes, noting that even though cash payments are still prominent among bribing companies, in order to avoid detection, other forms of compensation are increasingly used, such as covering travel expenses to tourist destinations, luxury gifts and entertainment, offering full employment to the corrupt official and his or her relatives, or covering course tuition fees and expenses.

As a second step, I analyzed the briber's pursued advantage, finding a huge variety of goals. While the most common purpose is to secure high-value contracts for supplies or for public works, I also found evidence of bribes paid to secure favorable results in tax controls, to enable the import of irregular goods or simply to facilitate customs procedures, and to obtain authorizations and accreditations. Bribing companies also sought to achieve an advantage over competitors by obtaining confidential or classified information, an unfavorable test result for competitor products, an adjustment in the rules of a public tender, or discounted fees to use public infrastructures.

[158] See Transcript of Status Conference, *USA v. Goncalves* (Feb. 21, 2012).

Section 5 examined the financial aspects of bribery. I first discussed the methods adopted to obtain the money necessary to compensate the public official, with specific reference to the creation of slush funds, the overpricing of the services provided to the public customer, and the use of legitimate funds to pay invoices submitted by third parties for totally or partially sham services.

I went on to illustrate the huge variety of means used to funnel the money without drawing the attention of control agencies, making detailed reference to specific cases that are illuminating in this regard. One notable feature that came to light as part of this process was the central role played by intermediaries, usually hired as agents or consultants; also noteworthy was the use of secret accounts for cash payments, and the simulation of arbitration with the sole intent of settling the dispute and thus creating a legal basis on which to make a payment. Nevertheless, the most important finding here is that no definitive list of payment methods exists: On the contrary, bribers and bribees are always looking for new—and often creative—ways to evade discovery, and as a consequence, internal controls cannot be directed only towards the most common and best-known techniques.

I then specifically assessed the problem of how corrupted payments are disguised in the company's books and records, trying to build a list of the varied expressions or phrases commonly used to divert controls. Consistent with previous findings on the participation of third parties as consultants or intermediaries, in most cases the use of vague terms like "commissions" or "payments" for consulting or other general services was documented.

In the section that followed, I analyzed the qualifications and functions of corrupt public officials, discovering that nearly every category usually included in legal definitions of "public official" is present in the set of examined cases. In particular, I noted the recurrence of bribery payments in favor of high-ranking members of national governments, and I discussed the problems related to the fact that the employees of state-owned enterprises are frequently beneficiaries of bribery agreements.

Sections 7 and 8 were dedicated to the study of the role played in bribery schemes by intermediaries and by managers or employees of the incriminated company. With regard to intermediaries, I found that their participation in bribery schemes is not limited to serving as a conduit through which payments can be funneled; rather, they often negotiate in the name of the briber or of the bribee, guaranteeing that they will fulfill the terms of the agreement, and even paying the amount of the bribe to the corrupt official in advance. In addition, I found that they usually act or simply appear to act as consultants, local agents, custom brokers, marketing advisers, and other kinds of outside agents.

With regard to the individuals involved, I assessed their position in the company's organizational chart, and learnt that—at least in foreign bribery cases—a member of the board of directors or a senior manager almost always participates in or is well aware of the ongoing bribery scheme.

Finally, I collected information about the ways in which the bribery cases examined have come to the attention of enforcement agencies. In this regard, I found that, at least in the USA, a major source of information can be the company itself, when it decides to disclose the misconduct to enforcement agencies. Knowledge of the facts is generally acquired through an internal investigation, prompted by a trigger event that is most likely the submission of an internal report by an employee.

The systematization of the information about bribery practices collected in the course of my research may serve as an important tool for compliance program designers: In fact, it represents a strong empirical basis both for the risk-assessment process and for the structuring of internal preventive protocols and procedures. It therefore constitutes a major source of empirical knowledge for the theoretical elaboration and practical construction of the ABC Model.

Table of FCPA Enforcement Actions

In Re Alliance One International, Inc. (Aug. 6, 2010)
In Re Aon Corp. (Dec. 20, 2011)
In Re Faro Technologies, Inc. (June 4, 2008)
In Re Helmerich & Payne, Inc. (July 29, 2009)
In Re UTStarcom Inc. (Dec. 31, 2009)
In Re Westinghouse Air Brake Technologies Corporation. (Feb. 14, 2008)
In the Matter of American Rice, Inc., et al., Admin. Proc. File No. 3–11024. (Sec. Ex. Act Rel. 47286/AAER No. 1710/January 30, 2003)
In the Matter of Baker Hughes Inc., SEC Administrative Proceeding File No. 3–10572. (2001)
SEC v. ABB, Ltd., No. 10-cv-1648. (D.D.C. Sept. 29, 2010)
SEC v. Akzo Nobel N.V., No. 07-02293. (D.C. Cir. 2008)
SEC v. Alliance One International, Inc., No. 10-cv-1319. (D.D.C. Aug. 6, 2010)
SEC v. Avery Dennison Corp., No. CV09- 5493. (C.D. Ca. July 28 2009)
SEC v. BellSouth Corp., No. 02–0113. (N.D. Ga. 2002)
SEC v. Comverse Technology, Inc., No. 11-cv-1704. (E.D.N.Y. 2011)
SEC v. Elkin et al., No. 1:10-cv-00661. (D.D.C. Apr. 28, 2010)
SEC v. Helmerich & Payne, Inc. (July 30, 2009)
SEC v. Innospec, Inc., 1:10-cv-00448. (D.D.C. 2010)
SEC v. Jennings, No.1:11-cv-00144. (D.D.C. 2011)
SEC v. Johnson & Johnson, No. 11-cv-686. (D.D.C. Apr. 8, 2011)
SEC v. Magyar Telekom Plc., et al., No. 11-cv-9646. (S.D.N.Y. Dec. 29, 2011)
SEC v. Meza, No. 1:09–01648. (D.D.C. 2009)
SEC v. Monsanto Co., No. 05-cv-14. (D.D.C. Jan. 6, 2005)
SEC v. Nature's Sunshine Products, Inc. et al., No. 09–0672. (D. Utah 2009)
SEC v. Pride International, Inc., Civil Action No. 4:10-cv-4335. (S.D. Texas, November 4, 2010)
SEC v. Sharef et al., n. 11-CIV-9073. (S.D.N.Y. Dec. 13 2011)
SEC v. Siemens Aktiengesellschaft, Civil Action No. 08 CV 02167. (D.D.C. December 12, 2008)
SEC v. Summers, No. 04:10-cv-02786. (S.D. Tex. 2010)
SEC v. UTStarcom, Inc., No. 09-cv-6094. (N.D. Cal., Dec. 31, 2009)

SEC v. Willbros Group, Inc., No. 4:08-cv-01494. (S.D. Tex. 2008)
SEC vs. Aon Corporation, Civil Action No. 1:11-cv-02256. (D.D.C. 2011)
SEC. v. Turner et al., No. 1:10-cv-01309. (D.D.C. 2010)
United States and SEC. v. KPMG Siddharta Siddharta & Harsono et al., Civ. No. 4:01-cv-03105. (S.D. Tex. 2001)
United States v. Aguilar, et al., No. 10-cr-1031. (C.D. Cal. October 21, 2010)
United States v. Alcatel-Lucent France, S.A., Alcatel-Lucent Trade International, A.G., and Alcatel Centroamerica S.A., No. 10-cr-20906. (S.D. Fla. 2010)
United States v. Alcatel-Lucent, SA, No. 10–20907. (S.D. Fla. December 27, 2010)
United States v. Amoako, No. 05–1122. (D.N.J. 2007)
United States v. BAE Sys. Plc., No. 10-cr-35. (D.D.C. Mar. 1, 2010)
United States v. Baker Hughes Svcs. Int'l, No. 07-cr-129. (S.D. Tex. Apr. 11, 2007)
United States v. Basurto, No. 09-cr-00325. (S.D. Tex., June 10, 2009)
United States v. Biomet, Inc., No. 1:12-cr-00080. (D.D.C. 2012)
United States v. Bistrong, No. 1:10-cr-0021. (D.D.C. 2010)
United States v. Bourke, No. 05-cr-518. (S.D.N.Y. July 2009)
United States v. Bridgestone Corp., No. 11-cr-00651. (S.D. Tx. October 5, 2011)
United States v. Caceres et al., No. 1:10-CR-20881. (S.D. Fla. 2010)
United States v. Carson et al., No cr-00077-JVS. (C.D. Ca. April 8 2009)
United States v. Chodan et al., No. 09-098 (S.D. Tex. 2009)
United States v. Control Components, Inc., No. 09-cr-162. (C.D. Cal. July 22, 2009)
United States v. Covino, No. 08-336. (C.D. Ca. 2008)
United States v. Daimler AG, No. 10-cr-63. (D.D.C. Mar. 22, 2010)
United States v. DaimlerChrysler Automotive Russia SAO, No. 10-cr-54. (D.D.C. 2010)
United States v. DaimlerChrysler China Ltd., No. 10-cr-66. (D.D.C. 2010)
United States v. Diaz, No. 09-cr-20346-JEM. (S.D. Flo. April 22, 2009).
United States v. Esquenazi, et al., n. 09-CR-21010. (S.D.Fla. 2009)
United States v. Giffen, No. 03-cr-663. (S.D.N.Y. 2003)
United States v. Goncalves, No. 09-cr-335. (D.D.C. 2009)
United States v. Granados, et al., No.10-20881. (S.D. Fla. 2010)
United States v. Innospec, Inc., 10-cr-00061. (D.D.C. 2010)
United States v. JGC Corp., No. 11-cr-260. (S.D. Tex. Apr. 6, 2011)
United States v. Johnson & Johnson, n. 1:11-cr-00099. (D.D.C. Aug. 4, 2011)
United States v. Kay and Murphy, No. 01-cr-914. (S.D. Tex. Oct. 6, 2004)
United States v. Kellogg Brown & Root LLC, No. 09-cr-71. (S.D. Tex. Feb. 6, 2009)
United States v. Latin Node, Inc., No. 09-CR-20239-PCH. (S.D. Fla. March 23, 2009)
United States v. Lindsey Manufacturing Company et al., No. 2:10-cr-01031-AHM. (C.D. of Cal. April 20, 2011)
United States v. Magyar Telekom, Plc., No. 11-cr-597. (E.D. Va. Dec. 29, 2011)
United States v. Maxwell Technologies Inc., No. 11-cr-329. (S.D. Cal. Jan. 31, 2011)
United States v. Morlok, No. 09–05. (C.D. Ca. 2009)
United States v. Novak, No. 05-CR-180-LRS. (E.D. Wa. March 2005)
United States v. Ott, No. 07–0608. (D.N.J. 2008)

United States v. Perez, 1:09-cr-20347-JEM. (S.D. Fla. 2009)
United States v. Pride International, Inc., No. 10-CR-766. (S.D. Tex. November 4, 2010)
United States v. Randock et al., No. 05–180-LRS-3. (E.D. Wa. March 2005)
United States v. Salvoch, No. 10–20893. (S.D. Fla 2010)
United States v. Shell Nigeria Exploration and Production Company Ltd., No. 4:10-cr-767. (S. D. Tex. 2010)
United States v. Siemens S.A. (Argentina), No. 08-CR-368. (D.D.C Dec. 15 2008)
United States v. Smith, No. 8:07-cr-00069. (C.D. Ca. 2007)
United States v. Snamprogetti Netherlands B.V., No. 10-cr-460. (S.D. Tex. Jul. 7, 2010)
United States v. Stanley, No. 08-cr-597. (S.D. Tex. 2008)
United States v. Tannenbaum, 1:98-cr-00784. (S.D.N.Y. 1998)
United States v. Tesler et al., No. 09-CR-098. (S.D. Tx. February 17, 2009)
United States v. Tidewater Marine Int'l, Inc., No. 4:10-cr-770. (S.D. Tex. 2010)
United States v. Vasquez, 10-CR-20894. (S.D. Fla. 2010)
United States v. Willbros Group, Inc. and Willbros International, Inc., No. 4:08-cr-028. (S.D. Tex. May 14, 2008)
United States v. Young, No. 07-0609. (D.N.J. 2008)

References

Andelman, D. A. (1998). Bribery: The new global outlaw. *Management Review, 87*(4), 49–51.
Bayar, G. (2005). The role of intermediaries in corruption. *Public Choice, 122,* 277–298.
Brown, L. (2001). Extraterritorial jurisdiction under the 1998 amendments to the Foreign Corrupt Practices Act: Does the government's reach now exceed its grasp? *North Carolina Journal of International Law and Commercial Regulation, 26,* 239–260.
Calderon, R., Álvarez-Arce, J. L., & Mayoral, S. (2009). Corporation as a crucial ally against corruption. *Journal of Business Ethics, 87*(1), 319–332.
Cregar, Z. D. (2011). Foreign corruption by payment of legal bills: Guidance on proactive detection of FCPA violations via payments to outside legal counsel. *Duquesne Business Law Journal, 14,* 1–143.
Davigo, P., & Mannozzi, G. (2007). *La corruzione in Italia: Percezione sociale e controllo penale*. Roma: Laterza.
Della Porta, D., & Vannucci, A. (2007). *Mani impunite: Vecchia e nuova corruzione in Italia.* Roma: Laterza.
DOJ [US Department of Justice]. (1997). *United States attorneys' manual.* http://www.justice.gov/usao/eousa/foia_reading_room/usam/. Accessed 28 June 2013.
DOJ [US Department of Justice]. (2005). U.S. announces charges in massive scheme to bribe senior government officials in the Republic of Azerbaijan. Press Release, 6 October. http://www.justice.gov/usao/nys/pressreleases/October05/kozenyetalindictmentpr.pdf. Accessed 28 June 2013.
DOJ [US Department of Justice]. (2010). Twenty-two executives and employees of military and law enforcement products companies charged in foreign bribery scheme. Press Release, 19 January. http://www.justice.gov/opa/pr/2010/January/10-crm-048.html. Accessed 28 June 2013.

DOJ & SEC [US Department of Justice, Criminal Division and US Securities and Exchange Commission, Enforcement Division]. (2012). A resource guide to the U.S. Foreign Corrupt Practices Act. http://www.sec.gov/spotlight/fcpa/fcpa-resource-guide.pdf. Accessed 28 June 2013.

Finder, L. D., McConnell, R. D., & Mitchell, S. L. (2009). Betting the corporation: Compliance or defiance? Compliance programs in the context of deferred and non-prosecution agreements—Corporate pre-trial agreement update—2008. *Corporate Counsel Review* 28. http://papers.ssrn.com/sol3/papers.cfm?abstract_id=1332033. Accessed 8 October 2013.

Flyvbjerg, B., & Molloy, E. (2011). Delusion, deception and corruption in major infrastructure projects: Causes, consequences and cures. In S. Rose-Ackermane, et al. (Eds.), *International handbook on the economics of corruption, volume two*. Cheltenham: Edward Elgar Publishing.

Forti, G. (2000). *L'immane concretezza: Metamorfosi del crimine e controllo penale*. Milano: Raffaello Cortina Editore.

Forti, G. (2003). Il diritto penale e il problema della corruzione, dieci anni dopo. In G. Forti (Ed.), *Il prezzo della tangente: La corruzione come sistema a dieci anni da "mani pulite"*. Milano: Vita e Pensiero.

Forti, G. (2007). Civic education in universities: Understanding the need for rules. In N. Passas, et al. (Eds.), *The United Nations convention against corruption as a way of life*. Milan: ISPAC.

Géneaux, M. (2004). Social sciences and the evolving concept of corruption. *Crime, Law and Social Change, 42*(1), 13–24.

Greenblum, B. M. (2005). What happens to a prosecution deferred? Judicial oversight of corporate deferred prosecution agreements. *Columbia Law Review, 105*(6), 1863–1904.

Hall, R. F. (2009). Deferred prosecution and non-prosecution agreements. In J. T. O'Reilly, et al. (Eds.), *Punishing corporate crime: Legal penalties for criminal and regulatory violations*. Oxford: Oxford University Press.

Henning, P. J. (2007). The organizational guidelines: R.I.P.? *Yale Law Journal Pocket Part, 116*(2007), 312–316.

Johansen, P. O. (2010). An invoice for all seasons. *Journal of Scandinavian Studies in Criminology and Crime Prevention, 11*(1), 86–99.

Koehler, M. (2010a). The façade of FCPA enforcement. *Georgetown Journal of International Law, 41*(4), 907.

Koehler, M. (2010b). The Foreign Corrupt Practices Act in the ultimate year of its decade of resurgence. *Indiana Law Review, 43*(2), 389–422.

Koehler, M. (2012). 2011 Foreign Corrupt Practices Act year in review: Scrutiny, reform, and individual prosecutions are key issues. *White Collar Crime Report* 7.

Law Commission. (2011). *The law commission, consultation paper no. 185: Reforming bribery*. London: Stationery Office. http://lawcommission.justice.gov.uk/docs/cp185_Reforming_Bribery_report.pdf. Accessed 28 June 2013.

Lindsey, C. (2009). More than you bargained for: Successor liability under the U.S. Foreign Corrupt Practices Act. *Ohio Northern University Law Review, 35*, 959–986.

Mark, G. (2012). Private FCPA enforcement action. *American Business Law Journal, 49*(3), 419–506.

OECD. (1997). Commentaries on convention on combating bribery of foreign public officials in international business transactions. http://www.justice.gov/criminal/fraud/fcpa/docs/combatbribe2.pdf. Accessed 28 June 2013.

OECD. (2004). *Implementing the OECD Anti-Bribery Convention: Report on the United States 2003*. Paris: OECD. doi:10.1787/9789264101142-en.

OECD. (2007). *Bribery in public procurement, methods, actors and counter-measures*. Paris: OECD. http://www.oecd.org/investment/anti-bribery/anti-briberyconvention/44956834.pdf. Accessed 28 June 2013.

OECD. (2009). *Typologies on the role of intermediaries in international business transactions, final report, 9 October 2009*. Paris: OECD. http://www.oecd.org/investment/anti-bribery/anti-briberyconvention/43879503.pdf. Accessed 28 June 2013.

OECD. (2011). OECD Convention on Combating Bribery of Foreign Public Officials in International Business Transactions and related documents. http://www.oecd.org/corruption/oecdantibriberyconvention.htm. Accessed 28 June 2013.

Oesterle, D. A. (2004). Early observations on the prosecutions of the business scandals of 2003–03: On sideshow prosecutions, Spitzer's clash with Donaldson over turf, the choice of civil or criminal actions, and the tough tactic of coerced cooperation. *Ohio State Journal of Criminal Law, 1,* 443–485.

Orland, L. (2006). The transformation of corporate criminal law. *Brooklyn Journal of Corporate, Financial & Commercial Law, 1,* 45–86.

Pieth, M. (2011). *Harmonising anti-corruption compliance: The OECD practice guidance 2010.* Zürich: Dike.

Rabl, T. (2008). *Private corruption and its actors: Insight into the subjective decision making processes.* Lengerich: Pabst Science.

Ryznar, M., & Korkor, S. (2011). Anti-bribery legislation in the United States and United Kingdom: A comparative analysis of scope and sentencing. *Missouri Law Review, 76*(2), 415–453.

SEC [US Securities and Exchange Commission]. (2012). *Annual report on the Dodd-Frank whistleblower program, fiscal year 2012.* http://www.sec.gov/about/offices/owb/annual-report-2012.pdf. Accessed 28 June 2013.

SFO [Serious Fraud Office]. (2010). BAE fined in Tanzania defence contract case. Press Release, 21 December. http://www.sfo.gov.uk/press-room/press-release-archive/press-releases-2010/bae-fined-in-tanzania-defence-contract-case.aspx. Accessed 28 June 2013.

Sharman, J. C., & Chaikin, D. (2009). Corruption and anti-money-laundering systems: Putting a luxury good to work. *Governance, 22*(1), 27–45.

Shihata, I. (1997). Corruption: A general review with an emphasis on the role of the World Bank. *Journal of Financial Crime, 5*(1), 12–29.

Spahn, E. (2010). Nobody gets hurt? *Georgetown Journal of International Law, 41,* 861–905.

Spalding, A. B. (2010). Unwitting sanctions: Understanding anti-bribery legislation as economic sanctions against emerging markets. *Florida Law Review, 62,* 351–427.

Spivack, P., & Raman, S. (2008). Regulating the "new regulators": Current trends in deferred prosecution agreements. *American Criminal Law Review, 45,* 176–190.

Thompson, B., & Yong, A. (2012). Corporate criminal liability. *American Criminal Law Review, 49*(2), 489–522.

TRACE. (2013). TRACE Compendium. http://www.traceinternational.org/Knowledge/Compendium.html. Accessed 28 June 2013.

Transparency International. (2008). *Bribe payers index 2008.* Berlin: Transparency International. http://archive.transparency.org/policy_research/surveys_indices/bpi/bpi_2008. Accessed 28 June 2013.

Transparency International. (2011). *Bribe payers index 2011.* Berlin: Transparency International. http://www.transparency.org/whatwedo/pub/bpi_2011. Accessed 28 June 2013.

UNODC [United Nations Office on Drugs and Crime]. (2004). *United Nations convention against corruption.* New York: United Nations. http://www.unodc.org/documents/treaties/UNCAC/Publications/Convention/08-50026_E.pdf. Accessed 28 June 2013.

UNODC [United Nations Office on Drugs and Crime]. (2006). *Legislative guide for the implementation of the United Nations convention against corruption.* New York: United Nations. http://www.unodc.org/documents/treaties/UNCAC/Publications/LegislativeGuide/UNCAC_Legislative_Guide_E.pdf. Accessed 28 June 2013.

US Courts. (2010). *Federal rules of criminal procedure.* Washington: US Government Printing Office. http://www.uscourts.gov/uscourts/RulesAndPolicies/rules/2010%20Rules/Criminal%20Procedure.pdf. Accessed 28 June 2013.

US Government Accountability Office. (2009). Corporate crime: DOJ has taken steps to better track its use of deferred and non-prosecution agreements, but should evaluate effectiveness. http://www.gao.gov/new.items/d10110.pdf. Accessed 28 June 2013.

Vannucci, A. (2003). La corruzione nel sistema politico italiano a dieci anni da "mani pulite." In G. Forti (Ed.), *Il prezzo della tangente: La corruzione come sistema a dieci anni da "mani pulite"*. Milano: Vita e Pensiero.

Weismann, M. F. (2009). The Foreign Corrupt Practices Act: The failure of the self-regulatory model of corporate governance in the global business environment. *Journal of Business Ethics, 88*(4), 615–661.

Wray, C. A., & Hur, R. K. (2006). Corporate criminal prosecution in a post-Enron World: The Thompson Memo in theory and practice. *American Criminal Law Review, 43*(3), 1095–1188.

[illegible]

Part IV
The ABC Model and International Legal Framework: Rules, Controls, and Sanctions

Chapter 11
Corporate Anti-Bribery Self-Regulation and the International Legal Framework

Juliette Tricot

Contents

J. Tricot (✉)
University Paris Ouest Nanterre La Défense, France
e-mail: j.tricot@u-paris10.fr

S. Manacorda et al. (eds.), *Preventing Corporate Corruption*,
DOI 10.1007/978-3-319-04480-4_11, © Springer International Publishing Switzerland 2014

11.1 Introduction: The Internationalization of Anticorruption Strategies

The international framework on corruption has two faces. It is commonly presented as a success story: Commentators point to the ever-growing quantity and diversity of the norms, actions, and initiatives at global or regional levels, by way of evidence that the fight against corruption is a "model" of successful internationalization of (criminal) law. Nearly all the international organizations have added fighting corruption to their agenda, and international standards have progressively solidified. However, as soon as one tries to clarify and map this framework, another reality arises—not entirely divergent from nor in contradiction with the former, but different nevertheless. To say the least, a glance at the international legal framework on corruption reveals a complex and evolving picture. Thus, if one is to understand it, it appears necessary to look deeper than the success story.

The observer is confronted with a general framework which, after a number of failed attempts and setbacks followed by successful initiatives, seems to be settled as regards its general features. Yet the details of the picture keep changing. As a result, a proper understanding of the international framework on corruption must overcome the necessity for constant follow-up of an increasing number of actors and actions, combined with the difficulty of articulating legal instruments of strikingly different natures, forms, and scopes—multiple instruments that are intertwined yet distinct. Even at this stage, the challenges of consistency and effectiveness represent a complex nest of issues which blurs the image of a simple success story.

In fact, a new era may already have started, one which is based upon this success story but which takes account of the limitations of the preceding phase. Progress notwithstanding, however, much remains to be done. In particular, the consolidation of the international legal framework has been insufficient, and has failed to curb corruption. Criminalization, and traditional legal instruments more generally, seems to have revealed its limit in the present globalized environment. However, the common will remains set upon greater accountability for the actors—and "beneficiaries"—of globalization. This new chapter in the international anticorruption enterprise is based on several shifts in strategies and methods which are designed to reach a goal that has also transformed itself along the way. Just as the last 30 years had witnessed a fundamental change in the approach to fighting corruption, from a focus on the demand-side to the supply-side of corruption and from domestic corruption to transnational corruption, at present the attention has shifted from a repressive and reactive approach to preventive actions, from prescription to effective enforcement. At no phase, however, do the changes exclude or abandon former concerns; rather, it is the order of priority that is modified.

Today the horizon remains to a large extent constituted by criminal law mechanisms and norms. However, the focus has shifted from ex post condemnation and sanction to ex ante prevention and compliance, which means not only special attention on the private sector, but also new roles and functions for the private sector. Notably, it means that the law-making process now includes diverse forms of privatization: In the absence of a global governance structure,[1] the traditional system of public international negotiation is more and more combined with self-regulation and self-discipline. This contributes to the increasing and evolving nature of the legal framework; but, more importantly, it implies new actors (Sect. 2), new actions (Sect. 3), and new enforcement mechanisms (Sect. 4) within the international legal framework on corruption.

11.2 The Private Sector and the International Anticorruption Institutional Framework: New actors Within a Multilevel Institutional Framework

The history of the internationalization of anticorruption tools is well known:[2] the attempts—and failures—of the 1970s and 1980s; the crucial role of the US legislature; and finally the growing successes since the mid-1990s. Since then, and especially recently, the process of internationalization of the so-called fight against corruption has had three major characteristics: first, the spread of actions targeting corruption, leading to the abundance—and, potentially, dispersion or redundancy—of legal initiatives; second, the diversification of the locales (regional, universal) and the senses (criminalization of passive or active bribery, of public or private bribery, etc.) of the internationalization efforts (Tricot 2005); and third, as both a consequence and a cause of the two former phenomena, the multiplication of actors carrying out anticorruption initiatives.

This evolution, which has taken place over the past 15 years, is linked to a shift in emphasis toward the private sector. Progressively, the focus has shifted toward—or, more precisely, it has extended and welcomed—a business-related approach. Initially, this approach relied on building a consensus to criminalize international/transnational active bribery. Following an unfair competition agenda—the "levelling the playing field" argument—the attention has focused on the definition of conduct eligible for criminal sanctions: Under this rubric, the private sector is considered and targeted as a perpetrator (or a victim) of the offence. In contrast, however, the business-related approach has developed on the basis of multiple attempts to implicate the private sector within and associate it with the fight against corruption. Here, attention focuses on preventing corrupt practices through the involvement of those who may be potential authors or victims of such practices. As a result, the private sector is offered the possibility to change its role, from a negative one (as author or victim) to a more positive one: being part of the solution as opposed to the problem—in other words, to shift from being subjects/objects of anticorruption policies to become actors within those policies.

This section describes this process, based, first, on the development and consolidation of the regulatory framework (Sect. 2.2) which has subsequently been

[1] In the sense of Mean (2011). See also Ghérari (2011), in the same volume.

[2] See, among many others, Small (1994), Stessens (2001), Tricot (2001).

completed by the contribution of the self-regulatory framework (Sect. 2.3), favoring a new path for the law-making process and law-enforcement strategies, called co-regulation (Sect. 2.4).

11.2.1 The Development and Consolidation of the Regulatory Framework: A Set of Binding Instruments to Curb Corruption

This section briefly describes the international anti-bribery regulatory framework within which corporate self-regulation must operate. This framework consists of a significant number of binding international (both regional and universal) agreements specifically dedicated to corruption.[3] It provides, primarily, for a set of obligations addressed to the state parties. The private sector is far from absent from the picture, however, but is targeted directly or indirectly by certain provisions and, more generally, is necessarily present through the approach which launched the successful process of internationalization. Such an approach can be characterized as a business- or economics-related approach as opposed to a more human-rights-based or democratic approach (Tricot 2001). However, the exclusive business/economics-related approach has been complemented with a development agenda coupled with a good-governance approach. This has led to the extension of the scope of the instruments negotiated. Public and private bribery are now addressed within this framework, as well as international and domestic cases. The scope of the agreements even goes beyond bribery, and includes the demand side as well as the supply side. Finally, the move toward criminalization is complemented by the establishment of preventive measures, frameworks for international cooperation, and private law provisions or mechanisms. The international legal framework can thus be pictured as a set of concentric circles: The first circle comprises the Organisation for Economic Co-operation and Development (OECD) convention, limited to the supply side and to international bribery and framed on the basis of a strict competition agenda (Pieth 2011b). This minimum standard has been completed, and then extended first at the regional level and then at the universal level. Each subsequent circle thus represents a chronological step in the development of the process and partially fills the gaps left by the preceding circle.

11.2.1.1 The Launch of the International Process: The OECD Convention

The starting point of the universal process came through the adoption of an international convention which emerged, contrary to expectations, from the OECD, an

[3] However, a complete overview should also take account of other international instruments aimed at preventing and "sanctioning" corruption, especially those developed by multilateral development banks. Because of their peculiar nature, they will be dealt with in Sect. 4.

organization which traditionally promoted self-discipline and self-regulation rather than hard law. However, under the strong influence of the USA, the OECD offered the first[4] forum for the negotiation and adoption of such an instrument (Pieth 2011b). On 21 November 1997, the Convention on Combating Bribery of Foreign Public Officials in International Business Transactions was adopted. It entered into force on 15 February 1999. It establishes binding standards to criminalize bribery for the 34 OECD member states[5] and five nonmember states.[6] Its main characteristics are its territorial scope of application (since states parties are the home states of most major international corporations), its focus on the "supply side" of the bribery transaction, and the monitoring mechanism established by the convention (an open-ended, peer-driven monitoring mechanism that ensures the thorough implementation of the international obligations that countries have taken on under the convention).

11.2.1.2 The Regional Input to Consensus Building: American, European and African Conventions on Corruption

In 1996, the member states of the Organization of American States (OAS) adopted the first regional anticorruption legal instrument,[7] which entered into force in 1997. It was completed in 2002 with a mechanism that evaluates the degree to which it had been fulfilled.

In the same year, the Council of the European Union adopted the first protocol to the convention on the protection of the European Communities' financial interests.[8] This limited original scope was then exceeded with the adoption by the Council of the Convention on the Fight Against Corruption involving officials of the European Communities or officials of member states of the European Union (EU).[9] This

---

[4] Since the failure within the UN in the 1970s and the 1980s. See Tricot (2001).

[5] Australia, Austria, Belgium, Canada, Chile, Czech Republic, Denmark, Estonia, Finland, France, Germany, Greece, Hungary, Iceland, Ireland, Israel, Italy, Japan, Korea, Luxembourg, Mexico, Netherlands, New Zealand, Norway, Poland, Portugal, Slovak Republic, Slovenia, Spain, Sweden, Switzerland, Turkey, the UK, the USA.

[6] Argentina, Brazil, Bulgaria, Russia, South Africa.

[7] See Inter-American Convention Against Corruption, The Organization of American States (OAS), http://www.oas.org/juridico/english/treaties/b-58.html, accessed 13 July 2013.

[8] See Council Act of 27 September 1996 drawing up a Protocol to the Convention on the Protection of the European Communities' Financial Interests [Official Journal C 313 of 23.10.1996], European Union, http://europa.eu/legislation_summaries/fight_against_fraud/protecting_european_communitys_financial_interests/l33019_en.htm, accessed 13 July 2013.

[9] See Council Act of 29 November 1996 drawing up, on the basis of Article K. 3 of the Treaty on European Union, the Protocol on the Interpretation, by way of Preliminary Rulings, by the Court of Justice of the European Communities of the Convention on the Protection of the European Communities' Financial Interests [Official Journal C 151 of 20.5.1997], European Union, http://europa.eu/legislation_summaries/fight_against_fraud/protecting_european_communitys_financial_interests/l33019_en.htm, accessed 13 July 2013.

framework was completed with the adoption of the council framework decision (2003/568/JHA) of 22 July 2003 on combating corruption in the private sector.[10]

In 1999, the Council of Europe adopted, first, the Criminal Law Convention on Corruption,[11] which entered into force in 2002 and was completed by an additional protocol[12] which extends the scope of application of the convention; and, second, the Civil Law Convention on Corruption,[13] which entered into force in 2003. Notably, the latter provides for the invalidity of contracts and the protection of whistleblowers. For both instruments, a specific body is entrusted with monitoring compliance with Council of Europe anticorruption standards: the Group of States against Corruption (GRECO).[14]

In 2001, the Southern African Development Community (SADC) and the Economic Community of West African States (ECOWAS) both launched the process in Africa, with the adoption of protocols against corruption attached to their constitutive treaties, respectively. In July 2003, the Convention on Preventing and Combating Corruption was adopted in Maputo, within the framework of the African Union,[15] and it entered into force in August 2006.

11.2.1.3 The Universal Turning Point: The UNCAC

The international framework has been completed with the adoption of a genuine universal instrument: the United Nations Convention against Corruption (UNCAC),[16] which was adopted in Merida and entered into force on 14 December 2005.

As of 29 May 2013, UNCAC has 140 signatories and 167 parties, including key players in international trade such as China, Russia, India, and Indonesia, in addition to the major OECD countries. It relies on a comprehensive approach to corruption, addressing both the demand and the supply sides, at both international and domestic levels and in public and private contexts, and adopts preventive, punitive, as well as restorative approaches.

---

[10] See Council Framework Decision 2003/568/JHA of 22 July 2003 on Combating Corruption in the Private Sector, European Union, http://europa.eu/legislation_summaries/fight_against_fraud/protecting_european_communitys_financial_interests/l33019_en.htm, accessed 13 July 2013.

[11] See Criminal Law Convention on Corruption, Council of Europe, http://conventions.coe.int/Treaty/EN/Treaties/Html/173.htm, accessed 13 July 2013.

[12] See Additional Protocol to the Criminal Law Convention on Corruption, Council of Europe, http://conventions.coe.int/Treaty/EN/treaties/html/191.htm, accessed 13 July 2013.

[13] See Civil Law Convention on Corruption, Council of Europe, http://conventions.coe.int/Treaty/en/Treaties/Html/174.htm, accessed 13 July 2013.

[14] See Group of States against Corruption (GRECO), Council of Europe, http://www.coe.int/t/dghl/monitoring/greco/default_en.asp, accessed 13 July 2013.

[15] See African Union Convention on Preventing and Combating Corruption, Council of Europe, http://www.africa-union.org/root/au/Documents/Treaties/Text/Convention%20on%20Combating%20Corruption.pdf, accessed 13 July 2013.

[16] See Sandage, "The Universal Approach of the United Nations Convention against Corruption," in this volume.

In less than 5 years, six international agreements have been adopted, concerning the whole spectrum of corruption and covering almost the entire globe. The acceleration of the internationalization process is remarkable. It has led to a consolidated international legal framework (even though some argue that effective and efficient monitoring and reporting mechanisms are lacking and wish in this respect for a new treaty: see Dugard 2013). There are undoubtedly many reasons for such acceleration and success. Several complementary approaches have played a role. However, it seems that the trigger has been the rise of the trade-related approach. It is very tempting to agree with Mark Pieth in this sense when he says:

> It may seem odd, but from the perspective of someone who has experienced the last twenty years of regulation in corruption, I firmly believe that "an unfair competition" agenda has initiated the current struggle against the age old phenomenon of corruption. (Pieth 2011a, p. 5)

If this interpretation is correct, then the increasing place and role of (business) self-regulation within the anticorruption international framework is simply a logical consequence of such a process.

11.2.2 The Contribution of and Support from the Self-Regulatory Framework: A Set of Voluntary Commitments to Prevent Corrupt Practices

Since the 1970s, acting on its own initiative, the private sector has produced several instruments for self-discipline aiming at preventing and curbing corruption, either through traditional channels or via new actions. The chronological ordering of those initiatives, designed by the private sector for the private sector, reveals the spread of the (self-) involvement of the business sector[17] in the area of anticorruption policies and programs: from the specific or sectoral forum to the global forum, and from traditional initiatives to innovative proposals.

11.2.2.1 The Traditional Fora of Self-Regulation

OECD In 1976, the OECD issued its guidelines for multinational enterprises (Plaine 1977), paving the way for progressive international attention to multi-

[17] This chapter focuses on business actors, though the private sector also includes civil society actors which play a great role in the design and implementation of anticorruption policies. It will suffice to mention the well-known work of Transparency International: founded in 1993, it has become the main civil society organization combating corruption. It issues an annual Global Corruption Report, highlighting corruption in specific areas. In 2009, the report focused on the private sector. It also issued the "Business Principles for Countering Corruption," currently under revision. See Business Principles for Countering Bribery, Transparency International, http://www.transparency.org/whatwedo/tools/business_principles_for_countering_bribery, accessed 13 July 2013. In the legal literature, see Hodess 2013. Concerning "Hunter Alliance" and "Global Witness," see also Rose-Ackerman and Carrington 2013.

national corporations. The guidelines are a set of voluntary recommendations addressed collectively by governments to multinational enterprises. They state best practices consistent with applicable laws. Compliance with the guidelines is voluntary, as they have no binding effect on the enterprises concerned. Signatory governments, however, are committed to promoting the guidelines, handling enquiries, and assisting in the resolution of specific instances through a network of National Contact Points. With these initiatives, multinational companies were thus invited not only to respect legal constraints but also to adopt a behavior consistent with ethical principles, interests of stakeholders, environmental concerns, and local working conditions. Slowly, the notion of corporate social responsibility (CSR) would take form and progressively become a point of attention for business leaders.

The guidelines were updated in 2011,[18] this being the fifth update since they were first adopted. On this occasion, the rules of the section on Combating Bribery, Bribe Solicitation, and Extortion were consolidated, with a special attention to compliance programs (this being a rewording of Sect. VII). In 2009, to mark the tenth anniversary of the entry into force of the OECD Anti-Bribery Convention, the OECD Council issued a Recommendation for further Combating Bribery.[19] It includes recommendations on the tax deductibility of bribes (which should be clearly disallowed); channels for reporting bribery without fear of reprisals; accounting requirements; external audit and internal controls; ethics and compliance; public procurement; officially supported credits; and international cooperation.

Of particular interest is Annex II of the recommendation, which provides for good practice guidance on internal controls, ethics, and compliance, and aims at providing business with guidance on how to structure an anti-bribery program. Though not legally binding, it has been adopted by the council of the OECD and is subject to the peer-review system of the OECD working group on bribery. This guidance is flexible, and intended to be adapted by companies, in particular small- and medium-sized enterprises, according to their individual circumstances, including their type, legal structure, and geographical and industrial sector of operation, as well as the jurisdictional and other basic legal principles under which they operate. Those OECD instruments are complemented by various other related instruments, concerning corporate governance, public procurement, conflict of interest, etc.

International Chamber of Commerce (ICC) Founded in 1919, the ICC[20]—the "world business organisation," as it describes itself—is a private organization for the business sector which gathers together hundreds of thousands of member

[18] See Guidelines for Multinational Enterprises, The Organisation for Economic Co-operation and Development (OECD), http://www.oecd.org/daf/inv/mne/oecdguidelinesformultinationalenterprises.htm, accessed 13 July 2013.

[19] See OECD Recommendation for Further Combating Bribery of Foreign Public Officials in International Business Transactions, The Organisation for Economic Co-operation and Development (OECD), http://www.oecd.org/investment/anti-bribery/anti-briberyconvention/oecdantibriberyrecommendation2009.htm, accessed 13 July 2013.

[20] See, inter alia, Mantovani, "The Private Sector Role in the Fight Against Corruption," in this volume. See also Vincke (2007).

companies and associations from over 120 countries. The ICC has promoted self-discipline and has a long experience of self-regulatory instruments. The relevant texts result from private initiatives and are adopted on a voluntary basis. The ICC has played an important role within the process of internationalization of the fight against corruption, accompanying both its failures and successes. Under the aegis of the OECD, in 1976 it first participated in the drafting of the Guidelines for Multinational Enterprises. The ICC also constituted an ad hoc committee responsible for drafting a report on Rules and Recommendations on Bribery and Corruption in International Transactions. This committee drafted self-regulatory rules,[21] directed at all ICC member companies, which show a strong resemblance to the US Federal Act of 1977. In so doing, the ICC would become the first international organization to ban all forms of corruption, be it active or passive, public or private, national or international. The ICC intended these rules to be complied with by all enterprises, large and small. The rules have been revised several times, the latest revision dating to 2011.[22] The rules fall into three parts: part I states the rules proper; part II deals with policies which enterprises should enact to support compliance with the rules; part III lists the suggested elements of an effective corporate compliance program. To complement the rules, the ICC has issued a handbook entitled "Fighting corruption" (Vincke and Heimann 2008) which provides practical insights into combating corruption in business. The ICC Anticorruption Commission has also issued several guidelines (guidelines on Agents, Intermediaries and other Third Parties;[23] guidelines on Whistle-blowing[24]) and a guide to responsible sourcing.[25] Most recently, the ICC has issued its latest addition to its "suite of anti-corruption tools," as a

[21] Rules of Conduct to Combat Extortion and Bribery in International Business Transactions.

[22] See ICC Rules on Combating Corruption, International Chamber of Commerce (ICC), http://www.iccwbo.org/Data/Policies/2011/ICC-Rules-on-Combating-Corruption-2011/, accessed 13 July 2013.

[23] See ICC Guidelines on Agents, Intermediaries and Other Third Parties, International Chamber of Commerce (ICC), http://www.iccwbo.org/Advocacy-Codes-and-Rules/Document-centre/2010/ICC-Guidelines-on-Agents,-Intermediaries-and-Other-Third-Parties/, accessed 13 July 2013.

[24] See Whistleblowing, International Chamber of Commerce (ICC), http://www.iccwbo.org/advocacy-codes-and-rules/areas-of-work/corporate-responsibility-and-anti-corruption/whistleblowing/, accessed 13 July 2013. ICC France has taken the initiative to issue guidelines on the important question of putting into place whistle-blowing mechanisms in enterprises. The purpose of these guidelines is to help companies establish and implement internal whistle-blowing programs, by setting forth practical indications that can serve as a useful point of reference, while meeting, as much as possible, the objections formulated in certain countries about certain aspects of a whistle-blowing system. These guidelines are inspired by international and national legal provisions.

[25] See Guide to Responsible Sourcing, International Chamber of Commerce (ICC), http://www.iccwbo.org/advocacy-codes-and-rules/areas-of-work/corporate-responsibility-and-anti-corruption/Guide-to-Responsible-Sourcing/, accessed 13 July 2013. The ICC guide on responsible sourcing focuses mainly on social and environmental responsibility, but it also refers to the necessity to comply with anticorruption principles.

response to the G20 anticorruption call: this is the ICC Anticorruption Clause,[26] designed for inclusion in any contract.[27]

11.2.2.2 Innovative and Ad Hoc Proposals

This strategy for the prevention and enforcement of anti-bribery policies has spread beyond those traditional fora of self-regulation. It has reached new fora and even penetrated certain international fora and organizations with no tradition of self-regulation, as well as those which are reluctant to use or acknowledge soft law.

In 2004, during the annual meeting of the World Economic Forum, chief executive officers from engineering and construction, energy, and metals and mining industries launched the Partnering Against Corruption Initiative, known as PACI, which has rapidly become a multi-sector initiative. It is based on principles for countering bribery[28] which are strongly inspired by the Transparency International Business Principles for Countering Bribery (Mean 2011, p. 84). The principles rely on the commitment of chief executive officers to zero tolerance of bribery and develop and implement a practical and effective anticorruption compliance program. As of April 2012, 171 companies had signed the PACI commitment; and as of May 2013, 126 companies were PACI members.

PACI's overall objective is to facilitate the alignment and acceptance of international anticorruption norms at the corporate and country level. The strategy is defined by three pillars: first, shaping the evolving corporate best practice in implementing effective anticorruption programs to prevent, detect, and address corruption; second, enabling collective action through public–private partnerships to address the root causes of corruption and develop scalable model process solutions; and third, helping to define the international anticorruption architecture through influencing public policy and the effective enforcement of laws and regulations, as well as through alignment and scaling of private-sector engagement in fighting corruption. Several tools and guides have been issued: in 2005, the Principles for Countering Bribery, a practical guide for developing internal anticorruption programs; the PACI Self-Evaluation Tool, which is a comprehensive self-assessment tool to evaluate the effectiveness of internal anticorruption programs; and in 2013, the Good Practice Guidelines on Conducting Third Party Due Diligence.[29]

In parallel with these initiatives, the G20 launched a comprehensive initiative at the Toronto summit in June 2010 and established its Anticorruption Working Group

[26] See ICC Anti-Corruption Clause, International Chamber of Commerce (ICC), http://www.iccwbo.org/Data/Policies/2012/ICC-Anti-corruption-Clause/, accessed 13 July 2013. See below, Sect. 4.

[27] In the future, the ICC plans to release an Ethics and Compliance Training Handbook.

[28] See Partnering Against Corruption Initiative (PACI), Principles for Countering Bribery, World Economic Forum, http://www.weforum.org/pdf/paci/PACI_Principles.pdf, accessed 13 July 2013.

[29] See Good Practice Guidelines on Conducting Third-Party Due Diligence, World Economic Forum, http://www.weforum.org/reports/good-practice-guidelines-conducting-third-party-due-diligence, accessed 13 July 2013.

chaired by Indonesia and France, which released an Anticorruption Action Plan,[30] subsequently approved at the Seoul G20 Summit in November 2010. As a continuation of these initiatives, the B20 released a final report in November 2011.[31] It makes key recommendations for governments and corporations, including a strong call for co-regulation through public–private partnership.[32]

Co-regulation and public–private partnership, along with the idea of a shared responsibility for all stakeholders, represent the key features of the emerging paradigm in the development of the international legal framework.

Before describing its main features, a few words should be said about the mechanism of "collective action," which represents another innovative way to envisage the role and action of the private sector toward corrupt practices. The World Bank Institute "Fighting Corruption through Collective Action" 2008 guide defines "collective action" as a collaborative and sustained process of cooperation among stakeholders that increases the impact and credibility of individual action, brings vulnerable individual players into an alliance of like-minded organizations, and levels the playing field between competitors. Collective action is conceived as a mechanism that can complement or temporarily substitute for and strengthen weak local laws and anticorruption practices. As Mark Pieth says, collective action is now a broad term for all sorts of joint activities by competitors, of companies with their clients, with trade associations or even the public sector, to prevent bribery (Pieth 2011a, p. 106). It accompanies—and also illustrates—the rise of co-regulation, constituting as it does a "complex form of hybrid regulation" (Pieth 2012).

11.2.3 The Rise of Co-regulation: The Case for Soft Law Revisited

The rise of a new paradigm, as called for by the G20 and the B20[33] (within the framework of the action plan against corruption), may be measured and observed through the example of the Global Compact (GC). The GC is an initiative proposed to business by former UN secretary-general Kofi Annan at the 1999 session of the Word Economic Forum. It sets out a principle-based framework for business. The GC illustrates the opening of the UN toward the private sector in general, and enterprises in particular.[34] As a UN initiative (it has been endorsed by the general as-

[30] See Group of Twenty (G20), Group of Twenty Official website, http://www.g20.org, accessed 13 July 2013.

[31] See Anti-Corruption, The Business 20 (B20), http://www.b20businesssummit.com/themes/anti-corruption, accessed 13 July 2013.

[32] The G20 Anti-corruption Action Plan 2013–2014, adopted in November 2012, renews the commitments and recommendations made in 2010. See G20 website, www.g20.org/load/781360452, accessed 13 July 2013.

[33] See Kett, "The Role of the G20 and B20 in the Fight Against Corruption," in this volume.

[34] "As recently as the late 1990s, indifference and mutual suspicion characterized the relationship between the UN and business.... This began to change with the launch of the Global Compact."

sembly of the UN),[35] it may be considered an institutional/public initiative. But at the same time it relies on the entirely voluntary involvement of the private sector. This combination both presupposes and favors a public–private partnership.

By extension, it also illustrates the opening of the international legislative scene to the business sector. This orientation—which presumably can be assumed to be long lasting—should certainly be read and assessed from the perspective of the effects of globalization of the economy and the withdrawal of states.

There is no doubt that the complementary relationship between corporate self-regulation and the efforts of governments and international organizations remains to be refined. But the GC already attempts to organize the circulation of common standards from hard law to soft law and vice versa. It relies on the idea that a common strategy (the GC itself) may lead to the building of a common point of reference: in the case of corruption, that common reference would be the UNCAC, through the tenth principle of the GC. The tenth principle on anticorruption was added in 2004 after the adoption of UNCAC. Businesses adhering to the GC commit "to work against corruption in all its forms including extortion and bribery." This includes committing to: "introduce anti-corruption policies and programs within their organizations and their business operations"; "report on the work against corruption in the annual Communication on Progress (COP) and share experiences and best practices through the submission of examples and case stories"; and "join forces with industry peers and with other stakeholders." The peculiarity of the GC as a form of co-regulation, in comparison for instance with the OECD's guidelines, is the incentive for corporations to join the GC and the "quasi sanctions" that may follow noncompliance with the reporting requirement attached to membership to the GC (see Sect. 4, below).

Another form of public–private partnership may be found in the Extractive Industries Transparency Initiative (EITI).[36] This began as a campaign by civil society organizations for the publication of payments by extractive companies to host governments, taken up in a speech made by the then British prime minister Tony Blair in 2002. Following this, the British government convened a group of resource-rich countries, extractive companies, and civil-society organizations, which started to develop the EITI methodology. At a conference in London in 2003, a set of principles (the EITI Principles) was agreed and then, in 2005, a set of criteria (the EITI Criteria). The EITI Source Book was published in the same year; this is an illustrative guide to assist countries implementing the EITI. The 2013 edition of the EITI standard[37] brings together the policy documents that together comprise the rules of the EITI.

See Georg Kell, UN Global Compact Executive Director Addresses Private Equity Community, CSR Press Release, http://www.csrwire.com/press_releases/27662-UN-Global-Compact-Executive-Director-Addresses-Private-Equity-Community, accessed 13 July 2013.

[35] See resolution adopted by the General Assembly (on the report of the Second Committee (A/60/495 and Corr.1)) 60/215, Towards Global Partnerships, United Nations Information Centre Prague, http://www.osn.cz/soubory/n0550050.pdf, accessed 13 July 2013.

[36] See Extractive Industries Transparency Initiative (EITI), Extractive Industries Transparency Initiative official website, http://eiti.org, accessed 13 July 2013.

[37] See EITI Standard, Extractive Industries Transparency Initiative (EITI), http://eiti.org/document/standard, accessed 13 July 2013.

The EITI sets a global standard for transparency in oil, gas, and mining. It promotes revenue transparency through monitoring and reconciling company payments and government revenues at the country level. Each implementing country creates its own EITI process which is overseen by participants from the government, companies, and national civil society. The international EITI Board and the International Secretariat are the guardians of the EITI methodology internationally.

Finally, the combination of hard law and soft law may also be observed within regional organizations such as the EU and the Council of Europe,[38] where binding instruments on corruption are employed alongside nonbinding recommendations and guidelines.

Such a multilevel institutional framework, wherein the private sector has become a key actor, has necessarily led to changes in the actions planned and carried out against corruption. The next section presents these new actions, as characterized according to the role assigned to corporate rules.

11.3 Corporate Rules and the International Legal Framework on Corruption: New Actions Within a Consolidated and Diversified Legal Framework

Whereas no international binding instrument refers to the adoption or existence of corporate anti-bribery rules, the "privatization" of the fight against corruption (Nieto Martín 2013) reveals that, though still limited, the role of such rules has potential to grow within that framework. Indeed, the increasing number of provisions addressed directly or indirectly to the private sector is not only a sign of this privatization but also, more importantly, offers a possible basis for the acknowledgment and taking into account of corporate anti-bribery rules. This, in turn, is paving the way for the generalization of such rules and the intensification of their adoption by companies around the world, as well as increasing the legitimacy of international and—notably—universal organizations which are seeking to conceive provisions for an adequate co-regulatory framework.

The anticorruption framework seems to be moving toward a "mutual recognition process" of hard-law instruments vis-à-vis soft-law guidelines and vice versa. This is leading to the building of an anticorruption framework made up of a complex

[38] See, for instance, Resolution (97) 24 on the Twenty Guiding Principles for the Fight Against Corruption, Council of Europe, https://wcd.coe.int/wcd/ViewDoc.jsp?id=593789&, accessed 13 July 2013. Recommendation No. R(2000)10 on Codes of Conduct for Public Officials, Council of Europe, http://www.coe.int/t/dghl/monitoring/greco/documents/Rec%282000%2910_EN.pdf, accessed 13 July 2013. Recommendation Rec(2003)4 on Common Rules against Corruption in the Funding of Political Parties and Electoral Campaigns, Council of Europe, http://www.coe.int/t/dghl/monitoring/greco/general/Rec%282003%294_EN.pdf, accessed 13 July 2013. Resolution (99) 5 Establishing the Group of States against Corruption-GRECO, Council of Europe, http://conventions.coe.int/Treaty/EN/PartialAgr/Html/Greco9905.htm, accessed 13 July 2013.

combination of both, where voluntary commitments may become enforceable obligations, universally recognized as such.

11.3.1 The Combination of Imposed Obligations with Voluntary Commitments

11.3.1.1 The Acknowledgment of Corporate Rules by Legal Instruments

As the most recent binding instrument adopted at the international level, and as the sole universal convention on corruption, UNCAC represents the best case through which to assess the reality and extent of the acknowledgment by the international regulatory framework of corporate rules, and their possible role.

From a general point of view, the UNCAC pays special attention to the private sector. It contains a number of provisions that, while addressed to states, have a direct impact on the corporate world. Most of the offences established by the convention involve the private sector either as a victim (to be protected) or the perpetrator (to be punished) of a given crime. For the two most well-known corruption offences (bribery and embezzlement), the convention introduces articles specifically directed at the private sector, thereby recognizing that neither the crime of bribery nor embezzlement requires involvement of a public administration and can be committed "private-to-private." As well as this, the chapter on prevention of corruption devotes an entire article to the private sector as such (Article 12). In this context, states parties are called upon to establish a variety of measures to ensure, among others, transparent procurement systems, simplified administrative procedures, enhanced accounting and auditing standards, and the participation of individuals and groups outside the public sector in the prevention of corruption and the decision-making processes of public administrations.

Another key element is the provision on corporate criminal liability. Article 26 makes it obligatory to establish the criminal, civil, or administrative liability of legal persons and to make such liability independent of the criminal liability of the natural persons committing an offence of corruption. The importance of such a provision is self-evident, considering the rapid development of the acknowledgment of compliance programs and other corporate rules of the same kind within the framework of criminal or para-criminal law proceedings.[39]

More specifically, however, the special attention to the private sector in the "UNCAC system" may be observed in the documents issued by the conference of the state parties. Pursuant to Article 63 of the convention, such a conference was established to improve the capacity of states parties to cooperate in order to achieve the objectives set forth in the convention and to promote and review its implementation.

[39] Cf. Pieth (2011a, p. 393). For reflections from the European perspective, see Manacorda and Giudicelli-Delage (2013).

During its second session, the Bali business declaration[40] was adopted, which considers that fighting corruption is "a shared responsibility that involves all stakeholders" and reaffirms the support for the tenth principle of the GC, which states that the private sector should work against corruption in any form and manifestation, including bribery and extortion. The declaration recalls that the voluntary character of the principle does not prevent companies from being put at risk in case of failure to implement them. It provides for a commitment to work toward the alignment of business principles with the fundamental values enshrined in the UNCAC; to ensure that anticorruption polices and strategies include effective whistle-blower protection and due diligence in the selection of agents and intermediaries, and that they address "facilitation payments"; to work toward developing mechanisms to review companies' compliance with the realigned business principles; and to strengthen private–public partnerships for combating corruption in business. During its third session (Doha, 9–13 November 2009), the conference adopted a resolution on the prevention of corruption, underscoring the role of the private sector in preventing and fighting corruption. In its fourth sessions (Marrakech, 24–28 October 2011), the conference adopted Resolution 4/3, the Marrakech Declaration on the Prevention of Corruption, which recognized that

> while the implementation of the Convention is the responsibility of States parties, the promotion of a culture of integrity, transparency and accountability and the prevention of corruption are responsibilities to be shared by all stakeholders and sectors of society, in accordance with Articles 7 to 13 of the Convention

and called upon states parties

> to promote the business community's engagement in the prevention of corruption by, inter alia, developing initiatives to promote and implement, where appropriate, anti-corruption measures within public procurement, consistent with Article 9 of the Convention, and by working with the business community to address practices that generate vulnerability to corruption in the private sector.

Though implicit or indirect in the conventions, and incomplete or too general in the texts adopted in parallel, the acknowledgment of corporate rules by international legal instruments does appear to be in progress. In this regard, the role of the domestic legal context as a key link should not be underestimated.[41]

11.3.1.2 The Establishment of Corporate Rules from Legal Standards

The observance of soft-law instruments and guidelines by enterprises is voluntary. Nevertheless, some matters covered by such instruments and guidelines may also

---

[40] See Business Coalition: The United Nations Convention against Corruption as a New Market Force, United Nations Global Compact, http://www.unglobalcompact.org/docs/issues_doc/Anti-Corruption/Bali_Business_Declaration.pdf, accessed 13 July 2013.

[41] See Nieto Martín and Muñoz de Morales, "Compliance Programs and Criminal Law Responses: A Comparative Analysis," in this volume. See also Goossens (1999).

be regulated by international instruments. As recalled by the OECD Guidelines for Multinational Enterprises:

> obeying…laws is the first obligation of enterprises. The guidelines are not a substitute for nor should they be considered to override…law and regulation.

But international guidelines show a growing attention to the international regulatory framework, upon which they aim to build and further deepen the legal context of anticorruption policies. This attention is the result of a preoccupation with the consistency of the applicable framework. At the same time, this serves as a very efficient tool for the circulation (and spreading) of common standards. References to the international legal framework by international guidelines may bring about their integration and assimilation into corporate programs and rules, leading to their "private enforcement."

For instance, the Bali Business declaration (cited above) has recognized the need to align existing business principles to the provisions of UNCAC. The PACI Principles are said to

> contribute to the goals of good governance and economic development and give practical effect to the OECD Convention on Combating Bribery of Foreign Public Officials in International Business Transactions and other similar governmental and private sector initiatives. These include the ICC Rules of Conduct to Combat Extortion and Bribery and the anti-bribery provisions of the revised OECD Guidelines for Multinationals.

Among the major relevant changes made in the 2011 edition of the OECD Guidelines for Multinational Enterprises, there is the mention of compatibility and consistency with the international legal framework. The reference to "internationally recognized standards" is added to the former (sole) reference to "applicable laws" in the preface[42] and in the guidelines themselves.[43] The ICC guidelines on whistle-blowing (2007) duly recall the relevant legal provisions "as they serve as valuable indications for the organizing of reporting within companies," and among them are the provisions of several international conventions. These are only a few examples from among the many cross-references from soft-law instruments to hard-law provisions.

In the background to this progressive process of mutual recognition and acknowledgment is the need for an articulation of the rules of soft law and hard law. This need is all the more pressing given that it is reinforced by another process: the refinement of the degree of precision of those rules, which tend to be more precise and as a result more binding.

11.3.2 The Transformation of Voluntary Commitments into Enforceable Obligations

As François Vincke writes, "enforcement of anti-bribery laws and adoption of corporate integrity programs play an interdependent and reinforcing role" (Vincke and

[42] "The Guidelines provide voluntary principles and standards for responsible business conduct consistent with applicable laws and internationally recognised standards."

[43] See Concepts and Principles: "[Guidelines] provide principles and good practice consistent with applicable laws and internationally recognised standards."

Heimann 2008, p. 210). This is all the more the case where general declarations give way to increasingly refined commitments.

From these ever-more-refined provisions emerges a web of commitments and obligations, whose scope, contents, and enforceability vary according to the legal framework, both international and domestic.

This suggests the limits of the distinction between soft law and hard law and highlights the necessity to go beyond questions of "legal nature" and focus instead on the degree of precision of the principles or rules concerned—in other words on the degree of commitment and/or obligation. The degree of commitment/obligation also depends on the legal domestic and international context.

In this respect, it is possible to draw out from the self-regulatory framework the scale of the commitments that are to be voluntarily assumed by corporations as well as the functions that corporate rules may fulfill.

11.3.2.1 Typology of Commitments[44]

The impact of the commitment may vary according to its target: For its author (the firm), it might be weakly coercive where the corporation originates from a country where legislation already imposes numerous harsh obligations. In such contexts, the commitment amounts to little more than simple confirmation of the existing legal framework that the corporation has to respect. In fact, this also depends considerably on the decisions on criminal law made at the national level and whether those commitments are taken into account for the purpose of criminal proceedings, with significant consequences for the firm. For the partners of the firm, on the contrary, the commitment might well be more coercive. In this sense, it could be seen as a tool to level the playing field. In this case, such a commitment does amount to an increase in the level of obligations, provided that the commitment in question is not too vague or general. Through the preventive and/or punitive contractual sanction, the idea is to use the economic strength of a large corporation to impose alignment upon its partners. Large companies are thus vested with functions or powers akin to a sort of private legislator and/or private enforcement agency, and for this reason there is a need to organize the (public) control of the obligations imposed in that way. But at the same time, those powers may well have (or come to have) a flip-side which is the liability of the firm itself. Finally, for the employees of the firm, the commitment might be properly and effectively coercive, through disciplinary mechanisms and whistle-blowing procedures, which have become a common standard among hard-law instruments, guidelines, and other soft-law initiatives.

11.3.2.2 Functions Expected from Corporate Rules

The importance of the first function of such corporate rules—including for criminal enforcement purposes—should not be underestimated. This first function is didacti-

[44] This typology is inspired by analysis in Deumier (2011).

cal, centering on the diffusion of legal knowledge. The focus on training programs, and also on clear and simple provisions which are easily accessible and widely distributed, illustrates this function perfectly.

The second function concerns enforcement. As well as corporate social responsibility (CSR) being born out of the limits of public/state enforcement, the development of corporate rules is closely linked to the limits of effectiveness of legal provisions, both international and national. The function of corporate anti-bribery rules is then to participate in the enforcement of national anti-bribery laws and international standards and to increase their effectiveness.

Yet it is hardly surprising, and is even perhaps to be expected, that compliance actions and voluntary commitments should have an ambivalent nature. These are tools of risk prevention, but at the same time are sources of risk—the risk of judicial proceedings against illegal provisions within corporate rules, such as codes of conducts or ethics codes, which are not mere voluntary commitments but may be seen as binding internal rules; and, more generally, the risk of judicial proceedings resulting from false commitments. Indeed, it should be recalled that voluntary commitment does not mean voluntary enforcement or voluntary respect of the commitment.[45] In a nutshell, the nature of such commitments is similar to *obligation de moyens:* An obligation that does not consist in achieving the goal (preventing corruption) but rather in carrying out and enforcing actions aimed at achieving this goal. Therein lie the legal obligations. However, it is a matter for the legal context—international and national—to ensure the enforceability of such commitments and acknowledge their ability to become true obligations.

But the issue of enforcement also requires taking account of other enforcement mechanisms. These are also business oriented, and specially designed for the private sector, but they have the advantage—or, at least, the particular characteristic—of being external mechanisms.

11.4 Consequences for the Private Sector in the International Legal Framework: New Enforcement Mechanisms for the Private Sector

Anticorruption policies have effected a transformation in the approach toward enforcement, and this is equally so concerning the follow-up in the implementation of international instruments. Within this framework, innovative mechanisms were designed and put in place for the public sector such as the OECD monitoring mechanism for the OECD convention,[46] the follow-up GRECO system for the Council of

[45] False commitment, for instance, may be (and indeed has been) subject to proceedings for false publicity or illicit commercial conducts. See Directive 2005/29/CE, which explicitly mentions the noncompliance of codes of conducts and qualifies such behavior as an illicit commercial practice.

[46] See Country Reports on the Implementation of the OECD Anti-Bribery Convention, The Organisation for Economic Co-operation and Development (OECD), http://www.oecd.org/daf/anti-

Europe Conventions,[47] etc. Yet this is also true for the private sector. New enforcement mechanisms have been created and more traditional ways to take account of the consequences of corruption for the private sector have returned to the forefront of the international legal debate. Both present two common characteristics. First, they are noncriminal law mechanisms—indeed, their legitimacy lies precisely in their (supposed) ability to surmount or overcome the fault lines of criminalization, both as regards the structural gaps in the internationalization of criminal law and the insufficient attention paid to the consequences of successful acts of bribery. However, paradoxically enough, this does not prevent those mechanisms from eventually resulting in criminal proceedings, and indeed they also have notable features in common with criminal law. Second, they are specifically designed for the business sector.

Two main enforcement mechanisms for "sanctioning" corruption in the private sector may be distinguished: the development of administrative sanctions (Sect. 4.1) and the renewal of private sanctions (Sect 4.2).

11.4.1 The Development of "Administrative" Sanctions at the International Level: Exclusion and Debarment

The development of administrative sanctions enforced by international organizations has increased considerably in the past 15 years. International organizations have been exposed to new demands and in response they have developed regulatory activities and established compliance and sanctions procedures. In this respect, since the mid-1990s anticorruption policy has represented a particularly well-adapted field.

The philosophy is based on a rationale of exclusion and stigma. Corporations proven to have engaged in corruption are publicly ("naming and shaming") excluded (by debarment or quasi-debarment systems) from specified programs implemented by such organizations. The sanction may be essentially reputational, as for instance within the framework of the GC or present more direct legal and financial consequences, as is the case within the World Bank Sanctions System.

11.4.1.1 The Global Compact

The GC is based on two principles: corporate transparency and accountability. Information and accountability are supposed to open a dialogue aimed at promoting the common values and principles as listed in the GC. Dialogue is thus considered

bribery/countryreportsontheimplementationoftheoecdanti-briberyconvention.htm, accessed 13 July 2013.

[47] See Group of States Against Corruption (GRECO), http://www.coe.int/t/dghl/monitoring/greco/default_en.asp.

an incentive to respect those principles. However, with a view to answering criticisms of—and indeed skepticism about—the GC related to its absence of sanctions, a condition of periodic reporting has been added to the commitment of the corporations. Hence, the GC does not only rely on dialogue but also on pressure. As a result, the philosophy of the GC remains a logic of voluntary commitment, where there is dialogue instead of obligation, and pressure instead of sanctions or controls (Boisson de Chazournes and Mazuyer 2011).

In their annual report or similar corporate documentation, participants are expected to publish a description of the ways in which they are supporting the GC and its ten principles. The GC is thus more like a guide dog than a watchdog;[48] however, it does contain a mandatory disclosure framework—the COP. Business participants are required to communicate their progress to their own stakeholders on an annual basis and to post a copy on the GC website. Failing to communicate progress on an annual basis results in a downgrading of participant status from active to noncommunicating. Participants who do not communicate progress for 2 years in a row are delisted and the GC publishes their name. Noncommunicating companies can return to the status of active participant by posting their COP. Companies that have been expelled need to reapply to join, and their application must be accompanied by their COP.

The weaknesses or limits of the GC reporting obligation should nevertheless be kept in mind. It is only the declaration that is controlled, not its sincerity, nor the effectiveness of the actions carried out. Still, it is a source of pressure to set up external controls.

11.4.1.2 The World Bank Sanctions System

Since a 1996 speech by former World Bank president James Wolfensohn, governance and anticorruption have been considered as development issues that fall within the World Bank's mandate, on the basis that the World Bank Articles of Agreement require the organization to ensure that its funds are used for their intended purposes.[49] Since this date, the organization has created, reformed,[50] and enforced anticorruption procedures.[51] In accordance with the Articles of Agreement, the World Bank ensures that either the Procurement or Consultant Guidelines are included in any grant or loan agreement between the World Bank and a borrower country, and that the borrower country includes the relevant guidelines in its request for propos-

[48] See The United Nations Global Compact—Frequently Asked Questions, United Nations Global Compact, http://www.unglobalcompact.org/AboutTheGC/faq.html, accessed 13 July 2013.

[49] The "fiduciary responsibility" of the bank to its shareholders upon which the sanction procedure is built is based on Article III, 65(b) IBRD Articles of Agreement.

[50] Established in 1998, the Sanction Process progressively evolved through four rounds of reforms successively conducted in 2004, 2006, 2007, and 2009–2010.

[51] See Zimmerman, "Globalizing the Fight against Corruption," in this volume; Heilbrunn, "The Fight Against Corruption: The World Bank Debarment Policy," in this volume.

als and the contracts that implement the purpose of the loan or grant. A sanctions process has also been set up, the steps of which are laid out in the World Bank's Sanctions Board Statute and Sanctions procedures. This was framed as a technique of exclusion or debarment,[52] and has the power to exclude a company or individual, at any time, temporarily or permanently, from any bank-financed contract, and to shut off the possibility of being selected as a subcontractor, consultant, supplier, or service provider to any company that may be awarded finance by the bank.[53] Since 2001, the World Bank has publicly sanctioned over 500 firms and individuals.[54] These sanctions include banning them from bidding on any World-Bank-financed project indefinitely or for a period of time[55] (i.e., debarment), nondebarment contingent on improved practices, sending a public letter of reprimand, or debarment with conditional release or restitution. When the World Bank learns about possible sanctionable conduct (from its own staff, the local government, or other bidders, for instance), the Integrity Vice Presidency (INT) is responsible for the investigation procedure concerning firms and individuals. Since 2004, a two-tiered structure has been established. The first level consists of the Evaluation and Suspension Officer. INT refers the case to the Evaluation and Suspension Officers,[56] who, on the basis of the Statement of Accusations and Evidence drafted by INT, assess the allegations and determine whether the evidence is sufficient to support a finding of sanctionable conduct. The second level is the Sanctions Board. It intervenes upon appeal of the respondent, which happens in about two-thirds of the cases. The Sanctions Board may also sanction Affiliates.

In addition, a Voluntary Disclosure Program (VDP) was established in 2006. According to this procedure, firms not being investigated by INT may report past behavior to the bank that may be sanctioned. If the firm is eligible for this program, the bank agrees not to sanction the said firm and to keep its identity confidential. Consequently, the firm must implement a compliance plan to prevent future misconduct and run an internal investigation. In the case of the emergence of new practices, the firm would be debarred for a statutory period of 10 years.

---

[52] "An administrative remedy utilized to disqualify contractors from obtaining public contracts or acquiring extensions to existing contracts for alleged breaches of law or ethics," Schooner (2004), cited in Boisson de Chazournes and Fromageau (2012, p. 7).

[53] See Guidelines Procurement under IBRD Loans and IDA Credits, 2011, The World Bank, http://siteresources.worldbank.org/INTPROCUREMENT/Resources/Procurement-Guidelines-November-2003.pdf, accessed 13 July 2013.

[54] See Sanctions System at the World Bank, The World Bank, http://www.worldbank.org/sanctions, accessed 13 July 2013.

[55] Almost all sanctions adopted between March 1999—the date of the first debarment order—and April 2001 were made for an indefinite period. The majority of the sanctions since then have been for an average period of 3 years. This might be seen as a follow-up of recommendations made by the Thornburgh Report.

[56] There are four EOs, one for the International Bank for Reconstruction and Development and International Development Association (who focuses on this work exclusively) and three part-time EOs for the Multilateral Investment Guarantee Agency, International Finance Corporation, and Bank Guarantee Projects.

A prohibition in bidding for projects and the associated negative publicity can be a serious business setback, and the negative consequences can be increased considerably through domino or "knock-on" effects. Indeed, since 2010, five multilateral development banks have participated in a cross-debarment arrangement.[57] As a result, if a firm or an individual is debarred by the World Bank, they will also be debarred from the other four banks. Proceedings before the World Bank also have other collateral effects, notably domestic consequences resulting in judicial proceedings. Moreover, since 2008 INT has initiated the practice of sending referral reports to member states where the evidence indicates that the laws of a member country have been violated. The idea is to inform the member states of the alleged practices as well as to induce them to pursue civil, criminal, or administrative cases against an individual or a company so as to determine whether any laws have been violated, and to take appropriate action under their own sovereign laws.[58] In 2011, INT issued 52 referral reports to member states and donor agencies; 32 referrals were made to national authorities in 2012.[59]

11.4.2 The Renewal of Private Remedies and Sanctions at the International Level?

Criminal law remains the weapon of choice for the fight against corruption. Yet corruption also has direct consequences at the level of private law. The validity of contracts may be questioned and compensation and may be claimed for the resulting damages. The contractual side of corruption has long been the object of attention, especially within arbitration law (Kahn & Kessedjian 1996); however, attention on the consequences of corruption from a private law perspective has recently increased and been extended beyond arbitration. The considerable sums of money which are potentially at stake, and the necessity of strengthening the connection between public deterrence through criminal law and the private consequences, have both played an important role in this regard.

The case of the UNCAC is an illustration of this attention, providing as it does for what can be considered minimum standards. UNCAC sets out a framework for private law intervention from two points of view: transaction validity and private claims

---

[57] See Agreement for Mutual Enforcement of Debarment Decisions, 9 April 2010, European Bank for Reconstruction and Development (EBRD), http://www.ebrd.com/downloads/integrity/Debar.pdf, accessed 13 July 2013.

[58] See Integrity Vice Presidency (INT) Annual Reports 2010, The World Bank, http://web.worldbank.org/WBSITE/EXTERNAL/EXTABOUTUS/ORGANIZATION/ORGUNITS/EXTDOII/0,,contentMDK:22203443~menuPK:5372841~pagePK:64168445~piPK:64168309~theSitePK:588921,00.html, accessed 13 July 2013.

[59] See Integrity Vice Presidency (INT) Annual Reports 2011 and 2012, The World Bank, http://web.worldbank.org/WBSITE/EXTERNAL/EXTABOUTUS/ORGANIZATION/ORGUNITS/EXTDOII/0,,contentMDK:22203443~menuPK:5372841~pagePK:64168445~piPK:64168309~theSitePK:588921,00.html, accessed 13 July 2013.

in case of corruption. As regards transaction validity, Article 34 addresses the enforceability of contracts resulting from corrupt activity.[60] Although it does not introduce a new legal regime regarding contract validity for contracts tainted by corruption, it does introduce a new level of convergence for contract law doctrine by instilling the notion of corruption as an independent vitiating factor for contracts tainted by corruption (Makinwa 2013, p. 267). As regards private remedies, Article 35 requires states to provide the right to institute legal proceedings.[61] Though it does not ease the requirements for standing and causality necessary for legal proceedings to be instituted, and only favors direct victims, Article 35 articulates the notion of a private claim for corruption in a global instrument (Makinwa 2013, p. 267).

It has long been recognized that corruption often takes the form of agreements and transactions. The consequences in private law for a contract tainted by corruption are not, however, unequivocal, but can be considerable for the party(ies) involved—as well as, in some cases, for third parties.

Domestic courts commonly do not enforce bribe transactions. They follow the principle that those who operate outside the law cannot claim its protection. The nullity of the bribe transaction often entails a further legal consequence: Bribes cannot be reclaimed, irrespective of whether or not the promised corrupt favor was delivered. This increases the risks of engaging in corrupt activities. Some argue that both the bribe transaction and the main contract should be nullified, while others debate whether contracts induced by bribery should be annulled *ex nunc* or *ex tunc*. Some, however, have emphasized the downsides to nullity: It is a binary choice that cannot be calibrated to the gravity of the offense, and may be counterproductive for the company that was not involved in the bribe but party to the tainted transaction. As regards anticorruption compliance programs, nullity may also act as an adverse incentive in detecting corrupt practices within the company. And, finally, only companies which have been successful in bribing are sanctioned. With these considerations in mind, some commentators have proposed maintaining the validity of contracts and instead imposing fines on bribe-paying companies, in order to fight corruption while simultaneously securing investments. At the international level, they suggest that the World Bank or International Monetary Fund might consider allowing for a general validity of contracts, contingent on substantial fines that are to be negotiated (Lambsdorff 2013, p. 226). Similar debates have been pursued with

[60] "Article 34. Consequences of acts of corruption: With due regard to the rights of third parties acquired in good faith, each State Party shall take measures, in accordance with the fundamental principles of its domestic law, to address consequences of corruption. In this context, States Parties may consider corruption a relevant factor in legal proceedings to annul or rescind a contract, withdraw a concession or other similar instrument or take any other remedial action."

[61] "Article 35. Compensation for damage: Each State Party shall take such measures as may be necessary, in accordance with principles of its domestic law, to ensure that entities or persons who have suffered damage as a result of an act of corruption have the right to initiate legal proceedings against those responsible for that damage in order to obtain compensation."

respect to arbitration case law,[62] which, in fact, has often been the place where such issues have first emerged.

Where multinational firms are parties, the typical forum for these legal issues is international arbitration. Consequently, arbitral tribunals also play a significant role in the global anticorruption network. They are called upon to enforce different existing preformulated anticorruption standards (domestic, international, and transnational) and, in some cases, to contribute to the creation of new standards.[63] The ban on corruption is part of the transnational *ordre public,* which arbitrators have progressively created and enforced. As early as 1963, Judge Lagergren denied enforcement of an agreement involving the transfer of bribe money. Today, the nullity of a contract proven to be a bribe transaction is part of the transnational *ordre public*—it is the solution laid down in the civil law convention (Article 8), and is also a rule in the list of transnational principles.[64]

Most cases concern conflicts between foreign bidders and their intermediaries, where the bidder, after getting the contract, refuses to pay the intermediary, arguing that the consultancy agreement was actually the legal cover for bribes. Arbitral case law has long established that no claim for bribe transaction should be executable. Nevertheless, the invalidation of the contract is contested in its consequences because it finally benefits the bidder.

The legal consequences concerning cases where the "main" contract was obtained by bribery are even more debated—since the issues at stake (and the possible collateral effects) are even more important. The question of the validity of such contracts remains unsettled. The three main positions within the debate are complete invalidity, voidability by judgment of the contractual partner, and maintaining the contract along with adjustment of the equilibrium of obligation and counter performance (Meyer 2013). But the few international standards available are either subject to criticism or do not allow a conclusive solution.

More generally, arbitration has a number of limitations as an anticorruption tool. First, and self-evidently, arbitration requires an arbitration agreement as normally found in a contract between two parties. Third-party claims are usually not possible in arbitration in the absence of an arbitration agreement.[65] Second, establishing proof of bribes, and especially of proof of intent to bribe, is often a major obstacle.

However, the contractual side of corruption is undoubtedly a crucial dimension of anticorruption policies, and has recently been recognized as such by the ICC

---

[62] For a recent and comprehensive retrospective of the arbitral approach toward corruption, see Meyer (2013).

[63] In this respect, a definition of the term "corruption" has not been established so far. But such a definition has not been necessary because the legal condemnation of the alleged behavior was not the issue, which consisted, on the contrary, mostly in problems of proof or concerned the appropriate consequences for a finding of corruption.

[64] See No. IV.7.2—Invalidity of Contract due to Bribery, Trans-Lex Law Research, accessed July 14, 2013, http://www.trans-lex.org/938000.

[65] However, an arbitration clause may be included in integrity pacts initiated by Transparency International in which all bidders agree not to pay bribes (see TI website, Integrity Pacts). It could then be possible that unsuccessful applicants would bring claims in arbitration against the successful bidder.

through its anticorruption clause.[66] Designed for inclusion in any contract, the new clause provides a contractual basis for parties to commit to complying with ICC's voluntary Rules on Combating Corruption or to implement a corporate anticorruption compliance program.

Finally, beyond the weapon of the contract, and taking into account all stakeholders including civil-society actors, other proposals and initiatives are attempting to design new enforcement mechanisms from a private law approach. In this respect, a recent proposal has been to establish at the international level a "model law empowering private citizen-relators to sue those guilty of corrupt practices in national court in the name of their governments, invoking jurisdiction where ever the offender or its assets might be found" (Carrington 2013, p. 292).

11.5 Conclusion: A Laboratory for Legal Globalization?

By way of conclusion, we may consider that this brief survey has largely confirmed the pioneering role—*d'avant-garde*—of anticorruption law (Tricot 2005). This is where the processes of internationalization are particularly well developed, and where limits and controversies have also arisen. Today, it is also the legal sector which is generating innovation concerning the creation and production of anticorruption law and legal enforcement, while also subjecting these innovations to questioning and criticism. It is, moreover, a witness to the ever-enhanced interdependence—be it of an economic, social, or legal nature—among the problems of corruption, and among the solutions proposed to address them, whether these be local, national, regional, or universal. As a consequence, it is also a witness to the need for the deployment of further legal imagination to help think of this interdependence as a form of global "intersolidarity" (Passet et al. 2013).

References

Boisson de Chazournes, L., & Fromageau, E. (2012). Balancing the scales: The World Bank sanctions and access to remedies. *European Journal of International Law, 23*(4), 963–989.

Boisson de Chazournes, L., & Mazuyer, E. (2011). *Le Pacte mondial des Nations Unies 10 ans après/The global compact of the United Nations 10 years after*. Brussels: Bruylant.

Carrington, P. D. (2013). Private enforcement of international law. In S. Rose-Ackerman, et al. (Eds.), *Anti-corruption policy, can international actors play a constructive role?* (pp. 285–299). Durham: Carolina Academic Press.

Deumier, P. (2011). La question de la sanction dans le pacte mondial. In L. Boisson de Chazournes & E. Mazuyer (Eds.), *The global compact of the United Nations 10 years after* (pp. 155–166). Brussels: Bruylant.

[66] See ICC Anti-Corruption Clause, http://www.iccwbo.org/Data/Policies/2012/ICC-Anti-corruption-Clause/.

Dugard, J. (2013). Corruption: is there a need for a new convention? In S. Rose-Ackerman, et al. (Eds.), *Anti-corruption policy, can international actors play a constructive role?* (pp. 159–168). Durham: Carolina Academic Press.

Ghérari, H. (2011). Le profil juridique et politique du pacte mondial. In L. Boisson de Chazournes, et al. (Eds.), *The global compact of the United Nations 10 years after*. Brussels: Bruylant.

Goossens, W. (1999). National and international anti-bribery regulations: Practical implications for multinational companies and compliance programs. *International Business Law Journal, 1*, 19–46.

Hodess, R. (2013). Civil society and nongovernmental organizations as international actors in anti-corruption advocacy. In S. Rose-Ackerman, et al. (Eds.), *Anti-corruption policy, can international actors play a constructive role?* (pp. 75–90). Durham: Carolina Academic Press.

Kahn, P., & Kessedjian, C. (1996). *L'illicite dans le commerce international*. Paris: LGDJ.

Lambsdorff, J. G. (2013). Securing investor confidence or fighting corruption? How intergovernmental organizations may reconcile two opposing goals. In S. Rose-Ackerman, et al. (Eds.), *Anti-corruption policy, can international actors play a constructive role*? (pp. 215–228). Durham: Carolina Academic Press.

Makinwa, A. O. (2013). Defining a private law approach to fighting corruption. In S. Rose-Ackerman, et al. (Eds.), *Anti-corruption policy, can international actors play a constructive role?* (pp. 267–283). Durham: Carolina Academic Press.

Manacorda, S., & Giudicelli-Delage, G. (2013). *Responsabilité pénale des personnes morales: perspectives européennes et internationales*. Paris: Société de Législation Comparée.

Mean, J. -P. (2011). The actors in the fight against corruption. In L. Boisson de Chazournes, et al. (Eds.), *The global compact of the United Nations 10 years after*. Brussels: Bruylant.

Meyer, O. (2013). The formation of a transnational ordre public against corruption: lessons for and from arbitral tribunals. In S. Rose-Ackerman, et al. (Eds.), *Anti-corruption policy, can International actors play a constructive role?* (pp. 229–245). Durham: Carolina Academic Press.

Nieto Martín, A. (2013). La privatización de la lucha contra la corrupción. In L. A. Zapatero, et al. (Eds.), *El Derecho Penal Económico en la Era de la Compliance* (pp. 191–210). Valencia: Tirant lo Blanch.

Passet, R., Hessel, S., Morin, E., Rocard, M., Sloterdijk, P., Delmas-Marty, M., et al. (2013). *Le monde n'a plus de temps à perdre*. Paris: Les liens qui libèrent.

Pieth, M. (2011a). Final remarks: criminal liability and compliance programs. In M. Pieth, et al. (Eds.), *Corporate criminal liability, emergence, convergence, and risk*. New York: Springer.

Pieth, M. (2011b). *Harmonising anti-corruption compliance: The OECD good practice guidance 2010*. Zurich: Dike Verlag AG.

Pieth, M. (2012). Collective action and corruption. Basel Institute on Governance, Working Paper Series 13.

Plaine, D. J. (1977). The OECD Guidelines for multinational enterprises. *International Lawyer, 11*(2), 339–341.

Rose-Ackerman, S., & Carrington, P. D. (2013). *Anti-corruption policy, can international actors play a constructive role?* Durham: Carolina Academic Press.

Schooner, S. L. (2004). The paper tiger stirs: Rethinking exclusion and debarment. *Public Procurement Law Review, 5*, 211–215.

Small, C. Y. (1994). Les paiements illicites dans le commerce international et les actions entreprises pour les combattre. *Annuaire français de droit international, 40*, 792–803.

Stessens, G. (2001). International fight against corruption. *International Review of Penal Law, 71*(3), 891–937.

Tricot, J. (2001). Inventaire des instruments internationaux: le processus de construction du cadre juridique international. In M. Delmas-Marty (Ed.), *Criminalité économique et atteintes à la dignité de la personne, Volume VII: Les processus d'internationalisation*. Paris: Maison des sciences de l'homme.

Tricot, J. (2005). La corruption internationale. *Revue de science criminelle et de droit pénal comparé, 4*, 753–765.

Vincke, F. (2007). Putting in place integrity programs to fight economic crime, ICC's Role. *International Business Law Journal, 5*, 681–712.
Vincke, F., & Heimann, F. (2008). *Fighting corruption, international corporate integrity handbook*. Paris: ICC Publishing.
Zapatero, L. A., & Nieto Martín, A. (2013). *El Derecho Penal Económico en la Era de la Compliance*. Valencia: Tirant lo Blanch.

Chapter 12
An Anticorruption Ethics and Compliance Program for Business: A Practical Guide

Dimitri Vlassis

Contents

12.1 The United Nations Convention Against Corruption

During the past decade, an international legal framework has been developed to tackle corruption. This framework includes the United Nations Convention Against Corruption (UNCAC) which entered into force in 2005 and is nearing universal ratification.[1] UNCAC is the only global legally binding anticorruption instrument. The convention's far-reaching approach and the mandatory character of many of its provisions make it a unique tool for developing a comprehensive response to a global problem.

The key objectives of UNCAC are to promote and strengthen measures to prevent and combat corruption more efficiently and effectively; to promote, facilitate, and support international cooperation and technical assistance in the prevention of and fight against corruption (including in asset recovery); and to promote integrity, accountability, and proper management of public affairs and property.[2]

---

[1] The convention has been adopted by the UN General Assembly in October 2003 (Resolution 58/4) and entered into force in December 2005. As of today (October 2013) the Convention has 168 parties. See United Nations Convention against Corruption, United Nations Office for Drugs and Crime (UNODC), http://www.unodc.org/unodc/en/treaties/CAC/signatories.html, accessed 16 July 2013.

[2] See Technical Guide to the United Nations Convention against Corruption—New York 2009, United Nations Office for Drugs and Crime (UNODC), http://www.unodc.org/documents/corruption/Technical_Guide_UNCAC.pdf, accessed 16 July 2013.

D. Vlassis (✉)
United Nations Office on Drugs and Crime-UNODC, Vienna, Austria
e-mail: dimitri.vlassis@unodc.org

S. Manacorda et al. (eds.), *Preventing Corporate Corruption*,
DOI 10.1007/978-3-319-04480-4_12,

Like all international treaties, UNCAC is only legally binding on states that have ratified or acceded to it. States that are parties to the convention are required to implement its provisions through the adoption of national legislation, policies, and practices. However, UNCAC contains a number of provisions that, while addressed to the states, will have a direct impact on the corporate community. The overall goal of these provisions is to avert market distortions and combat unfair competition.

Article 12(1) of the convention calls on states parties to

> take measures, in accordance with the fundamental principles of its domestic law, to prevent corruption involving the private sector, enhance accounting and auditing standards in the private sector and, where appropriate, provide effective, proportionate and dissuasive civil, administrative or criminal penalties for failure to comply with such measures.

Other areas that are directly relevant to the private sector include: public procurement (Article 9); money-laundering (Article 14); criminalization of offences of corruption (Articles 15–19, 21–25); liability of legal persons (Article 26); protection of witnesses, experts, and victims (Article 32); protection of reporting persons (Article 33); consequences of acts of corruption (Article 34); cooperation with law-enforcement authorities (Article 37); cooperation between national authorities and the private sector (Article 39); and bank secrecy (Article 40).

The private sector has a vested interest in contributing towards universal ratification and implementation of UNCAC. Companies operating in highly competitive markets need to be assured of the fairness and equity of their business relations. By working in partnership with states and international organizations and by investing in countries that need assistance, businesses can help achieve these competitive but fair markets.

Furthermore, UNCAC's values and principles are applicable to the widest spectrum of society, including the private sector. The principles enshrined in UNCAC do not only impact the countries in which businesses operate, but can also directly serve as inspiration for companies adopting or reviewing their anticorruption policies and practices.

The United Nations and its member states have given the United Nations Office on Drugs and Crime (UNODC) the responsibility to help translate the commitments of UNCAC into actions. An important part of UNODC's mission is to help the private sector strengthen its involvement with anticorruption activities globally and level the playing field for businesses around the world.

12.2 An Anticorruption Ethics and Compliance Program: UNODC's Practical Guide for Business

Over the years, a number of regional and international initiatives, standards, and principles have been developed to provide guidance for companies on how to fight corruption in their business operations by upholding enhanced integrity standards.

These initiatives, standards, and principles, together with the evolving international legal framework, are now prompting companies to focus on anticorruption measures as an essential component of their mechanisms to protect their reputation and the interests of their investors and shareholders. Increased costs due to corrupt payments, unfavorable dependencies between the supply and demand side of a corrupt act (resulting in recurring extortion requests), and missed business opportunities in distorted markets are further examples of negative consequences of corruption for companies. But, most significantly, corruption is illegal and companies face serious consequences if caught in engaging in such acts. Such consequences, going beyond legal penalties, have a strong impact on companies.

UNODC has developed an Anti-Corruption Ethics and Compliance Programme for Business: A Practical Guide.[3] The guide provides practical considerations of the various steps companies may take to prevent corruption in their operations by developing, implementing, and continuously improving an effective anticorruption ethics and compliance program. It concludes that while the approach to how an anticorruption ethics and compliance program is implemented may vary from company to company, there are some basic elements that need to be addressed. The guide also emphasizes specific challenges and opportunities for small and medium-sized enterprises (SMEs) and provides practical information for companies of all sizes regarding public disclosure of their anticorruption endeavors to demonstrate commitment to the fundamental values of integrity, transparency, and accountability. What follows is a short description of the main elements of the establishment and implementation of an effective ethics and compliance program as outlined in the guide.

An increasing number of companies are demonstrating leadership by implementing effective anticorruption ethics and compliance programs within their companies. Before companies start developing their own program, they need to assess the risks relevant to their business. The guide outlines typical corruption-related risk areas for companies and describes how risks can be identified and mitigated.

When developing an anticorruption ethics and compliance program, companies should ensure that it meets legal requirements under the international legal framework, including UNCAC.

In the spirit of Article 12 of UNCAC, the guide provides practical considerations of the various steps companies may take to prevent corruption in their operations by establishing an effective anticorruption system. Article 12 does not dictate to companies how this should be done and thus the guide does not seek to impose mandatory requirements. In addition to UNCAC, the guidance provided is derived from the business principles of major organizations.[4]

---

[3] The guide is available at the United Nations Office on Drugs and Crime's corruption homepage at: http://www.unodc.org/unodc/en/corruption/publications.html and will be launched during the fifth session of the Conference of the States Parties to the United Nations Convention against Corruption, Panama City, 25–29 November 2013.

[4] The Asia-Pacific Economic Cooperation (APEC) Anti-Corruption Code of Conduct for Business (2007); the International Chamber of Commerce (ICC) Rules on Combating Corruption (2011); the Organisation for Economic Co-operation and Development (OECD) Good Practice Guidance on Internal Controls, Ethics, and Compliance (2010); the World Economic Forum Partnering Against Corruption Initiative (PACI) Principles for Countering Bribery (2005); Transparency International's (TI) Business Principles for Countering Bribery (2009); and the World Bank Group Integrity Compliance Guidelines (2010).

Step 1: Support and Commitment from Senior Management for the Prevention of Corruption: An effective anticorruption program must be based on strong, explicit, and visible support and commitment from the senior management of the company. Even a well-defined program will fail to reduce the risk of corruption if employees and business partners perceive that senior management is not committed to preventing corruption.

This commitment must start at the top of the company. Senior management must clearly articulate a zero-tolerance attitude to corruption, supported by policies and practices that will put this commitment into action. Such a commitment plays a critical role in establishing a culture which is based on fundamental values such as integrity, transparency, and accountability.

Step 2: Developing an Anticorruption Program: An anticorruption program, comprising detailed policies and practices, puts commitment into action.

When establishing and continuously improving an anticorruption program, companies are encouraged to consider a set of underlying characteristics that support the program in being effective, efficient, and sustainable. These characteristics should be reflected in all elements of the anticorruption program and applied in the development and continuous improvement of the program.

Step 3: Oversight of the Anticorruption Program: The development and implementation of an anticorruption program require the active participation of every employee and relevant business partner. In order to manage the engagement of the entire organization in the program, a number of specific responsibilities should be assigned. The responsibilities should ensure that the program is implemented, executed, and overseen on an on-going basis. Oversight is important to guarantee that every employee and relevant business partner of the organization complies with and supports the program. Oversight of the program is also important to ensure that the different elements of the anticorruption program are carried out effectively and efficiently.

Step 4: Clear, Visible, and Accessible Policy Prohibiting Corruption: The commitment of senior management to preventing corruption, the development of an anticorruption program and its oversight, need to be translated into a policy prohibiting corruption. The clear, visible, and accessible policy prohibiting corruption represents the operational foundation for all other practical elements of the anticorruption program. It prescribes principles and rules to which all employees and relevant business partners need to adhere. A policy prohibiting corruption formalizes the company's engagement to prevent corruption. The guide describes how detailed policies can be provided and how companies can deal with different jurisdictions.

UNCAC is an innovative anticorruption instrument as it addresses not only major manifestations of corruption, such as bribery and embezzlement, but also acts carried out in support of corruption, such as obstruction of justice, trading in influence, and the concealment or laundering of the proceeds of corruption.[5] Further-

[5] See Legislative Guide for the Implementation of the United Nations Convention against Corruption—New York 2006, United Nations Office for Drugs and Crime (UNODC), http://www.unodc.org/pdf/corruption/CoC_LegislativeGuide.pdf, accessed 16 July 2013.

more, the convention covers not only corruption in private-to-public relationships (business relationship with public officials, including state-owned enterprises), but also private-to-private relationships (relationships among companies only).

The convention calls on state parties to establish a number of offences as crimes in their domestic law. Companies that operate in countries which have become parties to the UNCAC should therefore address the following manifestations of corruption and acts supporting corruption in their anticorruption policies:

- Bribery of national public officials
- Bribery of foreign public officials and officials of public international organizations
- Bribery in the private sector
- Embezzlement of property in the private sector
- Trading in influence
- Abuse of function
- Illicit enrichment
- Laundering of proceeds of crime
- Concealment of proceeds of crime
- Obstruction of justice

A policy which provides information on manifestations of corruption and the scope of application of the policy helps to translate the overarching commitment of zero tolerance of corruption into concrete and understandable elements. This approach further reduces the room for misinterpretation (e.g., by defining a "public official" or facilitation payments).

A policy addressing the above manifestations of corruption should be comprehensive in covering different forms and challenges. For example, bribery can take on a variety of forms (such as kickbacks, extortions, facilitation payments). Legitimate expenditures can also be misused as a subterfuge to a corrupt act (e.g., gifts, hospitality, travel payments, entertainment, sponsorship, charitable contributions, and/or political contributions).

Companies need to consider that while UNCAC addresses a variety of manifestations of corruption, countries have the discretion to go beyond the scope of this convention and could establish additional corruption-related offences, such as collusion.

Step 5: Detailed Policies for Particular Risk Areas: It is both an important and challenging endeavor to address the various manifestations of corruption through policies and practices. This is true for activities that are typically perceived as a violation of policies, such as bribing a public official to win a contract. However, it is especially difficult in cases where the borderline between legal practices and corrupt ones is not distinctively defined. For instance, while in some environments providing gifts in order to maintain good business relationships is common practice and allowed, gifts that influence a decision are strictly forbidden. Hence, there are many gray areas. Some cases may in fact constitute a corrupt act but are not perceived as such. Furthermore, the variety of different customs and business practices from one region to another make it difficult to distinguish between legal and illegal practices (see UNODC 2007, 2012). Companies should address these gray areas by drawing a clear line between legitimate and non-legitimate business practices.

When differentiating between legitimate and non-legitimate business practices, companies often face the following challenges:

- Business practices that are illicit but perceived as normal or even required (e.g., facilitation payments)
- Business practices that are legal but bear the risk of being misused to disguise corruption (e.g., misuse of political contributions, gifts, or hospitality as bribe for a national public official)
- Business practices that are based on biased decisions (conflicts of interest)

Step 6: Application of the Anticorruption Program to Business Partners: Companies operate in complex environments, engaging on a daily basis with a variety of business partners, such as suppliers, contractors, agents, subsidiaries, and joint ventures. The level of interaction with these partners varies, and could include informal relationships, single contractual relationships, or tight integration of business activities. The level of influence that a company has on its partners also varies. While some business partners remain fully independent, others may act on behalf of the company or are financially linked in the form of minor or major investments.

While engaging with business partners is a necessity for doing business, it can also present a considerable risk for companies as regards corruption. Companies that engage with business partners who have lower anticorruption standards may face the risks of corruption inquiries or even be held accountable for inappropriate behavior by their partners. National laws increasingly hold companies liable for the misconduct of their business partners. Additionally, a company's reputation can suffer considerably if it is associated with a corrupt partner.

Step 7: Internal Controls and Record Keeping: Business conduct should be based on mutual trust. Trust between a company's management and its employees is essential for a motivating work environment. In a similar way, it is important that there be trust between a company and its business partners. Management, employees, and business partners should conduct their activities in accordance with the company's ethical values, even in situations that are not clearly defined by policies and practices.

A company should ensure that all of its business activities are executed properly, especially those in high-risk processes such as financial reporting, procurement, sales, and marketing. However, relying completely on trust that business processes and activities will be properly executed can expose the company to significant negative consequences, such as severe legal fines, due to the commission of corrupt acts by a single rogue employee. Negative consequences can also occur due to carelessness, lack of awareness, or simple human errors. In order to mitigate these risks, companies should not only continuously strive to foster a working environment that is based on its ethical values, but also establish a system of internal controls (Brauer et al. 2009). The main objective of a system of internal controls is to provide reasonable assurance as to the effectiveness and efficiency of a company's operations, the reliability of its financial reporting, and its compliance with applicable laws, regulations, and internal policies.[6]

As part of the overall anticorruption program, the system of internal controls helps to ensure that anticorruption policies and practices are carried out as intended by the senior management of the company. Internal controls are therefore not only a means of reducing the risk of corruption, but also a way to support the management's responsibility to safeguard a company's assets and protect its employees and business partners from negative consequences.

Step 8: Communication and Training: Companies which establish anticorruption programs must not only ensure that their employees and relevant business partners are aware of their policies and practices, but also that they have the necessary information and skills to identify and counter corruption-related challenges. Regular communication and training activities play a key role in increasing awareness and obtaining commitment to anticorruption programs.

Step 9: Promoting and Incentivizing Ethics and Compliance: Commitment from employees and relevant business partners to the company's policies and practices is a key determinant of the program's success. In practice, companies often design and implement the anticorruption program according to good practice standards, but fall short in terms of encouraging employees and business partners to comply with its values and norms.

Incentive schemes are an option that can be employed to support the acceptance of the overall anticorruption program and sustain its major objective: to reduce corruption.

Step 10: Seeking Guidance—Detecting and Reporting Violations: Even companies with effective anticorruption programs may face violations of their policies and practices from employees or business partners. Recent years have also seen an increase in legal and reputational risks for companies which are associated with violations by business partners. Companies must therefore establish effective and efficient ways of detecting violations, while balancing risk and controls. Companies also need to provide opportunities for employees and business partners to seek guidance or to report violations, either committed by that person or by others.

Step 11: Addressing Violations: When violations of the company's anticorruption policies and practices are reported or detected, it is crucial to address these violations in order to demonstrate the company's commitment to zero-tolerance of corruption. How a company addresses violations or irregular practices determines the credibility of the anticorruption program among employees and business partners. Effective processes to deal with violations also help companies to avoid negative consequences by law enforcement and any reputational damage to the company. Companies should address violations as possible learning and improvement opportunities for their anticorruption program.

---

[6] See "Internal Control—Integrated Framework—1992," Committee of Sponsoring Organizations of the Treadway Commission (COSO), http://www.coso.org/ic-integratedframework-summary.htm, accessed 16 July 2013.

When violations are discovered, companies also need to decide whether to co-operate with law enforcement authorities, not only in the country where the alleged corrupt act has been discovered, but also with the authorities of other jurisdictions in which the company operates.

Step 12: Periodic Reviews and Evaluations of the Anticorruption Program: The implementation of an anticorruption program should be regarded as a continuous learning and improvement process. Periodic reviews and evaluations keep policies and practices up-to-date and relevant for employees and business partners.

Furthermore, reviews and evaluations help to identify shortcomings, weaknesses, or opportunities to optimize and simplify the overall anticorruption program.

References

Brauer, M. H, Steffen, K.-D., Biermann, S., & Schuler, A. H. (2009). *Compliance intelligence*. Stuttgart: Schäffer-Poeschel Verlag.

UNODC. (2007). *Corruption prevention to foster small and medium-sized enterprise development* (Vol. 1). Vienna: UNODC. http://www.unodc.org/documents/corruption/Publications/2012/UNIDO-UNODC_Publication_on_Small_Business_Development_and_Corruption_Vol1.pdf. Accessed 16 July 2013.

UNODC. (2012). *Corruption prevention to foster small and medium-sized enterprise development* (Vol. 2). Vienna: UNODC. http://www.unodc.org/documents/corruption/Publications/2012/Corruption_prevention_to_foster_small_and_medium_size_enterprise_development_Vol_2.pdf. Accessed 16 July 2013.

Chapter 13
The Role of the G20 and B20 in the Fight Against Corruption

Paul Kett

Contents

As one of the cochairs (with Mr. Joel Salas) of the G20 Anti-corruption Working Group (ACWG) in 2012, I am honored to contribute to the International Scientific and Professional Advisory Council (ISPAC) conference, *Anti-bribery Compliance Model: New International Approaches in Preventing and Fighting Corruption.* In this contribution, I provide some background to the work of the G20 in relation to anticorruption, its progress to date—including the emergence of the role of the B20—and next steps.

Before discussing the background, I wanted to share a reflection made as the year spent as the cochair came to an end. An *Economist* article[1] published the week before the conference commented on international efforts to tackle corruption. The article commented that the "working group set up in 2010 by the G20 (the world's largest economies) has done more than many observers expected," but highlighted the view of some commentators that "such efforts are 'steady, slow boring stuff', but still important."

[1] "The politics of corruption—Squeezing the sleazy," *The Economist*, 15 December 2012.

This contribution summarizes a presentation made at the International Scientific and Professional Advisory Council (ISPAC) conference, *International Strategies Against Corruption: Public–Private Partnership and Criminal Policy,* Courmayeur, Mont Blanc, 14–16 December 2012.

P. Kett (✉)
UK Ministry of Justice, London, UK
e-mail: paul.kett@justice.gsi.gov.uk

S. Manacorda et al. (eds.), *Preventing Corporate Corruption,*
DOI 10.1007/978-3-319-04480-4_13,

It was pleasing to see recognition of the progress that has been made, and that it has to some extent exceeded expectations—even if described as boring! Though that perhaps reflects the nature of the work the group has been leading. The starting point for the work of the group was largely based on the United Nations Convention Against Corruption (UNCAC) and the Organisation for Economic Co-operation and Development (OECD) Convention on Combating Bribery of Foreign Public Officials. These conventions have set the legal framework for the work the group has pursued in combating corruption and bribery globally. While these conventions have provided the framework, the reality has been that in addition to providing strong political leadership in securing their implementation, some of the most significant work of the group has focused on sharing best practice, and, increasingly, improving effective implementation of the measures supporting individual national governments' efforts in combating corruption. So, yes slow and steady, but this approach has seen the working group make significant and practical progress.

13.1 Background

The G20 ACWG was created under the Canadian presidency of the G20 at the Toronto Summit in June 2010,[2] where it was tasked with bringing forward recommendations for how the G20 could lead and support international efforts to combat corruption. Under the South Korean G20 presidency, an Anti-corruption Action Plan was put forward to leaders at the G20 Seoul Summit in November 2010, which saw its approval and a 2-year mandate established for the working group.[3] Under the Mexican G20 presidency, the working group's mandate was renewed at the Los Cabos Summit in June 2012,[4] where the group was tasked with bringing forward a renewed action plan, which was then agreed and published in November 2012.[5]

The G20, and therefore the ACWG, represents an intergovernmental process. The ACWG is additionally supported by the strong involvement of a number of international organizations including the OECD, UNODC, the World Bank, International Monetary Fund, and the Financial Action Task Force (FATF).

The ACWG has also seen increasingly effective collaboration with the business community and civil society groups, in particular through the emergence of the

[2] See Government of Canada, The G-20 Toronto Summit Declaration—June 26–27, 2010, paragraph 40, http://canadainternational.gc.ca/g20/assets/pdfs/g20_declaration_en.pdf, accessed 16 July 2013.

[3] See University of Toronto—G20 Information Center, G20 Anti-Corruption Action Plan—G20 Agenda for Action on Combating Corruption, Promoting Market Integrity, and Supporting a Clean Business Environment, Seoul, 12 November 2010, http://www.g20.utoronto.ca/2010/g20seoul-anticorruption.html, accessed 16 July 2013.

[4] See the G20, G20 Leaders Declaration—Los Cabos (Mexico) 18–19 June 2012, paragraphs 77–80, http://www.g20.org/load/780987820, accessed 16 July 2013.

[5] See G20—Mexico 2012,The G20 Anti-Corruption Action Plan 2013–2014, http://g20mexico.org/images/stories/docs/canalsherpas/anticorrup/01actionplan1.pdf, accessed 16 July 2013.

B20. The B20 brings together representatives from the international business community to contribute to the G20 process. It has been widely commented that corruption is bad for business. It is bad for growth, development, and market access. Our language around anticorruption need not be based only on the moral case: Tackling corruption is about ensuring sustainable economic growth and makes good business sense. Finding the right way of ensuring effective public–private action to combat corruption is one of the areas we must increasingly focus on.

As an intergovernmental process, the G20 operates by consensus and through leadership by example. The leadership role of the G20 has helped ensure that anticorruption efforts are regularly on the agenda of political leaders and has maintained the strong focus on international action to combat corruption. It is the role of the ACWG to seek to drive progress on the action plan and share best practices and country experience, and regularly report to leaders. In practice, this has seen the ACWG meeting about three times a year, with country delegates joined by representatives from the international organizations noted. The holder of the G20 presidency and one other country cochair the group. I pay tribute to my colleagues from France and Indonesia who cochaired the ACWG in 2011, and to my colleague from Mexico, Mr. Joel Salas, with whom I had the honor of cochairing in 2012.

13.2 The Seoul Action Plan

The Seoul Action Plan set out an ambitious agenda, central to which was providing a strong push on the UNCAC, which included a commitment to ratify and accede, and to strengthen reviews in line with the review mechanism. It also provided strong leadership in support of the other leading instrument: the OECD Convention on Combating Bribery, calling for engagement and promoting its implementation. In summary, the action plan called upon the ACWG to drive forward work:

- Ratify and implement UNCAC and strengthen individual reviews in line with the current terms of reference of the review mechanism
- Adopt and enforce laws and other measures against international bribery, such as the criminalization of bribery of foreign public officials
- Prevent corrupt officials from accessing the global financial system and laundering the proceeds of their corruption, and update and implement the FATF standards
- Prevent corrupt officials from travelling abroad with impunity and consider how to deny entry and safe haven
- Support the recovery of the proceeds of corruption abroad
- Protect whistle-blowers who report suspected corruption
- Strengthen the effective functioning of anticorruption bodies or enforcement authorities
- Promote integrity, transparency, accountability, and the prevention of corruption in the public sector

The action plan also highlighted the important role for business and opened the way for dialogue, which I discuss below.

Crucially, as well as requiring the group to update leaders at each G20 summit, the action plan sets out a clear approach to monitoring progress. This involved establishing an annual monitoring report, which provided transparency, and also offered a mechanism which served a further practical purpose, as it has led to a productive means of sharing of experiences, approaches, and lessons learned—both in the final reports and in the discussions in the ACWG which consider them. It is also fair to say, the publication of such reports has focused these discussions.

The monitoring reports highlight both individual country and overall G20 progress, and in practice have also provided a useful mechanism for countries to give more detail on particular initiatives or progresses made at national levels. The first monitoring report was published in 2011,[6] and the second in November 2012.[7]

13.3 The B20

The Seoul Action Plan provided a basis for opening dialogue between the ACWG and the business community. In the first year of taking forward the action plan under France's G20 presidency, a B20 of business leaders was established with a task group on anticorruption and transparency. In its first year, a core part of this dialogue took the form of a successful conference (which also included civil society participation).[8] Informed by the discussions at this conference, the B20 then prepared a report provided to the G20 at the end of the year.

Under Mexico's G20 presidency, the B20 task group on anticorruption and transparency continued, though the nature of the dialogue evolved and strengthened further, leading to considerable alignment and greater focus in areas of shared priorities. In practice, this saw B20 representatives joining the ACWG for dialogues as well as a second successful conference in Puerto Vallarta in April 2012. As a result, the ongoing dialogue informed the work of the G20, with shared priorities reflected in the Los Cabos declaration, the monitoring report, and the renewed action plan. In taking up the G20 presidency, Russia has indicated its intention to continue this maturing dialogue and collaboration with business in tackling corruption.

---

[6] See G20, First Monitoring Report of the G20 Anti-Corruption Working Group to G20 Leaders on Individual and Collective Progress made by G20 Countries in the Implementation of the Seoul Action Plan, http://www.g20.org/load/781360421, accessed 16 July 2013.

[7] See G20—Mexico 2012, G20 Anti-Corruption Working Group 2012 Monitoring Report, http://g20mexico.org/images/stories/docs/canalsherpas/anticorrup/02monitoringreport1.pdf, and http://g20mexico.org/images/stories/docs/canalsherpas/anticorrup/03g20acwgparis.pdf, accessed 16 July 2013.

[8] See OECD, G20–OECD Conference: Joining Forces against Corruption: G20 Business and Government—27–28 April, 2011, http://www.oecd.org/daf/anti-bribery/g20-oecdconferencejoiningforcesagainstcorruptiong20businessandgovernment.htm, accessed 16 July 2013.

Tackling corruption is not something that one actor alone can undertake—all have a role to play, and can achieve that much more when there is dialogue and collaboration. The dialogues that have been established between government, business, and civil society have shown clear impacts arising from the sharing of experience and approaches, and have informed efforts to tackle corruption across all sectors.

13.4 Where We Are Now: Progress During 2012

During 2012, the ACWG has made considerable progress against the Seoul Action Plan, as well as securing a renewed 2-year mandate and updated action plan. In particular, the ACWG has endorsed principles for the denial of entry of corrupt officials, having also convened discussions of national experts.[9] In pursuit of commitments to promote integrity, the ACWG has endorsed principles for financial and asset disclosure systems for public officials to prevent, identify, and appropriately manage conflict of interests.[10] The ACWG has also published a comprehensive Mutual Legal Assistance (MLA) Guide for G20 countries, which was no small undertaking given the complexity of arrangements—which of itself highlights its importance.[11] Continuing efforts to ensure effective cooperation and to promote transparency were furthered by the publication of country-by-country information on asset-tracing profiles.[12]

As well as broader engagement with business in the fight against corruption, the ACWG agrees that, in accordance with the Terms of Reference of the UNCAC review mechanism, G20 countries will involve the private sector and civil society in the UNCAC review process on a voluntary basis. The involvement of the private sector was a recommendation made by the B20. A number of G20 countries that have completed or are currently undergoing a review of their implementation of UNCAC have already involved the private sector both in the production of the self-assessment and during country visits, and state parties have reported the positive contribution that has resulted.

[9] See G20—Mexico 2012, G20 Common Principles for Action: Denial of Safe Haven, http://g20mexico.org/images/stories/docs/canalsherpas/anticorrup/g20denial-1.pdf, accessed 16 July 2013.

[10] See G20—Mexico 2012, G20 High-Level Principles on Asset Disclosure by Public Officials, http://g20mexico.org/images/stories/docs/canalsherpas/anticorrup/g20assetdisclosure.pdf, accessed 16 July 2013.

[11] See G20—Mexico 2012, Requesting Mutual Legal Assistance in Criminal Matters from G20 Countries: A Step-By-Step Guide, 2012, http://g20mexico.org/images/stories/docs/canalsherpas/anticorrup/g20mla.pdf, accessed 16 July 2013.

[12] See G20—Mexico 2012, Assets Tracing—Country Profiles—Anti-Corruption Working Group, June 2012, http://g20mexico.org/images/stories/docs/canalsherpas/anticorrup/g20assettracing.pdf, accessed 13 July 2013.

The revised FATF standards were adopted in February 2012,[13] and G20 leaders welcomed the adoption of the revised standards and looked forward to their implementation, as well as to progress made by FATF in identifying and monitoring high-risk jurisdictions with strategic Anti-money Laundering (AML) and/or Countering Financing of Terrorism (CTF) deficiencies and the use of AML/CFT tools in the fight against corruption, improving transparency of corporate vehicles, increasing cooperation against tax crimes, and addressing the risks posed by tax havens. The ACWG also held its second joint meeting with FATF anticorruption experts in Paris in October 2012. The discussion focused on specific issues relating to international cooperation, specifically in the context of money-laundering cases involving the proceeds of corruption and asset recovery.

Finally, the ACWG secured a renewal of its mandate for a further 2 years, and a renewed action plan which was published in November 2012.

13.5 Where Next? The Renewed Mandate and New Action Plan

The renewed mandate agreed by leaders at the Los Cabos G20 Summit was followed by the agreement of a new G20 Anti-corruption Action Plan 2013–2014, published in November 2012. The new action plan builds on the commitments already made, as the G20 renews its pledge to implement fully the commitments in the Seoul Anti-corruption Action Plan, the Cannes Monitoring Report and subsequent leaders' declarations adopted at the summits in Cannes and Los Cabos.

The particular focus of the renewed action plan is on closing the implementation and enforcement gap—building on past progress, and continuing to push forward implementation of the UNCAC and OECD convention. In closing this gap, the action plan includes commitments to sharing best practice, guidance, and information on enforcement and asset recovery, the establishment of a denial of entry experts' network, and building on international cooperation efforts and MLA guidance.

The action plan also builds on the progress made in strengthening the dialogue with business, identifying where there are opportunities to work with the private sector, in particular the B20. Accordingly, it identifies a number of areas in which that dialogue with business can be built upon: seeking views, collaborating, and calling for action—including identifying best practice for encouraging voluntary self-reporting, and in identifying enforcement measures which are effective in changing the behavior of bribe payers.

More generally, in relation to public–private action, the ACWG will identify best practices from sector-based initiatives, including those previously highlighted by

[13] See the Financial Action Task Force (FATF), International Standards on Combating Money Laundering and the Financing of Terrorism & Proliferation—the FATF Recommendations, Paris, 16 February 2012, http://www.fatf-gafi.org/topics/fatfrecommendations/documents/internationalstandardsoncombatingmoneylaunderingandthefinancingofterrorismproliferation-thefatfrecommendations.html, accessed 16 July 2013.

the G20—the Extractives Industries Transparency Initiative (EITI) and Construction Sector Transparency Initiative (CoST). It will also carry out a risk-mapping study, which will include input from business, to identify those areas and sectors at greatest risk of corruption.

Russia assumes the G20 presidency in 2013, with Canada as their cochair, and the renewed Action Plan will then conclude at the end of Australia's G20 presidency in 2014. It is therefore clear that while progress has been steady, and more considerable than some commentators predicted, there remains an important role for the G20 in leading and supporting international efforts to combat corruption, and the next 2 years provide a particular opportunity to close the implementation and enforcement gap.

Chapter 14
Emerging Control of and Sanctions Against Corruption: The International Chamber of Commerce

François Vincke

Contents

14.1 International Chamber of Commerce, the Business Pioneer in the Fight Against Bribery

Control of and sanctions against corruption is not necessarily the monopoly of public authorities. Corruption is an offense of such seriousness, and a social evil with such obnoxious ramifications, that the private sector cannot remain on the sidelines when it comes to fighting it.

F. Vincke (✉)
International Chamber of Commerce-ICC, Paris, France
e-mail: francoisvincke@gmail.com

S. Manacorda et al. (eds.), *Preventing Corporate Corruption*,
DOI 10.1007/978-3-319-04480-4_14, © Springer International Publishing Switzerland 2014

Fighting corruption consists not only of prohibiting and condemning all corruptive practices, but also, and maybe even more essentially, of implementing all reasonably available measures to avoid or prevent these practices. Public authorities play a role in matters of prevention, but the private sector (and civil society) cannot avoid taking a proactive stance as well.

Indeed, the private sector has long understood that corruption not only undermines the very foundations of democracy through breach of the public trust vested in public (national and foreign) officials and the private trust in corporate executives, but that it also undercuts the very basis of sound corporate governance, fair competition, and ultimately, the liberal economy (Vincke 1998, p. 192).

14.1.1 The First Report in 1977

Back in 1975, the International Chamber of Commerce (ICC), the world business organization, created a Committee on Extortion and Bribery (Heimann and Hirsch 2000, p. 170). The committee, called the Shawcross Committee[1] after its Chairman, issued a report in 1977, setting out Rules of Conduct on Extortion and Bribery,[2] written under the influence mainly of the US Foreign Corrupt Practices Act (FCPA).[3] The report was welcomed as a breakthrough, although not universally.[4] The ICC rules nevertheless had an effect in the longer term, if one may judge by the number of corporate documents, such as corporate codes of conduct and corporate integrity programs, which either refer to it or use its terminology (Vincke 1996, p. 119).

By issuing this report, the ICC became the first non-governmental organization to produce rules of conduct on matters as sensitive as extortion and bribery. In the years to follow, ICC would be joined in its endeavors by a number of other business and civil society organizations, such as Transparency International (TI),[5] the United

---

[1] Hartley William Shawcross (1902–2003), British barrister and politician. Lord Shawcross served as Member of Parliament from 1945 to 1958 and held the position of Attorney-General from 1945 to 1951. He was the (much-respected) lead British prosecutor at the Nuremberg War Crimes Tribunal.

[2] Another famous member of this committee was Lloyd Cutler (1917–2005), an American attorney who served as a White House Counsel during the democratic administrations of Presidents Carter and Clinton. In 1962, Lloyd Cutler cofounded the Washington, D.C.-based law firm Wilmer Cutler & Pickering.

[3] See US Government Printing Office, *91 Stat. 1494 Public Law 95–213—Dec. 19, 1977,* http://www.gpo.gov/fdsys/pkg/STATUTE-91/pdf/STATUTE-91-Pg1494.pdf, accessed 16 July 2013.

[4] Some criticism was voiced against the ICC document, e.g., Draetta (2010); Black and Witten (1997, Chap. 9 at item 5): "[T]here is no evidence that the ICC Rules of Conduct had any tangible impact on international practices"; and Pieth (2007, p. 9): "Similarly, the rules of conduct developed by the International Chamber of Commerce (ICC)…, and aiming to supplement an international public standard, were finalised. They too remained, however, a more or less dead letter without the public backing of the Convention, until new efforts in the 1990s proved more successful."

[5] Transparency International (TI) was founded as a nongovernmental organization in 1993 mainly by a group of former World Bank executives. TI has its international headquarters in Berlin and

Nations Global Compact,[6] and the Partnering Against Corruption Initiative (PACI)[7] of the World Economic Forum (WEF).[8]

The ICC report[9] condemned in no uncertain terms all forms of corruption, but also encouraged companies to draft their own codes of conduct (Trochon and Vincke 2006, p. 309) and to establish a corporate compliance program to avoid extortion and bribery (Heimann 1997). Right from the start, the question was asked: Does the ICC need to have some form of control and sanctioning power over compliance with its rules? Would the newly issued rules lack credibility if the ICC could not organize some kind of control, monitoring, or overview?

14.2 Emerging Control in the First ICC Report

In fact, the ICC report issued by the Shawcross Committee did not limit itself to proclaiming strong prohibitions in its Rules of Conduct; it also established an International Panel of Experts[10] as a monitoring mechanism for the Rules of Conduct, and wrote bylaws defining its role.[11] As I have explained in another publication (Vincke 1997), the panel was established by the ICC "to interpret, promote and oversee the application of the...Rules of Conduct." It had four main tasks: (1) periodic review of matters relating to the Rules of Conduct; (2) interpretation, clarification, and possible suggestion of modification to the rules; (3) periodic reporting to the council of the ICC on its activities; and (4) considering, in appropriate circumstances, alleged infringements of the Rules of Conduct. Article 5 of the panel's bylaws provided in substance that the expert panel could, upon request of any member or national committee (of the ICC) or of any other enterprise or public authority which, in the opinion of the panel, had a bona fide or commercial or other legitimate interest, examine any alleged infringement of the Rules of Conduct by any party, including non-members of the ICC and any public author-

has, since its foundation, created national chapters in about 100 countries. In June 2003, TI published its Business Principles for Countering Bribery.

[6] The United Nations Global Compact was launched in 1998, as the result of an invitation by UN Secretary-General Kofi Annan to the world's enterprises to commit to comply with the provisions of international instruments in the fields of human rights, labor law, and the protection of the environment. At a later stage, the fight against corruption was added, as "a tenth principle," to the list.

[7] Together with Transparency International and the Basel Institute on Governance, the World Economic Forum launched the document "Principles for Countering Bribery" of the Partnering against Corruption Initiative.

[8] The World Economic Forum was founded in 1971 as an independent international organization having its seat in Geneva.

[9] International Chamber of Commerce, *Extortion and Bribery in Business Transactions: Report Adopted by the 131st Session of the Council of the ICC, 29 November 1977* (Paris: The Chamber, 1977).

[10] Article 11 of the Shawcross Report, as well as Part IV of the same document containing the bylaws of the panel.

[11] Bylaws adopted by the 132d session of the Council of the ICC, 20 June 1978.

ity or official thereof. It was further provided that the panel would not proceed (absent special circumstances) with the examination of a case without the explicit consent of the party against whom an infringement was alleged.

14.3 A New Lex Mercatoria?

The ICC is known for its competence in matters of self-regulation.[12] In the banking world, the ICC Uniform Customs and Practice for Documentary Credits (UCP)[13] are in use everywhere. Everybody across the world who is involved in international trade uses the International Commercial Terms (INCOTERMS®).[14] In the field of marketing and advertising, of note is the ICC International Code of Advertising Practice, which later became the ICC Code of the Consolidated Advertising and Marketing Communication Practice (the ICC Code).[15,16] The ICC Code seeks, through effective self-regulation, to build trust with consumers by ensuring advertising that is honest, legal, decent, and truthful, and provides quick and easy redress when transgressions occur.[17]

The various texts mentioned above are based on best international practice, are drafted by the policy commissions of the ICC, and are processed through a lengthy, involved, and critical procedure of internal approval involving the national ICC committees, the individual experts who serve as members of the relevant policy commissions, and the top governance bodies of the organization.

These documents are part of what one considers to be "soft law," i.e., they are adopted in the framework of a professional association on a purely voluntary basis,[18] and their enforcement will not be pursued by the courts of any jurisdiction.[19] They are not compulsory but enjoy a status bordering customary law, as they are often and on

---

[12] ICC usually describes itself by saying: "It makes rules that govern the conduct of business across borders."

[13] The UCP were issued for the first time in 1933 and their sixth and latest revision (under the name 'UCP 600') dates from 1 July 2007.

[14] The INCOTERMS were first issued in 1936 and their latest revision (under the name "INCOTERMS® 2010") dates from 1 January 2011. See ICC, *The New Incoterms® 2010 Rules,* http://www.iccwbo.org/products-and-services/trade-facilitation/incoterms-2010/, accessed 16 July 2013.

[15] This code was first published in 1937, it has been revised seven times, the last being in 1997.

[16] See also the Business Action for Responsible Marketing and Advertising (BARMA), where advertisers, agencies, media, and other major stakeholders are brought together to promote greater application and reach of the ICC Code of the Consolidated Advertising and Marketing Communication Practice, which has served as the global gold standard for self-regulation in this field since 1937. The ICC Code sets the bar for ethical guidelines and responsible marketing practices globally, and is the reference for most nationally applied self-regulation.

[17] In addition to different codes, the ICC also produces an impressive number of model contracts, based on best business practice.

[18] The ICC report of 1977 provided that the ICC rules were "of a general nature constituting what is considered good commercial practice in matters to which they relate but without direct legal effect."

[19] Even if a certain number of courts refer to the ICC provisions in their rulings.

a constant basis used by professionals and trades people around the world. Over the years, these ICC documents have gradually transformed into a kind of *lex mercatoria,* becoming another source of law in the international business environment.

14.4 Seeking Redress in Anticorruption?

The Shawcross Committee thought that it was not only possible to set the rules for combating extortion and bribery in international business transactions, it also wanted to provide members and non-members of the ICC with a tool to fight effectively any attempt to commit malpractice. This was particularly relevant, as the business community often complained of being the victim of attempts at solicitation or extortion by greedy officials or politicians in a number of host countries, or of foul play by unscrupulous competitors who were not bound or believed themselves not bound by strict anticorruption provisions.

For the business community, having recourse to a discreet, efficient, and fast-working expert panel could potentially have worked smoothly. Such a panel, based on self-regulation, should have been a simple solution to a vexed issue. Where else could companies, pestered by solicitation attempts, or wronged by unfair competitors in a public or private procurement process, be better helped than in a privately organized process, led by internationally recognized experts? Was this not an opportunity to organize the rules for free and unfettered competition unhampered by illicit—or, at least, unethical—behavior by public officials or unruly competitors?[20]

14.5 The Panel, a Generous Idea, a Practical Failure

The time was not ripe, however. The FCPA was still in its infancy. The USA stood alone in its attempt to confront the evils of corruption (Glynn et al. 1997, p. 18). The USA launched an effort to "internationalize" the FCPA. But America's competitor nations were not so bothered about adopting similar or comparable legislation.[21,22]

[20] For a very critical comment on the ineffectiveness of the Panel, see Heritier (1981, p. 137; quoted by Oppetit 1987, p. 17): "one should ask the question whether the acceptance of very strict rules, laid down in the articles 1 to 5 of the [ICC] Code of Conduct [together with] the refusal of control and sanctions, has a meaning or if it is only a means to react in front of external pressure [and] a way to create a good conscience."

[21] Oppetit commented in the above-mentioned article (1987, pp. 5–21) that the positions taken in French criminal, civil, and tax law on corruption were particularly lenient, and noted that "the legal system [of the country concerned], far from pronouncing a condemnation free from any ambiguity, … appear[ed] to adopt an attitude of indifference, not to say of pure and simple acceptance: as soon as the matter turn[ed] around the conquest of markets outside the national territory, the moral reprobation of corruption weaken[ed] considerably or even vanishe[d]."

[22] On the "benign neglect" shown by the competitors of the USA, see Sacerdoti (2000, p. 30).

Meanwhile, the US initiative to prompt the United Nations into considering the matter of corruption in an international context[23] failed. A draft convention prepared by the United Nations Commission on Transnational Companies (UNTC), called the International Agreement on Illicit Payments, was not taken into consideration by the General Assembly of the organization.

The intention behind the creation of the Panel of Experts was excellent, but the results did not even meet the most minimal expectations. In the 17 years that elapsed between the adoption of the bylaws and their official repeal, little action was taken to implement the provisions of Article 11 of the ICC report, or Part IV of the same document containing the bylaws of the panel. Although the panel met on one or two occasions, only one case came before it. As a consequence, it last met in 1981 and gradually became completely inactive.

14.6 Why was the Panel of Experts a Failure?

The Panel of Experts, which could have been an innovative control instrument and a means to ensure equality of treatment for all companies facing allegations of extortion and bribery, never became effective. It eventually disappeared completely when the ICC issued a new report[24] which no longer contained any reference to the panel. This report was adopted by an ad hoc committee at the end of 1995 and approved by the executive committee of the ICC on 26 March 1996 (Argandona 1997).

The silent exit of the Panel of Experts can be explained by a lack of interest on the part of the business community: It seemed difficult for the enterprises to bring forward allegations of extortion or solicitation by officials (in the countries where they intended to do business), or to cast doubt on the fairness of a competitor. Moreover, nobody was certain about the competence of a private body to adjudicate on matters which would hinge on criminal law. Self-regulation, as we have seen, is accepted and welcomed, but self-adjudication seemed too far reaching and it appeared difficult to fathom how a "decision" of the panel would be made effective in the real world (Vincke 1997, p. 101).

14.7 A New Initiative: Reporting Solicitation to CCS

The panel disappeared, but the entrepreneurs' concern about solicitation did not. After the Organisation for Economic Co-operation and Development (OECD) Convention on Combating Bribery of Foreign Public Officials in International Business

[23] United Nations, Economic and Social Committee, *Report of the Ad Hoc Intergovernmental Working Group on the Problem of Corrupt Practices, July 5, 1977,* UN Doc. E/6006.

[24] International Chamber of Commerce, *Extortion and Bribery in International Business Transactions, Exec. Bd., 83rd Sess.* 26 March 1996.

Transactions was adopted, the ICC, together with other international organizations such as the Business and Industry Advisory Committee (BIAC),[25] would regularly and passionately argue with the OECD Working Group on Bribery for the need to give companies support and protection against solicitation or passive corruption. This was necessary, as the OECD convention gives only scant attention to passive corruption[26] and criminalizes only active corruption. Changing the OECD convention would have been a gigantic undertaking. So companies had to try to cope with solicitation by their own means. It was time to come up with a new initiative.

The ICC proposed to entrust its specialized division, located in the London area, ICC Commercial Crime Services (CCS), with a special task in relation to solicitation. Created in the 1980s in the form of a nonprofit organization, CCS provides technical support to enterprises confronted with economic crime. CCS enjoys an excellent reputation and its first-rate services give it access to numerous international organizations, governments, and police services (Vincke 2006, p. 188, 189; Vincke 2007; Juvin 2007, p. 609).

The ICC commission on anticorruption formulated the project to centralize all information pertaining to extortion or solicitation; enterprises participating in the project would report to CCS any solicitation or extortion attempt directed at them. CCS would then register the information received, compile the data, analyze any recurrent patterns, and, on that basis, establish a map of extortion and solicitation hot spots, which would thus be exposed to the reprobation of the international community. This process, based on the efficient naming and shaming technique, would also have the advantage of alerting potential investors to the risks they would incur by investing in certain countries, regions, or activities. Needless to say, CCS would ensure absolute confidentiality of its sources and would make sure that the documents emanating from its informants would be protected against any interference.

14.8 The CCS Project Was Not Seen as an Opportunity

This proposal, which had initially received a favorable appraisal from certain international institutions, had little or no success with the ICC members. Why was this? Was it the cost necessarily related to it, or was it the possibility that only situations which were already widely known would be revealed, or was it the fear of confronting extortion mafias? One of the most plausible explanations for the lack of traction of the project was that certain companies feared that the project would impose on

[25] BIAC is an independent international business association devoted to advising government policy-makers at OECD and related fora on the many and diverse issues of globalization and the world economy.

[26] See *Commentaries on the Convention*, item 1: "This Convention deals with what, in the law of some countries; is called 'active corruption' or 'active bribery', meaning the offence committed by the person who promises or gives the bribe, as contrasted with 'passive bribe', the offence committed by the official who receives the bribe.... In fact, in a number of situations, the recipient will have induced or pressured the briber and will have been, in that sense, the more active."

them another kind of constraint (having to report all extortion/solicitation attempts), rather than offering them a new opportunity.

14.9 RESIST, a Success Story

Was it then impossible to achieve a form of "emerging control" in the field of anticorruption? Both the above-mentioned initiatives could have led to such a conclusion. Fortunately, a new initiative would be brought forward which, although not bringing about a means to exercise a form of control over solicitation attempts, would at least address the issue seriously.

The project Resisting Extortion and Solicitation in International Transactions (RESIST)[27,28] was set up by the ICC, the Global Compact, PACI, and Transparency International. Based on 21 real-life scenarios, RESIST was designed as a training tool to provide practical guidance for company employees on how to prevent and/or respond to an inappropriate demand by a client, business partner, or public official in the most efficient and ethical way. RESIST, which was translated into French, Spanish, German, Mandarin, and Arabic, is used worldwide and offers a practical, easy, and user-friendly tool[29] to train and teach co-workers how to oppose illicit demands.

14.10 Good Practice Guidance

During the last decade, it became gradually clear that every individual company has a duty to establish an efficient corporate anticorruption program. Such a program should be adapted to the enterprise's particular circumstances, and be set up with the aim of preventing and detecting corruption and of promoting a culture of integrity.[30] Among the pioneer countries in imposing this requirement to install an

[27] In its first phase, the RESIST project was led by Mr. François Georges, at the time an executive of EDF and presently Secretary-General of ICC France, while the second phase was led by Mr. Iohann Le Frapper, General Counsel Networks Group at Alcatel-Lucent and recently appointed Vice-Chair of the ICC Commission on Social Responsibility and Anticorruption.

[28] See ICC, *Resisting Extortion and Solicitation in International Transactions (RESIST),* http://www.iccwbo.org/products-and-services/fighting-commercial-crime/resist/, accessed 16 July 2013.

[29] ICC France is preparing a number of practical instruments to make RESIST an even easier means to spread among company employees the recommended attitudes when facing solicitation and extortion.

[30] Compare Article 10 of the ICC Rules on Combating Corruption (2011).

effective corporate compliance program, one should mention the USA,[31] Italy,[32] and the UK.[33]

The OECD Working Group on Bribery, which oversees the regular monitoring of the implementation by member countries of the convention's provisions, adopted on 18 February 2010 a *Good Practice Guidance on Internal Controls, Ethics, and Compliance*. Such guidance is an integral part of the *Recommendation of the [OECD] Council for Further Combating Bribery of Foreign Public Officials in International Business Transactions* of 26 November 2009.

From the point of view of the ICC, as a business organization, it is interesting to note that the OECD considers that:

> Business organizations and professional associations may play an essential role in assisting companies, in particular SMEs, in the development of effective internal control, ethics, and compliance programs or measures for the purpose of preventing and detecting foreign bribery.[34]

14.11 Is There a Possible "Emerging Sanction"?

Traditional wisdom has it that sanctions against any form of corruption will be meted out only by the criminal courts. Sanctions on the basis of self-regulation would only be possible as a matter of internal discipline in the (limited) framework of the enterprise and in the context of labor relations.

---

[31] The US Federal Sentencing Guidelines contain a guideline entitled "Effective Compliance and Ethics Program." The program described in the guideline contains seven items, also often referred to as the Seven Steps: (1) setting up of a compliance program capable of preventing criminal or prohibited acts, (2) assigning specific high-level personnel to oversee compliance, (3) exercising care not to hire individuals or to delegate substantial discretionary authority to them if they are likely to participate in illegal activities or conduct inconsistent with an effective compliance and ethics program, (4) effectively communicating standards and procedures to all employees, (5) implementing reasonable compliance measures, such as monitoring, auditing, and reporting, (6) using disciplinary mechanisms to consistently enforce standards and procedures, and (7) taking all reasonable steps to respond appropriately after an offense has been detected, including modifying the compliance program.

An organization which can evidence effective compliance with a corporate compliance and ethics program meeting the above criteria, may expect this to have a bearing on the penalties and probation terms if it is convicted and sentenced for a criminal offense. See also Vincke (1999, pp. 21–25).

[32] See the Italian Legislative Decree N. 231 of 8 June 2001, which foresees an exemption for entities which can provide evidence that they meet certain compliance conditions. I note, in particular, in this context, that the management model adopted by an entity may be based on a code of conduct, established by a professional association, and notified to the Minister of Justice and to other departments.

[33] See Article 7 of the UK Bribery Act 2010 and the guidance about procedures which relevant commercial organizations can put into place to prevent persons associated with them from bribing.

[34] OECD, *Good Practice Guidance,* Sect. B.

This would leave out all possibility of disciplining unethical contractual parties, dishonest intermediaries, or business partners. In the business community, we have tried to overcome this obstacle.

14.12 A New and Innovative Forum: The B20

In the wake of the G20 Summit in Seoul, the G20 leaders asked experts of the business world, gathered in the Business 20 (B20), to give them help and advice on a number of issues, among which was the fight against corruption. In preparation for the Cannes Summit, the B20 anticorruption working group formulated six areas in which it believed urgent action was necessary and possible: (1) public procurement procedures; (2) the fight against corruption on the basis of sector-based initiatives; (3) private-sector involvement in monitoring reviews; (4) training and education in enterprises on anticorruption initiatives; (5) the drafting and implementation of codes of conduct and compliance programs, especially in small and medium-sized enterprises (SMEs); and (6) the fight against solicitation.

ICC decided to focus on two main subject matters: (1) training and education and (2) the preparation of instruments especially for SMEs. On the first subject, an ambitious program was set up in the ICC Commission on Corporate Responsibility and Anti-corruption to draft an *Ethics and Compliance Training Handbook*, which has been published by ICC Publishing, Paris, on December 9, 2014. The handbook will be the building block of a vast ethics and compliance training and education program conducted by the ICC.

14.13 The ICC Anti-corruption Clause (2012)

On the second subject, the ICC took the initiative to come forward with a new instrument to be used by companies of all sizes, but particularly by the smaller ones:[35] the *ICC Anti-corruption Clause.*[36] This clause is meant to be a strong instrument in the civil sanctioning of corruption. How did we arrive at this idea?

The basic reasoning at the origin of this initiative is as simple as a Columbus' egg. Let us imagine a businessman who starts negotiating with a potential customer, supplier, or any other business partner. Everything proceeds smoothly, but when our businessman comes close to concluding the deal, his or her advisors induce him into broaching some of the most sensitive subjects, such as an anticorruption

[35] See ICC, *ICC Anti-corruption Clause,* http://www.iccwbo.org/Advocacy-Codes-and-Rules/Document-centre/2012/ICC-Anti-corruption-Clause/, accessed 16 July 2013.

[36] See ICC, "New ICC Tool Responds to G20 Anti-corruption Call," http://www.iccwbo.org/News/Articles/2012/New-ICC-tool-responds-to-G20-anti-corruption-call/, accessed 16 July 2013.

provision. Our businessman will not be enthusiastic about the idea; though delicate, it is unavoidable to start talking about such subjects and to ask prospective partners:

> Have you bribed in the context of these negotiations, will you make sure nobody among your people is going to bribe during the implementation of the contract, have you put into place serious means to avoid any attempt at bribing, etc.?

Nobody likes to hear his or her reputation being questioned, nobody fancies being interrogated on such matters. In addition, smaller companies will feel dwarfed by larger ones, whom they will suspect of patronizing them, while bigger companies will fear that the resistance of a small company against their model clause may hide some desire to continue dodgy practices. Therefore, ICC wanted to create a clause usable by any kind of company in all circumstances.

The other idea underlying the new instrument was that hitting the corruptors and/or corruptees in their wallet, by terminating (or suspending)—under strict and fair conditions—their contract, was a sure way to mete out a strong, appropriate, and dissuasive sanction. Punishing malfeasance through affecting the material benefit the perpetrator expected to gain from malpractice is a relevant and adequate sanction.

14.14 A Neutral Solution

To avoid the difficult dialogue sketched above, parties may prefer to opt for a neutral solution: the *ICC Anti-corruption Clause*. The ICC clause offers truly equitable treatment to both sides in a negotiation. The clause is built on the most common practice in business and allows both parties to move from corporate compliance to contractual compliance.

A party to a contract containing the ICC clause will not only comply, within its organization, with the prevailing anticorruption provisions as summarized in Part I[37] of the ICC Rules on Combating Corruption (2011),[38] it may also expect the counter-party to do the same, failing which the first party may either suspend or terminate the contract.

Alternatively, the commitment of both contractual parties is that each of them has put into place (or is about to do so) a corporate anticorruption compliance program, as described in Article 10 of the ICC Rules on Combating Corruption.

---

[37] Part I of the *ICC Rules on Combating Corruption* expresses a prohibition of all forms of corruptive practices.

[38] See ICC, *ICC Rules on Combating Corruption,* http://www.iccwbo.org/advocacy-codes-and-rules/areas-of-work/corporate-responsibility-and-anti-corruption/ICC-Rules-on-Combatting-Corruption/, accessed 16 July 2013.

14.15 The Sanctity of Contracts

The authors of the clause wanted to eradicate corruption in commercial relations, but did not want this to happen at the expense of the sanctity of contracts. To ensure a balance between both objectives, the clause provides as follows:[39]

1. To be considered relevant under the clause, an infringement by one of the parties should consist of material or several repeated breaches of Part I of the ICC Rules on Combating Corruption. In other words, a minor or isolated occurrence would not trigger the sanctioning effect.
2. The infringement in question will be in the context of the very contract and not be related to another contract between the same parties or to a contract with other parties.
3. Evidence of the infringement can be (a) based on the conclusions of a contractually provided audit (but ICC hastens to say in the commentaries to the clause that it does not necessarily recommend an audit clause be included in the contract) or (b) by bringing other kind of evidence, which does not have to be corroborative in nature, but which has to be such that there would be no suspicion that it is invoked in a vexatious or otherwise unjustified manner.
4. The party suspected of having infringed an anticorruption provision will be allowed to take remedial action curing the situation in a reasonable time after having been notified by the other party.
5. The suspected party may invoke as a defense that, by the time the evidence of an infringement was invoked, it had put into place adequate anticorruption preventive measures, as described in Article 10 of the ICC Rules on Combating Corruption.

14.16 An Early Recognition

Many leading companies have expressed their interest in using the new ICC Anticorruption Clause extensively. The hope is that the clause will be so frequently and universally used that it becomes part-and-parcel of international customary law. In this way, ICC would have contributed in a significant way to the (alternative) sanctioning of breaches of anticorruption provisions.

[39] See also the commentaries, which are a part of the *ICC Anti-corruption Clause*.

References

Argandona, A. (1997). The 1996 ICC Report on extortion and bribery in international business transactions. *Business Ethics, 6*(3), 134–146

Black, S. F., & Witten, R. M. (1997). *Complying with the foreign corrupt practices act*. San Francisco: Lexis Nexis Matthew Bender.

Draetta, U. (2010). The European Union and the fight against corruption in international trade. In H. Lange (Ed.), *Working across cultures: Ethical perspectives for intercultural management*. New York: Springer.

Glynn, P., Kobrin, S. J., Naim, M. (1997). The globalization of corruption. In K. A. Elliott (Ed.), *Corruption and the global economy*. Washington: Institute for International Economics.

Heimann, F. F. (1997). Combating international corruption: The role of the business community. In K. A. Elliot (Ed.), *Corruption and the global economy*. Washington: Institute for International Economics.

Heimann, F. F., & Hirsch, M. (2000). How international business combats extortion and bribery: Anti-corruption efforts by the International Chamber of Commerce. In *No longer business as usual: fighting bribery and corruption*. OECD

Heritier, A. (1981). *Les pots-de-vin*. Genève: Georg.

Juvin, H. (2007). *L'entreprise mondialisée face aux risques répressifs: de nouvelles exigences de prévention et de gouvernance*. Paris: Jouve.

Oppetit, B. (1987). Le paradoxe de la corruption à l'épreuve du commerce international. *Journal de Droit International, 114*.

Pieth, M. (2007). Introduction. In M. Pieth, et al. (Eds.), *The OECD convention on bribery: A commentary*. Cambridge: Cambridge University Press.

Sacerdoti, G. (2000). To bribe or not to bribe? In *No longer business as usual, fighting bribery and corruption*. OECD.

Trochon, J., & Vincke, F. (2006). *L'entreprise face à la mondialisation: opportunités et risques, Stratégies juridiques*. Brussels: Bruylant.

Vincke, F. (1996). La communauté des affaires face à la corruption, un nouveau rapport de la CCI. *Revue de Droit International et de Droit Comparé, 73,* 119–134.

Vincke, F. (1997). How effective is the business community in combating corruption? In *Implementation, compliance and effectiveness: proceedings of the 91st Annual Meeting*, 9–12 April 1997, Washington, DC, The American Society of International Law-ASIL. Washington: The American Society of International Law-ASIL.

Vincke, F. (1998). The business community's attitude towards corruption, special focus on private-to-private corruption. In A. Benoit-Moury, et al. (Eds.), *Liber Amicorum: Commission Droit et Vie des Affaires*. Brussels: Bruylant.

Vincke, F. (1999). Responsibilities of enterprises. In F. Vincke, et al. (Eds.), *Fighting bribery, a corporate practices manual*. Paris: ICC Publishing.

Vincke, F. (2006). Le rôle et le potentiel de la Chambre de Commerce International (CCI) dans le domaine de l'anti-corruption. In P. Montigny (Ed.), *La corruption, un risque actuel pour les entreprises*. Paris: Secure Finance.

Vincke, F. (2007). La mise en place de programmes d'intégrité en matière de lutte contre la criminalité économique, le rôle de la CCI. *Revue de droit des affaires internationales*, *5,* 681–712

Chapter 15
Globalizing the Fight Against Corruption

Stephen Zimmermann

Perhaps not many people are familiar with what the World Bank is, or more specifically why the World Bank cares about corruption and what its role is with respect to it; but the World Bank takes the fight against corruption very seriously, and we try to approach it at a very practical level.

The World Bank is a public institution. We are first and foremost a development organization. We are an organization that finances projects in infrastructure, health, education, transport, and so on, in developing parts of the world. We provide loans and grants and development assistance to build things, to improve things, to fight poverty. The World Bank therefore operates at the intersection between the public and the private sector in some of the most difficult environments. And as a result, the integrity of those projects and the integrity of the people with whom we do business are of paramount importance.

The bank is a treaty organization. Between 1947 and today, the various institutions that make up the bank have each had in the region of 180 signatories. Each of these members has helped to create the bank.

Collectively, the bank has an obligation to ensure that the funds it lends are used for the purposes intended, and this is actually what distinguishes the World Bank from a traditional bank. The World Bank provides loans, credits, and grants, not for profit, but for the purpose of development, with the ultimate objective of a world free of poverty.

About 15 years ago, the World Bank first acknowledged that fighting corruption must be a critical part of any development agenda. You cannot pursue development without also fighting corruption. In the late 1990s, the bank launched its own Governance and Anticorruption (GAC) strategy, which combats corruption in bank-

This contribution summarizes a presentation made at the International Scientific and Professional Advisory Council (ISPAC) conference, *International Strategies against Corruption: Public–Private Partnership and Criminal Policy*, Courmayeur, Mont Blanc, 14–16 December 2012

S. Zimmermann (✉)
The World Bank, Washington, DC, USA
e-mail: szimmermann@worldbank.org

S. Manacorda et al. (eds.), *Preventing Corporate Corruption*,
DOI 10.1007/978-3-319-04480-4_15, © Springer International Publishing Switzerland 2014

financed operations and supports work with clients to strengthen their corruption-fighting capacity.

What we have learned over these years is that fighting corruption while also pursuing ambitious development goals is a challenging undertaking. I think there are parallels with the private sector, in the challenge of meeting corporate objectives and increasing profitability while at the same time addressing the risks, rooting out the practices, and avoiding the pitfalls of corruption in the places you operate. Yes, it can be done, but it takes diligence, creativity, innovation, and perseverance.

The bank lends more than US$ 50 billion a year, and has hundreds of billions of dollars in outstanding loans around the world in some of the most difficult environments. So, what do we do to protect the integrity of the World Bank's financing and operations?

The World Bank has created its own internal anticorruption program that includes my office, the World Bank's Integrity Vice-Presidency (INT). INT is the office responsible for receiving, investigating, and pursuing sanctions in cases of corruption in projects that we finance. This last point is very important: Our jurisdiction is limited to the projects that we finance. But that is more than enough.

Although my office has some parallels with national law enforcement entities, we look only at administrative violations of the bank's own rules. We do not conduct criminal investigations. We do not enforce the laws of any country; we only enforce the anticorruption policy of the bank. In some sense, this administrative regime has filled a vacuum and supports the work of local authorities and jurisdictions in difficult environments to tackle fraud and corruption.

I have a team of people in my office that includes investigators, prosecutors, forensic auditors, and analysts from around the world, who investigate these cases, determine whether the bank's policies have been violated, and then prosecute those cases within the bank's own adjudicative and sanctions system. We litigate internally and determine whether or not a firm should be sanctioned. We do not rely on national court systems. Where violations have occurred, the bank imposes its own sanctions on firms and individuals.

The sanctions that the bank imposes are periods of ineligibility—or debarment—from participating in bank-financed projects. That means, if you are found to have violated the World Bank's rules, if you engage in corruption as the World Bank defines it, the World Bank will say that you, or your company, may not participate in future World-Bank-financed projects for a period of time. So that is a sanction that can be quite powerful, given that many companies that do business with the World Bank or are contractors in World-Bank-financed projects rely quite extensively on similar projects in the developing world.

So, if you commit corruption in a bank-financed activity in one country, you may be debarred from doing any business with the World Bank, anywhere in the world. But that is not all. Under the cross-debarment regime that we negotiated several years ago with our sister regional multilateral development banks (MDBs), you will also be debarred from doing business with any of these other MDBs. I return to this below.

At the World Bank, we have now adopted high-level guidelines to govern what we believe is acceptable behavior for a company doing business in a bank-financed project. These guidelines were developed in consultation with a number of other organizations. We are now working with the United Nations Office on Drugs and Crime (UNODC) and the Organisation for Economic Co-operation and Development (OECD) to come up with a unified handbook to bring together the guidelines, because I think one of the great challenges for the private sector is the perceived variance in guidance and rules that may govern their behavior. Through this exercise, we have discovered just how similar the various pieces of guidance actually are. We have also created an Integrity Compliance Office to work with companies to ensure that, when they come off the bank's debarment list, they have a sound and dependable integrity mechanism in place.

In cases where we substantiate a finding—meaning where we find there was a violation of the World Bank's anticorruption policy—we present that finding to the national authorities that would be interested in that case. So, for example, we send the report to the UK Serious Fraud Office, or the US Justice Department, or the Prosecutor's Office in Bangladesh, depending on the companies and the countries that are implicated. And if it is a company that operates in one country and is executing a project in another, then we refer the case to both jurisdictions.

So, what are the rules of the World Bank?

The World Bank has defined five sanctionable practices: fraud, corruption, collusion, coercion, and obstruction. We heard the cries of the private sector asking for harmonization and these five definitions are now uniformly accepted by each of the leading MDBs. This effort at harmonization has become critical as more and more often there is more than one international institution financing a particular development project, so consistency in the applicable integrity policies is crucial.

Sanctions imposed by the bank are public. There are several reasons for this. First is the power of naming and shaming. The bank's debarment list has also become a tool for companies conducting their own due diligence for future transactions. In other words, before a company invests or enters into a business relationship, it may look to the World Bank's ineligibility list to see if its potential business partner has been debarred by the World Bank for fraud or corruption.

The debarment list is also made public because we must rely on our 187 member states to implement this program. Ultimately, the governments who are executing our loans are responsible for checking this list before they award a particular contract to a firm or individual.

And finally, and no less importantly, the sanctions are public because increasing the spotlight on these issues, calling those responsible to task, and bringing attention to these kinds of violations is crucial to a credible effort to leverage our results in order to deter future misconduct.

There have been some who have said that many global enforcement mechanisms have not been very successful. However, I believe that the World Bank's integrity program has been quite helpful in globalizing the fight against corruption, although not without some challenges.

For example, if you debar the leading suppliers of particular items, it may become harder to obtain those items for critical projects. This raises a very fundamental question for the World Bank, which is how do we continue to pursue our development agenda if we debar key players because they have engaged in fraud and corruption?

Moreover, we may end up leveling the playing field for some, but at the same time are we making the field more advantageous for others who have also engaged in fraud and corruption but simply have not been caught? That is one of the proverbial problems in fighting corruption, and one of the motivations behind the OECD conventions discussed earlier.

Any of you familiar with the world of development will be familiar with multilateral development banks, because rarely is there a significant development project in which one of these banks is not involved. They are the African Development Bank, the Asian Development Bank, the European Bank for Reconstruction and Development, the Inter-American Development Bank, and the World Bank. So, now all these banks recognize each other's sanctions, and "cross-debar." That is, if the World Bank debars a company, each of the other banks will debar that company for the same period of time. While it may seem a natural and obvious proposal to have undertaken, cross-debarment was actually very difficult to achieve, because each of the banks is an independent sovereign entity. However, cross-debarment has now become the first global enforcement mechanism and is an important benchmark for the World Bank and the other MDBs.

Most importantly, initiatives such as cross-debarment show that we are globalizing the fight against corruption to tackle this truly global challenge. Fighting corruption cannot be done at the national level alone. Yes, there are national corruption issues; but the cases we see at the World Bank are almost always global in nature. For example, we may find a company in country A, engaging in corruption and working with another company in country B, which is in a joint venture with a company from country C. As soon as you start crossing borders, the ability to pursue these cases, and the ability to come up with uniform mechanisms and to enforce these mechanisms, to collect evidence and prosecute, becomes very unwieldy.

So, to be truly effective and take the fight to the next level, we must come together and work towards global enforcement with continued innovation. To this end, at the World Bank we have expanded our use of settlements and voluntary disclosures; we encourage companies to come forward and work with us to identify corrupt actors in countries or among joint venture partners. At the end of the day, our goal is to have clean partners, to have companies that are executing our programs, and project officials who are implementing our projects, that are of the highest integrity. We do this through the power of deterrence, and we do this through creative prevention designed to mitigate future integrity risks.

We also work increasingly hand-in-glove with national authorities. Although we carry out administrative actions that determine only whether there has been a violation of the World Bank's policies, we recognize that the underlying facts and evidence we collect in our cases also may be relevant to proving violations of national laws. So, in almost every case where we conclude a violation of local law may have occurred, we refer our findings to national authorities and then work very closely with the authorities, to encourage them to take those cases forward.

We have also used the convening authority of the bank to create an International Corruption Hunters Alliance (ICHA) among different anticorruption enforcement officials around the world. ICHA members recognize that to be effective in their work and to be agile in a global context means that, in addition to treaties, and official mechanisms like mutual legal assistance, you must be able to pick up the phone and call for help. To do that you need a network of likeminded people; you have to know who your counterparts are; you have to know who to call.

ICHA is a network of interested, dedicated officials, who are engaged in the fight against corruption. Our efforts to create ICHA began regionally and were then scaled up to a global network. So, now officials in Costa Rica and Guatemala know each other, but now they also know the people in Europe as well, so that to the extent the money moves or the case involves actors from Latin America or Europe, New York, or Hong Kong, they know who to pick up the phone and call.

Finally, I would like to announce our most recent tool: a mobile integrity app. The World Bank's integrity app is meant to do two things: It gives you access to information about what the World Bank is doing—you can pull up a list of all the World Bank projects. So if you are somewhere in the world where the bank does business and you see an infrastructure project or a type of project that would be our concern and you are wondering if it is a World Bank project, this app will help you figure that out.

The app gives you information about the World Bank's integrity guidelines, sanctions decisions, and the list of debarred firms and individuals. More importantly, it gives you a mechanism to send a confidential report of fraud or corruption to my office. The app will ask you if you want to provide your name—although that is not required—and you can attach a picture to your report, if for example you want to send a picture of a school that is falling down or has not been built, or any other type of information that you would like to pass on to us. In this way, we hope to harness the power of mobile media and engage citizens of the world to help us identify any problems with corruption in our projects.

It is not just citizens who report allegations to my office, but companies, too. Companies across the world are calling for a level playing field. It is our job to create opportunities for integrity, not just through enforcement, but by harnessing all the tools and partnerships at our disposal.

Chapter 16
The Fight Against Corruption: The World Bank Debarment Policy

John R. Heilbrunn

Contents

16.1 Introduction

Since the mid-1990s, officials in international donor agencies and multilateral banks have increasingly perceived that good governance and efforts to reduce corruption are critical elements of development effectiveness. This sentiment crystalized after the then president of the World Bank, James Wolfensohn, delivered his oft-cited "cancer of corruption" speech at the 1996 Bank-Fund Annual Meetings in Hong Kong. As a result of that speech, governance and fighting corruption moved from the margins and became a critical part of project formulation, technical assistance, and lending instruments delivered by bilateral and multilateral organizations to low and middle-income countries. Although the issue remained controversial, officials at the World Bank debated what should be done when evidence demonstrated that individuals or firms had defrauded projects, embezzled project funds, engaged in

J. R. Heilbrunn (✉)
Colorado School of Mines, Golden, Colorado, USA
e-mail: jheilbru@mines.edu

S. Manacorda et al. (eds.), *Preventing Corporate Corruption*,
DOI 10.1007/978-3-319-04480-4_16,

misprocurement, or sought to impede or mislead audits or investigations. The decision was made to use a blacklisting mechanism called debarment. This choice was a difficult one to make; however, compliance with the 1944 Articles of Agreement left officials in the World Bank without any choice in how to respond to the allegations of corruption in its projects.

Development agencies have integrated efforts to control corruption in their lending, technical assistance, and post-conflict reconstruction operations. Still, the sensitive question of sanctions remains open for discussion, and despite efforts to ensure due diligence and probity in World Bank projects, the problem of how to deter dishonest behavior has been the subject of numerous discussions and position papers. In 2010, the then president of the World Bank Robert Zoellick articulated a new policy of cross debarment with the principle, "Steal and cheat from one, get punished by all." All multilateral development banks (MDBs)—the African Development Bank (AfDB), the Asian Development Bank (ADB), the European Bank for Reconstruction and Development (EBRD), and the Inter-American Development Bank (IADB)—thereafter adopted a policy that if one bank determined that a firm or individual had engaged in a sanctionable offense, then they would all debar that individual or firm. This harmonization of policy was a major step forward in the definition of new norms for sanctioning international corruption.

This chapter traces the evolution of thinking since the late 1990s among multilateral donors concerning governance, anticorruption, and debarment. It notes that a consensus has emerged, to the effect that corruption indicates poorly defined rules, a lack of transparency, and the absence of accountability. This chapter explores how rules, norms, and sanctions have emerged from this harmonization of policies. It also notes that although institutions gain credibility over considerable periods of time, the increasing number of firms the World Bank has debarred from participation in its projects demonstrates that the initiative launched in 1997 has gained considerable traction.

In making this argument, the chapter first considers the Articles of Agreement negotiated at the Bretton Woods meetings and signed by each of the 188 member countries of the World Bank. Having discussed the Articles of Agreement, the chapter turns to the process by which the concept of governance was first conceived and then integrated into World Bank programs. The purpose of this brief discussion is to demonstrate that the integration of governance into World Bank lending and technical assistance programs was incremental, and represented a shift in how the organization conducts its business. Third, the chapter analyzes the sanctions process, a two-tiered procedure that has a number of consequences. These consequences include both a deterrent effect and punishment for errant firms and individuals. To make this analysis, the chapter considers how allegations of corruption have contributed to a definition of the sanctions process. Finally, the chapter assesses the effectiveness of sanctions with a critical sense of the difficulties inherent in fighting corruption in the private sector.

Table 16.1 IBRD and IDA portfolios fiscal year (FY) 2008–2012 (US$ million). (Source: World Bank, Annual Report 2012 available at http://issuu.com/world.bank.publications/docs/annual_report_2012_en/14#print)

	FY 2008	FY 2009	FY 2010	FY 2011	FY 2012
IBRD (*N*=93)	US$ 13.5	US$ 32.9	US$ 44.2	US$ 26.7	US$ 20.6
IDA (*N*=81)	US$ 11.2	US$ 14.0	US$ 14.6	US$ 16.3	US$ 14.8
Total	US$ 24.7	US$ 46.9	US$ 58.8	US$ 43.0	US$ 35.4

16.1.1 What is the World Bank?

In July 1944, delegates from 44 countries assembled for 3 weeks at the United Nations Monetary and Financial Conference in Bretton Woods, New Hampshire. Under the stewardship of none other than Lord John Maynard Keynes and Harry Dexter White, delegates debated and approved the creation of the International Bank for Reconstruction and Development (IBRD) and the International Monetary Fund (IMF). These organizations commenced operations in 1946, on the basis of several key principles. Firstly, international finance would rest on the gold standard with the dollar as the de facto currency of international exchange. Secondly, exchange rates would be "fixed but adjustable," with substantial changes made only when faced with serious disequilibrium. Thirdly, the IMF would serve as the lender of last resort for governments experiencing balance-of-payment crises (Boughton 2006, pp. 6–7). Finally, the newly created financial organizations would have distinct roles; the IMF would correct balance-of-payment disequilibria and the IBRD would fund economic development (Skidelsky 2009, p. 116). This system has endured, and at the present time the World Bank Group includes the IBRD, the International Finance Corporation (IFC), the Multilateral Investment Guarantee Agency (MIGA), and the International Development Association (IDA).

The World Bank is an international financial organization that has 188 members. In terms of the size of its staff, its portfolio, and the extent of its operations, the World Bank is the largest MDB, vastly overshadowing other MDBs, including the ADB, AfDB, EBRD, and IADB. Finance for economic development is through either the IBRD, for middle-income countries, or the IDA, for low-income countries. Whereas the IBRD offers loans to middle-income countries, the IDA provides credits to the 81 poorest countries in the world, whose people live on an average annual per capita income of less than US$ 1,175. The World Bank's lending portfolio therefore includes financial and technical assistance to middle and low-income countries.

Since it is the largest MDB, the World Bank provides funding for the governments of its numerous member states. It functions largely as a cooperative; governments join the World Bank and their membership entitles them to borrow from the IBRD or to receive credits from the IDA. This particular structure resembles, in some important aspects, the lending decisions in American banks during the early nineteenth century, in which a small cadre of directors made decisions on loans that were often extended to the members (shareholders) of the bank (Lamoreaux

1991, p. 162). This management structure meant that the principal shareholders in the bank would decide upon the recipients of loans among themselves. Membership as determined by shareholdings was the crucial criterion. The insider lending evident in these practices reduced information asymmetries and, therefore, reduced the associated costs. It stands as a testimony to Harry Dexter White's influence at Bretton Woods that banking practices originally present in US firms were part of the procedures adopted by the IMF and IBRD. White's impact demonstrated that the growing influence of American political and economic power was a key element at the Bretton Woods meetings, as much as the drive to internalize information about the credit worthiness of its members and thereby reduce its costs (Boughton 1998).

The organization that Keynes and White created grew to become one of the world's major aggregations of development finance. As Table 16.1 displays, the combined portfolios of the IBRD and the IDA amount to substantial sums of finance for borrower governments. Although the sums reflect the volatility in international finance, the fact that governments of middle and low-income countries take loans and credits that disburse over years, means that the aggregate sums which the World Bank disburses shape growth.

16.2 Governance and Anticorruption: The Articles of Agreement

Work to reduce corruption in World Bank projects converged and, in some respects, collided with the Articles of Agreement that established the IBRD and, later, the other organizations that constituted the World Bank Group. Convergence was evident in the language concerning specific uses of funds. Keynes and White recognized the complexity of establishing an international organization that engaged in government-to-government lending. Hence, they drafted Articles which stipulated that the World Bank should provide funds for development, meaning that the money loaned to member governments should improve the living conditions of their citizens. According to Sect. 1 of the Articles of Agreement (below), the bank loans funds for the benefit of the client government's citizens. Delegates to the Bretton Woods meetings debated these particular stipulations about the intended purpose of the IBRD's lending operations:

> SECTION 1. Use of Resources
>
> a. The resources and the facilities of the Bank shall be used exclusively for the benefit of members with equitable consideration to projects for development and projects for reconstruction alike.
>
> b. For the purpose of facilitating the restoration and reconstruction of the economy of members whose metropolitan territories have suffered great devastation from enemy occupation or hostilities, the Bank, in determining the conditions and terms of loans made to such members, shall pay special regard to lightening the financial burden and expediting the completion of such restoration and reconstruction.

Over time it became evident that development assistance funds, whether in the form of grants, credits, or loans, are fungible (Dollar and Pritchett 1998). When donor agencies supplement fiscal budgets with development assistance, political leaders have unfortunate incentives to reduce their appropriations to that sector by the amount of the donor's assistance, and to use the funds for other purposes, including allocations for cronyism and politically driven investments (e.g., military spending). Efforts to ring-fence IBRD loans or IDA credits have therefore encountered resistance from leaders of borrower governments, who need to use fiscal revenues to satisfy political demands.

Prior to 1997, the immediate question was whether the misappropriation of funds by borrower governments constituted a breach of contract, as stipulated in Sect. 1 of the Articles of Agreement. However, World Bank officials consciously avoided any use of the term "corruption." They dismissed the problem with assertions that everything they did for borrower governments created greater efficiency, and thereby reduced opportunities for malfeasance. When faced with observations that in some borrower governments, corruption was both pervasive and persistent, senior officials would shrug and say that corruption was an internal police affair and was therefore beyond the World Bank's mandate. Inaction was the unfortunate consequence.

The Articles of Agreement specifically prohibited staff members from making lending decisions on the basis of political considerations. Negotiations among delegates at Bretton Woods had at times been quite testy, especially over language which the Soviet delegate, M. S. Stepanov, considered to be problematic.[1] This explicit interdiction placed on any political considerations in decisions regarding lending or programmatic assistance shows that Keynes and White realized that the financial organizations which emerged from the accord signed at Bretton Woods would have to be unambiguously apolitical. Hence, they assented to the language included in Sect. 10 (below) of the Articles, which states that political considerations are irrelevant in lending decisions:

> SECTION 10. Political Activity Prohibited
> The Bank and its officers shall not interfere in the political affairs of any member; nor shall they be influenced in their decisions by the political character of the member or members concerned. Only economic considerations shall be relevant to their decisions, and these considerations shall be weighed impartially in order to achieve the purposes stated in Article I.

Although this interdiction on political considerations seemed sensible at the time, an unanticipated and unintended consequence was that the World Bank would make loans to authoritarian governments whose leaders would use this financial support to prop up their brutal regimes. As Dollar and Pritchett show, the revenues from multilateral support enabled autocrats to divert funds for political purposes, to reward their supporting coalitions, to support their families in lavish style, and to otherwise ignore the World Bank's program objectives. In negotiations over different projects, the prohibition on politics compelled World Bank officials to negotiate loans with the knowledge that their counterparts across the table were agreeing to conditions which they had neither the ability nor the political will to respect.

[1] Minutes from the meetings at Bretton Woods are available in their entirety online. See Historic Documents and Memorabilia, Center for Financial Stability, http://www.centerforfinancialstability.org/brettonwoods_docs.php, accessed 16 July 2013.

The difficulties facing the reduction of inefficient behavior included the perverse incentives that drove lenders and borrowers in multilateral finance. Two different goals converged: World Bank officials, under pressure to either make loans or credits or see their careers languish, were willing to accept the assurances given by client governments that they would accept specific conditions. The national representatives were then under fiscal pressure to agree to conditions they could never honor. This was an equilibrium that continued until 1997, when the World Bank recognized that governance failures and corruption impeded development effectiveness.

The World Bank first presented governance as a development issue in a 1989 monograph entitled *Sub-Saharan Africa: From Crisis to Sustainable Growth* (World Bank 1989). This publication prompted an internal review of the concept, to determine whether it diverged from the World Bank's Articles of Agreement. In April 1991, Chief Counsel Ibrahim Shihata presented a paper to the World Bank's Board of Executive Directors which outlined his interpretation of the Articles of Agreement, and their relevance to questions of governance (Shihata 1991). This document traced the concept of governance back to its first usage in documents published in the Africa Region (AFR) and its subsequent employment in other areas of World Bank lending operations and technical assistance.

Shihata's exhaustive paper uses a wealth of materials to interpret the political clause in the World Bank's Articles of Agreement to "establish a legally sound framework for treating the issue of governance in the bank's work." Shihata repeatedly emphasizes that the World Bank may under no circumstances take political factors, events, or actions into consideration when assessing a government's eligibility for credit. The paper implies that whereas the Articles of Agreement expressly forbid a denial of credit based on political variables, an offer of credit which promotes incentives that lead to positive political change would be in compliance with the intentions of the Bretton Woods Agreements. Within 2 years of Shihata's paper, the World Bank had identified public-sector management, accountability, transparency, and building the institutions conducive for the rule of law as the four key areas of intervention for the improvement of governance. Under this conceptualization, the rule of law emerged as an "all-embracing concept" that was crucial for development (World Bank 1992, p. 28). Despite these changes in thinking about governance, the anticorruption initiative met with stiff resistance from both World Bank staff and borrower governments.

16.3 Governance and Corruption as Development Issues

According to the World Bank, corruption is the abuse of public position for personal gain. It is a form of behavior that indicates a breakdown in the rules, norms, and enforcement mechanisms in a public sector. Governance refers to the exercise of political power in the management of a country's economic and social resources for development. Good governance indicates that transparency and accountability are present in policy deliberations and implementation. Transparency means that debates about laws, policies, regulations, and legal texts are made available to the public. Citizens are aware of actions taken by the officials to whom they have delegated powers. Accountability implies that elected and appointed officials are answerable to a higher authority for their actions. The responsibilities of this higher authority include the elimination of impunity and the empowering of an independent judiciary capable of enforcing basic elements of the rule of law. Increasingly, development specialists recognize that the links between and interdependence of transparency and accountability are crucial attributes of good governance.

The application of governance as an organizing concept to explain efficiency in governments reflects an advance in thinking about development effectiveness. Anticorruption efforts were evident in the Organisation for Economic Co-operation and Development (OECD)'s anti-bribery convention, which extended many of the provisions in the US Foreign Corrupt Practices Act (FCPA) and criminalized the payment of bribes by national corporations to foreign officials. Further impetus came in September 1997 when the World Bank's board approved "Helping Countries Combat Corruption: The Role of the World Bank," which identified corrupt practices as a development issue and proposed a set of policies to reduce its incidence (World Bank 1997).

The first priority was to prevent corruption in World-Bank-financed projects. Hence, language was inserted into the World Bank's procurement codes in order to explicitly strengthen the anticorruption clauses. The Procurement and Consultant Guidelines were revised to include a new section on corruption. Loan disbursement procedures were reinforced, through the Loan Administration Change Initiative (LACI), which placed greater responsibility on borrower governments to manage disbursements and reinforce oversight. The Board of Governors approved the LACI reforms in July 1998. These operational assessments of borrowers' project financial management systems constituted a crucial step in the integration of the 1997 initiative into the World Bank's operations. Procurement reform and loan disbursement preceded initiatives in project preparation, analytic exercises, programmatic lending, and project appraisal, integrated by the Bank into its lending and non-lending programs through the Operational Core Service (OCS) Network. OCS became a formal vice-presidency in 1999, and worked on strengthening the control and prevention of corruption and fraud in bank projects. It collaborated with the Bank's audit department to ensure that due diligence was exercised in bank-funded projects.

Recognition that internal controls cannot fully ensure due diligence and probity in World Bank projects led to the creation of an oversight committee, a sanctions committee, and a hotline to receive reports of alleged incidents of corruption. The hotline was set up to accept calls 24 hours a day, with multilingual operators. At first, a selected number of managing directors sat on the Sanctions Committee. This committee had a mandate to investigate allegations of malfeasance in Bank-financed projects. If the Sanctions Committee determined that there was sufficient evidence of wrongdoing, it would publicize the names of individuals and firms found to have engaged in corrupt practices.

Officials working on the anticorruption initiative began to investigate a number of cases rapidly. In the first 2 years of the operation of this initiative (1998–2000), the World Bank investigated approximately 120 cases and debarred 14 firms, with sanctions ranging from a 3-year period to permanent status. To deter firms from engaging in sanctionable offenses, the World Bank formulated and publicized corporate codes of conduct for businesses bidding on projects. Embedded in these codes of conduct is a right to debar firms and individuals who defraud, steal, or cheat the World Bank. These reforms encountered resistance from staff members, which hindered their acceptance within the World Bank.

16.3.1 The Costs of Corruption

Once the informal silence that had veiled the issue of corruption had lifted, development practitioners inside the World Bank acknowledged that corruption was a high-cost behavior. A number of studies appeared that showed that governments which tolerated rampant venality suffered substantial losses in fiscal revenues (Shleifer and Vishny 1993). Systemic corruption fed into a cycle in which lost tax revenues deepened fiscal shortages and the inability to pay civil servants a living wage (Rose-Ackerman 1999). Worse, reputational costs were apparent in persistent misbehavior and in foreign investors' avoidance of markets known for their uncertainty (Tirole 1992; Mauro 1995). In effect, systemic corruption lowered rates of economic growth and the political system's perceived legitimacy.

International donors face a dilemma when they commence operations in circumstances of poor governance and systemic corruption. First, governments borrow funds from the World Bank, an organization owned and managed by sovereign governments. Borrowers are contractually obligated to use the loans for purposes intended. However, because revenues are fungible, as discussed above, project funds do not always have the intended impact. There may be incentives for political leaders to divert fiscal expenditures from sectors financed by multilateral banks. In the worst-case scenario, firms or individuals with links to the governing elite engage in graft, procurement fraud, or any of a number of illegal activities which divert funds provided by the World Bank finance. In low-income countries, these acts have a negative impact on the effectiveness of development assistance.

Corruption in low-income countries is a serious drag on their prospects for sustainable growth. This problematic behavior has been linked to organized crime (money laundering) and terrorist organizations. According to the World Bank's Sanctions Officer, Ms. Pascale Dubois, dishonest individuals and firms are responsible for over US$ 1 trillion in bribes and embezzled funds, as a result of corruption. The world economy stands at just over US$ 30 trillion, and these bribes amount to 3 % of this total. Even viewing these figures as rough estimates, it is evident that corruption constitutes a 20 % tax on foreign investment, which is a major impediment to global economic growth. Understandably, the major powers concur that international corruption, especially in World-Bank-funded projects, needs to be reduced to as close to zero as is economically feasible.

16.4 The World Bank's Sanctions Process

The World Bank provides development finance to middle and low-income countries through concessionary lending, credits, guarantees, and advisory services. As it became increasingly apparent that World Bank projects were not immune from dishonest behavior, initiatives were taken to minimize the incidence of such behavior in lending. After its initial strategy had been approved, the World Bank moved to establish the Integrity Vice Presidency (INT) and an independent sanctions board. Senior officials of the World Bank are appointed to these offices. Since their managers are staff members, their investigations are internal to the organization. However, their reports and decisions have a direct impact upon the external firms that participate in World Bank projects.

16.4.1 The Integrity Vice Presidency: Structure and Role

The first line of defense against corruption in World Bank projects is the INT. As an investigative unit, INT includes a staff of attorneys, accountants, and development specialists. A vice-president manages the overall operations undertaken by INT. Below the VP, INT engages a director of operations, lead specialists, investigators, and communications officers. In FY 2012, the investigation branch included 75 individuals, of whom 64 were investigators and specialists; the remainder included support staff. That year, INT received 110 complaints, resulting in 79 external investigations into alleged incidents of collusion (12), corruption (40), and fraud (27). Finally, an Independent Advisory Board provides crucial oversight of INT. The Independent Advisory Board assembles distinguished individuals who have been internationally active in anticorruption work.

16.4.1.1 The Sanctions Process: Integrity Vice Presidency

When INT receives complaints of corruption in projects for which the World Bank provides funding, it examines these complaints in order to determine whether the gravity of the alleged offense merits a formal investigation. If the offense is of a gravity that merits sanctions, INT forwards the materials from its investigation to World Bank staff members. The expectation is that World Bank's operational staff will undertake actions to reduce the opportunities for corruption that may have formed the basis of a complaint. However, if INT staff members determine that the complaint is valid, and that the transgressions violate one of the five World Bank sanctionable actions, an investigation is opened. The five sanctionable offenses are the following:

1. Offers, gifts, receipt, or solicitation of anything of value to influence improperly the actions of another party
2. Fraudulent practices such as misrepresentation that mislead or attempt to mislead a party to obtain financial or other benefit or to avoid an obligation
3. Collusive practices between two or more parties to achieve an improper purpose or influence the actions of another party
4. Coercive practices which either threaten or harm any party in order to influence the actions of that party
5. Obstructive practices which include deliberately destroying, falsifying, altering, or concealing evidence that pertains to an investigation into fraudulent, corrupt, coercive, or collusive practices or acts to impede the World Bank's right to audit or access information about performance on funded projects[2]

When INT first looks into allegations of corruption, it prepares a "Statement of Accusations and Evidence," announcing to both the concerned firm and World Bank staff members that an investigation has been launched. Two specific types of investigation are common—internal and external. Internal investigations involve World Bank staff members who are alleged to have been engaged in some form of illegal activity in a World Bank project. External investigations are inquiries into allegations of fraud, corruption, collusion, coercion, and/or obstruction by a firm or individual engaged on a World Bank project. A standard of proof is that a misdeed is "more likely than not" to have occurred.

When the evidence assembled during an investigation fails to substantiate the allegations, INT issues a report to that effect. However, if an investigation substantiates allegations of corruption, INT issues a public report that it transmits to the World Bank's senior management. In the event of misprocurement, a report is sent to the client government and the World Bank cancels all contracts. In principle, the client government then launches its own investigations and either reprimands or prosecutes the officials involved in dishonest activities. Within the World Bank, an investigation that substantiates allegations of corruption prompts INT to transmit a notice of sanctions proceedings to the Evaluations and Suspension Officer and the Sanctions Board. Between FY 2011 and 2012, INT increased its rate of substantiated investigations from 46 to 52%, and the number of new cases increased from 73 to 81. Finally, when INT investigations substantiate allegations of sanctionable offenses, INT submits a statement to the Evaluations and Suspension Officer.

[2] See "Guidelines on Preventing and Combatting Fraud and Corruption in Projects Financed by IBRD Loans and IDA Credits and Grants," The World Bank, http://siteresources.worldbank.org/INTRUSSIANFEDERATION/Resources/ibRD_IDA_AnticorruptionGuidelines.pdf, accessed 16 July 2013.

16.4.1.2 The Sanctions Process: Structure and Role

The sanctions process begins with INT and then, when allegations of fraud and corruption are substantiated, the Evaluations and Suspension Office and Sanctions Board get involved. The Evaluations and Suspension Office receives and reviews INT's Statement of Accusations. It notifies the accused firm or individual of the investigation and accusations. Once the Evaluations and Suspension Office takes this step, it suspends all finance from going to the individual or firm. On the basis of its review of the evidence, the Evaluations and Suspension Office makes a recommendation. The accused firm or individual has a right to contest the charges. The firm or individual may be summoned to hearings, at the discretion of the Evaluations and Suspension Office. On the basis of a review of the evidence and/or hearings, the Evaluations and Suspension Office forwards the evidence to the World Bank's Sanctions Board, which has the power to impose a sanction. Upon reviewing the evidence, the Sanctions Board may or may not follow the Evaluations and Suspension Officer's recommendation. Crucially, once the Sanction Board makes a decision, this decision is final and is not subject to appeal.

16.4.1.3 The Sanctions Board

The World Bank's Sanctions Board comprises seven members. Four of these are internationally distinguished individuals appointed by executive directors. The remaining three members are World Bank staff, appointed by the president. All Sanctions Board members serve renewable 3-year terms. Presiding over the Sanctions Board is an external member, who serves one term as chair. An independent secretariat coordinates the Sanctions Board's agenda. This agenda includes hearings and deliberations that occur 2–4 times a year. At these hearings, the Sanctions Board reviews cases "de novo," based on pleadings and hearings. It oversees the publication of its decisions, and these include the identity of each sanctioned party, the sanctions imposed, and the full text of decisions reached.

16.4.1.4 Sanctions: Debarment

For international firms that are contractors on World-Bank-funded projects, the prospect of debarment carries high costs in terms of lost income and damage to the firm's reputation. Given the potential severity of the possible sanctions, the Sanctions Board is careful in meting out punitive actions for corrupt firms and individuals. This care is evident in decisions that utilize different sanctions and methods to mitigate reputational damages. Regardless of potential damages, when evidence demonstrates egregious levels of corruption, the Sanctions Board has used the instrument of debarment to eliminate or suspend dishonest firms or individuals from participation in World Bank projects. When the outcome is debarment from MDB projects, the excluded individual or firm faces significant losses.

Sanctions vary according to the severity of the offense committed and the evidence presented by INT and the Evaluations and Suspension Office. The sanctions impose different costs on the concerned firms and individuals. Sanctions, as displayed below, have variable severity:

- Indefinite or fixed term
- Debarment with conditional release
- Conditional non-debarment
- Public letter of reprimand
- Restitution

Debarment may be indefinite or fixed term (without conditions). This is the most punitive action which the Sanctions Board imposes. When a firm or individual has engaged in a flagrant form of fraud or corruption, indefinite debarment excludes the entity from multilateral funded projects (see below on cross debarment). Next in punitive severity is Debarment with Conditional Release, which sets forth specific actions which must be undertaken by the individual or firm before the World Bank releases them from debarment. In these circumstances, the individual or firm must show evidence of the actions it has taken to prevent further incidents of sanctionable misbehavior. In the case of indefinite/fixed-term and conditional release debarment, the Sanctions Board publishes the names of the firms or individuals, the sanction they receive, and the period of debarment.

However, if the evidence neither demonstrates clearly illegal actions nor exonerates the firm or individual, the Sanctions Board may recommend Conditional Non-debarment. Again, the firm or individual is publicly identified, but sanctions are withheld. In less serious cases, the Sanctions Board may issue a Public Letter of Reprimand to state that a firm or individual may be implicated in a case of corruption. This public identification does not come without cost, for firms and individuals implicated in a letter of reprimand are at a disadvantage when competing for international contracts. The final sanction is that the firm or individual must make restitution for the costs associated with its questionable behavior. Restitution is nothing less than the reimbursement of costs associated with the firm's or individual's dishonest actions; it removes any illicit profits gained by corruption. Of these five sanctions, the default or "baseline" sanction is Debarment with Conditional Release.

16.4.1.5 Cross Debarment

In 2010, the multilateral banks adopted a policy that stipulated any firm or individual who defrauds one or another MDB will be debarred by all the others. The process often begins with a complaint to INT, the firm or individual receives notice of the Sanctions Board's decision. The firm or individual is given a ninety-day period in which to appeal against the sanction. If the firm or individual does not appeal, or if the appeal fails, debarment begins. The costs of debarment increased significantly after 7 December 2010, when World Bank President Zoellick announced a new policy of cross debarment. His proclamation was "cheat or steal from one of us, and you will be punished by all" (cross debarment). Cross debarment is applicable to firms and individuals implicated in trying to influence improperly the actions of another party, engaging in fraudulent practices, colluding with another party to gain advantage, coercing another actor, or trying to conceal illegal activity that might prejudice an investigation into their acts. These "sanctionable offenses," occurring over the past decade, have led MDBs to jointly debar more than 1,100 fraudulent and corrupt entities.

The impact of cross debarment is significant for the firm or individual concerned. Firstly, multilateral banks prohibit the individual, company, or firm excluded from participating in projects which they finance. In 2011, the sums invested by the individual banks were substantial—the World Bank group alone financed over US$ 50 billion and the other MDBs invested a combined total of over US$ 30 billion. Moreover, since most multilateral finance is disbursed in tranches, phased disbursement means that the loans and credits approved in any given year influence the financing of low and middle-income countries for extended periods of time. Hence, regardless of the precise amount the various banks disburse in a given year, a firm or individual subject to debarment loses considerable opportunities.

16.5 Analysis: Sanctions and Development Effectiveness

After the Cold War ended, multilateral banks and development agencies came under increasing pressure to demonstrate a return on their investments in low and middle-income countries. Governments, particularly those which were members of the OECD, articulated a demand for development effectiveness, or that aid recipient governments should use funds from donor agencies for the allocated purposes. In this regard, the anticorruption initiative, which gained international momentum after 1997, represented a significant shift. A second significant event was the September 2001 attack on the USA. After that event, corruption and illegal transfers of funds through money laundering were highlighted as acts which facilitated terrorist organizations. Corrupt regimes were vulnerable to rebellion and collapse. As a number of states in Africa descended into civil war, many identified corruption as a causal factor. Finally, corruption has enabled international criminal organizations to capture weak states in Latin America and Africa from which they are able to engage in drug smuggling, the illegal arms trade, and human trafficking. Without question, the sanctions process faces clear challenges in reducing corruption in multilateral-financed projects.

One problem is that individuals who own firms which are subjected to World Bank INT investigations have incentives to simply dissolve the firm, create a new company, and reengage in corrupt activities. The use of shell companies is not uncommon. Individuals may register a firm in an offshore location, give the company an untraceable name, open numbered bank accounts (also in offshore sites), and then engage in dishonest transactions. This practice affords a disreputable person the means to engage in any of the sanctionable offenses. If this company comes under investigation, it can be dissolved and another established. It is conceivable that the practice of linking firms and numbered bank accounts to specific individuals may be effective in limiting the strategy of opening and closing shell companies. The problem is complicated further when dishonest people use immediate and extended family members to serve as their front owners.

Dishonest individuals make their profits by staying one step ahead of law enforcement agencies. Given the sums available through multilateral finance, the attraction for international organized crime is clear. These organizations seek to acquire profits through fraudulent practices, coercion, and intimidation. Controlling criminal organizations is problematic. Worse, some individuals abuse their positions to demand bribes from contractors engaging in a project, such as occurred during the Lesotho Highlands Water Project. In this case, Lahmeyer International, a German firm, was found guilty of bribing Masupha Sole, the Lesotho Highlands Development Authority Chief Executive. The Sanctions Committee debarred Lahmeyer for 7 years, and subsequently investigated and debarred a number of other firms in relation to this project.

Despite multiple criticisms, the sanctions process at the World Bank provides a means for international organizations to limit the capacity of political leaders to encourage corrupt behavior; it has removed a possible source of funding for semi-formal terrorist organizations; it has brought greater stability to post-conflict reconstruction economies; and international criminal organizations learn that their capacity to engage in dishonest transactions may be short-lived. In effect, a consequence of the sanctions process has been an increase in transparency and accountability and, perhaps, an improvement in development effectiveness.

References

Boughton, J. M. (1998). Harry Dexter White and the International Monetary Fund. *Finance and Development* http://www.imf.org/external/pubs/ft/fandd/1998/09/boughton.htm (September 1998):*35*(3), 39–41.

Boughton, J. M. (2006). *American in the shadows: Harry Dexter White and the design of the International Monetary Fund.* Washington, DC: International Monetary Fund.

Dollar, D., & Pritchett, L. (1998). *Assessing aid: What works, what doesn't, and why*. New York: Published for the World Bank by Oxford University Press.

Lamoreaux, N. R. (1991). Information problems and banks' specialization in short-term commercial lending: New England in the nineteenth century. In P. Temin (Ed.), *Inside the business enterprise: Historical perspectives on the use of information*. Chicago: University of Chicago Press.

Mauro, P. (1995). Corruption and growth. *Quarterly Journal of Economics*. (August 1995):*110*(3), 681–712.

Rose-Ackerman, S. (1999). *Corruption and government: Causes, consequences, and reform*. New York: Cambridge University Press.

Shihata, I. (1991, Feb 5). *Issues of governance in borrowing members: The extent of their relevance under the bank's Articles of Agreement. Internal Board Document, Sec M91–131*. Washington, DC: The World Bank.

Shleifer, A., & Vishny, R. W. (1993). Corruption. *Quarterly Journal of Economics, 108*(3), 599–618.
Skidelsky, R. (2009). *Keynes: The return of the master*. New York: Public Affairs.
Tirole, J. (1992). Persistence of corruption, Institute for Policy Reform Working Paper 55 (October 1992).
World Bank. (1989). *The World Bank, Sub-Saharan Africa: From crisis to sustainable growth.* Washington, DC: The World Bank.
World Bank. (1992). *Governance and Development*. Washington, DC: World Bank.
World Bank. (1997, Sept). *Helping Countries Combat Corruption: The Role of the World Bank.* Washington, DC: Poverty Reduction and Economic Management, The World Bank.

Part V
The ABC Model and Criminal Justice: The National Legal Context

Chapter 17
Compliance Programs and Criminal Law Responses: A Comparative Analysis

Adán Nieto Martín and Marta Muñoz de Morales

Contents

17.1 Introduction

If a comparison with a coin were made when talking about corporate criminal liability, one side of the coin would be the model of imputation (the vicarious liability model, the principle of identification, the principle of collective knowledge, the theory of duty-based organizational liability, etc.), and the other side would be the role played by compliance programs.

A. N. Martín (✉) · M. Muñoz de Morales
University of Castilla-la-Mancha, Ciudad Real, Spain
e-mail: adan.nieto@uclm.es

M. M. de Morales
e-mail: marta.mmorales@uclm.es

S. Manacorda et al. (eds.), *Preventing Corporate Corruption*,
DOI 10.1007/978-3-319-04480-4_17, © Springer International Publishing Switzerland 2014

Compliance programs are usually defined as a form of corporate self-regulation, combining internal company-instituted rules and procedures, ethical codes, etc. These are informed by governmental guidelines and local, state, or international regulations or norms. Their aim is to prevent crimes and other violations of the law.[1] Much has been said about their effects, in both positive and negative terms. Positively, compliance programs have been said to aid the prevention and disclosure of crime (see Webb and Molo 1993, p. 375) and the dissemination of business ethics (Webb and Molo 1993, p. 377). Negatively, it has been argued that compliance programs are "cosmetic" or "window-dressing" (Laufer 2006, p. 99; Krawiec 2003, p. 491), that they are an invention of the business sector,[2] that implementation costs are high (Bowman 2004, p. 680), and that they are inefficacious even when enacted and implemented properly, etc. A lot has also been said about their role as a ground for exemption from corporate criminal liability (or as a mitigating factor; Walsh and Pyrich 1995, p. 606), and about their increased importance, at national[3] and international levels (Wulf 2012, p. 21; Murphy and Boehme 2012, p. 581; Jordan 2012, p. 89), in preventing bribery offenses (UN Global Compact,[4] OECD Guidelines for Multinational Enterprises).[5] Nevertheless, until now, there has been no worldwide, holistic, or detailed study of compliance programs as such, and, above all, no research into their practical effect on (international) bribery cases.

Part 3 of this book is a timely contribution to this issue, since it contains—in a wide sense—an analysis of case-law experiences in some of the most illustrative cases in countries where corporate criminal liability is recognized. To provide a context within which to introduce Part 3, this transversal report begins (in Sect. 17.2) by giving an overview of the role of compliance programs, both from a substantial point of view (as a ground for exemption or mitigation of liability) and a procedural point of view (probation, guilty plea agreements, or pretrial agreements). This chapter continues (Sect. 17.3) with an explanation of our reasons for deciding to focus our study on Italy, the UK, the USA, Switzerland, Canada, Australia, France, and China. The goals of the study and a discussion of the obstacles encountered in the development of the research are then presented. This chapter ends (Sect. 17.4) with a presentation of the key elements which a compliance program is supposed to include in order to be considered effective, and a survey of current best practices.

---

[1] This definition is based on Biegelman 2008, p. 8.

[2] In Spain, see Fiscalía General del Estado, Circular 1/2011, Relativa a la responsabilidad penal de las personas jurídicas conforme a la reforma del Código penal efectuada por la LO 5/2010, Madrid, 1 de Junio, 2011, available on the website of the Ministerio Fiscal, http://www.fiscal.es.

[3] See Cohen et al. 2008, p. 1,272. "Many companies, especially U.S.-based companies, have responded to heightened FCPA enforcement by installing comprehensive anti-corruption compliance programs."

[4] See "UN Global Compact & Transparency Intl., Reporting Guidance on the 10th Principles against Corruption (2009)," United Nations Global Compact, http://www.unglobalcompact.org/docs/issues_doc/AntiCorruption/UNGC_AntiCorruptionReporting.pdf, accessed 19 June 2013.

[5] For a comprehensive study, see Tricot, "Corporate AntiBribery Self-Regulation and the International Legal Framework," in this volume.

17.2 The Role of Compliance Programs

Explaining the role of compliance programs from a comparative point of view is not an easy task. First of all, the situation varies from one state to another, and even within a given country, the effects of a compliance program may differ, depending on several factors. One such factor is the model of imputation. At one end of the spectrum of possible situations, a compliance program has precious little to do when the legal framework relies on strict vicarious liability. Under this model, corporations are held criminally liable for the criminal acts of their agents, as long as they are acting within the scope of their authority and their conduct benefits the corporation. In such cases, it does not matter whether or not "the corporation has enacted and implemented internal controls and measures aimed to prevent or discover crimes" (Nieto Martín 2008, p. 85).In other words, exemption or mitigation of corporate liability is independent of the compliance program.

At the other end of the spectrum, the compliance program is decisive when the theory chosen is the prevent fault model of corporate criminal culpability. To put it differently, an effective compliance program enacted and implemented properly *before* and/or *after* the commission of the offense prevents the imposition of criminal sanctions on corporations, or may at least result in mitigation.

Obviously, there are intermediate situations and nuances between these two extremes. In a given country, the model of imputation may depend on the fault element of the offense. For example, in Canada, negligence offenses are imputed to corporations not only on the basis of the theory of vicarious liability but also the identification theory. For crimes other than negligence requiring proof of mens rea, the model chosen is the identification theory.[6] In the case of the former, a corporation could be held liable for crimes (including corruption) perpetrated by its employees or agents, among other circumstances, if one of the corporation's senior representatives, with an intent at least in part to benefit the corporation or organization knowing that a representative of the organization is or is about to be a party to the offense, "does not take all reasonable measures to stop [employees, agents, etc.] of the corporation from being a party to the offense e.g., corruption." This provision introduces "a limited version of the failing to prevent corruption offenses in jurisdictions like U.K." (Skinnider 2012, p. 6, 30). The determination of what amounts to "reasonable steps" is contingent on the nature of the offense, the specific industry involved, the risk-management techniques, and the individual circumstances of each case (Archibald et al. 2005). The expression "reasonable steps" is therefore a "due diligence defense" which could play a relevant role as the ground for exclusion from criminal liability when a corporation is charged with a serious criminal offense of subjective fault. The possibility of taking into consideration a "due diligence" defense in these cases blurs the line between regulatory offenses and mens rea crimes. But, on the other hand, it also permits the use of many of the factors pertaining to corporate conduct that are considered relevant for determining whether a company acted with

[6] See Muñoz de Morales, "Corporate Responsibility and Compliance Programs in Canada," in this volume.

due diligence in the case of regulatory offenses (Archibald et al. 2004, p. 384). Such factors would include the preventive system in place; the efforts made to address the problem; the promptness of the response; the industry standards; the foresight of the commission of the offenses; whether steps were taken to hire a responsible contractor; whether there were reasons to believe that corporate instructions would not be complied with, etc.—all these would now also be key issues in criminal offenses of subjective fault (e.g., intent).

Standards for holding organizations liable for the acts of their representatives and employees are also different in Australia, where in the case of negligence offenses the model of imputation is the result of a kind of "organizational failure." This is based on the fact that the prohibited conduct is substantially attributable to an "inadequate corporate management, control or supervision of the conduct of one or more of its employees, agents or officers" or a "failure to provide adequate systems for conveying relevant information to relevant persons in the body corporate" (Nieto Martín 2008, p. 132). However, in the case of offenses requiring intent, knowledge, or recklessness, the standard lies in the notion of "corporate culture." Corporations are held criminally liable, provided that it is proved that a corporate culture existed within the corporate body that "directed, encouraged, tolerated, or led to non-compliance with the relevant provision" or where the company "failed to create and maintain a 'corporate culture' that requires compliance with the law." "Corporate culture" is defined by the Commonwealth Criminal Code (CCC) itself as whatever "attitude, policy, rule, course of conduct or practice existing within the body corporate generally or in the part of the body corporate in which the relevant activities takes place." In order to determine the "corporate culture," courts could take into account both the specific corporate policies and programs for undertaking internal discipline or preventive reform and/or the "corporation's 'unwritten rule' and employment expectations, if these are at odds with formal documentation" (Hill 2000, p. 20; Hill 2003, p. 1).[7] Indeed, courts could also establish a culpable corporate culture if it could be shown that the corporation tolerated or encouraged bribery in the private sector (Brand 2000, p. 476). Therefore, if a corporation wants to avoid criminal sanctions for bribery committed by its employees, it will have to show not only that it has in place an "effective antibribery compliance system"[8] but also that such a compliance system has been maintained and enforced (Hill 2000, 2003). Stated differently, under Australian criminal law, compliance programs could be taken into account as a defense exempting the corporation from criminal liability (Baxt 2001, p. 4). However, taking into account what happens in other cases of breach of law (e.g., competition law), compliance programs are likely to play a

[7] See also "Criminal Code Bill 1994, Explanatory Memorandum," Australasian Legal Information Institute, http://www.austlii.edu.au/au/legis/cth/bill_em/ccb1994125/memo_0.pdf, accessed 19 June 2013.

[8] See Hill 2000, p. 16; Belcher 2007, p. 21: "Corporate responsibility for failing to create and maintain a corporate culture that requires compliance with the relevant provision…is likely to encourage companies to institute compliance programs and to give them importance."

more important role in the sentencing phase as a mitigating factor.[9] In other cases, it is also interesting to note that in Australia, because it is a federal state, the situation results in different approaches regarding corporate issues. This means that at federal level, there is a kind of organizational model, but that the situation varies at the state level.

In Switzerland, the imputation criterion works differently depending upon the nature of the offense. Article 102 of the Swiss Criminal Code (SCC)[10] introduces the following two alternative bases of corporate criminal liability: *subsidiary* and *primary/direct* corporate criminal liability.[11] As a general rule, corporate criminal liability seems to be *subsidiary*. In this regard, an enterprise can only be held liable if the offense is committed within the enterprise and in furtherance of business activity, and if the offense cannot be attributed to a specific individual due to a lack of organization.[12] In contrast, *primary* or *direct* criminal liability is imposed when a limited number of significant offenses, among them bribery of foreign public officials (Art. 322^{septies} SCC), is committed within the enterprise. In these cases, the enterprise can be held criminally liable even if the management had no knowledge of the offense, provided that not all necessary and reasonable organizational prevention measures have been taken. If a natural person is identified as the offender, both the offender and the enterprise can be held liable (cumulative criminal liability). The role to be played by the corporation in each system of corporate liability is likely to be different. When the offense is not included in the so-called system of primary liability, corporations are held criminally liable precisely because it can be proved that there is a causal link between the corporate mismanagement and the impossibility of identifying a natural person as the material author of the crime. However, under this system, it is not necessary to prove that the offense is due to a lack of organization (Villani 2012, p. 586). In the case of primary liability, the "blameworthiness" of the corporation is due to a "failure to prevent the commission of the offense." Therefore, corporate criminal liability requires "a link of causal derivation of the offense from organizational mismanagement" (Villani 2012, p. 590). The fact of having chosen an organizational model of corporate criminal liability means, in practice, that the legal entity will be convicted for not having an appropriate compliance program in place to counter offenses (e.g., corruption) provided that there is an explicit reference to these practices in the domestic or international legislation

[9] See Muñoz de Morales, "Corporate Responsibility and Compliance Programs in Australia," in this volume.

[10] See *Schweizerisches Strafgesetzbuch* (StGB), SR 311.0. The full text of the Swiss Penal Code is available on http://www.admin.ch/ in German, French, and Italian. For an English translation (provided for information purposes only) see "Swiss Criminal Code," The Federal Authorities of the Swiss Confederation, http://www.admin.ch/opc/en/classified-compilation/19370083/index.html, accessed 19 June 2013.

[11] For an overview of the Swiss system of criminal corporate liability, see Pestalozzi Lachenal Patry, "Switzerland," Lex Mundi Publication, http://www.lexmundi.com/images/lexmundi/PracticeGroups/BankFinance/Survey1/Switzerland.pdf; Livschitz 2011, p. 375; Perrin 2011, p. 193.

[12] See Cassani, "Corporate Responsibility and Compliance Programs in Switzerland," in this volume.

(e.g., money laundering legislation or international provision against bribery; Villani 2012, p. 594). In these cases, a legal entity could avoid criminal culpability by setting up and maintaining an effective (anticorruption) compliance program (Pieth 2004, p. 611).

In addition, even in those cases where the offense is of a specific nature (e.g., bribery), the imputation model will differ depending on the concrete nature of the conduct which is criminalized. For example, in the UK, the Bribery Act consolidates new bribery offenses: "active" bribery, "passive" bribery, and bribery of a foreign public official. When such offenses are committed by corporations, common law principles are applicable. Therefore, a person who represents the "directing mind" of the corporation has to possess the necessary fault element for the offense, and a director or senior officer who has consented or connived in the activity will also be liable (Wells 2012, p. 421). Compliance programs are not supposed to play such a relevant role. However, the prevent fault model presented in Section 7 of the Bribery Act states that commercial organizations will be held criminally liable if they have failed to prevent a bribe being paid on its behalf. What is new is that Section 7(2) affords organizations a defense of "adequate procedures" by which an effective compliance program can reveal its full effect.

The Italian approach is also particularly instructive in showing how the relevance of a compliance program can differ, depending upon when it is adopted and implemented. The Legislative Decree of 8 June 2001 (n. 231) introduced a form of administrative responsibility for corporations[13] related to the crimes committed by their agents and based on both objective and subjective standards. Firstly, the crime must either be committed *in the interest* of the corporation or should result in *a benefit* for the corporation. Furthermore, a kind of *structural culpability* of the corporation must be present. Therefore, the adoption and the effective implementation of a compliance program *before* the commission of the crime can exclude liability. Besides this, a kind of reactive culpability[14] is present in the Italian system as well, since the adoption and implementation of a compliance program *after* the commission of the crime can lead to a reduction in economic sanctions (Section 12 D. Lgs. 231/2001).[15] In Spain, a reaction from the corporation *after* the commission of the crime is also taken into account as a mitigating factor.[16] In this regard, Article 31*bis* Section 4 of the Spanish Criminal Code states that:

> Circumstances that mitigate criminal accountability of legal persons may only be deemed to concur when, after the felony is committed, they have [among others] established, prior to the trial itself, measures that are effective to prevent and discover felonies that might be committed in the future using the means or under the coverage of the legal person.

A similar mitigating factor is also provided under the Chilean system of corporate criminal liability (Matus Acuña 2013, p. 150).

[13] On the Italian system of corporate liability, see De Maglie 2011, p. 255 and Villani 2012, p. 14.

[14] On reactive culpability as the basis of corporate culpability, see Fisse 1983, p. 1,141.

[15] See Paludi and Zecca, "Corporate Responsibility and Compliance Programs in Italian Case Law," in this volume.

[16] On the Spanish model, see Nieto Martín 2012, p. 181.

It is interesting to note that in the Italian system, the role played by the compliance program differs depending on the person who commits the offense:

> When the crime is committed by *representatives*, *directors*, or *top managers*, the corporation is not responsible if it demonstrates that: (1) before the crime was committed, it had adopted and effectively implemented a compliance program suitable to prevent the kind of crime actually committed (Mongillo 2012a); (2) a supervisory body monitoring the functioning of, updating of, and respect for the compliance program had been appointed; (3) the crime was committed by *fraudulently circumventing* the compliance program; (4) the supervisory board had carried out its work properly (Section 6 D. Lgs. 231/2001). When the crime is committed by an *employee* of the corporation, subject to the control of the top management, the corporation is not responsible if: (1) a compliance program had been adopted and effectively implemented by the corporation before the crime was committed to prevent the kind of crime actually committed, and (2) the employee failed to comply with those rules.[17]

Curiously, a draft bill which is, in the relevant sense, a mere transposition of the Italian Decreto legge, is soon to be issued by the Spanish government.[18] If the draft is successful, Spanish judges will be likely to follow their Italian counterparts closely in terms of assessing the effectiveness of compliance programs.

In Portugal, the situation is different. If a crime is committed on behalf of the legal entity, and in the collective interest, by any of its members with decision-making powers, the model of imputation is one of vicarious liability;[19] in this case, the role of the compliance program is supposed to be insignificant. However, when the crime is committed by any person in a position subordinate to those with decision-making powers, the imputation model chosen is one of self-liability: In this case, it must be proved that the crime was committed due to a violation of the duties of supervision and control by the responsible members with decision-making powers.

Another issue which is relevant in distinguishing compliance programs concerns the onus of proof. In some states (such as the UK), a compliance program takes the form of an exculpatory clause, as in the 2010 Bribery Act,[20] particularly in the case of the above-mentioned defense of "adequate procedures."[21] Section 7 of the Act introduces the corporate failure to prevent an offense:

> (1) A relevant commercial organisation ('C') is guilty of an offence under this section if a person ('A') associated with C bribes another person intending—(a) to obtain or retain business for C, or (b) to obtain or retain an advantage in the conduct of business for C. (2) But

---

[17] See Paludi and Zecca, "Corporate Responsibility and Compliance Programs in Italian Case Law," in this volume.

[18] See "Anteproyecto de ley orgánica por la que se modifica la Ley Órganica 10/1995, del Código penal," Ministerio de Justicia, http://www.juecesdemocracia.es/pdf/legislacion/antProyCodPenal.pdf, accessed 19 June 2013.

[19] On the Portuguese model of corporate criminal liability, see Espinoza de los Monteros de la Parra 2012, p. 213.

[20] For a detailed discussion of the 2010 Bribery Act, see Mongillo 2012a, 304. On the corporate criminal liability system in England and Wales in general, see Wells 2011, p. 91.

[21] See Wells, "Corporate Responsibility and Compliance Programs in the United Kingdom," in this volume.

> it is a defence for C to prove that C had in place adequate procedures designed to prevent persons associated with C from undertaking such conduct.

As a defense, the burden of proof rests with the corporation.[22] Therefore, a corporation will be guilty unless it can prove that it had adequate procedures in place to prevent the conduct (e.g., the act of bribery) in question. Whether or not the corporation has implemented "adequate procedures" is decided by the court on a case-by-case basis. A single act of bribery does not necessarily imply that the organization's procedures were inadequate or deficient.[23] In Italy, the burden of proof also rests with the corporation. The wording of Article 22.2 (c) of the Canadian Criminal Code also appears to introduce a kind of due diligence defense, such that the corporation can avoid criminal liability if it is able to prove that adequate procedures were in place.

However, in other countries, it is the prosecution's responsibility to prove the lack of reasonable and effective preventive measures (e.g., in Switzerland), [24] or a violation of the duties of supervision and control (e.g., in Portugal). In other words, in other countries, there is no reversal of the burden of proof.

There is no substantial legal acknowledgment of compliance programs in France.[25] By requiring two conditions (the "condition of representation" and the "condition of interest"), the French model of imputation is indirect.[26] Therefore, the role played by compliance programs in the French case-law system is insignificant: "as far as the criminal system is concerned, enforcement authorities, and especially criminal courts, do not carry out any assessment of whether an organization has a compliance program." In addition, not only is there "no obligation to adopt such a program under criminal law, but, more generally, there is no legal incentive to do so (or interest in doing so) for the purpose of the application of French criminal law." Nevertheless, "recent developments in [French] case law, and the increasing number of proceedings against corporations for the bribery of foreign officials, might yet change the situation."[27] In the future,French judges could open the door to compliance programs as grounds for criminal exemption, or at least as a mitigating factor, by using a controversial notion: the "commercial policy" (*politique commerciale*) of the legal entity. This expression "allows judges to presume that the legal condition (that the offense has been committed by an organ or a representative of the corporation) is met, without having to identify the human agent…."[28] Another "fair wind" is the concept of the "intellectual offender" (*auteur moral*), used in cases of insider trading when the offense is considered to have been committed by an organ

[22] See Wells, "United Kingdom," in this volume.

[23] See "Bribery Act 2010, Joint Prosecution Guidance of The Director of the Serious Fraud Office and the Director of Public Prosecutions," Serious Fraud Office, http://www.sfo.gov.uk/, accessed 19 June 2013.

[24] See Cassani "Corporate Responsibility and Compliance Programs in Switzerland," in this volume.

[25] This is also the case in the Netherlands.

[26] On the French model of corporate criminal liability, see Tricot 2012, p. 132.

[27] See Tricot, "Corporate Liability and Compliance Programs in France," in this volume.

[28] See Tricot, "France," in this volume.

or a representative of the corporation. It should be noted that here we are moving into uncharted waters: To date, there have only been two published decisions of the Cour de cassation which have used such reasoning.[29] Another possibility under French law would be for judges to open the door to corporate social responsibility (CSR). The recent *Erika* case could be interpreted as an example of this. The Cour de cassation used the breach of obligations which had been voluntarily assumed by Total SA to establish the liability of the mother company and ascribe that liability to Total. Therefore, Total SA was held criminally liable for the offense of unintentional marine pollution, because it was found to have failed to carry out the required vetting procedures. In other words, Total was punished for the failure to inspect the vessel before it was chartered. This case can be interpreted as a way of supporting compliance programs by helping judges to establish "the objective component of the fault (in civil and criminal proceedings) as well as its subjective component (that the organs or representatives could not ignore/had to know/should have known)."[30]

There is no legal reference to compliance programs in China.[31] Under Chinese criminal law, there are no affirmative defenses such as "adequate procedures" in the sense of this term as used in the UK Bribery Act. However, the absence of "adequate procedures" is likely to be viewed unfavorably, according to *The Norton Rose Group Report*.[32] The report states that:

> in practice, the implementation of bribery prevention measures by a company may be presented to the authorities or the courts as evidence that the illegal actions of the company's agents were contrary to the company's regulations and serve to prevent a prosecution of individuals from becoming a prosecution of the company.

It remains to be seen, however, whether or not such a scenario materializes. An examination of Chinese case law reveals the fact (which is not surprising) that there is no trace of anything related to compliance program issues.[33]

Germany is halfway towards legal acknowledgment. German law punishes corporations with administrative sanctions (Espinoza de los Monteros de la Parra 2012, p. 419), but this has not presented any obstacle to the consideration of compliance issues. It is true that in Germany, legal entities do not have a general duty to implement a compliance system, but they do have to comply with the huge number of legal requirements from different legal fields, which leads them to establish compliance systems. In addition, the form or specific features or elements of these compliance systems are developed, above all, through case law.[34]

Compliance programs are not only important in exempting corporations from criminal liability, but they also serve to establish mitigating or aggravating circum-

[29] See Tricot, "France," in this volume.

[30] See Tricot, "France," in this volume.

[31] See Muñoz de Morales, "Corporate Responsibility and Compliance Programs in China," in this volume.

[32] See "Anti-corruption laws in Asia Pacific," Norton Rose Fulbright, http://www.nortonrosefulbright.com/, accessed 19 June 2013.

[33] See Muñoz de Morales, "China," in this volume.

[34] For a compilation of case law in this regards, see Greeve 2010, p. 514.

stances. In fact, this is what usually happens, and the US situation is a perfect illustration of this. There, based on the principle of aggregation or identification, compliance programs have found a place in the sentencing phase. Under the US Sentencing Guidelines, compliance programs can result in sentence reductions, provided certain requirements are satisfied (e.g., the implementation of adequate standards, the involvement of management and monitoring systems).[35] Mitigation through compliance also occurs in Italy and Spain, as previously mentioned. At the same time, compliance (or, rather, the lack of preventive measures) can also be taken into account as an aggravating factor, closely linked to recidivism. The fact that a corporation reoffends can be seen as a proof of the inadequacy of its internal organizational system. This happened in the famous *Siemens* case, for example.

The above explanation regarding the legal acknowledgment of compliance programs would not be complete without the mention of guilty plea agreements and pretrial agreements. This is the point at which the procedural analysis of the role of compliance programs begins. Primarily, when prosecutors have considerable room for discretion (as in the USA), they are even more likely than judges to assess internal corporate measures. In the USA, pretrial diversion is relevant in a number of respects. First of all, appeal to a well-designed and effective compliance program can result in a prosecutor's decision to bring charges against a corporation's employees only. Secondly, pretrial settlements impose penalties of a greater or lesser degree of severity on an enterprise, depending on how the compliance program has been designed and performed. Deferred prosecution agreements (hereinafter DPAs) and non-prosecution agreements (hereinafter NPAs)[36] are noteworthy examples of this. DPAs and NPAs are even more detailed than judgments: For this reason, they provide a potential framework for an effective compliance program and for the implementation of measures which will prevent future compliance-related failures.[37] Most employ the same formula, given the fact that when prosecutors have to evaluate any corporate compliance program, they use those provided by their manual (US Attorneys' Manual; USAM) as critical factors.[38]

The critical factors provided by the USAM are, in fact, criteria which are also provided by the US Sentencing Guidelines.[39] However, it is important to highlight

[35] See Fan, "An Analysis of Institutional Guidance and Case Law in the United States Pertaining to Compliance Programs," in this volume.

[36] For a definition of DPAs and NPAs see Dell'Osso, "Empirical Features of International Bribery Practice: Evidence from FCPA Enforcement Actions," in this volume. For further details, see Hall 2009, p. 119, and Epstein 2006, p. 38. For a general analysis of DPAs and NPAs dealing with bribery cases, see Muñoz de Morales Romero 2013, p. 220.

[37] Data on the number of DPAs or NPAs explicitly requiring compliance measures as part of a company's business reforms are provided in Martin et al. 2011, p. 509.

[38] See, for example, the United States Attorneys' Manual (USAM) Sect. 9–28.000, which directs federal prosecutors to consider compliance with respect to three of the nine factors prosecutors must weigh before filing criminal charges against a company, http://www.justice.gov/usao/eousa/foia_reading_room/usam/.

[39] See "US Sentencing Commission, Supplement to 2010 Guidelines Manual § 8B2.1 (2010)," United States Sentencing Commission, http://www.ussc.gov/Guidelines/2010_guidelines/Manual_PDF/2010_Guidelines_Manual_Supplement.pdf.

the fact that prosecutors sometimes use other criteria which go beyond these guidelines. DPAs and NPAs usually confirm that even where the corporation has implemented "a compliance and ethics program designed to detect and prevent violations of the FCPA, U.S. commercial bribery laws and foreign bribery laws throughout its operations, including those of its subsidiaries, affiliates, joint ventures, and those of its contractors and subcontractors...,"[40] such a compliance program is not enough. This is why corporations always agree "to adopt new or to modify internal controls, policies, and procedures."[41]

Pretrial agreements, a typical "US product," are likely to cross the pond. The director of the UK's Serious Fraud Office (SFO),[42] the counterpart to the US Department of Justice, has endorsed pretrial agreements, and encourages corporations to bring violations to light and to carry out internal investigations to uncover the practice of bribery (Cassell 2010, p. 6).

The fact of counting on an effective compliance program has also been taken into account in Switzerland as a ground for discontinuing the prosecution against a corporation, as in the recent *Alstom* case.[43] In this case, the Swiss attorney general (OAG) decided not to bring charges against the French parent company, Alstom S.A., because the company had made considerable efforts to observe the applicable rules and, from 2003 onwards, had improved its (anticorruption) compliance program.[44] The main reason why the OAG came to the conclusion that such improvements made the compliance program effective was the fact that the Alstom compliance program had been certificated by the ETHICH Intelligence Agency as good in 2008, and as the first of the CAC40 companies in 2009.[45] Certification has become an indicator of the "quality" or "effectiveness" of a compliance program

[40] See Deferred Prosecution Agreement, *United States of America v. Baker Hughes Incorporated*, April 2007, at 8; Deferred Prosecution Agreement, *United States of America v. Tidewater Marine International, Inc.*, November 2010, at 13; Deferred Prosecution Agreement, *United States of America v. Aibel Group Limited*, 2007, at 6; Deferred Prosecution Agreement, *United States of America v. Transocean Inc.*, October 2010, at 13.

[41] See, for example, Non Prosecution Agreement, Helmerich & Payne, Inc., 2009, at 10; Deferred Prosecution Agreement, *United States of America v. Snaprogetti Netherlands B.V.*, 2010, at 42.

[42] See "Bribery and Corruption," Serious Fraud Office, http://www.sfo.gov.uk/, accessed 19 June 2013.

[43] See Cassani, "Corporate Responsibility and Compliance Programs in Switzerland," in this volume.

[44] See Cassani, "Switzerland," in this volume. The charges against the French mother company were dismissed because "the company had made efforts to prevent corruption, although they were not sufficient, and because it had cooperated in the inquiry and made reparations in the form of a payment of one million francs to the International Committee of the Red Cross for projects in Latvia, Tunisia, and Malaysia."

[45] Both certificates are available at the ALSTOM website: in particular, see "Ethics rules rated at the best international standard," ALSTOM, http://www.Alstom.com/ethics/ethics-intelligence-certificate/, 19 June 2013.

and has therefore served as a proof, usually in the mitigation of liability, e.g., in Italy or Chile.[46]

On the other hand, it is worth mentioning the role played by compliance programs in the Department of Justice Opinion Releases. This procedure allows any corporation facing potential liability under the Foreign Corruption Practices Act (FCPA) "to obtain an opinion of the Attorney General as to whether certain specified, prospective—not hypothetical—conduct conforms with the department's present enforcement policy."[47] In other words, opinion procedure releases respond to "inquiries regarding compliance-related issues for organizations that wish to abide by the law."[48] Particularly relevant is the Opinion Release 04–02, where it is stated that one of the prerequisites for acquiring companies (and their assets) which have previously been convicted of FCPA violations is that the investment group adopt a rigorous compliance code.

Finally, compliance programs are particularly relevant in making probation orders (e.g., in the USA and Canada) and in determining the appropriateness or inappropriateness of imposing disqualification measures or suspending precautionary measures. As regards this last point, in Italy, an effective compliance program implemented *after* the commission of the crime does not avoid corporate liability. However, it does prevent judges from imposing disqualification measures.[49] Italian judges are also allowed to suspend any precautionary measure,[50] provided that the corporation asks, during the investigation, for time to adopt and effectively implement a compliance program.[51] Additionally, in Canada, corporations can be placed on probation, during which time steps must be taken to repair harms caused and ensure that the harms of the past are not repeated. In effect, under Article 732.1(3.1) of the Criminal Code, the court may prescribe probation in respect of an organization, which includes conditions such as one or more of the following: to provide restitution to a person for any loss or damage caused by the offense; to establish policies, standards, and procedures to prevent subsequent offenses; to report to the court on the implementation of these policies, standards, and procedures; to make a public announcement regarding the conviction, sentence; and to take any other measures needed to prevent further offenses.

---

[46] Despite a lack of case law on this matter in Chile, legal scholars support that certification would be only useful to mitigate liability and not as a way of exemption of corporate liability. See Matus Acuña 2013, p. 151.

[47] See "Foreign Corrupt Practices Act Opinion Procedure (28 C.F.R. § 80.1)," US Government Printing Office (GPO), http://www.gpo.gov/fdsys/granule/CFR-2010-title28-vol2/CFR-2010-title28-vol2-part80/content-detail.html, accessed 19 June 2013.

[48] See Fan, "United States," in this volume.

[49] Section 17 D. Lgs. 231/2001, see "DECRETO LEGISLATIVO 8 giugno 2001, n. 231," Normattiva – Il Portale della Legge Vigente, http://www.normattiva.it/uri-res/N2Ls?urn:nir:stato:decreto.legislativo:2001-06-08;231, accessed 18 June 2013.

[50] Ibid., Sect. 49.

[51] See Paludi and Zecca, "Corporate Responsibility and Compliance Programs in Italian Case Law," in this volume.

17.3 General Impressions on the Country Reports

The differing situations in which compliance programs may play a role and the varying roles they may play (as outlined above) give an idea of the difficulties involved in carrying out a holistic and exhaustive comparative analysis. For this reason, it has been necessary, in the present study, to stick to providing some general key elements. In addition, it is worthwhile recalling that one of the aims of the present research project was to make a selection, from the relevant case law on corporate criminal liability, concerning *international corruption in the specific area of energy companies*. Therefore, it was decided to analyze countries with a tradition of corporate criminal liability where case law dealing with compliance issues was supposed to be in place. It was also important to choose countries belonging to both the common law tradition (e.g., USA, Australia, and Canada) and the continental tradition (e.g., Italy and Switzerland). Given the focus on corruption, a report on the UK and the Bribery Act was obviously essential. It was also decided to explore the situation in a couple of countries where compliance programs were not legally acknowledged. For these purposes, France and China were chosen. Despite its lack of legal acknowledgment of compliance programs, France was selected because, as described above, expressions such as the "commercial policy" of the legal entity have been used recently by French judges, and this could result in the recognition of compliance systems through case law in the future. China was chosen due to the importance of Chinese corporations and the high levels of corruption in the country.

Having selected the countries, the main task was to analyze relevant rulings, in order to identify key elements which were useful for legal entities in configuring their compliance programs, and thereby avoiding or mitigating criminal liability. One drawback was the lack of relevant case law devoted to foreign bribery offenses. More generally, one problem was the lack of experience and specialized knowledge of criminal courts, particularly as regards corporate crime prevention systems. This lack of experience and specialized knowledge is linked to the fact that criminal courts often have a narrow concern for the different compliance program features or elements that have failed in a particular criminal case. In fact, courts "do not assess the full range of compliance program elements which are relevant in determining if a company operated a generally effective law compliance program" (Gruner 2007, p. 299). In other words, courts do not carry out a complete assessment of whether an organization had an effective program in place for the prevention and detection of violations of the law. Instead, courts "tend to allocate reduced corporate criminal penalties to firms that do not possess generally effective systems or fail to grant penalty reductions to firms that have such systems" (Gruner 2007, p. 299). Similar views are also expressed by law reform commissions such as the New South Wales Law Reform. According to this Australian body, "it is unclear…what factors the courts will look at in determining the capacity of a compliance program to be successful and effective."[52] The only thing which is certain is that the mere existence

[52] See "Report 102 (2003) – Sentencing: Corporate Offenders," NSW Government – Law Reform Commission Attorney General & Justice, http://www.lawreform.lawlink.nsw.gov.au/agdbasev7wr/lrc/documents/pdf/report_102.pdf, accessed 18 June 2013.

of a compliance program is not sufficient. Exemption from liability, or a more lenient penalty, is only feasible if the corporate compliance program is "a successful management tool with the demonstrated capacity to prevent, detect and remedy breaches that may occur in the daily conduct of the company's business."[53]

This initial shortcoming is exacerbated if one moves the discussion from the general arena, to a focus on corruption, to cases of international corruption primarily involving energy companies in particular. For example, in the USA, there have only been two such cases—and in neither of them was the defendant an energy company—in which the corporation went to trial for violation of the US FCPA. The first of these, which took place in 1990–1991, is the *Harris Corporation* case.[54] The company and its managers sought to obtain telecommunications contracts in Colombia by paying a portion of the commission to a foreign official, who was a member of the Cámara de Representantes (CDR). The trial resulted in the acquittal for all defendants, including the corporation. Acquittal was not based on the existence or inexistence of an effective compliance program; in fact, no mention of compliance was made. The second case was that of *Lindsey Manufacturing Co.,* where the company and the rest of the defendants' convictions were dismissed because the judge found that the prosecution had engaged in "flagrant" misconduct. There was no reference to compliance program issues in this case either.

The situation is not so different in other legal orders. Once again, there are very few cases of international corruption (particularly in the case of energy corporations). For example, there is a clear lack of enforcement of laws against foreign bribery in Australia. In this country, very few investigations and prosecutions have been carried out, and, worse, the number of investigations and prosecutions against corporations is even smaller.[55] This lack of prosecutions against corporations—and therefore of case law—is not surprising, since most of the prosecutions in this country are of individuals, not corporations; the provisions on "corporate culture" apply only to the Criminal Code Act 1995, not to other Commonwealth statutes, and most prosecutions of corporations occur under other statutes (e.g., the Australian Securities and Investments Commission Act 2001 and the Competition and Consumer Act 2010). Canada is another example of a country where very few prosecutions have been pursued by criminal law authorities against corporations for (foreign) bribery offenses, and very few of these have been successful. In fact, only two cases have so far been brought before the Canadian courts. In the first of these, *R v. Watts,* there was no mention of compliance programs issues. In the second, *R v. Niko Resources Ltd.,*[56] compliance program questions came to the surface in the probation order imposed on Niko. The court required the company to implement a compliance program for the prevention and detection of violations of the Corruption of Foreign Public Officials Act (CFPOA). Its requirements included the following: internal

[53] *Australian Competition and Consumer Commission v Australian Safeway Stores Pty Ltd* (1997) 75 FCR 238.

[54] See *United States v. Harris Corporation, John D. Iacobucci, and Ronald L. Schultz,* No. 3:90-cr-00456 (N.D. Cal. 1990), August 31, 1990.

[55] See Muñoz de Morales, "Australia," in this volume.

[56] R v. Niko Resources Ltd., Proceedings taken in the Court of Queen's Bench of Alberta, Judicial District of Calgary, on June 24, 2011.

accounting controls for fair and accurate books and records; a rigorous anticorruption compliance code designed to detect and deter violations; risk assessments; due diligence; etc. These were taken, almost verbatim, from an American civil action before the Securities and Exchange Commission (SEC) and from guilty plea agreements and DPAs.[57] The same holds for France: "More than twelve years since the entry into force of the offense of foreign bribery, there is still no final case law on the issue of liability of legal persons for this offense."[58] The situation is similar in China: there have been "a few convictions of companies for foreign bribery and for domestic bribery."[59] In Switzerland, it is nearly impossible to determine the number of convictions against corporations. As Perrin (2011, p. 222) and Cassani state, the criminal record does not include these,[60] and they are obscured by the published criminal and judicial statistics. So far, the most important bribery case in this country is the *Alstom* case.

There are various reasons for this lack of enforcement. Some of these can be attributed to the recognition of a limited jurisdiction for the prosecution of these offenses (e.g., in Canada);[61] others can be attributed to the fact that legislation does not judge a parent company liable for the actions of its subsidiaries, joint ventures, or agents (this is the case in Australia, for example).[62] The list of hindrances does not end here. Other substantial difficulties, mainly the need to prove the corruption pact and procedural obstacles—notably the monopoly of the public prosecutor's office over opening prosecutions in the case of foreign corruption—are the main reasons for lack of enforcement in France.[63] In other countries (e.g., China), the lack of enforcement in cases of bribery involving corporations is related to the following: insufficient resources or expertise for the purposes of conducting investigations and prosecutions of this nature; a belief that it is unimportant to go after companies; and the tendency to allow the USA and other countries to pursue the persons and corporations which pay the bribes (Bath 2012, p. 34). Finally, the lack of action is sometimes due (e.g., in Switzerland)[64] to the fact that public servants and/or national companies doing business in foreign markets do not have a reputation for being prone to bribe or to be bribed.

Given this lack of enforcement, a step forward in the global standardization on compliance issues is needed more than ever. This body of international standards

---

[57] See Muñoz de Morales, "Canada," in this volume.

[58] See Tricot, "France," in this volume.

[59] See "Liability of Legal Persons for Bribery," ADB/OECD Thematic Review – Final Report, *Anti-Corruption Initiative for Asia and the Pacific: The Criminalisation of Bribery in Asia and the Pacific*, p. 38, http://www.oecd.org/site/adboecdanti-corruptioninitiative/46485272.pdf.

[60] See Cassani, "Switzerland," in this volume.

[61] The Corruption of Foreign Public Officials Act (CFPOA) recognizes jurisdiction to prosecute foreign bribery offenses only when the offense is committed in whole or part in Canadian territory.

[62] See "Progress Report 2010: Enforcement of the OECD AntiBribery Convention," Transparency International, p. 13, http://www.transparency.org/whatwedo/publications, accessed 18 June 2013.

[63] See Tricot, "France," in this volume.

[64] See Cassani, "Switzerland," in this volume.

could feed on the guidelines which the present comparative analysis modestly offers. The country reports presented in the present volume have focused not only on *strictu sensu* judgments dealing with both foreign and domestic bribery (e.g., Italy,[65] USA[66]), but also on case law concerning other breaches of the law as competition (e.g., Australia,[67] Canada[68]). De facto case laws,[69] such as guilty plea and pretrial agreements (e.g., USA[70]) have also been studied, as well as specific guidelines coming from associations (e.g., Canada,[71] Australia[72]). The following section provides an overview of the main findings of the country reports.

17.4 Through an Effective Compliance Program—Country Reports: Analysis and Lessons Learned

Very briefly, the elements of an effective compliance program can be described as follows: (1) the need for proceeding to risk assessment; (2) the existence of an ethics code of conduct; (3) the existence of an appropriate training program; (4) the fact of setting up reporting methods, internal controls, and procedures including due diligence mechanisms; (5) the setting up of institutional channels (e.g., the appointment of a chief compliance officer) and tone at the top.[73] Not all the aspects mentioned have been addressed in the same degree of detail (e.g., risk assessment). However, in essential respects, this study offers some relevant guidelines which may help companies design their compliance programs to avoid or to mitigate liability.

17.4.1 The Need to Proceed to Risk Assessment

Basically, risk assessment means that an organization should assess the "nature and extent of its exposure" to potential external and internal risks.[74] Therefore, its goal is to identify how offenses (or misconduct) may be committed within the corpora-

[65] See Paludi and Zecca, "Corporate Responsibility and Compliance Programs in Italian Case Law," in this volume.

[66] See Fan, "United States," in this volume.

[67] See Muñoz de Morales, "Australia," in this volume.

[68] See Muñoz de Morales, "Canada," in this volume.

[69] This expression originates in Koehler 2010, p. 998.

[70] See Fan, "United States," in this volume.

[71] See Muñoz de Morales, "Canada," in this volume.

[72] See Muñoz de Morales, "Australia," in this volume.

[73] For ease of exposition we have followed, in essential respects, the compliance structure described by Moosmayer (2010) and, in Spain, by Lascuraín (2013, p. 129).

[74] This is the definition used by the Ministry of Justice. See "The Bribery Act 2010—Guidance about Procedures which Relevant Commercial Organisations can Put into Place to Prevent Persons Associated with them from Bribing (Sect. 9 of the Bribery Act 2010)," UK Government Ministry

tion, and in which part of the entity's structure the misconduct occurs (Selvaggi 2012, p. 23). The need to identify those activities more susceptible to misconduct is a crucial factor in tailoring a bespoke compliance program, in a wide sense. With this information available, a company could implement measures to protect itself from exposure to wrongdoing; it could train its employees to respond effectively and consistently if they encounter misconduct; it could introduce specific policies and training, appropriate to the political and business environments in which the company will be operating; and it could optimize available preventive resources where the company is more exposed to crime. In a nutshell: everything starts from risk assessment.

A focus on our comparative analysis directly leads to the Italian report. On the basis of the US guidelines, we know that in order to carry out a risk assessment it is necessary to take into account a range of factors, including the geographical organization of the corporation, the corporation's history, its interactions with foreign governments, and the specific industry in which the corporation operates. Italian case law provides further details concerning this issue. Risk assessments based on a generic approach (e.g., where there are no specific rules for the prevention of crimes, depending on the specific industry of the corporation) are not suitable. For example, in a decision made in 2004, the Court of Milan ruled that an analysis should have been more focused on financial sources, the creation of slush funds, participation in a competitive tender, the execution of contracts, etc. Another example worthy of mention in this respect is the Court of Bari's decision to judge a compliance program unsuitable because, among other reasons, there was no identification of the activities in relation to which offenses may be committed. In contrast, a compliance program adopted after the commission of the crime was judged suitable, according to the Court of Milan's decision of 2004, because it paid attention to accounting, the drawing up of balance sheets, intercompany billing, the relationship with Public Administration in relation to competitive tender, and participation in joint ventures and advisory services.

The lesson to be learnt from both cases is that risk assessment does not only involve an understanding of generic risks. The mere fact of indicating that there is a high risk of corruption when the company deals with bureaucracies in procurement is not enough. A further step is needed, which should consist in specifying the generic risk which has been identified. This is where the specific structure of the company involved plays a relevant role. It is obvious that there is a general risk in procurement, but that such a general risk becomes specific when a flaw in the company's internal processes is found (e.g., when practices relating to winning competitive tender are handled by those who are not involved in the compliance program). The detection of any possible flaws is what calls into question the pre-existing compliance program, and which leads to the demand for the program to be updated and upgraded. In this sense, risk assessments are a way of reviewing corporate compliance programs.

---

of Justice, http://www.justice.gov.uk/guidance/docs/bribery-act-2010-guidance.pdf, accessed 18 June 2013.

This raises another question: How often should risk assessments be carried out? Or, if one prefers, how often does a compliance program have to be updated? The general guideline is that the evaluation and testing of the effectiveness of a compliance program should be periodic. American cases speak of a constant updating, and the same is true in Australian competition cases. Therefore, it can be said that there is some margin of discretion in determining when to carry out a review. Nevertheless, under Italian law, the corporate compliance program should be amended "when significant violations of the prescriptions are discovered" (see Art. 6 of the Decree[75]). For this reason, Italian decisions "did not intend to forgive" a lack of modification once misconduct is detected. This was evident in the *Ordinanza di applicazione di misure interdittiva* and the *Ordinanza del Tribunale di Milano* (both dating from 2010), with reference to the case involving a multinational energy corporation (Siemens). Many months passed after the initial discovery of misconduct and no remedial action or revision of the compliance program was undertaken. This failure is reminiscent to one of the criteria provided by the US Sentencing Guidelines for considering a compliance program to be ineffective: "after criminal conduct has been detected, the organization shall not take reasonable steps to respond appropriately to the criminal conduct and to prevent further similar criminal conduct." The same is true in the analysis of competition cases in Canada (e.g., the *Sobeys Inc.* and *Robert Klein* cases).

Two final questions arise, both linked to the process of updating. The first question concerns how modifications must be decided. Italian case law gives a specific rule: Amendments to the compliance program must be passed by a qualified majority of votes by the board of officers (e.g., the Court of Rome's Ordinanza of 2003). The second question concerns which persons are competent to evaluate the compliance program. This is usually a decision taken by the members of the compliance office or the board of officers. However, American cases specify that external auditors can also carry out risk assessments and evaluate the effectiveness of compliance programs. However, we should note that the lack of working groups developing a step-by-step guide to the new compliance program is considered to be a failure, as is the absence of any improvement in financial controls.

The lesson to be learnt is that any misconduct detected must be followed by a decision of the compliance office or department indicating what has failed, and to what extent the compliance program must be modified. Obviously, this implies that any infringement must be investigated in order to draw lessons for the future.

[75] On other legal criteria for the amendment of the compliance model under Italian law, see Compagna (2012, p. 101).

17.4.2 The Existence of a Code of Conduct (Ethics)

A code of conduct[76] is the apex of any compliance system, and this is surely the reason why codes of conduct have received so much attention from the courts. A "code of conduct" is to be understood as the existence of "a clearly articulated" and "visible" corporate policy against illegal conduct of any kind. Generic codes of ethics are not enough to avoid conviction or mitigate liability. This idea is clearly demonstrated by the *Siemens* case in Italy. A similar sense of purpose can be detected in the 2005 Court of Bari's decision, where apart from underlining the fact that generic and theoretical rules are insufficient to avoid conviction, the court also stressed that the mere reproduction of laws or guidelines laid down by associations is not valid either. Very few exceptions to the rule can be identified. The first exception is the Court of Lucca's judgment of 2004, where the adoption of a code of ethics after the commission of the crime by the corporation, which contained a kind of generic compliance program, led the court to reduce the economic measures and exclude the imposition of a disqualification: In its view, "the suitability of the programs must be evaluated only in a theoretic and abstract way, on paper." Nevertheless, reproducing the guidelines of the sector seems to be relevant, if not for avoiding liability then at least for mitigating it. In a judgment of 11 December 2006, dealing with corruption involved in participating in and winning a competitive tender, the Court of Milan reduced the number of economic measures, and the compliance program was considered suitable for preventing future crimes because it was a code of ethics following the National Register of Building Contractors.

The analysis of strict liability offenses in Canada gives another perspective on the question of reproducing the sector guidelines, namely "that if a corporation follows (or, rather, thoroughly implements) the measures indicated in the check-list, it is not likely to be convicted."[77] At the same time, given the fact that such recommendations are simple suggestions, if the corporation does not implement all the measures this does not necessarily lead to a conviction.

Secondly, a code of conduct is binding. To put it differently, the infringement of the code's rules entails disciplinary sanctions. In this regard, the *Titan* case in the USA is worthy of mention. The corporation had a code of ethics stating that "employees must be familiar with and strictly adhere to such provisions as the Foreign Corrupt Practices Act that prohibit payments or gifts to foreign government officials for the purpose of influencing official government acts or assistance in obtaining business." However, this policy was never disseminated or enforced. The Italian report also provides specific guidelines, consisting in dismissing the legal represen-

---

[76] Ethics and compliance are often used as synonymous terms. They are, however, different. While "compliance emphasizes the need to follow written laws, regulations, or policies" (e.g., the US Sentencing Guidelines), "the emphasis in business ethics is on putting values such as honesty, fairness, integrity, and concern for others into practice in daily business relationships." Corporate codes of conduct must address both ethics and compliance. See Copeland 2000, p. 307.

[77] See Muñoz de Morales, "Corporate Responsibility and Compliance Programs in Canada," in this volume.

tative of the corporation (e.g., Court of Pordenone—Sentenza 4 November 2002). The *Robert Klein* case in Canada should be noted here as being in the same spirit, though more innovative. The case related to strict liability offenses, and sanctions such as receiving a warning for a first failure, a two-day suspension from work for a second failure, and dismissal for a third failure were considered suitable.

A different but closely related issue was addressed in the Court of Naples' Ordinanza of 2007, where an interesting indication running was provided, running in harmony with the principle of foreseeability. The judge stated that the compliance program had to give a specific indication of how particular forms of conduct determined a particular punishment, and that it must also specify the sanctions to be imposed on the directors (such as economic sanctions, revocations of the power of attorney, and the revocation of appointments).

Thirdly, (antibribery) compliance policies must be directed to all company employees and must reflect the strong, explicit, and visible support of and commitment to the policy by senior management. In this respect, Australian competition case law states that the mere provision of manuals or the setting up of material on the Intranet is not sufficient (e.g., *Coyne v. P & O Ports*).

Fourthly, the compliance program must also include specific and complete policies (for example gifts, hospitality, entertainment and expenses, customer travel, political contributions, charitable donations and sponsorships, facilitation payments, solicitation, and extortion). Furthermore, compliance policies contain not merely formal but also substantial rules (e.g., the Court of Naples' Ordinanza of 2007). Examples of substantial rules are the prohibition on accepting gifts from public officers, the use of the written form and the registration of all the communications with the public officers concerning competitive tender, the provision of self-restrictions on the participation in competitive tender for contracts in public works (which allow participation only under domestic law), the banning of information exchange with competitors in tender, or the banning of subcontracting with corporations in the same group.

Finally, compliance programs have to be clear. It is here that idiomatic issues may come to the surface. For example, in an Australian case on competition (*Coyne v. P & O Ports*), the printing of a booklet which explained corporate policy exclusively in the English language was considered a failure, as many of the staff came from non-English speaking backgrounds.

The lesson to be learnt is that compliance is not confined to mentioning prohibited conduct, and nor is it confined to the mere reproduction of laws or guidelines laid down by associations. Dissemination of the content of these laws and guidelines (clearly expressed) and the establishment of sanctioning policy and internal controls are also needed.

17.4.3 Training Programs

As regards the requirements for considering a training program appropriate, the following may be the most important factors: the training program has to result in employees learning to report incidents of suspected noncompliance without the fear of retribution, employees should be made aware of the imposition of disciplinary measures in cases of noncompliance, and training programs must be widely held and addressed to all employees of the corporation (e.g., directors, officers, and in some cases business partners, as raised in *Garth Peterson and Morgan Stanley* in the USA).

The analysis of competition cases gives some concrete examples. Firstly, training programs are not considered to have been held frequently when the last seminar took place approximately 6 years ago. Secondly, training programs must be targeted to all employers at risk regardless of their date of employment. In *Coyne v. P & O Ports*, for example, the judge did not accept the defense of "taking reasonable precautions," among other reasons because the training program implemented, although addressed to a large number of workers (49% of staff), was only targeted at employees taken on after 1996, whereas the offender had been employed prior to 1996.

Italian case law analysis also raises the mandatory nature of the training program (e.g., the Court of Naples' Ordinanza of 2007 or the Court of Milan's decision of 2004). Furthermore, in Italian case law it is considered important that training programs cover specific considerations, which differ depending on the employees' specific areas of employments. It is obvious that a training program followed by an employee working in the auditing department need not be the same as the program followed by an employee working in the sales department. The same applies as regards levels of seniority: The training program followed by a member of the supervisory board does not have to be the same as the program followed by an employee in a less senior position (e.g., the Court of Naples' Ordinanza of 2007 and Court of Milan's decision of 2004).

Lastly, courses have to be well organized, and their content and the number of training sessions, etc., must be clearly defined (e.g., the Court of Naples' Ordinanza of 2007 and Court of Milan's decision of 2004).

The main lesson to be emphasized in the present discussion is that training is not restricted to teaching/learning formal rules, but must include everything in the compliance program. In particular, it is necessary to provide information on the sanctions to be imposed in case of violation and on the internal procedures available for reporting misconduct. In addition, it must be made clear that no action may be taken against the staff in reprisal for reporting wrongdoing, providing information, or otherwise cooperating. In addition, the course content must be custom designed for its target group (taking into account positions and tasks performed, etc.).

17.4.4 Internal Controls and Procedures, Reporting Methods, and Due Diligence Mechanisms

Most of the case law we have analyzed sets up some standard internal controls and procedures to avoid bribery. This gives an idea of the importance these controls and procedures have acquired. In a nutshell: Having no internal procedures will result in conviction. In particular, a compliance program cannot be judged suitable if there is no mention of how to file the accountancy register and on what powers the supervisory board holds (e.g., Court of Milan's decision of 2004). Italian cases also refer to the imposition of specific rules of procedure in the various activities of the corporation, particularly in risk areas (e.g., the Court of Naples' Ordinanza of 2007; the Court of Rome's Ordinanza of 2003). It is important that every payment must be recorded in written form, in accordance with internal rules and tax law. Italian case law identifies the following failures: the compliance program does not provide for any specific direct protocols or implementation of decisions by the body regarding the prevention of offenses (e.g., Court of Bari's decision); practices for winning competitive tender are handled by people who are not involved in the compliance programs (e.g., the Court of Bari's decision); the compliance program does not provide specific rules concerning procedures for participation in competitive tenders, relations with public officers, execution of contracts, documentation of money flows in relation with public officers, selection of workers, etc. (e.g., the Court of Naples' Ordinanza of 2007); there is no individualization of responsible persons for risk operation (e.g., the Court of Naples' Ordinanza of 2007).

Further, positive elements which can be underlined are the use of the written form and the registration of all communications with public officers concerning competitive tender (e.g., the Court of Milan's decision of 2004), and the fact of providing for an internal procedure for managing external communication. As a result of this internal procedure, the participation of several individuals—minimally, the members of the accounting office and the communication department—must be guaranteed in the decision-making process, and in the arrangement of information and data. In the relevant Italian cases, these competent offices had prearranged the press release on the basis of real accounting and financial data (as per the 2009 Court of Milan and 2012 Court of Appeal of Milan decisions).

American cases provide some specific guidelines on internal accounting controls which ensure accurate books and records. A very concrete failure was identified in the *Aibel* and *Transocean* cases, where there were no internal procedures in place to guarantee limiting the use of suspicious payments: These were recorded in the books and records of the corporation's subsidiaries as "other services rendered," "freight and shipping charges," "courier charges," "after sale service fee," "consultation costs or commissions," "local processing fee," "administrative and transport fee," "extra/extraordinary expenses," "urgent processing/urgent dispatch," "custom processing," "customs facilitation," etc. A policy laid out in an email in which the use of these kinds of expenses are limited (and allowed as long as there is management preapproval and proof-of-duty payments) is not enough, if such a policy is not implemented. In contrast, relying on a payment-approval process (e.g., multiple layers of personnel authorization and review of transactions) was judged to be effective in the *Garth Peterson and Morgan Stanley* case.

The setting up of internal accounting controls and procedures is as important as their implementation. This was what failed in the *Alstom* case. The Alstom group had internal guidelines in place which prohibited payments to consultants for bribes or other illegal purposes. The consultants had to detail the contractual services they performed and to substantiate these with obligatory "proofs of rendered services." They had also to itemize amounts due and substantiate these with documentation. All payments were provided in written form and had to be checked by Alstom.Net. Yet, in the end, none of the above was enough, because in some of the prosecuted cases, none of these measures had been implemented.

A different question arises in cases where the corporation has adopted and effectively implemented internal procedures before the commission of the crime, but these procedures have occasionally (and exceptionally) been bypassed by high managers or directors. The decisions reached by the 2009 Court of Milan and the 2012 Court of Appeal of Milan are telling in this regard. The president and the director of the company fraudulently decided—independently, and in a covert manner—to change the content of press release and to communicate false and incomplete statements and data to the market. However, the corporation had always been law compliant:

> In fact, corporate governance and the internal audit procedures were both based on the principles stated by the Self-discipline Code of Borsa Italiana S.p.A. and this is considered as a signal of the existence of a culture of compliance within the organization.[78]

This is why the corporation was not convicted.

There are several lessons to be learnt from this. First, a compliance program cannot be judged as suitable without standard internal procedures. Second, occasional noncompliance with internal procedures does not automatically lead to conviction, if there are signs of the existence of a compliance culture. Third, it is important to set up special protocols when it comes to suspicious transactions. Fourth, a minimum rule is that every payment must be provided in written form, according to internal rules and tax law. Fifth, individualization of responsible persons for risk operations is crucial.

As far as due diligence is concerned, it must be emphasized that this is, in fact, an internal procedure implemented to mitigate the risk of bribery when a corporation is subject to a vetting process during merger and acquisitions, or during the establishment of business relationships. The former means that companies are also legally accountable for any other organization that could be seen to be acting on the company's behalf (e.g., subsidiaries, joint ventures, intermediaries, agent, subcontractors, etc.).[79]

---

[78] See Paludi and Zecca, "Corporate Responsibility and Compliance Programs in Italian Case Law," in this volume.

[79] On the doctrine, see Kochan and Goodyear 2011, p. 163; and Biegelman and Biegelman 2010, p. 250.

Unfortunately, there is very little input from the courts in this regard. The general rule is that compliance codes must include due diligence prior to engaging third-party business partners, as well as mechanisms to ensure that third parties are aware of a company's compliance code. The participation of a third party in the distribution chain usually hinders control and individualization of the source of payment. In *Siemens*, Italian judicial authorities considered that the Siemens AG compliance program had failed (among other reasons) because the modus operandi of misconduct consisted in using a third party as a way of complicating internal controls on payments.

Failures related to the lack of due diligence have also been detected in Australian and Swiss cases. As regards Australia, it is worth mentioning the *Securency and NPA* case. Two journalists showed that it was very easy to find out that people employed to win contracts abroad by these companies were corrupt, because the name of these people appeared on Google as persons charged and/or convicted for bribery in Africa. So, either there was no due diligence at all, or they knew these people were corrupt. In Switzerland, the *Alstom* case provides some further clues. According to Alstom's internal guidelines, there were measures in place "on paper" to prevent bribes, such as a prohibition on making payments to offshore companies and shell companies, rules specifying that consultants could not be individuals, that they must hold bank accounts in the relevant project country, and that they must be resident (or at least have a representative) in the country in which the project is to be carried out. Furthermore, services should preferably be performed via an "established company with all normal office facilities and records" and the internal threshold for consultancy fees (success fees) must be 3 % of the value of the contract. Again, such measures are useless if not enforced, and they were not in *Alstom*. Firstly, the payments of bribes in Tunisia were made via two offshore shell companies controlled by a son-in-law of the former president of that country, neither of whom had bank accounts in Tunisia, and their consultancy fees exceeded 3 % of the contract value. Secondly, in one of the countries where bribes were paid (Malaysia), the consultants were individuals and for this reason Alstom used its national companies as intermediary companies. Obviously, its national companies were neither resident in Malaysia, nor did they hold bank accounts there. In addition, the success fees amounted to more than 3 % of the contract value. Thirdly, in the case of the bribes investigated in Latvia, the main failure was related to "proofs of rendered services." Only 14 % of the payments made by Alstom were in line with the total services rendered by the consultancy companies.

The main lesson to draw from this research is that due diligence is crucial when considering whether a compliance program is suitable; even more importantly, due diligence "on paper" is useless without real enforcement.

The most general features of reporting systems relevant for present purposes, are the following: (1) to compel employees and directors to report any suspicion of violation to the supervisory board; (2) to have reporting systems sufficient to provide senior management and the board with timely and accurate information, such that they can make informed judgments concerning the corporation's compliance with the law, as well as its business performance (e.g., *Re Caremark*); (3) to impose sanctions in cases of violation of the obligation for employees and directors to report their suspicions of violations to the supervisory board; (4) to establish a confidential hotline; and (5) to respond to all requests and to act appropriately. A failure of this nature occurred in the *Titan* case in the USA, for example, where despite the fact that several high-level company employees had received several written allegations of violations, these were not investigated adequately.

The analysis of Italian case law also provides some guidance in this respect. As part of the Court of Bari's decision, it was stated that the compliance program had to specify the obligation to disclose information to the organization tasked with overseeing the implementation of and compliance with the program. Once again, the Court of Milan's decision of 2004 and the Court of Naples' Ordinanza of 2007 are interesting. In the first case, the fact that the compliance program does not contain specific obligations to report or explain how the reporting system works is perceived as a failure. In the Court of Naples' Ordinanza of 2007, this failure was identified as relating to the lack of sanctions.

17.5 Allocation of Compliance Responsibilities and Tone at the Top

The institutionalization of a compliance system requires identifying who deals with compliance issues. Compliance tasks are performed by a chief compliance officer (CCO) or by a compliance supervisory board (CSB). The preliminary thinking is that, contrary to other parts of the code of conduct, institutional channels have enjoyed a greater degree of legal regulation. This has implied a greater degree of legal certainty for corporations when designing their compliance programs.

The two major references are the Italian and the US models. In the USA, the Sentencing Guidelines refer directly to a particular person (or to specific individuals) within the high-level personnel who are responsible for the compliance and ethics program. However, compliance tasks are delegated to one or more CCOs, who oversee the implementation and are responsible for the continued oversight of remedial compliance measures. That is why the American cases underline the need to set up reporting lines between the CCO and the company's board of directors, as well as the need to audit committees or the company's legal counsels or legal directors. The company's board of directors performs the task of ensuring that the compliance program is being observed. But who watches the watchmen? In other words: Who ensures that the members of boards of directors also operate in compliance with the code of conduct? The answer is that nobody does.

This hindrance is what the Italian system tried to overcome by making the Compliance Supervisory Board independent of the board of directors (Mongillo 2012b, p. 58). That was made possible by preventing an officer from wearing two hats, and the criterion originates in the Court of Rome's Ordinanza of 2003, where it is indicated that the supervisory board must have effective powers to monitor the violations of the program, and that its members may not sit on the board of officers or other corporate bodies. This is also the case in the Court of Naples' Ordinanza of 2007.

The Italian cases also emphasize that there is no independence when the members of the CSB have operative or directive roles in the corporation or in the corporate group (e.g., when the corporation designates an officer as a CCO and who acts, at the same time, as a general counsel or in another analogous position). Last but not least, independence also requires a clear division of powers. This must be understood in terms of a clear indication of who holds the power to devise compliance programs, and who holds the power to execute the decisions. Of course, these cannot be the same individual or group of individuals (e.g., the Court of Naples' Ordinanza of 2007 and Court of Milan's decision of 2004).

In Australia, a lack of independence was identified in the *AWB* case, where payments to Iraqi authorities were supposed to be paid to secure the sale of Australian wheat. The majority of the AWB's board included people with a background in wheat farming. Therefore, the board saw itself as working on behalf of Australian wheat exporters, and the corporate culture was not to question the manager's decisions, because the most important thing was considered to be that the company kept selling wheat.

Another defining feature of the CCO or the members of the CSB is their honorableness. Their appointment has to take into account every sentence (including final and nonfinal judgments and pretrial agreements) for crimes previously committed, as well as every previous disqualification from managing public or private offices (e.g., the Court of Naples' Ordinanza of 2007). That relates to the so-called tone at the top doctrine (Schwartz et al. 2005, p. 79; Schroeder 2002, p. 260; Joseph 2002, p. 309; Vitell et al. 2000, p. 15). In addition, it is interesting to take into account the fact that judges detect a failure in the compliance program when violations are committed by high-level offenders, e.g., managers (see the Italian resolutions in *Siemens* and the competition cases analyzed in Australia). Tone at the top was lacking in *AWB*. Senior employees continuously ignored ethical guidelines which prohibited the payment of bribes. Therefore, a written set of guidelines means nothing if it is not supported by implicit signals from the board and senior management.

One last relevant characteristic is professionalism, which is not present when the members of the supervisory board have no specific experience in investigation and consultancy (e.g., as regards statistical techniques, knowledge of analysis procedures, skills in risk evaluation, interviewing people, and discovering frauds). It was this professionalism which was considered lacking by the Court of Milan's decision of 2004 and the Court of Naples' Ordinanza of 2007. In contrast, in *Siemens* it was highly valued as a remediation effort that Siemens' chief audit officer required every member of his 450 person staff to reapply for their jobs. In particular, the Court of Naples' Ordinanza of 2007 is very interesting in this respect, because it provides some specific guidelines which were evaluated positively but considered insufficient. The guidelines state that:

1. The supervisory board should be composed of at least three people, one of whom should act as the head of the internal audit. The other members of the board should be external to the corporate organization.
2. The activity of the supervisory board is regulated by a norm, approved by the board of directors, which states that the members of the supervisory board have the power of control and investigation but not the powers to direct the corporation, to modify its structure or punish its workers.
3. The supervisory board acts in cooperation with other corporate bodies, especially those which operate in risk areas: its members can ask for information, require the release of documents, and constantly receive information from managers working in risk areas.
4. The supervisory board can suggest that disciplinary measures be enforced.
5. The supervisory board assists the head of human resources in the preparation of training courses on respective compliance programs.
6. The supervisory board suggests updates to the compliance program if changes in corporate structure or law occur.
7. Every 6 months, the supervisory board sends an activity report to the board of directors and other formal bodies in the corporation, and informs the president of the board in case of the discovery of crimes.

The *Alstom* case in Switzerland is also telling in terms of the professionalism and independence of the persons dealing with compliance tasks. Taking into account that the Alstom group had a worldwide payroll of over 75,000 people, it was surprising for the Swiss attorney general (OAG) to discover that Alstom.Net had only two full-time employees, helped by a team of around ten/fifteen employees from their department in Paris. In short, the number of Alstom staff in the designated compliance function was disproportionately low in relation to its overall number of global employees. Furthermore, the director of the department in Paris, the two employees mentioned, and the vast majority of other employees had no relevant professional experience in the compliance sector. The latter were employees recruited from the operative divisions of Alstom due to the lack of an established compliance profession. Last but not least, it is true that Alstom offered its employees regular training on compliance issues, but this was inadequate. All in all, the levels of training and experience of Alstom's compliance staff were insufficient. With regard to the need for independence, Alstom.Net was obligated to report to the Representation and Compliance Division functionally attached to the International Network Department in Paris. The problem was that the members of that department also had other responsibilities (for example, they were charged with business development, lobbying in those countries where orders were sent, sales support, setting up and managing shared services, etc.). These responsibilities prevented independence, since the compliance department in Paris had other incompatible responsibilities in the corporation: for example, compliance officers also provided legal advice to the sales department, which included the drafting of agreements with consultants. Consequently, there was no clear division of powers.

Conversely, professionalism and the number of compliance officers were contributory factors in the Department of Justice declining to bring any enforcement against Morgan Stanley. In particular, the company was not prosecuted for the actions of its managing director (among other things) because "between 2002 and 2008, Morgan Stanley employed 500 dedicated compliance officers, including regional compliance officers responsible for evaluating region-specific risks." In the same vein, it was highly valued in *Siemens* (as a remediation effort) that "the number of compliance staff was increased to 600 individuals worldwide with added support for the legal department."[80]

Several general lessons must be learnt from this section. The first is the need to appoint a person or a group of people responsible for monitoring the implementation of the compliance program. Secondly, reporting lines between these people and the members of the board of directors (and other company bodies) is crucial. Thirdly, a compliance officer or a member of the supervisory board cannot wear two hats, and must be honorable (e.g., they must have no previous convictions) and they must be professional (e.g., they must have specific experience in investigation and consulting).

References

Archibald, T., Jull, K. E., & Roach, K. W. (2004). The changed face of corporate criminal liability. *The Criminal Law Quarterly, 48*(3), pp. 367–397.

Archibald, T., Jull, K. E., & Roach, K. W. (2005). *Regulatory and corporate liability: From due diligence to risk management*. Toronto: Canada Law Book, p. 1042.

Bath, V. (2012). China, international business, and the criminal law. *Asian-Pacific Law and Policy Journal, 13*(1), pp. 1–35.

Baxt, R. (2001). Ascribing civil and criminal liability for company employees and directors—Who carries the corporate can? Paper presented at Penalties; Policy Principles & Practice & Government Regulation. Sydney, Australia, 9 June 2001, pp. 1–25.

Belcher, C. (2007). Imagining how a company thinks: What is corporate culture? *Deakin Law Review, 11*(2), 1–21.

Biegelman, M. T. (2008). *Building a world-class compliance program: Best practices and strategies for success*. Hoboken: Wiley, p. 320.

Bowman, F. O. (2004). Drifting down the Dnieper with Prince Potemkin: Some skeptical reflections about the place of compliance programs in federal criminal sentencing. *Wake Forest Law Review, 39*, pp. 671–690.

Brand, V. (2000). Legislating for moral propriety in corporations? The Criminal Code Amendment (Bribery of Foreign Public Officials) Act 1999. *Company and Securities Law Journal, 18*(7), 476–492.

Cassell, B.-L. (2010). U.K. Fraud Office upgrades foreign-corruption fight. *The Wall Street Journal, 20*, pp. 1–6.

Cohen, J. M., Holland, M. P., & Wolf, A. P. (2008). Under the FCPA, who is a foreign official anyway? *The Business Lawyer, 63*(4), pp. 1243–1255.

[80] Fan, "United States," in this volume.

Compagna, F. (2012). The updating of the model. In A. Fiorella (Ed.), *Corporate criminal liability and compliance programs: Vol. 1, Liability "Ex Crimine" of legal entities in member states.* Napoli: Jovene, pp. 101–109.

Copeland, J. D. (2000). The Tyson story: Building an effective ethics and compliance program. *Drake Journal Of Agricultural Law, 5*(2), pp. 305–353.

De Maglie, C. (2011). Societas delinquere non potest? The Italian solution. In M. Pieth et al. (Eds.), *Corporate criminal liability: Emergence, convergence, and risk.* New York: Springer, pp. 255–270.

Epstein, R. A. (2006). Deferred prosecution agreements on trial. *Chief Executive (U.S.), General Business Magazines, 221,* pp. 38–61.

Espinoza de los Monteros de la Parra, M. (2012). Criminal liability of legal entities in Portugal. In A. Fiorella (Ed.), *Corporate criminal liability and compliance programs: Vol. 1, Liability "Ex Crimine" of legal entities in member states.* Napoli: Jovene, pp. 419–440.

Fisse, B. (1983). Reconstructing criminal law: Deterrence, retribution, fault and sanctions. *Southern California Law Review, 56*(6), pp. 1141–1246.

Greeve, G. (2010). Strafrechtliche Beratung und Compliance—Rechtsstaatlich bedenkliche Prävention und Kriminalitätsbekämpfung durch Private. In J. Wessels et al. (Eds.), *Strafverteidigung im Rechtsstaat: Die Straftat und ihr Aufbau.* Heidelberg: C.F. Müller, pp. 512–529.

Gruner, R. S. (2007). Preventive fault and corporate criminal liability: Transforming corporate organizations into private policing entities. In H. N. Pontell et al. (Eds.), *International handbook of white-collar and corporate crime.* New York: Springer, pp. 279–306.

Hall, R. F. (2009). *Deferred prosecution and non-prosecution agreements.* New York: Oxford University Press, pp. 119–154.

Hill, G. (2000). Laws prohibiting foreign bribery: The practicalities of legislating for integrity internationally. *Australian Mining and Petroleum Law Association Yearbook, 13,* pp. 13–34.

Hill, G. (2003). Corporate criminal liability in Australia: An evolving corporate governance technique? *Vanderbilt Law School, Law and Economics Research Paper Series No. 03–10, Journal of Business Law,* 1, pp. 1–40.

Jordan, J. (2012). The need for a comprehensive international foreign bribery compliance program, covering A to Z, in an expanding global antibribery environment. *Penn State Law Review, 117,* pp. 89–137.

Joseph, J. (2002). Integrating business ethics and compliance programs: A study of ethics officers in leading organizations. *Business and Society Review, 107,* pp. 309–347.

Kochan, N., & Goodyear, R. (2011). *Corruption: The new corporate challenge.* New York: Palgrave Macmillan, p. 295.

Koehler, M. (2010). The facade of FCPA Enforcement. *Georgetown Journal of International Law, 41*(4), pp. 907–1009.

Lascuraín, J. A. (2013). Compliance, debido control y unos refrescos. In L. A. Zapatero, A. Nieto Martín, & K. Tiedemann (Eds.), *El Derecho Penal Económico en la Era Compliance.* Valencia: Tirant lo Blanch, pp. 111–135.

Laufer, W. S. (2006). *Corporate bodies and guilty minds: The failure of corporate criminal liability.* Chicago: University of Chicago Press, p. 304.

Livschitz, M. M. (2011). Switzerland. In T. Gruetzner et al. (Eds.), *Anti-bribery risk assessment: A systematic overview of 151 countries.* Oxford: Hart Publishing, pp. 369–375.

Martin, J., McConnell, R. D., & Simon, C. A. (2011). Plan now or pay later: The role of compliance in criminal cases. *Houston Journal of International Law, 33,* pp. 509–587.

Matus Acuña, J. P. (2013). La certificación de los programas de cumplimiento. In L. A. Zapatero, A. Nieto Martín, & K. Tiedemann (Eds.), *El Derecho Penal Económico en la Era Compliance.* Valencia: Tirant lo Blanch, pp. 145–154.

Mongillo, V. (2012a). The Bribery Act 2010—Corporate criminal liability for bribery offences. In A. Fiorella (Ed.), *Corporate criminal liability and compliance programs: Vol 1, Liability "Ex Crimine" of legal entities in member states.* Napoli: Jovene, pp. 304–327.

Mongillo, V. (2012b). The supervisory body ("Organismo di Vigilanza") under Legislative Decree no 231/2001. In A. Fiorella (Ed.), *Corporate criminal liability and compliance programs: Vol. 1, Liability "Ex Crimine" of legal entities in member states*. Napoli: Jovene, pp. 57–82.

Moosmayer, K. (2010). *Compliance: Praxisleitfaden für Unternehmen*. München: C.H. Beck, p. 136.

Muñoz de Morales Romero, M. (2013). Programas de cumplimiento "efectivos" en la experiencia comparada. In L. A. Zapatero, A. Nieto Martín, & K. Tiedemann (Eds.), *El Derecho Penal Económico en la Era Compliance*. Valencia: Tirant lo Blanch, pp. 211–230.

Murphy, J., & Boehme, D. (2012). Commentary on the OECD Good Practice Guidance on Internal Controls, Ethics and Compliance. *Rutgers Journal of Law & Public Policy, 9,* pp. 581–623.

Nieto Martín, A. (2008). *La responsabilidad penal de las personas jurídicas: Un modelo legislativo*. Madrid: Iustel, p. 360.

Nieto Martín, A. (2012). Criminal liability of legal entities in Spain. In A. Fiorella (Ed.), *Corporate criminal liability and compliance programs: Vol. 1, Liability "Ex Crimine" of legal entities in member states*. Napoli: Jovene, pp. 181–211.

Perrin, B. (2011). La responsabilité pénale de l'entreprise en droit Suisse. In M. Pieth et al. (Eds.), *Corporate criminal liability: Emergence, convergence, risk*. New York: Springer, pp. 193–255.

Pieth, M. (2004). Risikomanagement und Strafrecht: Organisationsversagen als Voraussetzung der Unternehmenshaftung. In T. Sutter-Somm et al. (Eds.), *Risiko und Recht*. Basel: Festgabe zum Schweizerischen Juristentag, pp. 597–616.

Schroeder, D. (2002). Ethics from the top: Top management and ethical business. *Business Ethics: A European Review, 11*(3), pp. 260–267.

Schwartz, M. S., Dunfee, T. W., & Kline, M. J. (2005). Tone at the top: An ethics code for directors? *Journal of Business Ethics, 58*, pp. 79–100.

Selvaggi, N. (2012). The contents of a proper organization and the compliance programs. In A. Fiorella (Ed.), *Corporate criminal liability and compliance programs: Vol. 1, Liability "Ex Crimine" of legal entities in member states*. Napoli: Jovene, pp. 23–32.

Skinnider, E. (2012). *Corruption in Canada: Reviewing Practices from abroad to improve our response*. Vancouver: International Centre for Criminal Law Reform and Criminal Justice Policy, pp. 23–32.

Tricot, J. (2012). Corporate criminal liability in France. In A. Fiorella (Ed.), *Corporate criminal liability and compliance programs: Vol. 1, Liability "Ex Crimine" of legal entities in member states*. Napoli: Jovene, pp. 131–179.

Villani, E. (2012). Liability "ex crimine" of collective entities in the Italian legal system: An overview. In A. Fiorella (Ed.), *Corporate criminal liability and compliance programs: Vol. 1, Liability "Ex Crimine" of legal entities in member states*. Napoli: Jovene, pp. 14–22.

Vitell, S. J., Dickerson, E. B., & Festervand, T. A. (2000). Ethical problems, conflicts and beliefs of small business professionals. *Journal of Business Ethics, 28*(1), pp. 15–24.

Walsh, C. J., & Pyrich, A. (1995). Corporate compliance programs as a defense to criminal liability: Can a corporation save its soul? *Rutgers Law Review, 47*, pp. 605–689.

Webb, D. K., & Molo, S. F. (1993). Some practical considerations in developing effective compliance programs: A framework for meeting the requirements of the sentencing guidelines. *Washington University Law Quarterly, 71*(2), pp. 375–396.

Wells, C. (2011). Corporate criminal liability in England and Wales: Past, present, and future. In M. Pieth et al. (Eds.), *Corporate criminal liability: Emergence, convergence, and risk*. New York: Springer, pp. 91–112.

Wells, C. (2012). Who's afraid of the Bribery Act 2010? *The Journal of Business Law, 5,* 420–430.

Wulf, K. (2012). *Ethics and compliance programs in multinational organizations*. Berlin: Gabler, p. 411.

Chapter 18
An Analysis of Institutional Guidance and Case Law in the USA Pertaining to Compliance Programs

V-Tsien Fan

Contents

V.-T. Fan (✉)
Northeastern University, Boston, USA
e-mail: goheleth78@gmail.com

S. Manacorda et al. (eds.), *Preventing Corporate Corruption*,
DOI 10.1007/978-3-319-04480-4_18, © Springer International Publishing Switzerland 2014

18.1 Introduction

Compliance programs in the USA have been increasing in importance and number, due to the corresponding increase in the number and degree of enforcement of regulations aimed at preventing corporate misconduct (Biegelman and Biegelman 2010, p. 52; Ruhnka and Boerstler 1998, p. 313; Moohr 2007, p. 25). Compliance programs have also been integral in the pursuit of mitigating penalties for organizations convicted of breaking the law, and have been factored into government decisions whether to seek or decline prosecution (Huff 1996, p. 1253; Ruhnka and Boerstler 1998, p. 319). This chapter will first discuss compliance programs in general, including definitions, applicable legal frameworks, current models, and potential benefits and criticisms, and then it will turn to a discussion and analysis of current US institutional guidance and case law pertaining to compliance programs.

18.1.1 Definition of Compliance

"Compliance" generally means using a combination of procedures, programs, and policies in accordance with government guidelines, specifications, regulations, or legislation. The following examples are some of the definitions used in the field:

> Systematic procedures instituted by an organization to ensure that the provisions of the regulations imposed by a government agency are being met.[1]
>
> Compliance programs are established by corporate management to prevent and detect misconduct and to ensure that corporate activities are conducted in accordance with applicable criminal and civil laws, regulations, and rules.[2]
>
> Compliance means following the law and more. It's making sure organizations adhere to all applicable legal requirements. It is a detailed and complex process. For any particular situation one must be aware of all potentially applicable laws and regulations—federal, state, local, as well as internal company-instituted rules. State-of-the-art compliance involves a successful blending of compliance—following rules, regulations, and laws—with ethics—developing and sustaining a culture based on values, integrity, and accountability, and always doing the right things. True compliance ensures consistency of actions to eliminate, or at least lessen, opportunities for harm from criminal conduct or other compliance failures. (Biegelman 2008, p. 2)

[1] Compliance Program, Business Dictionary, http://www.businessdictionary.com/definition/compliance-program.html, accessed 14 July 2013.

[2] United States Attorneys' Manual, Chap. 9–28.800, United States Department of Justice (DOJ), http://www.justice.gov/usao/eousa/foia_reading_room/usam/, accessed 14 July 2013.

Table 18.1 The differences between legal and ethical mechanisms. (Arjoon 2005, p. 348)

Factors	Legal	Ethical
Ethos	Regards ethics as a set of limits and something that has to be done	Defines ethics as a set of principles to guide choices
Objectives	Geared toward preventing unlawful conduct	Geared toward achieving responsible conduct
Method	Emphasizes rules and uses increased monitoring and penalties to enforce these rules	Treats ethics as infused in business practice (leadership, core systems, decision-making processes, etc.)
Behavioral assumptions	Rooted in deterrence theory (how to prevent people from doing bad things by manipulating the costs of misconduct)	Rooted in individual and communal values (both material and spiritual)

Currently, almost all Fortune 500 companies and most large corporations have some type of compliance program (Aviram 2005, p. 766). Compliance programs in general have the following components:

- A well-developed and comprehensive code of ethics or conduct
- Clear policies and procedures against violations of the law
- A strong role for management and leadership in establishing, implementing, and supporting the compliance program
- Dedicated and skilled compliance staff, including a chief ethics and compliance officer or equivalent individual in charge of overseeing the compliance function
- Regular and effective training programs for employees
- Appropriate reporting systems for violations that preserves anonymity and confidentiality of reporting individuals
- Disciplinary measures for violators
- Performance incentives for staff contributing to a culture of compliance and integrity
- Ongoing monitoring and auditing of the compliance program
- Periodic reassessments and improvements of the compliance program. (Olsen 2010, p. 4; Murphy 2011, p. 201; Wulf 2011, p. 358; Biegelman 2008, p. 163–217)

18.2 The Relationship Between Compliance and Ethics

The evolution of compliance programs has started to incorporate the realm of ethics. The US Sentencing Guidelines originally referred solely to compliance programs, but later revisions have repeatedly emphasized ethics programs in addition to their original components. The relationship between compliance and ethics has practical implications in terms of the tension between laying down rules and respecting ethical principles. The advantage of rules is that they provide predictability as regards enforcement and obedience. Rules reduce discretion while providing a clear line of demarcation between legal and illegal behavior. On the other hand, addressing every possible scenario with rules may prove to be unwieldy, and could encourage would-be lawbreakers to seek loopholes and manipulate them for their own advantage. Principles, on the other hand, while seemingly more vague, can provide guidance in any ethical scenario. Focusing on ethics in addition to compliance helps prevent an overreliance on accountability in place of responsibility, as well as avoiding an overemphasis on legalism. Under the latter paradigm, managers' approaches to ethics and compliance could involve checking off a list of rules and regulations in lieu of making ethical judgments. The use of ethics sets the tone of an organization as one of achieving goals rather than preventing undesired conduct. It also has the possibility of building the decision-making skills of personnel in regards to identifying and resolving questionable scenarios (Gabel et al. 2009, p. 453; Trevino et al. 1999, p. 131; Fiorelli and Tracey 2007, p. 483; Arjoon 2005, p. 343; Coglianese et al. 2004, p. 11).

Table 18.1 (reproduced from the work of Surendra Arjoon) is useful to delineate the differences between legal and ethical mechanisms.

Compliance programs that use the traditional and more common approach tend to focus on preventing, detecting, and punishing, while an ethics-based approach defines organizational values and encourages ethical commitment. Relying on the former approach increases the risk of "moral mediocrity," while the latter can encourage more self-governance. A 1999 survey revealed that where employees perceived that their company implemented a value-based program, there was a lower incidence of unethical and illegal behavior and a higher likelihood of employees seeking ethical advice, reporting violations to management, and demonstrating more commitment to the organization. The study thus advocated a values-based approach with proper accountability and disciplinary systems. The needs of customers, suppliers, shareholders, and stakeholders should also be considered among the values to be emphasized. It is integral to the success of this approach that there be a strong follow-through once violations are detected or concerns are raised by employees, as well as consistency between company policies and practices, commitment by the leadership, open discussion of ethics and values, and rewards for ethical behavior.[3]

18.3 Compliance Programs and Legal Frameworks

There are several frameworks for how compliance programs fit within theories of legal liability. Under the most traditional framework, which relies on the principle of *respondeat superior*—whereby companies are generally liable for the conduct of their employees—the existence of compliance programs would not matter sig-

[3] See Trevino et al. (1999, pp. 135–144). The other orientations included in the study were a compliance-based, stakeholder-based, and protecting management approach.

nificantly in terms of preventing or mitigating prosecution and related penalties, even if they were targeted at preventing the misconduct. A second approach uses the existence of compliance programs as a "counterweight" to mitigate the criminal intent of an agent, by functioning as an "affirmative due diligence" defense. A third approach, as a counter to the strict vicarious liability framework, proposes a theory of duty-based organizational liability similar to the principle of negligence, where the presence of internal compliance structures are considered to be the "exercise of due care" in order to prevent and shield an organization from agent misconduct. Finally, the fourth approach (which is adopted in the USA) proposes a composite regime where compliance programs are considered by the government in decisions whether to prosecute organizations and mitigate penalties and fines in case of conviction or plea agreements (Gobert 1994, p. 393; Huff 1996, p. 1254; Krawiec 2005, pp. 575–579, 581–582, 584; Aviram 2005, p. 767).

Moreover, there is also a line of thinking that an effective compliance program should provide a complete affirmative defense to criminal liability. This view, however, comes with several potential problems. First, the burden of evaluating the effectiveness of a compliance program would be shifted from judges and prosecutors to juries, a task that would already be difficult for the former group due to the complexity of programs, and likely even more so for the latter. Next, the fact remains that even given the existence of a program, and even those that are effectively designed and implemented, instances of misconduct, violation, or crime may still occur. Accordingly, an affirmative defense would include liability for scenarios where the misconduct cannot be traced to a rogue agent acting without the knowledge or purview of the organization. Further, an affirmative defense would reduce the government's flexibility in charging and plea negotiations, and its corresponding discretion to seek avenues best suited for deterrence. Consequently, a company's motivation to cooperate will also be substantially reduced and the possibility of "window-dressing" programs, where purely nominal efforts are made toward program implementation, would increase. Finally, using the existence of a compliance program to act as a proxy for legal intent is problematic if the legislative framework does not encourage the optimal design of programs, leading again to the problem of nominally implemented programs (Wellner 2005, p. 524).

An alternative model to those stated above (which admittedly are more reactive than proactive in addressing misconduct) is an educational model whereby the government provides organizations with formal education and guidance on compliance programs. A possible example of such guidance is the Foreign Corrupt Practices Act (FCPA) opinion release procedure where companies can submit a query for legal advice from the US Department of Justice (DOJ) on compliance-related issues. There are several benefits to this approach. First, with improved education and guidance, companies would face reduced costs in instances of violation when they have to engage the services of an independent compliance monitor, which in many cases can be costly. Next, it would encourage the company and its employees to increase cooperation with the government in matters of compliance. On the government side, such a program would theoretically lead to evidence of higher quality in case of prosecution, a stronger case for proving legal intent in cases where companies ignore education and guidance, and ultimately fewer prosecutions and investigations (Podgor 2009, p. 1523).

18.4 Models of Compliance Programs

There are four typical models for compliance programs. In the first, the compliance program is a component of the risk-management office. This model is usually found in heavily regulated industries such as banking and financial services. Its main goal is to minimize risk and exposure for the company. Here, the chief compliance officer (CCO) reports to the risk officer along with several compliance directors responsible for oversight of business unit compliance programs. The main advantage of this model is the ability to quickly identify and respond to risks. This possibility of swift response is also due in part to the direct reporting line between the CCO and the risk officer. The disadvantages of this model are the lack of a direct reporting line to the chief executive officer (CEO) and less of an emphasis on ethics, which is related to the focus on risk aversion.

The second model involves a strong program supported by resources including a significant budget, and is found in highly regulated industries and those rebuilding after corporate governance crises. In this model, the CCO reports directly to the CEO. The advantages of this model are autonomy and freedom to design and implement compliance programs and initiatives as well as communicating a commitment to integrity by the company. The corresponding disadvantage is the increased pressure on the CCO and his staff to meet compliance goals to justify the expenditures involved.

The third model places a small compliance program within the auspices of the legal department, supported by a discretionary component of the latter's overall budget. While there is a CCO who reports to the general counsel, although not to the CEO, there are no dedicated compliance directors, and the system relies on part-time liaisons. The focus of this model is on legal priorities, training, and investigations. This model is found in companies with a lower degree of regulatory requirements. There are several disadvantages to this model, including lack of coordination of compliance activities, lack of quick response time to emerging issues, and limitations on CCO credibility with business unit heads and other staff due to the lack of a direct reporting line to the CEO.

The final model is a decentralized one, involving a compliance unit set within the legal department. Here, the CCO reports to the general counsel but the compliance unit functions generally as an internal advisory resource to business units, which are individually responsible for compliance responsibilities. The advantages of this approach are customization of training and ownership of initiatives by each business unit due to the assignment of responsibility. The decentralized approach, however, leads to conflicts between compliance prerogatives and other interests, inconsistency in implementation and content across business units, and the need for extensive partnering for compliance initiatives to work (Biegelman 2008, pp. 178–181).

18.5 Criticisms of Compliance Programs

There are multiple benefits for developing and implementing effective compliance and ethics programs, but potential drawbacks have also been identified. One of the main criticisms of compliance programs is the concern that organizations would enact largely ineffective compliance programs as "window dressing," without actually preventing the undesired behavior and activity. For example, there are multiple instances of organizations persisting in illegal behavior despite the existence of a compliance program on paper. Cosmetic compliance programs, lacking any real effect or influence, unsurprisingly lead to under-deterrence and under-detection of misconduct, as well as inefficient use of resources to implement costly programs. Underlying these criticisms are the ideas that organizations put too much stock in principal–agent explanations for misconduct, and that it is much easier to implement compliance programs than to change established business models based on unrestrained profit seeking and maximization (Krawiec 2005, p. 574; Biegelman 2008, p. 23; Berzins and Sofo 2008, p. 669).

Another criticism involves the possibility of management using a balancing test to weigh the value of compliance programs against the use of resources, efforts, and lost opportunities that are associated with their implementation. Here, companies might be tempted to accept instances of noncompliance by enacting programs that meet the expectations of management, but not the requirements of the regulator or the government (Parker and Nielsen 2009, p. 10). Conversely, from a regulator's perspective, a compliance framework implemented in conjunction and cooperation with the government is only effective when there is proper governmental and legal backing in terms of enforcement. Without proper backing, businesses and organizations are more likely to perceive regulatory enforcement as illegitimate and thus advocate for reduction in related staff and accountability mechanisms. This so-called compliance trap parallels the problem at the other end of the spectrum—the "deterrence trap"—whereby penalties are not significant enough to deter misconduct, or are considered so significant that they would damage a company's financial standing to the point of affecting innocent employees and creditors (Parker 2006, p. 591).

As regards the potential benefits of a compliance program in mitigating sentences and fines, several commentators argue that this benefit actually contributes to their ineffectiveness, and to the propensity for compliance programs to be "window dressing." First, by implementing compliance programs that actually detect misconduct, organizations would be exposed to both criminal and civil liability. Here, the conflict lies between implementing a program that fulfills the letter of the law, and incurring the attention of law enforcement and other parties which could result in further investigation and prosecution. Companies would want to implement compliance programs if their cost is outweighed by the potential decrease in liability, but if such programs lead to further liability, then the cost–benefit balance may be significantly altered. One logical but perverse effect of this line of thinking would be a pressure to enact compliance programs that reduce liability but do not actually detect or address instances of misconduct—thus leading to the "window-dressing" problem. Another potential problem arises if there is a lack of specific guidance given by the law in regards to development and implementation of compliance programs. Here, organizations are given the opportunity to devise their own compliance programs that may exploit loopholes in the law and veer toward window dressing rather than effectiveness (Wellner 2005, p. 510; Conway 1994, p. 622; Laufer 2008, p. 106; Krawiec 2005, pp. 576–577). An additional and related issue here is the potential inability of courts and agencies to properly evaluate compliance programs, and to distinguish the ones which are effective versus those which are created for cosmetic reasons.[4]

Accordingly, a proposed solution to mitigate the conflict between creating an effective compliance program and exposing an organization to increased legal liability is to create a legal self-evaluative privilege. This privilege would protect evidence and other information generated by investigations and audits from discovery in litigation, in addition to more established privileges such as those pertaining to the attorney–client relationship and work-product rules. The goal of this privilege is to provide a safe harbor in which organizations feel unburdened and so may implement programs without fear of increased liability. Such a privilege, however, must be granted carefully in order to improve compliance rather than provide a loophole for covering up misconduct. Regardless, this is a potential tool to add to the arsenal of compliance and should be seriously considered by organizations (Goldsmith and King 1997, pp. 31–32; Conway 1994, pp. 621–661).

Building on the issue of "window-dressing" programs, another less-than-stellar view of compliance programs is that they may be considered as a "commodity for purchase for risk management and insurance." While acknowledging that some companies are genuine in their desire to comply with the law and encourage a culture of integrity, others may be playing a "game" with or against the government. From the government end, its prerogatives are to use incentives to reward compliance and punish violations without increasing formal social controls. From the business end, the counterstrategy would be to "purchase" just enough compliance to minimize regulatory risk and liability. This "game," of course, makes a mockery of the purported goals and intent of compliance, which is detection of and reduction in misconduct. Further, the perspective of viewing compliance programs as insurance may have the unintended effect of increasing risk-seeking behaviors by the organization, which is again contrary to the goals of building a culture of integrity (Laufer 2008, pp. 99–129).

Finally, the most obvious drawback of a compliance program, especially one that is comprehensive, is its cost in terms of financial resources. The potential cost is great, especially in hiring compliance and related staff, conducting investigations, the use of time, and the possibility of lowering productivity and morale in cases of monitoring and discipline. The potential high cost of compliance programs thus

[4] See Krawiec (2005, pp. 580–581); Laufer (2008, p. 120). The counterargument here is provided by Aviram (2005, p. 769), that while identification of an effective compliance program is difficult, identifying sham programs is easier. Langevoort (2002, p. 115) also suggests that courts consult industry best practices to figure out what effective compliance looks like.

may deter some companies, especially smaller ones with lower levels of resources, from implementing an effective program, or even having one at all (Goldsmith and King 1997, p. 13; Wellner 2005, p. 508). A particular issue which arises in this regard is the proposed solution whereby companies overestimate the capacity of monitoring by line supervisors to detect misconduct. Their real capacity is, of course, due to other forces outside the supervisor's control, and this can lead to suboptimal monitoring. A potential problem arises here when companies overreact by resorting to unnecessary third-party compliance audits, which are expensive. Moreover, despite the upsurge in development and implementation of compliance programs in the private sector, there is virtually no empirical evidence that they actually reduce misconduct. In general, studies of ethics codes and compliance programs provide no evidence of a relationship with the curbing of illicit activities.[5]

18.6 Benefits of Compliance Programs

Notwithstanding the criticisms of compliance programs, there are strong theoretical reasons to advocate them, and their benefits have moreover been empirically demonstrated. In addition to the oft-cited practical reasons of mitigating liability and reducing the consequences for companies which are investigated and prosecuted by the government, the considerations in their favor include the increased ability to self-regulate, and the collateral benefits which accrue to compliance systems due to the institution of government regulations and the development of an organizational partnership with governmental entities. Other benefits related to the increased ability to evaluate an organization's civil and criminal liability, legal defense, assistance in making economic decisions, and exposing inefficient employees. On a societal level, compliance programs can avert crisis for the larger business community when problems in a particular company are identified, thus lowering the costs of goods and services by eliminating inefficiency and reducing attorneys' fees and fines related to investigations and prosecutions.[6]

Despite the aforementioned potential issues with conflicts of interest, underenforcement, and lack of specific governmental guidance associated with organizational compliance, there are some very powerful general benefits to the compliance framework. First, organizations by default enjoy greater proximity to their specific industries. This proximity affords better information and intelligence in identifying challenges and problems. Consequently, organizations are more sensitive to industry practices and constraints, possibly allowing for better compliance initiatives.

[5] See Krawiec (2003, pp. 510–511); Laufer (2008, p. 106); Langevoort (2002, p. 74); Krawiec (2003, pp. 528–537) also sets forth a cynical theory that legal compliance professionals have an economic interest in preserving incompleteness and vagueness in legal definitions of effective compliance programs in addition to business organizations resisting input from outside sources in designing compliance. In addition, she posits that legal compliance professionals encourage "alarmist" and "simplistic" constructions of the law and overstate risk to attract clients.

[6] Goldsmith and King (1997, pp. 12, 17); Huff (1996, p. 1270).

In addition, organizations can draw on the collective interests of their industries, adding to compliance effectiveness. Finally, because compliance programs are inherently self-established by individual organizations, there is greater flexibility to address problems as they arise and greater ability to marshal resources independent of governmental intrusion and constraint (Coglianese et al. 2004, pp. 5–10).

Although there are cogent criticisms of the legal repercussions and effects of compliance programs, based on the charge that they are not aligned with the aim of preventing corporate misconduct, some of the value of such programs lies outside the consequences as strictly defined by the legal realm. A significant possible benefit of compliance programs relates to avoiding reputational penalties and collateral consequences. Nonlegal sanctions, such as losing clients or customers who are averse to an organization's misconduct, may be greater in effect than legal sanctions. The credibility of an organization is affected by misconduct, leading to customer relationships and ties being severed. These nonlegal sanctions, which follow the announcement of misconduct allegations, usually precede the timing of the legal ones—since the latter often lag significantly due to the deliberative nature of the prosecution and judicial system. The effects of organizational reputation loss on employee loyalty and the recruitment of workers may also be quite significant, damaging both turnover and human resources. Finally, even in the event that a compliance program is not actually effective, there may be a placebo effect on public opinion, which capitalizes on the idea of the perceived risk of the effects of misconduct. Here, the placebo effect of enacting compliance programs, whether effective or not, reduces the perceived risk that victims will be harmed, resulting in a corresponding increase in social welfare through awareness of the issue (Aviram 2005, pp. 763–780; Moohr 2007, pp. 25–41).

Several studies have provided strong empirical support for the claim that there are reputational penalties for misconduct. In a 1999 study by an economist at the US DOJ, empirical analysis demonstrated that for certain offenses, including bribery, which primarily harm related parties, civil- or market-based sanctions are far more effective than criminal ones. Prior research had already estimated that 90 % of the equity loss following instances of misconduct is related to reputation and that instances of fraud were accompanied by loss of shareholder wealth. At the first news of criminal allegations, reports of negative consequences concerning customers, management, employees, and stock prices rapidly ensue. These include termination or suspensions of business dealings, closing of business units, and termination, suspension, or reassignment of personnel. Specifically, market-based penalties are estimated at four times the value of court-imposed penalties. On the other hand, offenses that harm third parties, such as in cases of environmental damage or infringement, are addressed primarily through legal penalties (Alexander 1999, p. 489).

In a study examining Securities and Exchange Commission (SEC) enforcement actions involving financial misrepresentation, the researchers found, on average, that "firms lose 41 % of their market value when news of the misconduct is revealed and estimate that of this loss, 24.5 % is related to the market's adjustment to more accurate financial information, 8.8 % reflects expected legal sanctions, and 66.6 % reflects market-imposed reputational penalties" (Karpoff et al. 2008, p. 581).

The effects of regulations resulting in compliance efforts have also been empirically demonstrated. A 2007 study found that the governance rules enacted by the Sarbanes–Oxley Act had an economically significant impact on firm value, at least as regards investor perceptions. A study of the conformity of big German publicly traded corporations to the German Corporate Governance Code (GCGC) demonstrated that firms that were more compliant with the GCGC enjoyed a 9 % premium on pricing in the capital markets with a 10 % increase in stock performance. The GCGC requires the management and supervisory board of companies to state annually the extent to which they are compliant with the code's recommendations. The GCGC study is particularly interesting as it demonstrates that a company's commitment to compliance may be underpinned by an economic incentive to adopt compliance programs. Further, it is important to note that the enforcement mechanisms in the GCGC are weak, and thus that compliance is driven by market pressures (Chhaochharia and Grinstein 2007, p. 1789; Goncharov et al. 2006, p. 432).

Finally, while the mandates of various regulatory frameworks may be costly and tedious to implement, some immediate practical benefits do accrue to the organization which adopts them. In the example of Sarbanes–Oxley compliance, the emphasis placed on internal controls for financial reporting has allowed some executives to improve their organization's financial management processes and capabilities while augmenting compliance. This approach not only has the purpose of curtailing misconduct, but also of increasing the available intelligence and information which would allow better decision making for their organizations (Wagner and Dittmar 2006, p. 1).

18.7 US Governmental Guidance Regarding Compliance Programs

In the USA, there are several governmental sources from which guidance regarding the design and implementation of compliance programs can be drawn. These include the Federal Sentencing Guidelines for Organizations, DOJ policies and pronouncements, and guidance from the SEC.

18.7.1 The Foreign Corrupt Practices Act: A Brief Overview

Established in 1977, the US FCPA contains provisions that address transparency in financial accounting as well as bribery of foreign officials.[7] It applies to enterprises and individuals with a connection to the USA who engage in foreign corrupt

[7] US Foreign Corrupt Practices Act, 15 U.S.C. § 78dd-1; US Department of Justice and US Securities and Exchange Commission (2012); FCPA, "A Resource Guide to the U.S. Foreign Corrupt Practices Act," http://www.justice.gov/criminal/fraud/fcpa/guide.pdf.

practices. Further, it applies to any issuers, and any domestic or foreign businesses, who trade securities in the USA. The accounting provisions require strong internal controls and the maintenance of accurate books and records. The anti-bribery provisions specifically prohibit monetary payments, offers, gifts, or anything of value to influence a foreign official, political party, or candidate for foreign political office in order to improperly influence or induce the obtaining, retaining, or directing of business.

Jurisdictionally, the FCPA applies to conduct inside and outside the USA if a defendant has used the US mail or any means or instrumentality of interstate commerce, defined as "trade, commerce, transportation, or communication among the several States or between any foreign country and any State or between any State and any place or ship outside thereof," in furtherance of a corrupt payment to a foreign official. Telephone calls, emails, text message, fax communications, and wire transfers from or to a US bank or using the banking system are all covered under the FCPA. Moreover, the alternative jurisdiction provision of the FCPA also includes US companies that act outside its borders.

The definition of "foreign official" is broad, applying to officers, employees, departments, agencies, instrumentalities, or any person acting in an official capacity for a foreign government or public international organization. The mens rea requirements under the FCPA are "corruptly," which requires intent to influence a foreign official to misuse his position, and "willfully" which implies voluntariness and purposefulness in the committing of a bad act. Traditional legal principles of liability based on complicity and conspiracy are also covered under the FCPA.

Corporate liability is attributed when a company's directors, officers, employees, or agents act within the scope of their employment to commit violations to benefit their company. Parent–subsidiary liability is applicable where a parent company is involved sufficiently in its subsidiary's conduct and under traditional principles of respondeat superior. Successor liability applies through the merger and acquisition process, which requires thorough due diligence pre-acquisition and strong compliance and internal controls post-acquisition.

Recognizing that there are a variety of inducements for corruption, the scope of improper benefits covered by the FCPA is also broad, including "the giving of anything of value." Offenses contemplated and covered by the FCPA include improper payments of cash, using the avenue of false charitable contributions, and inappropriate gift giving, travel, and entertainment expenses.

Penalties for violating the anti-bribery provisions of the FCPA include a fine of up to US$ 2 million for each violation by a company or business entity while individuals are subject to a fine of up to US$ 100,000 and 5 years' imprisonment. The US Sentencing Guidelines, of course, govern the precise penalties to be imposed, taking into consideration the nature of the offense, conduct of a company and their agents, quality of compliance programs, and other factors. Civil penalties of up to US$ 16,000 per violation may also be attributed to both business entities and individuals. Collateral consequences for violations may include debarment by the government and banks as well as suspension of certain privileges and contracts.

The FCPA also contains several affirmative defenses, including scenarios where the defendant must demonstrate that a payment was legal under the foreign official's country's laws and where there is a legitimate connection of expenses to demonstration of a product or contractual obligations. Further, there is an exception for "facilitating and expediting" payments which is applicable only in circumstances furthering "routine governmental action." The DOJ and SEC are responsible for enforcement of the FCPA.

18.7.2 Federal Sentencing Guidelines for Organizations

The US Federal Sentencing Guidelines at § 8B2.1 emphasize the role of compliance programs in mitigating the effects of investigation and prosecution, including sentence and fine reductions. To be considered effective, these programs must, at the minimum, provide for adequate standards, involve management in oversight and implementation, ensure effective communication, and establish adequate monitoring systems, discipline, and reporting.

It is important to note here that this section of the guidelines has been amended several times. The original version provided that the *mere* existence of a compliance program would be sufficient to mitigate liability for an offense. The updated and current version of the guidelines addresses potential problems with the original set of factors by emphasizing the need for proper design, implementation, and enforcement. The guidelines, however, do not explicitly provide specific guidance to organizations regarding developing and implementing their compliance programs. The strength of this approach lies in the fact that various industries have different needs and practices; but it does, however, open up questions of what exactly a compliance program should look like and so may provide windows of opportunity for organizations to obey the letter of the law but not the spirit.

The benefits of enacting compliance programs in response to the guidelines are significant; conversely, organizations which do not may suffer severe consequences. Federal criminal fines for compliant organizations (i.e., those that are cooperative, accept responsibility, and have enacted an effective compliance and ethics program) have been estimated to be reduced by up to 95%, while noncompliant ones may face a fourfold increase in their penalties. Further, as discussed in this chapter, the presence of an effective and thorough compliance program may even completely absolve an organization of liability for the actions of its employees or agents (Fiorelli and Tracey 2007, p. 467).

18.7.3 Department of Justice Guidelines for Prosecuting Corporations and Other Business Organizations

The DOJ has also provided guidance for the design and implementation of compliance programs through a series of memoranda authored by various deputy attorneys general. The latest of these memoranda reiterated and updated the standards for government corporate prosecutions that had been discussed and disseminated by prior administrations. These charging standards, which are based on various memoranda, were also recently incorporated for the first time into the US Attorneys' Manual. The list of these standards to be weighed by prosecutors in deciding to bring charges or negotiate a plea include the following (no single factor is dispositive, but there may be those that override the others):

- The existence and effectiveness of the corporation's preexisting compliance program
- The corporation's remedial actions, including any efforts to implement an effective corporate compliance program or to improve an existing one, to replace responsible management, to discipline or terminate wrongdoers, to pay restitution, and to cooperate with the relevant government agencies[8]

In regards to advice on the content and implementation of compliance program, the guidelines first state the following:

> Compliance programs are established by corporate management to prevent and detect misconduct and to ensure that corporate activities are conducted in accordance with applicable criminal and civil laws, regulations, and rules. The Department encourages such corporate self-policing, including voluntary disclosures to the government of any problems that a corporation discovers on its own. However, the existence of a compliance program is not sufficient, in and of itself, to justify not charging a corporation for criminal misconduct undertaken by its officers, directors, employees, or agents. In addition, the nature of some crimes, e.g., antitrust violations, may be such that national law enforcement policies mandate prosecutions of corporations notwithstanding the existence of a compliance program.[9]

The commentary to this section then goes on to list the critical factors that prosecutors should consider in evaluating whether a compliance program is effective in preventing and detecting wrongdoing and whether corporate management is in support of the program. These three main factors are as follows:

- Adequate design of the compliance program
- Earnest application of the compliance program in good faith
- Effectiveness of the compliance program

Sub-factors to be considered in determining the presence of the main ones are as follows:

- Comprehensiveness of the compliance program
- Extent, pervasiveness, seriousness, duration, and frequency of the criminal misconduct
- Number and level of the corporate employees involved
- Remedial actions, including disciplinary action against past violators uncovered by the compliance program
- Revisions to the compliance program in light of lessons learned

[8] See United States Attorneys' Manual, Title 9, US DOJ, Chap. 9–28.300, http://www.justice.gov/usao/eousa/foia_reading_room/usam/.

[9] Ibid., Chap. 9–28.800.

- Effective corporate governance mechanisms, such as independent review by directors, adequate audit functions to ensure independence and accuracy, and a reasonable information and reporting system to provide management and directors with timely and accurate information for compliance purposes

The task for prosecutors, therefore, is to determine whether a compliance program was adequately enacted and staffed, and whether the corporation educated and convinced its employees regarding the components and importance of the program. Further, compliance programs should be designed to detect and address the particular types of misconduct that are industry specific and in the corporation's line of business. While the difficulty for prosecutors here is obvious—evaluating whether an organization's compliance code exists solely on paper is a very delicate process—the guidelines encourage consultation with experts in order to assist in this determination.[10]

18.7.4 Department of Justice Opinion Release 04–02

The DOJ also issues FCPA Opinion Procedure Releases in response to inquiries regarding compliance-related issues for organizations that wish to abide by the law. While only binding on the DOJ and the requesting party for the instant scenario presented, the Opinion Procedure Release provides instructive advice and guidance. One in particular, Opinion Release 04–02, gives useful insight into what is expected of the contents of a compliance program. The context of this Opinion Release involved an investment group seeking to acquire companies and assets from another company that was previously convicted of FCPA violations. Part of the prerequisites for acquisition was the adoption of a rigorous compliance code by the investment group. The contents of this code are as follows:

- Clearly articulated corporate policy against violations of the FCPA and foreign anti-bribery laws
- Establishing compliance standards and procedures to be followed by all directors, officers, employees, and all business partners
- Assigning to at least one senior corporate official the responsibility, implementation, and oversight of the compliance program
- Direct reporting by senior official in charge of compliance program to the board of directors
- Effective communication of compliance program to all shareholders' representatives, directors, officers, employees, agents, and business parties through regular training and annual certifications of compliance
- Establishing a reporting system, including a helpline, for suspected violations of the compliance code and criminal conduct
- Appropriate disciplinary procedures

[10] Ibid.

- Clearly articulated corporate procedures for business relationships with reputable and qualified business partners and for preventing the granting of substantial discretionary authority to individuals whom corporation knows, or should know through due diligence, to have a propensity to engage in illegal or improper activities
- Extensive pre-retention due-diligence requirements and post-retention oversight for agents and business partners, as well as maintenance of due-diligence records
- A committee of senior corporate officials reviewing and recording retention, contracting, and payment of agents
- Agreements, contracts, and renewals to contain anticorruption standards, allowance for internal and independent audits of books and records of agents and business partners, and provision for termination
- Maintenance of a system of internal accounting controls
- Independent audits by outside counsel and auditors

18.7.5 Enhanced Compliance Programs

Recent FCPA cases have also involved the concept of enhanced compliance. Generally, companies who have agreed to and taken steps to augment the DOJ's prescriptions for their compliance programs benefit in their plea agreements, especially by not being required to appoint an independent compliance monitor, which can be very expensive and intrusive.[11] The components of these enhanced programs include the following:

- Appointing a senior corporate executive with significant experience with FCPA compliance to serve as chief compliance and risk officer
- Appointing other senior staff to serve as heads of compliance for business units
- Appointing of an executive compliance committee
- Appointing an anticorruption program office
- Enacting a global anti-bribery and anticorruption policy and international anti-bribery and anticorruption policy tailored for market, region, and function
- Establishing an international investigations group responsible for global compliance issues and remedial measures
- Enacting heightened due diligence for mergers and acquisitions as well as hiring of agents

[11] Prior to 2010, independent compliance monitors were regularly appointed for most FCPA cases. Between 2010 and 2012, there was a significant reduction in appointments of monitors, with no clear pattern for why some cases required them and others did not. The most recent cases have evinced the pattern stated above—taking on enhanced compliance, and in some cases, remediation such as termination of employees and agents responsible for misconduct. The DOJ and SEC FCPA Resource Guide lists six factors that are considered in whether a compliance monitor is required: seriousness of the offense, duration of the misconduct, pervasiveness of the misconduct, nature and size of the company, quality of the company's compliance program at the time of the misconduct, and subsequent remediation efforts.

- Enacting heightened risk-assessment reviews including "proactive reviews" targeting high-risk markets
- Requiring annual certifications from senior managers
- Requiring strong, explicit, and visible support from directors and senior management[12]

18.7.6 Securities and Exchange Commission Seaboard Report

In one of its agency enforcement decisions, the SEC also shed light on the factors it considers in mitigating organizational liability. In a case known as the Seaboard Report, a former controller of a company's subsidiary contributed to the presence of inaccurate books and records and subsequent concealment of this prohibited activity. The SEC declined to take action against the parent company due to its remedial actions in response to the controller's behavior. Shortly after discovering the controller's misconduct, the company's internal auditors conducted a preliminary review and reported their findings to management. The internal auditors in turn reported to the board of director's audit committee. Subsequently, the board of directors hired an outside law firm to conduct an independent inquiry. As a result of the independent inquiry, the controller, and two other employees who were found to have inadequately supervised the controller, were swiftly terminated (within days). The company also publicly disclosed this information and restated its earnings. Significantly, the company provided full cooperation with investigators, including all results of the internal investigation and waiving all privileges, including the attorney–client and work-product ones. The company also took steps to augment its financial reporting processes, including "developing a detailed closing process for the subsidiary's accounting personnel, consolidating subsidiary accounting functions under a parent company certified public accountant (CPA), hiring three new CPAs for the accounting department responsible for preparing the subsidiary's financial statements, redesigning the subsidiary's minimum annual audit requirements, and requiring the parent company's controller to interview and approve all senior accounting personnel in its subsidiaries' reporting processes." In announcing its decision to decline further action, the SEC provided thirteen general principles

---

[12] Deferred Prosecution Agreement, United States of America v. Pfizer H.C.P. Corporation, 12 CR 169 (D.C. 2012); see United States v. Pfizer H.C.P. Corporation, Court Docket Number: 12-CR-169, Deferred Prosecution Agreement, US DOJ, http://www.justice.gov/criminal/fraud/fcpa/cases/pfizer.html, accessed 14 July 2013. Deferred Prosecution Agreement, United States of America v. Data Systems & Solutions LLC, 12 CR 262 (E.D. Va 2012); see United States v. Data Systems & Solutions LLC, Court Docket Number: 12-CR-262-LO, US DOJ, http://www.justice.gov/criminal/fraud/fcpa/cases/data-systems.html, accessed 14 July 2013. Deferred Prosecution Agreement, United States of America v. Bizjet International Sales & Support, Inc. 12 CR 61 (N.D. Okla. 2012); see United States of America v. Bizjet International Sales & Support, Inc., Case No 12-CR-61-CVE, University of Virginia, School of Law, http://lib.law.virginia.edu/Garrett/prosecution_agreements/pdf/bizjet.pdf, accessed 14 July 2013. Non-Prosecution Agreement, The Nordam Group Inc. (6 July 2012); Non-Prosecution Agreement, Tyco International, Ltd. (20 September 2012).

that it said it would take into consideration in crediting the behavior of an organization. The pertinent ones to compliance are listed below:

- How did the misconduct arise? Is it the result of pressure placed on employees to achieve specific results, or a tone of lawlessness set by those in control of the company? What compliance procedures were in place to prevent the misconduct now uncovered? Why did those procedures fail to stop or inhibit the wrongful conduct?
- How was the misconduct detected and who uncovered it?
- What processes did the company follow to resolve many of these issues and ferret out necessary information? Were the audit committee and the board of directors fully informed? If so, when?
- Did the company commit to learn the truth, fully and expeditiously? Did it do a thorough review of the nature, extent, origins, and consequences of the conduct and related behavior? Did management, the board, or committees consisting solely of outside directors oversee the review? Did company employees or outside persons perform the review? If outside persons, had they done other work for the company? Where the review was conducted by outside counsel, had management previously engaged such counsel? Were scope limitations placed on the review? If so, what were they?
- What assurances are there that the conduct is unlikely to recur? Did the company adopt and ensure enforcement of new and more effective internal controls and procedures designed to prevent a recurrence of the misconduct? Did the company provide our staff with sufficient information for it to evaluate the company's measures to correct the situation and ensure that the conduct does not recur?[13]

[13] In the Matter of Gisela de Leon-Meredith, Exchange Act Release No. 44970 (23 October 2001); Report of Investigation Pursuant to Sect. 21(a) of the Securities Exchange Act of 1934 and Commission Statement on the Relationship of Cooperation to Agency Enforcement Decisions, Exchange Act Release No. 44969. In its statement, the SEC provided the following caveats:

> First, the paramount issue in every enforcement judgment is, and must be, what best protects investors. There is no single, or constant, answer to that question. Self-policing, self-reporting, remediation and cooperation with law enforcement authorities, among other things, are unquestionably important in promoting investors' best interests. But, so too are vigorous enforcement and the imposition of appropriate sanctions where the law has been violated. Indeed, there may be circumstances where conduct is so egregious, and harm so great, that no amount of cooperation or other mitigating conduct can justify a decision not to bring any enforcement action at all. In the end, no set of criteria can, or should, be strictly applied in every situation to which they may be applicable.
>
> Second, we are not adopting any rule or making any commitment or promise about any specific case; nor are we in any way limiting our broad discretion to evaluate every case individually, on its own particular facts and circumstances. Conversely, we are not conferring any "rights" on any person or entity. We seek only to convey an understanding of the factors that may influence our decisions.
>
> Third, we do not limit ourselves to the criteria we discuss below. By definition, enforcement judgments are just that—judgments. Our failure to mention a specific criterion in one context does not preclude us from relying on that criterion in another. Further, the fact that a company has satisfied all the criteria we list below will not foreclose us from bringing enforcement proceedings that we believe are necessary or appropriate, for the benefit of investors.

18.7.7 *Department of Justice and Securities and Exchange Commission Resource Guide to the Foreign Corrupt Practices Act*

In November 2012, the Criminal Division of the US DOJ and the Enforcement Division of the US SEC released a nonbinding and informal resource guide for businesses and individuals regarding the FCPA. The guide discusses, among other issues, the history of the FCPA and explication of each of its provisions, including coverage, jurisdictional issues, principles of liability, defenses, and penalties. The guide also provides an in-depth discussion of the hallmarks of an effective compliance program, all of which are detailed in this chapter, including commitment from senior management, a clearly articulated policy against corruption, effective code of conduct, appropriate policies and procedures, proper oversight by management, incentive and disciplinary measures, adequate third-party due diligence, thorough risk assessment, and continuing training and improvement. Further, the guide also confirms the role of compliance programs in influencing government action.

More importantly, the guide is particularly helpful in providing hypothetical and real-life scenarios and examples pertaining to FCPA issues. Included in these real-life scenarios are anonymized cases in which the DOJ and SEC has declined further investigation and prosecution of companies where there were appropriate precautions to prevent or address illegal conduct, including the proper design and implementation of an effective compliance program. Specific measures taken and corresponding results by these companies included:

- Immediate and thorough internal investigation once allegations of misconduct were brought to light
- Termination and discipline of implicated individuals following the company's investigation
- Ability of effective internal controls and due diligence procedures to detect misconduct
- Self-reporting of discovered misconduct to DOJ and SEC
- Full cooperation and voluntary disclosure of results of company's investigation
- Extensive review and improvement of company's compliance program
- Comprehensive company-wide FCPA training

18.8 Legal Cases

The following cases provide insight into what constitutes effective components and implementation of compliance programs and related issues.

18.8.1 In Re Caremark

The seminal *Caremark* case is one of the most important cases in the discussion of compliance programs. Here, shareholders brought a derivative lawsuit against Caremark International, Inc., alleging that the company had participated in a kickback scheme. As a result, the company was fined and subsequently suffered financial losses. The shareholders based their lawsuit on the theory that Caremark's board of directors breached their fiduciary duty of care by failing to monitor their employees. Both parties agreed to settle and brought the matter before the Delaware Chancery Court. The court in its judgment allowing for the settlement recognized that boards of directors had such a duty to monitor their employees, and that one such avenue was the establishment of some type of compliance program. The court explained:

> I note the potential impact of the federal organizational sentencing guidelines on any business organization. Any rational person attempting in good faith to meet an organizational governance responsibility would be bound to take into account this development and the enhanced penalties and the opportunities for reduced sanctions that it offers.
>
> [C]orporate boards may satisfy their obligation to be reasonably informed concerning the corporation, [by] assuring themselves that information and reporting systems exist in the organization that are reasonably designed to provide to senior management and to the board itself timely, accurate information sufficient to allow management and the board, each within its scope, to reach informed judgments concerning both the corporation's compliance with law and its business performance.
>
> [N]o rationally designed information and reporting system will remove the possibility that the corporation will violate laws or regulations, or that senior officers or directors may nevertheless sometimes be misled or otherwise fail reasonably to detect acts material to the corporation's compliance with the law. But it is important that the board exercise a good faith judgment that the corporation's information and reporting system is in concept and design adequate to assure the board that appropriate information will come to its attention in a timely manner as a matter of ordinary operations, so that it may satisfy its responsibility. [O]nly a sustained or systematic failure of the board to exercise oversight—such as an utter failure to attempt to assure a reasonable information and reporting system exits—will establish the lack of good faith that is a necessary condition to liability.[14]

Thus, compliance programs play an integral part in determining whether a board has exercised its duties, including a making good-faith attempt to implement adequate information and reporting systems. Although there has been commentary[15] highlighting the diminished results of this decision when compared to its goals,

---

[14] In Re Caremark International Inc., 698 A.2d 959 (Del. Ch. 1996).

[15] Biegelman (2008, pp. 75–77) argues that after the decision, boards rushed to create compliance programs that emphasized the limiting of legal liability at the cost of neglecting building an ethical culture. Biegelman also quotes Elson and Gyves (2004, p. 692) in explaining the post-Caremark phenomena:

> The more actions taken by the corporation to create compliance procedures and regimes, the better record for liability preclusion upon judicial review. This led to a substantial increase in the size and scope of corporate compliance activities and ultimately the creation of vast compliance bureaucracies within the organization. As the motivation for these actions was primarily liability-driven, their actual impact on corporate activities was questionable.

[16] See Roman v. US, 2000 US App. LEXIS 9025 (holding that compliance programs have to be effective, not perfect; training, internal reviews, and termination of violators are substantial evidence

especially the strategy of boards absolving themselves of liability by haphazardly investing in and developing compliance programs, the case is still important in setting the precedent for the role of corporate leadership in ensuring compliance and integrity.

18.8.2 Successful or Adequate Compliance Initiatives

The following set of cases provides useful insight into what can be considered an effective compliance program despite imperfection in results[16]—active involvement by management, appointments of skilled personnel and managers dedicated to compliance functions, drawing on the expertise of independent consultants and experts, constant communication between compliance units and management, and regular compliance-related meetings and discussions.

18.8.2.1 Stone v. Ritter

Stone v. Ritter[17] is the Delaware Supreme Court case that reaffirmed the holdings in the *Caremark* case, stating that liability for failure to monitor employees would occur where

> (a) the directors utterly failed to implement any reporting or information system or controls; *or* (b) having implemented such a system or controls, consciously failed to monitor or oversee its operations thus disabling themselves from being informed of risks or problems requiring their attention.

In this case, a bank and corporation paid fines for failing to file suspicious activity reports, in violation of the Bank Secrecy Act. The bank and corporation, however, took several steps that absolved it of *Caremark* liability despite failures in compliance. After their violations were discovered, the bank and corporation were required to engage an independent consultant to review and improve its compliance program. Consequently, the independent consultant's report found that the corporation "dedicated considerable resources and systems to ensure compliance." Among the many components of the compliance program enacted and supported by numerous employees and other staff, it included:

- Appointment of an officer responsible for training, communications, reporting, and presenting policy and program changes to the board of directors and management
- Long-standing presence of a compliance department staffed with 19 professionals, including a compliance manager and compliance reporting manager

---

of an effective program); In Re Citigroup, Inc., 2009 U.S. Dist LEXIS 75564 (large losses despite having monitoring system does not mean that directors breached fiduciary duties)

[17] 911 A.2d 362 (Del. 2006)

- Presence of a corporate security department responsible for detection and reporting of suspicious fraudulent activity led by and experienced head who had served in the US Secret Service for two decades
- Presence of a suspicious activity oversight committee responsible for active oversight of the compliance program

The court, in considering the various components above, found that the directors not only had discharged their oversight responsibility to establish an information and reporting system, but also held that the system was designed for appropriate monitoring. The court also noted that the directors were involved in the monitoring process through enacting written compliance policies and procedures, including directing employees to report all suspicious behavior to the appropriate authorities.[18]

18.8.2.2 South v. Baker

In *South v. Baker,* a mining company suffered two accidents causing loss of life and reduced production. The plaintiffs brought a shareholder derivative suit charging the board of directors with failing to implement a reasonable information and reporting system. In dismissing the complaint with prejudice, the court stated that the plaintiffs' claim was baseless and that the opposite had actually happened, that the company made an "evident effort" to establish a reasonable system. In support of their holding, the court cited the company's establishment of:

> [a] Safety Committee in charge of (i) reviewing health, safety and environmental policies; (ii) discussing annually with management the scope and plans for conducting audits of the Company's performance in health and safety; (iii) reviewing and discussing with management any material noncompliance with health or safety laws and management's response to such noncompliance; and (iv) receiving and reviewing updates from management regarding the Company's health and safety performance [with the] members of the Safety Committee [who] were the four outside directors with the most mining industry experience.[19]

18.8.2.3 Wylie v. Stipes

In *Wylie v. Stipes,* the court dismissed the plaintiff's derivative shareholder suit as baseless, holding that the defendant corporation's "information systems appear to have represented a good faith attempt to be informed of relevant facts." The court cited the establishment of an Auditing Committee with four directors that met regularly with outside auditors, the board of directors receiving regular updates on financial results, and the presence of a Senior Credit Committee in charge of approving loans over a certain amount. The court instead stated that for the plaintiff to prevail, he had to cite examples of substandard monitoring such as a lack of an

[18] Ibid.

[19] 2012 Del. Ch. LEXIS 229.

audit committee, sporadic meetings and inadequate time for work, and ignoring or encouraging of irregularities.[20]

18.8.2.4 Collins and Aikman Corporation v. Stockman

In *Collins and Aikman Corporation v. Stockman,* the court held that the plaintiff's claim that company had inadequate controls was baseless even in presence of illegal behavior. Here, the company's audit committee conducted investigations, was aided by independent counsel and auditors who were "frequently present," had "continual access" to company records, "actively participated" in reviewing financial information, and were "primarily responsible" for reviewing financial results. The company's audit committee also twice initiated internal investigations and retained prominent independent counsel and auditors for assistance.[21]

18.8.3 Failure of Oversight and Compliance

18.8.3.1 Pereira v. Cogan

In *Pereira v. Cogan,* the plaintiff, a trustee, alleged that the controlling shareholder of a company was in default of promissory notes and engaged in self-dealing in breach of his fiduciary duty by receiving excess compensation. At trial, expert testimony was presented that the board of directors did not have adequate monitoring practices and procedures, which led to the misconduct of the shareholder. Such a program should have included regularly scheduled meetings, adequate documentation, and audit and compensation committees. Instead, the company did not have procedures for financial officers to make reports to the board of directors and relied on informal discussions between these two sets of employees. The company also did not have either a compliance program or officer. Further, the company's general counsel never advised the board on its obligations, responsibilities, and duties, including the need for compliance, monitoring, auditing, and supervision of employees. Although the company belatedly established a compensation committee, it never actually convened in person. In holding that the plaintiff was entitled to all his claims, the court justifiably held that the company's corporate governance practices were "sadly deficient."[22]

The lesson for compliance in this case is clear—establish a well-supported compliance program with adequate monitoring, reporting procedures, appropriate committees, and education of all employees, especially upper management and the

---

[20] 797 F. Supp. 2d 193 (D.P.R. 2009).

[21] 2009 U.S. Dist. LEXIS 43472. See also Kanter v. Barella, 489 F. 3d. 170 (3rd Cir. 2007) (plaintiff failed to plead existence of any facts that should have alerted directors of problems; rather the company had functioning audit committee that met properly and the presence of a responsive board).

[22] 294 B.R. 449 (SDNY 2003).

board of directors. Not doing so will almost certainly lead to liability and damaging consequences.

18.9 Case Studies

18.9.1 Siemens: *Evolution of a Compliance Program*

The *Siemens* case is a seminal one in the arena of anticorruption and compliance, especially in exemplifying the perils of conducting business without a compliance program. Here, Siemens and its various subsidiaries engaged in widespread bribery, involving projects in many countries. For years, Siemens and its subsidiaries made thousands of illegal payments (totaling approximately US$ 1.4 billion) to various government officials while engaging in various methods of concealing the nature of these bribes. Among the illicit practices that Siemens and its subsidiaries used were direct payments to consultants, cash desks where employees could withdraw sums for corrupt payments, use of special "Barschecks" and bearers checks for corrupt payments, use of intermediaries for payments, slush funds, a confidential payment system outside the normal accounts payable process, internal commission accounts, and sham supplier agreements, resale transactions, and receivables manipulation. In its prosecution, Siemens's lax compliance function and internal controls were emphasized in contributing to the company's indefensible actions.[23]

First, Siemens had a long history of questionable behavior. Prior to 1999, its project cost calculation sheets referenced a common tax term partly understood by many employees to mean "bribes." Only in 2001 did the company establish a position for a Corporate Officer for Compliance and expanded its antitrust compliance program to cover anticorruption matters. The newly appointed Corporate Officer for Compliance, however, worked part time, and until 2004 only had a staff of two lawyers. Siemens also ignored multiple warnings from various sources, including legal staff, that it was exposing itself to a great deal of liability due to its practices. In particular, by their lackadaisical approach to compliance, senior management did not set the correct "Tone at the Top." On learning about various troubling practices

[23] Information and Statement of Offense, United States v. Siemens Aktiengesellschaft, Court Docket Number: 08-CR-367-RJL, US DOJ, http://www.justice.gov/criminal/fraud/fcpa/cases/siemens-aktiengesellschaft.html, accessed 14 July 2013; Complaint, Securities and Exchange Commission v. Siemens Aktiengesellschaft, 1:08-CV-02167 (D.C. 2008), U.S. Securities and Exchange Commission (SEC), http://www.sec.gov/litigation/complaints/2008/comp20829.pdf, accessed 14 July 2013; see Information and Statement of Offense, United States v. Siemens S.A. (Venezuela), Court Docket Number: 08-CR-370-RJL, US DOJ, http://www.justice.gov/criminal/fraud/fcpa/cases/siemens-venezuela.html, accessed 14 July 2013. Information and Statement of Offense, United States v. Siemens Bangladesh Limited, Court Docket Number: 08-CR-369-RJL, US DOJ, http://www.justice.gov/criminal/fraud/fcpa/cases/siemens-bangladesh.html, accessed 14 July 2013. Information and Statement of Offense, United States v. Siemens S.A. (Argentina), Court Docket Number: 08-CR-368-RJL, US DOJ, http://www.justice.gov/criminal/fraud/fcpa/cases/siemens-argentina.html, accessed 14 July 2013.

worldwide, neither investigations nor disciplinary actions against involved personnel were carried out. Due diligence on business consultants was also not performed and there was no appropriate training on anticorruption and to prevent bribery of foreign government officials.[24]

Despite the bleak nature of this case as related to the weak nature of Siemens's prior commitment to compliance, the turnaround that the company then implemented is nothing short of impressive. The lesson here is that with increased commitment and willingness to invest in compliance, a company with poor or nonexistent measures can become a leader in establishing a culture of integrity in the private sector. After a thorough investigation involving interviewing thousands of employees and examining millions of documents, Siemens implemented the following measures in building its compliance program and culture of integrity:

Replacement of Top Management The company brought in experienced individuals with strong corporate governance and compliance backgrounds to replace their senior management, including the CEO, general counsel, chief audit officer, and chief compliance officer. Further, the company established a compliance committee within the supervisory board and a corporate disciplinary committee made up of the general counsel, labor director, chief compliance officer, head of human resources, and other heads of business units where violations occur.

Increased Support for Compliance Functions and Clear Reporting Lines Direct reporting to top management was granted to the compliance function with the CCO reporting directly to the general counsel and CEO. The number of compliance staff was increased to 600 individuals worldwide with added support for the legal department. The company also established a compliance investigative unit headed by a former Interpol officer and a forensic audit unit headed by a former professional services firm investigations leader. In addition, the company strengthened its audit functions by adding hundreds of staff and appointed an experienced individual with anticorruption experience to oversee this department.

Increased Emphasis on Training and Communication The company established training programs using a variety of methods including specialized training for senior management, compliance officers, employees with signing authority, and individuals responsible for dealing with government officials. Included in the training program was a robust anti-compliance program, an anticorruption handbook, and ongoing meetings and conferences. The company also created an anticorruption toolkit that details its controls used to implement its compliance initiatives.

Ombudsman Program and Compliance Helpdesk The company established a confidential and anonymous ombudsman program to handle complaints from individuals, including employees and third parties that may not want to contact the company directly. The company retained an attorney from a prominent law firm to act as an external ombudsman. In addition, the company established a confidential and

[24] See Information, United States v. Siemens Aktiengesellschaft; Complaint, Securities and Exchange Commission v. Siemens Aktiengesellschaft.

anonymous helpdesk that could be reached by email, telephone, and other means available 24/7 in 150 languages for questions and reporting of misconduct.

Enhanced Internal Controls The company also instituted new policies regarding its internal controls including:

- Increased monitoring of company bank accounts
- Clarifying prohibitions on company funds held in the name of employees or third parties
- Enhancing rules for signature authorization for payments and other transactions
- Strengthening restrictions on cash advances and disbursements
- Using automation and data assurance processes as further controls

Increased Due Diligence and Monitoring In light of the company's problems with consultants, agents, and other business partners, the company implemented a more rigorous review and due diligence process, including stricter controls on payments to such parties. The company also instituted a new code of conduct for its suppliers emphasizing compliance and a prohibition on bribery and corruption (Biegelman and Biegelman 2010, p. 122).

18.9.2 Garth Peterson and Morgan Stanley: A Successful Compliance Program Saves the Company

This case is unique as it represents the principle that an effective compliance program can potentially absolve a company of all liability. Garth Peterson, a managing director with Morgan Stanley, falsely represented to the company that the real-estate interest it was selling was to a legitimate organization. In fact, the interest was sold to a shell company controlled by Peterson and his coconspirators, a Chinese government official and a Canadian attorney. Based on the false representation, Morgan Stanley sold the interest at a discount, resulting in a paper profit of more than US$ 2.5 million for Peterson and his coconspirators. Over the following years, the interest also generated equity distributions and appreciated in value. Upon being investigated and charged with violating the FCPA, Peterson pled guilty. For the first time in FCPA enforcement history, however, the DOJ declined to bring any enforcement against the company associated with its agent. In doing so, the DOJ specifically emphasized the high quality of Morgan Stanley's compliance program. Morgan Stanley's program contained the following:

Substantial Compliance Staff and Resources Between 2002 and 2008, Morgan Stanley employed 500 dedicated compliance officers, including regional compliance officers responsible for evaluating region-specific risks. These compliance staff had direct lines to the board of directors and regularly reported through the chief legal officer to the CEO and senior management committees. They were also responsible for drafting and maintaining policies and procedures, coordinating with business units firm-wide to provide anticorruption-related advisory services; evaluating the retention of agents; preclearing expenses involving non-US government officials, and working with outside counsel to conduct due diligence into potential business partners. Compliance officers were also responsible for monitoring client and employee transactions and randomly auditing selected personnel in high-risk areas while regularly auditing and testing Morgan Stanley's business units.

Stringent Payment-Approval Process and Anticorruption Policy Morgan Stanley's payment-approval process included multiple layers of personnel authorization and review to ensure that transactions were in accordance with management's authorization and to prevent improper payments, including the transfer of things of value to officials of foreign governments and foreign government officials instrumentalities. The company's anticorruption policy also addressed the FCPA and risks associated with gift giving, business entertainment, travel, lodging, meals, charitable contributions, and employment. Employees were also required to certify annually their adherence to the code of conduct, which contained provisions for FCPA compliance.

Emphasis on Training There were frequent trainings of employees through various methods, including live training presentations. Between 2002 and 2007, Morgan Stanley conducted at least 54 training sessions for Asia-based employees—including Peterson, who was trained seven times, including at certain points by the global head of litigation and the global head of the anticorruption group. Peterson was also provided with 35 FCPA reminders, including written training materials, circulars, and reminders of the company's code of conduct, policies of gift giving and entertainment, global anti-bribery policy, guidance on engagement of consultants, and policies for high-risk events such as the Olympics. Peterson also certified on multiple occasions that he was in compliance with the FCPA, which were kept on his permanent employment record.

Compliance Hotline Morgan Stanley maintained a 24-h, 7-days-a-week toll-free compliance hotline staffed to field calls in every major language.

Constant Evaluation and Improvement Morgan Stanley constantly evaluated and improved their compliance program and internal controls. In 2007, the company instituted risk-based auditing to detect risks of FCPA violations in addition to regular internal audits, desk reviews, and meetings between compliance personnel and other staff to discuss anticorruption risks. Compliance staff also kept themselves updated on regulatory developments and changing risks. Finally, the company conducted an annual formal review with independent legal counsel.[25]

In short, this case provides an excellent argument for the utility of developing and implementing a state-of-the-art compliance program. As stated previously, this case was the first of its kind in terms of preventing further liability for the company for the actions of one of its employees. In all other FCPA cases, including those involving companies with varying degrees of compliance programs, benefits were limited to mitigation of penalties. This case, however, not only highlights the incen-

[25] Information, United States v. Garth Peterson, Court Docket Number: 12-CR-224, US DOJ, http://www.justice.gov/criminal/fraud/fcpa/cases/petersong.html, accessed 14 July 2013.

tives for a compliance program, but also its necessity in order to prevent damage to companies and their shareholders, especially in scenarios where rogue agents manage to circumvent internal controls.

18.9.3 Bonny Island Cases: Failure of Existing Compliance Programs

The Bonny Island Project set of cases involves a complex and drawn-out scheme of bribery intended to win a series of contracts worth billions of dollars from the Nigerian government. The parties, Snamprogetti Netherlands B.V., Technip S.A., JGC Corporation, and Kellogg, Brown & Root, Inc.,[26] formed a four-company venture named TSKJ in order to execute a strategy involving high-level executives and management, multiple international bank accounts, shell companies, agents, tactics to avoid liability, and hundreds of millions of dollars worth of bribes.

Over the period of almost a decade, from 1995 to 2004, several members of the Nigerian government awarded the TSKJ joint venture a series of contracts worth US$ 6 billion. To obtain these contracts, through its agents and shell companies TSKJ promised and paid tens of millions of dollars of bribes to various levels of the Nigerian government. The members of this conspiracy planned and executed a complex and multipronged strategy in furtherance of their scheme. Through "cultural meetings," senior executives, employees, and agents of TSKJ discussed their plan to obtain Bonny Island Project contracts. The amounts of the bribes were previously negotiated between Albert J. Stanley, a director and officer of Kellogg, Brown & Root, Inc. and other members of TSKJ with a top-level office in the executive branch of the Nigerian government.[27]

---

[26] KBR, Inc. was formed in March 2006 and was a wholly owned subsidiary of Halliburton, a Delaware energy services corporation, until November 2006. KBR's senior directors consisted solely of Halliburton officials who had authority over KBR's senior officials and their salaries and performance goals. After Halliburton acquired Dresser Industries, Inc., the parent company of M.W. Kellogg Company in September 1998, KBR's financial statements were consolidated into Halliburton's and its profits reported to investors as Halliburton's.

[27] Information United States v. JGC Corporation, Docket No: 11-CR-260, US DOJ, http://www.justice.gov/criminal/fraud/fcpa/cases/jgc-corp.html, accessed 14 July 2013; Complaint, Securities and Exchange Commission v. Halliburton Co. and KBR, Inc., 4:09-CV-399 (S.D. Tex. 2009), US SEC, http://www.sec.gov/litigation/complaints/2009/comp20897.pdf, accessed 14 July 2013; Information and Plea Agreement, United States v. Kellogg Brown & Root LLC, Court Docket Number: 09-CR-071, US DOJ, http://www.justice.gov/criminal/fraud/fcpa/cases/kellogg-brown.html, accessed 14 July 2013; Information and Deferred Prosecution Agreement, United States v. Marubeni Corporation, Court Docket Number: 12-CR-022, US DOJ, http://www.justice.gov/criminal/fraud/fcpa/cases/marubeni.html, accessed 14 July 2013; Complaint, Securities and Exchange Commission v. ENI, S.p.A. and Snamprogetti Netherlands B.V., 4:10-CV-2414 (S.D. Tex. 2009), US SEC, http://www.sec.gov/litigation/complaints/2010/comp-pr2010-119.pdf, accessed 14 July 2013; Information and Deferred Prosecution Agreement, United States v. Snamprogetti Netherlands B.V., Court Docket Number: 10-CR-460, US DOJ, http://www.justice.gov/criminal/fraud/fcpa/cases/snamprogetti.html, accessed 14 July 2013; Complaint, Securities and Exchange

During the subsequent investigation, the SEC determined that Halliburton's Legal Department had actually conducted a due-diligence investigation of the agent used by TSKJ to obtain the contracts through bribery prior to one of the awards. According to the SEC complaint:

> Halliburton's policies required that the investigation be "reasonable under the circumstances," and required that a number of factors be considered, including the "reasonableness of the fees" and the "business and cultural environment" in which the agent would be operating. The policies did not require, however, any specific description of the agent's duties, or that the agent agree to any accounting or audit of fees received, nor did the policies specify what steps needed to be taken in conducting the investigation.

Pursuant to the due diligence investigation, the legal department also learned of the existence of a shell company and that the only active official related to it was the aforementioned agent. Despite this information, the legal department did not conduct a follow-up investigation on the identity of the beneficial owner of the shell company's shares, how the agent was going about his work to seek contracts with the Nigerian government, or check the references provided by the agent, some of which turned out to be false. Further, a senior Halliburton legal officer reviewed the results of the due diligence investigation, realized the lack of information gleaned, and yet still Halliburton approved the agent's use and role. Halliburton also conducted minimal follow-up and due diligence, in violations of its policies, prior to the final phase of contracts with the Nigerian government. As the SEC complaint details:

> At the time that Nigeria LNG awarded the contract for [the final phases of the contract], Halliburton required that a form called "B-2 Agent Approval Request" be prepared for any agent contract. This document needed to be signed by senior Halliburton officials before the agent contract was entered into. Senior KBR officials prepared a form B-2 for the proposed UK Agent contract. The document contained false statements as to, among other things, the UK Agent's place of business (falsely stated to be Monaco) and number of employees (falsely stated to be four). The document was signed for approval by senior Halliburton officials for finance and administration, as well as senior KBR officials. None of the senior Halliburton or KBR officials who signed the document undertook any independent review or asked any questions concerning the UK Agent.

Further, Halliburton also failed to conduct due diligence regarding Marubeni, an intermediary company used to funnel bribes to Nigerian government officials. Although KBR hid the true nature of its and TSKJ's relationship to Marubeni by char-

---

Commission v. Albert Jackson Stanley, 08-CV-02680 (S.D. Tex. 2008), US SEC, http://www.sec.gov/litigation/complaints/2008/comp20700.pdf, accessed 14 July 2013; and Deferred Prosecution Agreement, United States v. Albert Jackson Stanley, Court Docket Number: 08-CR-597, US DOJ, http://www.justice.gov/criminal/fraud/fcpa/cases/stanleya.html, accessed 14 July 2013; Complaint, Securities and Exchange Commission v. Technip, 4:10-CV-02289 (S.D. Tex. 2010), US SEC, http://www.sec.gov/litigation/complaints/2010/comp-pr2010-110.pdf, accessed 14 July 2013; Information and Deferred Prosecution Agreement, United States v. Technip S.A., Court Docket Number: 10-CR-439, US DOJ, http://www.justice.gov/criminal/fraud/fcpa/cases/technip-sa.html, accessed 14 July 2013; Indictment and Plea Agreements, United States of America v. Jeffrey Tesler and Wojciech J. Chodan, 09 CR 098 (S.D. Tex 2009), US DOJ, http://www.justice.gov/criminal/fraud/fcpa/cases/tesler/tesler-indict.pdf, accessed 14 July 2013.

acterizing it as a "services" contract, Halliburton's polices, procedures, and internal controls could not have properly identified the relationship as an illicit one. Finally, the multiple payments made by KBR for bribery purposes were falsely characterized as "consulting" and "services" fees in KBR's books, which were also reflected in Halliburton's corporate books and records.[28]

The SEC also assigned liability to Snamprogetti and Technip for not conducting due diligence on either the agent or Marubeni. Further, Snamprogetti's parent company Eni failed to monitor its subsidiary or conduct due diligence on the joint ventures in which Snamprogetti participated, leading to the failure of internal controls to detect, deter, or prevent the TSKJ scheme. Finally, the multiple payments made by Snamprogetti for bribery purposes were falsely characterized as "consulting" and "services" fees in Snamprogetti's books, which were also reflected in Eni's corporate books and records. In regards to Technip, the SEC specifically stated:

> Technip did not adopt due diligence procedures as to agents that were adequate to detect, deter or prevent the payment of bribes by agents. The due diligence procedures adopted by Technip only required that potential agents respond to a written questionnaire, seeking minimal background information about the agent. No additional due diligence was required, such as an interview of the agent, or a background check, or obtaining information beyond that provided by the answers to the questionnaire. A senior executive of Technip admitted that the due diligence procedures adopted by Technip were a perfunctory exercise, conducted so that Technip would have some documentation in its files of purported due diligence. In fact, Technip executives knew that the purpose of the agreements with the UK Agent was to funnel bribes to Nigerian officials, and therefore certain answers by the UK Agent to the questionnaire were false.[29]

The failure of existing controls and the implementation of such for each of the joint venture companies is obviously indefensible. As is clear from the lack of due diligence performed on the TSKJ scheme, including the active investigation by Halliburton attorneys that was cursory at best, this scenario reveals either willful negligence or a breakdown in the system of compliance. It is also unclear whether JGC even had a compliance program in place during the course of the scheme. More troubling is the absolute lack of a commitment to ethics and integrity shown by the top leadership and management of the joint venture companies. The "top–down" approach of providing an example for the entire organization was turned on its head, instead providing an example of encouraging a "whatever it takes" approach to business. As also stated previously, the so-called gatekeepers among the legal and financial staff of each company not only did not pose a barrier to the planning and implementation of misconduct, but also actively participated as coconspirators.

---

[28] Complaint, Securities and Exchange Commission v. Halliburton Co. and KBR, Inc., 4:09-CV-399 (S.D. Tex. 2009), US SEC, http://www.sec.gov/litigation/complaints/2009/comp20897.pdf, accessed 14 July 2013.

[29] Complaint, Securities and Exchange Commission v. ENI, S.p.A. and Snamprogetti Netherlands; Complaint, Securities and Exchange Commission v. Technip.

18.9.4 Titan Corporation: Absence of a Compliance Program

Titan Corporation and its subsidiaries contracted with the government of Benin to build and operate a wireless telephone network. Titan was compensated for their work through a management fee. Involved in the negotiation of the contract was an agent hired by Titan who claimed to be a business advisor to the then president of Benin and had access to him. Titan did not perform any due diligence on this agent, and over the course of several years paid him US$ 3.5 million. These payments were used to influence the presidential election in Benin under the label of "social payments" which were processed under false invoices as "consulting services" in violation of the FCPA. These payments were also used to raise Titan's management fee by a factor of four. Titan also violated federal tax laws by claiming these disguised bribes as deductible business expenses.[30]

During the course of these activities, an independent Benin auditor informed Titan that it was unable to substantiate several payments in the country and that there was a lack of internal controls. Titan's external auditor, Arthur Andersen, had also previously warned the company of "the need to establish standard policies and procedures to be followed by the entities reporting into [the project]," and noted a "lack of controls related to inventory tracking and reconciliation to the General Ledger." Another Arthur Andersen process review also noted "there is no accounting system set up in the company" and that it was not "reliable." This review also identified several risks including: "intentional mistake: loss of cash," "fraud," and "loss of data." These issues were never seriously considered or addressed by Titan's management and not brought to the attention of its audit committee. Further, several company employees including senior staff and executives had received several written allegations of forged invoices, bills, and bribery in Benin, which were also inadequately investigated. In its complaint, the SEC stated the following about Titan's lack of oversight and compliance:

> Despite utilizing over 120 agents and consultants in over 60 countries, Titan never had a formal company-wide FCPA policy, failed to implement an FCPA compliance program, disregarded or circumvented the limited FCPA policies and procedures in effect, failed to maintain sufficient due diligence files on its foreign agents, and failed to have meaningful oversight over its foreign agents.

The only (negligible) "policy" that Titan had was a code of ethics stating "employees must be familiar with and strictly adhere to such provisions as the FCPA that prohibit payments or gifts to foreign government officials for the purpose of influencing official government acts or assistance in obtaining business"—and even this was neither disseminated nor properly enforced. There was also no evidence that Titan conducted any due diligence in regards to retaining foreign agents or consultants.[31]

---

[30] Unrelated to the Benin investigation, Titan also was involved in falsifying documents linked to under-reporting of commission payments in other countries.

[31] Information and Deferred Prosecution Agreement, United States v. Titan Corporation, Court Docket Number: 05-CR-314-BEN, US DOJ, http://www.justice.gov/criminal/fraud/fcpa/cases/

The lesson from the Titan case is clear—the absence of an adequate compliance program has severe consequences. Here, without a formal program and assigned responsibilities, the company's activities and actions went unchecked, leading to misconduct not only in Benin but in multiple other jurisdictions. Even with the supposed safeguards of independent auditors, their warnings went unheeded while allowing the widespread existence of illicit activities. While not providing a complete guarantee that these activities would not have occurred even with a compliance program, components of a compliance program would have drastically reduced the likelihood of their occurrence.

18.10 Conclusion

The USA's contribution to the development of compliance programs through its governmental policies and case law is insightful in terms of legal and practical considerations. Further, legal frameworks, purpose, models, and corresponding strengths and weaknesses should be considered in the development and implementation of such programs. Nonetheless, it is evident that the use of compliance programs has become increasingly widespread and that further analysis and consequent improvements and innovations will be the norm. As this field of compliance develops in the future, with corresponding input from the stated sources above, the future for combating and preventing crime and corruption in the private sector seems promising.

References

Alexander, C. R. (1999). On the nature of the reputational evidence for corporate crime: Evidence. *Journal of Law and Economics, 42*(1), 489–526.

Arjoon, S. (2005). Corporate governance: An ethical perspective. *Journal of Business Ethics, 61*(4), 343–352.

Aviram, A. (2005). In defense of imperfect compliance programs. *Florida State University Law Review, 32*(2), 763–780.

Berzins, M., & Sofo, F. (2008). The inability of compliance strategies to prevent collusive conduct. *Corporate Governance, 8*(5), 669–680.

Biegelman, M. (2008). *Building a world-class compliance program: Best practices and strategies for success*. Hoboken: Wiley.

Biegelman, M., & Biegelman, D. (2010). *Foreign Corrupt Practices Act compliance guidebook: Protecting Your organization from bribery and corruption*. Hoboken: Wiley.

Chhaochharia, V., & Grinstein, Y. (2007). Corporate governance and firm value: The impact of the 2002 governance rules. *The Journal of Finance, 62*(4), 1789–1825.

titan-corp.html, accessed 14 July 2013; Securities and Exchange Commission v. Titan Corporation, 05-CV-0411 (D.C. 2005), US SEC, http://www.sec.gov/litigation/complaints/comp19107.pdf, accessed 14 July 2013.

Coglianese, C., Healey, T. J., Keating, E. K., & Michael, M. L. (2004). The role of government in corporate governance. *New York University Journal of Law and Business, 1,* 219 (Kennedy School of Government Research Working Paper 04–045).

Conway, J. C. (1994). Self-evaluative privilege and corporate compliance audits. *Southern California Law Review, 68,* 621–690.

Elson, C. M., & Gyves, C. J. (2004). In Re Caremark: Good intentions, unintended consequences. *Wake Forest Law Review, 39,* 691–702.

Fiorelli, P., & Tracey, A. M. (2007). Why comply? Organizational guidelines offer a safer harbor in the storm. *The Journal of Corporation Law, 32*(3), 483.

Gabel, J. T. A., Mansfield, N. R., & Houghton, S. M. (2009). Letter vs. spirit: The evolution of compliance into ethics. *American Business Law Journal, 46*(3), 453–486.

Gobert, J. (1994). Corporate criminality: Four models of fault. *Legal Studies, 14*(3), 393–410.

Goldsmith, M., & King, C. W. (1997). Policing corporate crime: The dilemma of corporate compliance programs. *Vanderbilt Law Review, 50*(1), 31–32.

Goncharov, I., Werner, J. R., & Zimmerman, J. (2006). Does compliance with the German corporate governance code have an impact on stock valuation? An empirical analysis. *Corporate Governance: An International Review, 14*(5), 432–445.

Huff, K. B. (1996). The role of corporate compliance in determining corporate criminal liability: A suggested approach. *Columbia Law Review, 96*(5), 1252–1298.

Karpoff, J. M., Lee, D. S., & Martin, G. S. (2008). The cost to firms of cooking the books. *Journal of Financial and Quantitative Analysis, 43*(3), 581–612.

Krawiec, K. (2003). Cosmetic compliance and the failure of negotiated governance. *Washington University Law Quarterly, 81,* 510–511.

Krawiec, K. (2005). Organizational misconduct: Beyond the principal–agent model. *Florida State University Law Review, 32,* 571–615.

Langevoort, D. C. (2002). Monitoring: The behavioral economics of corporate compliance with law. *Columbia Business Law Review, 71,* 77–117.

Laufer, W. S. (2008). *Corporate bodies and guilty minds: The failure of corporate criminal liability.* Chicago: University of Chicago Press.

Moohr, G. S. (2007). On the prospects of deterring corporate crime. *Journal of Business and Technology Law, 2*(1), 1–18 (University of Houston Law Center No. 2007-A –37).

Murphy, A. G. (2011). *Foreign Corrupt Practices Act: A practical resource for managers and executives*. Hoboken: Wiley.

Olsen, W. P. (2010). *The anti-corruption handbook: How to protect your business in the global marketplace*. Hoboken: Wiley.

Parker, C. (2006). The "compliance" trap: The moral message in responsive regulatory enforcement. *Law and Society Review, 40*(3), 591–622.

Parker, C., & Nielsen, V. L. (2009). Corporate compliance systems—Could they make any difference? *Administration and Society, 41*(1), 3–37.

Podgor, E. (2009). Educating compliance. *American Criminal Law Review, 46*(4), 1523–1534.

Ruhnka, J. C., & Boerstler, H. (1998). Governmental incentives for corporate self regulation. *Journal of Business Ethics, 17*(3), 309–326.

Trevino, L. K., Weaver, G. R., Gibson, D. G., & Toffler, B. L. (1999). Managing ethics and legal compliance: What works and what doesn't. *California Management Review, 41*(2), 128–142.

Wagner, S., & Dittmar, L. (2006). The unexpected benefits of Sarbanes-Oxley. *Harvard Business Review, 84*(4), 133–140.

Wellner, P. A. (2005). Effective compliance programs and corporate criminal prosecutions. *Cardozo Law Review*, 27(1), 497–528.

Wulf, K. (2011). *Ethics and compliance programs in multinational organizations*. New York: Springer Gabler.

Chapter 19
Corporate Responsibility and Compliance Programs in Italian Case Law

Alessia Paludi and Mattia Zecca

Contents

19.1 Introduction

In order to elaborate a self-regulation model in the field of international corruption which is sufficient to become a point of reference for multinational corporations and international institutions, a preliminary evaluation of certain important elements is required. These elements include the features of compliance programs actually adopted and implemented by corporations,[1] the internal legislative discipline concerning corporate responsibility in the specific country in question, and the guidelines

[1] For analysis of the economic impact of the compliance programs, see Centonze 2009, p. 219. For a social analysis of corporate liability, see Grillo 2009, p. 205. (Manacorda 2012)

A. Paludi (✉) · M. Zecca
LUISS Guido Carli University, Rome, Italy
e-mail: alessia.paludi@alice.it

M. Zecca
e-mail: m.zecca@penalistiassociati.com

S. Manacorda et al. (eds.), *Preventing Corporate Corruption*,
DOI 10.1007/978-3-319-04480-4_19,

and other initiatives on this subject promoted by the international organizations. While in the past prevention was prominently a matter for law-enforcement agencies, today the private sector is called upon to play a direct role in the fight against corruption.

In order to identify common standards in the elaboration of compliance programs suitable to prevent corruption, it is of capital importance to examine the relevant judicial decisions. The aim of this chapter is to select the most relevant decisions of the Italian courts concerning corporate responsibility, and evaluate them in order to get a clear view of the essential prerequisites of any compliance program that will be suitable to tackle corruption. We begin by providing a brief explanation of the Italian law concerning corporate responsibility and compliance programs, before turning to the analysis proper.

19.2 Corporate Responsibility and the Role of Compliance Programs in Legislative Decree no. 231/2001

With the Legislative Decree of 8 June 2001, n. 231, a form of administrative responsibility for corporations was introduced into the Italian system, related to the crimes committed by their officers, directors, managers, or employees.[2] This type of responsibility is based on both objective and subjective standards. First, the crime must either be committed *in the interest* of the corporation, or it should bring the corporation *a benefit* (Section 5 D. Lgs. 231/2001). In addition, a kind of *structural culpability* (Paliero and Piergallini 2006, p. 167; Giunta 2009) of the corporation must be present (De Maglie 2001, p. 1348; Mucciarelli 2010, p. 1247). The corporation's liability is based on a simple mechanism: the adoption (Bartolomucci 2010) and the effective implementation of a compliance program *before the commission of the crime* can exclude liability (Lunghini and Musso 2010, p. 300). This rule operates in a different way according to the type of person who committed the crime.

In fact, when the crime is committed by *representatives, directors,* or *top managers,* the corporation is not responsible if it demonstrates that: (1) before the crime was committed, it had adopted and effectively implemented a compliance program suitable to prevent the kind of crime actually committed (Pisani 2006, p. 5422); (2) a supervisory body monitoring the functioning of, updating of, and respect for the compliance program had been appointed; (3) the crime was committed by *fraudulently circumventing* the compliance program; (4) the supervisory board had carried out its work properly (Section 6 D. Lgs. 231/2001). When the crime is committed by an *employee* of the corporation, subject to the control of the top management, the corporation is not responsible if: (1) a compliance program had been adopted and effectively implemented by the corporation before the crime was committed to pre-

[2] See Di Giovine 2005, p. 3; De Vero 2008; De Vero 2001, p. 1126; Marinucci 2007, p. 445; Stile 2012, p. 37. On the subject of Corporate Group liability, see Scaroina 2006.

vent the kind of crime actually committed, and (2) the employee failed to comply with those rules (Section 7 D. Lgs. 231/2001).

The compliance program also plays a role if it is adopted and effectively implemented *after* a crime is committed: in this case, the corporation is liable, but disqualification measures cannot be imposed (Section 17 D. Lgs. 231/2001) and the economic sanctions can be reduced (Section 12 D. Lgs. 231/2001). Moreover, the precautionary measures can be suspended if the corporation asks for time during the investigation to adopt and effectively implement a compliance program suitable to cover the organizational deficiencies (Section 49 D. Lgs. 231/2001).

The law sets out the basic elements that a compliance program must contain, with regards to the extension of delegated powers and the risk of committing offenses. The legislator is aware of the impossibility of predetermining the specific contents of the compliance programs, given the wide range of forms such a program can adopt relative to the structure of the corporation, its business, and its dimensions.

However, according to Decree no. 231/2001 there is a minimal requirement that an acceptable compliance program be able to:[3]

(a) *Identify the activities in relation to which offenses may be committed.* This is a vital preliminary requirement for creating a suitable compliance program. Indeed, the adoption and implementation of the program must be preceded by a specific analysis of the corporate structure, in order to identify the different crimes which might be committed across its various arms.
(b) *Provide for specific direct protocols regarding training and implementation of decisions to be adopted by internal bodies.* The compliance programs must state specific rules for every activity and these must be observed by managers and employees. It is also important to establish who is responsible in every area and to separate out the roles which pertain to risky operations.
(c) *Identify procedures for the management of financial resources which are fit to prevent the commission of offenses.* Every financial flow must be registered, documented, and justified, in order to avoid the creation of hidden funds for criminal activities.
(d) *Provide for obligations to pass information to the supervisory body.* The body that is tasked with monitoring the functioning and updating of the compliance program must be provided with all pertinent information regarding the activities of the corporation. The privacy of the employees that pass information to that body must be protected as well.
(e) *Introduce a disciplinary system to punish noncompliance with the measures set out in the program.* The rules imposed by compliance programs must be enforced by specific sanctions for top management and other employees alike.

Effective implementation of the program also requires regular verification and, where appropriate, amendment when significant breaches of rules are discovered or when changes are otherwise made to the functioning of the corporation.

[3] On this point, see Assumma 2010, p. 193. The author has some doubts about assigning every decision on the suitability of the program to the judge.

It is important to note that the judicial evaluation of compliance program's suitability will differ according to the *time of adoption* of the compliance program (Assumma 2010). As already mentioned, the compliance program can be adopted before or after the commission of the crime. In the latter case, the compliance program must be more concrete and pragmatic, and must refer specifically to the risk area already identified. The corporation must clear up the causes of the offense charged and address the associated deficiency within the organization, and the *ex post* compliance program must propose specific measures able to prevent the same offense being committed again.[4]

While the above mentioned points comprise the legal foundations in this area, the Italian courts have added further specific requirements for compliance programs in their decisions concerning corporate responsibility. This is why it is so important to examine the case law.

19.3 The Study of Italian Case Law: A Brief Statistical Introduction

The study of Italian case law concerning the violation of Decree no. 231/2001 comprises about 120 decisions. Especially in the first phase of the enforcement of Decree no. 231/2001, Italian judges explained what was expected in terms of compliance, and indicated the key elements to be used to evaluate a program. However, very few decisions comprise a complete assessment of whether a corporation has a compliance program sufficient to detect and prevent the offense charged to the corporation. This is due to the fact that most corporations charged with violating Decree no. 231/2001 had not adopted a compliance program before the crime was committed.

The most relevant decisions concern crimes of internal corruption; certain others relate to different crimes such as false statements on balance sheets, defrauding the Italian State, market abuse, etc. There is no decision concerning compliance programs in relation to the crime of international corruption.[5]

Few decisions are final judgments, and in only one of them is the corporation acquitted thanks to its compliance program. Rather, most of the rulings are orders passed during the preliminary investigations which decide on the imposition of precautionary measures, such as disqualification or seizure. Nonetheless, some of these decisions involve issues relevant to the enforcement of Decree no. 231/2001: in order to apply a precautionary measure, the judge must also investigate the adoption and effective implementation of a compliance program and evaluate it.

[4] See the decision of judge of the preliminary investigations of Rome of 4 April 2003, concerning a corporation charged with corruption, and the decision of Court of Milan of 20 September 2004.

[5] The decisions passed by the judge of the preliminary investigation of Milan and by the Court of Milan, both of April 2004, refer to an energy company for the crime of internal corruption, although the evaluation of the compliance program is also made in relation to the conduct of corruption in a foreign country. On this point, see Sect. 19.3.5.

Our purpose here is to examine the most relevant decisions issued by the Italian courts which have evaluated the compliance programs adopted by corporations, thus providing useful information regarding their adoption and implementation, and focusing on their key elements.

19.3.1 Decision of 20 September 2004, Court of Milan[6]

The Court of Milan's decision of 20 September 2004 concerns certain corporations, belonging to the same group, which specialized in providing security services. The crimes alleged to have been committed involved corruption of public officers of the Ministry of Defense in order to win competitive tenders concerning security for military buildings; corruption of public officers of Regione Lombardia in order to win competitive tenders concerning night urban security; and defrauding the city of Milan by making false certifications about the number of workers employed in security.

No compliance program had been adopted and implemented by the corporations before the crimes were committed. However, according to section 17 of Legislative Decree no. 231/2001, the corporation could avoid the application of the disqualification measure if it adopted and effectively implemented a compliance program suitable to prevent the kind of crime previously committed, thus resolving the "organization deficiency which makes the commission of the crime possible."

The public prosecutor asked for the application of the precautionary measure of disqualification for 1 year. The judge appointed a special administrator over the corporations in order to allow their business to continue for 1 year, since he considered that an interruption of their commercial activities would be dangerous for the workers (who could lose their jobs) and for the community (who could lose as fundamental a service as security). The corporations asked for and obtained a suspension of the precautionary measure for 2 months, in order to set up the compliance programs. The precautionary measure for the holding corporation was then revoked by the Court of Milan after the appeal of 20 December 2004 on the grounds that the court did not recognize the persistence of a danger that could justify its application.

The corporations adopted the compliance programs after the crimes were committed but before the hearing. The judge therefore evaluated the compliance program, stating the following principles. A compliance program is suitable if it is:

- Concrete, specific, and developed in a dynamic fashion
- Elaborated from a concrete and economic substantive point of view and not from a purely legal or formal one
- Tailored to the specifics of the corporation's business and to its previous history; and it should therefore be constantly updated
- Based on a deep risk analysis, in order to enable the specific prevention of crimes, while also developing formal procedures for decision making

[6] The decision is published on Foro it., 2005, II, 528 .

This ruling is important not only in that it is the first to focus on compliance programs, but also because it provides recommendations on how to elaborate them in order to prevent crimes. The judge thus gave very important indications not only on what a compliance program should not contain, but also on what it must contain in order to be deemed suitable. The judge considered that there is no structural difference between a program adopted after the commission of the crime and one adopted beforehand. In the elaboration of every compliance program, it is thus important to consider the corporation history and the eventual crime-risk warning highlighted by that history.

In particular, the judge underlined the positive and negative elements of the compliance programs adopted by the corporations involved in the criminal proceedings and suggested some basic rules for a suitable program. These rules make up what is called the Decalogo 231, the name of which highlights the number of the legislative decree which introduces corporate responsibility and the topic of compliance programs into the Italian system. The following points sketch the judge's requirements as suggested in his Decalogo:

1. *Risk Analysis.* A suitable compliance program requires a deep and specific risk analysis and must not merely recapitulate legal or very general rules. In the decision, the judge stated that the risk analysis in this case had failed because of its overly generic approach. The rules issued in order to prevent crimes were not sufficiently specific, and the analysis should have been more focused on the specific issues of sources of finance, the creation of slush funds, participation in competitive tendering, and the execution of contracts. The corporation must be organized in order to make the creation of slush funds very difficult. A good compliance program must prevent the creation of unregistered money, which is often paid to corrupt officers.
2. *Qualification of the supervisory board's members.* The members of the supervisory board must have specific experience in investigation and consulting. The members must have statistical training, knowledge of analysis procedures, and skills in risk evaluation, interviewing people, and discovering fraud. A weak supervisory board cannot perform its task properly, the judge confirmed.
3. *Reputation of the supervisory board's members.* The appointment of the members of the supervisory board must consider every sentence (not only the definitive ones, but also the ones which are not definitive, and the pre-trial agreements as well) for crimes previously committed and every previous disqualification from managing public or private offices. The members must be independent from all the workers and managers of the corporation.
4. *Training courses.* The compliance program must impose training courses on all workers, which are tailored to specific areas in which they work with a particular focus on risk areas. Special training programs must be provided for the members of the supervisory board and the internal audit committee.
5. *Contents of the training courses.* The training courses must be well organized: the content and number of lessons should be defined, and attendance compulsory. Moreover, there should be constant controlling of participation and

course quality. In the case in question, the training course established as part of the compliance program by one of the corporations involved in the criminal proceedings only contained general considerations on workers' and managers' respect for compliance. The judge thought that training should be more specific, and should correspond to the workers' roles in the corporate system.

6. *Disciplinary measures*. The compliance programs must state the disciplinary measures that should be applied to officers, directors, or managers who do not recognize, try to eliminate, and punish violations.
7. *Procedures to discover risks*. A suitable compliance program must elaborate procedures to discover and map risks, especially when particular circumstances happen (i.e., when coming out of previous violations, or in case of a high turnover of human resources).
8. *Monitoring system*. The compliance programs must impose control and monitoring systems over their own working and effectiveness, while periodically verifying procedures (including by surprise checks) in the risk areas, and constant updating.
9. *Obligation of reporting*. A suitable compliance program must state that employees and directors are obliged to report any suspicions of violation to the supervisory board. In the case in question, the judge highlighted that the compliance programs provided by the corporations contained only a general obligation to report, without explaining how it should be done. The importance of this point is also underlined by the associations who wrote guidelines on elaborating the compliance program.
10. *Procedures*. A suitable compliance program must be based on specific and concrete procedures. Prevention procedures must be elaborated not in a general but in a specific way. For example, the compliance programs provided by the corporations involved in the proceedings stated that filing accountancy registers must foresee an easy way to collect information. A suitable program must indicate how to file the registers and what powers the supervisory board has on this point.

The rules affirmed by the judge in this case, which are based on legal principles, involve a range of relevant matters that will be developed by the Italian courts in future cases.

19.3.2 Decision of 18 April 2005, Court of Bari[7]

In Court of Bari decision of 18 April 2005, the public prosecutor asked for the application of the precautionary disqualification measure of the prohibition of the involved corporations from every activity. According to the public prosecutor, the corporations were under investigation for the following crimes: fraud against the state on the basis of Section 24 of Decree no. 231/2001 for perjured statements

[7] The decision is published on www.rivista231.it.

about community service in some hospitals of Regione Puglia, and corruption of many public officers in participating and winning competitive tenders regarding cleaning services on the basis of Section 25 of Decree no. 231/2001.

The judge of the preliminary investigations approved the prosecutor's request. He applied the precautionary disqualification measure of prohibition from every activity, and appointed a special administrator for the corporation. On appeal, the court reduced the disqualification measure term (to 6 months) and appointed a special administrator only as regards corruption.

The offenses had been committed by people serving as representatives of the corporation, or holding administrative or senior executive positions within it, as well as by people actually exercising management and control and by people under the direction or supervision of the above. The fraud and the corruption were committed in the corporations' interest to win profitable contracts without legal tender, obtain illegal follow-up of cleaning works, and pay the public officers back for their favors.

As for the compliance programs, the public prosecutor pointed out that two of the corporations in question did not have a suitable compliance program in place to prevent offenses of the same type occurring again. Additionally, if the offenses' commission was a tool to achieve corporate aims, the simple adoption of compliance programs on the part of the corporation would not be sufficient to remove the precautionary measure requirements (indeed, Section 6 parts (b)–(e), Section 49 concerning suspension of precautionary measures, and Section 50 on their revocation, confirm the judge's assumption).

The compliance programs filed in the proceedings on 14 April 2000 were judged completely unsuitable at first sight because they did not fulfill the following requirements:

(a) Identify the activities in relation to which offenses may be committed.
(b) Provide for specific direct protocols and schedule training and implementation of decisions by the corporation regarding offenses to be prevented.
(c) Identify procedures for the management of financial resources which are fit to prevent the commission of offenses.
(d) Provide for obligations to disclose information to the organization tasked with overseeing the working of and compliance with the program.
(e) Introduce a new disciplinary system to punish noncompliance with the measures set out in the program.

The judge's criticism of the compliance programs is clear and is able to give important indications: the contents were generic, abstract, and tautological. There were no internal protocols in relation to scheduled practices in the corporations. The management did not even remove the words "Guidelines" from the document's title, underlining how informal and merely cosmetic the adoption of the programs was. In addition, the judge noted that the compliance programs adopted by the two corporations were completely identical, even though the bodies themselves were dissimilar. And, finally, the compliance programs were not enacted effectively because the practices for winning competitive tenders were handled by people who were not involved in the compliance programs, and a disciplinary system to punish noncompliance with the measures set out in the compliance program was missing, even though it is essential and required by law.

19.3.3 Decision of 26 June 2007, Court of Naples[8]

The Court of Naples decision of 26 June 2007 concerns certain corporations which formed a joint venture and won the competitive tender concerning contracts for urban garbage disposal in the Regione Campania. The contracts in question concerned, in particular, the construction and management of some industrial establishments for garbage disposal and related transport services, with an express ban on subcontracts.

The crime charged to all the defendants was defrauding public entities (the Italian Government, Civil Defense Department, and many Cities of Regione Campania) by giving a false representation of whether the requirements set out in the contract had been respected. The corporations declared themselves to have correctly executed those contracts, when in fact they had not performed their obligations. There had been serious deficiencies in garbage disposal in the Regione Campania, with damage having resulted; nevertheless, the corporations continued to collect the garbage disposal fees.

The public prosecutor asked for the application of the precautionary measure of disqualification from negotiating with public officers, and judicial attachment. The judge applied the stated precautionary measure for 1 year, but only as regards the specific business of garbage disposal and only for some of the corporations involved in the proceedings. The judicial attachment was applied.

In the judge's opinion, the crime was committed by executing the "specific instructions of the management" of the corporations: The crime was not the outcome of someone's decision, but the execution of a corporate policy, common to all the corporations who were part of the joint venture. The crime was inspired by the corporate strategy.

The proceeding was in a precautionary phase, so the judge had to recognize the existence of the risk of the new commission of crimes by the corporations. On this point, the judge evaluated as positive the change in the corporation's top management, but he considered that it was only a formality, without any real break with the past or the previous policy.

Some of the corporations involved in these criminal proceedings had formally adopted compliance programs before the crime was committed. However, the judge considered that these programs had not been effectively implemented, stating that they were not suitable to prevent crimes. His arguments referred to all the corporations, since their compliance programs were almost the same.

A compliance program, in the judge's opinion, is suitable if it is:

[8] The decision is published on www.rivista231.it.

- Concrete, specific, and developed in a dynamic fashion
- Elaborated from a concrete and economic point of view and not from a purely legal or formal one
- Tailored to the specifics of the corporation's business and to its previous history and constantly updated

The judge also explained what features a suitable compliance program is expected to have. The indications contained in this decision can be collated and divide into the following points:

1. *Documentation.* The judge stated that documentation is very important in order to evaluate the suitability of a compliance program, as is investigation of its effective implementation in the corporation. The documentation is also important in order to spread the compliance program throughout the corporation, and if the compliance program is explained in a document, it is also easier for the corporation to verify when it needs to be updated.
2. *Update.* In the judge's opinion, the updating of compliance programs is very important, in order to adapt the program to changes in corporate structure and to the evolution of the law.
3. *Procedures.* A suitable compliance program must contain specific rules and impose particular procedures for every part of its organization, especially in the areas where there is a greater possibility of the commission of crimes, as well as in the light of the corporation's history. For this reason, a deep risk analysis is of fundamental importance. The procedures must be carefully enumerated and specific, especially in those areas which concern the making and execution of a decision. Those who have the powers to make and those who have the power to execute each decision must be *exactly indicated by the program.* Furthermore, the people involved in the different phases of the process should be different. This requires that *the person who decides must be different from the one who executes the decision, as well as from the one who monitors it.*

Every step of the decision-making process must be accounted for in specific registers or documents: authorizations, the drawing up of formal documents, power of attorneys, privacy of information, and the filing of documents are some of the elements that a suitable compliance program must address.

Given the procedures, it is very important to monitor the respect of the rules and to punish every violation. In this case, for example, the judge considered that the procedures should be more specific in the following areas: participation in competitive tenders, relations with public officers, execution of contracts, documentation of money flows in relation to public officers, and selection of workers. The person responsible for these risky operations must be individuated, in order to specify that the rules of the program fall under his responsibility and supervision.

1. *Supervisory board.* The judge regarded as positive some elements of the compliance program adopted by the company, especially those points which concerned the supervisory board:

- The compliance program required that the members of the supervisory board be independent, professional, and well respected. There must be three or more of them, and include the head of internal audit, while the others should be external to the corporate organization.
- The supervisory board must adopt rules for its own activity which are approved by the board of directors. Its members must have power of control and investigation, but not the powers to direct the corporation, modify its structure, or punish its workers.
- The supervisory board acts in cooperation with other corporate bodies, especially with ones which operate in the areas of risk. Its members can ask for information, require the exhibition of documents, and should constantly receive information from the managers in the areas of risk.
- The supervisory board can suggest that disciplinary measures be applied.
- The supervisory board helps the head of human resources with the preparation of training courses on the respect of compliance programs.
- The supervisory board suggests updates to the compliance program if there are any changes in corporate structure or law.
- Every 6 months, the supervisory board sends the board of directors and the other formal bodies of the corporation a report on its activity and informs the president of the board in case of the emergence of crimes.

Although the judge evaluated the above elements as positive, he stated that they were not sufficient to make a compliance program suitable. The compliance program must specify what is required of the members of the supervisory board in terms of professionalism. It must require specific experience in investigation and consulting. It must also be set down that a person cannot become a member of the body if he has been convicted in a previous sentence (not only the definitive ones, but also the ones which are not definitive and the pretrial agreement as well) for crimes already committed, or in case the person has been disqualified from managing public or private offices. Moreover, the members of the supervisory board should not have operative or directive roles in the corporation or in the corporate group. For example, in this case a member of the supervisory board of a corporation was also on the board of directors of another company of the group: this fact was considered a negative element.

2. *Reporting*. In the case in question, the compliance programs stated an obligation for employees and directors to report any suspicions of violation to the supervisory board. But the judge said that it is important also to introduce disciplinary measures in case of violation of this specific obligation.
3. *Disciplinary measures*. On this topic, the judge underlined some missing elements in the compliance program:

- The compliance programs must contain disciplinary measures, with specific indication of the conduct that determines the punishment.

- Different measures, such as economic sanctions, revocation of the power of attorney, and, in the worst cases, revocation of appointment, can be imposed on directors.
- A disciplinary measure should be present which punishes the director in case he fails to supervise the workers properly.

4. *Training*. The compliance programs must impose on all workers training courses which are tailored to the specific area in which they work, especially in areas of risk. Particular training programs must be imposed on the members of the supervisory board and of the internal audit committee.

The training courses must be well organized. Their contents, the number of lessons, the compulsory attendance regime, and system for monitoring the level and quality of participation must be defined in the compliance program.

The rules set in this case are a kind of enhancement of the Decalogo 231, and certainly comprise a reference point for corporations in elaborating their programs.

19.3.4 Decision of 17 November 2009, Court of Milan[9]; Decision of 21 March 2012, Court of Appeal of Milan[10]

The Court of Milan decision of 17 November 2009 is the first case in which a corporation has seen acquittal due to a suitable compliance program. For the first time, a decision of an Italian Court excluded the liability of the corporation because—before the offense was committed—it had adopted and effectively implemented an "organization and management model" (the compliance program) suitable to prevent the offense actually charged. Recently, the Court of Appeal of Milan confirmed this judgment, with a decision in favor of the suitability of the corporation's compliance program.

The case concerns an offense of market abuse (false statements to the financial market). Even though the offense was actually committed by its president and the director, the company was exempted from liability. Its structural culpability was excluded because the compliance program was effective to prevent the kind of crime actually committed. The culprits, in fact, had eluded the internal procedures and the control system. In other words, they had not followed the standard procedures.

It was proven that the program adopted was not only formally compliant with the standards of Decree no. 231/2001, but also contained specific measures to prevent the conduct of market abuse. Moreover, the compliance program was adopted in accordance with the Confindustria[11] Guidelines, as approved by the Italian Ministry of Justice.[12]

---

[9] The decision is published on *Foro padano*, 2010, 2, I, 360.

[10] The decision is published on www.rivista231.it.

[11] Confindustria is the most important industrial association in Italy.

[12] Sect. 6, paragraph 3, D. Lgs. 231/2001.

After having determined the compliance with the decree, the judge stated that the management had adopted the compliance program before the offense was committed; the responsibility for the monitoring of the program and for its updating had been assigned to a supervisory board with specific skills and with suitable powers to make decisions and to monitor it; an information flow from and to the supervisory board had been implemented; and the compliance program was effective as implemented, as it had been incorporated into the company procedures and in its internal control systems.

It was seen as positive that the corporation had been law-compliant even before Decree no. 231/2001 had been passed. In fact, corporate governance and the internal audit procedures were both based on the principles stated by the Self-discipline Code of Borsa Italiana S.p.A. and this is considered as a signal of the existence of a culture of compliance within the organization.

It is important to underline that the court admits exemption from corporate liability even when a compliance program is not formally adopted. In fact, one of the criminal conducts dates back to just before the compliance program was adopted, but the corporation was nevertheless found not guilty because it had systems in place suitable to prevent the offense of market abuse.

In other words, no matter what name is given to the compliance program (ethics code, self-discipline code, organization and management model, corporate governance model, etc.), a corporate organization which meets all the requirements of Decree no. 231/2001 can be excluded from corporate liability. In the present case, the decisions stated that the compliance program and the internal procedures, if observed, could have avoided the offense. The company, in fact, was able to demonstrate that preventive measures specifically directed to avoid the conduct of market abuse had been set up in its compliance program and implemented in the organizational and control system. In particular, the company had adopted an internal procedure to manage external communications. This procedure required the participation, in the decision-making process and in the management of information and data, of several individuals working in different areas, including the accounting office and the communications department. These competent offices had, as a matter of fact, prearranged the relevant press release on the basis of real accounting and financial data. The president and the director fraudulently eluded this internal procedure, deciding—independently and in a covert manner—to change the content of the press release and to communicate false and incomplete statements and data to the market.

On one hand, if the directors had respected the compliance program—the court believed—it would have been impossible to commit the crime. On the other, although the crime was committed, we cannot automatically affirm that the compliance program was not suitable to prevent that crime. Otherwise, in case of crimes, no corporation could ever avoid liability. It is important to highlight that no compliance program and no supervisory board can, in every time and every place, exclude the commission of fraud.

19.3.5 Decisions of April 2004, Court of Milan[13]

The decision (*ordinanza*) in favor of the application of a disqualification measure passed by the judge of the preliminary investigation of Milan, and the decision passed by the Court of Milan with reference to the case involving a multinational energy corporation, both adopted in April 2004, are relevant for two reasons. First, these rulings are among the few cases of corruption which involve energy companies; second, the court found that the corporation's compliance program was fragmentary and incomplete.

The judge of the preliminary investigation ordered the application of precautionary measures consisting in a prohibition from entering into contracts with the public administration for 1 year. The measure was then confirmed by the court competent for the precautionary measures.

The two judges, both focused on the corporation's compliance programs and the concomitant adoption of measures, concluded that the corporation's failure to implement an effective compliance program led to its becoming an instigator of or an accomplice to the corruption.

The Italian judicial authorities used the standards elaborated by Confindustria in March 2002 as well as the US Sentencing Guidelines to identify failures in the compliance program. The compliance program was judged as not suitable because it allowed the participation of a third party in the distribution chain to hinder controls on and individualization of the sources of payment, and because the misconducts (the illegal payments and commissions) were frequent and not occasional, and were made at the managerial level by the same persons.

Furthermore, the preexistence of funds available for and used to commit the offense made the compliance program ineffective, not only because the bodies charged with the task of verifying law enforcement did not do anything when the offense was detected (in the words of the US Sentencing Guidelines, they evinced passiveness with regard to misconduct and lack of oversight with respect to the implementation and effectiveness of the compliance and ethics program), but also because the *modus operandi* of misconduct was reinforced by the creation of slush funds.

The lack of modification of the compliance program after detecting criminal misconduct is one of the most important points raised in this case, and it is even more significant given that many months had passed since the misconduct was detected and no remedial actions or revisions of the compliance program were enacted (in the words of the US Sentencing Guidelines, "after criminal conduct has been detected, the organization shall not take reasonable steps to respond appropriately to the criminal conduct and to prevent further similar criminal conduct"). In this regard, the corporation did not take any remedial actions such as disciplinary actions; nor did it implement training systems, set incentives to perform in accordance with laws (disciplinary sanctions), conduct risk assessments, or open up channels

[13] The decisions are published on www.rivista231.it.

of information inside the corporation, etc. (according to the US Sentencing Guidelines: conduction of effective training programs, communication of its standards and procedures, etc.). Furthermore, it did not plan which financial resources should be devoted to preventing criminal offenses, nor how many. Last but not the least, the improper recording of certain funds was highlighted.

The corporation did not establish any appropriate standards and procedures to detect and prevent criminal misconduct under the terms provided by Italian law. The mere fact of having a generic ethics code (also known as Business Conduct Guidelines) designed to inspire employees' conduct is not enough, even though Italian courts leave a large margin of discretion for companies to determine what specific actions are necessary to respect those general requirements provided by law or other guidelines.

19.3.6 Other Decisions

The decisions analyzed above are the richest in terms of indications about what a compliance programs should have or should not have. However, there are some other interesting decisions which should be noted. One of the most recent is the decision by the Court of Appeal of Milan of 7 February 2012,[14] in a case involving a bank charged with the crime of market abuse and posing an obstacle to the activity of a public authority, committed by the chief executive officer and the chief financial officer. Confirming the first instance ruling, the Court of Appeal convicted the bank on the grounds that the crime committed by its managers was a direct expression of the corporate policy and because the bank had not adopted or implemented any compliance program apt to prevent the crimes actually committed.

The court affirmed that even if a compliance program did not exist, the corporation's liability could be evaluated by looking at the facts of the way it is organized. In this case, the bank's organizational structure was found lacking as regards measures and instruments relevant to evaluating criminal risks. Furthermore, the corporation did not have an appropriate governance system for defining the roles and duties of the managers, nor a body which could oversee the manager's activities. For these reasons, the commission of the crimes was possible and the corporation was convicted.

As mentioned above, most of the interesting decisions are passed during the preliminary investigations in order to verify whether the corporation warrants a precautionary measure. Among these, a notably relevant judgment is the one passed by the judge of the preliminary investigations of Rome, 4 April 2003,[15] concerning a corporation charged with corruption. In this case, after the commission of the crime, the corporation asked for and obtained the dismissal of the president of the holding

[14] The decision is published on www.penalecontemporaneo.it.

[15] The decision is published on Foro it., 2004, II, 317 and Riv. trim. dir. pen. economia, 2004, 293.

company, and adopted a compliance program.[16] The judge stated that it is important to evaluate the suitability of the compliance program adopted by the corporation, engaging an expert advisor if necessary. This evaluation is necessary in order to verify whether the company's structure is well organized. In this way, the application of a precautionary disqualification measure can be avoided. In the judge's opinion, the evaluation of a compliance program adopted after the commission of the crime is different from the evaluation of one adopted before. In the first case, the evaluation must be more penetrating and must consider the conditions that made the commission of the crime possible—not only in hypothetical terms—but concretely. It is stated by the National Association of Building Contractor's Guidelines (this being the corporation's area of business in this case) that, in relation to the adoption of compliance programs, it is important to focus on participation in competitive tendering and the execution of related public works, as well as possible areas of committing crimes. The corporation's new compliance program contains a kind of self-restriction regarding participation in competitive tenders for contracts in public works: the participation is allowed only if it falls under Law no. 109/94 (the "Merloni" law). The compliance program demands clarity in relations with public officers and bans information exchange with other competitors in the tender. Another risk area is related to the restrictions on subcontracting in public works: a suitable compliance program must ban subcontracting to corporations of the same group. Moreover, according to the judge, the supervisory board must have effective power to monitor the violations of the program, and its members must not also be members of the board of directors of other relevant corporate bodies. It must be stated that there is a duty to report any suspicions of violation of the compliance program to the supervisory board. Every payment must be approved in written form, according to internal rules as well as to tax law. It would also be appropriate to require a stated majority of the vote among the board of directors in order to amend the compliance program. The judge imposed the appointment of a special administrator on the corporation as a precautionary measure.

A point often underlined by the Italian courts in their decisions concerning corporate responsibility is the role of ethics codes in relation to the compliance programs required by Decree no. 231/2001. In its decision of 20 March 2007,[17] the Court of Milan convicted a corporation of corruption and, in this case, no compliance program had been adopted before the crime was committed. After the commission of the crime, the corporation adopted an ethics code, but the court considered this insufficient to avoid conviction. Even though the court did not refer to the formal adoption of the compliance programs, the corporation had not demonstrated that it had an organizational structure suitable for the prevention of crimes.

[16] Another decision evaluated as positive the dismissal of the legal representative in a corporation charged with the crime of instigation of corruption committed by him. In the decision of 4 November 2002, the judge of the preliminary hearing of Pordenone convicted the corporation but reduced the amount of the financial measure because a compliance program suitable to prevent future crimes had been adopted and effectively implemented.

[17] The decision is published on Giur. www.rivista231.it.

In a decision of 15 April 2011,[18] the Crown Court of Turin convicted a corporation of manslaughter in an industrial accident. The corporation was charged with an offense regulated by Section 25^{septies} of Decree no. 231/2001, because the legal representative committed the crime in the interests of the company, or at least to its benefit. No compliance program had been adopted by the corporation before 6 December 2007; a compliance program was, however, adopted afterwards, but it did not contain any protocol equal to preventing the crime with which the corporation was charged. As in the preceding case, the court did not refer to the formal adoption of the compliance program, but at least required a demonstration that the corporate organization was suitable to prevent crimes.

On this topic, the decision of 26 October 2004 passed by the judge of the preliminary hearing of Lucca is very interesting.[19] In this case, the top managers of the corporation corrupted the town mayor in order to obtain favors with respect to some measures concerning urban planning. No compliance program was adopted before the crime was committed; after the commission of the crime, however, the corporation adopted an ethics code which contained a kind of generic compliance program. The judge said that, according to the law, the suitability of the programs must be evaluated only on paper, in a theoretical and abstract manner. Accordingly, the judge reduced the amount of the financial measure and excluded the imposition of disqualification.

Instead, in the decision of 11 December 2006 passed by the Court of Milan,[20] the corporation was charged with corruption in participating in and winning a competitive tender. No compliance program was adopted before the crime was committed. After the commission of the crime, the corporation adopted an ethics code following the National Register of Building Contractors. The court reduced the amount of the financial measure because the compliance program was considered suitable to prevent future crimes.

19.4 Conclusion

As shown in the previous paragraphs, the international policy on anticorruption has changed its face, affecting both the legal and the reputational liability of companies for acts of bribery. If, previously, prevention was prominently a matter for law-enforcement agencies, today the private sector is called upon to play a more direct role. For this reason, companies both large and small are swamped by rules and guidelines emanating from various institutions and trade associations, while at the same time they are under the scrutiny of different country authorities as never before (for example the UN, OECD, GRECO (Council of Europe Anti-Corruption Group), and WGB (OECD Working Group on Bribery)).

[18] The decision is published on www.rivista231.it.

[19] The decision is published on www.rivista231.it.

[20] The decision is published on www.rivista231.it.

The huge and unprecedented legal production both in domestic and international legal systems has created high expectations for the possibility of tackling the plague of corruption. Nevertheless, the rate of bribery scandals is not likely to diminish, even though corporations are exposed to the risk of colossal, or even lethal, sanctions and losses if they fail to prevent the commission of misconduct.

Institutions must fight against corruption because the interests at stake are of primary importance: the stability and growth of economic systems, integrity of democracy, protection of the economic and human capital generated by commercial enterprises, and social justice and fair competition as bases on which to promote investment and development. We must not forget that European corporate law was born to prevent international corruption and, more deeply, to seek for fair competition rulings between corporations in the global market.

Sustaining a virtuous network between crime prevention, fair competition, and the observance of rules is a strategy of fundamental importance for governments. There is therefore an urgent need for assessment and revision in order to clarify the role played by the private sector in this field, and to make it definite and—above all—effective. But this requires that the rules and domestic legislation be homogeneous (Severino 2012, p. 427). More than hard legislation, soft law in this field has a strong appeal to corporations and could encourage them to invest the relevant assets into compliance.

Today, the deregulation model is realizing itself with the introduction of compliance programs that are more flexible than the ones used in the past. The rulings analyzed in this chapter are not only a helpful guide for the elaboration of compliance programs, but are also useful to determine whether an extant compliance program is well elaborated and effective.

The Italian experience shows that this is a system of responsibility based heavily on what has gone before in other parts of the world, and which is characterized by openness to models already tried elsewhere. It is a system that, again in the light of Italy's experience, has distinguished itself by dint of its capacity to develop and, over time, has enjoyed increasingly widespread application. It is also a system which is helping to fuel the debate on possible punitive models for entities.

In general terms, the Italian courts have affirmed that the adoption of an ethics code is not enough to avoid conviction, since such a document only provides for generic and theoretical rules. This is true also for a compliance program which only reproduces the law or other guidelines: the rules must be specific and contain substantial prescriptions. It is considered that compliance programs must be elaborated from an economic and substantive point of view and not from a merely legal/formal one. The last conclusion is strictly related to another issue: the importance of the prevention measures set forth in the compliance program, and of the internal procedures which implement the program. The judges have pointed out that effective prevention measures must be based on a selective and targeted process of risk assessment; both these elements have to be continuously monitored and updated, especially when an offense has been discovered or is being prosecuted. The importance of developing formal and specific procedures for the management of financial resources and the making and execution of corporate decisions is also underlined.

Every step of the decision-making process, in particular, must be accounted for in specific registers or documents.

When the courts analyze the effectiveness of compliance programs, they pay particular attention to the following elements: the supervisory board, the disciplinary system, the information reporting system, and the training programs. The composition and the powers of the supervisory board are often seen as key elements of the compliance program. All the members of the board must be independent and professional, and this feature means that none of the members should have operational duties in the company or in another entity belonging to the same corporate group. All the members of the supervisory board should also have professional duties and competencies to investigate and monitor the implementation of the compliance program. Furthermore, each member must be respected, and must prove that he has not previously been prosecuted or convicted. Case law also provides guidance on the supervisory board's powers and duties, and on information flows from and to the supervisory board. In particular, the Italian courts have stated that a suitable compliance program must impose, on employees and directors, a requirement to report any suspicions of violation to the supervisory board, and should explain how this reporting is to be done.

As a second issue, the decisions of the Italian courts have indicated which elements of the disciplinary system may impact upon the effectiveness of the compliance program. In some cases courts go into detail, stating, for example, that the compliance program should specify which kind of conduct should call for the application of a disciplinary measure, or that the compliance program should punish the violation of the obligation to report to the supervisory board an event that constitutes or may constitute a violation of the compliance program, or that violates the procedures established for its implementation.

Finally, all the relevant decisions pay particular attention to the training system: the contents, the number of lessons, the degree of compulsory attendance, and the oversight of participation are all key elements which contribute to the effectiveness of the compliance program.

Europe is going to move toward an integration of disciplinary systems; and so it seems that the challenge now is to develop an approach that actually takes account of the way models "circulate" in order to draw on common features. By analyzing best practices and the experience gained in applying the various systems, it will be possible to prepare the ground for setting out "model" guidelines.

References

Assumma, B. (2010). Il ruolo delle linee guida e della best pratice nella costruzione del modello di organizzazione e di gestione e nel giudizio di idoneità di esso. *Rivista, 231*(4), 193–200.

Bartolomucci, S. (2010). Il modello di organizzazione e gestione con finalità penal-preventiva. *Corriere Giuridico: IPSOA.*

Centonze, F. (2009). La co-regolamentazione della criminalità d'impresa nel D.Lgs. 231/2001. Il problema dell'importazione dei „compliance programs" nell'ordinamento italiano. *Analisi Giuridica dell'Economia, 2*, 219–242.

De Maglie, C. (2001). Principi generali e criteri di attribuzione delle responsabilità. *Diritto penale e processo, 11*, 1348–1352.

De Vero, G. (2001). Struttura e natura giuridica dell'illecito di ente collettivo dipendente da reato. Luci ed ombre nell'attuazione della delega legislativa. *Rivista italiana di diritto e procedura penale, 44*(4), 1126–1167.

De Vero, G. (2008). La responsabilità penale delle persone giuridiche. In F. G. Carlo et al. (Eds.), *Trattato di diritto penale*. Milano: Giuffré.

Di Giovine, O. (2005). Lineamenti sostanziali del nuovo illecito punitivo. In L. Giorgio (Ed.), *Reati e responsabilità degli enti. Guida al D.Lgs. 8 giugno 2001, n. 231*. Milano: Giuffré.

Giunta, F. (2009). Il reato come rischio d'impresa e la colpevolezza dell'ente collettivo. *Analisi Giuridica dell'Economia, 2*, 243–264.

Grillo, M. (2009). La teoria economica dell'impresa e la responsabilità della persona giuridica: considerazioni in merito ai modelli di organizzazione ai sensi del D.Lgs. 231/2001. *Analisi Giuridica dell'Economia, 2*, 205–217.

Lunghini, G., & Musso, L. (2010). I modelli di organizzazione ai sensi dell'art. 6, D.Lgs. n. 231/2001: un caso di assoluzione della società. *Il Corriere del Merito, 3*, 296–304.

Manacorda, S. (2012). Appunti sulle potenzialità e i limiti di applicazione territoriale delle norme in material di responsabilità degli enti. In F. Antonio et al. (Eds.), *Corporate criminal liability and compliance programs: First colloquium*. Napoli: Jovene.

Marinucci, G. (2007). La responsabilità penale delle persone giuridiche. Uno schizzo storico-dogmatico. *Rivista italiana di diritto e procedura penale, 50*(2–3), 445–469.

Mucciarelli, F. (2010). Una progettata modifica al d.lgs. n. 231/01: la certificazione del modello come causa di esclusione della responsabilità. *Le Società Rivista di diritto e pratica commerciale societaria e fiscale, 1247*.

Paliero, C. E., & Piergallini, C. (2006). La colpa di organizzazione. *Rivista, 231*, 167–184.

Pisani, M. (2006). La responsabilità amministrativa delle persone giuridiche: i modelli organizzativi. Fisco, *35*, 5422–5430.

Scaroina, E. (2006). *Il problema del gruppo di imprese. Societas delinquere potest*. Milano: Giuffré.

Severino, P. (2012). „Omogeneizzazione" delle regole e prevenzione dei reati: un cammino auspicato e possibile. In F. Antonio et al. (Eds.), *Corporate criminal liability and compliance programs: First colloquium*. Napoli: Jovene.

Stile, A. M. (2012). La natura giuridica della responsabilità dell'ente e i suoi rapporti con la responsabilità individuale. In F. Antonio et al. (Eds.), *Corporate criminal liability and compliance programs: First colloquium*. Napoli: Jovene.

Chapter 20
Corporate Responsibility and Compliance Programs in Australia

Marta Muñoz de Morales

Contents

20.1 Introduction

Australia is a federal system. Under the Australian Constitution, the Commonwealth has no legislative power in respect of general criminal law. Therefore, most criminal law in Australia is State law; however, Commonwealth law does provide for criminal offenses in respect to certain matters in which it does have legislative power.

M. Muñoz de Morales (✉)
University of Castilla-la-Mancha, Ciudad Real, Spain
e-mail: marta.mmorales@uclm.es

S. Manacorda et al. (eds.), *Preventing Corporate Corruption*,
DOI 10.1007/978-3-319-04480-4_20, © Springer International Publishing Switzerland 2014

Bribery of Commonwealth and foreign public officials are both federal offenses.[1] Furthermore, the Commonwealth Criminal Code (CCC) Part 2.5, and in particular Section 12.3(2), introduces provisions holding corporations directly liable for criminal offenses. There are also various provisions in individual federal statutes setting out models of corporate liability as they apply to particular offenses. This is the case, for example, of the Competition and Consumer Act 2010 (CCA, the former Trade Practices Act 1974) which will be discussed later on. At the state level, bribery of state foreign public officials is obviously also punished.[2]

20.2 Legal Acknowledgment of Compliance Programs

Since December 2001, the CCC has employed an organizational model of corporate criminal liability[3] in which concepts of due diligence, organizational blameworthiness, corporate culture, and enforced self-regulation through effective compliance programs, are meaningful.

The CCC provides for two kinds of models of corporate criminal liability: a model for offenses committed with negligence on one hand, and a model for offenses in which the mens rea is other than negligence (e.g., intent). Given the fact that bribery is an offense committed with intent, this contribution will focus on the latter model,[4] particularly in relation to its implications for compliance strategies.

Section 12.3 CCC makes companies criminally liable in circumstances where the organizational nature of a corporation directed, encouraged, tolerated, or led to the commission of an offense[5] (such as the bribery of foreign public officials).

---

[1] Bribery of a Commonwealth or foreign public official is a federal offence and, when committed by a body corporate, is punishable on conviction by a fine of up to whichever is the greatest of 100,000 penalty units (US$ 11 million), three times the value of benefits obtained as a result of the bribe, or 10% of the annual turnover. See "Commonwealth Criminal Code Act 1995," Australian Government, http://www.comlaw.gov.au/Series/C2004A04868, s. 70.2(5) "Bribery of a foreign public official" and 141.1 (6) "Bribery of a Commonwealth public official." Initially, the maximum penalty for a corporation was set at 30,000 penalty units. The 2010 Crime Legislation Amendment increased the fine and left the sanction as already mentioned. See "Crimes Legislation Amendment (Serious and Organised Crime) Act (No. 2) 2010," Australian Government, http://www.comlaw.gov.au/Details/C2010A00004, accessed 6 July 2013.

[2] For an overview of the regulation of corporate criminal liability in State criminal codes, see Wolff (2011, p. 11).

[3] The organizational model of corporate criminal liability is applied to all federal offenses save for those offenses created under acts retaining specific regimes of corporate responsibility.

[4] On the differences between the two models and how the model for negligent offenses is equivalent to a model based on an organizational failure, see Nieto Martín (2008, p. 132).

[5] Section 12.3 CCC: The fault elements of a criminal offence, insofar as they are attributed to a company, are achieved if the company "expressly, tacitly or impliedly authorised or permitted the commission of the offence." The "means" by which such an authorization or permission may be established include:

In addition, under Australian law, a company can be criminally liable where it can be proved "that a corporate culture existed within the body corporate that directed, encouraged, tolerated or led to non-compliance with the relevant provision" or that the company failed to create and maintain a "corporate culture"[6] that requires compliance with the law.[7] These provisions relating to "corporate culture" have significantly extended the scope for corporate criminal responsibility beyond the current position in common law,[8] and have been described as "the most sophisticated model of corporate criminal liability in the world" (Clough and Mulhern 2002, p. 138).

A definition of "corporate culture" is provided by the CCC itself: Any "attitude, policy, rule, course of conduct or practice existing within the body corporate generally or in the part of the body corporate in which the relevant activities takes place." Therefore, there is a connection between "corporate culture" and "blameworthiness" at an organizational level: The company is blameworthy if its practices and procedures are found to have contributed in some way to the commission of the offense.[9] To put it differently, the key issue is whether the organizational structure

---

"(a) proving that the body corporate board of directors intentionally, knowingly or recklessly carried out the relevant conduct, or expressly, tacitly or impliedly authorised or permitted the commission of the offence; or (b) proving that a high managerial agent of the body corporate intentionally, knowingly or recklessly engaged in the relevant conduct, or expressly, tacitly or impliedly authorised or permitted the commission of the offence; or (c) proving that a corporate culture existed within the body corporate that directed, encouraged, tolerated or led to non-compliance with the relevant provision; or (d) proving that the body corporate failed to create and maintain a corporate culture that required compliance with the relevant provision."

"Letter (b) does not apply if the body corporate proves that it exercised due diligence to prevent the conduct, or the authorisation or permission. Besides, in determining whether the relevant corporate culture of non-compliance existed or whether no corporate culture of compliance exists, a court may have regard to: (a) whether authority to commit an offence of the same or a similar character had been given by a high managerial agent of the body corporate; and (b) whether the employee, agent or officer of the body corporate who committed the offence believed on reasonable grounds, or entertained a reasonable expectation, that a high managerial agent of the body corporate would have authorised or permitted the commission of the offence."

[6] On the reasons why the organization model was based on "corporate culture," see Allens Arthur Robinson (AAR) report (2008, p. 11).

[7] For a commentary on the new provisions, see Leader-Elliott (2002, p. 231).

[8] As a rule, before 1995, corporate criminal liability followed the House of Lords decision in Tesco Supermarkets Ltd v. Nattrass, A.C., 153 (1972). That meant that corporate criminal liability was only attributed where mental and conduct elements could be traced to the board of directors, managing director, or someone to whom full management powers have been delegated. However, since 1995, the key issue has been whether the organizational structure of the corporation was such that the relevant act of noncompliance could occur at any level of the corporation, not only at a high level. See Hill (2003, p. 17) and Hill (2000, p. 16).

[9] This provision allows prosecutors to offer evidence that "the company's written rules tacitly authorised non-compliance or failed to create a culture of compliance. It would catch situations where, despite formal documents appearing to require compliance, the reality was that non-compliance was expected [f]or example, employees who know that if they do not break the law to meet production schedules (e.g., by removing safety guards or equipment), they will be dismissed. The company would be guilty of intentionally breaching safety legislation. Similarly, the corporate

of the corporation was such that the relevant act of noncompliance could occur at any level of the corporation and not only at a high level.

Section 12.3(4) of the CCC provides two relevant factors which determine whether or not a tainted corporate culture existed within the corporation. The first one focuses on the existence or nonexistence of the authority to commit an offense of the same or similar character by a high managerial agent of the corporate body. The second factor concerns whether the employee, agent, or officer of the corporate body who committed the offense had reasonable cause to believe or entertain an expectation that a high managerial agent of the corporate body would have authorized or permitted the commission of the offense. The issue here is to what extent "authority" could also include "hypothetical authorization," that is to say, those cases in which a high managerial agent simply turns a blind eye to criminal conduct (Brand 2000, p. 476, 480).

Between them, the above factors do not seem to provide an exhaustive numerus clausus, but rather offer somewhat simplistic examples, which have been criticized by legal scholars. For instance, it has been stated that "corporate culture" is "an extraordinarily wide and vague" concept (French 2003, p. 5) and "provide[s] little guidance to companies and their lawyers about what is required" (Parker 2002, p. 6). As such, it is left to judges to determine the existence of a corporate culture within the corporation. Some scholars have also pointed out that judges should pay attention to a corporation's failure to react ex post to the commission of an offense (Fisse 1991, p. 227; Fisse 1983, p. 1141; Fisse and Braithwaite 1993, p. 146). If this were the case, then specific corporate policies and programs for undertaking internal discipline or preventive reform adopted before the commission of the offense would become significant factors. *Sensu contrario,* for Fisse and Braithwaite, the company's general polices of compliance existing prior to the commission of the offense should be relegated to a lower priority in determining that a corporate culture existed within the corporation.

In the case of foreign bribery offenses, a corporation could be held criminally liable with respect to "bribes paid by any employee, if it can be shown that the practices and policies, which constituted its 'corporate culture', encouraged, tolerated, or at a minimum, did not discourage such conduct" (Hill 2000, p. 20; Hill 2003). It is not clear whether in such cases a demonstration of culpability based on corporate culture alone is enough, or whether it is also necessary to prove that a particular agent of the corporation actually acted with the requisite mens rea.

To determine the "corporate culture," courts may take into account both the specific corporate policies and programs for undertaking internal discipline or preventive reform, and/or the "corporation's 'unwritten rules' and employment expectations, if these are at odds with formal documentation" (Hill 2000, p. 20).

culture may tacitly authorise reckless offending (for example, recklessly disregarding the substantial and unjustifiable risk of causing serious injury by removing the equipment guards). The company would be guilty of a reckless endangerment offence." See Explanatory Memorandum to the Criminal Code Bill 1994. Commonwealth of Australia Explanatory Memoranda, 7.126 http://www.austlii.edu.au/au/legis/cth/bill_em/ccb1994125/memo_0.html. Accessed 6 July 2013.

Indeed, courts can also establish a culpable corporate culture if it can be shown that the corporation tolerated or encouraged bribery in the private sector (Brand 2000, p. 476). Therefore, if a corporation wants to avoid criminal sanctions for bribes committed by its employees, it will have to show not only that it has in place an "effective anti-bribery compliance system" (Hill 2000, p. 16)[10] but also that its compliance system has been maintained and enforced (Hill 2000, p. 20; Hill 2003, p. 21). To put it differently, under Australian law, the existence of compliance programs can be taken into account as a defense exempting the corporation from criminal liability (Baxt 2001, p. 4). However, taking into account what happens in other breaches of law (such as competition law), compliance programs are likely to play a more important role in the sentencing phase as a mitigating factor.

In any case, the key question is what constitutes an effective compliance program. In general terms, "effective" means compliance programs which are updated and properly enforced or implemented. But by what standards should this updating and enforcement be judged? The first problem we come upon is that there is a lack of case law on bribery cases. Relatively, few investigations[11] and prosecutions[12] into bribery have ever been carried out, and of these, the number of investigations and prosecutions against corporations is even smaller.[13] That has led to criticisms of Australia's enforcement of its international obligations (Heimann and Dell 2009, p. 18; Heimann and Dell 2010, p. 19). However, this lack of prosecutions against corporations and the resultant paucity of case law are unsurprising in the case of foreign bribery. The general tendency in Australia is that whatever the criminal

[10] In the same sense, see Belcher (2007, p. 18): "Corporate responsibility for failing to create and maintain a corporate culture that requires compliance with the relevant provision…is likely to encourage companies to institute compliance programs and to give them importance."

[11] As of June 2008, the Australia Federal Police had conducted only six foreign bribery cases. See OECD (2006, p. 3). In fact, the first charges were not laid until 2011, over a decade after the foreign bribery offence was enacted (see Barker 2012, p. 8). According to Wee (2012, p. 372), Australia has launched nearly 200 investigations for the period between 2000 and 2004, but it is not clear whether these 200 investigations refer both to domestic bribery offences and foreign bribery. He also points out that the number of investigations launched after the year 2004 is unclear, as shown by the lack of information in the Australian Federal Police (AFP)'s annual reports.

[12] According to the last report of the Office of the Commonwealth Director of Public Prosecutions (CDPP), the number of Criminal Code 1995 charges dealing with bribery and related offences in 2011–2012 was only 6. The number was not much higher in 2010–2012 (9 charges). Nevertheless, it was a little bit higher in 2009–2010 (15 charges). See "Annual Reports 2011–2012, 2010–2011, 2009–2010," Commonwealth Director of Public Prosecutions (CDPP), http://www.cdpp.gov.au/Publications/Annual-Reports/, accessed 6 July 2013.

[13] For instance, in 2005, the AFP investigated two Australian companies for bribing officials in Bangladesh and the Democratic Republic of Congo. See "Annual Report 2005–2006," AFP, http://www.afp.gov.au/media-centre/publications/annual-reports.aspx, accessed 6 July 2013. In 2006, AWB was also under investigation, followed by civil action as will be explained later in this chapter. Investigations have been also carried out in relation to Woodside Petroleum, a firm supposed to have paid bribes to the former Mauritanian oil minister Zeidane Ould H'Meida for oil exploration. See Wee (2012, p. 373), and Barker (2012, p. 10). Unfortunately, the CDPP Annual Report (2011–2012) does not indicate how many corporations were prosecuted.

offense, most prosecutions are of individuals, not corporations. The provisions for "corporate culture" apply only to the Criminal Code Act 1995, and not to other Commonwealth statutes; most prosecutions of corporations occur (as highlighted below) under other statutes, such as the Australian Securities and Investments Commission Act 2001 and the CCA.

At the federal level, the first Australian prosecutions for foreign bribery were initiated on 1 July 2011. The prosecution was against seven individuals for bribery of foreign officials and two Australian companies, Securency International Pty. Ltd. and Note Printing Australia (NPA) Ltd. (Australian Federal Police 2011). The charges related to the bribes allegedly paid to public officials in Indonesia, Malaysia, and Vietnam between 1999 and 2005. Senior managers from Securency and NPA stood accused of using international sales agents to bribe foreign public officials in order to secure bank note contracts. One of the accused, chief financial officer David Ellery, pleaded guilty to one charge of false accounting.[14] He admitted to concealing a US$ 79,502 payment to a Malaysian agent, saying that the money was a reimbursement for "marketing expenses." The method employed to divert sums of money for bribery was in this case an extremely popular one: that is, the use of the company's financial resources to cover apparently legitimate expenses.[15] The judgment makes it perfectly clear that the offender was "acting within the culture which seems to have developed within Securency, whereby staff were discouraged from examining too closely the use of, and payment arrangements for, overseas agents" and also that "secrecy, and a denial of responsibility for wrongdoing…seem to have been part of the corporate culture at Securency at that time" (at 28).

In relation to Securency and NPA, both companies entered pleas on 27 October 2011 at the Melbourne Magistrate's Court[16] to three charges each of bribing or conspiring to bribe foreign officials in order to obtain a business advantage.[17] Six months later, the Australian Securities and Investment Commission (ASIC) decided not to prosecute Securency for securities offenses, such as the breach of fiduciary duty by company directors (Australian Securities & Investments Commission 2012). Both companies remain under investigation for possible corruption offenses in Vietnam, Indonesia, Malaysia, and Nigeria.

Securency and NPA's plea agreements are not publicly available. Despite this, it is possible to use this case to highlight one of the most predominant and recurrent causes of failure in an effective compliance program: the failure to exercise due diligence prior to engaging third-party business partners. Both companies are

[14] The Queen v. David John Ellery, Supreme Court of Victoria, at Melbourne Criminal Division, 20 August 2012.

[15] On methods to collect sums for bribery see in this book Dell'Osso, "Empirical Features of International Bribery Practice: Evidence from FCPA Enforcement Actions," in this volume.

[16] Neither plea agreement is available to the public.

[17] See TRACE International, *The Trace Compendium–Note Printing Australia Limited*, 2, https://www.traceinternational2.org/compendium/pdf.asp?id=414, accessed 6 July 2013.

subsidiaries of the Reserve Bank of Australia.[18] In the wake of an investigation by Australian journalists into individuals employed by the Reserve Bank of Australia companies to win contracts abroad,[19] it was found that one of those people was corrupt:

> I simply Googled it and found out he was charged with corruption in Africa, and convicted. And that's one of many breakthroughs. We said: "Wow the Reserve Bank of Australia is employing a guy that is corrupt, convicted in court, to work for us. As journos, we'd just done a Google search and found out, how can they not know that?" Now of course they knew it. The reason they were going to employ the guy was because he was going to pay bribes. And to this day the question remains: where was the Reserve Bank of Australia's due diligence? It appears to have been non-existent….How come [the Reserve Bank] didn't know, how come [it] didn't know what was going on? (Vatsikopoulous et al. 2012, p. 32).

The journalist goes on to explain why it is highly likely the Reserve Bank was aware of the agent's history:

> Particularly because they get a list every year—the board of Securency and Note Printing Australia. They would get a list of the agents and how much money they were getting paid, and often where they were getting paid. So it's mind-boggling to think that this went on, and the claims of ignorance are pretty incredible really. (Vatsikopoulous et al. 2012, p. 33)

The lack of Australian case law related to foreign bribery could mean, as some scholars have pointed out (Wyld 2010, p. 13), either that Australian corporations and individuals do not bribe foreign public officials or that Australia conceals its involvement in bribery and corruption of foreign officials. In my opinion, the situation is more complicated than this and cannot be reduced to these two possibilities. The Australian authorities had tried to prosecute cases of foreign bribery prior to the Securency and NPA cases. The 2009 Rio Tinto bribery scandal is just one example of this. Rio Tinto's top executives were accused of accepting bribes on iron ore trades with China. One of them, Stern Hu, was a Chinese-born Australian citizen and was the Shanghai-based head of Rio Tinto's iron ore operations in China. He allegedly accepted bribes amounting to ¥ 1.5 million and was further accused of stealing commercial secrets. He was found guilty by the Shanghai courts of taking bribes and stealing trade secrets, and was sentenced to 10 years in prison.[20] Australia failed to prosecute Stern Hu for his actions because the offense did not fall within the scope of the Organisation for Economic Co-operation and Development (OECD) Convention:

> The obligation to prosecute the bribery offence under Article 5 of the OECD Convention only applies where a person offers a bribe to another. In this instance, Stern Hu accepted the bribes instead of offering the bribes to a foreign public official. Prima facie, there is no offence falling within the ambit of Article I of the OECD Convention and accordingly, there cannot be an offence under section 70.2 of the Bribery Act. However, the scope of a

[18] Securency is 50 % owned by the Reserve Bank of Australia: it makes plastic metal. NPA prints money and is 100 % owned.

[19] This investigation was carried out by Richard Baker and Nick McKenzie. See Vatsikopoulous et al. 2012.

[20] See Muñoz de Morales, "Corporate Responsibility and Compliance Programs in China," in this volume.

> foreign bribery offence under the United Nations Convention against Corruption (UNCAC) is slightly different to the OECD Convention in that UNCAC also places an obligation upon States to punish those who accept bribes. As such, we can conclude that while Australia may be obliged to prosecute Stern Hu for accepting bribes under UNCAC, it has in fact, acted in accordance with its obligation to prosecute under Article 5 of the OECD Convention. (Wee 2012, p. 388)[21]

An additional hindrance is that Australian legislation does not allow a parent company to be liable for the actions of its subsidiaries, joint venture partners, or agents (Heimann and Dell 2010, p. 13). This prevented Australia from prosecuting Rio Tinto for the actions of its subsidiary Chinese company in the 2009 Rio Tinto bribery scandal, and also prevented Australian prosecutors from charging the Australian Reserve Bank for acts committed by its subsidiaries, Securency and NPA.

A further issue is that corporate liability cannot be established under the organizational provisions of the CCC unless there is also the conviction of an individual.[22]

A last barrier to criminal prosecutions has been the defense provided under Section 70.3 of the CCC. This defense allows an exemption to the bribery offense where the conduct is lawful in the foreign public official's country.

In Iraq, bribes are not known to be expressly illegal. This can be deduced from the Cole's (2006) inquiry into the payments made by the Australian Wheat Board (AWB) to secure the sale of Australian wheat. The AWB was a government body until 1999, when it was transformed into a private company owned by wheat growers. The AWB was the only Australian buyer of wheat. In late 2005, it was alleged that AWB had knowingly paid kickbacks to the Iraqi government, defrauding the United Nations (UN) and violating sanctions. The UN had, in the period from 1996 to 2003, operated an "Oil for Food" program which was set up to help Iraqis facing hardship due to UN sanctions. Under this program, Iraq was allowed to sell oil in order to buy humanitarian goods like wheat. AWB's internal investigation, entitled "Project Rose," revealed that trucking fees paid to the Jordanian trucking company Alia varied from US$ 12 to 47.75 per tonne for shipments of wheat within Iraq between July 1999 and December 2002.[23] These bribery payments to the Iraqi government were investigated in the Victorian Supreme Court, where Mr. Lindberg, the former AWB chief executive, and Mr. Ingleby, the former chief financial officer, faced civil charges. Mr. Lindberg agreed to admit to contraventions of the Corporations Act and accept civil sanctions (a fine of AU$ 100,000 and disqualification

---

[21] Another reason was that Australia had no jurisdiction to prosecute Stern Hu for his actions.

[22] See Allens Arthur Robinson report (2008, p. 16): "In circumstances in which it is difficult to prosecute an individual, either because the individual is not identifiable, or is out of the jurisdiction, or for some other reason, it is not clear how the provisions might operate."

[23] The Jordanian company was a shell company used by the Iraqi government. AWB was exporting wheat to the Iraqi Grain Board (IGB), and their contract included a provision whereby a "trucking fee" was added to the CIF price paid by IGB. AWB then paid the trucking fee to a Jordanian trucking company nominated by IGB. See TRACE International, *The Trace Compendium—Australian Wheat Board*, https://www.traceinternational2.org/compendium/view.asp?id=145, accessed 6 July 2013.

from managing corporations until 15 September 2014).[24] Mr. Ingleby also accepted a fine of AU$ 40,000 and was disqualified as a director for 15 months.[25]

So far, no criminal charges for bribery have been laid against any AWB executives[26] or the corporation itself.[27] Criminal investigations were halted on 28 August 2009 because the Victoria Police did not anticipate any likelihood of success. One of the reasons for their pessimism may have been that these payments were permissible because they were not expressly illegal under Iraqi law; this fact would have constituted a defense to any accusations of bribery (see Section 70.3 CCC; Buckley and Danielson 2008, p. 92; Wee 2012, p. 374). Fortunately, since the 2006 Cole inquiry, Section 70.3 CCC makes such a defense available only where there is a written law in force, either in the foreign country or in the place where the headquarters or central administration of a public organization is located, which permits bribery (Australian Government 2007). This means that law enforcement in such cases should be easier in the future.

Despite the lack of a criminal judgment on the AWB case, legal scholars have made efforts to deduce what failed in the AWB corporate culture. The first failure refers to the term "tone at the top" (Schwartz et al. 2005; Schroeder 2002, p. 260; Joseph 2002, p. 107; Vitell et al. 2000, p. 15). From this perspective, there was a failure within the organization's leadership to promote an ethical atmosphere in the workplace. To put it another way, the fact that corporate managers appeared unconcerned with ethics and focused solely on the bottom line led employees to be more prone to commit contraventions of the company's compliance program and to feel that ethical conduct was not a priority within the corporation. In the AWB case, the corporation had, of course, established ethical guidelines that prohibited the payment of bribes, but these were ignored by senior employees. The company's culture focused on maximizing returns to wheat growers. One of AWB's former employees, Mark Rowland, said in a statement to the Cole Inquiry:

> There was certainly a culture of pushing the business of AWB as far as possible for the highest return. My perception was that on occasion, this might mean that the company moved into what some might describe as "grey areas," where the legality of the position adopted by AWB might be open to doubt. If the commercial imperative justified the position adopted, in my experience, the company adopted that position in order to vigorously protect its customers and markets from overseas competitors. All of AWB management, as far as I could discern, were driven to ensure that the company maximised its trading capacity on behalf of Australian wheat growers. (Exhibit 0009 AWB.5035.0337, quoted in Botterill 2007, p. 11)

[24] Australian Securities & Investments Commission [ASIC] v Lindberg [2012] VSC 332 (9 August 2012), available at http://www.austlii.edu.au/au/cases/vic/VSC/2012/339.html.

[25] Australian Securities & Investments Commission [ASIC] v Ingleby [2012] VSC 339 (10 August 2012), available at http://www.austlii.edu.au/au/cases/vic/VSC/2012/339.html.

[26] Mr. Lindberg could be the only one to face court proceedings over the secret payments.

[27] AWB agreed, in a settlement with its shareholders on February 15 2010, to pay AU$ 39.5 million for their losses on the company's kickbacks.

The first lesson to be learnt from this failure is that "a written set of guidelines [disapproving illegal payments and instructing employees not to make payments that were unethical] means nothing if it is not supported by the implicit signals from the board and the senior management" (Parker 2007, p. 30; quoted in Steytler 2010, p. 153). On the contrary, if there is "a clash between a code of conduct and an ingrained corporate culture, the latter is nearly certain to prevail" (Parker 2007).

A second lesson can be drawn from the failures resulting from a lack of monitoring or supervision. The corporate board neither questioned nor ensured oversight of management decisions. Indeed, AWB's board remained unaware of what had happened for a very long time, and when its suspicions were eventually aroused, took far too long to discover the truth (Steytler 2010, p. 137).

In addition, a lack of independence in the corporate board was also demonstrated. The majority of AWB's board included people with a background in wheat farming. It is, therefore, unsurprising that a culture of maximizing returns to wheat growers developed. As some authors have suggested, the board saw its role as working on behalf of Australian wheat exporters, and that is why its members "had no incentive to question their managers, so long as wheat kept being sold" (Bartos 2006, quoted in Parker 2007, pp. 28, 29). The affinity with growers is also supported by the fact that, "when put up for re-election on 23 February 2006, six of the directors who had been on the board during the period in which bribes of more than $ 300 million had been paid were re-elected" (Botterill 2007, 11, quoted in Steytler 2010, p. 140).

20.3 Seeking Guidance from Australian Jurisprudence on Nonbribery Cases

Given the lack of case law related to (foreign) bribery in Australia, research has been extended to other areas: mainly trade practices (particularly in relation to competition and consumer protection law). It should be noted that most cases analyzed in this chapter deal with strict liability offenses rather than mens rea offenses. Nevertheless, an analysis of such cases is relevant due to their use of an exculpatory concept directly linked to compliance issues: the defense of due diligence.

Under Section 44ZZ0 of the CCA[28] it is stated:

> Any conduct engaged in on behalf of a body corporate: (a) by a director, servant or agent of the body corporate within the scope of the person's actual or apparent authority; or (b) by any other person at the direction or with the consent or agreement (whether express or

[28] In January 2011, the Trade Practices Act 1974 (TPA) became the Competition and Consumer Act 2010 (CCA) (available at http://www.comlaw.gov.au/Details/C2011C00003). The new act repealed the TPA consumer protection provisions (unconscionable conduct, consumer protection and liability of manufacturers and importers for defective goods) and reenacted them in Schedule 2 devoted to Australian Consumer Law (ACL). As far as we are concerned, all the commentaries on the TPA and TPA case law are still applicable because the defense based on due diligence and the obligation of establishing a compliance program when a probation order is made by a court are also provided by the new acts.

> implied) of a director, servant or agent of the body corporate, if the giving of the direction, consent or agreement is within the scope of the actual or apparent authority of the director, servant or agent; is taken for the purposes of this Part to have been engaged in also by the body corporate, *unless the body corporate establishes that the body corporate took reasonable precautions and exercised due diligence to avoid the conduct.*

This defense covers cartel contraventions. The same is provided under Section 208 CCA devoted to Australian Consumer Law (ACL):[29]

> "(1) In a prosecution for a contravention of a provision of this Chapter, it is a defence if the defendant proves that: (b) the defendant took reasonable precautions and exercised due diligence to avoid the contravention". The Chapter covers a number of criminal offences i.e. unfair marketing practices, offences relating to product safety, product information, etc.[30]

Specific defenses related to compliance program issues (i.e., procedures to follow prior to embarking on any high-risk activity) are also provided under Section 76A CCA regarding contraventions of Section 95AZN (providing false or misleading information). The defense is applicable when "the contravention in respect of which the proceedings were instituted was due to reasonable reliance on information supplied by another person."

When such defenses are not successful (and this is what usually happens), compliance programs are taken into account in assessing the penalty as a mitigating or aggravating factor.

Last but not the least, courts may make "probation orders" pursuant to ensure corporations do not engage in the contravening conduct, similar conduct, or related conduct during the period of the order.[31] These "probation orders" may oblige corporations:

> to establish a compliance program for employees or other persons involved in the person's business, being a program designed to ensure their awareness of the responsibilities and obligations in relation to the contravening conduct, similar conduct or related conduct (a); and an order directing the person to establish an education and training program for employees or other persons involved in the person's business, being a program designed to ensure their awareness of the responsibilities and obligations in relation to the contravening conduct, similar conduct or related conduct (b); and an order directing the person to revise the internal operations of the person's business which lead to the person engaging in the contravening conduct (c).[32]

For instance, in *Australian Competition and Consumer Commission (ACCC)*[33] *v. Real Estate Institute of Western Australia Inc. & Drs.,* the court ordered the appointment

---

[29] See previous note.

[30] Chapter 4 ACL includes offenses relating to unfair practices (i.e., false or misleading representation about goods, services, sales; misleading conduct relating to employment; multiple prices; etc.); offenses related to consumer transactions (i.e., negotiating unsolicited consumer agreements); offences related to safety of consumer goods and product-related services (i.e., supplying consumer goods that do not comply with safety standards); and offenses related to information standards (i.e., supplying goods that do not comply with information standards).

[31] A "probation order" cannot be longer than 3 years (Section. 86C(2)(b) CCA and Section 246(2)(b) ACA).

[32] See Section. 86C(4) CCA and Section 246(2)(b)(i)(ii)(iii) ACA.

[33] The Australian Competition and Consumer Commission (ACCC) is a law-enforcement body whose primary responsibility is "to ensure that individuals and businesses comply with the Com-

of both internal and external compliance officers with the responsibility for maintaining and securing compliance, legal review of all business documentation, the establishment of an effective complaints handling system, four training sessions over 3 years in trade practices compliance, the dissemination of ACCC publications on compliance issues, annual audits of the program, detailed record keeping subject to review by the ACCC, and a best endeavors approach to comply with AS 3806[34].

The following sections will examine the role of compliance programs in case law related to competition breaches and also in other areas, such as discrimination and environmental protection.

20.3.1 "Reasonable Precautions" and "Due Diligence" Defenses in Competition Law[35]

20.3.1.1 As a Ground for Exemption from Liability

The defenses of "reasonable precautions," "due diligence," and "reasonable reliance on information supplied by another person," as they are provided under the CCA (Competition and Consumer Act), may be raised on the basis of the existence of compliance systems designed to avoid the kind of contravention that occurred. For instance, in *Gilmore v. Poole-Blunden,*[36] the corporate compliance program included a policy of obtaining legal advice prior to embarking on any high risk activities. The company successfully put forward the defense of "reasonable reliance on information supplied by another person" in relation to a charge of pyramid selling, having obtained legal advice sanctioning the conduct prior to undertaking the activity (Godfrey 2002, p. 24).

In practice, however, it is quite rare to be successful in maintaining a due diligence defense before courts; the general trend in the cases analyzed here is that such a defense is not usually accepted. Above all, it is considered inapplicable when there is evidence of a lack of supervision and control over the implementation of corporate policies (Fisse 1989; Shafron 1998). For instance, in *Universal Telecasters (Queensland) Ltd v. Guthrie,*[37] in which the broadcaster appealed against its conviction under s53(e) of the TPA 1974[38] in *Guthrie v. Doyle Dane & Bernbach*

monwealth competition, fair trading and consumer protection laws." See http://www.accc.gov.au/content/index.phtml/itemId/3744.

[34] For further examples, see Parker (1999, p. 183).

[35] To draw up this section, I have made use of the list and explanation of a number of cases provided by *Inhouse* at http://www.austlii.edu.au/.

[36] Gilmore v Poole-Blunden & Ors, No. SCGRG-98–1731, SCGRG-98–1732 Judgement No. S186 [1999] SASC 186 (12 May 1999), available at http://www.austlii.edu.au/.

[37] Universal Telecasters (Qld) Ltd v Guthrie [1978] FCA 9; (1978) 32 FLR 360 (4 April 1978), available at http://www.austlii.edu.au/.

[38] For a commentary on the case, see Davidson and Harkness (1979, p. 98).

Pty Ltd.,[39] the company was found to have falsely represented that tax savings on new car sales would end after a certain date.[40] In relation to the reasonable precautions taken and due diligence used by the corporation, the Federal Court of Australia (FCA) stated that:

> [I]n order to establish this defence, [it should be shown that Universal Telecasters] had laid down a proper system to provide against contravention of the Act and that it had provided adequate supervision to ensure that the system was properly carried out.[41]

The court found that Universal had established a proper system for "vetting advertisements" before they were televised and also that such a system had been adequately supervised. Particularly, it was shown that the general manager of the company provided instructions to the sales service manager in relation to the vetting of advertisements for compliance with the TPA prior to their being screened. Nevertheless, the court found failings in procedures for logging and responding to customer complaints after the commission of the contravention (that is to say, after the advertisement had been screened). In particular, the court held that although a system had been devised to deal with viewer complaints, it was not sufficiently rigorous, and further, there was no adequate supervision of it, stating:

> It is necessary to make a judgement about the system and the provision for supervision. The system of having advertisements checked by Mr. Yardley before transmission appears to have been basically a sound one, although it would have been stronger if it had not placed so much weight upon his mere personal knowledge and reaction to the advertisements which he viewed. However, I would not be prepared to hold that the system was defective in not requiring an advertisement, such as that in the present case, to be checked with the relevant government department or in not requiring the advertisement to be verified by the advertiser. The failure to provide a better system of dealing with telephone complaints made at the time, in the evening, when the advertisement was to be broadcast, raises a more difficult question. It is, in my opinion, not enough for Universal Telecasters to show that it had a careful system of vetting advertisements before it put them to air. In the case of advertisements which are to be broadcast during the evening period on more than one day, I think a proper system should include some procedure whereby a complaint made during this period that an advertisement is misleading or otherwise contravenes the Trade Practices

---

[39] *Guthrie v. Doyle Dane and Bernbach Pty Ltd* [1977] FCA 13; (1977) 30 FLR 116 (21 September 1977), available at http://www.austlii.edu.au/. In this case the Court held that the agency had not taken reasonable precautions or exercised due diligence sufficient to establish the defense. Further, it was held that whatever system the agency had implemented was not devised for the purposes of avoiding a contravention of the Act: "In addition to there having been no precautions taken there is also no evidence of the exercising of any diligence. The incidence of sales tax and the treasurer's intentions in relation to it are matters of public knowledge available to those who took the trouble to inquire. No reasonable explanation could be advanced as to why…the defendant company could not have made its own inquiries as to the incidence of sales tax and the duration of any sales tax cuts. There is no evidence of specific attention being given to avoiding contravention of Sect. 53(e) of the Act."

[40] The announcement made by Telecasters on prime-time viewing was: "Dr Jim's lovely tax cuts are guaranteed till only April 30…Metro Ford offer immediate delivery of automatic Falcon 500 sedans that save you $ 335.00. If you don't take delivery by April 30 you're up for an extra 335 bucks in tax."

[41] *Universal Telecasters (Qld) Ltd v. Guthrie, at 9.*

> Act will be referred promptly to an appropriate officer. No system had been established which made adequate provision for this. In this respect I think the company failed to make out the defence under s85(1).

An interesting point highlighted by this case is that even where the corporate system and supervision have been shown to be inadequate, this "does not necessarily" mean that the corporate system "is defective" because "even the best systems may break down due to human error."

In *Videon v. Barry Burroughs Pty. Ltd.,*[42] a case of misleading land sales brochures, there was no clear evidence whether or not the published brochure had been approved by the corporation before printing. The corporation, Beneficial Finance, argued that the due diligence defense provided by s85(1)(c) TPA was applicable to this case. However, the judge found that:

> [R]easonable precautions and due diligence were not taken by the officers of the State Branch in that they failed to carry out the instructions of Head Office to approve the brochure prior to printing. Such officers included the Branch Manager and the Real Estate Manager and it was not disputed that they were "core personnel" and, no limitation on their authority having been proved; they are "the company" for the purposes of such default.... Beneficial Finance laid down an effective procedure in an attempt to ensure that no misleading material appeared in its brochure. However it failed to supervise and "police" this procedure, in that it failed to take steps to ensure that the procedure was followed. By failing to ensure that a draft brochure was presented for approval and, when presented, approved and any misleading statements excised, Beneficial Finance has denied itself the benefit of the defence. It did not take reasonable precautions and it did not exercise due diligence to avoid the contravention.

Ali v. Hartley Poynton Ltd.[43] dealt with a claim against Hartley Poynton for improper trading on a client's discretionary account. The judge found that there was no proper supervision or control of the way in which the employee managing the account had carried out his trading activities, notwithstanding that the employer was aware the employee needed close supervision because of earlier misconduct. The judge considered that even though "a stockbroker employing brokers cannot supervise each dealing they make as they make it," he can, however, set down policies. It is true that the defendant had set down policies but they had not been properly enforced, nor checked from time to time:

> The compliance officer and Committee do not appear to have done anything effective to protect the interests of the clients. To promote itself publicly, in the way the defendant did, and to recognise the need for, and develop, policies which will address the rights and interests of clients but do nothing effective to enforce them, shows a contempt for the rights and interests of all clients. (§ 618 a)

---

[42] *Re John Graham Videon v. Barry Burroughs Pty. Ltd. v. Beneficial Leasing Pty. Ltd. v. Beneficial Finance Corporation Ltd.* [1981] FCA 168; (1981) 53 FLR; 425 (30 October 1981), available at http://www.austlii.edu.au/.

[43] *Ali v. Hartley Poynton Limited* [2002] VSC 113 (16 April 2002), available at http://www.austlii.edu.au/.

20.3.1.2 "Due Diligence" and "Reasonable Precautions" Defenses as Mitigating or Aggravating Factors in Determining the Penalty

Although it is very difficult to succeed in satisfying the requirements for "due diligence" or "reasonable precautions" defenses in court, the existence and enforcement of a compliance program may at least assist in mitigating the ultimate penalty that may be imposed. One of the first and most important cases in which a court took "corporate culture" and compliance programs into consideration as a factor in determining the level of penalties[44] was *Trade Practices Commission v. CSR Ldl. 1991.*[45] The offense under investigation was whether CSR, a building products company, had taken advantage of its market power over the supply of ceiling materials in an anticompetitive way. The corporation tried to prove the existence of a corporate culture of compliance, arguing that since 1980 it had retained a copy of the Guide to the Trade Practices Act for internal use and that its staff had attended seminars before the commission of the contravention in 1985. However, these two elements were judged to be insufficient by the court, mainly because the Guide had not been updated since it was introduced some 11 years earlier and because no staff training had been conducted since a seminar held some 6 years earlier. No indication of any corrective measures or revitalization of that program was offered in the wake of the discovery of the breach by the Australian Trade Practices Commission (now the ACCC) (at 48). The compliance program was, stated the FCA, "less than vigorous" (at 36). In short, the court highlighted the need for the periodic review and updating of compliance procedures.

More of the same was stated in *ACCC v. Rural Press Ltd.,*[46] but the court also added here that the company's undertaking to establish a proper compliance program after a breach was also a relevant factor in assessing penalties.[47]

In *ACCC v. Australian Safeway Stores Pty. Ltd.,*[48] the court underlined that compliance programs should be examined in two respects. Firstly, it is necessary to establish whether there had been a substantial compliance program in place at the time of the contravention. In this case there was: the compliance guide made quite clear that the Trade Practices Act could not be ignored and that "severe pecuniary penalties" would be involved if the act were contravened, and staff seminars had been conducted on the subject. Secondly, it is necessary to determine whether the compliance program had been successfully implemented. It was not so in this case:

---

[44] For an exhaustive list of case law in this regard, see Parker and Nielsen (2006, 446n18).

[45] *Trade Practices Commission v. CSR Limited* [1990] FCA 521; (1991) 13 Atpr 41–076 (20 December 1990), available at http://www.austlii.edu.au/.

[46] *ACCC v. Rural Press Ltd* (Includes Corrigendum dated 8 August 2001) [2001] FCA 1065 (7 August 2001). Available at http://www.austlii.edu.au/.

[47] Note that where assessing the penalties, courts have tended to focus more on whether the compliance system had been adequately reviewed (or a new compliance system had been implemented) after the discovery of the contravention, instead of analysing the type of the compliance program in place at the time of the breach. See Parker and Nielsen (2006, 446n17).

[48] *ACCC v. Australian Safeway Stores Pty Ltd & Ors* [1997] FCA 450 (30 May 1997), available at http://www.austlii.edu.au/.

> [A]ll [corporate] officers who participated in the contraventions were well aware, or ought to have been well aware from the documentation that they had received and seminars some had attended, that what they were doing was a clear contravention of the Act which may involve severe pecuniary penalties.

In this regard, then, the compliance program failed, and has since been revised. The failure in question was not an isolated incident; it occurred on different occasions and with different officers. The court stated that the level of penalties should take these failures into account. Furthermore, the contraventions were blatant, implicating the top Victorian management of the relevant corporate division. In summary, although a compliance program was in place, it was not effective—rather, it was disregarded or ignored.

20.3.2 Failures in Compliance Programs in Other Areas

20.3.2.1 The Compliance Program Fails in Almost Everything

In *EPA v. Great Southern Energy,*[49] a company was prosecuted for the spillage into waterways of oil contaminated with polychlorinated biphenyl (PCB). It pleaded guilty, but in assessment of the penalty the corporation tried to show that it was a responsible environmental operator. The corporation had spent over AU$ 1 million in obtaining accreditation of its environmental management program under ISO 14001. However, the court said:

> Despite the defendant's enormous expenditure on accreditation, there were numerous failings in the system or practices adopted by the defendant at the time of the incident. Whilst obviously directing attention to its general concern for the environment the defendant appears to have overlooked the most basic and elementary requirements, namely of ensuring that its employees were adequately trained in all handling, safety and emergency procedures, and familiar with the defendant's voluminous Codes of Practice. The employees involved had received a copy of a publication entitled Technical Response Group Operating Manual prior to the incident but neither had been instructed concerning its contents nor application. At least one of the operators has said that he did not receive any written instruction concerning oil spill procedures nor been given any training in oil spill response prior to receiving the manual. There is no evidence that the contents of the manual was ever brought to the attention of the employees by specific instruction.…A bund was not provided around the oil treatment operation and there is no explanation before the Court for such deficiency. The spill kits available on the site were completely inadequate to deal with the oil spillage problem and no pumps exist for any emergency. There is no evidence before the court which suggests any proper audit had been made of emergency equipment nor awareness by employees of the emergency procedures.

The court also criticized the defendant for not having adequate escalation procedures:

> Upon the leak having been discovered a strict code ought to have been implemented which was fail-safe. This occurrence has revealed a difficulty in communication at all levels.

[49] *Environment Protection Authority v Great Southern Energy* [1999] NSWLEC 192 (31 August 1999), available at http://www.austlii.edu.au/.

> Within the company's own operations there was no access to a central authority which was available to provide expert advice and assistance. Instead contact was attempted with Mr. Donaldson who did not receive the message for some four hours after it was given that an oil spill had occurred. The message did not suggest urgency and his attention was already diverted with another problem. The fact that he was uncontactable and there was nobody else in senior management to take charge of the emergency operations is alarming.

A final criticism related to the fact that the defendant had complex and "voluminous" staff manuals:

> [T]he complexity of the Codes of Practice suggests that unless explicit instruction was provided they would be bewildering to most employees.

20.3.2.2 Failures Related to Monitoring and Auditing

In *Adams v. Eta Foods Ltd*[50] the ACCC prosecuted Eta Foods for describing pies as beef pies when they contained mutton. Eta claimed to have brought the meat from a reputable supplier who had stated that the mince supplied was beef. It had systems in place for testing and controlling the quality of pies but none that tested for species substitution. Despite that, the court said that Eta's procedures to deal with fat and gristle content and excessive moisture levels were not enough. Eta had not taken adequate precautions or exercised due diligence in avoiding the risk of species substitution in raw mince supplied to it as minced beef, and appeared to have no cognizance of there being any such risk. Accordingly, the defense was not admitted.

20.3.2.3 Failures Referring to Communication

In a case of sexual harassment and discrimination, *Evans v. Lee,*[51] a corporation sought to avoid liability saying that it had taken "all reasonable steps" to prevent its employees from any contravention. Indeed, the corporation had in fact developed relevant antidiscrimination policies and a code of conduct, as well as a system of performance-related audits by managers of their responsibility in this regard. However, the corporate compliance system failed because the corporation had a duty to ensure that its policies were communicated effectively to its executive officers, and that they accepted the responsibility for promulgating the policies and for advising on remedial action when breached. In the Human Rights and Equal Opportunity Commission's view, the corporate policies did not "focus on sexual discrimination/sexual harassment in the provision of banking services":

> [T]here was clearly no instruction to the staff at the [relevant] branch about these matters nor, it seems, was there any check through the audit process that the [corporate] policies, limited as they were, were communicated to the staff. In particular, there does not appear

[50] *Re Ronald Edwards Adams v. Eta Foods Limited* [1987] FCA 402 (6 November 1987), available at http://www.austlii.edu.au/.

[51] *Evans v. Lee* [1996] Human Rights and Equal Opportunity Commission [HREOCA] 8 (3 May 1996), available at http://www.austlii.edu.au/.

to have been clear guidelines as to how the staff ought to handle a problem where conduct was engaged in by a manager which might be classified as unlawful under the discrimination legislation. (§ 3 *in fine*).

20.3.2.4 Failures Regarding the Clearness and Form of the Compliance System

The policies and procedures that make up a compliance system must be committed to writing and must be clear and easily understandable by relevant staff, as was stated, for instance, in the above-mentioned *EPA v. Great Southern Energy,* as well as in *Chapel Road Pty Limited v. Australian Securities and Investments Commission*[52] judgments. The latter case involved an action by a banned securities dealer to have the ban set aside in the Administrative Appeals Tribunal. In the course of the Tribunal's judgment, an observation was made about the obligation of the dealer, under its license, to establish and maintain adequate training, supervision, and compliance procedures, noting that "as a matter of practicality and good management, this would ordinarily require that those procedures should be set out in writing."

20.3.2.5 Neither the Provision of Manuals Nor the Setting up of Material on the Intranet is Sufficient

In *Coyne v. P & O Ports,*[53] a woman working in a canteen at a wharf was sexually assaulted by a waterside worker. The issue was whether his employer had exercised reasonable precautions against sexual harassment in the workplace so as not to be vicariously liable for the employee's misconduct. The court stated:

> [T]he preventive measures to be taken [by the employer] would ordinarily include the implementation of adequate educational programmes on sexual harassment issues and monitoring of the workplace to ensure compliance with its sexual harassment policies. [Besides, the employer] must have taken appropriate steps to communicate its sexual harassment policies to all employees, the objective being that they become aware of what may constitute sexual harassment and that it is unlawful.

The employer's corporate policy prohibited sexual harassment. The corporate policy was contained in hard copy in its staff manual. A copy of the staff manual was kept in the office near the canteen and was also available on the Intranet. The corporate policy also included an induction training program that all new employees had to undertake that went through their obligations in this area, and a booklet which was mailed to all staff explaining the policy prohibiting harassment. However, all these things were judged insufficient by the court. Reasons cited for why the system failed were as follows:

---

[52] Chapel Road Pty Limited and Australian Securities and Investments Commission [2003] AATA 660 (14 July 2003), available at http://www.austlii.edu.au/.

[53] *Coyne v. P &O Ports* [2000] VCAT 657 (31 March 2000), available at http://www.austlii.edu.au/.

First, the new staff training program had only been in operation since 1996 and had only reached 49 % of staff. The offender in this case had been employed before 1996 and had not received the training.

Secondly, none of the employees had any recollection of receiving the booklet explaining the policy. Besides, the booklet was only printed in English and there was evidence that many staff came from non-English speaking backgrounds. The court said that it had no evidence before it whether the protagonist in this case had received the booklet or whether he had understood it.

Last but not the least, the court said that it was very likely that the offender would not have had access to a computer to view the policy on the Intranet. In general terms, it was stated that very few employees had ever consulted the staff manual in the office.

20.4 Guidelines Coming from Associations: Is their Implementation Enough to Mitigate Penalties?

Another important aspect which has been stressed in relation to compliance programs is whether a compliance program which simply reproduces the law or guidelines coming from associations should be enough to mitigate penalties.[54]

In Australia, there is a recognized standard for compliance programs which covers the structural, operational, and maintenance elements that must be included in any program. The standard is known as the *Australian Standard AS3806.*[55] It does not focus on specific elements of international corruption compliance; on the contrary, it applies to programs across all areas of compliance. However, a look at the AS3806[56] is relevant because it highlights the essential components of an effective compliance program: to prevent and, where necessary, identify and respond to breaches of laws, regulations, codes, or organizational standards occurring within the organization; to promote a culture of compliance within the organization; and to assist the organization in remaining or becoming a good corporate citizen.

The key elements featured by AS3806 are common to those in other countries:[57] (1) commitment, (2) compliance policy, (3) management, (4) management responsibility and supervision, (5) resources, (6) record keeping and reporting, (7) education and training, (8) visibility and communication, (9) monitoring and assessment,

---

[54] See Paludi and Zecca, "Corporate Responsibility and Compliance Programs in Italian Case Law," and Muñoz de Morales and Nieto Martín, "Compliance Programs and Criminal Law Responses: A Comparative Analysis," in this volume.

[55] An index of the last version (2006) is available at http://www.austlii.edu.au/. The first version is dated 1998 (AS3806–1998).

[56] For a historical perspective on the introduction of AS 3806, see Carroll and McGregor-Lowndes (2001, p. 178).

[57] See, for instance Muñoz de Morales, "Corporate Responsibility and Compliance Programs in Canada," in this volume.

(10) review, (11) accountability, (12) systems for handling compliance failures, (13) continuous improvements, and (14) identification of compliance issues.[58]

Given the fact that the AS3806 provides useful guidelines to configure an (effective) compliance program, it is worth analyzing the value of such guidelines in competition case law. It must be pointed out that most judicial resolutions on the AS3806 focus on orders sought by the ACCC forcing the corporation to set up a trade practices compliance program which conforms to AS3806, and not on assessment of the effectiveness of the compliance program as a ground for exemption of criminal liability or as a mitigating factor.

Firstly, compliance with the AS3806 is not mandatory. The AS3806 does not have statutory recognition. It is only a text providing guidelines. That means basically two things: (1) individual corporations should use the system best suited to their operations, and (2) the AS3806 is not necessarily superior to a tailored compliance program prepared by an independent expert for a particular entity.[59]

Secondly, the AS3806 imposes standards which are aspirational in their expression and not readily measured in application. That was stated in *ACCC v. Real Estate Institute of Western Australia,*[60] a case where several corporations were prosecuted for alleged price fixing on property transactions. The procedure was resolved by agreement between the parties and a consent order was placed before the court for approval. The order forced the corporation to set up a trade practices compliance program complying with AS3806. Recognizing the aspirational character of the AS3806, the court amended the order and so limited the requirement for compliance with the AS3806 to a "best endeavors" undertaking.

---

[58] For a comparative analysis on the standards to be met by corporations in order to have an effective compliance program, see Muñoz de Morales and Nieto Martín, "Compliance Programs and Criminal Law Responses: A Comparative Analysis," in this volume.

[59] *ACCC v. Rural Press Ltd* (includes Corrigendum dated 8 August 2001) [2001] FCA 1065 (7 August 2001), available at http://www.austlii.edu.au/. In this case, it was proved that "Rural Press has retained independent solicitors to advise it about what steps it should take to procure and implement a trade practices 'training tool' to develop a trade practice compliance culture within that group and to prevent conduct which might contravene the Act." It was also proved that not all the features of AS3806–1998 had been included or implemented by the corporation but that did not mean that its program was not a sound or sensible one. Since the compliance program was genuinely directed to ensuring a culture of compliance with the Act within its organisation, "there [was] no reason to think that the quality of the advice given is other than professional and competent or that the program is not comprehensive in relation to the structure and needs of Rural Press…."

In this regard, see also Australian Competition & Consumer Commission v Wizard Mortgage Corporation Limited [2002] FCA 1317 (25 October 2002), available at http://www.austlii.edu.au/. In this case, the Federal Court refused to grant an injunction sought by the ACCC requiring the defendant to implement a trade practices compliance program for 3 years complying with AS 3806. Since the aim of a compliance program is to avoid the repetition of a contravening conduct, such a goal can be reached by the corporation by setting in place a formal process, based on the recommendations of its legal advisers. Therefore, it was not necessary to impose a program based on AS 3806 on the corporation.

[60] *Australian Competition & Consumer Commission v. Real Estate Institute of Western Australia Inc* (includes corrigendum dated 2 February 1999) [1999] FCA 18 (18 January 1999), available at http://www.austlii.edu.au/.

In conclusion, the stipulations of AS3806 are not compulsory but "any business ignoring them does so at its peril" (Clark 2000, p. 2; Shafron 1998 §33–000, §100–000, §100–010; both quoted in Godfrey 2002, p. 33).

20.5 Conclusions

The Australian formula assigning liability to companies on the basis of corporate culture can be read as giving legislative force to the emphasis placed on the development and implementation of legal compliance programs. To put it differently, it could be read as a ground for exemption of liability. In other areas where case law on corporate (criminal) liability is more abundant (i.e., competition law), there is no express reference to compliance programs providing a way to avoid criminal liability. However, cross-cutting concepts such as "due diligence," "reasonable precautions," and "corporate culture" might lead to this result.[61] Said differently, given that the Australian model of criminal culpability is a preventive-fault one, corporations will be found criminally liable when they fail to assert and implement an adequate internal system of controls to prevent the commission of a crime. An express reference to compliance programs does not appear, but it can be deduced from the spirit of the text. Less controversial is that courts take into account compliance programs in the sentencing phase as a mitigating factor.

In the case of bribery offenses, courts have said almost nothing yet. We await forthcoming cases!

References

Allens Arthur Robinson. (February 2008). 'Corporate culture' as a basis for the criminal liability of corporations. http://198.170.85.29/Allens-Arthur-Robinson-Corporate-Culture-paper-for-Ruggie-Feb-2008.pdf. Accessed 6 February 2014.

Australian Federal Police. (2011). Foreign bribery charges laid in Australia. http://www.afp.gov.au/media-centre/news/afp/2011/july/foreign-bribery-charges-laid-in-australia.aspx. Accessed 6 July 2013.

Australian Government. (2007). International Trade Integrity Act 2007, 1. http://www.comlaw.gov.au/Details/C2007A00147. Accessed 6 July 2013.

Australian Securities & Investment Commission. (2012). 12-47AD Statement on Securency International and Note Printing Australia. http://www.asic.gov.au/asic/asic.nsf/byheadline/1247AD+Statement+on+Securency+International+and+Note+Printing+Australia. Accessed 6 July 2013.

Barker, C. (2012). Australia's implementation of the OECD Anti-Bribery Convention. Parliament of Australia, Department of Parliamentary Services. http://www.aph.gov.au/About_Parliament/

[61] For doubts regarding the notion of "corporate culture" giving legal acknowledgement to "compliance programs," see Belcher (2007, p. 18): "proving that the body corporate failed to create and maintain a corporate culture that required compliance with the relevant provision…does not require the organisation to have a 'compliance program' as such."

Parliamentary_Departments/Parliamentary_Library/pubs/BN/2011-2012/AntiBribery. Accessed 6 July 2013.

Bartos, S. (2006). *Against the grain: The AWB scandal and why it happened.* Sydney: University of New South Wales Press.

Baxt, R. (2001). Ascribing civil and criminal liability for company employees and directors—Who carries the corporate can? Paper presented at Penalties: Policy Principles & Practice & Government Regulation conference. Sydney, Australia: 9 June 2001.

Belcher, A. (2007). Imagining how a company thinks: What is corporate culture? *Deakin Law Review, 11*(2), 1–21.

Botterill, L. C. (2007). Doing it for the growers in Iraq? The AWB, oil-for-food and the Cole Inquiry. *Australian Journal of Public Administration, 66*(1), 4–12.

Brand, V. (2000). Legislating for moral propriety in corporations? The Criminal Code Amendment (Bribery of Foreign Public Officials) Act 1999. *Company and Securities Law Journal, 18*(7), 476–492.

Buckley, R. P., & Danielson, M. (2008). Facilitation payments in international business: A proposal to make section 70.4 of the criminal code workable. *Australian Law Journal, 2,* 92–104.

Carroll, P., & McGregor-Lowndes, M. (2001). A standard for regulatory compliance? Industry self-regulation, the courts and AS3806–1998. *Australian Journal of Public Administration, 60*(4), 80–91.

Clark, E. E. (2000). Legal risk management. In E. Clarke et al. (Eds.), *Marketers and the law*. Sydney: LBC Information Services.

Clough, J., & Mulhern, C. (2002). *The prosecution of corporations*. Melbourne: Oxford University Press.

Cole, T. R. H. (2006). Inquiry into certain Australian companies in relation to the UN Oil-For-Food Programme. http://www.oilforfoodinquiry.gov.au. Accessed 6 July 2013.

Davidson, I., & Harkness, A. (1979). Universal Telecasters Queensland Ltd. v. Guthrie. *Federal Law Review*, 10(1–2), 98–107.

Fisse, B. (1989). Corporate compliance programmes: The trade practices act and beyond. *Australian Business Law Review, 17,* 356–399.

Fisse, B. (1991). The attribution of criminal liability to corporations: A statutory model. *Sydney Law Review, 13,* 277–297.

Fisse, B., & Braithwaite, J. (1993). *Corporations, crime and accountability*. Melbourne: Cambridge University Press.

French, J. R. (2003). The culture of compliance: A judicial perspective. Paper presented at Australian Compliance Institute National Conference, Culture is Critical, World Legal Information Institute, 3–5 September 2003. http://worldlii.austlii.edu.au/au/journals/FedJSchol/2003/16.html. Accessed 1 July 2013.

Godfrey, K. (2002). Trade practices compliance programs—Ignore them at your peril! Part 1. *Australian Construction Law Newsletter, 83,* 21–30.

Heimann, F., & Dell, G. (2009). Progress Report 2009: Enforcement of the OECD Convention on Combating Bribery of Foreign Public Officials in International Business Transactions. Transparency International USA. http://www.transparency-usa.org/news/documents/FinalOECD-ProgressReport2009.pdf. Accessed 1 July 2013.

Heimann, F., & Dell, G. (2010). Progress Report 2010: Enforcement of the OECD Anti-Bribery Convention. Transparency International. http://www.transparency.org/whatwedo/pub/progress_report_2010_enforcement_of_the_oecd_anti_bribery_convention. Accessed 1 July 2013.

Hill, J. G. (2000). Laws prohibiting foreign bribery: The practicalities of legislating for integrity internationally. *Australian Mining and Petroleum Law Association Yearbook*, p. 13–34.

Hill, J. G. (2003). Corporate criminal liability in Australia: An evolving corporate governance technique? Vanderbilt Law School, Law and Economics Research Paper Series No. 03–10, http://ssrn.com/abstract_id=429220, 1–41. Accessed 6 February 2014.

Joseph, J. (2002). Integrating business ethics and compliance programs. *Business and Society Review, 107*(3), 309–347.

Leader-Elliott, I. D. (2002). Elements of liability in the Commonwealth Criminal Code. *Criminal Law Journal, 26*(1), 28–42.
Nieto Martín, A. (2008). *La responsabilidad penal de las personas jurídicas: Un modelo legislative*. Madrid: Iustel.
OECD. (2006). Australia Phase 2—Follow-up report on the implementation of the Phase 2 Recommendations, application of the Convention on Combating Bribery of Foreign Public Officials in International Business Transactions and the 1997 Rrevised Recommendation on Ccombating Bribery in International Business Transactions. http://www.oecd.org/dataoecd/57/42/35937659.pdf. Accessed 6 July 2013.
Parker, C. (1999). The emergence of the Australian compliance industry: Trends and accomplishments. *Australian Business Law Review, 27*(3), 178–195.
Parker, C. (2002). Is there a reliable way to evaluate organisational compliance programs? Paper presented at Current Issues in Regulation: Enforcement and Compliance conference, convened by Australian Institute of Criminology, Regulatory Institutions Network, RSSS, Australian National University, and the Division of Business and Enterprise, University of South Australia, Melbourne, 2–3 September 2002.
Parker, C., & Nielsen, V. L. (2006). Do businesses take compliance systems seriously? An empirical study of the implementation of trade practices compliance systems in Australia. *Melbourne University Law Review, 30*(2), 441–494.
Parker, D. (2007). Management Today article—Lessons learned? Australian Institute of Management. http://www.aim.com.au/DisplayStory.asp?ID=648. Accessed 1 July 2013.
Schroeder, D. (2002). Ethics from the top: Top management and ethical business. *Business Ethics: A European Review, 11*(3), 260–267.
Schwartz, M. S., Dunfee, T. W., & Kline, M. J. (2005). Tone at the top: An ethics code for directors. *Journal of Business Ethics, 58*(1–3), 79–100.
Shafron, P. (1998). *Australian Trade Practices Compliance*. Sydney: CCH Australia Limited.
Steytler, C. (2010). James Hardie, NAB and AWB Ltd.—What have we learned? *The University of Notre Dame Australia Law Review, 7*(12), 123–170.
Vatsikopoulous, H., Baker, R., McKenzie, N., et al. (2012). Panel discussion—Investigative case studies. *Pacific Journalism Review, 18*(1), 30–45. (http://www.pjreview.info/articles/panel-discussion-investigative-case-studies-723.)
Vitell, S. J., Dickerson, E. B., & Festervand, T. A. (2000). Ethical problems, conflicts and beliefs of small business professionals. *Journal of Business Ethics, 28*(1), 15–24.
Wee, S. Y. (2012). The OECD Convention on Combating Bribery of Foreign Public Officials and its effectiveness in Australia: Are we doing enough? *International Trade and Business Law Review*, 15, 360–379.
Wolff, A. (2011). Australia. In T. Gruetzner et al. (Eds.), *Anti-bribery risk assessment: A systemic overview of 151 countries*. Munich: C. H. Beck.
Wyld, R. R. (2010). Anti-corruption regulation in Australia—Myth or Reality? Presentations slides from International Serious & Organised Crime Conference 2010. Documents & Resources for Small Businesses and Professionals. http://www.docstoc.com/docs/70201094/Presentation-slides--Anti-Corruption-Regulation-in-Australia. Accessed 24 July 2013.

Chapter 21
Corporate Responsibility and Compliance Programs in Canada

Marta Muñoz de Morales

Contents

21.1 Introduction

Corporate crime liability in Canada is an issue of "before and after" the entry into force of Bill C-45, which amended the Canadian Criminal Code[1] in March 2004.[2]

[1] Bill C-45: An Act to Amend the Criminal Code (Criminal Liability of Organizations), S.C., chap. 21 (2003). Bill C-45 amended the Canadian Criminal Code to create new duties and possible criminal liability for individuals and organizations, which include corporations. It became law in March 2004. For a full explanation, see *A Plain Language Guide Bill C-45– Amendments to the Criminal Code Affecting the Criminal Liability of Organizations* (Government of Canada, Department of Justice), http://www.justice.gc.ca/eng/rp-pr/other-autre/c45/.

[2] Bill C-45 is also known as the *Westray Bill*. In 1992 the Westray coal mine exploded, killing twenty-six workers in Pictou County, Nova Scotia. The corporation as well as some of its managers

M. Muñoz de Morales (✉)
University of Castilla-la-Mancha, Ciudad Real, Spain
e-mail: marta.mmorales@uclm.es

S. Manacorda et al. (eds.), *Preventing Corporate Corruption*,

DOI 10.1007/978-3-319-04480-4_21,

Before Bill C-45, the attribution of liability to corporations in Canada was based solely on the identification doctrine.[3] According to this doctrine, a corporation could be convicted of a crime when the criminal behavior was carried out by individuals who were the "directing minds" of the corporation (Little and Savoline 2003). Directors and senior managers were considered the corporation's "directing mind and will," and their conduct and state of mind were thus the conduct and state of mind of the corporation itself.[4] In this regard, a distinction was made between those who decided corporate policy and those who, once policy had been decided by others, were charged with its implementation. The former had "governing executive authority" and were designated directing minds in those spheres; the latter were not.

Corporate criminal liability in Canada was dramatically affected after the entry into force of Bill C-45.[5] Since that date, the Canadian Criminal Code has contained general standards for holding organizations liable for the acts of their representatives, distinguishing between the standards applicable to negligence offences (Sect. 22.1)[6] and those requiring a higher mental state (Sect. 22.2). In the first

---

and executives were charged with manslaughter; however, these charges were dropped due to lack of evidence. See Recommendation 73 of the Report of the Public Inquiry: "The Westray Story: A Predictable Path to Disaster," wherein Commissioner K. Peter Richard recommends amendments to establish criminal law accountability for workplace safety on the part of officers and directors.

[3] See Rhone (The) v. Peter A.B. Widener (The), [1993] 1 S.C.R. 497 at 521 [The Rhone]; Canadian Dredge and Dock Co., [1985] S.C.J. No. 28.

[4] For further details, see MacPherson 2004, p. 253. "A person could have governing executive authority and be a directing mind for some purposes, but not for others. For example, assume that a fraud is perpetrated against a third party by the vice-president of marketing, using the corporation's advertising department to line both the company coffers and his own pockets. The corporation will be liable, provided the vice-president for marketing sets policies for the advertising department (which he or she presumably would). The company would be criminally liable in addition to the human perpetrators of the fraud. If, however, the vice-president of research and development perpetrated the same fraud using the advertising department, it is unlikely that the corporation would be liable. The vice-president of research and development generally does not set corporate policy with respect to advertising. Since the vice-president of research and development is only a directing mind for the areas where he or she has the discretion to set policy, and the fraud related to the advertising department, the corporation would not be liable for the actions of the vice-president of research and development….Middle managers do not usually set policy; rather, they are the instruments to implement the policy set by others. This means that, at common law, the corporation is generally immune from criminal sanction for the actions of mid- to low-level managers and other employees."

[5] See Jennings 2012, p. 6: "The Legislature has taken Canada beyond the confines of the directing mind concept of liability and we have entered a new era." See also Keith 2010, p. 253: "Sections 22.1 and 22.2 of the Code—for the first time—provided a statutory framework for the *mens rea* and of organizations, including corporations."

[6] On corporate criminal liability for crimes requiring negligence, see Bittle and Snider 2006, p. 470.

case (Esakov 2010, p. 181), the Code codifies both the theory of vicarious liability (Sect. 22.1(a))[7] and the identification theory (Sect. 22.1(b)).[8]

For crimes requiring proof of mens rea other than negligence the code uses the identification theory (Archibald et al. 2004, p. 370; see also Esakov 2010, p. 181), stating that a corporation could be held liable for the crimes (including corruption) committed by its employees or agents, "if a senior officer, with intent at least in part to benefit the corporation or organization, (a) acting within the scope of their authority, is a party to the offence; (b) having the mental state required to be a party to the offence and acting within the scope of their authority, directs the work of other representatives of the organization so that they do the act or make the omission specified in the offence; or (c) knowing that a representative of the organization is or is about to be a party to the offence, does not take all reasonable measures to stop [employees, agents, etc.] of the corporation from being a party to the offence."

"Senior officer" is understood to mean "a representative who plays an important role in the establishment of an organization's policies or is responsible for managing an important aspect of the organization's activities and, in the case of a body corporate, includes a director, its chief executive officer and its chief financial officer."[9]

The above definition has a number of consequences which are detailed hereunder. Firstly, a corporation will not be held liable unless senior officers act with intent at least in part to benefit the organization (Edwards and Conlin 2005, p. 47). Therefore, in those cases where a senior officer has no intent to benefit the organization, criminal liability of the organization will not exist "even though his or her actions may have unintentionally benefited the organization" (Archibald et al. 2004, p. 379). Secondly, the wide definition of "senior officer" includes—contrary to the identification doctrine—both the person who is the directing mind or acting within the scope of his authority and those officers who are not properly directing minds (i.e., operational-level officers).

Another major change made by Bill C-45 is that the new system applies to more than just corporations: "organization" means "(a) a public body, body corporate, society, company, firm, partnership, trade union or municipality, or (b) an association

[7] Section 22.1: "In respect of an offence that requires the prosecution to prove negligence, an organization is a party to the offence if (a) acting within the scope of their authority (i) one of its representatives is a party to the offence, or (ii) two or more of its representatives engage in conduct, whether by act or omission, such that, if it had been the conduct of only one representative, that representative would have been a party to the offence…."

[8] Section 22.1: "In respect of an offence that requires the prosecution to prove negligence, an organization is a party to the offence if…(b) the senior officer who is responsible for the aspect of the organization's activities that is relevant to the offence departs—or the senior officers, collectively, depart—markedly from the standard of care that, in the circumstances, could reasonably be expected to prevent a representative of the organization from being a party to the offence."

[9] On the new provision of expanded organizational criminal liability through Bill C-45, see Archibald et al.2004, p. 367; MacPherson 2004, p. 253; Dusome 2007, p. 98. For particular reference to foreign bribery offences, see Jennings 2012, p. 6.

of persons that (i) is created for a common purpose, (ii) has an operational structure, and (iii) holds itself out to the public as an association of persons."[10]

For our present purposes, Sect. 22.2(c) is probably the most interesting provision since it introduces "a limited version of the failing to prevent corruption offences in jurisdictions like U.K." (Skinnider 2012, p. 6). Under this paragraph, if any senior officer becomes aware that any representative is or is about to be a party to an offence, then the corporation would be criminally liable, subject to a "due diligence" defense. Differently stated: organizations will be held liable for the offence when the senior officer is aware that a representative is or is about to be party to the offence, but he or she "does not take all reasonable measures to stop [the representatives] from being a party to the offence." Under this section a corporation would be criminally liable, for example, when a senior officer is aware that an employee is going to get a kickback from thieves for getting the organization to buy stolen goods and he or she has done nothing to set up the transaction, because the organization will benefit from the lower price.[11] The determination of what amounts to "reasonable steps" will be contingent on the nature of the offence, the specific industry involved, risk-management techniques, and the individual circumstances of each case (Archibald et al. 2005). The expression "reasonable steps" is therefore a "due diligence defense" which could play a relevant role as ground for exclusion of criminal liability when a corporation is charged with a serious criminal offence of subjective fault. On the one hand, the possibility of taking a "due diligence" defense into consideration in these cases blurs the line between regulatory offences and mens rea crimes;[12] but, on the other hand, it also makes it possible to employ in the case of regulatory offences, many of the factors relating to corporate conduct that are considered relevant to determining that a company acted with due diligence (Archibald et al. 2004, p. 384). Factors[13] such as the kind of preventive system in place, the efforts made to address the problem, the promptness of the response, the industry standards in force, the degree of foresight regarding the commission of the offences,[14] whether steps were taken to hire a responsible contractor, whether there are reasons to believe that corporate instructions would not be complied with,[15] etc., will all be key issues in the case of criminal offences of subjective fault (i.e., intent).

Besides this, Sect. 718.21 of the Canadian Criminal Code (Bill C-45) cites a number of aggravating and mitigating factors for sentencing organizations. For our purpose, the following aggravating factors are relevant: "(b) the degree of planning involved in carrying out the offence and the duration and complexity of the offence"

---

[10] For criticisms in this regard, see MacPherson 2004, p. 256, and MacPherson 2010, p. 329.

[11] The example is taken from *A Plain Language Guide Bill C-45*; see n. 1.

[12] The due diligence defense was made available to a new category of regulatory or strict liability offences in the late 1970s. See Supreme Court of Canada in *R v. Sault St. Marie* [1978] 2 S.C.R 1299; 5 D.L.R. (3d) 161.

[13] For an overview of the factors that determine the due diligence defense in regulatory offences, see Nelson and Sulek 2006.

[14] See *R v. Bata Industries Ltd.* [1992] O.J. no. 236, 9 O.R. (3d) 329, (Ont. Court Provincial Division).

[15] See *R v. Pacifica Papers Inc.* [2002] B.C.J. no. 1639 (B.C. Prov. Court).

and "(g) whether the organization was—or any of its representatives who were involved in the commission of the offence were—previously convicted of a similar offence or sanctioned by a regulatory body for similar conduct."

Although in Canada there are no guidelines that speak to the importance of a compliance program for sentencing purposes, the above-mentioned factors are reminiscent of the US Sentencing Guidelines wherein, among the elements which can lead to a compliance program being considered inefficient, we find passiveness with regard to misconduct or recurrence of similar misconduct ("Recurrence of similar misconduct creates doubt regarding whether the organization took reasonable steps to meet the requirements of this guideline…"), as well as the fact that any individual with substantial authority has previously engaged in illegal activities or other conduct.

Among the mitigating factors, Sect. 718.21 includes: "(h) any penalty imposed by the organization on a representative for their role in the commission of the offence"[16] and "(j) any measures that the organization has taken to reduce the likelihood of it committing a subsequent offence."

Both mitigating factors pay attention to adequate organization and reaction once the offence has been committed. Therefore, contrary to the US Sentencing Guidelines, they are not proactive requirements. Clause (h) refers to one of the classic elements which a compliance program is supposed to include: the implementation of appropriate disciplinary procedures to address violations. To put it differently, penalties can be reduced if internal controls are put in place imposing disciplinary action against the offenders after the crime has been committed. Clause (j) is much wider in scope, including other kinds of remedial actions implemented after discovering the misconduct.[17] Its basis is that, "large and competent organizations may often be in the best position to know how to improve their risk management techniques" (Archibald 2004, p. 391). In this regard, new policies and practices (i.e., spot audits or changes in personnel) can be seen as a signal of the fact that the corporation has learned its lesson.

Concerning bribery offences, bribery of Canadian public officials is punishable under the Canadian Criminal Code (Sects. 119, 120), while in the case of bribing a foreign public official the Corruption of Foreign Public Officials Act (hereinafter CFPOA)[18] is applicable.[19] In both cases corporations may be held liable. In particular,

[16] This mitigating factor also has a close connection with the guidelines already analyzed in other legal orders to determine whether the compliance program is effective. See e.g., the Siemens case in Italy, where Italian judicial authorities considered that the Siemens AG compliance program had failed, among other reasons because "since the misconduct was detected … no remedial actions or revision of the compliance program were enacted …. In this regard, the corporation did not take any remedial actions such as disciplinary actions … ," Paludi and Zecca, "Corporate Responsibility and Compliance Programs in Italian Case Law," in this volume.

[17] And this serves as a reminder of remedies such as the implementation of training systems, incentives to perform in accordance with laws, risk assessment, or channels of information inside the corporation, etc.

[18] The CFPOA entered into force on 14 February 1999, and was amended in 2001.

[19] See Section 3 of the CFPOA: "(1) Every person commits an offence who, in order to obtain or retain an advantage in the course of business, directly or indirectly gives, offers or agrees to

the CFPOA, which is limited to criminal enforcement, states that, the offence of bribing a foreign public official can be committed not only by individuals "but also by public bodies, corporations, firms, partnerships trade unions, municipalities or other associations of persons." Although the act is silent on the mental element of the offence, there is a consensus that the accepted standard of intention and knowledge must be proven, consistent with Canadian criminal law (Jennings 2012). That means that proof of negligence is not sufficient for a conviction under the CFPOA (Monk 2011).

Another relevant issue is that the CFPOA does not make any provisions to encourage companies to introduce and follow compliance programs.[20] This should not present a serious problem since bribery offences fall under the regimen applying to fault other than negligence, that is to say, under Article 22.2(c) of the Canadian Criminal Code (Lafontaine 2006, p. 10). Therefore, organizations would be criminally liable when senior officers, with intent at least in part to benefit the corporation or organization, do "not take all reasonable measures to stop" employees, agents, etc. of the corporation from being a party to the offence (e.g., corruption).

The problem is, as some legal scholars have pointed out, that corporations are seldom charged with crimes—and particularly not if the charges are related to subjective intent offences.[21] Besides this, an affirmative due diligence defense is not likely to be taken into account (Skinnider 2012, p. 6). However, as already mentioned—and as already occurs in other legal orders—the implementation of an effective compliance program is likely to be more successful as a mitigating factor. In this sense, Sect. 718.21 of the Canadian Criminal Code is applicable. It is interesting to note that the fines that can be imposed do not have prescribed maximums. That means that the quantum is left to the discretion of the court.[22]

Corporations can also be placed on probation, and be required to take steps to repair harms that they have caused and ensure that the harms of the past are not repeated (Douglas 2011, p. 48). In effect, under Article 732.1(3.1) of the Criminal Code, the court may prescribe probation, in respect of an organization, which includes conditions such as one or more of the following:

1. Provide restitution to a person for any loss or damage caused by the offence.
2. Establish policies, standards, and procedures to prevent subsequent offences.

---

give or offer a loan, reward, advantage or benefit of any kind to a foreign public official or to any person for the benefit of a foreign public official (a) as consideration for an act or omission by the official in connection with the performance of the official's duties or functions; or (b) to induce the official to use his or her position to influence any acts or decisions of the foreign state or public international organization for which the official performs duties or functions."

[20] "Canada's *Foreign Anti-Bribery Act* does not contain a due diligence defense or 'adequate procedures' provision. As a result, a Canadian business cannot demonstrate that they have a code of conduct, require agents and representatives to not engage in prohibited foreign bribery activities in contracts, have training, have a compliance officer, engage in internal audits, and similar preventative measures" (Todgham Cherniak 2011, p. 144).

[21] "In Canada, charges against corporations for subjective intent offences are relatively rare. Post-Enron, it is perhaps easier to envisage a corporation being charged with such a crime" (Archibald et al. 2004, p. 378).

[22] See Sects. 734 and 735 of the Canadian Criminal Code.

3. Report to the court on the implementation of these policies, standards, and procedures.
4. Make a public announcement regarding the conviction, sentence, and any measures being taken to prevent further offences.

Notably, the wording of Sect. 732.1(3.1) is "the Court may prescribe…"; the imposition of probation orders is thus a discretionary judicial power. On the other hand, however, courts may also delegate the task of supervising the development and implementation of the corrective standards and policies to another regulatory body with more expertise, or to one which is better positioned to regulate quality control and effective risk-management practices.[23] Although probation orders have been considered "a primary vehicle by which CSR [Corporate Social Responsibility] standards" (Tatum 2012a, p. 16) are met, the truth is that there are very few cases where probation provisions have been used to rehabilitate corporate offenders (ibid.). However, the Niko case, analyzed later in this chapter, could change this situation.

Last but not least, it is curious that the automatic legal disbarment from contracting with the government upon conviction of corruption offences is limited to certain domestic corruption offences, and is not applicable in the case of a conviction for foreign bribery (Skinnider 2012, p. 31).

21.2 Case-Law Analysis

In the Transparency International Reports on the Organisation for Economic Co-operation and Development (OECD) Anti-bribery Convention, Canada is listed within the group of countries with little or moderate enforcement. To date there have been very few investigations[24] and only three prosecutions under the CFPOA. Furthermore, the Canadian process does not contain as an option a possibility for the corporation to negotiate under (non-) deferred prosecution agreements, as does occur in the United States.

This, then, provides an indication of the lack of enforcement; the comments to be made on compliance program issues are therefore unfortunately very few.[25]

[23] See Sect. 732.1(3.1.) of the Canadian Criminal Code.

[24] According to the last report by Transparency International, only 34 investigations are underway (TI 2012, p. 40). Previous reports have shown an even lower level of enforcement (e.g., in 2010 only 23 investigations, and between 2008 and 2009 only two investigations). See Progress Reports 2009, 2010, and 2011.

[25] Among the reasons for the lack of enforcement, it has been pointed out that Canada's jurisdiction is relatively narrow in contrast to the jurisdiction provided by the UK and US Acts. The Act recognizes jurisdiction to prosecute foreign bribery offences only when the offence is committed in whole or part in Canadian territory. See *The Corruption of Foreign Public Officials Act—A Guide* (May 1999), available online at http://www.justice.gc.ca/eng/dept-min/pub/cfpoa-lcape/guide.pdf. This limitation has been criticized by legal scholars and also in the TI Reports. Among legal scholars see, with further references, Tatum 2012b; among the TI Reports, see Heimann and Dell 2013, p. 23, in which Canada is recommended to adopt the newly proposed legislation providing for nationality jurisdiction in addition to the existing territorial jurisdiction. This would cover

The first case on foreign bribery brought before the Canadian courts was *R. v. Watts*.[26] The corporation Hydro-Kleen Group Inc. (hereinafter Hydro-Kleen) was involved. Hydro-Kleen pleaded guilty in 2005 under Sect. 3(1)(a) of the CFPOA and was ordered to pay a fine of US$ 25,000 for bribing a US immigration officer who worked at the Calgary International Airport. Bribes were paid to facilitate the entry of Hydro-Kleen's employees into the USA and to delay the entry of its competitors' employees. The OECD (2011, p. 8) criticized the guilty plea because the size of the penalty imposed (US$ 25,000) was pretty small[27]—and therefore neither effective, proportionate, nor dissuasive—compared to the size of the bribe (US$ 30,000).[28] As far as we are concerned here, no mention of compliance issues was made, perhaps because Bill C-45 had only just entered in force.

The first significant Canadian CFPOA[29] case is *R. v. Niko Resources Ltd.*[30] The corporation Niko Resources Ltd. (hereinafter Niko), a Canadian oil and gas company, was charged under the CFPOA for having bribed[31] the Bangladesh Minister of Energy and Mineral Resources in order to obtain or retain an advantage in the course of Niko's business. In particular, it was alleged that the bribes were made to persuade the minister to exercise his influence to ensure that Niko was able to secure a gas purchase and sales agreement acceptable to Niko and to ensure that Niko was dealt with fairly in relation to claims for compensation related to industrial accidents, which potentially represented very large amounts of money.[32] As a result, a US$ 9.5 million penalty and a probation order for a period of 3 years were

the activities of foreign subsidiaries and third-party agents where Canadian nationals are involved; see also Transparency International's progress report for 2012, where Canada is again advised to amend the CFPOA and to introduce nationality jurisdiction because, under the current situation, the prosecution is required to devote scarce resources to establish that the facts disclose a "real and substantial link to Canada…" (TI 2012, p. 17).

[26] *R. v. Watts* [2005] A.J. no. 56.

[27] For a different point of view, see Todgham Cherniak 2011, p. 163: "The low amount of the fine in the plea… does not represent a lack of commitment by Canada to preventing bribery of foreign public officials; it was merely a small provincial case that involved small payments to a U.S. official in unusual circumstances."

[28] The Canadian authorities pointed out that because the court in the Hydro-Kleen case deemed that the sentence agreed to by the prosecution and the defense was fit, other sanctions, such as those outlined in subsection 732.1(3.1) of the Criminal Code, were therefore not considered by it.

[29] There are further cases involving compliance issues, but these are currently in the prosecution or police investigation stage. The first one involves Blackfire Exploration Ltd. for allegedly making 14 payments to the Mayor of Chicomuselo, Mexico, for protection from anti-mining protests. The second one is the SNC Lavalin Group case, based on allegations of corruption in the bidding process for the World-Bank-funded Padma Bridge Project in Bangladesh.

[30] *R. v. Niko Resources Ltd.*, proceedings taken in the Court of Queen's Bench of Alberta, Judicial District of Calgary, on 24 June 2011.

[31] Bribes consisted in, e.g., gifting a vehicle (costing US$ 190,984) and paying the Minister's travel and accommodation expenses of approximately US$ 5,000 to Calgary to attend the Gas and Oil Exposition, then onward to New York and Chicago to visit his family who lived there.

[32] For further details, see http://www.fcpaprofessor.com/category/securency-international.

imposed against Niko on 24 June 2011. The Probation Order was aimed at reducing the likelihood of Niko committing a subsequent related offence.

This case is very interesting regarding the challenges of corporate compliance in Canada. Firstly, several aggravating and mitigating factors already mentioned above were considered during sentencing; secondly, a probation order was imposed.

In setting the fine, the court took into consideration among other factors (see Sect. 718.21 of the Canadian Criminal Code) the frequency of the illegal payments (two incidents of bribery having been admitted by Niko).[33]

The probation order, meanwhile, gives specific details on what an effective compliance program is supposed to include (Appendix A). The court required the company to implement a compliance program to detect and prevent violations of the CFPOA. This compliance program was tailored to the company's bribery risk and included the following key elements: (1) internal accounting controls for fair and accurate books and records; (2) a rigorous anticorruption compliance code designed to detect and deter violations of CFPOA and other anticorruption laws; (3) risk assessments in order to develop these standards and procedures; (4) review and updating at least annually; (5) assignment of responsibility to senior corporate executive(s) with direct reporting to independent monitoring bodies; (6) periodic training and annual certification of directors, offices employees, agents, and business parties; (7) systems for guidance, advice, and confidential reporting; (8) protection against retaliation; (9) disciplinary procedures for violations; (10) due diligence and compliance requirements on agents and business partners, including documentation, informing them, and seeking reciprocal commitment; (11) standard provisions in agreements, contracts, and renewals thereof with all agents and business partners to prevent violations of anticorruption laws.

All these requirements were taken, almost verbatim, from *Securities and Exchange Commission v. Siemens Aktiengesellschaft*[34] and the *United States v. Panalpina World Transport (Holding) Ltd.*[35]—the latter being a case in which Panalpina, a Swiss-based freight company, admitted to paying over US$ 27 million in bribes to foreign officials (TI-Canada 2012, p. 6). The structure of this plea agreement also indicates significant parallels with attachment C to typical US Department of Justice FCPA deferred prosecution agreements, which sets forth a company's agreement to revise or strengthen its corporate compliance program. In this sense it could be

---

[33] Note the similarities with the *Siemens* case and the failures there found by the Italian authorities; see Paludi and Zecca, "Corporate Responsibility and Compliance Programs in Italian Case Law," in this volume.

[34] Civil Action No. 8, CV 02167 (D.D.C.). On the parallels between the *Siemens* and *Niko* cases, see Chang 2012, *ad fine*: "When one reviews the undertaking contained in the Siemens court order, it becomes clear that the court in the Niko case borrowed liberally from it when drafting its own probation order. In fact, the Siemens undertakings are virtually identical to the terms and conditions imposed in Niko."

[35] See the *USA v. Panalpina, Inc.*, Docket Number 10-CR-765, in particular Attachment C, available at http://www.justice.gov/criminal/fraud/fcpa/cases/panalpina-inc.html.

said that "with Niko Plea, Canada Joins the Club,"[36] in the global implementation of anticorruption compliance in accordance with the OECD benchmarks. Some scholars have even commented that "Canada has adopted US guidelines, at least for the purpose of assessing the effectiveness of anticorruption compliance programs" and "as a result, US Cases that address the effectiveness of anticorruption compliance programs should have relevance in Canada as well" (Chang 2012, *ad fine*).

21.3 Compliance Programs and Competition Law

The lack of case law on bribery makes it necessary to look at the question from the perspective of other branches of law, and in particular of competition law.

21.3.1 The Role of a Compliance Program

In Canada, the act governing competition is a federal statute known as the Competition Act.[37] Its purpose is to maintain and encourage competition in Canada. The Act is administered and enforced by an independent law enforcement agency, the Competition Bureau of Canada (hereinafter CBC),[38] under the direction of the Commissioner of Competition, which investigates anticompetitive practices and promotes compliance with the laws under its jurisdiction. In criminal cases, the CBC works together with the Director of Public Prosecutors (DPP), who is responsible for prosecuting individuals and companies for violations of the criminal provisions under the Act, and punishing individuals for serious and deliberate misconduct.[39]

As far as the topic of this chapter is concerned, "the existence of a program does not immunize businesses or individuals from enforcement action by the commissioner or from prosecution by the DPP."[40] However, the compliance program may play a role as a ground of exclusion of liability in offences containing a due diligence defense[41]

[36] The expression is taken from *Global Convergence on Anti-corruption Compliance: A Canadian Example* (Shearman & Sterling LLP, November 2011), available via http://www.shearman.com/publications/.

[37] For an overview of the Act, see Lowman et al. 2008, p. 691.

[38] The CCB is also responsible for the administration and enforcement of the Consumer Packaging and Labelling Act, the Textile Labelling Act, and the Precious Metals Marking Act.

[39] See "Policy Round-tables—Promoting Compliance with Competition Law," OECD, available via the OECD website at http://www.oecd.org/daf/competition/latestdocuments/.

[40] See "Bulletin—Corporate Compliance Programs" (henceforth, "Bulletin"), Government of Canada—Competition Bureau, available via the website of the Competition Bureau, http://www.competitionbureau.gc.ca/eic/site/cb-bc.nsf/eng/03280.html, 14.

[41] See Sect. 52.1, deceptive telemarketing, Sect. 53, deceptive notice of winning a prize, and Sect. 55, multi-level marketing plans. Certain provisions of the Consumer Packaging and Labelling Act, the Textile Labelling Act, and the Precious Metals Marking Act also contain a due diligence defense. Available at http://laws-lois.justice.gc.ca/eng/acts/.

and also—most commonly—as a mitigating factor.[42] Last but not least, the existence of a compliance program (rather the nonexistence of a compliance program, or the existence of a merely cosmetic compliance program[43]) may be taken into account as an aggravating factor for sentencing purposes or any other form of resolution, including administrative monetary penalties (Bulletin, 17).

Regarding the defense of due diligence, it is important to stress two points. Firstly, very few sections of the Competition Act contain a defense of due diligence (Bulletin, 16). This means that an effective compliance program is not as rule a ground for exclusion of criminal liability. Secondly, the pre-existence of a program is not, in and of itself, a defense against allegations of wrongdoing under any of the acts. So, only a credible and effective program can enable a business to demonstrate that it took reasonable steps to avoid contravening the law.

Despite this, the commissioner "may give weight to the pre-existence of a credible and effective program in making sentencing recommendations to the DPP" (Bulletin, 16). In other words, the presence of a credible and effective program, or the fact of taking verifiable steps to strengthen an existing one in response to a violation of the Act, may be seen as a mitigating factor warranting a reduction in the penalty. It must be pointed out that the commissioner may recommend that the DPP reduce the penalty, justifying such a reduction by reference to the existence of an effective compliance program, but the DPP has ultimate discretion as to whether to accept or reject the Commissioner's recommendation (Bulletin, 15).

Last but not least, having an effective compliance program in place also allows the determination of which regimen (civil or criminal) is the most appropriate for addressing misleading representations and deceptive marketing practices.[44]

21.3.2 Towards an Effective Compliance Program: Guidance from the CBC

On 27 September 2010, the Canada's Competition Bureau (hereinafter CCB) published a revised version of its Information Bulletin on Corporate Compliance Programs (hereinafter the Bulletin),[45] wherein it sets out its views with respect to corporate programs designed to ensure compliance with the Competition Act, the

[42] Further positive impacts of establishing a credible and effective program or of taking verifiable steps to strengthen an existing one in response to a violation are visible in the remedy sought by the Commissioner in civil re-viewable matters and in leniency programs. See Bulletin, 14. In the scholarship, see Goldman and Katz 1999, p. 33.

[43] Regarding the expression "cosmetic compliance programs," see Krawiec 2003, p. 487.

[44] See Goldman and Bodrug 2009; R v. Benlolo [June 2006], Ontario Court of Appeal. See also "Misleading Representations and Deceptive Marketing Practices: Choice of Criminal or Civil Track under the Competition Act," Government of Canada—Competition Bureau, http://www.competitionbureau.gc.ca/eic/site/cb-bc.nsf/eng/01223.html.

[45] The first version is dated 3 July 1997. For a general and brief overview of the Bulletin, see Baldanza and Di Padova 1999, p. 241.

Consumer Packaging and Labelling Act, the Textile Labelling Act, and the Precious Metal Marking Act. This regulatory compliance guidance bears in mind the US guidelines' recommendations for an effective compliance program but sets things out in more detail.

The preface to the Bulletin highlights the key issues for consideration:

> This Bulletin describes measures that businesses should consider in order to prevent or minimize their risk of contravening the Acts, and to detect contraventions, should they occur. The Bulletin also provides tools to help Canadian businesses develop their own compliance program….
> Implementing a program is not required by the Acts, but can, in certain circumstances, be ordered by a court [competition tribunal]….This Bulletin outlines the essential components of such a program. To be credible, a program must demonstrate the company's commitment to conducting business in conformity with the law. To be effective, it needs to inform employees about their legal duties, the need for compliance with internal policies and procedures as well as the potential costs, actual and opportunity (i.e., the cost of not complying with the law) of contravening the law and the harm it may cause to the Canadian economy. A good corporate compliance program helps to identify the boundaries of permissible conduct, as well as identify situations where it would be advisable to seek legal advice. Moreover, in some cases, courts have recognized a credible and effective compliance program as a mitigating factor when assessing remedies in the event of a breach.
> The Bureau recognizes that certain businesses may already have a program in place and encourages them to take the opportunity to ensure that the essential components highlighted in this Bulletin are reflected in their program.

First of all, as a rule the decision to implement a program is voluntary. There are, however, cases where it is compulsory: (1) when a prohibition order has been issued by the commissioner (Sect. 34 of the Competition Act); (2) when a court issues a probation order (here the above-mentioned Sect. 732.1 of the Criminal Code is applicable); and (3) when a consent agreement is reached (Sects. 74.12 and 105 of the Competition Act).

Secondly, given the fact that businesses are not all alike, businesses "must tailor their program to address the compliance issues specific to their industry or market" (Bulletin, 1). Therefore, the relevant components described in the bulletin "are neither industry nor company-specific, and are recommended as the baseline for the development of any in-house program" (Bulletin, 1). That means that the guidance must be interpreted as "a general guide only and the Bureau will not deem a compliance program deficient or non-credible if a company deviates from the Framework, where the deviation is reasonable in the circumstances." Besides this, "the Framework is not binding on the Commissioner of Competition" (Bulletin, 20).

Regarding the content of the guidelines, there are five fundamental elements considered crucial in a proper compliance program (Bulletin, 7):

1. Senior management involvement and support
2. Corporate compliance policies and procedures
3. Training and education
4. Monitoring, auditing, and reporting mechanisms
5. Consistent disciplinary procedures and incentives

The first element, senior management involvement and support, on the one hand requires senior management to identify and assess the principal risks faced by the business, and on the other requires them to implement appropriate systems to manage such risks. Furthermore, senior management must foster a culture of compliance within the business organization by playing an active and visible role in promoting its program. This concerns the "tone at the top" doctrine.[46] By demonstrating its commitment to compliance, senior management is conveying the message that contraventions of the acts are not acceptable as legitimate business practices. In this regard, fluent communication between senior management and the board of directors, and reports on compliance program issues such as progress and breaches, are also very important.

The board should also be involved in the appointment of the person or group responsible for compliance, the endorsement of the business compliance program, and any disciplinary actions resulting from a breach. The involvement of the board serves as an additional protection where senior managers may be the perpetrators of a contravention of the law (Bulletin, 7).

The second element refers to the need for up-to-date publication of the substantive content of a corporate compliance program. The document, and its updates, must be available to all employees in a readily (and easily) accessible format. The document can include examples, such as a list of "do's" and "don'ts" in particular cases (i.e., bid submission), or "Red Flag" issues which make it clear to employees what they should do in a given situation. Another important measure is to request employees to sign a certification letter stating that they have read and understood the compliance program in place.[47]

Concerning training and education, the Bulletin encourages corporations to provide an ongoing training component focusing on compliance issues for staff at all levels who are in a position to potentially engage in, or be exposed to, conduct in breach of the Acts.

Employees must be trained to detect prohibited conduct and educated about the range of penalties and remedies for noncompliance. In other words, the training method must make employees aware of the imposition of disciplinary measures in cases of noncompliance.

As examples of training methods, the Bulletin cites the use of small-group seminars, manuals, email messages, online training, workshops, descriptions of prohibited conduct, and the issuance of regular Bulletins discussing current compliance issues. According to the bulletin, experts (i.e., knowledgeable legal counsel or a compliance officer) are best positioned to deliver effective training courses.

---

[46] On this doctrine, see Schwartz et al. 2005, p. 79; Schroeder 2002, p. 260; Joseph 2002, p. 309; Vitell et al. 2000, p. 15.

[47] Bulletin, 8. The bulletin offers a sample: "I, …. Of the City of … , am employed by … in the capacity of … I acknowledge that I am subject to and am required to comply with…'s Corporate Compliance Program, including its Policies and Procedures (the 'Program'). This is to advise that I have read and understand [Company X]'s Program, the goal of which is to promote compliance with the [specify: the acts] generally and [list specific sections of the act] that are relevant to the business]. I understand that compliance with [Company X]'s Program is a condition of my continued employment with [Company X] and that failure to comply with the Program may result in disciplinary action, including termination of employment. I also understand that this certification letter is not a guarantee of continued employment with [Company X]."

It is also highlighted that senior management should play an active role by delivering compliance messages to employees, reinforcing their support for the program, undertaking the necessary compliance training themselves, sending emails supporting the compliance program, and referring to the program in presentations and during other speaking opportunities. Again and again, this concerns the tone at the top doctrine.

Training programs must be regularly evaluated by the business's compliance officer or equivalent (e.g., by regularly testing the employees' knowledge of the law, as well as the company's compliance policies and procedures, to determine whether the program needs to be updated or modified). It is recommended that all employees be trained at an early stage (for instance, during an initial orientation session); that senior management and staff be trained as required in particular circumstances to recognize and address compliance issues; that employees' knowledge of compliance policies and procedures be regularly assessed; and that all training sessions be documented (Bulletin, 9).

Regarding monitoring, auditing, and reporting mechanisms, such procedures should enable companies to identify areas of risk, areas where additional specific training is required, and areas where new compliance issues may require new policies to be developed (Bulletin, 10). Monitoring refers to the ongoing procedures implemented to prevent contravention of the Acts. Evidence of such efforts may also support a due diligence defense should litigation arise. Depending on the risks, periodic or continuous monitoring may be necessary. A business could take the opportunity to verify whether any of its internal or external practices may potentially contravene the Acts.

Audits may be periodic, ad hoc, or event triggered, and should be designed to determine whether a contravention has occurred. Audits are designed to identify whether a contravention of the law has occurred and, if so, to ensure that it has been dealt with appropriately.

Last but not least, an internal reporting procedure encourages employees to provide timely and reliable information that can be the basis for further investigation by the business. Employees must be encouraged to freely report conduct that they believe contravenes the Acts or company policy. The program should clearly identify which actions require reporting, and when and to whom they should be reported.

An effective reporting system can be achieved in different ways, for example by implementing a confidential reporting system, endorsing an open-door policy, promoting an anonymous hotline, or by identifying legal counsel as compliance resources (Bulletin, 10).

While an internal reporting mechanism is important, there may be situations where the use of an external reporting mechanism would be more appropriate. A program should also educate employees who are in a position to engage in, or be exposed to, conduct in potential breach of the Acts on the Bureau's Immunity Program and the whistle-blowing provisions.

By way of illustration, the Bulletin suggests the following measures: monitor business activities continuously or periodically, as appropriate, to ensure compliance; review the program when issues arise or are detected; plan formal audits, either by appointment or unannounced, to check for actual contraventions; use surveys, focus groups, and exit interviews to assess the effectiveness of the compliance program; conduct audits to confirm whether a business is fully complying with the Acts, where an audit may include a review of paper and computer files (especially emails) of staff who are in a position to engage in, or be exposed to, conduct in potential breach of the Acts; take immediate action to stop any contravention of the Acts; cooperate with the government where a breach has occurred (which involves self-reporting); put in place a confidential reporting procedure (for instance, inform senior management when an incident occurs and report to legal counsel); identify employees who are exposed to a heightened risk (for instance, based on roles and responsibilities, previous issues, and misconduct); and document all compliance efforts (this will also assist a company in advancing a defense of due diligence, where available) (Bulletin, 12).

Notably, the list above refers to disciplinary procedures and incentives: "A credible and effective program should explicitly state that disciplinary actions (for example, suspension, demotion, dismissal, and even legal action) will be taken where an employee contravenes the Acts" (Bulletin, 12). On the other hand, incentives are also crucial (i.e., compliance could be considered for the purposes of employee evaluations, promotions, and bonuses). All disciplinary actions and procedures should be recorded since proper documentation can support a claim of due diligence defense where a business is found to be in contravention of the Acts. Proper disciplinary actions should also be taken against managers who fail to take reasonable steps to prevent or detect misconduct.

21.3.3 Towards an Effective Compliance Program: Guidance from Case law

The Bulletin states that "courts have recognized a credible and effective compliance program as a mitigating factor," which bodes well for finding interesting cases concerning this point. Nevertheless, a thorough analysis of different databases[48] yielded no cases in which compliance programs figure as a ground for exclusion of liability (that is to say, as a full due diligence defense) or as a mitigating factor.

Furthermore, most of the cases on compliance program issues found are consent agreements.[49] To put it differently: they are alternative case resolutions (ACRs).

[48] All databases containing judgments, court orders, and consent agreements related to cases involving the Bureau of Competition. This includes the following: Alberta Courts (http://www.albertacourts.ab.ca/); Competition Tribunal (http://www.ct-tc.gc.ca/CasesAffaires/Cases-eng.asp); Federal Court of Canada (http://decisions.fct-cf.gc.ca/en/index.html); Nova ScotiaCourts (http://www.courts.ns.ca/); Ontario Superior Court of Justice (http://www.canlii.org/en/index.html); and Quebec Courts (http://www.jugements.qc.ca/). Westlaw International and V-Lex have been also used to this end but without success.

[49] A consent agreement is signed by the Commissioner and a person in respect of whom the Commissioner has applied or may apply for an order of the court. Such an agreement may be filed with the court for immediate registration. If so, the proceedings, if any, are terminated and the consent agreement has the same force and effect, and proceedings may be taken, as if it were an order of the court. In some cases, the court may rescind or vary a consent agreement that it has registered or an order on application by the Commissioner or the person who consented to the agreement, or the

Nevertheless, they deserve to be analyzed since the factors considered by the commissioner in signing such consent agreements are related to compliance measures implemented by the corporation after the commission of the breach. Thus, it is important for the commissioner's decision whether the business terminated the conduct in breach of the Acts as soon as it was detected or whether it attempted to remedy the adverse effects of the conduct (Bulletin, 16).

In most of the consent agreements analyzed, the Competition Tribunal (CT) required the corporation to establish and maintain a compliance program, and in doing so it refers the corporation to the above-mentioned Commissioner's Information Bulletin on "Corporate Compliance Programs."[50] As well as this, the elements of the compliance program that are to be included are indicated in the majority of cases:[51]

---

person against whom the order was made. See Competition Act R.S.C., 1985, c. C-34, Sects. 74.12 and 74–16, available on the Government of Canada—Justice Laws Website, http://laws-lois.justice.gc.ca/eng/acts/c-34/.

[50] See Competition Tribunal (CT), *Commissioner of Competition v. Brent Marsall,* Dynasty Spas and Games Rooms, Rochelle Marsall, Dynasty Spas Inc. and 1232466 Alberta Ltd., decided: 17 January 2011; CT, *Commissioner of Competition v. Sleepwise Inc.,* [2009]; CT, *Commissioner of Competition v. Elkhorn Ranch & Resort Ltd.,* [2009], CarswellNat 4781; CT, *Commissioner of Competition v. Phonetime Inc.,* [2009] CarswellNat 4782; CT, *Commissioner of Competition v. Polar Spas (Edmonton) Ltd.,* [2009] CarswellNat 4790; CT, *Commissioner of Competition v. Metron* [2009] CarswellNat 4787; CT, *Commissioner of Competition v. 6474675 Canada Inc.,* [2009] CarswellNat 4794; CT, *Commissioner of Competition v. Dynastyspasregina Inc.,* [2009] CarswellNat 4785; CT, *Commissioner of Competition v. Valley Spas Invermere* [2009] CarswellNat 4786; CT, *Commissioner of Competition v. Avonnlee Pies and Fine Baking,* [2009] CarswellNat 4795; CT, *Commissioner of Competition v. 1327974 Alberta Ltd.,* [2009] CarswellNat 4835; CT, *Commissioner of Competition v. Premium Wholesale Home and Leisure,* [2009] CarswellNat 5854; CT, *Commissioner of Competition v. Valley Spas Invermere,* [2009] CarswellNat 5855; CT, *Commissioner of Competition v. Curry's Art Store Ltd.,* [2009] CarswellNat 4797; CT, *Commissioner of Competition v. Northern Response International Ltd.,* [2008] CarswellNat 5947; CT, *Commissioner of Competition v. Premier Fitness Clubs,* [2007] CarswellNat 4171; CT, *Commissioner of Competition v. Grafton-Fraser Inc.,* [2006] CarswellNat 6432; CT, *Commissioner of Competition v. Media Syndication Global,* [2006] CarswellNat 6426; CT, *Commissioner of Competition v. McNabb,* [2006] CarswellNat 6419; CT, *Commissioner of Competition v. Walsh,* [2006] CarswellNat 6429; CT, *Commissioner of Competition v. Media Syndication Global, Havas S.A. and Interactive Marketing Group ULC,* decided 14 June 2006; CT, *Commissioner of Competition v. Grattan,* [2005] CarswellNat 7059; CT, *Commissioner of Competition v. Grattan,* [2005] CarswellNat 7056; CT, *Commissioner of Competition v. Stothers,* [2005] CarswellNat 7060; CT, *Commissioner of Competition v. 3283312 Canada Inc.,* [2005] CarswellNat 7057; CT, *Commissioner of Competition v. Goodlife Fitness Clubs Inc.,* [2005] CarswellNat 7055; CT, *Commissioner of Competition v. Performance Marketing Ltd.,* [2004] CarswellNat 6905; CT, *Commissioner of Competition v. Urus Industrial Corp.,* [2004] CarswellNat 6908; CT, *Commissioner of Competition v. Forzani Group Ltd.,* [2004] CarswellNat 6904; CT, *Commissioner of Competition v. Suzy Shier Inc.,* [2003] CarswellNat 6105; CT, *Commissioner of Competition v. Urus Industrial Corporation o/a Koolatron,* decided: 22 July 2004.

[51] The level of detail in this regard has grown over the time. For example, a 2000 consent agreement consulted contained a little information about the elements of the compliance program. It states only that the corporation has to develop a Corporate Compliance Policy Manual with respect to the respective act. See, e.g., *Commissioner of Competition v. 1376535 Ontario Limited,* Tadros & Tadros Limited, Ibrahim & Tadros Inc. and Tadros and Mina Limited, operating as fine gold

- The designation of a Corporate Compliance Officer
- The development of a written Corporate Compliance Policy in respect of…(this varies depending on the provision breached, i.e., deceptive marketing practices, ordinary prices provisions, advertising, etc.) of the Act (the "Compliance Policy") which will include, among other things:
- — A statement by senior management stressing the company's commitment to the policies and procedures contained therein
- — A reference to the purpose of the Act, a general description of the Act, as well as a description of those provisions of the Act that are most relevant to [the corporation], including the enforcement, penalty, and remedy provisions
- — Clear examples to illustrate the specific practices that are prohibited, so that [the corporation's] personnel at all levels can easily understand the potential application of the Act to their own duties; a practical code of conduct that identifies activities that are illegal or open to question; a statement outlining the consequences of breaching corporate policies; procedures that detail exactly what an employee should do when concerns arise out of certain situations, or when possible violations of the Act are suspected; and training sessions to ensure that all persons, to whom this agreement applies, understand the terms of this Agreement and the Compliance Policy
- The distribution of the Compliance Policy to its personnel
- The inclusion of the Compliance Policy in any and all marketing policy manuals and retail store operations manuals or in the corporation's intranet network[52]
- The development of and delivery to its personnel of a mandatory Compliance Program/Compliance Policy education session
- The development and delivery of an annual refresher Compliance Program/Compliance Policy education session for the corporation's personnel
- The annual acknowledgment, in writing, by its personnel, of their awareness and comprehension of the Compliance Program and Compliance Policy as provided in Appendix "F" of the Agreement
- An annual review of the Compliance Program and Compliance Policy
- Some consent agreements are even more detailed,[53] requiring in addition the promulgation of a practical code of conduct (the "Code") that identifies activities that are illegal or open to question and includes the following features at a minimum:
- A message from the respective President/CEO of the corporation explaining the importance of the code and the requirement for adherence by all employees as a condition of employment
- Employee responsibilities under the code

---

jewelers and the Diamond Co., and Mansour Tadros and Isis Tadros, at 3, decided: 20 December 2002. Since 2003 consent agreements have started to become more detailed.

[52] See, e.g., *The Commissioner of Competition v. Forzani Group Ltd.*, [2004] CarswellNat 6904, at 8.

[53] Canada (Commissioner of Competition) v. Media Syndication Global, [14 June 2006] CarswellNat 6426.

- Penalties for violation and ways of reporting any violation of the code to management and/or company legal counsel
- Examples of activities that fall under the criminal and civil provisions of the Act regarding false or misleading representations and deceptive marketing practices in promoting the supply or use of a product or any business interest
- A statement outlining the consequences of breaching corporate policies
- Procedures that detail exactly what an employee should do when concerns arise out of certain situations, or when possible violations of the Act are suspected
- Training sessions to ensure that all persons to whom this Agreement applies understand the terms of this Agreement and the Compliance Policy

21.4 Compliance Programs in other Areas

A particularly interesting area of study is the sector of strict liability offences. As has been said, the possibility of taking into consideration a "due diligence" defense in these cases blurs the line between regulatory offences and mens rea crimes. Therefore, many of the factors concerning corporate conduct which are considered relevant to determining that a company acted with due diligence in the case of regulatory offences could also be taken into account in criminal offences of subjective fault (i.e., intent).

In particular, situations of noncompliance with the Tobacco Act are illustrative here. In these cases a corporation is accused of supplying cigarettes to young persons in different locations. Sometimes the corporation is also accused of failing to post, in the prescribed place and manner, signs in the prescribed form and with the prescribed content that inform the public that the sale of a tobacco product to a young person is prohibited.

For our purpose, these judgments are interesting mainly because they focus on the key elements of every compliance program—in particular, on the existence of an appropriate training program and on monitoring and reviewing measures. Thus, the following analysis examines the standard of "having taken reasonable steps to train corporate employees and meet the standards of due diligence."[54] In any case, what is incontestably clear is that the due diligence defense may not be successful when the corporation has not instructed its employees regarding the appropriate procedures for selling tobacco,[55] or indeed has never conducted any training sessions

[54] Section 54 of The Tobacco Act 1997, Chap. 13, and similar acts in other states, provide as follows: "54. In a prosecution for an offence under this Act, it is sufficient proof of the offence to establish that it was committed by an employee or agent, of the accused, whether or not the employee or agent is identified or has been prosecuted for the offence, unless the accused establishes that the offence, was committed without the knowledge or consent of the accused and that the accused exercised all due diligence to prevent its commission."

[55] See R. v. Yung [1997], A.J. n. 547.

at all.[56] Nor will it be successful when the corporation failed to inform sales staff of the content of warning letters previously received from governmental agencies.[57]

21.4.1 Cases of Successful Due Diligence Defenses

21.4.1.1 R v. Robert Klein Enterprises Inc.[58]

To establish the defense of due diligence in *Robert Klein Enterprises Inc.,* the corporation called a number of witnesses. Among them, the corporation office manager indicated that "on tobacco issues there was a policy and procedure manual and employee contracts were signed which acknowledged the obligation of each employee to comply with The Tobacco Act." It was also highlighted that "the employees were required to sign a statement *on receipt of pay cheques*, approximately once a month, to the effect that they understood the requirements of and would comply with The Tobacco Act" (*Robert Klein Enterprises Inc.,* at 13, emphasis added).

As the same time, it was proved that a company policy manual and employees' policy manual instructions given to all employees required them to sign memos acknowledging instructions. It was described how, at managers' weekly meetings, information was given to managers which was to be disseminated to employees. Managers signed memos acknowledging instructions regarding compliance with age checks under the Tobacco Act. Employees were also required to sign documents acknowledging familiarity with the policies and instructions with respect to the tobacco sales (*Robert Klein Enterprises Inc.,* at 14).

Furthermore, the manager exhibited "a test Mystery Shopper Program, where a shopper in the employ of the Corporation would be sent to test compliance with The Tobacco Act in stores" (*Robert Klein Enterprises Inc.,* at 15). When the test shopper tested an employee, the employee would be advised with respect to failures or successful incidents of verifying age.

At the same time, store managers and store employees were also phoned to remind them with respect to the requirements of complying with age verification: "The phone calls were described as being twice a day but did not necessarily cover all stores each day." Besides this, "employees were made aware of this policy and on occasion employees were disciplined" (*Robert Klein Enterprises Inc.,* at 16). The corporate policy was that "employees who failed to comply with the requirements for checking would receive a warning for a first failure and for a second failure they would be given a 2-day suspension from work. A third occasion would result in dismissal" (*Robert Klein Enterprises Inc.,* at 15).

[56] See R. v. Taylor's Pharmacy [unreported], Alberta Provincial Court decision, 3 September 1997.

[57] See R. v. Yung [1997], A.J. n. 547.

[58] *R. v. Robert Klein Enterprises Inc.,* Saskatchewan Provincial Court, Henning Prov. J., Judgment: February 13, 2004.

It was also proved through an employee called as a witness that when someone was hired by the corporation, he or she was given written information and a manual of procedures that were to be followed which covered the Tobacco Act (*Robert Klein Enterprises Inc.,* at 7). Assessments had indicated that the instructions in this manual were understandable (ibid.). Indeed, employees were supposed to sign a document indicating that they had read the various instructions.

To sum up: the accused corporation had a policy of compliance and had emphasized the need for that policy through their management system: (1) all employees were given written and verbal instructions regarding compliance with the Tobacco Act; (2) regular, though not necessarily daily, phone calls were made to each store to remind them of the need for compliance; (3) sanctions were in place for employees who were found not to be complying with the corporation policy; (4) the owner of the chain visited all stores daily or at least two or three times a week and emphasized compliance; (5) a test shopper program, though limited in frequency, was in place; and (6) appropriate signs were distributed.

Could that be considered enough to establish a due diligence defense? Before answering this question, the court stated that "what is reasonable and effective compliance to amount to due diligence will depend on the nature of the subject matter, the harm sought to be contained or managed by the legislation, the measures and resources that may reasonably be available and applied, and the actual measures taken for compliance" (*Robert Klein Enterprises Inc.,* at 23). The size of the store chain itself, as well as the stores which comprised it, is also an important criterion to consider.[59] In this case—stores of relatively small size—the aforementioned measures were judged sufficient,[60] even though some failures were underlined. For example, the Court highlighted regarding the instructions given to employees once they were hired, that they did not receive any formal training with respect to the sale of tobacco products. Although employees were sporadically tested for compliance with the Tobacco Act (*Robert Klein Enterprises Inc.,* at 7, 15, 21), "further measures in

[59] This element is reminiscent of the US Sentencing Guidelines. See § 8B2.1. Effective Compliance and Ethics Program: "Factors to Consider in Meeting Requirements of this Guideline.—(i) In General…in determining what specific actions are necessary to meet those requirements, factors that shall be considered include:…(ii) the size of the organization…." See "USSC Guidelines Manual," United States Sentencing Commission, available via http://www.ussc.gov/.

[60] *Robert Klein Enterprises Inc.,* at 29. Bear in mind that the Court dismissed the charges related to supplying cigarettes to young persons. However, it found the accused corporation guilty of the offence of failing to post prescribed signage. "Notwithstanding that it was the policy of the Accused Corporation to display signage, I conclude that there was no sign displayed where it was 'conspicuous' reasonably visible. If there was a sign in the store in question, the evidence discloses it was not to be seen by reasonable inspection at the store entrance of the check-out counter. It is not sufficient compliance for a sign to be located at the back of store where it might be discoverable but not readily noticeable. It must comply with the descriptor 'conspicuous and not obstructed' contained in the Regulations. Appropriate signage must always be displayed and in the absence of some explanation, for example, that the omission was extraordinary and temporary due to some unusual occurrence, the required level of due diligence is not met" (ibid., at 32).

conducting employee training sessions might have been possible,"[61] but that does not mean that "such sessions are a necessity to establish due diligence."

Last but not least, it is also worth mentioning as regards this case that the Court used the "reasonable check-list" issued by Health Canada[62] for compliance with the Tobacco Act as a parameter to assess whether all reasonable steps to avoid misconduct had been taken. It was determined that "not all things in this check-list were actually carried out. For example, training sessions that included role playing exercises were not carried out nor were there reminders attached to cash registers" (*Robert Klein Enterprises Inc.*, at 26). It is important to note that the Court does not assign the force of law to such standards as issued by a governmental agency. That means that it is not necessarily the case that a failure to comply with all of these recommended measures should constitute a lack of due diligence. Nevertheless, there is no doubt that the checklist is "a useful guide to retailers" and "it appears to represent the most exhaustive possible list of measures that may be undertaken to ensure compliance." Most importantly, it indirectly becomes "the legal standard by which due diligence is to be determined" (ibid.). What this boils down to is that "a retailer who complies with all measures would not likely be held liable for non-compliance with the Act when, as inevitably will happen at least occasionally, an employee fails to comply with the Act." This is a very strong assertion[63] because it virtually means that if a corporation follows (or, rather, thoroughly implements) the measures indicated in the checklist, it is not likely to be convicted. But, at the same time, because the recommendations are only persuasive suggestions, the corporation is not necessarily lacking in due diligence if it does not employ all of the measures recommended (*Robert Klein Enterprises Inc.*, at 26).

21.4.1.2 Domo Gasoline Corp.[64]

This case highlights the utmost importance of conducting "spot checks and surprise inspections" by persons unknown to the employees in order to determine whether the policy was being adhered to. Given the fact that the corporation had conducted such a control policy, the defense of due diligence was applicable. It would be interesting to transfer this idea to the scope of bribery offences and so to promote surprise audits as an effective tool in the fight against corruption.

[61] *Robert Klein Enterprises Inc.*, at 30: "I do not suggest that the Accused Corporation cannot make improvements in their compliance program, and they might indeed still wish to do so."

[62] Health Canada is the Federal department responsible for helping Canadians maintain and improve their health, while respecting individual choices and circumstances: "About Health Canada," Health Canada website, http://www.hc-sc.gc.ca/index-eng.php.

[63] In other cases, Courts have only said that "the defence of due diligence does not depend on the regulatory body establishing the guidelines, but rather on whether the vendor has established reasonable procedures, both in respect to establishing a policy and in respect to ensuring its observance." See *R. v. Sobeys Inc.,* [2000] 181 N.S.R. (2d) 263 (N.S. S.C.), 62.

[64] See *R. v. Domo Gasoline Corat,* [1997] Provincial Court decision, A.J. No. 1298.

21.4.2 Cases in which the Defense of Due Diligence was not Established

21.4.2.1 Sobeys Inc.

When the store chain, and the stores which comprise it, are large, the standard to determine that the corporation exercised due diligence to comply with the Tobacco Act is higher. In these cases structured and continuous training and monitoring programs for employees are required.

In the Sobeys case, it was shown that the corporation had already taken the first step of instructing its employees about the appropriate procedures to be followed. It had also implemented a regular system where employees were continuously reminded of the proper procedures to be followed (*Sobeys Inc.,* at 42). But in this case this was not enough, mainly because managers had notice of prior violations communicated by the Division Vice-President and they had not done anything to prevent future misconduct. It is not enough, therefore, "to simply repeat that the policy must be reviewed with all employees. Something further is then required."[65] Effective monitoring policies were thus lacking.

21.4.2.2 R v. Van Gard Drugs Ltd.[66]

The defense of due diligence was not established in this case because in spite of having a policy requiring its employees to ask anyone appearing to be under the age of 25 years for identification, and providing employees with a policy manual maintained in respect to dealing with the sale of tobacco products to minors, there was no requirement for the employees to sign the policy in order to indicate they had read and understood the manual. Another pertinent factor was that only oral training occurred when the employee was first hired, and there was no evidence of any additional training. In addition, the store had recently received a warning from the Department of Health that it had failed a compliance check and could be subject to more formal action and penalties in the event of another violation. Although the corporation had notice of prior violation, no "alarms bells" sounded in the "mind of management" such as to alert managers that the system in place was not working and required further testing.

[65] *Sobeys Inc.*, at 61–62: "Merely to ask the store managers to review with staff the existing policies or procedures is not sufficient to establish due diligence in the event of a subsequent violation…."

[66] *R. v. Van Gard Drugs Ltd.,* [11 March 1997] Alberta Provincial Court decision.

21.5 Conclusions

The attribution of conduct to a corporation in Canada is based mainly on a variation of the identification doctrine. In the case of mens rea offences other than negligence the Canadian Criminal Code states that a corporation could be held liable for the crimes (including corruption) committed by its employees or agents, "if a senior officer, with intent at least in part to benefit the corporation or organization, (a) acting within the scope of their authority, is a party to the offence; (b) having the mental state required to be a party to the offence and acting within the scope of their authority, directs the work of other representatives of the organization so that they do the act or make the omission specified in the offence; or (c) knowing that a representative of the organization is or is about to be a party to the offence, does not take all reasonable measures to stop [employees, agents, etc.] of the corporation from being a party to the offence."

The reference to the expression "reasonable steps" in (c) opens the doors to a due diligence defense which could play a relevant role as ground for exclusion of criminal liability when a corporation is charged with a serious criminal offence of subjective fault, for instance bribery offences.

Unfortunately, very few prosecutions have been pursued by criminal law authorities against corporations for (foreign) bribery offences, and even fewer have been successful. To date only two cases have been brought before the Canadian Courts. In the first one, *R. v. Watts,* there was no mention of compliance programs issues; in the second, *R. v. Nikon Resources Ltd.,* compliance programs questions came to the surface in the probation order imposed on Nikon. It is remarkable that all the requirements included in the probation order were taken from a US plea agreement and a deferred prosecution agreement. This setting foreshadows a trend towards adopting US practices related to compliance programs. Next time, perhaps, a corporation compliance program will be used expressly as a mitigating factor in sentencing in Canada. Section 718.21 of the Canadian Criminal Code is an important step in this direction.

References

Archibald, T., Jull, K., & Roach, K. (2004). The changed face of corporate criminal liability. *Criminal Law Quarterly, 48,* 367–96.

Archibald, T., Jull, K., & Roach, K. (2005). *Regulatory and corporate liability: From due diligence to risk management*. Toronto: Canada Law Book.

Baldanza, A.F., & Di Padova, A. (1999). Recent developments in Canadian competition law. *Canadian Business Law Journal, 32*(2), 241–290.

Bittle, S., & Snider, L. (2006). From manslaughter to preventable accident: Shaping corporate criminal liability. *Law & Policy, 28*(4), 470–496.

Chang, H. (2012). Establishing an anti-corruption compliance program in Canada. Blaney McMurtry Barristers and Solicitors LLP, August 2012. http://www.blaney.com/articles/. Accessed 23 July 2013.

Douglas, L.M. (2011). Canada. In T. Gruetzner et al. (Eds.), *Anti-bribery risk assessment: A systematic overview of 151 countries*. Oxford: Hart Publishing.

Dusome, P. (2007). Criminal liability under Bill C-45: Paradigms, prosecutors, predicaments. *Criminal Law Quarterly, 53*(2), 98–148.

Edwards, C.A., & Conlin, R.J. (2005). *CLV special report: Corporate and organizational liability for OH & S under Bill C-45*. Toronto: Carswell.

Esakov, G.A. (2010). Corporate criminal liability: A comparative review. *City University of Hong Kong Law Review, 2,* 181.

Goldman, C.S. & Bodrug, J.D. (Eds.). (2009). *Competition law of Canada*. New York: Juris Publishing, Inc.

Goldman, C.S., & Katz, M. (1999). International cartel cases: A Canadian perspective. *Antitrust, 15,* 33.

Heimann, F., & Gillian, D. (2009). Progress report 2009: Enforcement of the OECD convention on combating bribery of foreign public officials in international business transactions. Transparency International USA, http://www.transparency-usa.org/news/documents/FinalOECDProgressReport2009.pdf.

Jennings, G. (2012). Anti-corruption and bribery compliance US, UK, EU and Canada: How does it all fit together? Gowling Lafleur Henderson LLP, January 2012. http://www.gowlings.com/KnowledgeCentre/.

Joseph, J. (2002). Integrating business ethics and compliance programs. *Business and Society Review, 107,* 309.

Keith, N. (2010). Evolution of corporate accountability: From moral panic to corporate social responsibility. *Business Law International, 2*(3), 253.

Krawiec, K.D. (2003) Cosmetic compliance and the failure of negotiated governance. *Washington University Law Quarterly, 81,* 487–544.

Lafontaine, L. (2006). Canada's experience with the implementation of international conventions against corruption. Paper presented at the Seminar on International Cooperation on Anti-Corruption Including Fair Investigation Practices, Beijing, P.R. China, June 5–6, 2006. http://www.icclr.law.ubc.ca/.

Little, C.M., & Savoline, N. (2003). Corporate criminal liability in Canada: The criminalization of occupational health & safety offences. Filion Wakely Thorup Angeletti LLP Annual Firm Seminar, June 2003. http://www.docstoc.com.

Lowman, J., Boughs, S., Strekaf, J., & Riley, B. (2008). A practical guide to competition act compliance in the oil and gas industry. *Alberta Law Review, 45*(3), 691–734.

MacPherson, D.L. (2004). Extending corporate criminal liability: Some thoughts on Bill C-45. *Manitoba Law Journal, 30*(3), 253.

MacPherson, D.L. (2010). "Organizational" criminal liability of partnerships in Canada: Constitutional and practical impediments. *Manitoba Law Journal, 33*(2), 329–390.

Monk, A. (2011). The cost of doing business? Laws against bribery of foreign public officials in international business transactions. Fraser Milner Casgrain LLP, November 2011. http://www.dentons.com/.

Nelson, L., & Sulek, L. (2006). Due diligence defence in regulatory prosecutions: Developmental trends and current interpretation. Fasken Martineau DuMoulin LLP, November 2006. http://www.fasken.com/en/publications/.

OECD. (2011). Canada: Phase 3 report on the application of the convention on combating bribery of foreign public officials in international business transactions and the 2009 revised recommendation on combating bribery in international business transactions. OECD Directorate for Financial and Enterprise Affairs, March 18, 2011.

Schroeder, D. (2002). Ethics from the top: Top management and ethical business. *Business Ethics: A European Review, 11*(3), 260–267.

Schwartz, M.S., Dunfee, T.W., & Kline, M.J. (2005). Tone at the top: An ethics code for directors. *Journal of Business Ethics, 58,* 79–100.

Skinnider, E. (2012). *Corruption in Canada: Reviewing practices from abroad to improve our response*. Vancouver: ICCLR.

Tatum, J. (2012a). Enhancing corporate accountability under the criminal code through enforcing corporate social responsibility (May 1, 2012). http://papers.ssrn.com/sol3/papers.cfm?abstract_id = 2143940. Accessed 23 July 2013.

Tatum, J. (2012b). Revisiting Canada's commitment to the fight against global corruption and the need for nationality jurisdiction under the corruption of foreign publics officials act. (March 20, 2012). http://papers.ssrn.com/sol3/ papers.cfm?abstract_id = 2026442. Accessed 23 July 2013.

TI [Transparency International]. (2012). Exporting corruption? Country enforcement of the OECD anti-bribery convention. Transparency International Progress Report 2012. http://www.transparency.org/whatwedo/publications.

TI-Canada [Transparency International, Canada]. (2012). Second annual spotlight on anti-corruption: Current issues day of dialogue, 19 April 2012. http://www.transparency.ca/9-Files/Older/2012-Events/201207-TI-Dialogue_Rapporteur_Reports.pdf.

Todgham Cherniak, C.D. (2011). Canada's anti-foreign bribery regime requires a balancing act. *The Law and Development Review, 4*(3), 130–174.

Vitell, S.J., Dickerson, E.B., & Festervand, T.A. (2000). Ethical problems, conflicts and beliefs of small business professionals. *Journal of Business Ethics, 28*(1), 15–24.

Chapter 22
Corporate Responsibility and Compliance Programs in China

Marta Muñoz de Morales

Contents

In China, corporations can be held liable for the acts of their employees, directors, and officers under criminal, administrative, and civil regulations.[1]

Under civil regulations, Article 43 of the General Principles of the Civil Law of the People's Republic of China (PRC) provides that "an enterprise as a legal person shall bear civil liability for the operational activities of its legal representatives and other personnel." In addition, Article 63 of the same document provides that corporations shall also be liable for acts of their appointed agents.

In the field of criminal law, Article 30 of the PRC Criminal Law[2] punishes corporations[3] for the commission of crimes: "Companies, enterprises, institutions, state organs, and social organisations when committing acts endangering the society shall assume criminal liability when prescribed by law."[4]According to PRC Criminal Law and its amendments, issues concerning corporate criminal liability are also addressed by the valid judicial interpretations of the Chinese Supreme Court. These interpretations can be considered a source of law (Zhang 2012, p. 104). One of these

[1] For an account of the historical evolution of corporate criminal liability in China, see Liu 2000, p. 569; Zhang 2012, p. 103.

[2] The PRC Criminal Law came into force on 1 October 1997.

[3] The term used is criminal liability of "units," including not only any companies, enterprises, institutions, and organizations, but also entities in the public sector (e.g., state organs). See Zhang 2012, p. 103.

[4] Before the enactment of the Criminal Code, similar provisions punishing corporations through criminal law were included into special laws such as the 1987 Customs Law.

M. Muñoz de Morales (✉)
University of Castilla-la-Mancha, Albacete, Spain
e-mail: marta.mmorales@uclm.es

S. Manacorda et al. (eds.), *Preventing Corporate Corruption*,
DOI 10.1007/978-3-319-04480-4_22,

interpretations, issued in December 2012,[5] is focused on "several issues concerning the application of law for handling criminal cases of bribe offering."[6]

There has always been some confusion concerning the scope of corporate criminal liability in China. In fact, in recent decades legal scholars have not agreed even on the number of offences in the Criminal Code which allow for corporate criminal liability.[7] The question is still problematic today, but according to Zhang, after eight amendments to the PRC Criminal Law, the number of offences which can be committed by corporations has increased to 124 (Zhang 2012, p. 104). Most of them are found in Chap. 3 of the PRC, devoted to "crimes of disrupting the order of the socialist market economy," and Chap. 6 focused on "crimes of obstructing the administration of public order." Bribery offences are also crimes which can be committed by corporations.

The Supreme Court of the PRC has interpreted this broadly, stating that any crimes committed by the officers, employees, and agents of an entity can be treated as crimes committed by the entity itself, if certain conditions are fulfilled: (a) the crime is committed on behalf of the entity; (b) the crime is committed for the benefit of the entity, and (c) there is a gain of illegal income by the entity (Norton Rose Group 2012, p. 21).

The Chinese model of corporate criminal liability seems to be based on the "identification" approach. That is why, the unit crime is committed as a result of a decision made by the unit collectively or by a person in a position of responsibility, and reflects the will of the unit (Liu 2000, p. 574). Offences committed by ordinary employees would not amount to a unit crime. In other words, only the actions of senior and relatively senior management—such as the chairman of the board, general manager, or factory director—are relevant to whether a corporation is criminally liable (Liu 1999, p. 71). The fact of imputing the crime as a result of a decision made by the unit collectively appears to be an aggregate form of identification in which the acts of a number of individuals can be found to have a collective *mens rea* imputable to the unit (Allens 2008, p. 52). What is not clear is whether the Chinese corporate liability regime "would also cover situations where persons in position

[5] An english translation at "Interpretations of the Supreme People's Court on Bribe Offering," Ethic Intelligence, http://www.ethic-intelligence.com/compliance-tools/31-anti-bribery-and-anti-corruption-strategy/268-interpretations-of-the-supreme-people-s-court-on-bribe-offering, accessed 24 June 2013.

[6] Other interesting interpretations of the Supreme People's Court dealing with corporate criminal liability are the Supreme Court Interpretation on the Specific Issues Related to the Application of Criminal Law in Hearing Criminal Cases Involving Crimes Committed by Units (Supreme Court Interpretation no. 17/1999, adopted 18 June 1999, http://www.law-lib.com/law/law_view.asp?id=460), and the Supreme Court Interpretation on the Question of Whether or Not, in Hearing the Case of a Crime Committed by a Unit, One Should Distinguish Between Principal Criminal and Accomplice for the Persons who are Directly in Charge and the Other Persons who are Directly Responsible for the Crime (Supreme Court Interpretation no. 31/2000, adopted 28 September 2000, http://www.lawtime.cn/info/xingfa/fzdwfz/20110214111629.html).

[7] According to Chen, about 81 offences in the Criminal Code allow for corporate criminal liability; Liu puts the figure at 129. See Chen 1999, p. 181 and Liu 1999, p. 71, both as cited in Allens 2008, p. 51.

of responsibility knowingly failed to prevent an employee from committing [the crime], or if the lack of supervision or control by such persons made the commission of the crime possible" ("P.R. China," in ADB/OECD 2010).

On a separate issue, Article 31 of the Chinese Criminal Law makes reference to the dual punishment of the offence:

> Where a unit commits a crime, it shall be fined, and the persons who are directly in charge and the other persons who are directly responsible for the crime shall be given criminal punishment. Where it is otherwise provided for in the Specific Provisions of this Law or in other laws, those provisions shall prevail.[8]

Regarding bribery offences,[9] the PRC Criminal Law punishes domestic bribery and since 1 May 2011[10], it has also set out a clear prohibition on the payment of bribes to "foreign officials" and to "officials of international public organizations."[11] Bribery offenders can be either individuals or companies.[12]

Article 393 of the PRC Criminal Law punishes any unit offering rebates or service payments to state functionaries for the purpose of securing illegitimate benefits or in violation of state regulations.[13]

Since May 2011, bribery of foreign public officials has also been criminalized.[14] The offence is applicable to PRC nationals both inside and outside the PRC, and all PRC companies (and their managers) which carry out business overseas (including Sino–foreign joint ventures[15] and wholly foreign-owned enterprises). However, it must be borne in mind that as a rule under PRC law, a company is legally independent from its subsidiary, and is not liable for any of its subsidiary's actions, unless

[8] On the so-called "double punishment-based responsibility," see Zhang 2012, p. 106.

[9] For an historical overview of bribery regulations, see Zhigang 2011, p. 128.

[10] The Amendment was passed on 25 February 2011 by the PRC National People's Congress and came into effect on 1 May 2011. It states: "Whoever provides property to a foreign official or an international public organisation for the purpose of seeking an improper commercial benefit, will be punished in accordance with the provisions applicable to commercial bribery."

[11] The new provision derives from Article 16 of the UN Convention Against Corruption (UNCAC) on "the promise, offering or giving to a foreign public official or an official of a public international organization, directly or indirectly, of an undue advantage." The amendment has been considered to be a manifestation of "the Chinese government's zero tolerance of corruption and its determination to develop international cooperation ….." It also represents the Chinese compromise designed to meet international obligations. In this regard, see Zhigang 2011, p. 14.

[12] See "China," in Herbert Smith 2012, p. 20; Carlson et al. 2011, p. 517.

[13] For an overview of corruption and bribery offences in Hong Kong and Guangdong, see Independent Commission Against Corruption—Hong Kong (China) 1999, pp. 1–30.

[14] The 8th Amendment to the PRC Criminal Law was enacted on 1 May 2011. Since then Chinese anti-bribery provisions have covered foreign government officials and officials of international public organizations. With this amendment China has fulfilled the requirements of the United Nations Convention Against Corruption.

[15] This means that although the new provision does not directly affect non-PRC companies, a joint venture between a PRC company and a foreign company could also be held liable where the joint venture is organized under PRC law. The provision is also applicable in the case of a representative office in China of a non-PRC company that is involved in sales outside of China. See Carlson et al. 2011, p. 517.

the parent company is itself involved in such action (i.e., a parent company may be held liable if it authorized or instructed its subsidiary to commit bribery or if it had knowledge that its subsidiary was involved in such criminal conduct).[16] Along with the general offence of bribery, there is also the offence of "commercial bribery," understood as an act of unfair competition that is committed by private individuals or companies (that is to say, cases not involving state employees, or in other words bribery in the private sector). Such behavior may be punished by both criminal and noncriminal sanctions. Commercial bribery is an offence only when the value of the transaction exceeds RMB 10,000 (approx. US$ 1,600) where committed by an individual, or RMB 200,000 (approx. US$ 32,000) where committed by a company or other organization.

Under the Unfair Competition Law, criminal sanctions for corporations are the same as the ones provided for individuals. Noncriminal penalties for corporations may consist of a fine ranging from RMB 10,000 to RMB 200,000. Illegal income can be confiscated and business competitors can also bring a civil claim for unfair competition (Tang 2011, p. 63).

In the case of domestic bribery offences in the public sector, the above mentioned interpretation of the Supreme People's Court of December 2012 clarifies the penalties associated with different levels of official corruption.[17] It remains to be seen, however, whether or not such thresholds will be also taken into consideration in cases against corporate perpetrators (Fava et al. 2013, p. 2). In contrast, fines imposed on bribers in foreign cases have been clarified by the Supreme People's Procuratorate and the Ministry of Public Security: RMB 10,000 for individual bribe payers and RMB 200,000 for companies that pay bribes (Herbert Smith 2012, p. 21).

On another level, it is interesting to note the collateral consequences (i.e., reputational damage) for corporations for the commission of bribery offences both in the public and private sector. For instance, the Supreme Procuratorate[18] has a public database of criminally convicted bribe payers which is expected to soon be connected to local databases nationwide; and in many industries and regions, the authorities have set up blacklists that prohibit entities that have been convicted of bribery from being involved in public tenders.

As far as compliance issues are concerned, PRC antibribery regulations do not state that the implementation of antibribery measures by a company can be

---

[16] See Clifford Chance Report 2013, p. 16. Here the rules on principal–agent relationships under PRC civil law may be so applied.

[17] The Interpretation clarifies what range of payments constitutes a "serious case," a "very serious case," and a "major loss to the national interest," as well as the penalties associated with each. For example, a "serious case" carries a penalty of imprisonment for 5–10 years. A bribery case is considered to be "serious" where the amount of the bribe falls between RMB 200,000 and RMB 1 million or where the amount of the bribe is between RMB 100,000 and RMB 200,000 and aggravating factors occur (e.g., the bribe is offered to more than three persons). For further details, see Fava et al. 2013, p. 2.

[18] The People's Procuratorate is the body with primary responsibility for the prosecution of all criminal cases in China. See Article 5 of the Organic Law of the People's Procuratorate (promulgated by the National People's Congress in 1983).

considered as a defense against prosecution by local authorities and the courts. In other words, under PRC Criminal Law there are no affirmative defenses such as "adequate procedures" in the sense of the UK's Bribery Act (Clifford Chance Report 2013, p. 16). Does this mean that antibribery compliance programs may not have any effect at all? As is remarked in the Norton Rose Group Report:

> Since 2009, the PRC Government has initiated a new anticorruption campaign, targeted indiscriminately at officials, state-owned enterprises, and domestic and foreign private companies. All business operators will be expected to have taken adequate measures in response to this campaign, including codes of conduct, employee policies, training, etc. *The absence of such measures will be viewed unfavourably by local authorities, from both a political and legal perspective*. (Norton Rose Group 2012, p. 22; emphasis added)

Notably, the Norton Report also predicts that:

> In practice, the implementation of bribery prevention measures by a company may be presented to the authorities or the courts as evidence that the illegal actions of the company's agents were contrary to the company's regulations and serve to prevent a prosecution of individuals from becoming a prosecution of the company (Norton Rose Group 2012).

However, it remains to be seen whether or not such a scenario materializes. So far, the only step in that direction, albeit a small and timid one, is the above mentioned 2012 Interpretation of the Supreme People's Court on Several Issues Concerning Application of Law for Handling Criminal Cases of Bribe Offering. The 2012 Interpretation sets forth several incentives for preprosecution and postprosecution confessions from both entities and individuals. Preprosecution confessions can lead to mitigation or exemption from penalties,[19] while postprosecution confessions may only result in lighter penalties.[20] These provisions could be interpreted as a way of encouraging whistleblowing channels and voluntary disclosure. This reveals "a very modern and practical approach to the prosecution of bribery" (Hong et al. 2013). The 2012 Interpretation does not force corporations to disclose knowledge of bribery but it will likely influence "how corporate representatives of multinationals weigh their options in determining when and whether to proactively disclose compliance issues to regulators" (Fava et al. 2013, p. 3). In any case, as Nieto indicates in this volume, incentives awarded to offenders (whether natural or legal persons)

[19] Article 7: "A briber shall not be awarded for a 'meritorious act' under Article 68 of the Criminal Law when his/her voluntary confession, before the prosecution of his crime of bribery, leads to successful discovery of the corresponding crime of receiving the bribe. Instead the briber may be granted a reduced or exempted punishment in accordance with Paragraph 2, Article 390 of the Criminal Law."If the briber is an entity, and the entity or the responsible person for the entity initiates a confession before being prosecuted, the entity and the responsible person may be allowed a reduced or exempted punishment in accordance with Paragraph 2 of Article 390 of the Criminal Law. A person entrusted to give a bribe for an entity, who on his own initiative confesses his knowledge of the acts of bribery by the entity, may be allowed a reduced or exempted punishment in accordance with Paragraph 2 of Article 390 of the Criminal Law."

[20] Article 8: "A briber who has been prosecuted and confesses truthfully to his or her crimes may be sentenced with lighter penalties from within the applicable spectrum in accordance with Paragraph 3, Article 67 of the Criminal Law; where the confession of the briber prevents his crime from having significantly serious consequences, the briber can be given a reduced punishment."

cooperating or confessing their crimes are independent of the question of whether a corporation has implemented a compliance program before the commission of the crime. A corporation can confess and the penalty to be imposed could be mitigated even though the corporation policy is for the commission of offences. To put it differently, the 2012 Interpretation cannot be understood as a duty for corporations to adopt and implement compliance programs. As mentioned above, compliance programs do not lead to exemption from criminal liability nor mitigation. However, self-reporting mechanisms and voluntary disclosure do have a link with “confession incentives” and therefore, they can have some influence on how corporations are to organize themselves.

The last part of this contribution will be devoted to the study of some cases on corporate criminal liability for foreign bribery offences. Given that in China “having adequate procedures” is not a defense, it is not surprising that no trace of anything related to compliance program issues was to be found in Chinese case law.

According to the ADB/OECD Anticorruption Initiative for Asia and the Pacific (ADB/OECD 2010, p. 37), there have been “only a few convictions of companies for foreign bribery and none for domestic bribery.” The reasons for such low numbers of antibribery cases involving corporations can be summed up as follows: insufficient resources or expertise to conduct investigations and prosecutions of this nature; a belief that it is unimportant to go after companies (ADB/OECD 2010, p. 39); and above all the great discretion of regulatory agencies as to how they deal with noncomplying companies (especially private enterprises) combined with the fact that many companies are partially or wholly state owned (Donghua et al. 2011, p. 14).

The aforementioned reasons, together with the common Chinese prosecutorial trend of allowing the USA and other countries to pursue the persons, officials, and corporations which pay the bribes (Bath 2011, p. 34), give us some idea of the difficulties of finding relevant information on the role of compliance programs in case law.

In fact, the most high profile cases compiled either on bribery or commercial bribery usually make reference to corporate employees (Warin et al. 2012; Heimann and Dell 2013, p. 66). Examples of this include:

1. The *Rio Tinto* case[21] in which four employees were convicted by a Shanghai court for stealing state secrets and taking bribes from Chinese steel mills seeking to secure iron ore. They were given sentences of between 7 and 14 years in prison and ordered to pay hundreds of thousands of dollars in fines. The Shanghai No. 1 Intermediate People’s Court said that “the four have seriously damaged the interests of the Chinese steel enterprises and put those enterprise[s] in an unfavorable place in the iron ore negotiations and led to the suspension of the negotiations in 2009.” Although the corporation itself was not prosecuted, companies operating in China were paying attention to the case for some guidance on

[21] See Muñoz de Morales, “Corporate Responsibility and Compliance Programs in Australia,” in this volume.

this issue. Unfortunately, there is very little to say because the court proceedings on this topic were closed.[22]

2. The *Siemens* case. A number of former senior executives of state-owned Chinese enterprises were convicted and sentenced for accepting bribes from Siemens. Some of the offenders have even received suspended death penalties (Luo and Zhao 2011; Bushell-Embling 2011).

Regarding corporations themselves, there are a few cases worth mentioning, but unfortunately no information on compliance programs has been found.

Although it is not a criminal case but rather a civil one, the *Toyota* case of 2010 is interesting to consider. Chinese authorities fined Toyota Motor Corp.'s finance unit for bribing car dealers. Toyota disputes the charge. An official at the Jianggan Administration for Industry and Commerce in Hangzhou said the bribes took the form of rebates meant to encourage dealers to use Toyota's in-house finance wing rather than retail banks to finance customer purchases. The official Xinhua News Agency reported that authorities would fine the company RMB 140,000 (US$ 20,650) and have confiscated RMB 426,352 (US$ 65,500) in "illegal earnings" from 49 car sales (The Economic Times 2010) Toyota tried to legitimize these payments by saying that they were paid to the dealers for introducing customers to Toyota's finance unit.

The second case was against Guangzhou Pepsi Cola Beverage Co., Ltd. (hereinafter Pepsi), a subsidiary of PepsiCo. It was fined RMB 700,000 (approx. € 79,200) for the commission of a commercial bribery offence. According to the *China Food and Beverage Newsletter*(September 2009), the subsidiary offered bribes to 47 chain retailers, stores, and supermarkets in Foshan, asking them to display its products following certain requirements.[23] Pepsi Guangzhou got revenue of 3.05 million yuan and enjoyed a profit of 650,000 yuan. China's official judicial explanation concerning commercial bribery pointed out that commercial bribery referred to "bribery by business entities and their employees in order to buy or sell products and services (China Market Research 2009)."

To conclude, it can be said that compliance program issues are not still a main concern for corporations in the PRC. However, the door has been opened to confessions on the part of not only physical persons but also corporations. This, and the encouragement of whistleblowing channels and voluntary disclosure, could lead in the future to an increase in the importance of compliance programs in bribery cases.

[22] See "CS Newsflash," Compliance Strategists LLC, accessed 25 June 2013, http://compliancestrategists.net/newsflash.html.

[23] See "Chinese Anti-Corruption Law Amendment and the FCPA: One Year Later; Best Practices for Responding to a Chinese Government Commercial Bribery Investigation," Strafford, accessed 25 June 25 2013, http://www.straffordpub.com/products/chinese-anti-corruption-law-amendment-and-the-fcpa-one-year-later-2012–08-16.

References

ADB/OECD. (2010). Thematic review—final report, "P.R. China." In the criminalisation of bribery in Asia and the Pacific. http://www.oecd.org/site/adboecdanti-corruptioninitiative/46485272.pdf. Accessed 24 July 2013.

Allens, A. R. (2008). 'Corporate culture' as a basis for the criminal liability of corporations. February 2008. http://198.170.85.29/Allens-Arthur-Robinson-Corporate-Culture-paper-for-Ruggie-Feb-2008.pdf. Accessed 24 July 2013.

Bath, V. (2011). China, international business, and the criminal law. *Asian-Pacific Law & Policy Journal, 13*(1), 1–35.

Bushell-Embling, D. (2011). Ex-China Mobile exec sentenced to death. Telecom Asia Net, 25 July 2011. http://www.telecomasia.net/content/ex-china-mobile-exec-sentenced-death. Accessed 24 July 2013.

Carlson, E., Eliasoph, E., & Stratford, T. (2011). China amends criminal law to cover foreign bribery: Bribery of non-PRC government officials criminalized. *Financial Fraud Law Report, 3*(6), 517–521.

Chen, J. (1999). *Chinese law: Towards an understanding of Chinese law, its nature and developments*. The Hague: Kluwer Law International.

China Market Research. (2009). China food and beverage industry newsletter (September 2009). http://www.chinamarketresearch.com/sample3.pdf. Accessed 25 June 2013.

Clifford Chance Report. (2013). Anti-corruption legislation in the People's Republic of China. In a guide to anti-corruption legislation in Asia-Pacific, 9 May 2013. http://www.cliffordchance.com/publicationviews.html#/featuretopic1. Accessed 24 July 2013.

Donghua, C., Dequan, J., Shangkun, L., & Fangping, W. (2011). Selective enforcement of regulation. *China Journal of Accounting Research, 4*(1–2), 9–27.

Fava, P., Martin, A., & Li, H. (2013). 2013 guidance on PRC anti-bribery law focuses on bribe givers. Paul Hastings LLP, January 2013. http://www.paulhastings.com/publications-items/details/?id=f7c52a26-8aa5-6986-8b86-ff00008cffc3. Accessed 9 February 2014.

Heimann, F., & Dell, G. (2013). Progress report 2010: Enforcement of the OECD anti-bribery convention. Transparency international. http://www.transparency.org/whatwedo/pub/progress_report_2010_enforcement_of_the_oecd_anti_bribery_convention. Accessed 24 July 2013.

Herbert Smith, L. L. P. (2012). Asia anti-corruption report, "China." In Asia Anti-corruption, no. 1, Summer 2012. https://www.icsaglobal.com/assets/files/AsiaanticorruptionreportIssue1.pdf. Accessed 25 June 2013.

Hong, S., Ye, G., & Diot, R. (2013). China reinforces its anti-bribery arsenal. Norton Rose Fulbright. http://www.nortonrose.com/knowledge/publications/74721/china-reinforces-its-anti-bribery-arsenal. Accessed 25 June 2013.

Independent Commission Against Corruption—Hong Kong (China). (1999). *"Observing the law": A guide for businessmen in Guangdong and Hong Kong*. Hong Kong: Guangdong Provincial People's Procuratorate.

Liu, J. (1999). The legislation and judicial practice on punishment of unit crimes in China. In E. Albin et al. (Eds.), *Criminal responsibility of legal and collective entities*. Freiburg: Iuscrim.

Liu, X. (2000). Responsabilité et sanctions pénales des danweis en Chine. *Revue de science criminelle et de droit pénal comparé,* 3, pp. 569–584.

Luo, J., & Zhao, H. (2011). Siemens bribery scandal ends in death sentence. Caixin online, 30 June 2011. http://english.caixin.com/2011-06-30/100274546.html. Accessed 23 July 2013.

Norton Rose Group. (2012). Anti-corruption laws in Asia Pacific. January 2012. http://www.nortonrosefulbright.com/files/anti-corruption-laws-in-asia-pacific-63559.pdf. Accessed 24 July 2013.

Tang, C. (2011). China. In G. Thomas et al. (Eds.), *Anti-bribery risk assessment: A systematic overview of 151 countries*. Oxford: Hart Publishing.

The Economic Times. (2010). China fines Toyota finance arm for alleged bribery. http://articles.economictimes.indiatimes.com/2010–09-21/news/27629744_1_finance-unit-china-and-japan-xinhua-news-agency. Accessed 25 June 2013.

Warin, J. F., Austin, K. S., Pathak, J. S., & Schwarz, B. (2012). Webcast: FCPA trends in the emerging markets of China, India, Russia and Central and Latin America. Gibson Dunn & Crutcher LLP, January 2012. http://www.lexology.com/library/detail.aspx?g=b865fcf4-240b-439f-aa9e-c097340fcf06. Accessed 24 July 2013.

Zhang, Y. (2012). Corporate criminal responsibility in China: Legislations and its deficiency. *Beijing Law Review, 3*(3), 103–108.

Zhigang, Y. (2011). China's system of anti-corruption charges: The tightening-up process and future development. *Social Sciences in China, 32*(4), 128–147.

Chapter 23
Corporate Liability and Compliance Programs in France

Juliette Tricot

Contents

23.1 Is the French Criminal Justice System a Counter-model?

The remarkable and extremely rapid development of corporate antibribery rules is an undisputable feature of the modern international criminal policy on corruption, and, presumably, destined to be long lasting.[1] This trend is, however, not easily accommodated within all legal orders at the national level, as it does not immediately appear to be consistent or even compatible with all national legal cultures or criminal policy options.

France seems to be a good example of this problem, since it does not present a very welcoming prospect for the development, promotion, and acknowledgment of

[1] An assumption confirmed by the international regulatory framework. See Tricot, "Corporate Antibribery Self-Regulation and the International Legal Framework," in this volume.

J. Tricot (✉)
University Paris Ouest Nanterre La Défense, Paris, France
e-mail: j.tricot@u-paris10.fr

S. Manacorda et al. (eds.), *Preventing Corporate Corruption*,
DOI 10.1007/978-3-319-04480-4_23, © Springer International Publishing Switzerland 2014

the "doctrine" and correlative techniques of compliance within its criminal justice system. The French legal order might even represent an island of resistance in opposition to what is otherwise a global trend, a role which France likes to consider itself as playing in many other sectors—in other words, in this area we could be facing another illustration of the so-called "French exception."

The two basic legal requirements for compliance programs to play a role as effective tools of anticorruption policy are indeed present in France: namely, a system of punitive—and more precisely criminal—corporate liability on the one hand, and a comprehensive legal framework of prevention of foreign/international corruption on the other. However, such a role is not only not recognized by law or favored explicitly in any way by the criminal justice system, but is in fact completely ignored. As far as criminal liability is concerned, compliance programs appear to be irrelevant to the French legislative and enforcement authorities.[2] In this sense, compliance programs and corporate antibribery rules are a "nonobject" as well as a "nonsubject" as far as French criminal law is concerned.[3]

It could, then, be said that the French criminal system as applicable to international corrupt practices constitutes a counter-model as regards the role of compliance programs. However, this total absence of acknowledgment of corporate antibribery rules on the part of the French criminal justice system does not entirely rule out the existence of possible relationships in the future. This assumption, which I will try to demonstrate, rests on an apparent paradox. The present situation concerning corporate criminal liability for acts of corruption in France is the result of what can be seen as weaknesses in the French criminal system, and for this very reason, may also be seen as the possible source of future transformations in the direction of acknowledgment of compliance programs for the purposes of criminal law. If this direction is to be taken, however, certain adverse headwinds must be dealt with (see Sect. 21.2); once this is done, we may consider how best to take advantage of the favorable—albeit unreliable—winds (Sect. 21.3).

23.2 Adverse Winds

The acknowledgment of corporate anti-bribery rules for the purposes of criminal law, if not entirely foreclosed, is surely hindered by two considerable obstacles: first, the French antiforeign bribery legal regime and, second, the French model of criminal liability for legal entities.

[2] Concerning the acknowledgment of compliance programs in French competition law, see Sect. 21.3.2.

[3] But, as we will see and try to explain, the same is not true for criminal lawyers and scholars.

23.2.1 The Anticorruption Framework in French Law

The role, or more precisely the lack thereof, played by anticorruption compliance programs should be first put in the context of the French legislation on foreign bribery, the influence of which should not be underestimated.

Due to poor application, foreign bribery law is not a sector in which legal innovation, or even simple development of the legal framework, has had an occasion to occur. It has not been a sector wherein new configurations have had the opportunity to emerge through diverse and constructive interpretation, drawing on input from other disciplines (such as corporate law, competition law, or elements of labor law in which compliance programs may play a role) or other legal orders (international or foreign); see Sect. 21.3.2.

More than 12 years after the entry into force of the offense of foreign bribery,[4] there is still no final case law on the issue of liability of legal persons for this offense. Although the number of cases has recently been increasing, it remains rather low in comparison with the legal tools offered by the French legal system and with the number and size of French corporations operating worldwide—and especially so given that some of these corporations are involved in foreign or international proceedings for bribery.[5]

Several reasons have been given as to why rules on corruption, especially in its international dimension, are commonly perceived as poorly effective, despite the existence of a very comprehensive legal framework. In brief, these reasons concern substantial difficulties concerning the requirement of a corruption pact, abandoned only recently with the 2011 Act on corruption,[6] and procedural obstacles, notably the monopoly of the Public Prosecutor's office on opening prosecutions in cases of foreign corruption.[7] While those difficulties do not directly impact on the place and role of corporate rules in French criminal law, they favor procedural strategies aimed at circumvention, which do indeed have an impact.

As a consequence of the obstacles posed by the laws on foreign bribery, cases dealing with corrupt practices are prosecuted and judged in France through the medium of other offenses which are easier to prove, for both substantial and procedural reasons. In this respect, the offense of misuse of corporate assets (*abus de biens sociaux*)[8] plays a prominent role. French law enforcement authorities tend to describe acts of bribery as a misuse of corporate assets (Dekeuwer 1998, p. 310), relying on the case law of the Cour de cassation (De Leyssac and Mihman 2009) in

---

[4] Ex-Article 435–3 CP, modified several times, introduced by Law no. 2000–595, 30 June 2000, and which explicitly referred to the OECD Convention. The version in force no longer includes such a reference to the convention.

[5] See US proceedings against Alcatel-Lucent (Spalding 2013, p. 44) and other cases cited in the OECD 2012 Report on France (OECD 2012).

[6] Law no. 2011–525, 17 May 2011. For commentary, see Segonds (2011, p. 879).

[7] Article 435–6 CP, with the exception of cases involving agents from the EU.

[8] See article L241–3 of the Commercial code, applicable to limited liability companies, and article L242–6, applicable to public limited companies.

order to ensure the punishment of acts which would otherwise go unpunished (being time-barred, for example), or which would be more difficult and take longer to prove. Although investigations may be initiated on both counts—bribery of foreign public officials and misuse of corporate assets—converging reasons, essentially for purposes of proof, result in charges of misuse of corporate assets being the only one to be brought forward. Whereas the establishment of a corruption pact may often represent a diriment obstacle, no such proof is required to establish misuse of corporate assets, and the interpretation of "corporate interest" by the courts is very broad. Besides, the onus of proof is partially reversed since the mere proof that funds were misappropriated or removed from the company, covertly imposes on the company director the obligation to prove that they were used on the company's behalf and in its interest.

However, and as highlighted in the last Organisation for Economic Co-operation and Development (OECD) report on France, this judicial strategy has consequences. It is evident that these two offenses do not protect the same social values, and also that the framing in terms of misuse of corporate assets ignores both the democratic dimension and the particular economic dimension of corruption. The offense of bribery of foreign public officials implies a serious violation of the duty of probity and of the authority of the state. Some authors even consider foreign bribery to be, per se, a breach of human rights (Spalding 2013). Misuse of corporate assets, on the other hand, is an expression of mismanagement (Rebut 2002). But one may, in passing, reflect that this notion of mismanagement is reminiscent of, or at least not entirely disconnected from, the compliance approach to corruption.[9] Furthermore—and this is particularly significant for our concerns here—excepting very specific situations (Matsopoulou 2009, p. 81), only natural persons can commit the offense of misuse of corporate assets (Rebut 2002). Moreover, the application of this offense in cases of corruption results in the company being made the victim, rather than being held liable. Although liability may be established on the basis of a separate offense subsequent to the natural person being charged or convicted of the offence of misuse of corporate assets, there is no case law in which legal persons have been prosecuted following convictions of individuals for misuse of corporate assets (OECD 2012).

Hence, the French criminal law on foreign bribery plays an important role in the current situation of underenforcement of corporate criminal liability for corrupt acts, and, as a consequence, is also partly responsible for the lack of recognition of compliance programs in French law.

However, the underenforcement and lack of recognition is also a result—and here perhaps the connection is even more firm—of the model of corporate liability chosen by the French legislature.

[9] Although the penalties are not at all comparable (5 years' imprisonment and a fine of € 375,000 for misuse of corporate assets compared to 10 years' imprisonment and a fine of € 150,000 for bribery under Article 435–3 CP).

23.2.2 The French Model of Corporate Criminal Liability

Criminal liability for legal persons was introduced into French law in 1994 with the entry into force of the new Criminal Code.[10] At first, the legislature chose to limit the scope of the new mechanism to specific offenses. It was necessary for express provision for corporate liability to be made in each specific offense. Corporate liability for acts of transnational bribery was introduced in June 2000,[11] in order to comply with the international obligations undertaken by France, especially the OECD Convention, signed 3 years earlier in Paris. But, 10 years after the entry into force of the reform, the legislature abandoned the *spécialité* principle (Cartier 2006, p. 97, 105; Matsopoulou 2009), and the criminal liability of legal persons is now applied generally.[12]

The French legislature opted to give corporate criminal liability relatively wide scope: it applies, in principle, to all offenses and to all legal persons, with the exception of the state and of local public authorities in their exercise of public prerogatives (Tricot 2012a; see also Tricot 2012b). As Deckert notes (2011, p. 151; see also Giudicelli-Delage 2005, p. 187), corporate criminal liability was introduced predominantly for practical reasons; it was seen as necessary for improving law enforcement through targeting a new type of criminality, and it was also thought to allow a more just imputation of criminal liability. The objective was not only to limit the personal liability of directors,[13] but also to ensure greater respect for the general principles of personal liability (*responsabilité personnelle*) and individual nature of penalties (*personnalité des peines*) (Deckert 2011, p. 147). However, the model of imputation chosen at the time has to a very large extent proven unable to live up to such expectations.

The choice of an indirect imputation mechanism has considerably limited the impact and significance of the reform. The criminal code requires two conditions to be met in order to establish the criminal liability of the legal entity. The first is what some French scholars call the "condition of representation" (Saint-Pau 2003, p. 71): this requires that it be established that the offense was committed by an organ or a representative of the legal person. Second, the "condition of interest": the offense must have been committed "on the behalf" or "on the account" (the French Criminal Code says: *pour le compte*) of the entity.

---

[10] Adopted in 1992 (Law no. 92–683, 1992–07-22).

[11] Article 435–3 CP; see n. 5 to this chapter.

[12] Article 121–2 CP: "Legal persons, with the exception of the state, are criminally liable for the offenses committed on their account by their organs or representatives, according to the distinctions set out in articles 121–4 and 121–7. However, local public authorities and their associations incur criminal liability only for offenses committed in the course of their activities, which may be exercised through public service delegation conventions. The criminal liability of legal persons does not exclude that of any natural persons who are perpetrators or accomplices to the same act, subject to the provisions of the fourth paragraph of article 121–3."

[13] French minister of justice Robert Badinter said that the introduction of criminal liability of legal persons would remove the presumption of liability that directors are subject to, for offenses the very existence of which they sometimes ignore.

Those two conditions circumscribe the French model of the indirect criminal liability of the legal person. The French legislature has clearly rejected a mechanism that allows for the direct imputation of criminal acts to legal persons;[14] and despite attempts by a few scholars and local judges to address the organizational failure (see Sect. 21.3.1), the Cour de cassation seems to maintain a rather narrow interpretation of the criminal code, one which is in line with the principle of legality but is entirely closed to organizational issues and theories.

As regards the preventive role of compliance programs vis-à-vis the corrupt practices of legal persons, those conditions have proven to be strong hindrances. The choice of a model of indirect liability has indeed prevented compliance programs, and more generally, mechanisms of corporate social responsibility from being taken into account, and thus has discouraged—or at the very least has not encouraged—their adoption.

Notably, this situation stands in complete contrast to the attention traditionally paid, especially by French criminal judges, to the preventive function of criminal liability within legal entities; it is in especial contrast to the fact that judges, acting on their own initiative, have developed incentives which favor virtuous organizational structures, such as the exonerating effect of the delegation of power (Robert 2001, p. 383; Robert 2012, p. 740; Cœuret 2009, p. 101; Mauro 2009, p. 61).

As regards proceedings concerning transnational corrupt practices, the reform adopted in 1992 is plagued by two additional fundamental weaknesses: first, the choice to build the model of corporate liability on the exclusive criteria of legal personality, subsequently excluding from its scope of application the case of groups of companies (Pariente 1993, p. 247); second, the absence of adaptation of the rules on jurisdiction. Despite their being several possible ways to remedy this (e.g., the use of rules on instigation or of presumption of participation; Mauro (2012, p. 12)), the mother company has remained immune to criminal proceedings (OECD 2012) while foreign subsidiaries are protected by the specific rules on jurisdiction. The latter confers a monopoly to the public prosecutor, and the criterion of double jeopardy which is applicable in cases where the personality principle also applies might block proceedings if the law of the country of the subsidiary does not provide for the criminal liability of legal entities (Mauro 2012, p. 12). The last OECD report on France harshly underlined the inability of the French enforcement authorities to tackle the strategies of circumvention developed by large companies, which consist of decentralizing their compliance activities, and the payment of consultants' commissions to their foreign subsidiaries—those strategies being a final illustration of the weakness of the model of corporate liability and the ease with which it is exploited by corporations.

Finally, another expression of "resistance" to the compliance movement (set in motion notably by the USA and UK legislatures) is the so-called blocking statute,[15]

[14] For a clear account of this by an author who has been one of the foremost promoters of direct imputation, see Saint-Pau (2011, p. 8).

[15] The Act of 26 July 1968 dealing with the communication of documents and information of an economic, commercial, industrial, financial, or technical nature to foreign natural or legal persons,

which prohibits[16] sending documents or information of an economic, commercial, industrial, financial, or technical nature to foreign authorities, except in cases specified in international treaties (Haeri 2012, p. 7; De Vauplane 2010, p. 78). This aims to protect French companies against discovery efforts by foreign authorities seeking access to information without using judicial cooperation. The blocking statute can put French companies in a difficult position, facing conflicting obligations resulting in possible sanctions either in France or abroad.[17]

In sum, several and strong adverse winds need to be overcome if French law is to be rendered more favorable to compliance programs: as far as the criminal system is concerned, enforcement authorities, and especially criminal courts, do not carry out any assessment of whether an organization has a compliance program. Not only is there no obligation to adopt such a program under criminal law, but more generally, there is no legal incentive to do so (or interest in doing so) for the purpose of the application of French criminal law.[18]

However, favorable winds are also blowing across the French criminal justice system, which might eventually change (or even already be changing) its course.

23.3 Fair Winds

Although French criminal law does not seem to present favorable conditions for the development of anticorruption compliance programs, recent developments in case law, and the increasing number of proceedings against corporations for the bribery of foreign officials, might yet change the situation.[19]

More generally, certain discreet changes occurring both within and outside criminal law favor their progressive recognition, and at the same time the weaknesses underlined by the OECD in its October 2012 report on France, concerning the enforcement of the French criminal law on foreign bribery, might also push in the direction of compliance, as is thought to have happened in the UK.

---

as amended by the Act of 16 July 1980.

[16] Breaches of the prohibition are punishable by 6 months in prison and/or a fine of € 18,000. Article 2 of the text stipulates that persons to whom such a request is addressed are required to inform the Ministry of Foreign Affairs without delay.

[17] According to the OECD 2012 report on France, the blocking statute has been applied in a transnational bribery case, in relation to which several cases had been opened abroad, notably in Germany and the USA, and internal investigations conducted by the accused company in multiple countries. See OECD (2012).

[18] The French version of plea bargaining, applicable since 2011 to offenses of corruption, is not likely to change the situation. The public prosecutor may suggest that the defendant agree to appear on prior admission of guilt whereby the defendant accepts one or more of the principal or additional penalties for which he or she is liable, which exposes companies to exclusion from national, foreign, or international public procurement procedures.

[19] At least three cases will be tried in 2013, involving companies operating worldwide, for their alleged corrupt practices abroad (OECD 2012).

23.3.1 The Criminal Implications of CSR: New Openings

A closer look at case law may shed some light on the otherwise rather murky picture concerning both corporate criminal liability for corrupt practices and the role of compliance programs in this framework. Although still rather limited and uncertain, it is possible to observe a tendency in France towards addressing corporate organizational failure more closely, and designing a more direct or autonomous system for corporate criminal liability. These could turn out to be a first step towards the positive acknowledgment of compliance programs.

The case law of local criminal judges on corporate criminal liability provides several examples of attempts to take into account corporate culture or commercial policies in order to attribute liability to the corporation.

Where intent is required (as is the case for bribery), judges have used a controversial notion—the commercial policy of the legal entity (*politique commerciale*)—in order to attribute criminal liability to the corporation.[20] This notion allows judges to presume that the legal condition (that the offense has been committed by an organ or a representative of the corporation) is met, without having to identify the human agent (*l'agent humain*) or "human substratum." This notion of commercial policy has been compared to the concept of corporate culture. But to date there is only a single published decision of the Cour de cassation which acknowledges such reasoning. At the same time, the notion (and its use) has been the object of severe criticism related to the mechanism of presumption and the vagueness of the notion itself. For these reasons, the future of this notion remains rather uncertain; yet the fact that it exists at all is illustrative of the need for legal tools to address dysfunctional corporate cultures which result in offences, as well as the awareness of this need on the part of French criminal judges.

Judges have also used the controversial concept of "intellectual offender" (*auteur moral*) in a case of insider trading in order to presume the establishment of that condition (Stasiak 2010, p. 156). The decision, however, has not been published and the reasoning within it is only implicit. In addition, it has not since been renewed. On the basis of this concept, scholars have interpreted this decision as meaning that because the organ in question had vested the employee with the power (or even the mandate) to commit the offense, the organ is presumed to have committed the offense or to have permitted the offense to be committed.

More generally, concerning offenses requiring intent as well as offenses of negligence, case law has provided for an open interpretation of the condition that the offense be committed by an organ or a representative, a condition which appears to be more or less demanding depending on the type of the offense in question. The wording of the rule describing the appropriate conduct and the nature of the violation

[20] "Les infractions retenues s'inscrivent dans le cadre de la politique commerciale des sociétés en cause et ne peuvent, dès lors, avoir été commises, pour le compte des sociétés, que par leurs organes ou représentants": Cour de cassation (Chambre criminelle), 25 June 2008, *BC* 167; Fortis (2009, p. 89) Crim., 28 January 2009, no. 07–81.674.

may locate the offender in the person of the employer, and hence the organ, or, in the case of a delegation of powers, in the representative of the legal entity. In this case, the mere occurrence of the violation has been considered sufficient to attribute criminal liability to the legal entity, and the reasoning has been extended to other offenses on the basis of a presumption of imputation to the organ or representative of the legal person.[21]

Nevertheless, the Cour de cassation has recently blocked this case law, indicating that criminal judges are becoming increasingly inclined towards corporate social responsibility and addressing organizational failures through criminal proceedings and sanctions. These recent decisions (October 2011 and April 2012)[22] are limited to offenses of negligence. Up to the present, there is no comparable decision concerning offenses requiring intent. However, offenses of negligence were the main area where the presumption (of imputation) was used in order to sanction organizational failure. For now, the legal debate primarily concerns two opposing interpretations of the recent case law. The *minimalist* interpretation considers that it has only excluded—albeit for good—any possibility of direct and autonomous liability on the part of the corporation, on the basis of the principle of legality and a strict interpretation of Article 121–2 CP (Saint-Pau 2012, p. 1381). The mechanism of presumption, however, remains valid, although it requires careful use and precise grounds. The *maximalist* interpretation sees in these decisions the outright abandonment of the system of presumptions and the return to the orthodoxy of indirect liability where the identification of the peculiar organ or representative is always necessary (Robert 2012, p. 740).

In any case, the possibility that, when assessing criminal liability, judges could take corporate rules and compliance programs into consideration remains not only fragile but also quite narrowly drawn.

However, in parallel to this another, path could be taken. This consists of taking the avatars of corporate social responsibility (CSR) seriously, and turning CSR against corporate practices that are inconsistent with it.

In the recent *Erika* case,[23] resoundingly significant for both the scope and the intensity of its impact on civil and criminal liability for environmental offenses (among many others: Delebecque 2012, p. 2711; Neyret 2010, p. 2238; Montas and Roussel 2012, p. 574), the Cour de cassation has used the breach of obligations voluntarily assumed by Total SA to establish the liability of the mother company and ascribe liability to it. The Cour de cassation has confirmed the judgment of the Court of Appeal, which held Total SA criminally liable for the offense of unintentional marine pollution because it failed to carry out the vetting procedure (i.e., the inspection the company may make of a vessel before it is chartered) it had voluntarily adopted.

[21] For a retrospective on this case law, see Tricot (2012a).

[22] Cour de cassation, 11 October 2011, no. 10–87.212 (see also Robert 2011, p. 1385). Cour de cassation, 11 April 2012, no. 10–86.974.

[23] Cour de cassation, 25 September 2012, no. 10–82.938.

The decision is crucial for three reasons. First, it was issued in September 2012, that is to say within the context of the narrow interpretation described above of the conditions of corporate liability. However, in this case, the identification of the representative of the corporation—located in the person of the manager of a specialized division of Total SA responsible for the approval of charter-parties—did not seem problematic. Second, the decision was highly anticipated and, for this reason, can be presumed to have been carefully thought through before being published. Third, it is an explicit acknowledgment that possible punitive implications can be deduced from obligations voluntarily adopted by a corporation.

This decision illustrates something which scholars had already warned of: that whereas the existence of compliance programs may never exonerate from liability or mitigate penalties, it may increase the severity of judges when it is established that the requirements of the program have not been met. It may help in establishing the objective component of the fault (in civil and criminal proceedings) as well as its subjective component (that the organs or representatives could not ignore/had to know/should have known).

23.3.2 Multiplication of Incentives Favoring Compliance

Although, for all the reasons indicated above, searching for the expression "compliance program" (or its equivalents) within French criminal case law remains—for now—a largely quixotic enterprise,[24] there is no doubt that large French corporations have implemented compliance programs and, notably, anticorruption programs. Not only are they obliged to do so in order to comply with US, and now UK legislation (see, inter alia, Mattou 2011; Todorov and Huten 2010, p. 4), but they are also strongly encouraged to carry out such actions by national bodies, both public (the Central Service of Corruption Prevention; see Ministère de la Justice 2011) or private (such as the French employers' organization MEDEF).

As well as this, the development of indirect incentives from outside criminal law to adopt and enforce compliance programs could also hasten their progressive acknowledgement within the criminal justice system. Those incentives are either of a general nature, calling for taking into consideration the adoption of compliance programs, or specific, aiming to promote the adoption of particular elements of an eventual anticorruption compliance program.

As far as general incentives are concerned, competition law on the one hand, and civil law on the other, could play a definite, albeit limited, role. As regards competition law, from a general point of view, the links and relationships between antitrust and anticorruption policies and practices should not be underestimated. However, a rapid overview of French competition law shows that compliance programs continue to play a rather limited role, and are entirely confined to leniency procedures.

[24] At least as far as the decisions of the Cour de cassation are concerned; access to first- and second-tier tribunals decision is too limited to extend this affirmation further.

Outside the framework of leniency requests, compliance programs have no exonerating effect, nor are they even mitigating factors. But while the existence of a compliance program which has proved to be ineffective by the mere existence of the proceedings is of no use as regards the establishment of liability, the French Financial Market Authority has clearly established that the existence of such a program may not be an aggravating cause of liability. However, such a categorical and general affirmation may be met with skepticism (Cretenet et al. 2011).

As regards civil law, Article 4 § 1 of the Council of Europe Civil Law Convention on Corruption should be kept in mind. It reads that:

> Each Party shall provide in its internal law for the following conditions to be fulfilled in order for the damage to be compensated: (i) the defendant has committed or authorised the act of corruption, or failed to take reasonable steps to prevent the act of corruption….

Significantly, the explanatory report indicates that:

> those who failed to take the appropriate steps, in the light of the responsibilities which lie on them, to prevent corruption would also be liable for damage. This means that employers are responsible for the corrupt behaviour of their employees if, for example, they neglect to organise their company adequately or fail to exert appropriate control over their employees.

Though the Cour de cassation has refused to allow that the victim of private corrupt practices committed by an employee can be compensated by the employer, consideration of the Civil Convention could lead to another solution (Segonds 2012, p. 13). In a case ruled by the Cour de cassation on 25 January 2012, the victim argued—in vain—that the employer had been lenient vis-à-vis the activities of his/her employee, and had not enforced the code of good conduct in force in the company.[25]

As far as incentives for the adoption of elements of compliance program are concerned, recent reforms of French law should be taken into account. First, whereas it does not yet include any reference to the anticorruption sector, the development of nonfinancial reporting obligations should be mentioned.[26] Second, the adoption of special provisions designed to protect whistle-blowers[27] and to control the whistle-blowing procedures adopted by French companies are also of special interest (Lefebvre-Dutilleul et al. 2010). As far as the private sector is concerned, provisions on whistle-blowers remain controversial (Ayela and Bihannic 2011, p. 68). They are limited to the introduction of a right to report for private sector employees.[28] The 2007 Act has introduced into the Labor Code provisions for the protection of employees who, in good faith, disclose or report acts of bribery. Article 1161–1 of the code provides that:

---

[25] Cour de cassation, Chambre criminelle, 25 January 2012, no. 10–88.511.

[26] See the adoption of the Decree (2012–557) of 24 April 2012; Malecki (2012, p. 590).

[27] For a synopsis of the existing French legal framework, concerning both the public and the private sector, see Ministère de la Justice (2011).

[28] The provisions on witness protection (Article 706–60 of the Code of Criminal Procedure) are limited to cases of harm or risks to life, and by procedural limits which make those provisions applicable only to very specific cases.

> no employee may be punished, dismissed or subjected to any discriminatory measure, direct or indirect, in particular with respect to remuneration, training, transfer, assignment, qualification, classification, professional promotion, amendment or renewal of contract for having reported or disclosed in good faith, either to his/her employer or to the judicial or administrative authorities, acts of corruption of which s/he becomes aware in the exercise of his/her functions.

No obligation, and certainly no criminally or otherwise sanctioned one, is placed on employees to report illicit conduct to the enforcement authorities. On the contrary, the Commission Nationale de l'Informatique et des Libertés (CNIL)—the independent authority responsible for the enforcement of the Data Protection Act[29]—has considered that only a nonmandatory whistle-blowing system would be compatible with the French legal order (CNIL 2005). However, although questions are raised concerning whether the whistle-blowing systems already in place in major French groups are in compliance with French law (especially labor law and computer law), such systems are increasingly regulated by legal texts[30] and are addressed by a growing case law (Ministère de la Justice 2011). This illustrates the difficulties that the French legal system poses for those whistle-blowing procedures, as well as the limits it sets; but it also shows that they are legally acknowledged. In other words, despite the persistent mistrust of such systems, they are being adopted by French companies and, as a result, are becoming subject to legal requirements and restrictions which, though they may conflict with foreign requirements, also contribute to their progressive development and recognition.[31]

23.4 The French Criminal Justice System vis-à-vis Corporate Antibribery Rules: An Antimodel?

Having presented this analysis of the French criminal system, the initial impression that it may represent a counter-model as regards the role of corporate antibribery rules seems to be fading away. Rather, it seems like a model still in the making, in search of its identity. Should it, then, be for the time being considered an antimodel, a nonmodel from which nothing can be learnt? That seems like a step too far. Lessons could be drawn from the difficulties, the conflicting options, and the hesitations which are manifested in the texts and case law, and these could help to consolidate and expand the emerging role of corporate antibribery rules while eluding the criticism addressed to the process of internationalization of law, which may

[29] Act no. 78–17 of 6 January 1978 on Data processing, Data files, and Individual liberties.

[30] See "Circulaire DGT 2008/22 du 19 novembre 2008 relative aux chartes éthiques, dispositifs d'alerte professionnelle et au règlement intérieur," Wolters Kluwer, http://www.wk-rh.fr/actualites/upload/circnov2008-signa.pdf, accessed 7 July 2013. See also the Act of 16 April 2013 (loi no. 2013–316 relative à l'indépendance de l'expertise en matière de santé et d'environnement et à la protection des lanceurs d'alerte).

[31] See, especially for whistle-blowing systems concerning corrupt practices, "Autorisation unique n° AU-004," http://www.cnil.fr/documentation/deliberations/deliberation/delib/83/, Art. 1.

seem hegemonic if it is to impose a single and exclusive conception of criminal liability. In any event, the first lesson is undoubtedly that if the acknowledgment of the role of corporate antibribery rules is yet to come (and while a few precursors—uncertain and fragile—are perceptible in case law, there is still no sign that the law will move in this direction, and the rare incentives that do exist all stem from outside the field of French criminal law), international input will play a significant role in promoting this development, and in defining the modalities in which it is expressed, and the scope it eventually comes to have.

References

Ayela C., & Bihannic, K. (2011). Nouveau coup de sifflet contre le whisleblowing: quel avenir en France pour les alertes éthiques? Recherche sur l'apport de l'alerte professionnelle au regard de la coopération en matière pénale. *Lamy Droit des affaires, 112*(65), 68–72.

Cartier, M.-E. (2006). De la suppression du principe de spécialité de la responsabilité pénale des personnes morales: Libres propos. In F. Alt-Maes et al. (Eds.), *Les droits et le Droit: Mélanges dédiés à Bernard Bouloc*. Paris: Dalloz-Sirey.

CNIL. (2005). Autorisation unique n° AU-004—Délibération n°2005–305 du 8 décembre 2005 portant autorisation unique de traitements automatisés de données à caractère personnel mis en œuvre dans le cadre de dispositifs d'alerte professionnelle. http://www.cnil.fr/documentation/deliberations/deliberation/delib/83/. Accessed 7 July 2013.

Cœuret, A. (2009). La responsabilité pénale en droit pénal du travail: vers un nouvel équilibre entre personnes physiques et personnes morales. In M. Daury-Fauveau et al. (Eds.), *Dépénalisation de la vie des affaires et responsabilité pénale des personnes morales*. Paris: Presses Universitaires de France.

Cretenet, I., Laurent-Moulin, B., & Trochon, J.-Y. (2011). Dossier Spécial—Programmes de compliance: un must pour les enterprises! *Juriste d'Entreprise Magazine,* 8. http://www.afje.org/JEM-08-v09.pdf. Accessed on August 2013.

De Leyssac, Lucas M.-P., & Mihman, A. (2009). *Droit pénal des affaires: Manuel théorique et pratique*. Paris: Economica.

De Vauplane, H. (2010). Les entreprises européennes face à l'extraterritorialité du droit américain. *Revue Banque , 724,* 78–83.

Deckert, K. (2011). Corporate criminal liability in France. In M. Pieth et al. (Eds.), *Corporate criminal liability: Emergence, convergence, and risk*. New York: Springer.

Dekeuwer, A. (1998). Défense et illustration de l'incrimination d'abus de biens sociaux dans un système de corruption. *La Semaine Juridique Entreprise et Affaires*, 9.

Delebecque, P. (2012). L'arrêt 'Erika': un grand arrêt de droit pénal, de droit maritime ou de droit civil? *Le Dalloz*, 40.

Fortis, E. (2009). Chronique de jurisprudence. Droit pénal général: la responsabilité pénale des personnes morales. *Revue de science criminelle et de droit pénal comparé*, 1.

Giudicelli-Delage, G. (2005). La responsabilité pénale des personnes morales en France. In R.-N. Schultz et al. (Eds.), *Aspects nouveaux du droit de la responsabilité aux Pays-Bas et en France*. Paris: LGDJ.

Haeri, K. (2012). Laissez la loi de blocage tranquille! *La Gazette du Palais*, 7–9.

Lefebvre-Dutilleul, V., Naftalski, F., Estelle, C. (2010). Le déploiement des programmes de conformité: une étape crucial. *Option Finance*.

Malecki, C. (2012). Le décret du 24 avril 2012 relatif aux obligations de transparence des entreprises en matière sociale et environnementale. *Bulletin Joly Sociétés*.

Matsopoulou, H. (2009). Responsabilité pénale des personnes morales et infractions du droit pénal des affaires. In M. Daury-Fauveau et al. (Eds.), *Dépénalisation de la vie des affaires et responsabilité pénale des personnes morales*. Paris: Presses Universitaires de France.

Mattou, J. (2011). Le Bribery Act ou les choix de la loi britannique en matière de lutte contre la corruption: un danger pour les enterprises françaises? *Journal du droit international*, 138(4).

Mauro, C. (2009). Éléments de droit comparé. In M. Daury-Fauveau et al. (Eds.), *Dépénalisation de la vie des affaires et responsabilité pénale des personnes morales*. Paris: Presses Universitaires de France.

Mauro, C. (2012). Application dans l'espace de la loi pénale et entreprises multinationales. *Actualité Juridique Pénal*, 1.

Ministère de la Justice. (2011). Annual Report 2011—Service Central de Prévention de la Corruption [The central service for the prevention of corruption]. Website of the Ministère de la Justice. http://www.justice.gouv.fr/multilinguisme-12198/english-12200/the-central-service-for-the-prevention-of-corruption-24860.html. Accessed 7 July 2013.

Montas, A., & Roussel, G. (2012). Les principaux apports de la décision de la Cour de cassation dans l'affaire Erika. *Actualité Juridique Pénal*.

Neyret, L. (2010). L'affaire Erika: moteur d'évolution des responsabilités civile et pénale. *Le Dalloz*.

OECD (2012). Phase 3 report on implementing the OECD anti-bribery convention in France—October 2012. Website of the OECD. http://www.oecd.org/daf/anti-bribery/Francephase3reportEN.pdf. Accessed 7 July 2013

Pariente, M. (1993). Les groupes de société et la responsabilité pénale des personnes morales. *Revue des sociétés*.

Rebut, D. (2002). Abus de biens sociaux. *Répertoire Dalloz de droit pénal*, 2.

Robert, J.-H. (2001). Les préposés délégués sont-ils les représentants de la personne morale? In P. Couvrat et al. (Eds.), *Mélanges offerts à Pierre Couvrat: La sanction du droit*. Paris: Presses Universitaires de France.

Robert, J.-H. (2011). Resserrement des conditions de la responsabilité pénale des personnes morales. *La Semaine Juridique Edition Générale*, 50.

Robert, J.-H. (2012). Vers une refondation de la responsabilité pénale des personnes morales. *La Semaine Juridique Edition Générale*, 25.

Saint-Pau, J.-C. (2003). La responsabilité des personnes morales: réalité et fiction. In P. Conte et al. (Eds.), *Le risque pénal dans l'entreprise*. Paris: Litec.

Saint-Pau, J.-C. (2011). La responsabilité pénale des personnes morales sans représentation. *La Gazette du Palais*.

Saint-Pau, J.-C. (2012). Imputation directe et imputation présumée d'une infraction à une personne morale. *Le Dalloz*, 21.

Segonds, M. (2011). Loi de simplification et d'amélioration de la qualité du droit. *Revue de science criminelle et de droit pénal comparé*, 4, 879–885.

Segonds, M. (2012). Un an de droit pénal du travail. *Droit pénal*, 11.

Spalding, A. B. (2013). Corruption, corporations and the new human right. Website of SSRN (13 March). http://papers.ssrn.com/sol3/papers.cfm?abstract_id=2232670. Accessed on August 2013.

Stasiak, F. (2010). Infractions boursières. *Revue de science criminelle et de droit pénal comparé*, 1.

Todorov, P., & Huten, S. (2010). L'émergence d'une norme internationale de lutte contre la corruption. *Actes pratiques et ingénierie sociétaire* (2012).

Tricot, J. (2012a). Le droit penal à l'épreuve de la responsabilité des personnes morales; l'exemple français. *Revue de science criminelle et de droit penal comparé*, 1, 19–46.

Tricot, J. (2012b). Corporate criminal liability in France. In A. Fiorella (Ed.), *Corporate criminal liability and compliance programs*. Napoli: Jovene.

Chapter 24
Corporate Responsibility and Compliance Programs in Switzerland

Ursula Cassani

Contents

24.1 Introduction

This chapter describes the mechanisms of Swiss criminal law that encourage companies to develop compliance programs in order to prevent corruption. Although the application of individual criminal liability and sanctions is potentially harmful to a company's reputation, and therefore also calls for preventive action, it was the

I would like to express my gratitude to my assistants Hadrien Mangeat and Lorenzo Palestini, for their much-appreciated help in drafting this chapter. Last update of source: 31 Jan 2013.

U. Cassani (✉)
University of Geneva, Geneva, Switzerland
e-mail: Ursula.Cassani@unige.ch

S. Manacorda et al. (eds.), *Preventing Corporate Corruption*,
DOI 10.1007/978-3-319-04480-4_24,

introduction of corporate criminal liability that established a direct link between criminal sanctions and the obligation to introduce preventive measures in the form of anticorruption compliance programs.

Before addressing the role of compliance programs in Swiss criminal law, this chapter briefly describes the provisions defining the offenses of active and passive bribery and the impact of corruption in Switzerland.

24.1.1 Swiss Anticorruption Law in a Nutshell

Bribery of Swiss officials has been a federal offense since the enactment of the Swiss Criminal Code of 1937 (SCC),[1] and was punishable even before that, under the cantonal penal laws. The provisions of the SCC governing corruption have been amended twice, in 1999 and 2005.

The first revision was undertaken in order to allow Switzerland to ratify the Organisation for Economic Co-operation and Development (OECD) Convention on Combating Bribery of Foreign Public Officials in International Business Transactions (1997). Accordingly, its main feature was the creation of a criminal offense prohibiting active bribery of public officials of foreign states and international organizations (Article $322^{septies}$ SCC). The provisions involving national public officials were also amended, with the general aim of punishing active bribery, considered a lesser offense in the SCC of 1937, as harshly as passive bribery (Articles 322ter to 322^{sexies} SCC).

The 2005 revision was launched in order to comply with the obligations set out in the Council of Europe Criminal Law Convention on Corruption of 1999; among other amendments, passive bribery of foreign public officials was also made a crime (Article $322^{septies}$ (2) SCC).

The United Nations Convention Against Corruption of 2003 (Merida Convention) did not necessitate any revision of the Swiss legislation, since the catalog of offenses is the same as in the Council of Europe Convention. Furthermore, the idea of restituting assets to the victim states, which contributed to making the Merida Convention a success among third world countries, was already well established in Swiss law and practice.[2] So far, Switzerland has returned more assets stolen by

[1] An English translation of the SCC is provided by the Swiss Federal Administration. However, it is not an official version of the legal text, and hence has no legal force. In Switzerland, all legislative acts have three official versions deemed equally authoritative: German, French, and Italian. See "Swiss Criminal Code," The Federal Authorities of the Swiss Confederation, http://www.admin.ch/ch/e/rs/311_0/index.html, accessed 31 Jan 2013.

[2] Article 74a of the Federal Act of 20 Mar 1981 on International Mutual Assistance in Criminal Matters allows the restitution of assets before confiscation. See "Mutual Assistance Act (IMAC)," the Federal Authorities of the Swiss Confederation, http://www.admin.ch/ch/e/rs/c351_1.html, accessed 31 Jan 2013. This provision was interpreted broadly by the Swiss Federal Tribunal in the case of the funds of the Abacha family, allowing the reversal of the burden of proof (Article 72 SCC) regarding the illicit source of the assets on the grounds that the Abacha clan was a criminal organization (see Arrêt du Tribunal fédéral (ATF) 131 II 169); accessible online at http://www.

politically exposed persons to the victim states than any other country: 1.7 billion Swiss francs over the past 15 years.[3]

Some weak points remain in the definition of corruption under Swiss law:[4]

- Facilitation payments remain a gray area. Very small sums (up to approximately 50 or 100 francs according to authority) are not considered undue, as long as they correspond to common social practice (Article 322^{octies} (2) SCC). However, this exception must be construed narrowly and only includes what is common social practice in Switzerland, as opposed to a foreign and more permissive country's practice.
- The bribery of a foreign public official is only an offense if the act expected from him or her in return for the bribe is either contrary to his or her duties or dependent on his or her discretion (Article 322^{septies} SCC). Consequently, making improper payments to encourage foreign officials to actually perform their duties is not punishable. More importantly, if the payment cannot be matched with a particular act of duty on a do ut des basis, the act remains unpunished. For Swiss public officials, there is a subsidiary offense prohibiting soliciting or accepting "an advantage which is not due [to the official] in order that he carries out his official duties" (Articles 322^{quinquies} and 322^{sexies} SCC).
- Finally, corruption in the private sector remains one of the blind spots of Swiss criminal policy. Although both active and passive bribery of private agents are offenses under Article 4a of the Federal Act of 19 December 1986 on Unfair Competition, as amended in 2005,[5] offenses are not brought before the courts. Corruption of private agents is only prosecuted if a criminal complaint is lodged by the injured party ("délit sur plainte"; "Antragsdelikt"; "reato punibile solo a querela di parte"), who may prefer to avoid the publicity of a criminal trial.[6]

---

bger.ch/fr/index.htm). More recently, the Federal Act of 1 October 2010 on the Restitution of Assets of Politically Exposed Persons obtained by Unlawful Means was introduced as a subsidiary measure to allow the freezing, forfeiture, and restitution of the assets of politically exposed persons when the victim country is a failing state unable to cooperate in the procedure of international assistance in criminal matters. See "Restitution of Illicit Assets Act (RIAA)," the Federal Authorities of the Swiss Confederation, http://www.admin.ch/ch/e/rs/c196_1.html, accessed 31 Jan 2013. On this topic, see Pieth (2008); Cassani (2009); and Cassani (2010).

[3] For further information, see "Illicit assets of politically exposed persons (PEPs)," Federal Department of Foreign Affairs, http://www.eda.admin.ch/eda/en/home/topics/finec/poexp.html, accessed 31 Jan 2013.

[4] For a more extensive analysis of the strengths and shortcomings of Swiss law, see the GRECO Evaluation Report on Switzerland on Incriminations (ETS 173 and 191, GPC 2), Strasbourg, 17–21 Oct 2011. See "Evaluation Report on Switzerland on Incriminations (ETS 173 and 191, GPC 2)," Council of Europe, http://www.coe.int/t/dghl/monitoring/greco/evaluations/round3/GrecoEval3%282011%294_Switzerland_One_EN.pdf, accessed 31 Jan 2013; see also Cassani (2011, p. 33).

[5] The 2005 amendment was a consequence of the ratification of the Council of Europe Criminal Law Convention on Corruption of 1999. However, active bribery in the private sector became an offense as early as 1943.

[6] The federal administration has recently published a draft bill proposing, among other amendments, to replace the current provision in the Federal Act on Unfair Competition by offenses punishing the bribery of private agents in the SCC (Article 322^{octies} and 322^{novies}). The requirement of

24.1.2 Corruption in Switzerland: How Widespread is the Phenomenon?

Swiss public servants do not have a reputation for being particularly prone to soliciting or accepting bribes. In fact, Switzerland always ranks among the countries with very good scores in the Corruption Perception Index issued annually by Transparency International; in 2012, it was ranked sixth out of a total of 174 countries on a scale from the cleanest to the most corrupt.[7]

The reputation of Swiss companies doing business in foreign markets is also excellent, as evidenced by the first rank occupied in the 2011 Bribe Payers Index established by Transparency International, reflecting the perceived likelihood of companies from 28 leading economies to win business abroad by paying bribes.[8]

The ranking established by Transparency International only reflects perceptions and therefore does not allow any definitive conclusions to be drawn about the number of acts of corruption effectively committed. Nevertheless, it may be assumed that corruption is not endemic in Switzerland and that paying bribes to public officials is not considered a normal or ethically acceptable way of doing business and obtaining contracts. This does not mean that Swiss corporations are totally exempt from corrupt practices. In fact, a study published in 2012 shows that 40.3 % of Swiss companies active abroad are confronted with demands for "informal payments" from public and private agents. More importantly, 56 % of the companies which have received solicitations of this nature declare that they have indeed made such payments, representing about 5 % of their turnover (Becker et al. 2012, p. 17).

As for the number of criminal convictions on corruption charges, it is, predictably, not very high, that is, between 6 and 16 convictions per year (2007–2011) involving the corruption of Swiss public officials.[9] The total number of convictions on charges of corruption of foreign officials, since it became an offense in May 2000, is three so far, according to the data made available by the Federal Office of Statistics. There are no statistics showing the number of convictions for the bribery of private agents, but it is generally held that no such convictions have been handed down until now.[10]

---

a complaint by the injured party would be dropped; see "Rapport explicatif concernant la modification du code pénal et du code pénal militaire (Dispositions pénales incriminant la corruption)," http://www.ejpd.admin.ch/content/dam/data/kriminalitaet/gesetzgebung/korruptionsstrafrecht/vorentw-f.pdf, accessed 15 May 2013.

[7] See "Corruption Perception Index," Transparency International, http://cpi.transparency.org/cpi2012/, accessed 31 Jan 2013.

[8] See "Bribe Payers Index," Transparency International, http://bpi.transparency.org/bpi2011/, accessed 31 Jan 2013.

[9] Information provided by the Federal Office of Statistics. The statistics pertaining to recent years must be read with caution, as the convictions are only taken into account when they enter into force. This may take several years.

[10] There are some cases where the offense of mismanagement of funds (Article 158 SCC; "gestion déloyale," "ungetreue Geschäftsbesorgung," "amministrazione infedele") was applied to high-level employees who had betrayed the economic interests vested in them because they were bribed.

24.2 The Role of Compliance Programs in Criminal Liability of Natural Persons

Until 2003, Swiss criminal law applied the principle *societas delinquere non potest,* with the exception of some minor cases of administrative penal law. Companies could therefore not be criminally charged and convicted in Switzerland.

This does not mean that issues of corporate responsibility and governance were entirely absent from the criminal courts during the twentieth century. In fact, some very high-profile cases referred to those issues in recognizing the criminal liability of the head of a company ("responsabilité du chef de l'entreprise," "Geschäftsherrenhaftung"). A first case decided by the Federal Tribunal (Swiss Supreme Court) in 1970 involved the head of a weapons company (Mr. Bührle), who was found guilty of intentionally breaching the Federal War Material Act, because he failed to effectively prevent arms sales and exports to certain foreign countries by his employees in violation of an embargo decreed by the government.[11]

The second and most important decision was handed down in 1996 in the case of Von Roll, a group of companies manufacturing large steel parts such as pipes and presses.[12] The company sold products to Iraq that were purportedly destined for industrial purposes, whereas they were in fact bought as part of the project known as Saddam Hussein's Supergun. Von Roll had never been active in the arms trade, and the construction of the Supergun never succeeded and was ultimately abandoned. The chairman of the board of Von Roll, who was also the chief legal officer of the company, was nevertheless convicted for having negligently permitted an illegal arms deal, in spite of the fact that he had neither known about the sale of the steel parts to Iraq nor suspected that the parts could be used to build a gun. He was convicted, alongside the persons directly involved in the deal, for not having put control mechanisms in place which would have allowed him to detect the fact that there were suspicions about the legality of this contract.

Although he was the only member of the board held liable, the framing of the Federal Tribunal ruling makes it clear that ultimate responsibility for ensuring that preventive measures are effectively implemented is exercised collectively by the members of the board, who are under a duty to prevent risks which are typically linked to the business of the company. This includes the duty to ensure that any important event is brought to the attention of the board of directors and that any red flags are recognized as such and promptly reported to it.

The criminal liability of the head of a company is founded on *individual culpability,* that is, the fact that he or she omits measures which would have prevented his or her subordinates from committing the offense. Hence, the mens rea is defined by the particular offense. In the case of Von Roll, the offense under the Swiss War Material Act prohibited both intention and negligence. Therefore, the prosecution only had to show that the chairman of the board charged with the offense had been

---

[11] ATF 96 IV 155.

[12] ATF 122 IV 103.

negligent in not taking the necessary preventive measures. Whenever intention is required, as is the case for all bribery offenses, the prosecution must show that the head of the company acted at least with *dolus eventualis*.[13] Therefore, this type of liability only reaches its full scope for offenses punishing negligence.

24.3 Introduction of Criminal Liability of "Undertakings"

Corporate criminal liability was introduced as part of a general revision of the SCC adopted in 2002. This part of the revision was put into force on 1 October 2003, in order to enable Switzerland to ratify the 1999 United Nations Convention for the Suppression of the Financing of Terrorism. It may be assumed that without pressure from international conventions, including the OECD Convention on Combating Bribery of Foreign Public Officials in International Business Transactions of 1997, the general reticence of Swiss law makers towards corporate criminal liability would not have been overcome.

The same reluctance also characterizes the use of this new prosecutorial tool. During the first few years, convictions of companies were very rare and anecdotal at best. Only recently have there been any indictments in important cases. Two significant convictions have been handed down so far: A Swiss subsidiary of Alstom S.A. was convicted on corruption charges in November 2011 (See Sect. 24.4.), and the financial branch of the Swiss postal system (PostFinance) was convicted for money laundering in April 2011 by the District Court of Solothurn-Lebern. This sentence was not published and is currently on appeal.[14]

24.3.1 Article 102 SCC: Criminal Liability of "Undertakings"

The provision of the SCC governing the criminal liability of corporations and other businesses is Article 102, which reads as follows in English translation:[15]

Article 102 Liability under the criminal law

1. If a felony or misdemeanor is committed in an undertaking in the exercise of commercial activities in accordance with the objects of the undertaking and if it is not possible to attribute this act to any specific natural person due to the inadequate organization of the

[13] Under Swiss law, *dolus eventualis* is a form of intention and not of negligence. It is given whenever the perpetrator identifies the risk that the offense may be committed and accepts this eventuality.

[14] The Superior Tribunal of Solothurn handed down a preliminary decision on 17 April 2012. See "05.11.2012 Strafkammer," Kanton Solothurn, http://www.so.ch/gerichte/obergericht/praxis/05112012-strafkammer.html, accessed 31 Jan 2013.

[15] See note 1, above.

undertaking, then the felony or misdemeanor shall be attributed to the undertaking. In such cases, the undertaking shall be liable to a fine not exceeding 5 million francs.

2. If the offense committed falls under Articles 260ter, 260^{quinquies}, 305bis, 322ter, 322^{quinquies} or 322^{septies} paragraph 1 or is an offense under Article 4a paragraph 1 letter a of the Federal Act of 19 Dec 1986 on Unfair Competition, the undertaking shall be penalized irrespective of the criminal liability of any natural persons, provided the undertaking is responsible for failing to take all the reasonable organizational measures that were required in order to prevent such an offense.
3. The court shall assess the fine in particular in accordance with the seriousness of the offense, the seriousness of the organizational inadequacies and of the loss or damage caused, and based on the economic ability of the undertaking to pay the fine.
4. Undertakings within the meaning of this title are:

   a. any legal entity under private law;
   b. any legal entity under public law with exception of local authorities;
   c. companies;
   d. sole proprietorships.

Article 102 SCC provides for two different regimes of liability. The first paragraph of the article describes what is referred to as the *subsidiary model,* and the second paragraph describes the *direct model*. The first holds the company liable for any felony or misdemeanor committed in the course of its business activities if the individual perpetrator cannot be identified; the second sets out a limited list of specific crimes for which the company may be held liable even if an individual perpetrator has been identified and prosecuted.

24.3.2 Features Common to Both Regimes

The two regimes have in common a broad definition of the entity held liable, which is not referred to as a corporation but an *undertaking* ("Unternehmen," "entreprise," "impresa"), which is an economic rather than a legal notion. Article 102 (4) SCC mentions not only legal entities but also simple partnerships or sole proprietorships. Undertakings governed by foreign law may also fall within the scope of Article 102 SCC, as long as they are organized in one of the forms described. One of the most important questions discussed among scholars is whether a group of companies may be considered as a single economic unity seen as an "undertaking" or whether the separate legal personhood of the companies prevents the mother company from being held liable for offenses committed anywhere within the group.[16]

Another common feature lies in the fact that the undertaking is held liable for offenses committed by natural persons acting in the scope of its business as defined in the Commercial Registry. Therefore, (1) an act presenting the objective and subjective characteristics of a crime or misdemeanor must have been committed; (2) this offense must be connected to the business of the undertaking in accordance

[16] The broadest view on criminal liability in a group of companies is taken by Heiniger Matthias, Der Konzern im Unternehmensstrafrecht gemäss Article 102 StGB, Stämpfli Verlag, Bern 2011 (*in toto* and N 461 ff.).

with its objects; and (3) the person who has committed it must be integrated in the company's hierarchy. The perpetrator may be a member of the board, a director or officer, or even a simple employee. External agents such as independent attorneys, as opposed to in-house counsels, are not deemed as acting within the company.

The penalty is a fine not exceeding 5 million Swiss francs. Furthermore, illicit profits are subject to *confiscation* (criminal forfeiture) in accordance with Article 70 seq. SCC. Switzerland has a well-established system of criminal forfeiture of assets deriving directly or indirectly from any type of offense (Article 70 SCC). Bribes are undisputedly proceeds from the offense of bribery and must therefore be confiscated. The Swiss Federal Tribunal has recently held that illegal profits which the briber draws from the bribery, for example, the profits made from the underlying contract obtained through bribery, are also proceeds subject to confiscation.[17] This is a major step forward, as the offense of money laundering applies to proceeds of crime and is subject to confiscation. Therefore, financial intermediaries must file suspicious activities reports if they suspect that a company has gained money from business obtained through bribery (Article 9 Money Laundering Act).

When the proceeds are no longer available, other assets may be used to cover a claim for compensation attributed to the state (Article 71 SCC). More importantly, Article 72 SCC allows for the general confiscation of all assets which are subject to the power of disposal of a criminal organization. In the case of a person who participates in or supports a criminal organization (Article 260ter SCC), it is presumed that the assets are subject to the power of disposal of the organization until the contrary is proven. This reversal of the burden of proof may also apply to the assets held by a company if it is controlled by persons having participated in or supported a criminal organization or if the company itself is held criminally liable on this basis. This also triggers the obligation to file a suspicious activities report.

24.3.3 Distinctive Elements of the Two Models of Criminal Liability of the Undertaking

24.3.3.1 Subsidiary Liability (Article 102 (1) SCC)

The subsidiary model applies to all crimes and misdemeanors not listed in Article 102 (2) SCC. Although it is the general regime governing most offenses, this model leaves much to be desired as a basis for criminal liability.

The undertaking may be charged, prosecuted, and convicted only if the individual who actually committed the offense cannot be identified due to organizational inadequacies within the company ("it is not possible to attribute [the offense] to any specific natural person due to the inadequate organization of the company"). In other words, the liability of the undertaking is not triggered by circumstances which caused or permitted the commission of the offense but rather by circumstances

[17] ATF 137 IV 79.

which allowed the perpetrator not to be identified. Consequently, if the undertaking is able to point a finger at an individual perpetrator, only that person is prosecuted, thereby exempting the company from any criminal liability. The subsidiary model therefore literally invites manipulations of justice by sacrificing a person designated to assume criminal liability in order to protect the company.

The unsatisfactory nature of this regime has been pointed out by many scholars. Unsurprisingly, the business community, which is very influential with the Swiss legislative body, does not share this critique.

24.3.3.2 Direct Liability (Article 102 (2) SCC)

Fortunately, active bribery is not governed by the subsidiary model, but by the direct liability model described in Article 102 (2) SCC.

This model allows for a corporate liability which is *direct,* in the sense that it applies to the company on the basis of its organizational inadequacy, regardless of whether the individual who actually committed the crime is prosecuted. It is deemed *parallel* in the sense that the individual perpetrator and the undertaking may both be brought to trial on the basis of the same set of facts.

This model applies only to a restricted number of crimes listed in Article 102 (2) SCC: organized crime (Article 260ter SCC); financing terrorism (Article $260^{quiquies}$ SCC); money laundering (Article 305bis SCC); active bribery of public officials, whether they are Swiss, foreign, or international (Article 322ter, $322^{quinquies}$, and $322^{septies}$ (1) SCC); and active bribery in the private sector (Article 4a (1) (a) Unfair Competition Act).

The company is held criminally liable "for failing to take all the reasonable organizational measures that were required in order to prevent such an offense." This inadequacy replaces the notion of "fault" which is key to individual criminal liability. Although the lack of preventive measures seems to refer to negligence, the criminal liability of undertakings may be based on this approach even if the offense committed requires criminal intent.

It is for the prosecution to prove the lack of reasonable and effective preventive measures; there is no reversal of the burden of proof, and the fact that an offense was committed within the company does not trigger the presumption that the organizational measures put into place were insufficient. The prosecution must prove that the company failed to implement adequate preventive measures as well as the causal nexus between this inadequacy and the fact that the offense was committed.

Thus, *compliance programs are at the core of the criminal liability of undertakings*: if a company has taken the required organizational measures to prevent individuals from committing offenses such as corruption, it cannot be held criminally liable. Consequently, companies are encouraged to take preventive measures commanded by the specifications of their business, the size of the company, the nature of the commercial activity developed by it, the risks linked to the type of products or services sold, the markets targeted, cross-border risks, and so on.

Defining and implementing the necessary preventive measures is the responsibility of each company; the government has issued no legal guidance and the courts have yet to explore the matter. However, the recent case involving Alstom gives some indication as to the general principles defining the requirements of anticorruption compliance programs.

24.3.4 The Alstom Case

24.3.4.1 Facts

Alstom is a large French multinational conglomerate headquartered near Paris, involved in the power generation and transport markets. Many of its clients are states or state-controlled companies. The group appoints consultants to secure contracts on a success fee basis.

Alstom's Swiss subsidiary, Alstom Network Switzerland AG, was in charge of compliance procedures within the group, in collaboration with the mother company Alstom S.A. It handled the contractual relations with the consultants on behalf of other subsidiaries of the Alstom group of companies. In spite of efforts to regulate and oversee the consultancy agreements, some consultants "had forwarded a considerable part of their success fees to foreign decision makers and thereby had influenced the latter in favor of Alstom."[18]

In 2008, the Swiss Attorney General's Office indicted certain natural persons and both Alstom S.A. and Alstom Network Switzerland AG. In November 2011, the attorney general issued a "summary penalty order" (Article 352 Swiss Code of Criminal Procedure (SCCP); "Strafbefehl," "ordonnance pénale," "decreto d'accusa") against Alstom Network Switzerland AG, which the convicted company did not contest before a court as it could have chosen to do.[19] This conviction accepted by the company appears to have been preceded by negotiations between the prosecution and the Alstom group. Alstom Network Switzerland AG was convicted for failing to take all necessary and reasonable organizational precautions to prevent bribery of foreign public officials in Latvia, Tunisia, and Malaysia. The penalty was a fine of 2.5 million francs and confiscation of 36.4 million francs, representing the counter-value of illicit profits estimated on the basis of the operating profit margin. In fact, these profits were not earned by Alstom Network Switzerland AG but by

[18] Press release of the Office of the Attorney General of 22 November 2011. See "Criminal proceedings against Alstom entities are brought to a close," Federal Administration, http://www.news.admin.ch/message/index.html?lang=fr&msg-id=42300, accessed 31 Jan 2013.

[19] The original order in German was briefly published by the Swiss Attorney General's Office in its web page but is no longer publicly accessible. For an English translation see "Summary punishment order, Article 352 Swiss Code of Criminal Procedure," World Bank Group and the United Nations Office on Drugs and Crime (StAR), http://star.worldbank.org/corruption-cases/sites/corruption-cases/files/Alstom_Summary_Punishment_Order_Nov_22_2011.pdf, accessed 31 Jan 2013.

other operative subsidiaries of the group. Obviously, this was part of the bargain involving the whole group who most likely tried to keep the other subsidiaries out of the criminal proceedings and to have the charges against the mother company dropped.

This strategy seems to have paid off, as the Office of the Attorney General issued a second order on the same day, dismissing all charges against the mother company. A remarkable aspect of this order is that it holds the French mother company to be within the territorial reach of Swiss criminal law, as its employees had committed crimes on Swiss soil by cooperating with Alstom Network Switzerland AG. Due to the criminal liability of the mother company being engaged because of the acts attributed to its own employees, the Office of the Attorney General did not need to enter into the controversy of group liability.

In spite of the fact that jurisdiction over the French mother company could be established, the charges were dismissed because the company had made efforts to prevent corruption, although they were not sufficient, and because it had cooperated in the inquiry and made reparations in the form of a payment of 1 million francs to the International Committee of the Red Cross for projects in Latvia, Tunisia, and Malaysia. The Office of the Attorney General therefore held that the public and private interests at stake did not warrant further prosecution (Article 53 SCC). This argument is questionable, and there is no way of knowing if this or any other part of the deal would have stood if challenged before a court of law.

24.3.4.2 Alstom's Compliance Policy Under the Scrutiny of the Office of the Attorney General

During the investigations "the [Office of the Attorney General] established that the group had implemented a Compliance policy that was suitable in principle, but that it had not enforced it with the necessary persistence and therefore acts of bribery in Latvia, Tunisia and Malaysia were not prevented."[20]

The overall design of Alstom's compliance program was in principle, considered satisfactory. The fact that the group compliance function had been consolidated in one company of the conglomerate was considered acceptable. The company upheld a policy prohibiting corruption directed towards its employees and the consultants. The consultants retained by Alstom were under the obligation to detail the contractual services they performed in connection with contracts awarded to Alstom and substantiate them with required proofs of rendered services. There was a policy in force governing the selection of consultants: Only persons effectively residing or having offices and bank accounts in the country in which the project was carried out could be used as consultants. The consultants' services were preferably to be performed via an established company with all normal office facilities and records. There was a ban on signing consultancy agreements with offshore companies or shell companies.

[20] Press release of the Office of the Attorney General of 22 November 2011, see note 19.

However, although the policies defined were suitable, the Office of the Attorney General held that there were severe shortcomings in their implementation. Some consultancy agreements were signed in breach of the policy against offshore and shell companies and with consultants who were not well established and had no bank account in the target countries. No suitable organizational measures were imposed against consultants or employees, who had not respected the internal guidelines, to make sure that tainted deals would not continue. The compliance division was severely understaffed (less than 20 individuals for a workforce of about 75,000); the employees working there had no relevant professional experience in the compliance sector at the time they were hired and were not properly trained. Furthermore, the compliance division was given an insufficiently prominent role within Alstom's organizational structure to enforce compliance regulations.

24.4 Conclusion

The fact that only very few convictions imposing sanctions on the basis of Article 102 SCC have been handed down so far does not mean that this basis for criminal liability of undertakings has had no effect at all since it was introduced in 2003. The direct liability regime (Article 102 (2) SCC) encourages companies to develop policies and take measures against active bribery in order to avoid incurring criminal sanctions. Although this preventive effect of corporate criminal liability cannot be viewed, strictly speaking, as a partnership between the public and the private sector, the mechanism put in place institutes an obligation to identify and manage criminal risks which differ from one business to another and therefore are best addressed by the companies themselves.

It would be naïve, however, to think that the efficacy of preventive efforts made by the private sector is the sole explanation for the fact that criminal convictions of companies on corruption or any other charges have been so scarce so far. The fact that corporate criminal liability can only be established if the prosecution proves that there were organizational shortcomings, and that without them the offense could not have been committed, remains a difficult hurdle to overcome.

Forms of negotiated justice are therefore a necessary tool for the efficient handling of corporate crime. Swiss criminal procedure has been traditionally reluctant towards plea bargains, but the SCCP of 2007 introduced some instruments encouraging negotiation between the prosecution and the defense, in particular, a simplified procedure amounting to a plea bargain ("procédure simplifiée," "abgekürztes Verfahren," "procedura abbreviata"; Article 358 seq. SCCP).

Detecting corporate crime in general and corruption in particular remains a significant challenge. An important role is played by the financial intermediaries and their suspicious activities reports providing the criminal justice system with information about customers and transactions to which they have access (Article 9 Money Laundering Act). This source of financial intelligence is protected by a robust legal framework.

The contrary must be said about measures encouraging whistle-blowing. While whistle-blowers are viewed as heroes in some countries, the Swiss still show a cultural intolerance towards what is often perceived as a form of betrayal. Swiss labor law allows employers to terminate contractual relations without giving any reason, and even if the termination is considered to be an abuse of law, the remedy is only financial compensation without the right to reintegration into the working place. Government bills designed to improve the protection of whistle-blowers in the private sector have met with harsh criticism from industry. This attitude is short-sighted, as credible compliance programs must implement mechanisms which ensure the detection of corporate crime from within.

References

Becker, K., Hauser, C., & Kronthaler, F. (2012). *Korruptionsrisiken erfolgreich begegnen—Strategien für international tätige Unternehmen*. Chur: HTW Chur. http://www.osec.ch/de/filefield-private/files/42112/field_blog_public_files/8866. Accessed 31 Jan 2013.

Cassani, U. (2009). La confiscation de l'argent des "potentats": À qui incombe la preuve? *Semaine judiciaire, 2*(8), 229–256.

Cassani, U. (2010). Les avoirs mal acquis, avant et après la chute du "potentat". *Revue Suisse de Droit International et Européen, 20*(4), 465–482.

Cassani, U. (2011). La lutte contre la corruption: Vouloir, c'est pouvoir? In U. Cassani et al. (Eds.), *Lutte contre la corruption internationale: The never ending story*. Geneva: Schulthess.

Pieth, M. (Ed.). (2008). *Recovering stolen assets*. Bern: Peter Lang.

Chapter 25
Corporate Responsibility and Compliance Programs in the United Kingdom

Celia Wells

Contents

25.1 Introduction: The Bigger Picture

My aim in this chapter is to shed some light on the confused and changing picture of the UK bribery compliance requirements for corporations (legal entities). I will not discuss compliance strategies as such.

Common law jurisdictions have long recognized corporate criminal responsibility, but it has never been fully accepted, and it is often tolerated rather than encouraged. The UK Bribery Act, which was passed in 2010, introduces an offense of corporate failure to prevent bribery. The defense for a company against this liability is to prove that it had "adequate procedures" in place to prevent bribery.

C. Wells (✉)
University of Bristol, Bristol, United Kingdom
e-mail: celia.wells@bristol.ac.uk

S. Manacorda et al. (eds.), *Preventing Corporate Corruption*,
DOI 10.1007/978-3-319-04480-4_25, © Springer International Publishing Switzerland 2014

25.2 Common Law Framework in the United Kingdom

Criminal offenses in England and Wales first developed through the common law (in the sense of decided cases), although many have since been defined by statute and yet more are creatures of statute. The general principles of criminal law are also a mixture of common law and statute. So, for example, it is presumed that offenses require proof of mens rea, but statute can provide otherwise. Under the Interpretation Act, the word "person" in a statute is to be interpreted as including corporations unless otherwise stated.[1]

The *general* principles in relation to *corporate* liability are not in statutory form. They apply to all criminal offenses unless a statute specifically provides otherwise, as is the case with corporate manslaughter and bribery. We can look in vain for logic in all this. Corporate liability has emerged case by case, and more recently statute by statute. There has been no blueprint or underpinning design. Criminal law developed long before industrialization and corporatization, and used a limited conceptual vocabulary that needs to be adapted to the developing dominance of business corporations. Courts described the acts of corporations through a dualist anthropomorphic metaphor, namely the "brains" of management and the "hands" of workers.

This lack of conceptual language allowed a divergence between the US and the UK approaches to corporate criminal liability. The English courts had (or still have) difficulty in coping with the idea that a corporation can have mens rea (or mental element-based fault).

Two main types of corporate liability evolved, applying to different groups of offenses. Very roughly, we can say that agency or vicarious liability applies only to regulatory offenses, many of which are strict liability and do not require proof of fault. Where the vicarious route applies, the corporate entity will be liable for any offenses committed by its employees or agents. This is similar to the US approach.

The perceived difficulty of attributing mens rea to a legal entity such as a corporation was eventually overcome by the invention of the doctrine of identification (or controlling mind). This applies to nonregulatory fault-based offenses, attributing to the corporation only the acts and mens rea of the top-echelon senior officers of the company. As the so-called mind or "brain" of the company, the directors and other senior officers are "identified" with it. More significantly, of course, a company is then *not* liable for offenses carried out by any managers or groups of employees lower down the chain.

Until the enactment of the Bribery Act 2010, this was the restrictive principle that applied to offenses of bribery and corruption. The Bribery Act replaced the previous offenses and introduced a much wider form of corporate liability than would apply if this had been left to common law principles. The Organisation for Economic Cooperation and Development's (OECD) Working Group on Bribery put pressure on the UK to reform its bribery offenses. In particular it regarded the identification route

[1] Interpretation Acts have since 1827 stated that, in the absence of contrary intention, the word "person" includes corporations; see current Interpretation Act 1978 c. 30. Courts in fact were generous in finding contrary intention and rarely did so when the offense required proof of fault.

to corporate liability—which applied to bribery offenses—as wholly inadequate in meeting the UK's obligations under the 1997 Anti-bribery Convention.

25.3 The Bribery Act 2010 in Brief

The act is broader in some respects than the FCPA. It covers both bribes within the private sector and those paid to overseas government officials.

Three offenses replace the previous common law and statutory provisions with a new consolidated scheme of bribery offenses. The first two offenses cover the offering, promising, or giving of an advantage ("active" bribery, s. 1), and the requesting, agreeing to receive, or accepting of an advantage ("passive" bribery, s. 2). The third is a discrete offense of bribery of a foreign public official to obtain or retain business or an advantage in the conduct of business (s. 6). Without going into the detail of the elements of these offenses, it can be noted that each requires the prosecution to prove *intention, knowledge,* or *belief* on the part of the offender that the acceptance of the bribe constitutes improper performance.

These offenses may be committed by individuals *or corporations*. If committed by a corporation, the common law identification principle of attribution would apply. Under this principle, a person who represents the "directing mind" of the corporation has to possess the necessary fault element for the offense.[2] In addition, a director or senior officer who has consented or connived in the activity will also be liable (s. 14).

Jurisdiction for these three offenses extends to bribery committed anywhere in the world by persons with a close connection to the UK, which includes those ordinarily resident in the UK as well as UK nationals and UK corporate bodies (s. 12(4)). All three offenses are punishable by a maximum of 10 years' imprisonment and/or an unlimited fine (s. 11).[3]

Facilitation payments remain illegal. Serious Fraud Office Guidance on these and on hospitality was issued in 2012 (Serious Fraud Office 2012).

25.4 The Corporate Failure Offense

The act has been said to be the "toughest" anticorruption law in the world. That is because of an additional clause targeting commercial organizations which fail to prevent bribes being paid on their behalf. This has been described as an offense of

[2] The fault element for active bribery is satisfied by proof of intention to induce a person to perform improperly a relevant function or activity (as defined in s. 3) or knowledge or belief that acceptance of the advantage would constitute an improper performance (s. 1(2) and s. (3)).

[3] They can also be prosecuted summarily when the penalties would be subject to the statutory maxima, s. 11(1).

strict liability, although it would be more accurate to classify it as a hybrid offense. It contains a reverse onus of proof defense of having in place "adequate procedures designed to prevent" bribery (s. 7(2)). The act requires the Secretary of State to publish guidance on adequate procedures (s. 9). It has wide extraterritorial jurisdiction covering bribes committed anywhere by commercial organizations incorporated in the UK or "carrying on business" in the UK (s. 12).

25.5 The Corporate Failure to Prevent Offense in Detail

S. 7 provides: "(1) A relevant commercial organisation ('C') is guilty of an offence under this section if a person ('A') associated with C bribes another person intending—(a) to obtain or retain business for C, or (b) to obtain or retain an advantage in the conduct of business for C. (2) But it is a defence for C to prove that C had in place adequate procedures designed to prevent persons associated with C from undertaking such conduct."

Who can commit the offense? The offense only applies to "relevant commercial organizations." These include not only bodies incorporated in the UK but also those incorporated elsewhere if they carry on a business, or part of a business in any part of the UK. The meaning of "carries on part of a business" is crucial but undefined. The gloss placed on this phrase by the Bribery Act Guidance is that only entities with "demonstrable business presence" need to be concerned. I return to this point below.

For whose activities is the commercial organization responsible? An "associated person" is defined in s. 8 as a person who "performs services" for or on behalf of the organization and "may (for example) be [an] employee, agent or subsidiary" (s. 8(3); there is a rebuttable presumption that employees do perform services for their employer s. 8(5)).

This is clearly not an exhaustive list, and the association in each case has to be determined "without regard to the bribe under consideration" (s. 8(1) and "by reference to all the relevant circumstances and not merely by reference to the nature of the relationship between [the organization and the person]" (s. 8(4)). The meaning of this phrase is somewhat opaque. Sullivan has argued that it could be restrictive if the only evidence of service provision on the part of the associated person is the bribe or bribes which form the basis of the offense in the first place (Sullivan 2011, p. 96).

Another gray area is that of a non-UK parent with a UK subsidiary. The guidance states that this would not "in itself" mean that the parent company is carrying on a business in the UK, since a subsidiary may act independently of its parent or other group companies.[4]

[4] See Bribery Act 2010 Guidance, gov.uk, para. 36, http://www.justice.gov.uk/legislation/bribery, accessed 15 July 2013.

The guidance admits that the test of an associated person is a broad one but lays much emphasis on the limiting effect of the intention lying behind the associated person's activities. Although the two questions should be separate, as the intention clearly forms part of the offense definition in s. 7(1), the guidance merges them under the heading "associated person."[5] The next question to consider is which of the associated person's activities might trigger s. 7 liability of the commercial organization.

For what activities and with what intention? For this, we need to return to the offense definition in s. 7. The commercial organization commits the offense (subject to the adequate procedures defense) if an associated person (i.e., one performing services for them) bribes another intending to obtain or retain business for the organization or to obtain or retain an advantage in the conduct of business for the organization. Part of the prosecution's case will therefore need to be to prove the intention of the briber or associated person. To use a favorite expression from the guidance this *in itself* could be a difficult evidential hurdle. The guidance speculates:

> a bribe on behalf of a subsidiary by one of its employees or agents will not automatically involve liability on the part of its parent company, or any other subsidiaries of the parent company, if it cannot be shown the employee or agent intended to obtain or retain business or a business advantage for the parent company or other subsidiaries. This is so even though the parent company or subsidiaries may benefit indirectly from the bribe.[6]

Adequate procedures If we assume that the prosecution has proven the elements of the offense discussed above, the burden of proof then turns to the commercial organization. It will be guilty unless it can prove (on a balance of probabilities, the civil standard of proof) that it had in place adequate procedures to prevent the conduct (the bribe in question). The Secretary of State is required by s. 9 to publish guidance about procedures that relevant commercial organizations can put in place to prevent persons associated with them from bribing. The guidance was published in April 2011.

More than half of the guidance is devoted to explaining the act as a whole and much of this has informed the commentary above. The guidance sets out six principles which closely echo the OECD Working Group's own guidance on compliance (Organisation for Economic Co-operation and Development 2010). The underlying aim appears to be to reassure business that it will not be at risk of prosecution for isolated examples of bribery so long as it can show top-level commitment to preventing bribery, and has undertaken risk assessments, training, and monitoring.

The six principles comprise: proportionate procedures, top-level commitment, risk assessment, due diligence, communication (and training), and monitoring and review. Each is explained in detail with illustrative case studies (Organisation for Economic Co-operation and Development 2010; Transparency International UK 2010).

[5] Bribery Act 2010 Guidance, paras. 37–43.

[6] Bribery Act 2010 Guidance, para. 42

Jurisdiction The corporate failure offense applies to bribes offered anywhere in the world (s. 12) by associated persons of commercial organizations incorporated or "*carrying on business or part of a business*" in the UK (thebriberyact.com 2011a).[7]

"Carrying on business" is therefore a key phrase. The guidance suggests that "mere listing" would not be enough, that this would need a "demonstrable presence" in the UK. However, in a carefully worded statement which avoided contradicting the guidance outright, the then SFO Director Richard Alderman said that *while*

> a mere listing taken by itself with nothing else is unlikely to involve anything in the UK and certainly no economic engagement with the economy of the UK or a demonstrable business presence in the UK as it is put in the guidance. The position is likely to be different though when there is economic engagement. What constitutes economic engagement or carrying on business in the UK as the Act puts it? When is the engagement so insubstantial that it can be ignored and when does it cross the line and become substantial and demonstrable?

He suggested the SFO might probe why the company was listed, was it trading in the UK, was it raising finance, dealing with shareholders, and were any corporate functions carried out in the UK, "in order to see whether, on the natural construction of these words, the activity involved does satisfy the test" (thebriberyact.com 2011b).

25.6 Enforcement Procedures

The lead prosecutor for bribery is the Serious Fraud Office. Resources for the Serious Fraud Office have been severely pruned. Its budget fell from £ 51 million in 2008–2009 to £ 33 million in 2012–2013 and is set to fall to £ 29 million by 2014–2015 (Brady and Owen 2012).

There is an evidential threshold (a realistic prospect of conviction) and a public interest threshold (Crown Prosecution Service n.d.). Specific guidance on corporate prosecutions states that prosecution of a company should not be a substitute for individual liability. In assessing the public interest, prosecutors should take into account the value of gain or loss, the risk of harm to the public and unidentified victims, to shareholders, employees and creditors, and the stability of financial markets and international trade: "A prosecution will usually take place unless there are public interest factors against prosecution which clearly outweigh those tending in favor of prosecution."

Factors in favor of prosecution include the existence of previous criminal, civil, and regulatory enforcement actions against the company; evidence that the alleged conduct is part of the established business practices of the company; the ineffectiveness of any corporate compliance programs; the issuance of previous warnings to the company; and the company's failure to self-report within a reasonable time of its learning of the wrongdoing. Factors against prosecution include: proactive

[7] The Court of Appeal case of *Fradley* [2005] EWCA Civ 1183 was cited in support of this interpretation. http://www.bailii.org/ew/cases/EWCA/Civ/2005/1183.html, accessed 23 October 2013.

responses by the company, such as self-reporting and remedial actions; a clean record; the existence of a good compliance program; and "the availability of civil or regulatory remedies that are likely to be effective and more proportionate." This last factor suggests that, where there is an alternative regulatory offense, suspected corporate offenders continue to attract a hands-off, or rather kid-glove protective hand.

25.7 Concurrent Jurisdiction

See Sect. 25.3 of this chapter for jurisdiction for offenses under Act ss. 1, 2, and 6. See Sect. 25.5 of this chapter (*ad finem*) for jurisdiction under act s. 7 (corporate failure to prevent).

The DPP issued interim guidelines on cases with concurrent jurisdiction in October 2012 (Crown Prosecution Service 2012). There should be early sharing of information between prosecutors with an interest in the case; prosecutors should consult on cases and the issues arising from concurrent jurisdiction; in reaching a decision on whether a prosecution should take place in England and Wales, CPS prosecutors should apply the principles set out in these guidelines. Any decision on questions arising from concurrent jurisdiction should be, and should be seen to be, fair and objective. Each case should be considered on its own facts and merits.

The guiding principles:

a. So long as appropriate charges can properly be brought which reflect the seriousness and extent of the offending supported by admissible evidence, a prosecution should ordinarily be brought in the jurisdiction where most of the criminality or most of the loss or harm occurred.
b. Where potentially relevant material may be held in another jurisdiction, the prospects of the material being identified and provided to prosecutors in England and Wales for review in accordance with disclosure obligations in this jurisdiction will be an important consideration in deciding whether appropriate charges can properly be brought in England and Wales.
c. Provided it is practicable to do so and consistent with principles (a) and (b) above, where crime is committed in more than one jurisdiction, all relevant prosecutions should take place in one jurisdiction.

25.8 Summary

Corporate liability risk under the Bribery Act 2010 exists in two forms:

a. Applying general principles of statutory interpretation, a corporation can commit the bribery offenses under ss. 1, 2, and 6. "Corporation" here can include any incorporated or unincorporated association, commercial or otherwise. In such a case the prosecution would need to establish that a senior officer or "directing mind" of the corporation had the relevant intention and knowledge required by the offense definition. This would be possible to prove in a small company (there are many "one or two man" companies) or in a larger one which was corrupt in its higher management. This type of corporate liability could also trigger the liability of an individual director who was shown to have "consented or connived" in the corporate offense (s. 14).

b. Under s. 7, which provides a discrete failure to prevent offense that applies only to "commercial organizations," the prosecution needs to prove that an associated person undertook bribes that could amount to a s. 1 or s. 6 offense (i.e., "active" bribery). The organization will be guilty unless it can show adequate procedures to prevent such bribes. There is no *individual* liability under this section.

References

Brady, B., & Owen, J. (2012, July 1). Budget cuts killed off Libor inquiry. *The independent.* http://www.independent.co.uk/news/uk/politics/budget-cuts-killed-off-libor-inquiry-7901940.html. Accessed 15 July 2013.

Crown Prosecution Service. (n.d.). Corporate prosecutions. http://www.cps.gov.uk/legal/a_to_c/corporate_prosecutions/. Accessed 15 July 2013

Crown Prosecution Service. (2012). CPS launches concurrent jurisdiction consultation. http://www.cps.gov.uk/consultations/concurrent_jurisdiction_consultation.html. Accessed 15 July 2013.

Organisation for Economic Co-operation and Development. (2010). Good practice guidance on internal controls, ethics, and compliance. http://www.oecd.org/investment/anti-bribery/anti-briberyconvention/44884389.pdf. Accessed 15 July 2013.

Serious Fraud Office. (2012). Facilitation payments. http://www.sfo.gov.uk/bribery-corruption/the-bribery-act/facilitation-payments.aspx. Accessed 15 July 2013.

Sullivan, G. R. (2011). The Bribery Act 2010: (1) An overview. *Criminal Law Review, 2,* 87–100.

thebriberyact.com. (2011a). What amounts to carrying on business in the UK under the Bribery Act? http://thebriberyact.com/2011/01/20/what-amounts-to-carrying-on-business-in-the-uk-under-the-bribery-act/. Accessed 15 July 2013.

thebriberyact.com. (2011b). A mirage? The Bribery Act 'exemption' for overseas companies & subsidiaries. http://thebriberyact.com/2011/04/18/a-mirage-the-bribery-act-exemption-for-overseas-companies-subsidiaries/. Accessed 15 July 2013.

Transparency International UK. (2010). Adequate procedures—Guidance to the UK Bribery Act 2010. http://www.transparency.org.uk/our-work/publications/10-publications/95-adequate-procedures-guidance-to-the-uk-bribery-act-2010. Accessed 15 July 2013.

Appendix A

Questionnaire: Anti-Corruption Compliance Program Benchmarking Assessment

Anti-Corruption Compliance Program

Benchmarking Assessment

A. General information on the group
B. Anti-corruption compliance program
C. Facilitation payments
D. Gifts/benefits/hospitality
E. Political contributions/charitable contributions/donations
F. Sponsorship activities
G. Business partners
H. Other aspects of the anti-corruption compliance program

All the answers given to the present questionnaire will only be used in the framework of the research program conducted by ISPAC under the supervision of the United Nations Office for Drugs and Crime.

Before filling in the questionnaire, please answer the following question.

Does your Company wish to be listed as having participated in this survey?

- Yes
- No, the answers given to the present questionnaire must remain anonymous

S. Manacorda et al. (eds.), *Preventing Corporate Corruption*,
DOI 10.1007/978-3-319-04480-4, © Springer International Publishing Switzerland 2014

A. General Information on the Group

1. How many employees are in your corporate group?
   - Less than 10,000
   - Between 10,000 and 25,000
   - Between 25,001 and 40,000
   - Between 40,001 and 60,000
   - Between 60,001 and 90,000
   - Over 90,000

2. How many subsidiaries are in your corporate group?
   - Less than 25
   - Between 25 and 50
   - Between 50 and 100
   - Between 101 and 250
   - Between 251 and 400
   - Over 400

3. Please state the total amount of annual sales in your corporate group (specify whether in Euro or USD)
   - Euro
   - USD
   - Less than 1,000,000,000
   - Between 1,000,000,000 and 5,000,000,000
   - Between 5,000,000,001 and 10,000,000,000
   - Between 10,000,000,001 and 25,000,000,000
   - Between 25,000,000,001 and 50,000,000,000
   - Between 50,000,000,001 and 100,000,000,000
   - Over 100,000,000,000

4. In which geographical areas are your Company's subsidiaries located?
   - Europe
   - North America
   - South America
   - Middle East
   - North Africa
   - Sub-Saharan Africa
   - Asia
   - Oceania

B. Anti-Corruption Compliance Program

5. Has your Company implemented an anti-bribery compliance program?

   - Yes
   - No

6. Is the program aimed at preventing and fighting corruption in both the public and private sectors?

   - Public sector only
   - Both public and private sectors

7. Has that program been implemented on a worldwide basis?

   - Yes
   - No

If not on a worldwide basis, how has that program been implemented? (*Please circle one or more as appropriate*):

- Corporate headquarters
- On a regional or local basis
- All subsidiaries
- Business entities over which Company has effective control
- Other (please specify): _____

8. When did your Company implement an anti-bribery compliance program? Please specify the year of implementation:_____

9. Is your Company's compliance program based on the guidelines that belong to any of the following organizations? (*Please circle one or more as appropriate*):

   - International institutions
   - Industry associations
   - Chamber of Commerce
   - National public institutions
   - NGOs
   - Others (please specify): _____

10. Is your Company's compliance program inspired by one of the following anti-bribery guidelines adopted by International institutions? (*Please circle one or more as appropriate*):

    - OECD
    - Global Compact
    - World Bank
    - ICC
    - Others (please specify): _____

11. Does your Company's compliance program explicitly refer to international instruments/guidelines mentioned above?

 - Yes
 - No

12. Is your Company's compliance program inspired by the United Nations Convention Against Corruption?

 - Yes
 - No

13. Who is responsible for monitoring the implementation of your Company's compliance program? (*Please circle one or more as appropriate*):

 - Board of directors
 - Chief executive officer
 - Internal audit
 - Compliance officer
 - Ethics committee
 - Others (please specify): _____

14. For which of the following categories has your Company adopted specific compliance rules? (*Please circle one or more as appropriate*):

 - Whistle-blowing reports
 - Political contributions
 - Charitable contributions
 - Sponsorship activities
 - Gifts/hospitality/travel expenses
 - Joint ventures agreements
 - Intermediaries agreements
 - Consultants agreements
 - Acquisitions and disposals
 - Facilitation payments
 - Selection of personnel
 - Training of personnel in anti-bribery compliance program
 - Disciplinary actions/contractual remedies for breach of anti-bribery compliance program
 - Communication of the anti-bribery compliance program to stakeholders/ business partners
 - Record keeping and internal controls
 - Others (please specify): _____

15. Who is involved in the *risk assessment* process (identification of activities at risk, Company' functions managing the risk process, etc…) (*Please circle one or more as appropriate*):

 - Board of directors
 - Chief executive officer

- Chief financial officer
- Chief operating officer
- Internal audit
- Ethics committee
- Others (please specify): _____

16. Is there a reporting requirement for *employees* in cases of suspected violations of the anti-bribery compliance program or the anti-corruption laws (red flags)?

    - Yes
    - No

If yes, who is to be notified of these suspected violations?
Please specify: _____

17. Is there a reporting requirement for *business partners* in cases of suspected violations of your Company's anti-bribery compliance program or the anti-corruption laws (red flags)?

    - Yes
    - No

If yes, who is to be notified of these suspected violations?
Please specify: _____

18. If the answer to question 16 or 17 is yes, how many of these red flags have been reported in 2010 and 2011?

    - None
    - Less than 10
    - Less than 20
    - More than 20

19. Is there a mechanism for processing suspected violations of the anti-bribery compliance program or the anti-corruption laws (red flags) reported by employees or third parties?

    - Yes
    - No

20. Who is responsible for managing the violations or suspected violations (red flags) of the anti-bribery compliance program or the anti-corruption laws?

    - Legal unit or department
    - Chief executive officer
    - Chief operating officer
    - Internal audit
    - Ethics committee
    - Other (please specify): _____

21. In cases where there is evidence of a violation, does your Company implement any measures to prevent a reoccurrence of the reported violation?

    - Yes
    - No

22. Does your Company's compliance program have provisions for disciplinary actions in the case of violations?

    - Yes
    - No

23. If the answer is yes, could you indicate how many disciplinary sanctions have been imposed in the last year?

    - None
    - Less than 5
    - Less than 10
    - More than 10

24. Is there a body or a department in your organization which is responsible for appropriate support and interpretation on the anti-bribery compliance program and anti-corruption laws, and to update the compliance program after identification of gaps or issuance of new laws and regulations?

    - Yes
    - No

25. If yes, which body holds such responsibility:

    - Compliance officer
    - Ethics committee
    - Legal department
    - Others (please specify):

26. Is there a periodic report on the monitoring activity on the compliance program?

    - Yes
    - No

If yes, which corporate body is notified of this report? (*Please circle one or more as appropriate*):

- Board of directors
- Chief executive officer
- Chief financial officer
- Chief operating officer
- Internal audit
- Ethics committee
- Others (please specify): _____

27. How often is this periodic report performed?

   - Monthly
   - Quarterly
   - Annually
   - Other (please specify): _____

28. Does your Company's compliance program provide for external assessment of its anti-bribery program?

   - Yes
   - No

29. If the answer is yes, has this external assessment ever been carried out?

   - Yes. Frequency: _____
   - No

30. Does your Company provide training on its anti-bribery compliance program to (*Please circle one or more as appropriate*):

   - Directors
   - Senior management
   - Middle management
   - All employees
   - Business partners
   - Other (please specify): _____

C. Facilitation Payments

31. Does your Company explicitly forbid facilitation payments?

   - Yes
   - No

If yes, is the prohibition absolute or subject to exceptions (such as health and safety protection, depending on the country involved, etc.)?
Please specify: _____
If no, are those payments subject to conditions?
Please specify: _____

D. *Gifts/Benefits/Hospitality*

Public Officials

32. Does your Company permit provision of gifts, hospitality, or other benefits to public officials?

    - Yes
    - No
    - Yes, depending on stated criteria

Please specify: _____

33. Are there financial limits on the provision of gifts, hospitality, and other benefits to public officials?

    - Yes
    - No

34. Are these financial limits based on:

    - A singular monetary threshold (please specify value): _____
    - A cumulative monetary threshold (please specify value): _____
    - Both (depending on circumstances)
    - Other (please specify): _____

35. Does your Company require reporting of requests from public officials for gifts, hospitality, or other benefits?

    - Yes
    - No
    - Only if such requests are unreasonable or not bona fide

36. Are employees permitted to receive gifts, hospitality, or other benefits from public officials?

    - Yes
    - No
    - Yes, depending on stated criteria

Third Parties

37. Does your Company permit provision of gifts, hospitality, or other benefits to third parties?

    - Yes
    - Yes, depending on stated criteria
    - No

38. If your Company requires approval to provide gifts, hospitality, or other benefits, which of the following unit or departments is responsible for it? (*Please circle one or more as appropriate*):

  - Line management
  - Legal unit or department
  - Compliance unit or department
  - Human resource unit or department
  - Finance unit or department
  - Other (please specify): _____

39. Where does that unit or department principally reside?

  - Corporate headquarters
  - Subsidiary
  - Field/local office
  - Other (please specify): _____

40. If your Company permits the provision of gifts, hospitality, or other benefits to third Parties, are employees required to report such gifts, hospitality, or other benefits?

  - Yes (always)
  - Yes (sometimes depending on the value or other stated criteria)
  - No

41. Are there financial limits on the provision of gifts, hospitality, and other benefits to third parties?

  - Yes
  - No

42. Are these financial limits based on:

  - A singular monetary threshold (please specify value): _____
  - A cumulative monetary threshold (please specify value): _____
  - Both (depending on circumstances)
  - Other (please specify): _____

43. Are employees required to record in a register the provision of gifts/hospitality/other benefits to third parties?

  - Yes (always, even though refused)
  - Yes (sometimes, depending on the value or other stated criteria) (please specify): _____
  - No

44. If the Company requires the registration of gifts, hospitality, or other benefits to third parties, who maintains this register?

  - Legal unit or department
  - Compliance unit or department

- Finance unit or department
- Human resource unit or department
- Other (please specify): _____

45. At what level of the company is this register maintained?

- Corporate headquarters
- At the subsidiary level
- At the office level
- Other (please specify): _____

46. Are employees permitted to receive gifts, hospitality, or other benefits from third parties?

- Yes
- Yes (depending on stated criteria)
- No

47. If your Company so permits, do these employees require approval to accept such gifts, hospitality, or other benefits?

- Yes (always)
- Yes (depending on the value or other stated criteria)
- No

48. If so, who approves requests for receipt of gifts, hospitality, or other benefits from third parties?

- Line management
- Direct supervisor
- Human resource unit or department
- Finance unit or department
- Legal unit or department
- Other (please specify): _____

49. Are employees required to report such gifts, hospitality, or other benefits?

- Yes (always)
- Yes (sometimes depending on the value or other stated criteria)
- No

50. If yes, to whom must the report be made:

- Line manager
- Legal unit or department
- Human resource unit or department
- Finance unit or department
- Compliance unit or department
- Other (please specify): _____

51. Are there financial limits on the value of the gift, hospitality, or other benefit that an employee is permitted to receive from third parties?

   - Yes
   - No

52. Are these financial limits based on:

   - A singular monetary threshold (please specify value): _____
   - A cumulative monetary threshold (please specify value): _____
   - Both (depending on circumstances)

53. Are employees required to record in a register the receipt of gifts, hospitality, or other benefit from third parties (*including public officials*)?

   - Yes (always, even though refused)
   - Yes (sometimes, depending on the value or other stated criteria)
   - No

54. If yes, who maintains this register?

   - Legal unit or department
   - Human resource unit or department
   - Compliance unit or department
   - Other (please specify): _____

55. At what level of the company is this register maintained?

   - Corporate headquarters
   - At the subsidiary level
   - At the office level
   - Other (please specify): _____

E. Political Contributions/Charitable Contributions/Donations

56. Does your Company permit contributions to political parties, movements, committees, political organizations, or trade unions?

   - Yes
   - Yes, depending on stated criteria (please specify): _____
   - No

57. Does your Company permit charitable contributions?

   - Yes
   - Yes, depending on stated criteria (please specify): _____
   - No

58. If yes, do these charitable contributions require approval?

- Yes
- Yes (depending on value or other stated criteria)
- No

59. Who authorizes these charitable contributions? (*Please circle one or more as appropriate*):

- Line management
- Finance unit or department
- Human resource unit or department
- Legal unit or department
- Compliance unit or department
- Other (please specify): _____

60. Is there a due diligence process that is performed on the entity which receives the charitable contributions?

- Yes
- No

61. Does your Company provide restrictions on methods and terms of payment in favor of the entity which receives the contributions?

- Yes
- No

62. If so, which of the following payment terms are not allowed (*Please circle one or more as appropriate*):

- In cash
- To a numbered account
- To an account referring to a person other than the contractor
- Other (please specify): _____

F. Sponsorship Activities

63. Is approval required for undertaking sponsorship initiatives?

- Yes
- No

64. Who gives approval for sponsorship requests? (*Please circle one or more as appropriate*)

- Line management
- Compliance unit or department
- Legal unit or department

- Finance unit or department
- Human resource unit or department
- Other (please specify): _____

65. Does your Company perform a due diligence process on the entity which solicits the sponsorship?

    - Yes
    - No

66. Does your Company provide restrictions on methods and terms of payment in favor of the counterparty of a sponsorship agreement?

    - Yes
    - No

67. If so, which of the following payment terms are not allowed (*Please circle one or more as appropriate*):

    - In cash
    - To a numbered account
    - To an account referring to a person other than the contractor
    - Other (please specify): _____

G. Business Partners

68. As part of your Company's anti-bribery compliance program, does your Company require or encourage any of the following persons to have or to implement/adopt certain compliance programs to counter bribery/corruption? (*Please circle one or more as appropriate*)

    - Intermediaries
    - Consultants
    - Contractors
    - Joint venture partners
    - Business partners (including agents, distributors, dealers and franchisees)
    - Other (please specify): _____
    - None

69. As part of its anti-bribery compliance program, does your Company require compliance with relevant anti-bribery laws by any of the following? (*Please circle one or more as appropriate*):

    - Intermediaries
    - Consultants
    - Contractors
    - Joint venture partners

- Business partners (including agents, distributors, dealers and franchisees)
- Other (please specify): _____
- None

70. Which of the following third parties do subsidiaries require approval to sign contracts with? (*Please circle one or more as appropriate*):

- Intermediaries
- Consultants
- Contractors
- Joint venture partners
- Business partners (including agents, distributors, dealers and franchisees)

71. If so, who gives approval? (*Please circle one or more as appropriate*):

- Local subsidiary's top management
- Direct supervisor
- Headquarters' management

72. As part of its anti-bribery compliance program, does your Company require that due diligence be undertaken on any or all of the entities above?

- Yes, all of the above
- No
- Yes, some of the above (based on risk analysis or other stated criteria)

73. If yes, please specify which entities, stating where applicable 'potential' or 'actual—existing' or both:

	Potential	Actual (*Existing*) (*Specify frequency*)
Intermediaries		
Consultants		
Contractors		
Joint venture partners		
Business partners (including agents, distributors, dealers and franchisees)		
Other (please specify)		

74. Does your Company maintain a database of any or all of the relevant entities above?

- Yes, all of them
- Yes, some of them
- No

75. If yes, please specify (Please circle one or more as appropriate):

- Intermediaries
- Consultants
- Contractors

- Joint venture partners
- Business partners (including agents, distributors, dealers and franchisees)
- Other (please specify): _____

76. For which of the following third parties does your Company provide standard protection clauses in agreements?

- Intermediaries
- Consultants
- Contractors
- Joint venture partners
- Business partners (including agents, distributors, dealers and franchisees)
- Other (please specify): _____

77. If so, please specify the content of these anti-bribery compliance clauses (*Please circle one or more as appropriate*):

- Prohibition to make undue payments to public officials
- Prohibition to make undue payments to third parties
- The right to terminate or suspend the execution of the agreement in case of breach of the obligations
- The right to receive compensation for damages in case of breach of the obligations
- The right to audit the contractor in case of a reasonable suspicion of violation of the compliance program provisions and/or anti-corruption laws
- The extension of clauses over sub-contractors
- Other (please specify): _____

78. Which of the following third parties does your Company provide restrictions on methods and terms of payment in favour of? (*Please circle one or more as appropriate*):

- Intermediaries
- Consultants
- Contractors
- Joint venture partners
- Business partners (including agents, distributors, dealers and franchisees)

79. If so, which of the following payment terms are not allowed? (*Please circle one or more as appropriate*):

- In cash
- To a numbered account
- To an account referring to a person other than contractor
- Other (please specify): _____

80. With respect to your Company's *incorporated or unincorporated* joint ventures, does your Company's compliance program require the joint venture entity (or the third party operator) to have or to implement/adopt certain compliance programs to counter bribery/corruption?

   - Yes
   - Yes (only joint ventures in which the Company exercises control)
   - No

81. With respect to *incorporated or unincorporated* joint ventures in which your Company does not exercise control (or in which there is a third party operator), does your Company's compliance program encourage the joint venture vehicle/entity (or the third party operator) to have or adopt or implement certain compliance programs to counter bribery/corruption?

   - Yes
   - No

82. Does your Company require the monitoring of the activities of its joint ventures?

   - Yes
   - No
   - Sometimes (depending on risk analysis or other stated criteria)

83. Does the Company require its joint ventures representatives to report on their monitoring activities on the joint ventures?

   - No
   - Yes (*Please specify in which circumstances*): _____

84. If so, to whom is this report made? (*Please circle one or more as appropriate*):

   - Line management
   - Legal unit or department
   - Compliance unit or department
   - Human resource unit or department
   - Finance unit or department
   - Other (please specify): _____

H. Other Aspects of the Anti-Corruption Compliance Program

85. As part of its anti-bribery compliance program, in case of acquisition or disposal does your Company provide for due diligence on the acquired company or on the purchaser?

   - No
   - Yes

86. As part of its anti-bribery compliance program, does your Company include questions in its employment applications regarding an employee's personal relationship with public officials?

 - No
 - Yes

87. Does your compliance program require an audit on the degree/extent to which its own rules are observed or violated?

 - No
 - Yes

88. If yes, who performs such checks?

 - Internal audit
 - Third party
 - Other (please specify): _____

89. Are such checks performed periodically?

 - Yes (specify frequency): _____
 - No (specify when occurring): _____

90. Does your Company advertise its anti-bribery compliance program to customers?

 - No
 - Yes

91. Does your Company consider its anti-bribery compliance program to be an asset in its marketing strategy?

 - No
 - Yes

92. Does your Company take part in any (national or international/ public or private) campaigns or initiatives against bribery?

 - No
 - Yes

If yes, please specify the name of campaign or initiative: _____

Additional Comments (Please add any other information you consider relevant for the description of your Company's compliance program)

Documentation (Please attach all the documentation/internal procedures you consider relevant)

Index

S. Manacorda et al. (eds.), *Preventing Corporate Corruption*,
DOI 10.1007/978-3-319-04480-4, © Springer International Publishing Switzerland 2014

9783319044798